Ordnance Survey

STREE

Nottinghamshire

Contents

III	Key to map symbols
IV-V	Key to map pages
VI-VII	Route planning
VIII	Administrative and post code boundaries
1	Street maps
221	Town maps of Chesterfield and Lincoln
222	Extra-large-scale map of Nottingham town centre
224	Index of hospitals, industrial estates, railway stations, schools, shopping centres, street names and universities

PHILIP'S

First edition published 1994
First colour edition published 1999 by

Ordnance Survey® and   George Philip Ltd., a division of
Romsey Road   Octopus Publishing Group Ltd
Maybush   Michelin House
Southampton   81 Fulham Road
SO16 4GU   London SW3 6RB

ISBN 0-540-07543-4 (pocket)

To the best of the Publishers' knowledge, the information in this
atlas was correct at the time of going to press. No responsibility
can be accepted for any errors or their consequences.

The representation in this atlas of a road, track or path is no
evidence of the existence of a right of way.

**The mapping between pages 1 and 223 (inclusive) in this
atlas is derived from Ordnance Survey® Large Scale and
Landranger® mapping, and revised using OSCAR® and Land-
Line® data.**

Ordnance Survey, OSCAR, Land-line and Landranger are
registered trade marks of Ordnance Survey, the national mapping
agency of Great Britain.

Printed and bound in Spain by Cayfosa

Digital Data

The exceptionally high-quality mapping
found in this book is available as digital
data in TIFF format, which is easily
convertible to other bit-mapped (raster)
image formats.

The index is also available in digital
form as a standard database table.
It contains all the details found in the
printed index together with the National
Grid reference for the map square in
which each entry is named and feature
codes for places of interest in eight
categories such as education and
health.

For further information and to discuss
your requirements, please contact the
Ordnance Survey Solutions Centre on
01703 792929.

(22a)	**Motorway** (with junction number)	Walsall	**Railway station**
	Primary route (dual carriageway and single)	⊚	**Midland Metro**
	A road (dual carriageway and single)	Ⓜ	**Metrolink station**
	B road (dual carriageway and single)	⊖	**Underground station**
	Minor road (dual carriageway and single)	**D**	**Docklands Light Railway station**
	Other minor road (dual carriageway and single)	**M**	**Tyne and Wear Metro**
	Road under construction	🚂	**Private railway station**
	Pedestrianised area	⬤	**Bus, coach station**
		◆	**Ambulance station**
DY7	**Post code boundaries**	◆	**Coastguard station**
	County and Unitary Authority boundaries	◆	**Fire station**
	Railway	◆	**Police station**
	Tramway, miniature railway	✚	**Accident and Emergency entrance to hospital**
	Rural track, private road or narrow road in urban area	H	**Hospital**
	Gate or obstruction to traffic (restrictions may not apply at all times or to all vehicles)	✛	**Church, place of worship**
	Path, bridleway, byway open to all traffic, road used as a public path	**i**	**Information centre** (open all year)
	The representation in this atlas of a road, track or path is no evidence of the existence of a right of way	**P** **P&R**	**Parking, Park and Ride**
126		**PO** **PO**	**Post Office**
94	**Adjoining page indicators**	Prim Sch	**Important buildings, schools, colleges, universities and hospitals**
164	The map area within the pink band is shown at a larger scale on the page indicated by the red block and arrow	River Medway	**Water name**
			Stream

Acad	**Academy**	Meml	**Memorial**
Crem	**Crematorium**	Mon	**Monument**
Cemy	**Cemetery**	Mus	**Museum**
C Ctr	**Civic Centre**	Obsy	**Observatory**
CH	**Club House**	Pal	**Royal Palace**
Coll	**College**	PH	**Public House**
Ent	**Enterprise**	Recn Gd	**Recreation Ground**
Ex H	**Exhibition Hall**	Resr	**Reservoir**
Ind Est	**Industrial Estate**	Ret Pk	**Retail Park**
Inst	**Institute**	Sch	**School**
Ct	**Law Court**	Sh Ctr	**Shopping Centre**
L Ctr	**Leisure Centre**	TH	**Town Hall/House**
LC	**Level Crossing**	Trad Est	**Trading Estate**
Liby	**Library**	Univ	**University**
Mkt	**Market**	YH	**Youth Hostel**

	River or canal (minor and major)
	Water
	Tidal water
	Woods
	Houses
House	**Non-Roman antiquity**
VILLA	**Roman antiquity**

■ The dark grey border on the inside edge of some pages indicates that mapping does not continue onto the adjacent page ■ The small numbers around the edges of the maps identify the 1 kilometre National Grid lines

The scale of the maps is 3.92 cm to 1 km (2½ inches to 1 mile)	0	¼	½	¾	1 mile
	0	250m 500m	750m 1 kilometre		
The scale of the maps on pages numbered in red is 7.84 cm to 1 km (5 inches to 1 mile)	0	220 yards	440 yards	660 yards	½ mile
	0	125m 250m	375m ½ kilometre		

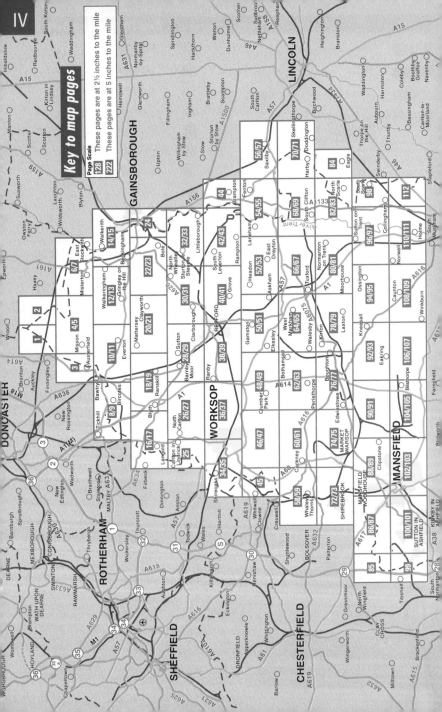

IV

Key to map pages

Page Scale	
128	These pages are at 2½ inches to the mile
222	These pages are at 5 inches to the mile

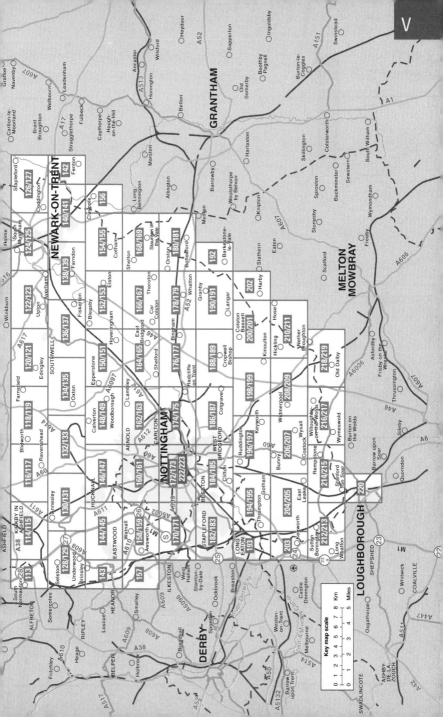

V

Route planning

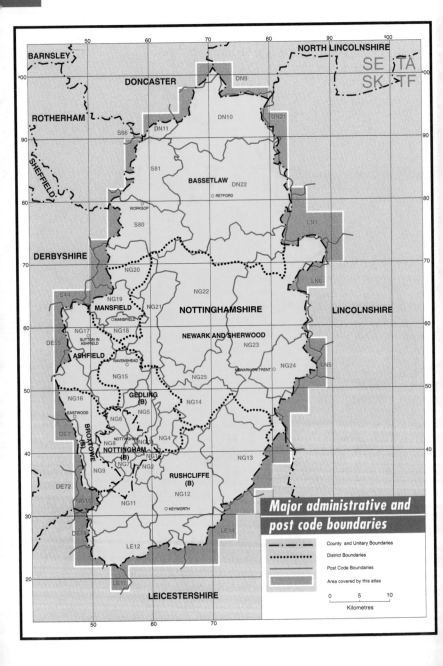

Major administrative and post code boundaries

	County and Unitary Boundaries
	District Boundaries
	Post Code Boundaries
	Area covered by this atlas

0   5   10
Kilometres

A   B   C

Thatch Carr Bank

Thorn Cottage Farm

Thorn Cottages

South Engine Drain

Wroot Grange

THORN BANK

Greenholm Bank Farm

4

Wroot

Birds Wood (Nature Reserve)

Charity Farm

Cove Farm

01

Snell Drain

Cove Farms

Westwoodside

Bull Hassocks

ONE RD

Bull Hassocks Farm

Folly Drain

3

DN9

IDLE BANK

Monkham Drain

00

Pelf Intax

B1396

Bank House

B1396

2

SANDERSON'S BANK

Birdlevels Cottage

DONCASTER RD

Levels Farm

99

Park Drain Hotel (PH)

BROOMSTON LANE

Warping Drain

LC

1

Chapel Baulk

DN10

LC

Snow Sewer

Broomston

Little Broomston Farm

Middle Broomston Farm

98

71   A   72   B   73   C

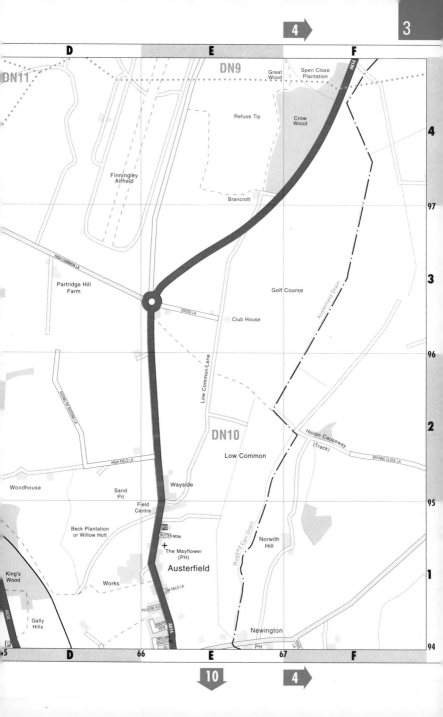

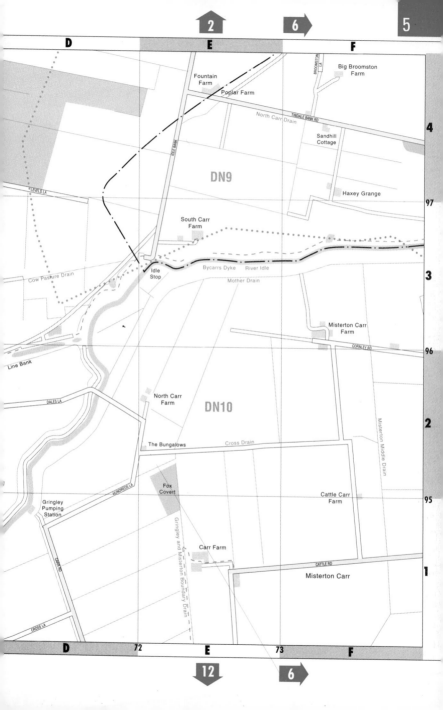

4

Fountain Farm

Poplar Farm

BRICKNELL TON LA

Big Broomston Farm

North Carr Drain

TINDALE BANK RD

Sandhill Cottage

97

W LEVELS LA

DN9

Haxey Grange

South Carr Farm

OLD BANK

Cow Pasture Drain

Idle Stop

Bycarrs Dyke   River Idle

3

Mother Drain

Misterton Carr Farm

CORNLEY RD

96

Line Bank

DALES LA

North Carr Farm

DN10

Misterton Middle Drain

2

The Bungalows

Cross Drain

Fox Covert

95

Gringley Pumping Station

HUNDREDS LA

Cattle Carr Farm

Gringley and Misterton Boundary Drain

Carr Farm

CATTLE RD

CROFT RD

1

Misterton Carr

CROSS LA

5

A   B   C

Warping Drain

Langholme

Langholme Wood

Haxey

DN9

Langholme Farm

4

Langholme

LC

Cornley Farm

TINDALE BANK RD

Langholme Manor

Cornley Lane

Richmond Farm

97

Hunter's Hill

North Carr

North Carr Farm

3

Mother Drain

River Idle

HAXEY GATE RD

Haxey Gate Bridge

Haxey Gate Inn (PH)

NORTH CARR RD

Debdhill Farm

Mother Drain Bridge

96

Cornley Farm

Cornley Carr Farm

Debd Hill

Cornley

Debdhill Road

DN10

CORNLEY RD

New Cemy

HAXEY RD

2

Red House

White House Farm

LAUREL AVE

PARK AVE

95

CHURCH ST

B1403

PO

Cattle Farm

Sandholes Lane

HIGH ST

CATTLE RD

Misterton

Liby

A161

1

Cooper's Bridge

GRINGLEY RD

Chesterfield Canal

Wh Brid

Trent Valley Way

GROVE WOOD TERR

GROVE

Green's Yard

B1403

GRAVELHOLES LA.

94

74   A   75   B   76   C

5

13

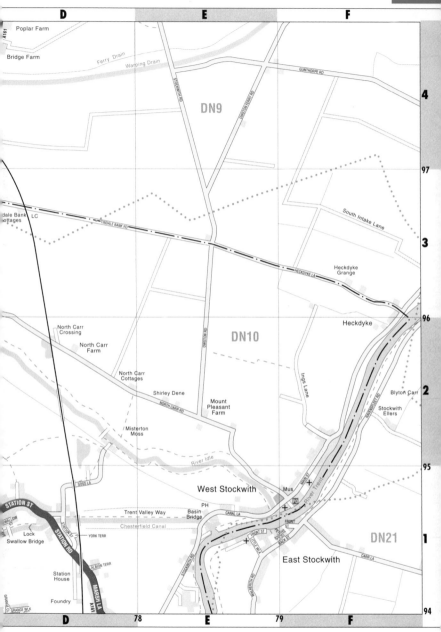

D 78 **E** 79 **F**

Poplar Farm

Bridge Farm

A161

Ferry Drain

Warping Drain

GUNTHORPE RD

STOCKWITH RD

OWSTON FERRY RD

DN9

4

97

dale Bank
ottages   LC

TINDALE BANK RD

South Intake Lane

3

HECKDYKE LA

Heckdyke
Grange

96

North Carr
Crossing

North Carr
Farm

North Carr
Cottages

Shirley Dene

NORTH CARR RD

Mount
Pleasant
Farm

DN10

Heckdyke

Ings Lane

OLD NORLAND

Blyton Carr

Stockwith
Ellers

2

Misterton
Moss

River Idle

95

SOSS LA

STATION ST

SWALLOW
CT

Lock
Swallow Bridge

STATION RD

JEROME ST

YORK TERR

Chesterton Canal

Trent Valley Way

Basin
Bridge

West Stockwith

PH

CANAL LA

Mus.

BANK ST

A20

FRONT ST

River Trent

BASKETTER RD

DN21

1

ALBION TERR

Station
House

MARSH LA

A161

Foundry

GRANGE WLK

STOCKWITH RD

FRONT ST

BELLE VUE

East Stockwith

WHARTON RD

CARR LA

94

D 78 **E** 79 **F**

Tickhill

Bog Hill

SHEEPWASH LA

HIGH COMMON LA

Bracken Croft Lane

Sewage
Works

STRIPE RD

Warehouses

Sandrock
Plantation

Sandrock
Park

Tollbar
Bridge

Goole
Bridge

BAWTRY RD

Sandrock
Farm

Spital
Hill

Tickhill
Spital

NORTH GATE

SUNDERLAND ST

Sch

Liby

PO

Castle
Folds Farm

A631   DAM RD

Tickhill
Castle

West Bank
Farm

Goole Dike or River Torne

Little Black Lane

Moorhouse
Farm

BLYTH RD

Harworth

MOOR TOP

RUTLAND
CRES

SANDROCK RD

GREENWOOD
AVE

Water Lane

Tickhill Low
Common

DN11

Sewage
Works

TICKHILL RD

DORSET

AMANDA RD

DEVONSHIRE RD

Cemy

Bagley
Green

Bagley
Farm

Bagley Dike

Rose
Cottage

COMMON LA

COMMON LA

BRAMBLE WAY

MAIN ST

PH

SCHOOBY RD

STYRRUP RD

Styrrup Carr

Banks Carr Drain

Industrial
Estate

SNAPE

River Torne

Grange
Farm

Hall

SELBY RD

OAKLANDS DR

MAIN ST

PH

Styrrup

PINFOLD DR

Conveyor

Spoil Heap

STYRRUP LA

BRASS

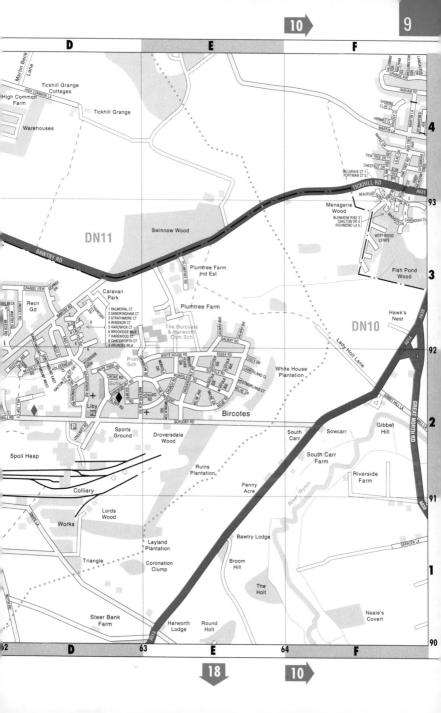

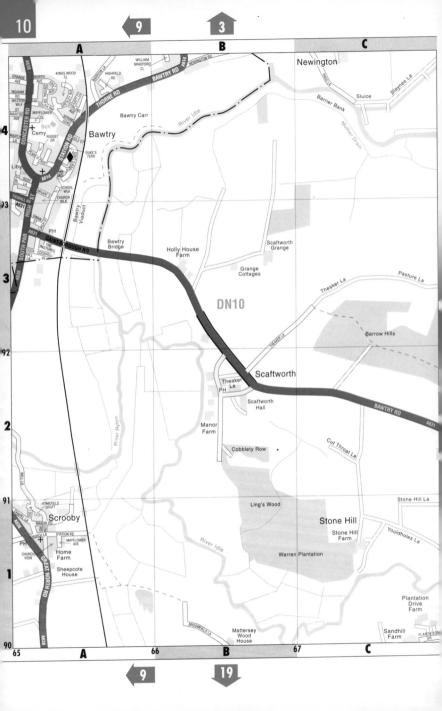

9

3

A **B** **C**

Newington

BAWTRY RD

NEWINGTON RD

THORNE RD

William Bradford CL

Kings Wood CL

Marsh La

Highfield RD

GRANGE AVE

NORTH AVE

INGHAM RD

WESTERN WLK

MARTINS AVE

MAYFLOWER AVE

Sch

Cemy

Bawtry Carr

Bawtry

RUSSET GR

DUKE'S TERR

Libry

A614

SCHOOL WLK

CHURCH WLK

A631

HIGH ST

SWAN ST

PH

GAINSBOROUGH RD

SOUTH PAR

A631

THE PASTURES

COCKHILL

Bawtry Viaduct

Bawtry Bridge

Holly House Farm

Scaftworth Grange

Grange Cottages

Barrier Bank

Sluice

Staynes La

Mother Drain

River Idle

DN10

Theaker La

Pasture La

Barrow Hills

4

93

3

92

Scaftworth

Theaker La

PH

Scaftworth Hall

Manor Farm

Cobblety Row

Cut Throat La

BAWTRY RD

A631

River Ryton

2

Ling's Wood

Stone Hill La

91

Scrooby

HOMEFIELD CROFT

MANOR RD

CHAPEL LA

VILLA

STATION RD

MAYFLOWER AVE

PH

CHURCH VIEW

Home Farm

Sheepcote House

Stone Hill

Stone Hill Farm

Youdholes La

Warren Plantation

GREAT NORTH RD

A638

River Idle

1

Plantation Drive Farm

BROOMFIELD LA

Mattersey Wood House

Sandhill Farm

PLANTATION DR

90

A 65 66 **B** 67 **C**

9

19

D
E
F

4

93

3

92

2

91

1

90

River Idle

Green La

Black Bank

CROSS
LA

Everton Carr
Farm

Clay Bank La

Mother Drain

Toft Hill La

Black Bank
Farm

Magnus Drain

Pasture
Farm

Claybank
Farm

Everton Carr

DN10

Black Bank

Farm
Cottages

Roe Lane
Farm

Black Bank Drain

Pasture La

Carr Hill
Farm

Harwell Slucie La

Roe La

Carr Hill

Middle Cross La

Everton Sluice La

Manor
Farm

Mansfield
Farm

Harwell

Harwell La

Gordon
House

OLD
POST OFFICE
ST

FERRY
LA

CHURCH ST

Everton
Cty Prim Sch

BREWERY

CARR
VIEW

Everton

Tethering La

Oatville
Broad View
Farm

BAWTRY ROAD

LONG
MEADOWS

PIKE LA

CROFT FARM
CLOSE

Stone Hill La

PH

PO

Field
House

GAINSBOROUGH RD

Chesterfield Canal

Haven
Croft

Cemetery

Drakeholes
Farm

A631

B6045

Broomhill La

Mattersey Rd

Mill La

Windmill
(disused)

Mill
Farm

Pusto Hill La

Rock La

PH

Drakeholes

Youdholes La

River Idle

PLANTATION
DR

NEWALL
DR

WAVELL
CRES

Sewage
Works

Pusto Hill
Farm

EEL POOL RD

B6045

Picnic
Site

8

D

69

E

70

F

CROSS LA

Portland Drain

Carr Road West Drain

Oatlands Farm

Carr Farm

Taylor Drain

Dukes Drain

Gringley Carr

Winkersley Farm

DN10

Cow Dale Lane

Ellicar Farm

Polly Bell Bank

Ellicar Farm

Trent Valley Way

Shaw Bridge

Ellicar Lane

Apple Tree Farm

Shaw Lock

Dunstan Farm

Woodlands Farm

Carrholme Farm

Middle Bridge Farm

Park Farm

Chesterfield Canal

Gringley Top Lock

Gringley Bridge

Middle Bridge

Sewage Works

Scott's Wood

Valley Farm

Prospect Hill Covert

Wood's Farm

HM Young Offender Institution

WEST WELLS LA

HUNTER'S DR

LOW ST

HIGH ST

Park House Farm

A631

Rose Cottage

MILL HILL

GAINSBOROUGH RD

Prospect Hill Farm

Gringley Windmill (disused)

Cemy

St Peter's CE Prim Sch

CLAYWORTH RD

B1403

A631

Cuckoo Hill

Wiseton Gardens

High Holme

Gringley on the Hill

Chesterfield Canal

Lady's Bridge

Bland's Wood

Taylor's Bridge

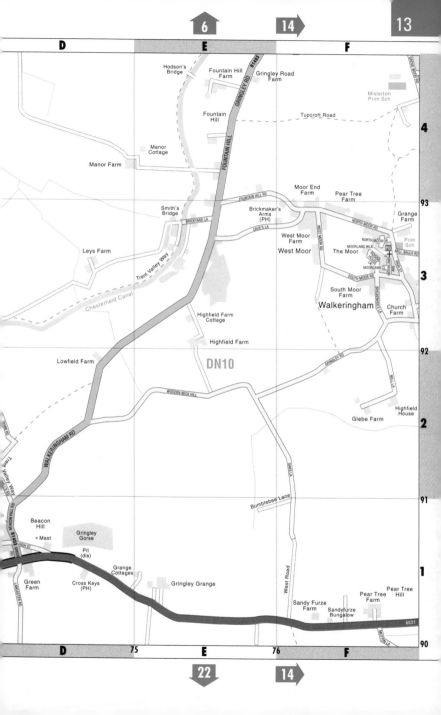

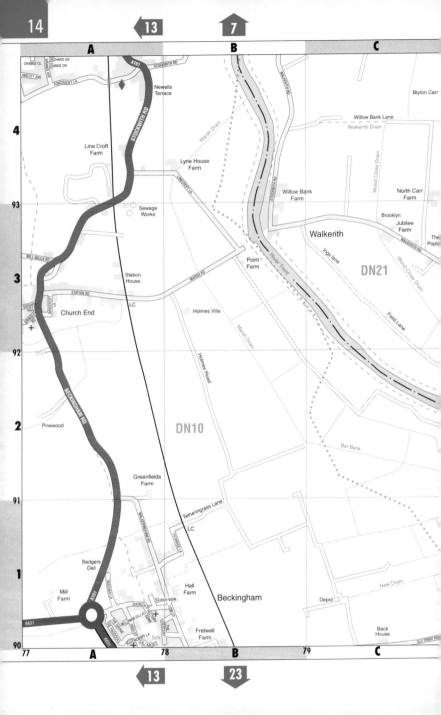

A
B
C

GRANGE CL
ORCHARD GR
GRANGE DR
GRANGE AV
AMCOTT AVE
FONCOVERT LA

A161
STOCKWITH RD

STOCKWITH RD

Newells Terrace

Blyton Carr

Willow Bank Lane

Walkerith Drain

4

Line Croft Farm

Marsh Drain

Lyne House Farm

LINCROFT LA

STOCKWITH RD

Willow Bank Farm

Wood Close Drain

North Carr Farm

93

Sewage Works

Brooklyn

Jubilee Farm

The Popla

Walkerith

WALKERITH RD

MILL BAULK RD

Point Farm

River Trent

Ings lane

DN21

Wood Close Drain

3

Station House

STATION RD

MARSH RD

Church End

LC

SIDGATE HILLS

ACROSS

Holmes Villa

Field Lane

92

Holmes Road

Marsh Drain

2

Pinewood

BECKINGHAM RD

DN10

Bar Bank

Greenfields Farm

MILL FIELD RD

91

Tetheringrass Lane

LC

YORDALE LA

Badgers Dell

New Drain

1

Mill Farm

A161

BECKS LA

Hall Farm

CHURCH VIEW

CHURCH LA

Beckingham

Depot

Back House

A631

WILLOUGHBY VILLAS

CHURCH LA

KATICOURT RD

HIGH ST

GROVE

THE

THE MEWS

Fretwell Farm

OLD TRENT RD

Sch

90

77
A
78
B
79
C

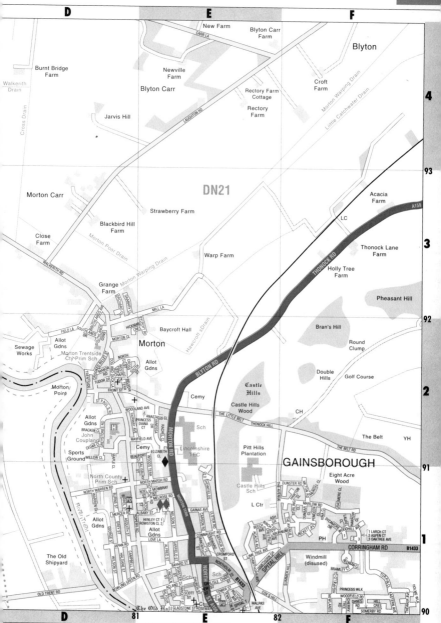

D **E** **F**

New Farm

Blyton Carr Farm

CARR LA

Blyton

Burnt Bridge Farm

Morton Warping Drain

Walkerith Drain

Newville Farm

Croft Farm

Little Catchwater Drain

4

Blyton Carr

Rectory Farm Cottage

Rectory Farm

Cross Drain

Jarvis Hill

LAUGHTON RD

93

DN21

Acacia Farm

A159

Morton Carr

Strawberry Farm

LC

THONOCK RD

Thonock Lane Farm

3

Blackbird Hill Farm

Morton Poor Drain

Close Farm

Holly Tree Farm

WALKERITH RD

Warp Farm

Morton Warping Drain

Pheasant Hill

92

Grange Farm

MILL LA

Bran's Hill

Round Clump

Sewage Works

FIELD LA

SOUTH SIDE

Baycroft Hall

Havcroft Drain

Castle Hills

Double Hills

Golf Course

2

Allot Gdns

HICKMAN RD

Morton

Morton Trentside Cty Prim Sch

BLYTON RD

Allot Gdns

Castle Hills Wood

CH

NORTH

MORTON TCE

Cemy

THE LITTLE BELT

THONOCK HILL

THE BELT RD

Morton Point

ST PAUL'S

TUDOR DR

CHAPEL

FRONT ST

WOODLAND AVE

ANASTASIA CL

Cemy

Sch

YH

The Belt

DIANA CT

PRINCESS

RACHEL CL

MORTON RD

Allot Gdns

BRACKEN CL

John Coupland

MAYFIELD AVE

Lincolnshire TEC

Pitt Hills Plantation

GAINSBOROUGH

91

Sports Ground

WILLOW CL

BEAUFORT

ELIZABETH CL

Eight Acre Wood

North County Prim Sch

MAPLE CL

NORTH MARSH RD

Sch

Castle Hills Sch

DUNSTER RD

L Ctr

MARLOW RD

MARTIN

MANOR DR

NOEL ST

MOWBRAY ST

LENTON RD

GAINAS AVE

ASH

GESMERE CL

BEECH

1

Allot Gdns

MERCER RD

ALBANY ST

HENLEY CT

ROWSTON CL

LOVE LA

COMMAUGHT RD

SYCAMORE

LAUREL

PACKETT ST

PH

1 LARCH CT
2 ASPEN CT
3 OAKTREE AVE

JAPAN ST

Allot Gdns

BAYARD ST

CROMFORD

LIME TREE RD

CORRINGHAM RD

B1433

The Old Shipyard

WILSON ST

NORTH ST

SPITAL HILL

Windmill (disused)

BRAMLEY

OLD TRENT RD

Sch

MALPAS AVE

PRINCESS WILK

WOODFIELD

DANES RD

HILL CRES

SOMERBY RD

The Old Hall

GLADSTONE

SCOTT

P

90

D **81** **E** **82** **F**

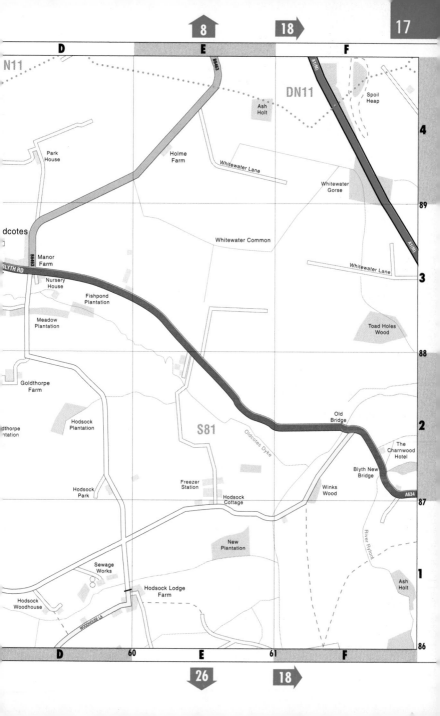

17
9

A   **B**   **C**

Nook Flatt Wood

Sunny Nook

Lodge

East Lodge

The Woodlands

GREEN LA

Elm Cottage

Serlby

4

Kirk View

The Laurels

Serlby Hall

Home Farm

CH

DN10

HARWORTH AVE

Serlby Park

89

THE WOODLANDS

Serlby Park Golf Course

Black Cat Plantation

Bishopfield House

BANTRY RD

ROMAN BANK LA

Bishopfield Farm

BISHOPFIELD LA

3

A1(M)

WHITEHOUSE LA

A614

Service Area

Decoy Pond

Roe Hill Plantation

B6045

A1

Blyth Wood

Hodgkinson's Holt

Brecks Wood

S81

88

Nornay

COMMON LA

River Ryton

Roman Bank La

NORNAY CL

Bridge Farm

South View

2

Blyth Hall

The Grange

DN22

PRIORY CL

Inn

THE MALTINGS

BLYTH RD

B6045

Blyth

SHERWOOD RD

RETFORD RD

The Manfles

PO

87

A634

Mill Farm

B6045

MOOR LA

Belmont

Do A

BAULK LA

B6049

HIGH ST

SHERWOOD CRES

BLYTHE CE Prim Sch

LAWSON SQ

GRAVES MOOR LA

WORKSOP RD

BRIBER RD

1

SPITAL RD

BRIBER HILL

LONG BECK LA

Sycamore La

B6045

Spital Farm

A1

A634

86

62   **A**   **63**   **B**   **64**   **C**

17
27

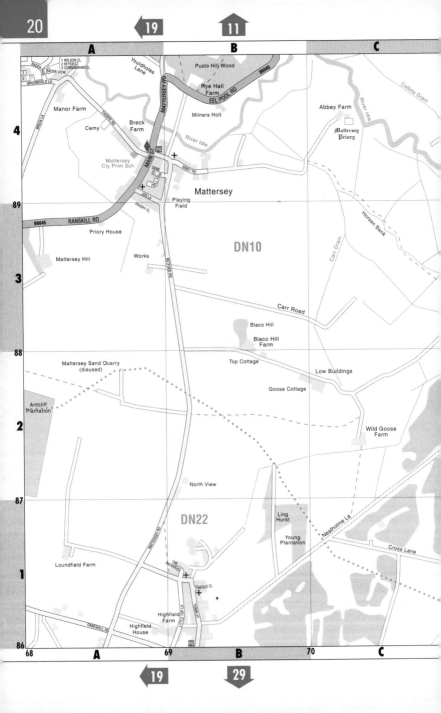

Mattersey

DN10

DN22

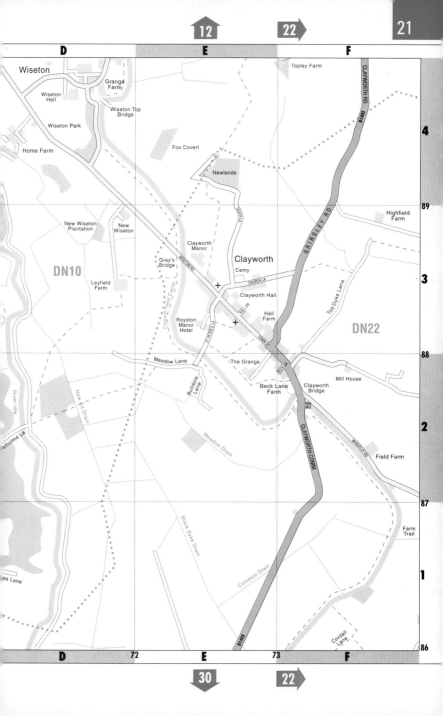

D   E   F

Wiseton

Grange Farm

Wiseton Hall

Wiseton Top Bridge

Wiseton Park

Fox Covert

Home Farm

Newlands

4

89

Highfield Farm

New Wiseton Plantation

New Wiseton

DN10

Clayworth Manor

Clayworth

Cemy

Gray's Bridge

Leyfield Farm

Church La

Clayworth Hall

3

Tott Dyke Lane

GRINGLEY RD

DN22

Royston Manor Hotel

Hall Farm

Meadow Lane

The Grange

Bulldole Lane

Beck Lane Farm

Mill House

Clayworth Bridge

88

River Idle

New Fox Drain

Meadow Drain

CLAYWORTH COMM

2

Field Farm

WHEATLEY RD

Heathholme La

87

Black Syke Drain

Farm Trail

Common Drain

1

ss Lane

Cordall Lane

86

D   72   E   73   F

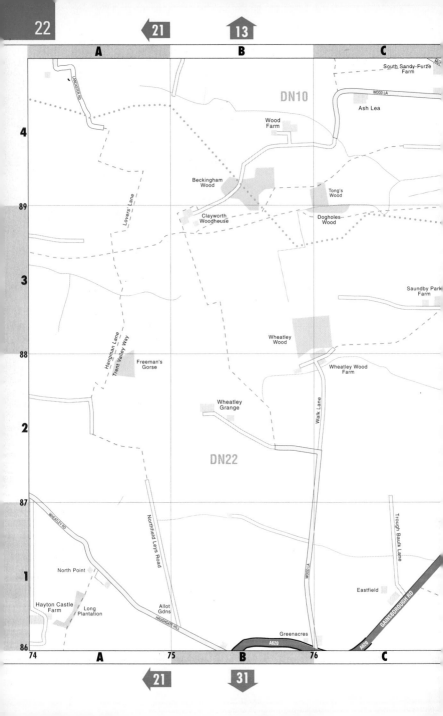

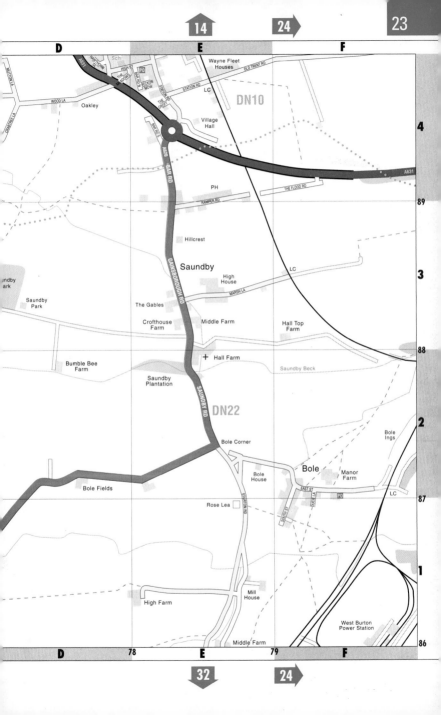

D   E   F

Acorn Piece

Miller Lands

WEST VIEW

Costhorpe

Ingham Bungalows

Langold Holt

Trading Estate

PINFOLD DR 1
COPPICE WAY 2
HARVEST CL 3
PLOUGH DR 4.

4

Woodland Farm

Buckwood Farm

ROTHERHAM BAULK

PH

CHILTERN WAY 1
PENTLAND DR 2
HAMBLETON CT 3
LOWTHER SQ 4
CLEVELAND CL 5
BEVERLEY WLK 6
CHICHESTER WLK 7
CHEVIOT CT 8
MENDIP CT 9
CANTERBURY WLK 10
LICHFIELD WLK 11
COTSWOLD CT 12

OAK TREE RISE

BEECH GR

LIME

LILAC

WILLOW AVE

PO

85

STEWART CL

Liby

STEWART RD

Oxford Rd

QUEENS RD

LONG LA

Schs

WARWICK AVE

Green Lane

WINDSOR GDNS

WINDSOR RD

ARUNDEL DR

Castle Garden

Wallingwells Wood

3

Carlton in Lindrick

Carlton Wood

Wallingwells

Wallingwells Hall

S81

Hollin Hills

The Lawns

Mus

+

lands Wood

Wallingwells Park

Carlton Lake

CARLTON HALL LA

84

Corn Mill Farm

The Ashes

Holme Wood

South Carlton

Field House Farm

2

The Bottoms

Owlands Wood Dike

Holme House Farm

Hardwick Ashes

83

Broom Farm

Woodsetts

Owday Wood

OWDAY LA

The Homestead

Owday Plantation

Nab's Ashes Wood

Little Broom Wood

1

Rough Piece

Whipman Wood

Sand Hill Plantation

ISOP

Fox Covert

Ashes Wood

Dog Kennel Plantation

Cocked Hat Wood

82

D   57   E   58   F

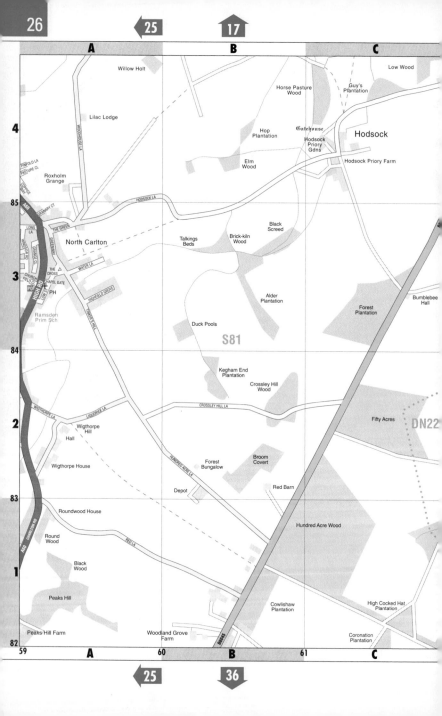

A   B   C

Willow Holt

Low Wood

Horse Pasture Wood

Guy's Plantation

Lilac Lodge

4

Hop Plantation

Gatehouse

Hodsock Priory Gdns

Hodsock

Elm Wood

Hodsock Priory Farm

WOODHOUSE LA

FINFOLD LA

PASTURE CL

COPPICE

Roxholm Grange

ROSEMARY CT

HODSOCK LA

85

A60

LONG LA

THE GREEN

GREENWAY

Black Screed

North Carlton

WINDSOR RD

GRANGE CL

WATER LA

Talkings Beds

Brick-kiln Wood

THE CROSS

CHAPEL GATE

HIGHFIELD GROVE

Alder Plantation

Forest Plantation

Bumblebee Hall

3

CHURCH FIELD CL

LOW ST

POS

HIGH RD

PH

FINNER'S HILL

Duck Pools

S81

Ramsden Prim Sch

Kegham End Plantation

84

Crossley Hill Wood

CROSSLEY HILL LA

Fifty Acres

DN22

2

WROTHORPE LA

LANGWISH LA

Wigthorpe Hill

Hall

Broom Covert

HUNDRED ACRE LA

Forest Bungalow

Wigthorpe House

A60

Depot

Red Barn

83

Roundwood House

RED LA

Hundred Acre Wood

CHARTERS RD

Round Wood

1

Black Wood

Peaks Hill

Cowlishaw Plantation

High Cocked Hat Plantation

Peaks Hill Farm

Woodland Grove Farm

B6045

Coronation Plantation

82

59   A   60   B   61   C

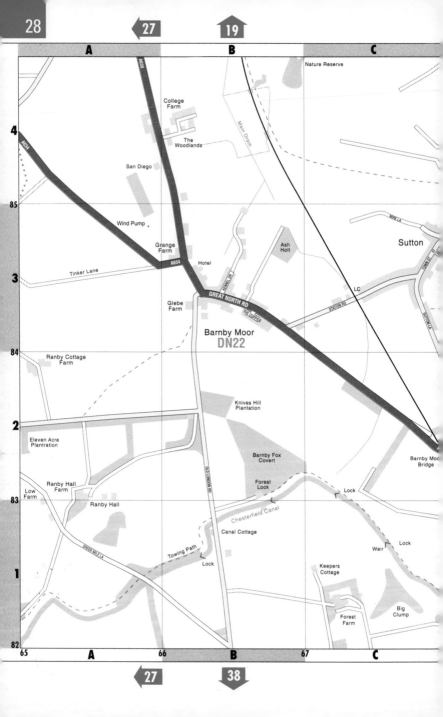

D E F

Lound

CHAINBRIDGE LA

Chainbridge Lane

Yew Tree Farm

TOWN ST

CHAIN BRIDGE RD

Sutton Grange

4

Low Farm

LOUND LOW RD

Waterfowl Reserve

85

CHURCH WAY

Ash Lagoon

PH

TWL ST

PORTLAND PL

Sutton-cum-Lound CE Prim Sch

Bellmoor Farm

3

Tiln Grange

DN22

Tiln

Whitehouse Farm

84

River Idle

Cross Road Farm

Works

2

Bolham Hall

TILN LA

Sutton Cross Roads

GREAT NORTH RD

83

LC

NORTH RD

SUTTON LA

Sewage Works

Bolham

Trinity Farm

SCOTTON SQ

HALLCROFT IND EST

AVILL DE WAY

HALLCROFT RD

HARDSTAFF

MILLMAN

RANDALL WAY

BIRCH CT

Bolham Manor

1

BADGERS CHASE

MEADOW

FALLOW

BOLHAM LA

REDFORD PARK RD

REDFORD PARK RD

RICHMOND RD

SHASH RD

EVINGTON CT

OLLAND CT

LOWELL RD

HIGHFIELD

PALMER RD

RICHMOND RD

RIVER CLOSE

HILL WAY

Lady Bridge Wood

Lady Bridge

BREWSTERS WAY

SILVERDALE

RICHMOND WAY

WHITSTER

MILNERCROFT GREEN

MILNERCROFT

CHERRY AVE

MILLBECK

CLEVELAND

SELBY

MAYFIELD CL

CAMBORNE CL

Sch

Sch

82

D 69 E 70 F

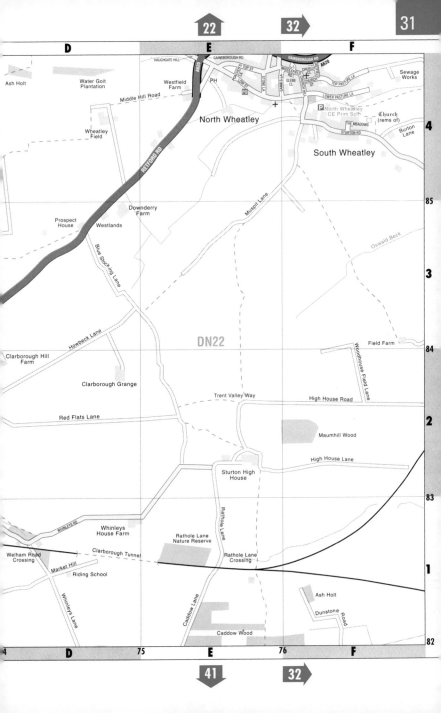

Ash Holt

Water Goit
Plantation

HAUGHGATE HILL

GAINSBOROUGH RD

Westfield
Farm

PH

Middle Hill Road

Wheatley
Field

North Wheatley

GAINSBOROUGH RD

A620

TOP ST

MACKLEY FIELD
CL

LOW ST

STONE LA

MAUDS FIELD
RD

GLEBE
CL

CHURCH
LA

CHURCH
ST

TOP PASTURE LA

LOWER PASTURE LA

P North Wheatley
CE Prim Sch

THE MEADOWS

STURTON RD

Sewage
Works

Church
(rems of)

Burton
Lane

South Wheatley

RETFORD RD

A620

Muspit Lane

Prospect
House

Westlands

Downderry
Farm

Blue Stocking Lane

Oswald Beck

Howbeck Lane

DN22

Clarborough Hill
Farm

Clarborough Grange

Red Flats Lane

Trent Valley Way

High House Road

Field Farm

Woodhouse Field Lane

Maumhill Wood

High House Lane

Sturton High
House

Whinleys
House Farm

WHINLEYS RD

Rathole Lane

Rathole Lane
Nature Reserve

Rathole Lane
Crossing

Welham Road
Crossing

Clarborough Tunnel

Market Hill

Riding School

Whinleys Lane

Caddow Lane

Ash Holt

Dunstone Road

Caddow Wood

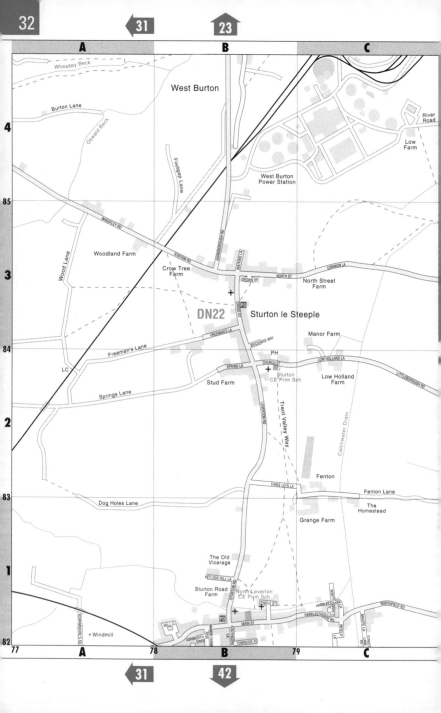

West Burton

West Burton
Power Station

River
Road

Low
Farm

Wheatley Beck

Burton Lane

Oswald Beck

Footgap Lane

WHEATLEY RD

Wood Lane

Woodland Farm

STATION RD

Crow Tree
Farm

GAINSBOROUGH RD

WATKING LA

CROWN CT

NORTH ST

COMMON LA

North Street
Farm

DN22

Sturton le Steeple

Manor Farm

FREEMAN'S LA

BRIDGINGS WAY

Freeman's Lane

LC

Springs Lane

Stud Farm

SPRING LA

PH

CHURCH ST

Sturton
CE Prim Sch

LOW HOLLAND LA

Low Holland
Farm

UTERLBOROUGH RD

LIVERTON RD

Trent Valley Way

Catchwater Drain

Fenton

Dog Holes Lane

THREE LEVS LA

Fenton Lane

The
Homestead

Grange Farm

The Old
Vicarage

KETLOCK HILL LA

Sturton Road
Farm

North Leverton
CE Prim Sch

TEMPLE ST

HABBLESTHORPE RD

NORTHFIELD RD

Windmill

MILL CL

ASHWORTH
CRES

MANOR FARM
LA

SOUTHSIDE
LA

MAIN ST

TOWNSIDE RD

PO

HABBLESTHORPE RD

STREET LANE
RD

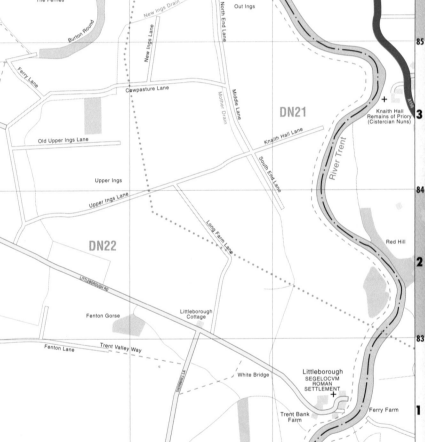

D · E · F

4

85

Ppg Sta

Knaith Reach

Lea Marshes Main Drain

GAINSBOROUGH RD

A156

River Road

Catchwater Drain

The Ferries

Burton Round

Ferry Lane

New Ings Lane

New Ings Drain

North End Lane

Out Ings

Cowpasture Lane

Mother Drain

Middle Lane

DN21

Knaith Hall Lane

South End Lane

Knaith Hall
Remains of Priory
(Cistercian Nuns)

A156

3

Old Upper Ings Lane

Upper Ings

Upper Ings Lane

River Trent

84

DN22

Long Farm Lane

Red Hill

2

LITTLEBOROUGH RD

Fenton Gorse

Littleborough
Cottage

83

Fenton Lane

Trent Valley Way

White Bridge

THORNHILL LA

Littleborough
SEGELOCVM
ROMAN
SETTLEMENT

Trent Bank
Farm

Ferry Farm

1

Smythe
Lane

NORTHFIELD RD

NORTH END RD

MARSH LA

82

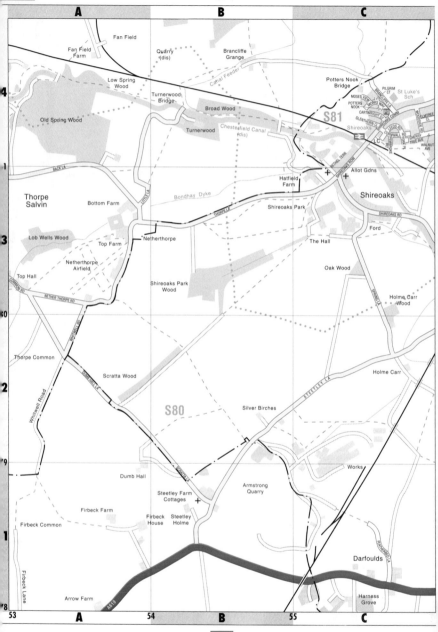

A   **B**   **C**

Fan Field

Fan Field Farm

Quarry (dis)

Brancliffe Grange

Canal Feeder

Low Spring Wood

Turnerwood Bridge

Broad Wood

Potters Nook Bridge

PILGRIM CT

St Luke's Sch

MOSES

POTTERS NOOK

CARTWRIGHT ST

GLENTHORN DR

S81

ELMTREE

Shireoaks

WOODLANDS

WALNUT AVE

Old Spring Wood

Turnerwood

Chesterfield Canal (dis)

BACK LA

Hatfield Farm

Allot Gdns

Thorpe Salvin

Bottom Farm

FIELD LA

Bondhay Dyke

THORPE LA

Shireoaks Park

Shireoaks

SHIREOAKS RD

Lob Wells Wood

Top Farm

Netherthorpe

The Hall

Ford

Netherthorpe Airfield

Oak Wood

SPRING LA

Holme Carr Wood

Top Hall

COMMON RD

NETHER THORPE RD

Shireoaks Park Wood

Thorpe Common

WHITWELL RD

Scratta Wood

DARFOULDS LA

Holme Carr

STEETLEY LA

Whitwell Road

S80

Silver Birches

Works

Dumb Hall

STEETLEY LA

Steetley Farm Cottages

Armstrong Quarry

Firbeck Farm

Firbeck House

Steetley Holme

Firbeck Common

Darfoulds

FICHERBECK LA

Firbeck Lane

Arrow Farm

A619

Harness Grove

53   **A**   54   **B**   55   **C**

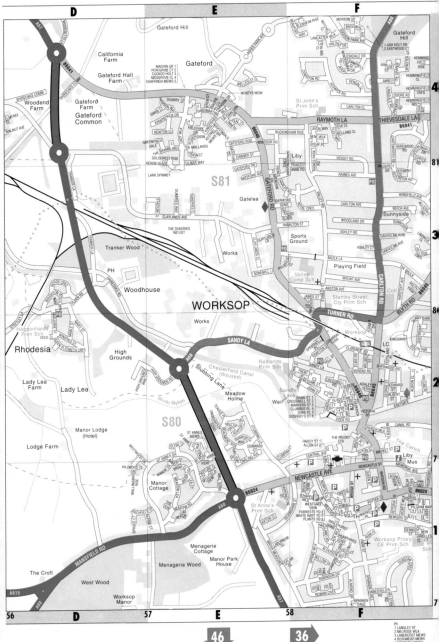

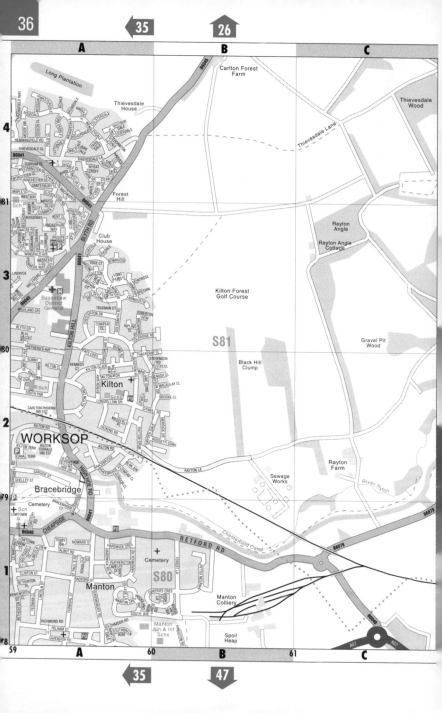

37
28

A   B   C

Green Mile Farm

4

Bowman Hill

Ranby CE Jun & Inf Sch

Ranby House Prep Sch

Sewage Works

81

H M Prison

New Plantation

PH

RETFORD RD

Ranby

STRAIGHT MILE

PILGRIM CL

OLD LONDON RD

GREEN MILE LA

BEECHWOOD CH

A620

Beech Wood Farm

Walker's Wood

The Rectory

3

Dunstons Clump

A620

Chestnut Hill

B6420

DN22

Morton Hall Gardens

Morton

80

Kaye's Wood

Rushey Inn Wood

GREEN LA

Morton Park

Forest Farm

LC

2

Mansfield Road Crossing

Works

MANSFIELD RD

OLD LONDON RD

79

Little Morton Farm

Morton Hill Farm

1

B6420

78

65   66   67

A   B   C

37
49

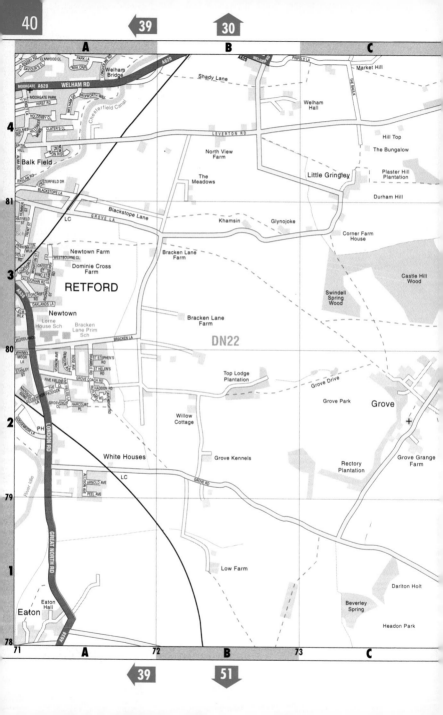

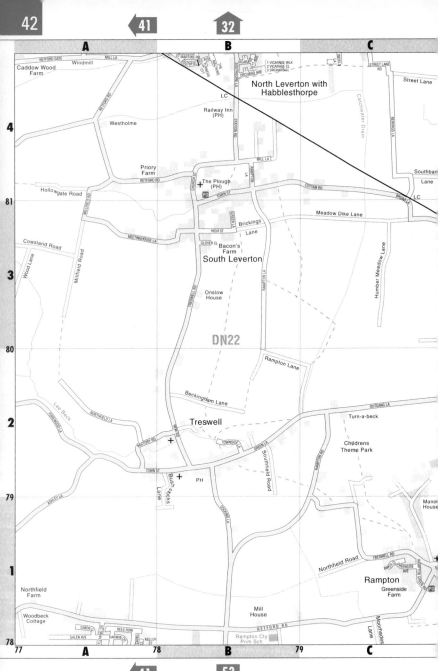

A
B
C

Caddow Wood Farm

Windmill

RETFORD GATE

MILL LA

ST MARTINS RD

SOUTH

ST RISE

THE

VICARAGE

ORCHARD AVE

1 VICARAGE WLK
2 VICARAGE CL
3 ORCHARD CL

INFIELD

LA

STREET LANE
RD

Street Lane

North Leverton with Habblesthorpe

Westholme

LC

Railway Inn (PH)

STATION RD

Catchwater Drain

NEWINGS LA

4

Priory Farm

RETFORD RD

CHURCH ST

The Plough (PH)

PO

TOWN ST

MILL LA

RAMPTON

COTTAM RD

Southbank Lane

Hollowgate Road

MILLFIELD RD

81

Meadow Dike Lane

BRABBLE

LC

MEETINGHOUSE LA

GREEN ST

HIGH ST

Brickings Lane

Cowsland Road

GLOVER CL

Bacon's Farm

South Leverton

Humber Meadow Lane

Wood Lane

Millfield Road

3

Onslow House

DN22

80

Rampton Lane

Lee Beck

TORKSEY RD

NORTHFIELD LA

TRESWELL RD

Beckingham Lane

OUTGANG LA

Turn-a-beck

2

VICTORY RD

NEW RD

Treswell

TOWNSIDE LA

GREEN LA

Childrens Theme Park

Southfield Road

RAMPTON RD

TOWN ST

Bush Dowks Lane

PH

DOCSEN LA

79

ASHLEY LA

Manor House

Northfield Road

TRESWELL RD

GREENSIDE AVE

BIRCH CL

1

Northfield Farm

Rampton

Greenside Farm

PO

RADFORD LA

Woodbeck Cottage

Mill House

RETFORD RD

Moorsides Lane

SIMON ST

REES ROW

GALEN AVE

DARWIN ST

KELLER CL

Rampton Cty Prim Sch

78

77

A

78

B

79

C

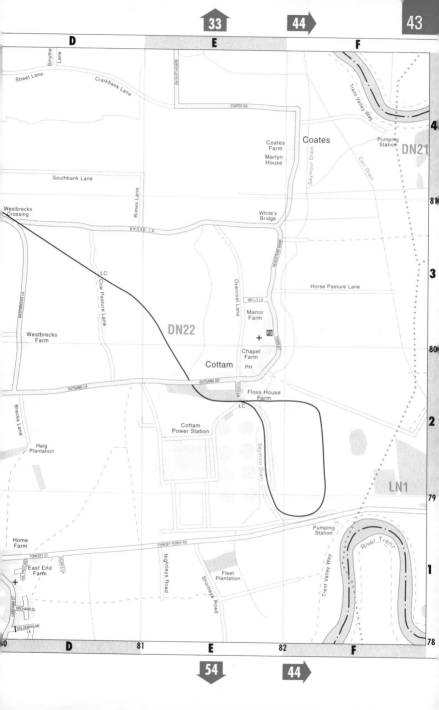

D

E

F

Smythe Lane

Street Lane

Craikbank Lane

COATES RD

Coates Farm

Coates

Marlyn House

Trent Valley Way

Pumping Station

DN21

4

Southbank Lane

Rimes Lane

81

Westbrecks Crossing

BROAD LA

White's Bridge

Seymour Drain

Carr Drain

LC

Cow Pasture Lane

Overcoat Lane

WELLS LA

Horse Pasture Lane

3

DN22

Manor Farm

+ PO

80

Westbrecks Farm

Chapel Farm

Cottam

PH

OUTGANG LA

OUTGANG RD

FOSS LA

Floss House Farm

Brecks Lane

LC

Cottam Power Station

Seymour Drain

2

Haig Plantation

LN1

79

Home Farm

Pumping Station

TORKSEY FERRY RD

Trent Valley Way

River Trent

TORKSEY ST

East End Farm

Nightley's Road

Fleet Plantation

Shortleys Road

1

+

THE PADDOCKS

ORCHARD CL

LARKHAM ST

GOLDENHOLME LA

80

D

81

E

82

F

78

43

A   B   C

THE OLD COURTYARD
Marton PH
PO
Cemy
Windmill
WAPPING LA
A1606
MOUNT PLEASANT CL
THE PADDOCKS
HILLSIDE
A156
TRENT PORT RD
Marton Cty Prim Sch
Trent View
ARM SPRAY
STAFFORD CL
STOW PARK RD
Marton Grange
A1500
LC
TILL BRIDGE LA

Marton Rack

4

Trent Port NTL
Ppg Sta
HIGH ST
Poplar Farm
Sewage Works
Marton Moor Farm
LC

DN21

81

Brampton Grange

Trent Valley Way

3

Bunker's Hill Warren

The Lodge

80

River Trent

Treswell Marsh
Road

Manor Farm

LN1

Brampton

West Lawn

2

Torksey Terminal

Golf Course

Ash Holt

CH

Torksey Viaduct

Castle Inn (PH)

The Grange Farm

STATION RD

Vicarage

79

Caravan Site

MAIN ST

PH
PO
Torksey
Torksey Common

Firs Cottage

Cemy

SAND LA

1

Firs Farm

Torksey Lock

A156

Caravan Parks

Fossdyke Navigation

78

Ppg Sta

83   A   84   B   85   C

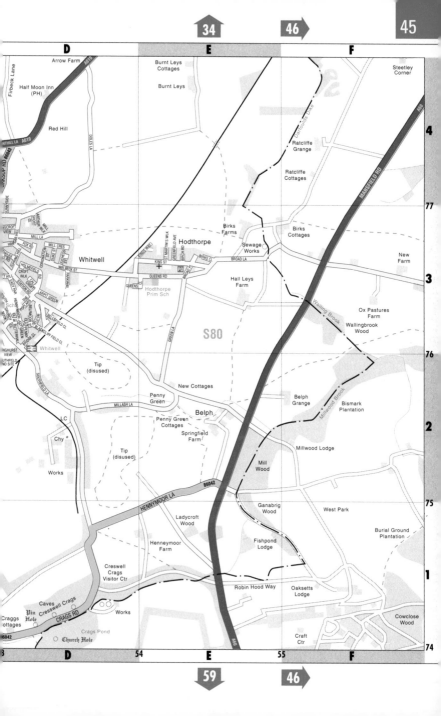

D
E
F

Upper Morton

MANSFIELD RD

B6420

S80

4

Top Farm

WORKSOP RD

77

Apley Head
Farm

Rough Hill
Wood

DN22

Forest Farm

The Table
Plantation

3

Works

76

Bracken Hill

Crookford
Farm

CROSS LA

COALPIT LA

2

Fox
Covert

River Poulter

Ford

BROUGH LA

Spitfire
Bottoms

Crookford Hill

75

S80

Spitfire
Hill

Normanton
Hill

Robin Hood Way

Patmore

1

Normanton
Larches

West Drayton Avenue

Haughton
Kennels
Farm

Normanton Larches
Farm

BASSET LA

D
66
E
67
F
74

OLD LONDON RD

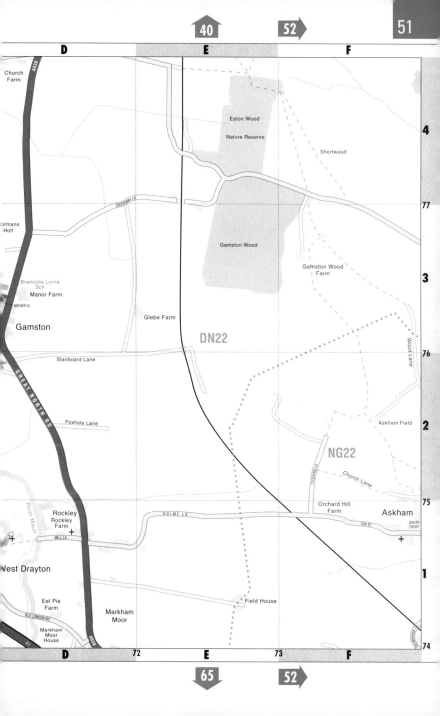

D
E
F

4

Church
Farm

Eaton Wood

Nature Reserve

Shortwood

77

ormans
Holt

CAUSEWAY LA

Gamston Wood

Gamston Wood
Farm

3

Bramcote Lorne
Sch

Manor Farm

HATHER CL

Glebe Farm

DN22

Wood Lane

Gamston

Stanboard Lane

76

GREAT NORTH RD

Foxhole Lane

Askham Field

2

NG22

STOCKING LA

Church Lane

75

Orchard Hill
Farm

Askham

River Maun

Rockley
Rockley
Farm

HOLME LA

TOP ST

SOUTH
CROFT

MILL LA

West Drayton

1

Eel Pie
Farm

Field House

OLD LONDON RD

Markham
Moor

A1

Markham
Moor
House

A638

D
E
F

74

51
41

A   B   C

Schoolhouse
Plantation

LADY WELL LA

Mill Hill

HASLEWOOD LA

Mill Hill
Farm

Headon
Wood

Nether
Headon

Magpie Hall
Farm

4

Headon Manor
Farm

THIEVES ST

Headon

77

Clover Close Lane

3

Upton

Brigg Lane

DN22

Dotegate Road

ASKHAM LA

76

Wood Lane

UPTON HILL

UPTON RD

Hawksley Lane

Drayton Field
Farm

RETFORD RD

Mill House

2

Ash Holt Lane

Hawksley Farm

Beast Wood

TOWN ST

Prospect Farm

75

PH

EASTCROFT LA

Nancy Fox Lane

Thornlea

Kirke's
Plantation

Kirke's
Ash Holt

1

NG22

ASKHAM RD

Meadow Cottage

Old Moorgate

74

74   A   75   B   76   C

51
66

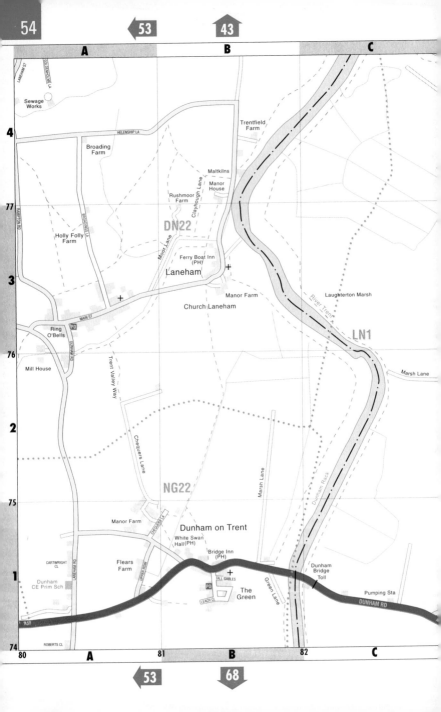

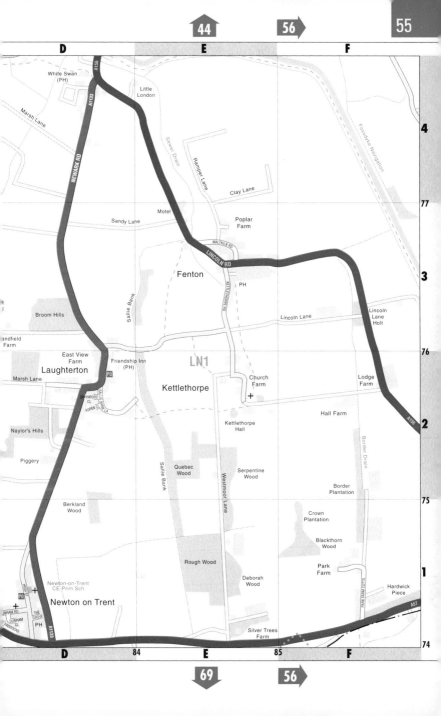

55

A **B** **C**

Highwood Farm

4

Saxilby Sykes

Highwood Farm

77

Sykes Junction

Sykes Farm

Hardwick Farm

Works

3

Foss Dyke Farm

LN1

Manor Farm

SYKES LA

CHURCH LA

76

Hardwick

LC

ST ANDREWS DR

Highfield Farm

Hardwick Wood Farm

Orchard Farm

WESTERN AVE

TORKSEY AVE

Saxilby

2

A156

WOODHALL CRES

75

Green Lane

WEST BANK

Drinsey Farm

A57

Rd

Whitehouse Farm

GAINSBOROUGH RD

1

A156

Tom Otter's Bridge

A57

B1190 TORKSEY LA

DRINSEY NOOK LA

Fossdyke Navigation

Drinsey Nook

74

86 **A** **87** **B** **88** **C**

D   E   F

B1214

Ingleby Hall

Ingleby Hall Farm

Manor Farm

4

STURTON RD

Ingleby Grange

CARLTON LA

Cornhills Farm

77

Broxholme

BROXHOLME LA

Wheelgate Farm

3

CHURCH LA

ST WILFRIDS LA

NORTHCROFT

MRS COURT DR

EASTHORPE

LN1

River Till

BROXHOLME LA

CHURCH LA

RUSSELL CT

MEADOW RD

76

SOUTH PARADE

MANOR RD

ALMOND GR

MILL LA

ARKNEY CL

KIRKSEY AVE

NURSERY CL

OTTER AVE

Eastfield House Farm

WILLOW LA

FOSSDYKE

BRIDGE CL

2

HIGHFIELD

MAYS LA

Saxilby CE Prim School

SYKES LA

SKUB LA

CHAPEL LA

WILLOW LA

PO

WILLIAM ST

FOSSE GR

Saxilby

RAILWAY CT

QUEENSWAY

BRIDGE PL

B1241

LC

QUEENSWAY

BRIDGE ST

Odder Farm

WEST BANK

PH

GAINSBOROUGH RD

LINCOLN RD

Odda Farm

Odder

75

The Old Mill

Fossdyke Navigation

A57

Moor House Farm

BROADHOLME RD

Crossing Cottage

LC

River Bank Farm

1

Broadholme

Whitehouse Farm

Bartons Farm

Birchwood Farm

Highland Farm

MOOR LA

Ouseness Farm

LN6

74

D   90   E   91   F

71

A   **B**   **C**

Markland Farm

Camp Hill

MODEL VILLAGE

DUCHESS ST

Fox Green

The Oaks

Creswell

4

Grange Farm

Elmton

S80

Colliery

Spoil Heap

OXCROFT LA

PH

Green Farm

FRITHWOOD LA

Elm Tree Farm

73

Frithwood Farm

The Old Hag

Frith Wood

DONSIDE LA

3

Whaley Moor

LC

Norwood Farm

MAG LA

72

Whaley Hall

WHALEY COMM

Whaley Common

MOORFIELD LA

NG20

PH

Whaley

Whaley Farm

2

Bolsover Moor Quarry

Grave Wood

Mill Pond

P

71

Mill Farm

Langwith Country Park

Scarcliffe Park

Owl Sick

P

Whaley Thorns Apsley Grange

S44

Owl Spring

BEVERLEY RD

PH

1

Scarcliffe Grange

Archaeological Trail

River Poulter

70

50   **A**   **51**   **B**   **52**   **C**

A
B
C

S80

The Roses

Wilderness

Landing Stage

Clown Hill Plantation

Wood Barn Plantation

4

Greendale Oak

Angling Garden Plantation

Battlefield Plantation

Lambing Cabin Clump

Moss Hall Plantation

Tichfield Hill

Deer Park

73

Common Piece Plantation

Fox Covert Plantation

Park Lodge

Kennel Plantation

Robin Hood Way

Bunker's Hill Plantation

Cat Hills Plantation

3

Bunker's Hill

Weir

Carburton Forge Dam

Milnthorpe Lodge

Harvest Dam Hill

Norton

River Poulter

Corunna Lodge

Mon

Corunna Hi Plantation

INFIELD LA

72

Bentinck Lodge

Battarain Plantation

WORKSOP RD

Sewage Works

Cuckney

Burn's Breck

2

Bridge House

Hatfield Grange

Lord Woodstock's Plantation

Old Mill House

NG20

GLOVERS RIVERSIDE

A616

Greendale Oak (PH)

MANSFIELD RD

BUDBY RD

BUDBY RD

CRESWELL RD

Cuckney House

A632

A6

71

Sedan Lodge

A616

High Hatfield

Gleadthorpe Bre Plantation

LANGWITH RD

A632

Sandy Lane

Hatfield Plantation

1

Presley's Plantation

Welbeck Colliery

Elkesley Hill

1 RUFFORD AVE

Spoil Heap

PORTLAND TERR

HATFIELD

NETHER

Warsop Hill Plantation

70

56

A
57
B
58
C

A   B   C

Weir

Clumber Bridge

Thorney Hill

Claypit Wood

Little Oak Square

Great Oak Square

Thoresby Border

Freeboard Lane

4

The Aviaries

Robin Hood Way

Blyth Corner

73

Catwhins

S80

Budby Corner Plantations

South Lodge

Carburton Corner

Morris Dancer's Plantation

Morris Dancer's Lodge

3

Shepherd's Lodge

Day's Corner

72

Piperwell Wood

Holders Grove

Charcoal Plantation

Osland Wood

2

Perlethorp

Mary's Grove

River Meden

Weir

NG22

Thoresby Hall

Thoresby Home Farm

Thoresby Park

71

Weir

✚

Cameleon Lodge

Weir

Weir

Deer Barn

1

Spready Oaks

Thoresby Lake

Pierrepoint Bridge

Kingston Island

Nelson's Grove

Nelson's Lodge

The Woodyard

70

A   63   B   64   C

A614

D
E
F

S80

Bothamsall

RUSSELL LA

CHURCH LA

MAIN ST

BANK

MEDEN BANK

4

VICTORIA LA

73

River Meden

Spittalmoor Forest
Farm

Mill House
Farm

Haughton

B6387

Ramillies
Plantation

DN22

3

Conjure
Alders

River Maun

Crow Park

Gosling Carr

Haughton Warren

72

ickin's
Bridge

Middle Ashes

Blackcliffe Hill
Plantation

Robin Hood Way

2

Oakham
Poultry
Farms

BLYTH RD

Forest Lane

FOREST LA

NG22

Anthony's
Orchard

Whitewater

71

Whitemoor
Farm

Robin Hood's
Cave

NEW HILL 1
KENNEDY RISE 2

Broom
Covert

RETFORD RD

Briers Lodge

MILL LA

1

Walesby
Forest

PH

Henrys
Grove

Druids Cottage

New
England

Breck Cottages

BRAKE RD

WHITEWATER LA

A614

The
White Lodge

Whitewater
Bridge

BRAKE RD

B6387

70

D
66
E
67
F

A
B
C

Haughton Park House Farm

Colliery

Lawn Covert

Gravel Pit Lane

4

River Meden

River Maun

Lound Hall Training Centre

DN22

Haughton Hall Farm

Earth Holme Plantation

73

Chapel (remains of)

P

3

The World of Robin Hood

Robin Hood Way

Bevercotes

Lower Ponds

Decoy House

72

NG22

Haughton Decoy

Leys Lane

Bevercotes Beck

Green Lane

2

Bevercotes Park Cottages

Farleys Wood

Bevercotes Park

71

Walesby CE Prim Sch

WILLOUGHBY WAY

Farleys House

NEW HILL

KENNEDY

CHAPEL

CL

ASH

MANOR

Willoughby

Hanging Hill Plantation

MAIN ST

1 THE HAWTHORNS
2 STANHOPE CL
3 THE BRAMBLES

FERN BANK AVE

Walesby

Nickerbush Plantation

Willoughby Hill

Mast

B6387

Willoughby Hill

OLLERTON R

A6075

70

68
A
69
B
70
C

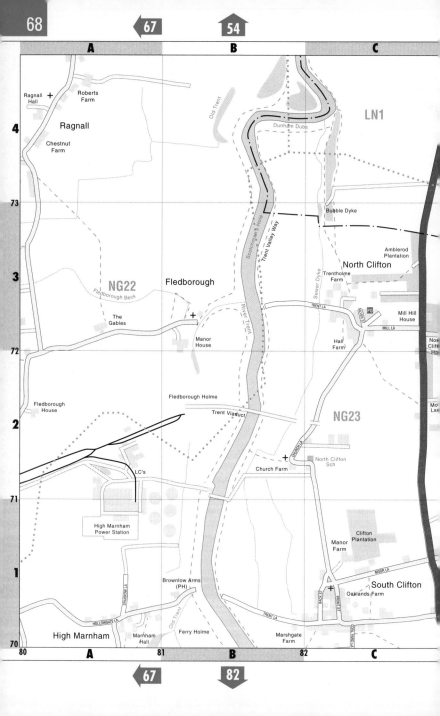

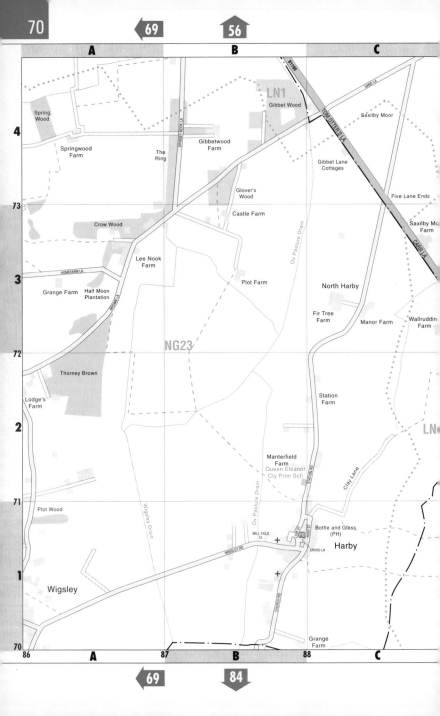

A
B
C

4

LN1

Spring Wood

Gibbet Wood

Saxilby Moor

DRINSEY NOOK LA

Springwood Farm

The Ring

Gibbetwood Farm

TOM OTTER'S LA

GARR LA

Gibbet Lane Cottages

73

Glover's Wood

Five Lane Ends

Crow Wood

Castle Farm

Saxilby Mo Farm

CARR LA

Ox Pasture Drain

3

HOMEFARM LA

Lee Nook Farm

Plot Farm

North Harby

Grange Farm

Half Moon Plantation

Fir Tree Farm

Manor Farm

Wallruddin Farm

B.

NG23

72

Thorney Brown

Station Farm

Lodge's Farm

2

LN

Manterfield Farm

Clay Lane

Queen Eleanor Cty Prim Sch

STATION RD

71

Plot Wood

Ox Pasture Drain

Wigsley Drain

Bottle and Glass (PH)

MILL FIELD CL

PO

Harby

WIGSLEY RD

CROSS LA

1

Wigsley

CHURCH RD

70

Grange Farm

86
A
87
B
88
C

D   E   F

Lound Farm

SAXILBY RD

Manor Farm

MANOR LA

Broadholme
House

LN1

4

Western Plantation

Broadholme
Gorse

73

Magtree Hill

Skellingthorpe Big Wood

3

Old Wood

Carr Farm

Woodbank Farm

Old Wood
House

LN6

72

Old Wood
Nursery

CARR LA

Skellingthorpe

Old Hag
Wood

2

JERUSALEM RD

QUEENSWAY

Old Hag
Farm

Ash Lound

71

Little Sale

Jerusalem
Farm

JERUSALEM

Birch Spring
Farm

1

Strunch Hill

Church
Farm
House

KENNEL LA

B1190 MAIN ST

BECK

Doddington
Hall

Doddington

Top House
Farm

70

D   90   E   91   F

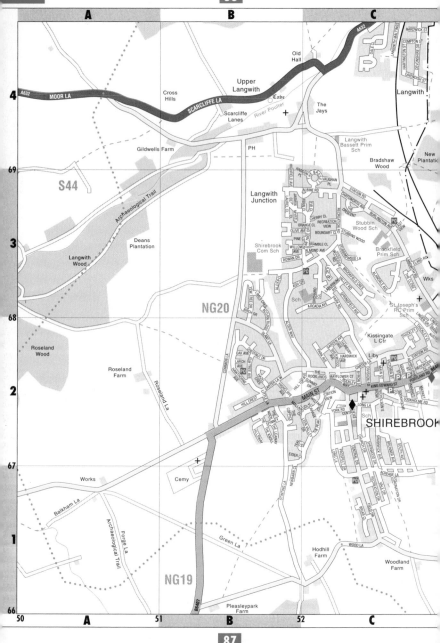

A   B   C

A632

MOOR LA

SCARCLIFFE LA

Old Hall

Upper Langwith

Cross Hills

Scarcliffe Lanes

River Poulter

The Jays

Langwith

Langwith Bassett Prim Sch

Bradshaw Wood

New Plantatio

PH

Gildwells Farm

S44

Archaeological Trail

Langwith Junction

Station Rd

Stubbin Wood Sch

Deans Plantation

Langwith Wood

Shirebrook Com Sch

Brookfield Prim Sch

NG20

Wks

Roseland Wood

St Joseph's RC Prim Sch

Kissingate L Ctr

Liby

Roseland Farm

Roseland La

Hardwick Ave

The Rocklands

Mayflower Ct

King Edward St

Main St

SHIREBROOK

Hill Crest

Central

York Rd

Long La

Sch

Works

Cemy

Green La

Balkham La

Forge La

Archaeological Trail

Eider

Hodhill Farm

Wood La

Woodland Farm

NG19

B6407

Pleasleypark Farm

A   B   C

50   51   52

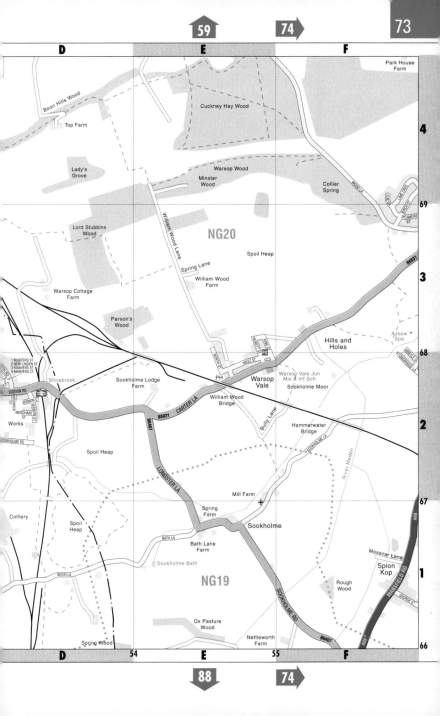

73
60

A   **B**   **C**

Park House Plantation

Hag's Plantation

Spoil Heap

Meden Vale

KIRTLE

BUSBY CRES

JACKSON TERR

Oakfield Plantation

MARSTON AVE

MARKET CT

EDMANTON RD

MANOR AVE

LAXTON AVE

EDMANTON RD

HEALTHORPE DR

EASTLAND TERR

Sch

PO

RUFFORD AVE

P

P

P

4

KNEESALL CL 1
CAUNTON CL 2
THORESBY CL 3
OSSINGTON CL 4

Poultry Houses

RETFORD DR LA

The Three Lions (PH)

Assarts Farm LC

LIME CRES

Church Warsop

Church Vale Prim Sch

Cemy

LAUREL AVE

SYCAMORE AVE

CALLFAX AVE

WEETMAN AVE

SWEETMAN AVE

DUKERIES DR

MANOR RD

ULANNIS SQ

The Bottoms

River Meden

Assarts Hill Plantation

Sewage Works

69

WOOD LA

B6031

BISHOP'S WLK

B6031

EASTLAND LA

MANOR CT

Burns Farm

Broomhill

Lane

CASTHORPE LA

CHURCH RD

P

1 OLD HALL CL
2 MOORFIELD PL
3 LEEMING CL

3

Meden Comp Sch

Sod Wall Plantation

Hetts Lane Inf Sch

Queen St

BIRKLANDS CL

68

CUMBERLAND AVE

SAVILLE WAY

STONEBRIDGE RD

YORK ST

NG20

SHERWOOD ST

MANSFIELD RD

2

Libly

PO

P

CLUMBER CT

Sherwood Jun Sch

LC

MARKET WARSOP

Mount Pleasant

SOOKHOLME LA

BRACKEN CL

OF SANDY LA

LANS VIEW

WENDY HOUSE

Ling Lane

67

A60

LEEMING LA

HODD AVE

FOREST RISE

Blakeley Hill

Norman's Plantation

ROSEWOOD AVE

OXHAY LA

COVENTRY LA

Blakeley Lane

Blakeley Hill Plantation

1

GAVELS LA

GALLOW HILL

Welbeck Colliery Junction

FOREST RD

Bradmer Hill

Windmill

Windmill Plantation

A60

B6035

66

PEAFIELD LA

A6075

56   **57**   **58**

A   **B**   **C**

D
E
F

4

69

3

68

2

67

1

66

South Farm

A616 WORKSOP RD

Experimental Husbandry Farm

River Meden

Holborn Hill Plantation

Ladysmith Plantation

NG22

Boundary Plantation

Budby South Forest

Gleadthorpe New Plantation

Hanger Hill Drive

NG20

Hanger Hill Wood

Assarts Wood

Hanger Hill

Seymour Grove

Sunnyside Wood

Sherwood Forest Country Park

Jerusalem Plantation

Railway Piece

Birklands

The Lings

Warsop Quarter

Fox Den Plantation

Robin Hood Way
Broad Drive

Robin Hood Way

Green Drive

Centre Tree

Turner's Plantation

Crook Dale Drive

NG21

NORMANTON CL 1
PERLETHORPE CL 2

...PER AVE

Cabin Plantation

Blackpool Plantation

GREENDALE AVE

PARKSIDE RD
...LIN AVE

Top Vals Hill

MANVERS CRES

THORESBY DR

...ough Piece

Clipstone Drive

The Sarts

Villa Real Farm

WELBECK DR

A6075

Clipstone Old Quarter

MANSFIELD RD

The Rufford Sch

A6075

FOURTH AVE

Nursing Home

King Edwin Prim Sch

Broomhill Grange

D
60
E
61
F

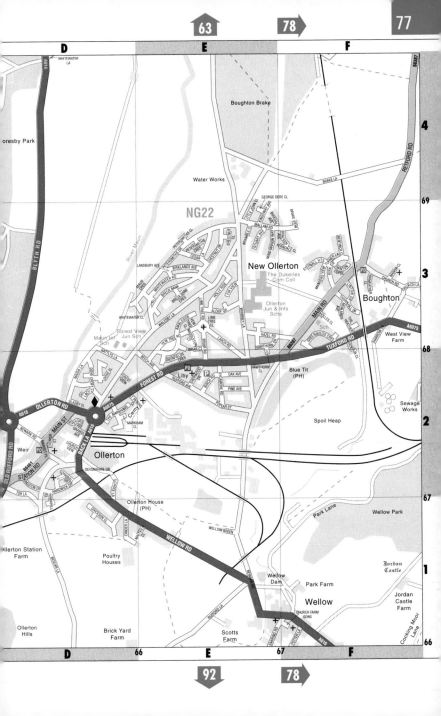

77
64

A   B   C

Collinridge Wood

TELFORD RD

A6075 OLLERTON RD

Priors Park Farm

Manor Farm

4

+

Pasture Farm
Carriage Mus

PH

Hall Farm

PO

RECTORY GDNS

Goosemoor Dyke

69

SANDFIELD LA

KIRTON LA

Kirton

Winson Hill

Doncaster Farm

CHARLOTTE CL

KIRTON CT

CHURCHILL CL

3

Manor Farm

MAIN ST

THE FURZE

Kirton Wood

PRIMROSE LA

NG22

A6075

BROUGHTON
IND EST.

68

Brick Works

Cocking Hill Farm

TRENT RD

ARTHUR RD

MAUN WAY

CASTLE WAY

BROUGHTON

Marl Pit

Norton Wood

COCKING TRL

Golden Hill

2

Birkhill Wood

West Field

Wellow Park

Laxton Common

67

Cocking Moor

Westwood Farm

ACRE EDGE RD

1

Jordan Castle Farm

Ompton Lodge

WESTWOOD LA

COCKING MOOR LA

66

68   A   69   B   70   C

77
93

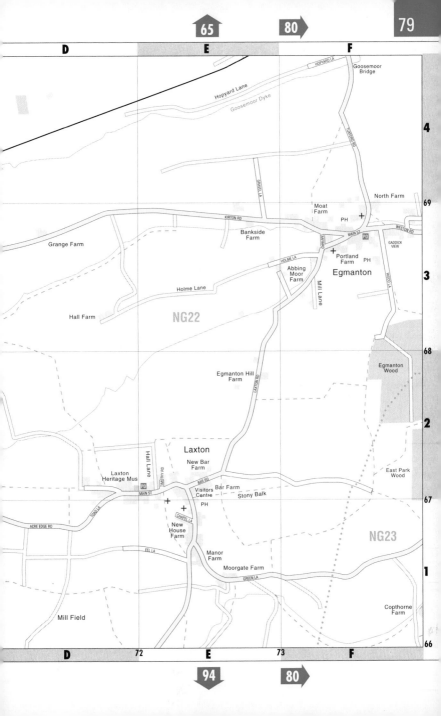

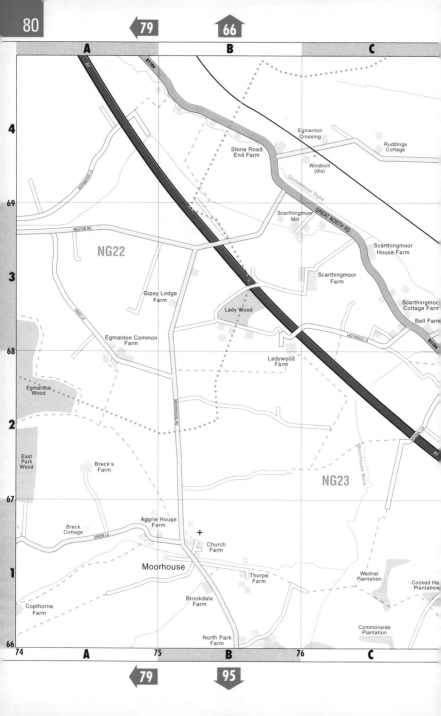

A   B   C

Low Marnham

The Grange   Holme
Farm

Marnham Holme

4

SPACEFIELD LA

HOLME LA
Church Farm

69

Holly
Farm

Marnham Meadow

BROTTS RD
HOPYARD LA

Meadow Lane

3
NG23

River Trent

Marnham Road
Farm

HOLME LA

Normanton
Holme

Marshgate
Farm
COAL YARD LA

Clifton Hill

Old Trent

Girton
Grange

68

Grassthorpe Beck

Trent Valley Way

2

Holme Lane

Green Lane

NEW LA

MEADOW LA

Highfield
Farm

Sand & Gravel Pit

GAINSBOROUGH RD

A1133

Grassthorpe Holme

Works

Boating Lake

67

Lower Girton Stakes

North
Holme

Upper Girton Stakes

Smithy Marsh

1

Cemy

CHURCH

Sch

Oak
Doors

The Fleet

TRENT LA

Weecar
Home
Farm

Girton

Baxter
Bridge

WEST LA
HIGH ST

PROCTERS DR

Baxter
Bridge
Farm

NEW LA

66
80   A   81   B   82   C

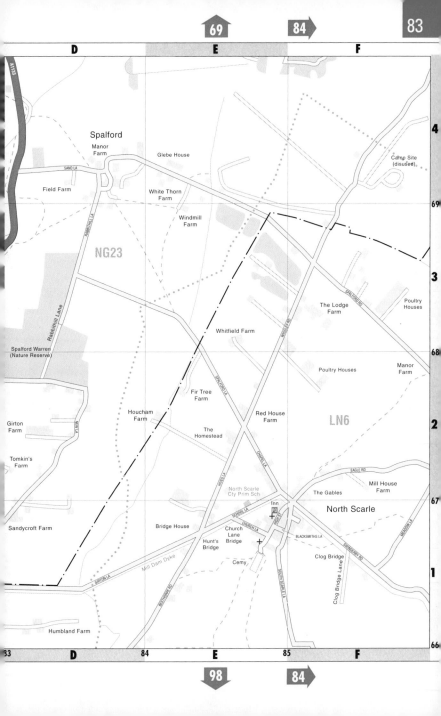

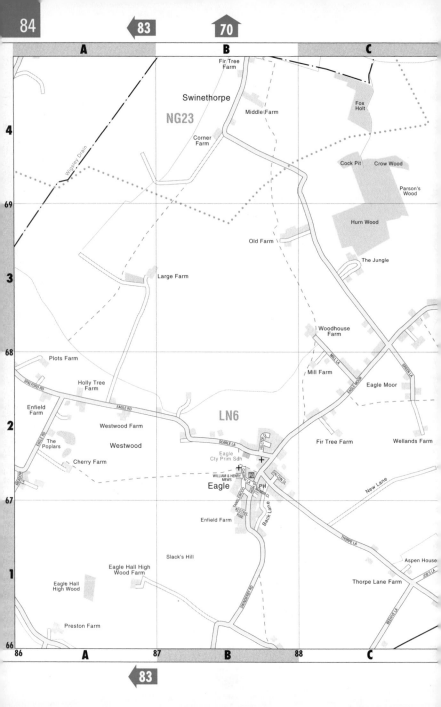

A B C

4

69

3

68

2

67

1

66

86 87 88

A B C

Fir Tree Farm

Swinethorpe

NG23

Middle Farm

Fox Holt

Corner Farm

Cock Pit Crow Wood

Parson's Wood

Hurn Wood

Old Farm

The Jungle

Large Farm

Woodhouse Farm

Plots Farm

MILL LA

Holly Tree Farm

Mill Farm

Eagle Moor

BECK LA

SPALFORD RD

EAGLE RD

Enfield Farm

EAGLE RD

Westwood Farm

LN6

Fir Tree Farm

Wellands Farm

The Poplars

Westwood

SCARLE LA

Cherry Farm

Eagle Cty Prim Sdh

WILLIAM & HENRY MEWS

PH

New Lane

Eagle

Enfield Farm

PRESTON RD

Back Lane

THORPE LA

Slack's Hill

Aspen House

BECK LA

Eagle Hall High Wood Farm

JOES LA

Eagle Hall High Wood

Thorpe Lane Farm

Preston Farm

Wigsley Drain

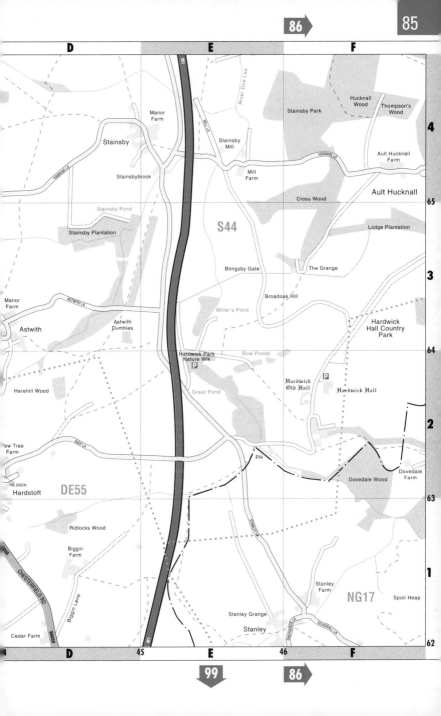

D E F

4

River Doe Lea

Manor Farm

Stainsby

Stainsbybrook

MILL LA

M1

Stainsby Park

Hucknall Wood

Thompson's Wood

Stainsby Mill

Mill Farm

HOOMIRE LA

Ault Hucknall Farm

Ault Hucknall

Cross Wood

65

S44

Stainsby Pond

Stainsby Plantation

Lodge Plantation

3

Blingsby Gate

The Grange

Broadoak Hill

Manor Farm

ASTWITH LA

Astwith Dumbles

Miller's Pond

Hardwick Hall Country Park

Astwith

64

Hardwick Park Nature Wlk
P

Row Ponds

Harehill Wood

Great Pond

Hardwick Old Hall

P

Hardwick Hall

2

ew Tree Farm

DEEP LA

PH

Dovedale Wood

Dovedale Farm

THE GREEN

Hardstoft

DE55

63

Ridlocks Wood

Biggin Farm

STREET LA

1

Stanley Farm

NG17

Spoil Heap

CHESTERFIELD RD

B6039

Biggin Lane

Cedar Farm

Stanley Grange

Stanley

SHERWOOD LA

SILVERHILL LA

62

D 45 E 46 F

A   B   C

BEECH CRES
MILES GR
POPLAR DR
LIME TREE AVE
HAWTHORN AVE
THE
GREEN
SYCAMORE AVE
CHURCH
VIEW
LILAC GR
OAK TREE AVE
ORCHARD
CRES
HARDWICK
AVE
PO

Glapwell

A617

MANSFIELD RD

GREEN LA

Hill Top
Farm

Works

ROTHERHAM RD

Longman
Nook

B617

New
Houghton

GARDEN CRES RD
PAVILION
GDNS
STANTON

VERNEY
WAY

CHESTERFIELD RD

4

Griff
Wood

Strickle Brook

AULT HUCKNALL LA

S44

Top Farm

ROW HORNE LA

DELTA

Anthony Bek
Prim Sch

65

Hall Farm

P

Rowthorne

FIELD LA

LONGMERE LA

Car
Plantation

Farfield Lane

Spoil Heap

NG19

3

DUKE'S DR

Car Ponds

Park Piece

Norcliff
Wood

Merril Sick

Batley Farm

64

Norwood

MILEY LA

Longedge Lane

MOORHAIGH LA

KEEPERS HILL LA

2

Hardwick
Park Farm

BAXTER LA

MOORHAIGH LA

Newbound
Farm

Newboundmill
Farm

63

Crossley
Plantation

NG17

Hare
Plantation

PLEASLEY LA

NEWBOUND LA

Baxterhill

TOP LA

1

Spoil Heap

Hill Farm

River Meden

Little Dawgates
Wood

ROUSTON LA

GREEN LA

62

47   A   48   B   49   C

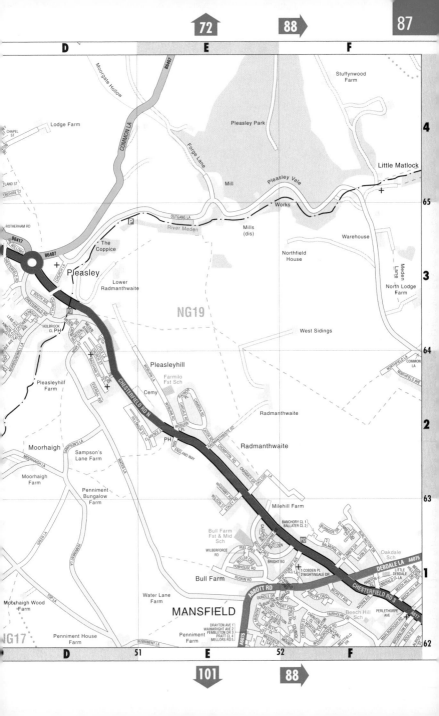

Moorgate Hollow

Lodge Farm

Stuffynwood Farm

Pleasley Park

CHAPEL ST

LAND ST

ONGHIPE ST

COMMON LA

B6407

Forge Lane

Mill

Pleasley Vale

Little Matlock

4

Works

65

ROTHERHAM RD

B6417

BILLINGS

B6407

OUTGANG LA

River Meden

Mills (dis)

Warehouse

The Coppice

Pleasley

Lower Radmanthwaite

Northfield House

Meden Lane

North Lodge Farm

3

NG19

West Sidings

64

HOLBROOK CL PH

Pleasleyhill

Farmilo Fst Sch

Pleasleyhill Farm

Cemy

CHESTERFIELD RD N

COMMON LA

NORTHFIELD AVE

Moorhaigh

Sampson's Lane Farm

PH

FOOTPATH AND WAY

Radmanthwaite

Radmanthwaite

2

Moorhaigh Farm

Penniment Bungalow Farm

Milehill Farm

63

BANCHORY CL 1
BALLATER CL 2

Bull Farm Fst & Mid Sch

WILBERFORCE RD

PEEL CRES

BRIGHT SQ

Oakdale Sch

A6075

DEBDALE LA

LITTLE DEBDALE

1

Bull Farm

Water Lane Farm

HOBHOUSE RD

RUSKIN RD

1 COBDEN PL
2 NIGHTINGALE DR

CHESTERFIELD RD S

Moorhaigh Wood Farm

ABBOTT RD

MANSFIELD

Beech Hill Sch

Perlethorpe Ave

NG17

Penniment House Farm

Penniment Farm

PENNIMENT LA

DRAYTON AVE 1
WAINWRIGHT AVE 2
PEMBLETON DR 3
PRATT CL 4
MELLORS RD 5

A6075

62

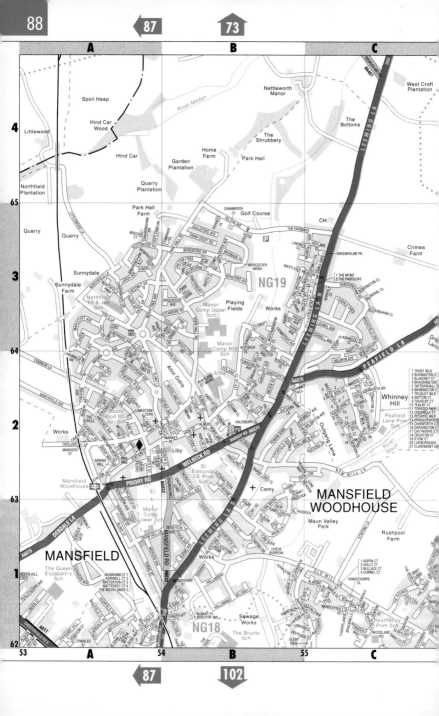

A   B   C

4

Spoil Heap

Nettleworth Manor

West Croft Plantation

Littlewood

Hind Car Wood

River Meden

The Bottoms

Hind Car

The Shrubbery

Home Farm

Park Hall

Northfield Plantation

Garden Plantation

65

Quarry Plantation

Park Hall Farm

CRANBROOK CT

FELTON AVE

Golf Course

CH

Crimea Farm

Quarry

Quarry

Quarry

GUILDFORD AVE

PEMBRIDGE CL

THE FAIRWAYS

LINDRICK CL

HOYLAKE

GREENHOLME PK

BERESFORD PL

BRISBANE CL

WORCESTER MEWS

WESTLEIGH

3

Sunnydale

Sunnydale Farm

Northfield Inf & Jun Sch

BROOKSIDE AVE

Manor Comp Upper Sch

Playing Fields

Works

HEREFORD AVE

NG19

SANDHILL

KENSINGTON CL

BELMORAL CL

BUCKINGHAM CL

64

Alfor Gdns

Manor Comp Mid Sch

NORWICH

ILKLEY CROFT

Schs

CL

C'ASHWOOD CL

LOWELL AVE

MARPLE

WELWYN AVE

PEAFIELD LA

Gre Lane

2

Works

Robin Hood Inf & Jun Sch

LIMESTONE TERR

ALBERT

Market Pl

Liby

SALISBURY RD

ROMAN BANK

WHINNEY LA

OUTGANG LA

Whinney Hill

Peafield Lane Prim Sch

River Maun

1 TRENT WLK
2 BURNASTON CT
3 BLAKENEY CT
4 BRASSINGTON
5 TATTERSHALL
6 BRIMINGTON
7 TRUSLEY WLK
8 REPTON CT
9 THURLBY CT
10 TEALBY CT
11 TORKSEY WLK
12 CRESWELL CT
13 RETFORD WLK
14 CHARLESWORTH
15 CHISWORTH CT
16 CARSINGTON
17 CASTHORPE CT
18 CROXTON CT
19 STOW CT
20 LUDBOROUGH
21 CLAREMONT CT

THE CIRCLE

MANVERS ST

OXCLOSE LA

Spring Hill

WELBECK RD

WARSOP RD A6075

St Edmunds CE Prim Sch

Mansfield Woodhouse

PRIORY RD

Cemy

MANSFIELD WOODHOUSE

63

DEBDALE LA

A6075

Manor Comp Lower Sch

LEEMING LA S

Maun Valley Park

Rushpool Farm

1 ASPEN CT
2 HOLLY CT
3 BULLACE CT
4 CORNEL CT

MANSFIELD

The Queen Elizabeth's Sch

MUSKHAM CT 1
NORWELL CT 2
MASTERTON CT 3
MATTERSEY CT 4
THE WOODLANDS 5

KINGSTHORPE CL

1

BEECH HILL CRES

MANSFIELD RD

CHESS BURROW

GLEN

Works

Heatherley Prim Sch

WOODLAND RD

A617

WOODHOUSE

HALLAM WAY

1 ALBANY PL
2 DOROTHY AVE

Sewage Works

NG18

The Brunts Sch

LONGDALE
DEEPDALE VIEW
GLEBE VIEW

62

53   A   54   B   55   C

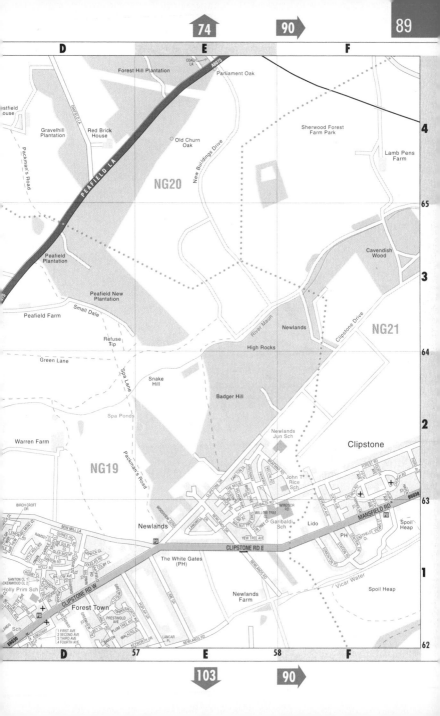

D
E
F

4

Forest Hill Plantation
Parliament Oak
COACH LA
A6075

stfield ouse

Gravelhill Plantation
Red Brick House

Old Churn Oak

Sherwood Forest Farm Park

Lamb Pens Farm

Packman's Road

PEAFIELD LA

New Buildings Drive

NG20

65

Peafield Plantation

Cavendish Wood

3

Peafield New Plantation

Small Dale

River Maun

Newlands

Clipstone Drive

NG21

Peafield Farm

Refuse Tip

High Rocks

64

Green Lane

Spa Lane

Snake Hill

Badger Hill

2

Warren Farm

Spa Ponds

Newlands Jun Sch

Clipstone

NG19

Packman's Road

John T° Rice Sch

FOREST RD

BIRCH CROFT DR

NEW MILL LA

WOODROW CT

CLIPSTONE DR

GARIBALDI RD

WINDSOR RD

Lido

MANSFIELD RD

B6030

Spoil Heap

63

Newlands

LANDMERE

WILLOW TREE

Garibaldi Sch

PH

Holly Prim Sch

The White Gates (PH)

YEW TREE AVE

CLIPSTONE RD E

1

SANTON CL 1 CKENWOOD CL 2

Vicar Water

Holly Prim Sch

CLIPSTONE RD W

Newlands Farm

Spoil Heap

Sch

Forest Town

1 FIRST AVE
2 SECOND AVE
3 THIRD AVE
4 FOURTH AVE

PRESTWOLD AVE

LANGAR PL

B6030

NEWLANDS RD

62

D
57
E
58
F

A   B   C

New Lodge
Plantation

Broomhill
Gorse

Robin Hood Way

Gorsethorpe

Forge
Bridge

4

Clipstone Junction

Halfmoon
Plantation

River Maun

Eastfield
Farm

Eastfield
Cottage

65

PH

Squires La

Cavendish
Lodge

Clipstone Dr

King John's
Palace
(rems of)

Old
Clipstone

SQUIRE CROSS

B6030

Cavendish
Wood

NG21

3

Mansfield Rd

Forest Walks
Cycle Route

Culloden
Farm

Intake
Wood

Waterfield
Farm

Culloden
Plantation

Culloden

64

Lindleys
Plantation

Vicar Water

Woodland Cl
Davis Cl
Sherwood
Pl
Baulker La
Greendale Cres

Cemy

Lib

Sch
THE CIRCLE

North Dr
Church Rd
Second
Third
South Cres

Forestry
Office

2

Colliery

Forestry
Holdings

Sherwood Pines
Forest Pk

B6030

63

Vicar
Pond

Clipstone Forest

Spoil
Heap

NG22

1

Sherwood Forest
Golf Course

62

59   A   60   B   61   C

D   E   F

B6030

King's Stand Farm

Ollerton Hills

Lidgett

ROBIN HOOD WAY

ABBEY RD

PELTON RD

SANDY LA

RUFFORD RD

A614

1 GAITSKELL CRES
2 BEARDSLEY RD
3 MERRYWEATHER CL

King's Stand Plantation

RUFFORD LA

P   Mill

4

GREENFIELD CL 1
HAWTHORNE WAY 2
OAKWOOD GR 3
PINEWOOD AVE 4
BROOKLEHURST DR 5
PORTLAND ROW 6

VEXATION LA

Rufford Lake

PH

NG21

Holly Farm

Amen Corner

The Wilderness

B6034

65

Broadoak Brake

Rufford Country Pk

Ash Tree Farm

Shooters Brake

P

Abbey (rems of)

South Forest Farm

Robin Hood Way

MAY LODGE DR

3

South Forest

Fir Tree Farm

Manor Farm

64

+

Pittance Park

Beech Hill

Rainworth Water

Sherwood Forest Holiday Village

Cremorne Wood

Beech Hill Wood

2

Blooms Gorse

Park Lodge

Clipstone Forest

NG22

Primrose Hill Farm

63

Blooms Gorse Farm

Primrose Hill

OLD RUFFORD RD

Rufford Stud Farm

Cutt's Wood

Bogs Farm

1

Toothill Wood

Robin Dam Bridge

A614

EAKRING RD

62

D   63   E   64   F

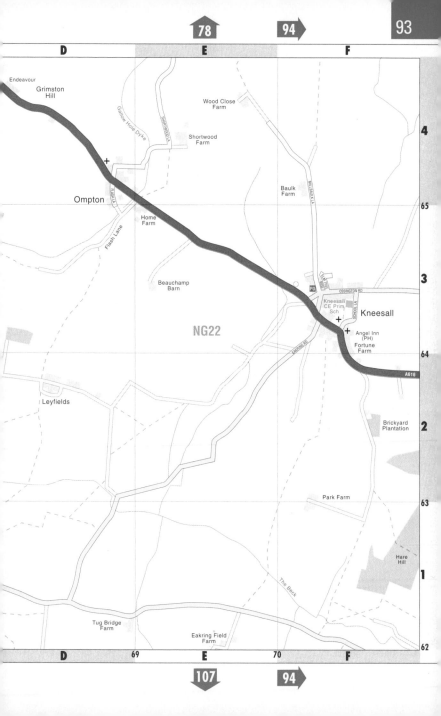

D
E
F

4

Primrose
Farm

North
Wood

Speaker's
Plantation

Primrose
Plantation

Lake
Plantation

The
Grange

Pamela
Plantation

65

+

Weir

Home
Farm

Ossington

Post Office
Farm

Hopbine
Farm

Highland
Farm

MAIN ST

Lady Elinor's
Plantation

3

Highland
Cottages

NG23

Springs
Farm

Highland La

64

Park
Lidget

Broadwaters
Farm

Broadwaters
Wood

2

63

w Tree
arm

Norwell
Lodge

Moat
Farm

Norwell Woodhouse

Lower Grove
Farm

1

Grange
Farm

Northfield
Farm

62

D
75
E
76
F

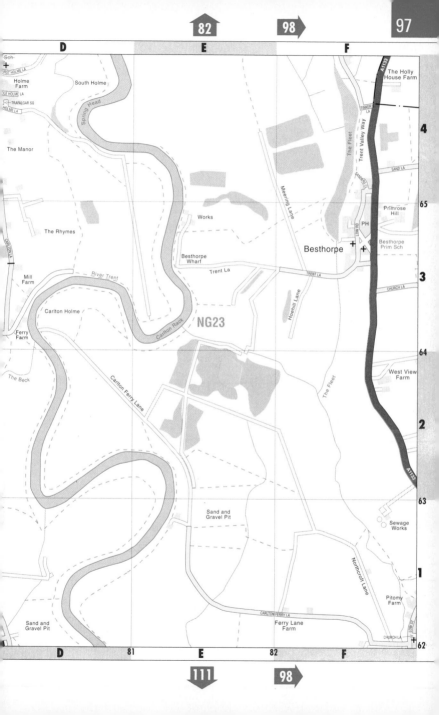

D

E

F

Sch

Holme Farm

TRENT HOLME LA

SLE HOLME LA

HOLME LA

TRAFALGAR SQ

South Holme

Spring Head

The Holly House Farm

A1133

TINKER LA

The Fleet

Trent Valley Way

4

The Manor

SAND LA

SANDBECK

Meering Lane

LOW RD

Primrose Hill

65

The Rhymes

Works

PH

Besthorpe

Besthorpe Prim Sch

Besthorpe Wharf

Trent La

TRENT LA

CHURCH LA

3

Mill Farm

River Trent

Carlton Holme

Hoehill Lane

Ferry Farm

Carlton Rack

NG23

64

The Beck

Carlton Ferry Lane

The Fleet

West View Farm

2

A1133

Sand and Gravel Pit

63

Sewage Works

Northcroft Lane

1

Pitomy Farm

Sand and Gravel Pit

CARLTON FERRY LA

Ferry Lane Farm

LOW ST

CHURCH LA

62

D

81

E

82

F

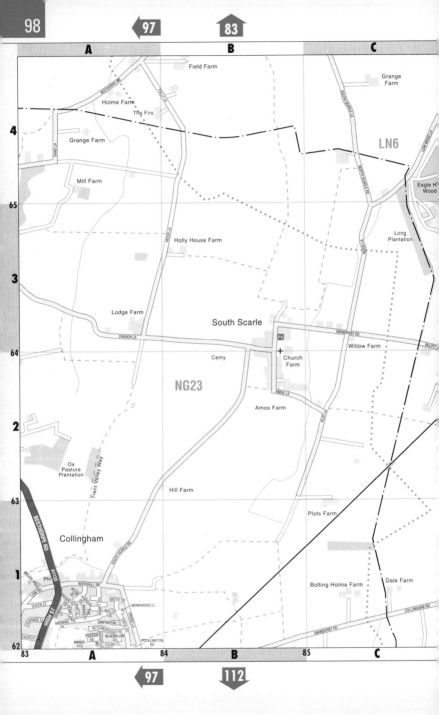

A B C

4

65

3

64

2

63

1

62

Field Farm

Grange Farm

BESTHORPE RD
Holme Farm
The Firs
Grange Farm

FEN LA

LN6

Eagle H
Wood

Mill Farm

SOUTH SCARLE LA
NORTH SCARLE RD
FEN RD
LOW WOOD LA

Long Plantation

Holly House Farm

MOOR LA

Lodge Farm

South Scarle

CHURCH LA
SWINDERBY RD
BULA RD
Willow Farm

Cemy

Church Farm

NG23

AMOS LA

Amos Farm

PLOT LA

Ox Pasture Plantation

Trent Valley Way

Hill Farm

Plots Farm

BESTHORPE RD

Collingham

SOUTH SCARLE RD

A1133

HIGH ST
CHURCH ST
QUEEN ST
WOODHILL RD
MOOR LA
MONKWOOD CL
BUTLER
CAWTHORNE CL
MEERING
PETERBOROUGH RD
FOSTER
BLACKBURN
POCKLINGTON RD
MANOR RD
FISHER CL

Bolting Holme Farm

Dale Farm

COLLINGHAM RD

SWINDERBY RD

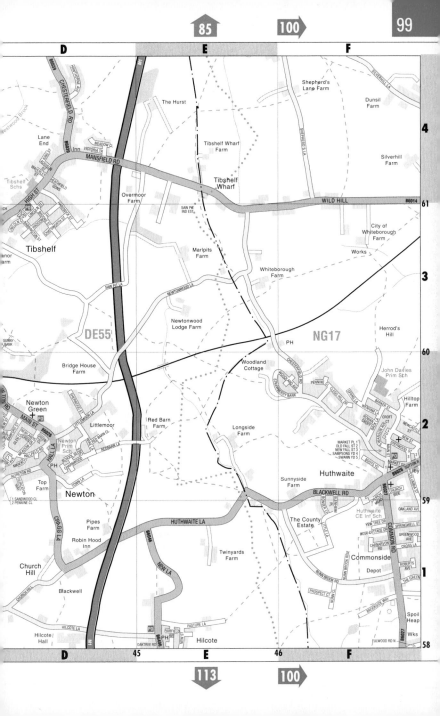

D E F

Chesterfield Rd
Whitehouse Av
B6039

Westwood Brook

The Hurst

Shepherd's
Lane Farm

Dunsil
Farm

4

Lane
End

Inn
MANSFIELD RD

Meadow Cl
Victoria Tr

Tibshelf Wharf
Farm

Silverhill
Farm

SILVERHILL LA

SHEPHERDS LA

Tibshelf
Schs

HIGH ST

HEATHFIELD
GDNS

Overmoor
Farm

Tibshelf
Wharf

WILD HILL

B6014

61

Tibshelf

Manor
Farm

SAW PIT
IND EST

Marlpits
Farm

Whiteborough
Farm

City of
Whiteborough
Farm

Works

3

SAW PIT LA

NEWTONWOOD LA

Newtonwood
Lodge Farm

PH

NG17

Herrod's
Hill

DE55

60

SUNNY
BANK

Bridge House
Farm

Woodland
Cottage

CHESTERFIELD RD

PENNINE

John Davies
Prim Sch

NW TWN RD

Newton
Green

MAIN ST

Littlemoor

SHERWOOD ST

ELMORE LA

HALL LA

Newton
Prim Sch

Red Barn
Farm

Longside
Farm

STRAWBERRY BANK

CLOSE HILL DR

GRANGE LA

Hilltop
Farm

MARKET PL 1
OLD FALL ST 2
NEW FALL ST 3
SAMPSONS YD 4
SWANN YD 5

NEWCASTLE
ST

CROFT
CT

2

PH

REDBARN LA

PH

Top
Farm

Newton

1 SANDWOOD CL
2 PENNINE CL

TOWN LA

Sunnyside
Farm

Huthwaite

BLACKWELL RD

BOOTS LA

MAIN ST

B6026

Liby

SUTTON RD

CHURCH
SIDE

OAKLAND AVE

59

CRAGG LA

Church
Hill

Pipes
Farm

Robin Hood
Inn

B6026

NEW LA

HUTHWAITE LA

Twinyards
Farm

The County
Estate

YEW TREE DR

ROSE COTTAGE CL

CARNARVON RD

Huthwaite
CE Inf Sch

COMMON RD

SPRINGWELL ST

GREENWOOD
AVE

CROSS LA

Commonside

ROBERTS
AVE

THE GREEN

1

Blackwell

GRINDLOW LA

HILCOTE LA

PASTURE LA

B6406

NEW LA

FAIRFIELD

PH

BRINDSIDE WAY

PROSPECT CL

BURN BROOK RD

BURN BROOK RISE

Spoil
Heap

B6027

FULWOOD RD N

Wks

58

Hilcote
Hall

OAKTREE RD

Hilcote

D 45 E 46 F

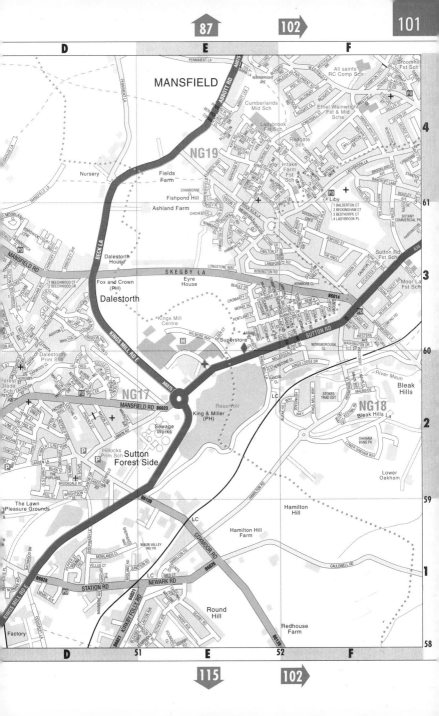

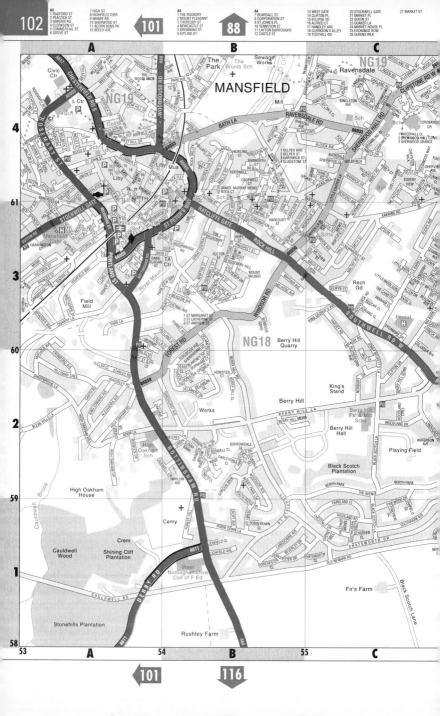

D   E   F

89
104

1 PRESTWOLD AVE
2 WALTON CL
3 STANLEY PL
4 LANGAR PL

NG19

Factory

Ind
Est

CROWN FARM WAY

Tip
(dis)

4

Sherwood Forest
Golf Course

CH

Clipstone Forest

EAKRING RD

61

1 STRAWBERRY WAY
2 FOX COVERT WAY

1 ECKINGTON WLK
2 HATHERSAGE WLK
3 HASSOP WLK
4 HADFIELD WLK
5 HEANOR WLK
6 HOLMERFIELD WLK

7 BARROWHILL WLK

Sch

NG18

The Links

Strawberry Hill

3

1 MAYFIELD CL
2 MORLEY CL
3 MACKWORTH CT
4 PINXTON CT

SOMERSBY CT
STANAGE CT

WHALEY BRIDGE
CL

PO

Ratcher Hill

NG21

60

Quarry

SOUTHWELL RD W

Dawn House
Sch

2

OAK TREE
BSNS PK

Clipstone Forest

3 WATERSON
AVE

BRAMCOTE
CT

BRADMORE
CT

BELLAMY RD

GREASLEY
CT

Old Newark Road

RANSOM RD

59

Rainworth
Nursery

THE CLOSE

LEEWAY CL

SOUTHWELL RD E

A617

Three Thorn
Hollow

1 SCARRINGTON CT
2 SHREOAKS CT
3 YEOVIL CT
4 RUDDINGTON CT
5 BODMIN CT
6 TUXFORD CT
7 TROWELL CT
8 THORNEY CT
9 TRESWELL CT
10 TITHEY CT
11 WILLOUGHBY CT
12 SHARRATT CT
13 CLAYWORTH CT
14 EPPERSTONE CT
15 WHATTON CT
16 CLAVERTON CT
17 EDWALTON CT
18 FARNSFIELD CT
19 EATON CT
20 FISKERTON CT
21 WALESBY CT

Three Thorn Hollow
Farm

Heathlands
Fst Sch

Bishopshill Plantation

1

Foulevil Brook

L Lake

Lindhurst Lane

Lake View
Prim Sch

58

D   57   E   58   F

D
E
F

Deerdale Farm

Clipstone Forest

Robin Hood Farm

Forest Walks Cycle Route

Letterbox Farm

Birch Belt

4

Sewage Works

Machin's Gorse

LANDSBURY RD
OAK RISE
NORTH DR
VALLEY RD
SPRING WAY

MICKLEDALE CL

MICKLEDALE LA

61

Featherstone House Farm

THE CRESCENT
ALMOND AV
NEW RD

PO
CHURCH S RD

Inkersall Farm

Bilsthorpe

CHERRY CL
CUL DE SAC
OLD DE SAC
CROSSHILL DR
LIME CL

Inkersall Manor

Bilsthorpe Inf Sch

3

Rainworth Water

Red Bridge

Hage's Wood

Damside Covert

NG22

60

Crifton Lodge

HIGHFIELD RD

2

OLD RUFFORD RD

Rook Wood

Forest Lane

Lockwell House Farm

RINGFIELD RD

59

Lockwell Hill Wood

A617

Cottage Farm

KIRKLINGTON RD

1

Lockwell Hill Farm

Cockett Plantation

COCKETT LA

Cockett Barn Farm

A614

58

2
D
63
E
64
F

A   B   C

SWAB LA

Mill Hill

Tenters Land

SIDE LA

TRIUMPH RD

BLACK LA

TRIUMPH CL

Mill Lane

Mill Lane

Robin Hood Way

4

Brail Lane

Depot

61

Eakring Brail Wood

Coultas Farm

CHURCH ST

BRAILWOOD RD

BLENCOW DR L

3

Long Springs Wood

Pudding Poke Wood

Manor Farm

FERN CL

KINGS WOOD LA

WOODRUFF LA

CHURCH HILL

CLUMBER WY

HERBERT GLADE

ARCHERS DR

ST MARGARET'S CL

Fox Holes

Whip Ridding

BENET DR

CHAPPEL GDNS

60

NG22

Redgate Wood

MAID MARION AVE

RUFFORD

Fox Holes

WYCAR RD

HIGHFIELD DR

COTTAM CR

FARMER RD

Whip Ridding Farm

2

Wycar Leys

Middle Plantation Farm

Bilsthorpe Moor

BRANDRETH LA

Belle Eau Park

Summer House Plantation

Egg Hatchery

59

Swiss Cottage

A617

KIRKLINGTON RD

Willows Farm

1

NG21

Upper Hexgreave

Hexgreave Park

Archway House

A617

58

Camp Hill

65   A   66   B   67   C

109
96

A   B   C

Model
Farm
Church
Farm

Beck Bridge
New Farm

Milestone Farm
Laurels Farm

NORWELL LA

LC

Cromwell House
Farm

PO
Sch
FAIR VALE
SCHOOL LA
OLD HALL

4

The Beck

Norwell

Cromwell

CHURCH LA

MAIN ST

GREAT NORTH RD

61

Fox
Covert

3

Foxholes Farm

NG23

Lodge
Farm

60

CAUNTON RD

Sunnybrook
Farm

Mousehole Corner

VICARAGE LA

Bracken
Farm

LC

Fallows End

Norwell
Crossing

Manor
Farm

2

THE PARK

THE GRANGE

Cogley Lane

Bathley

MAIN ST

CHAPEL LA

Northroad
Farm

GREAT NORTH RD

WILLOW DR

CHAPEL LA
PO

Trent
Farm

59

MUSKHAM LA

GREEN LA

Cordon
Lodge

BATHLEY LA

Lord
Nelson
Inn

MELTON 3 LA

MACKLEYS LA

TRENT

River Trent

The Cottage

Mill
House

LC

FERRY LA

PH

MELTON LA

EASTFIELD

Oak
Farm

Downside
Cottage

ST WILFRIDS CL

Muskham
Prim Sch

TEETS DR

The Old
Hall

MARSH LA

1

Hopyard Lane

Moorhouse Lane

Moor
House

BATHLEY LA

GREAT NORTH RD

North
Muskham

MEADOW CL

Mill Lane

Mill House

MILL LA

B6325

A1

CHURCH LA

58

77   A   78   B   79   C

109
124

D E F

WHITE HART LA
TEMPERANCE LA
BAPTIST LA

Horse Pool

WESTFIELD LA

Manor Farm

Westfield
Farm

THE GREEN

4

DYKES
END

SOUTH END

Cromwell Lock   Weir

61

WEST BROOK LA

The Ness

Trent Valley Way

Sand &
Gravel Pit

Willow Farm

Mill Close
Farm

3

River Trent

Coney
Green

Cottage Lane
Crossing

WHITEMOOR LA

NG23

60

Slough Dyke

Whitemoor
Farm

Lodge Farm

Grange Farm

LC

Trow
Bridge

2

South View
Farm

Lowfield
Farm

Holme

The Hall

LC

LANGFORD LA

HOLME LA

Gothic House Farm

59

The
d Hall

Manor House

Langford

1

Elmtree
Farm

NG24

Langford Home
Farm

58

D   81   E   82   F

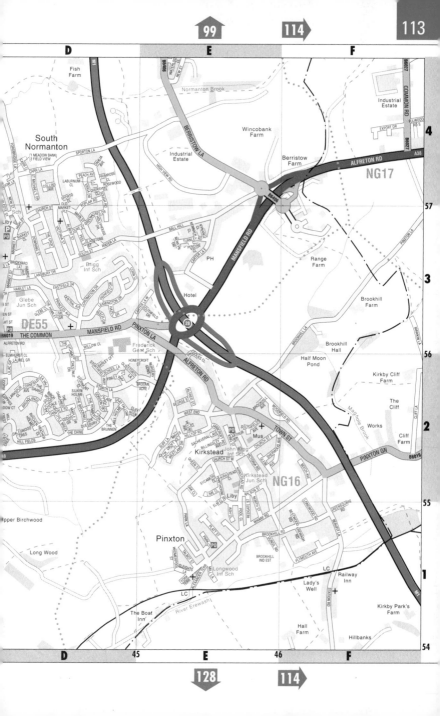

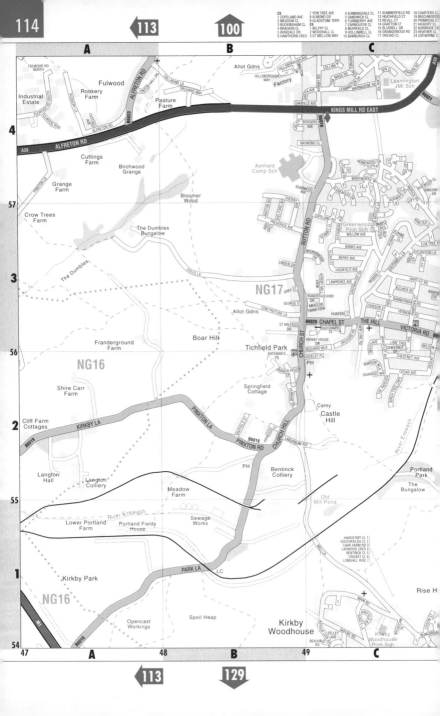

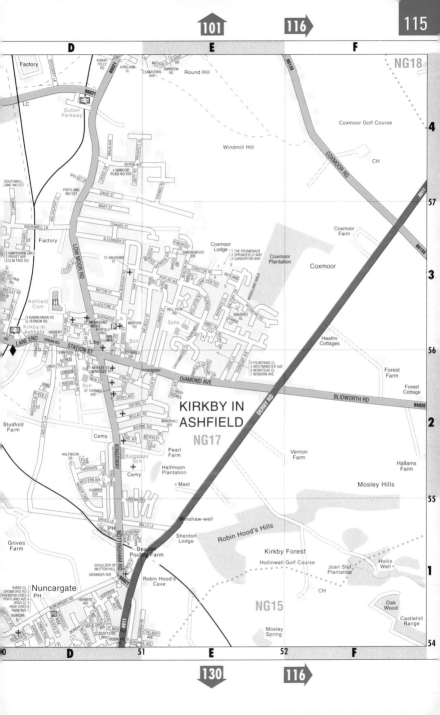

D **E** **F**

Lindhurst La

Lindhurst
Farm

NG18

Rainworth

The
Joseph Whitaker
Sch

Rainworth
Lodge

The Archer
(PH)

New
Farm

Cottage
Farm

4

57

Providence
Farm

High Park

Norwood Hill
Close

Fountain
Dale

Greenfields

Robin Hood Way

Copt Hill
Farm

Brick Kiln
Hill

3

Ling
Farm

RICKET LA

NG21

Redgate
Farm

Norwood Hill
Farm

56

Rock
Farm

PH

MAIN ST

PH

2

Silverland
Farm

PH
ROBIN HOOD
TERR

Fishpool
Farm

FISHPOOL RD

Tel Ex

MAIN RD

Cottage
Farm

1 CHERNSIDE
2 STANLEY CL
3 CASTLETON

55

Schs

SWINTON RISE

NG15

Bottom
Farm

PH

Woodland Rise 1
Ridgewood Gr 2

PH

Robin Hood Way

Jackson's
Hill

1

Sch

Ravenshead

BIRCHWOOD CL

Blidworth
Dale

54

D 57 **E** 58 **F**

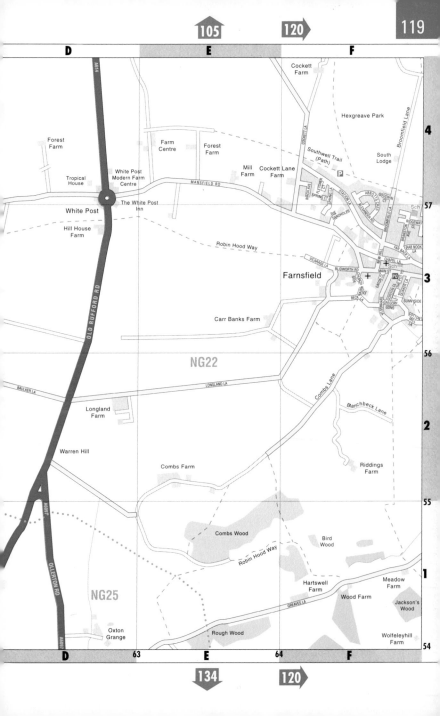

D
E
F

4

Forest
Farm

Cockett
Farm

Hexgreave Park

Broomfield Lane

Farm
Centre

Forest
Farm

Southwell Trail
(Path)

South
Lodge

Tropical
House

White Post
Modern Farm
Centre

MANSFIELD RD

Mill
Farm

Cockett Lane
Farm

P

COCKETT LA

BRICK LEYS

FLETCHER SPRINGFIELD

STATION RD

ABBOTTS CLO

GOLDING

Sch

57

White Post

The White Post
Inn

The CHRONICLES

RIDGEWAY

A614

OLD RUFFORD RD

Hill House
Farm

Robin Hood Way

VICARAGE LA

BLIDWORTH RD

HAZEL LA

FAR BACK LA

CRAB NOOK LA

Sch

Farnsfield

MAIN ST

PO

3

Carr Banks Farm

BECK

GREGORY GDNS

SUNNYSIDE

COTTON LA

NG22

56

BAULKER LA

LONGLAND LA

Combs Lane

Blanchbeck Lane

2

Longland
Farm

Warren Hill

Combs Farm

Riddings
Farm

55

A6097

OLLERTON RD

Combs Wood

Bird
Wood

Robin Hood Way

1

Hartswell
Farm

Meadow
Farm

NG25

Wood Farm

Jackson's
Wood

Oxton
Grange

GREAVES LA

Rough Wood

Wolfeleyhill
Farm

54

A6075

D
63
E
64
F

A   B   C

4

Lower Hexgreave
Farm

Hexgreave
Park

Home
Farm

NEWARK RD

Kirklington

Kirklington
Cty Prim Sch

Mill Farm

SCHOOL

Park
Plantation

River Greet

Moor Farm

Robin Hood Way

57

RIDGEWAY CL
D'AYNCOURT WLK

MEADOW CL

THE RIDGEWAY

WOODINGS

LONG MEADOW

MILLDALE RD

GREENWOOD CL

BRICKYARD LA

Osmanthorpe
Manor

Pumping
Station

Southwell Trail

Spring's
Farm

Collyeat
House

3

1 CRAB NOOK LANE
2 CHAPEL LA
3 MAIN ST

Cotton Mill Dyke

NG22

Edingley Beck

STATION RD

COTTON MILL LA

Sewage
Works

Edingley
Mill

Valley
Farm

PH

Edgehill
Prep Sch

Harlow
Fields

56

Cotton Mill
Farm

ALLISFORD LA

MANSFIELD RD

MAIN ST

Manor House
Farm

Edingley

LONGS LA

STATION RD

Diamond
Cottage
Farm

2

New Manor
Farm

GREAVES LA

LITTLE LA

Woodendale

Grange
Farm

Halam
Mill

Old
Hall
Farm

Halam
Beck

55

Littledale

ST HELEN ST A

New Hall
Farm

WINDLES LA

Halam
CE Sch

SCHOOL

1

DARKES HOLLOW

Little Turn Croft
Farm

Brockley
Farm

Middlebeck
Farm

GRAY LA

ST MICHAEL

Halam

PH
HALAM

Wolleyhill La

Machin's
Farm

CHURCH ST

DIXIE LA

Manor
Farm

Halam House
Farm

Turncroft
Farm

Cutlersforth

54

65   A   66   B   67   C

D
E
F

4

Rodney Sch

Hall Farm

Greet Farm

FB

Winkburn Park

Hockerton Moor Wood

Hockerton Road Farm

Intake La

Hockerton Moor Farm

A617

Brickfield Farm

Hockerton Dumble

NG25

Wyton Lodge Farm

57

3

Meadow Farm

Far Corkhill Farm

NG22

Cork Hill

CORKHILL LA

Norwood View

Middle Corkhill Farm

Little Corkhill Farm

Goldhill Cottages

56

Goldhill Farm

River Greet

The Old Silk Mill

Halam Park

Robin Hood Way

Maythorne Farm

Maythorne

2

Halam Osier Beds Wood

NG25

Chestnut Farm

55

Maythorn Orchard

Nurseries Normanton

Crow Wood

The Hall

Norwood Park

MERRYWEATHER

SOUTHWELL

1

Norwood Hill

Lodge Plantation

Nurseries

Norwood Park Farm

Jun Sch

Liby

Ct

ALLENBY RD

HALAM RD

WOODLAND VIEW

QUEEN ST

BULL YD

BURGAGE LA

BURGAGE LA

HEYWOOD CL

54

COOKS LA

8

69

70

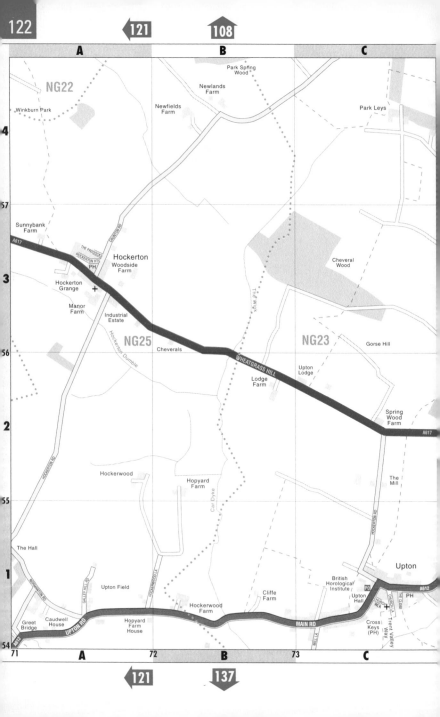

121
108
121
137

A
B
C

NG22

Winkburn Park

Park Spring Wood

Newlands Farm

Newfields Farm

Park Leys

4

57

Sunnybank Farm

A617

THE PADDOCKS
HOCKERTON HTS
PH

CHURCH ST

Hockerton

Woodside Farm

Cheveral Wood

3

Hockerton Grange

Manor Farm

Industrial Estate

Hockerton Dumble

NG25

Cheverals

Trent Wyk

NG23

Gorse Hill

WHEATGRASS HILL

Lodge Farm

Upton Lodge

56

Spring Wood Farm

A617

2

Hockerwood

Hopyard Farm

Car Dyke

The Mill

HOCKERTON RD

55

The Hall

Upton

SOUTHWELL RD

SALTER HALL RD

HOCKERWOOD LA

Upton Field

Cliffe Farm

British Horological Institute

Upton Hall

PO

A612

PH

1

CHURCH LA

THE CLOSE

Greet Bridge

A612

Caudwell House

UPTON RD

Hopyard Farm House

Hockerwood Farm

MAIN RD

BELL LA

Cross Keys (PH)

Trent Valley Way

54

71
A
72
B
73
C

125
112

A   B   C

NG23

Thorpe Field Farm

Danesthorpe Hill

NG23

Danethorpe Hill Farm

Little Danethorpe Farm

High Wood

LN6

4

57

Lingspot Farm

Langford Moor Farm

3

Langford Moor

Stapleford Wood

NG24

56

Newark Air Museum

Northlea

Drove Cottage Farm

The Bungalow

2

Moor Brats

The Cottage

Moor Plantation

Flawford Farm

55

Coddington

The Tinderbox

Hall Farm

PH

THE GREEN

Coddington Moor

SLEAFORD RD

1

Coddington CE Prim Sch

Manor Farm

Kelwick Wood

Vale Farm

Newark Golf Course

Club House

54

83   A   84   B   85   C

125
141

D
E
F

4

Kirkby
Park

PARK LA
B6018

Kirkby
Lane
Farm

RIDGE END
AVE

MANITOBA
WAY

Spoil Heap

Kirkby Park's
Farm

CHAPEL ST
VICTORIA RD

Selston
Holly Hill Sch

DEETELTON
CL

NEWSTEAD CL

HARDWICK
CL
UPPER
MEXBOROUGH

LOMAS CL
DR

MIDLAND
DRES

VICTORIA RD

HOLLYHILL RD
ANNIES EX CT

Selston
Common

Annesley
Lane End

BRENCASTER CT

Skegness

PH
Woodnook

NOTTINGHAM RD

Alma

ALMA RD

Middlebrook
Farm

Millington
Springs

NG16

Middlebrook
Bridge

MIDDLEBROOK LA

Middle Brook

New
Bagthorpe

Shipton Hill
Farm

Selston
Bagthorpe
Prim Sch

SCHOOL RD

ALFRETON RD

Bagthorpe
Plantation

LAWRENCE
PARK

BANKHILL
RD

BEECH RD

CHURCH LA

PH

B600

Friezeland

OLD CHAPEL LA

DE MORGAN
CL

PETTERSDALE RD

Underwood

MAIN RD

PO

FELLY MILL LA S

MILL CL DR

CORDY LA

B600

Willeylane
End

Willey
Spring

Haggs
Farm

Greasley Haggs

Felley
Farm

Felley Priory
Farm

Felley
Priory

FELLY MILL LA E

Felley
Mill

Bleak Hall
Farm

Cemetery

GREENHILL
LA

VICARAGE WAY

THORNHAM CRES

Annesley
Woodhouse

Nuncargate

MAIN ST

FOREST RD

PO

Salmon
Farm

Salmon La

NG17

Cuttail Brook

Two Dale
Farm

Boggs
Farm

53

Sherwood
Park

Davis's
Bottom

Works

3

Home
Farm

A608

52

27

MANSFIELD RD

Audrey
Wood

HEVERS LA

William
Wood

NG15

2

America
Farm

Pamela's
Larches

The
Dumbles

51

1

Park
Springs

M1

50

D
48
E
49
F

D E F

NG21

Far Tops

HAYWOOD OAKS

A614

Robin Hood Way

BLIDWORTH LA

Archer's Water Farm

OAKS LA

4

Forest Walk

Little Tithe Farm

Oakmere Park Golf Course

53

Club House

NG25

Darcliff Hill

G15

Big Tithe Farm

OLD RUFFORD RD

Salterford Farm

SALTERFORD LA

Salterford Dam

3

Salterford House Sch

LONGDALE LA

52

War Memorial

Gorse Covert

Sansom Wood Farm

Oxton Bogs

2

Watchwood Plantation

OLLERTON RD

Beanford Farm

BEANFORD LA

Bean Ford

hmond arm

NG14

WINKBURN LA

Spoil Heap

51

NOTTINGHAM RD

B6386

Lodge Farm

Whitehaven Farm

Thorndale Plantation

1

OXTON RD

DAGBELLY HOLLOW

B6386

Calverton Colliery

PEVERIL LA

NORTH GREEN

KYLES

MANSFIELD LA

CARRINGTON LA

50

D 60 E 61 F

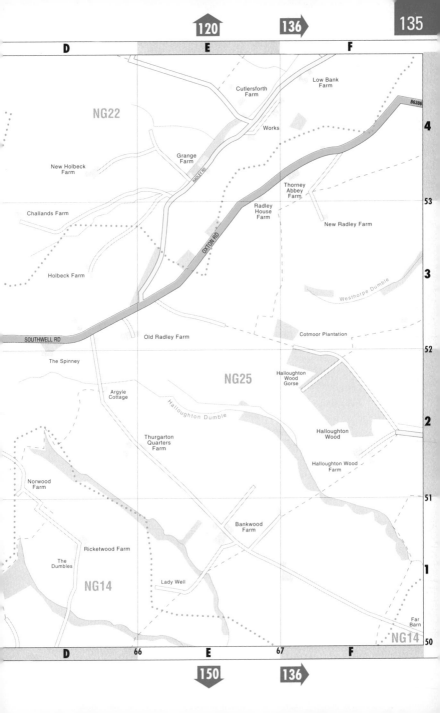

D
E
F

NG22

Cutlersforth
Farm

Low Bank
Farm

B6386

Works

4

Grange
Farm

New Holbeck
Farm

B6197 RD

Thorney
Abbey
Farm

53

Radley
House
Farm

New Radley Farm

Challands Farm

OXTON RD

Westhorpe Dumble

3

Holbeck Farm

SOUTHWELL RD

Old Radley Farm

Cotmoor Plantation

52

The Spinney

NG25

Halloughton
Wood
Gorse

Argyle
Cottage

Halloughton Dumble

2

Thurgarton
Quarters
Farm

Halloughton
Wood

Norwood
Farm

Halloughton Wood
Farm

51

Bankwood
Farm

Ricketwood Farm

The
Dumbles

1

NG14

Lady Well

Far
Barn

NG14

50

D
66
E
67
F

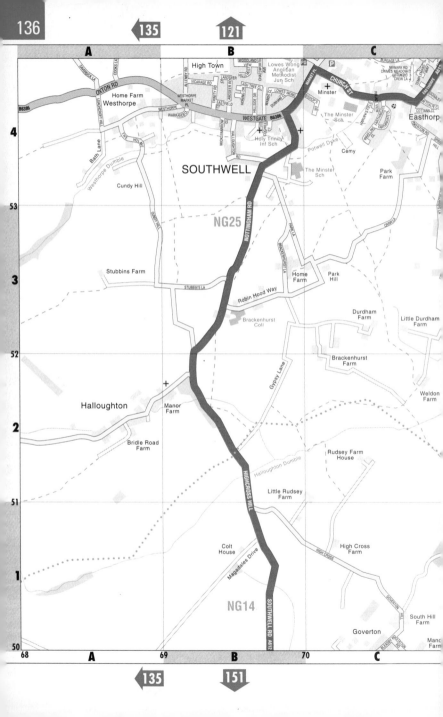

A

B

C

Staythorpe

PINGLEY CL

BERAY GDNS

4

LC

Staythorpe
Power Station

LC

53

CROFT FARM CL

MANOR CL · CROFT CL

STAYTHORPE RD

Greenaway

Rolleston
Gorse

Baggarley Rack

The
Crown Inn

Rundell Dyke

LC

SEATON RD

3

Rolleston

HOLL CT

Ferry
(foot)

Rolleston Field

The Lazy Otter
(PH)

Norwood
Farm

NG23

FISKERTON RD

River Greet

Trent Valley Way

52

Swillow Lane

CHURCH ST

PRIEST RD

NG24

River Trent

Fiskerton
Mill

WEST

ST PETER'S CL

SLEAFORD CL

Main St

2

NG25

A46

51

FOSSE RD

Gawburn Nip

1

Gawburn Holt

P

Wharf
Farm

Stoke
Hall

The Park

A46

Thorpe

CHURCH LA

50

74

A

75

B

76

C

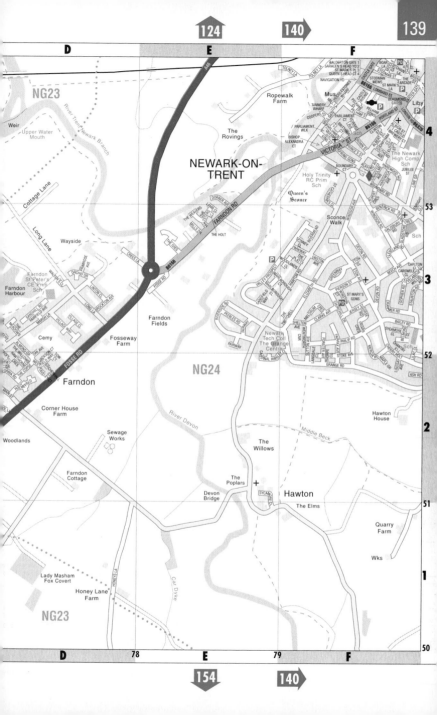

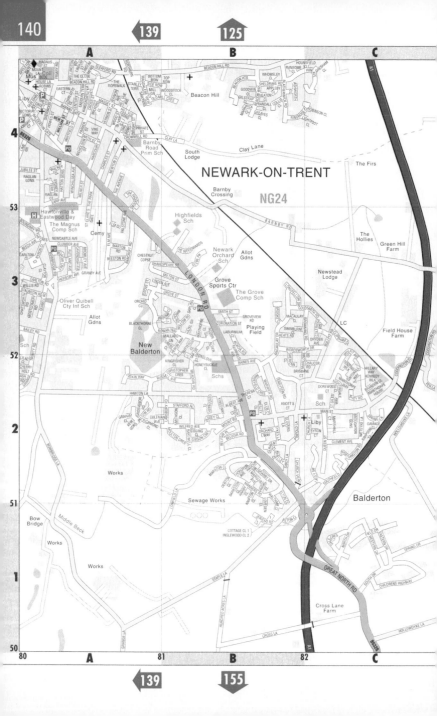

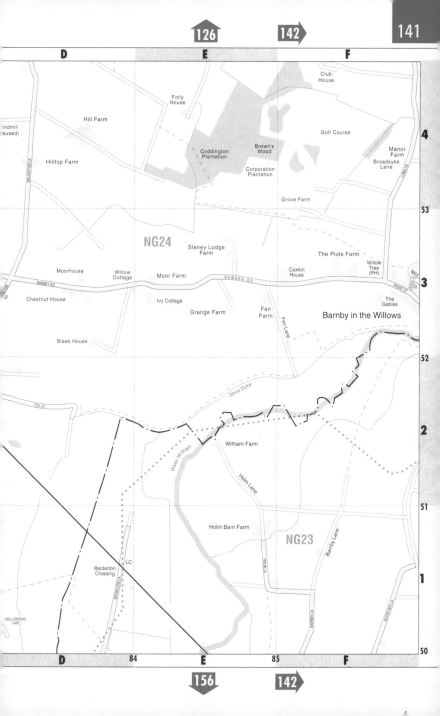

D
E
F

Club House

Folly House

Hill Farm

Golf Course

indmill (sused)

Coddington Plantation

Brown's Wood

Manor Farm

BALDERTON LA

Hilltop Farm

Corporation Plantation

Broadsyke Lane

FIRBECK LA

4

Grove Farm

53

NG24

Slaney Lodge Farm

The Plots Farm

Moorhouse

Willow Cottage

Moor Farm

NEWARK RD

Caxton House

Willow Tree (PH)

BACKLANE COVENT CLOSE

3

RD FLOW

BARNBY RD

FRONT ST

Chestnut House

Ivy Cottage

Grange Farm

Fen Farm

Fen Lane

The Gables

Barnby in the Willows

Bleak House

52

FEN LA

Shire Dyke

2

River Witham

Witham Farm

Holm Lane

51

Holm Barn Farm

NG23

Barnby Lane

1

HOLM LA

HOLLOWDYKE LANE

Balderton Crossing

LC

BRIDGE FEN LA

BARNBY LA

OUTER FEN LA

50

D
84
E
85
F

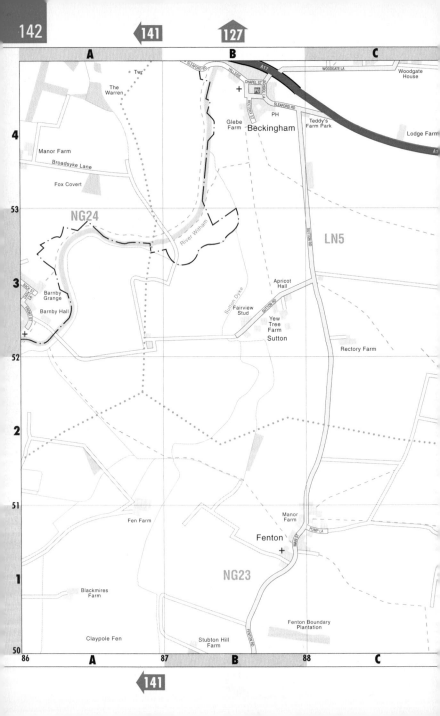

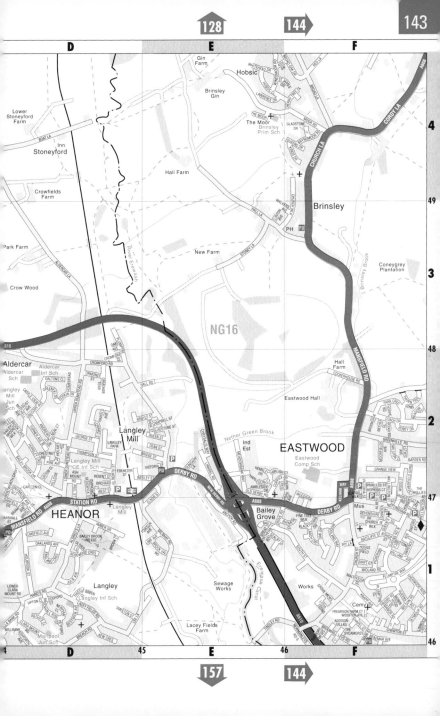

A   B   C

4

Willey Spring

Great Haggs Plantation

High Park Wood

Morning Springs

NG15

Willey Wood Farm

WILLEY LA

HUNT'S HILL

B6009

Oaks Farm

Moorgreen Reservoir

Beauvale House

Beauvale Priory (remains of)

Robin Hood's Well

49

Beauvale Abbey Farm

New Rd

Lamb Close

The Dumbles

Beauvale Lodge

Beauvale Manor Farm

3

Coneygrey Farm

NG16

48

Manor House

Moorgreen

PH

B6000 MOORGREEN

2

EASTWOOD

Greasley

Greasley Castle Farm

Sledder Wood

Bogend

DICKS LA.

CHURCH RD

47

PH

BEAUVALE

Greasley Beauvale Jun Sch

Beauvale

Robin Hood Way

Greasley Castle (remains of)

Cliff Brook

Hill Top

Newthorpe

NOTTINGHAM RD E

Brookhill Leys Inf Sch

Robin Hood Way

CHAWORTH AVE

B6010

DOVECOTE RD

Parkside Sch

Newthorpe Common

Reckoning House Farm

Watnall Wood

MAIN RD

B6010

LANCELOT DR.

46

47   A   48   B   49   C

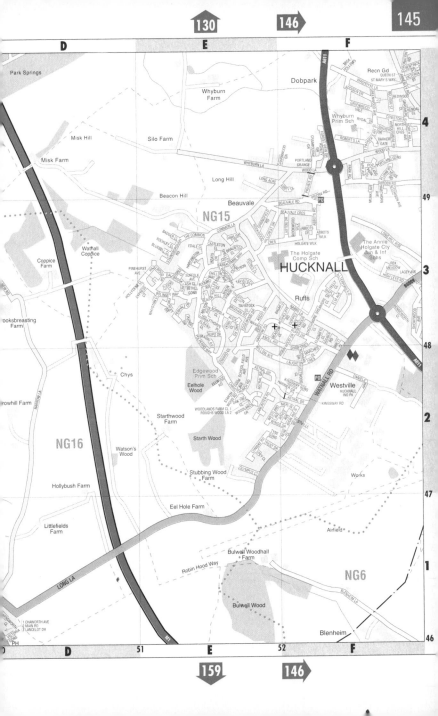

A B C

1 BROXTOWE DR
2 BENTINCK ST
3 NEWSTEAD TERR
4 VICTORIA ST

ST ANDREW'S CL

ST MARY'S CL

ST
JAMES'S
ST

ST
GEORGE'S

Sch

Leisure
Centre

1 KERSALL GDNS
2 KNEESALL GR

LC

Leen Mills
Sch

4

Liby

MKT
PL

The Connery

PO

BEECH
LA

LOYCROFT
AVE

Hucknall

HUCKNALL

The Duck Ponds

Sports
Ground

Robin Hood Way

COPELAND

49

WATNALL RD

Coll

NG15

Butler's
Hill

HATHS
LA

Hucknall Golf
Course

Hucknall
Golf Course

1 RUFFORD CL
2 CAVENDISH CL
3 BUTLERS CL

BAKER BROOK
IND PK

Cobbler's
Hill

MOOR RD

3

A6009

HIDDEN
CHATSWORTH

WOODFORD
RD

Park

WINFIELD

WHYBURN
ST

ASHDALE

Hazelgrove

Cemy

Butlers Hill
Sch

KAYNARD CL

LC

BROOMHILL PARK
VIEW

Allot
Gdns

Westhouse Farm

FORGE MILL
GR

48

GLENDON

ARLINGTON
CL

ELDER
GR

LIME TREE

SURTON GR

LEEN VALLEY WAY

Broomhill

The Bowman
(PH)

Mill Lakes
Country Park

THE
SPINNEY

CORONATION
RD

HILL RD

Schs

THE
MOUNT

BRIDGE VALLEY

**Bestwood
Village**

2

A611

Farley's Lane

SHELTON RD

Allot
Gdns

Broomhill
Farm

River Leen

MAYES
WLK

PARK RD

PO

P

**Broadvalley
Farm**

Shaft
(dis)

47

Airfield

Home
Wood

Robin Hood Way

Mills

Bestwood
Country Park

Nature
Reserve

NG6

NOTTINGHAM

1 COLINWOOD AVE
2 JENNESS AVE
3 CROWTHORNE GDNS
4 HOUSTON CL

HEXHAM GDNS 1
TITHE GDNS 2
MUIRFIELD RD 3
LYTHAM GDNS 4
MEREGILL CL 5
ECTON CL 6
TERTON RD 7
HELMSDALE GDNS 8
THORPGDNS 9
CARLSWARK GDNS 10

1

City Golf Course

Bulwell Hall Park

HOWDEN RD

LONGFORD CRES

GOODLIFF RD

HUCKNALL LA

ASTON
DR

CALDON
GN

BROWNLOW DR

WILLFIELD

MILLFIELD

BARDFIELD
GDNS

HAVERHILL CRES

WANSTEAD WAY

NG5

A611

BESTWOOD RD

Barker's
Wood

ACLE
GDNS

CH

Springfield
Prim Sch

LAWTON DR

NAOMI
CT

LEEN DR

HUCKNALL RD

REVELSTOKE
AVE

ARCH

ABBOTSBURY CL

CROWTHORNE WAY

REVELSTOKE WAY

BARRHEAD
CL

3W

PO

Rise Park

EARLSFIELD DR

ELMSHAM

RISE PARK

BRACKNELL

OLD FARM

PINE HILL CL

Liby

TOP VALLEY DR

Schs

46

MORRIVATH GDNS

CAMBERLEY RD

A6002

SANDHURST RD

A6002

BESTWOOD PARK DR W

LANGDALE
AVE

53 A 54 B 55 C

D · E · F

4

Goosedale Farm

Raceground Hill

Duke's Cottage

Cottage Wood

Robin Hood Farm

OXTON RD

B6386

49

Round Hill Plantation

Sunnyside Farm

Ramper Covert

Ramsdale House

GOOSEDALE LA

Twelve Acre Farm

MANSFIELD RD

Forest Farm

OLLERTON RD

Bottomhouse Farm

3

Six Ways Stables

Hundred Acre Boarding Kennels

NG6

Squires Drive

Knightwood Drive

Sunrise Avenue

Crimea Plantation

Mushroom Farm

B684

Tophouse Farm

48

Little Lime Lane

Limelane House

LAMINS LA

Lamins Lane

Robin Hood Way

LIME LA

B684

The Old Rectory

PARK RD

A60

OLLERTON RD

A614

Warrenhill Plantation

NG5

2

Alexandra Lodges

Violet Hill

Leapool

Garage

Big Wood

Country Park

Japanese Plantations

Red Hill

Stockings Farm

47

Gaunt's Hill

New Farm

BERRY HILL RD

A60

BROMPTON

Big Wood Sch

Fire Brigade HQ

Works

ARNOLD

COGENHOE WLK 1
SIBSON WLK 2

1

PENTLAND DR

CAIRNGORM DR

CHILTERN CL

Sch

FRENCHURCH

Bestwood Lodge

P

The Strip

CEDAR TREE

WOODCHURCH RD

Redhill

Sch

GLEN PARVA AVE

P

L Ctr

46

TOWNSEND

JACKLIN GDNS

BESTWOOD PK DR W

EVEDON WLK

1 MOSS CL
2 BULLINS CL
3 TREE VIEW CL

SALCOMBE DR
REDHILL LODGE DR
SALCOMBE CIRCUS
PENDINE CL

Cemy

THE MOUNT

CRANSTON

D1
1 HEXHAM GDNS
2 TITHE GDNS
3 BENEDICT CT
4 BONIFACE GDNS
5 WEARMOUTH GDNS
6 LINDISFARNE GDNS
7 MASSON CT
8 GOATCHURCH CT
9 HEATHINGTON GDNS

10 TREVINO GDNS
11 WHITCOMBE GDNS
12 CHEVIN GDNS
13 CROSSFIELD DR
14 COXMOOR CT
15 WOOD VIEW BSNS CTR
16 LOCKWOOD CL
17 PARKLANDS CL
18 SNOWDON CL

19 WHITTON CL
20 BESTWOOD PARK DR

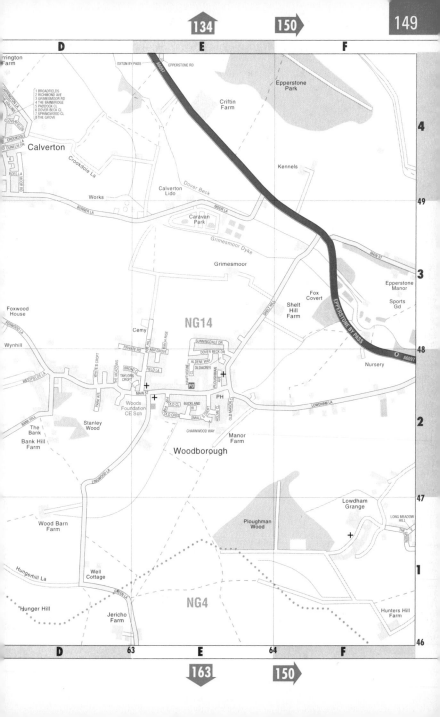

D E F

rrington
Farm

Oxton BY PASS EPPERSTONE RD

1 BROADFIELDS
2 RICHMOND AVE
3 GRIMESMOOR RD
4 THE BAINBRIDGE
5 PADDOCK CL
6 DOVER BECK CL
7 SPRINGWOOD CL
8 THE GROVE

Criftin
Farm

Epperstone
Park

Calverton

Crookdale La

Kennels

4

Works

Dover Beck

Calverton
Lido

49

Caravan
Park

MOOR LA

Grimesmoor Dyke

Grimesmoor

NG14

Epperstone
Manor

3

Fox
Covert

SHELT LANE

Shelt
Hill
Farm

Sports
Gd

MAIN ST

Foxwood
House

Cemy

EPPERSTONE BY PASS

Wynhill

FOXWOOD LA

PRIVATE RD
ASH GROVE
BIRCH RISE

SUNNINGDALE DR

DOVER BECK DR

ALDENE WAY

OLDACRES

WHITE'S CROFT

FIELD LA

BROWNS
TAYLORS
CROFT

HAWTHORNE

PLOUGHMAN AV

48

WESTFIELD LA

THE MEADOWS

PO

Nursery

Bank Hill

The
Bank

Stanley
Wood

PARK AVE

MAIN ST

OLD CL

OLD CRES

BUCKLAND
DR

SMALLS

PH

OLD MANOR CL

OLD MANOR GR

LOWDHAM LA

2

Bank Hill
Farm

LINGWOOD LA

CHARNWOOD WAY

Woodborough

Manor
Farm

47

Wood Barn
Farm

Ploughman
Wood

Lowdham
Grange

LONG MEADOW
HILL

THE GREEN

Hungerhill La

Well
Cottage

NG4

1

Hunger Hill

GREEN LA

Jericho
Farm

Hunters Hill
Farm

46

D 63 E 64 F

A   B   C

NG25

Hill Farm

Thurgarton Beck

Brockwood
Farm

Starling
Hall

Foxhole
Wood

4

Cottage
Farm

Thistly Coppice

Green
Acres

Souther
Wood

Southerw
Barn

Eastwood
Farm

49

Hagg Farm

Hagg Lane

Hagg
Cottage

Older Beck

Bentley
Wood

PHELPS CROFT
DAMES LA
CHURCH LA

Epperstone

PH
MAIN ST
DAMES LA

PARR LA

3

Netherfield
Farm

Older Beck

Playing
Field

Netherfield Farm
House

48

A6097

Wash Bridge

NG14

Leland's
Dumble

LOWDHAM LA

EPPERSTONE BY-PASS
OLD EPPERSTONE RD

Nursery

Car Holt
Farm

GONALSTON LA

Dover Beck

2

Nurseries

Lowdham
Mill

Eliment Hill
Farm

Vicarage

Carr B
Bar

The Hut

The
Hermitage

Cliff
Mill

47

LONG MEADOW HILL

Lowdham
CE Sch

EPPERSTONE RD
THE
LEVS

Cliff Mill
Farm

HILL SIDE

ROCKLEYS
VIEW

Grove
Farm

The
Old Hall

Liby

DR PARKER HILL

Barker Hill

SOUTHWELL RD

Norrisden

Cocker Beck

LAMBLEY RD

STATION RD

MAIN ST
ST
MARY'S

TON LA

MANOR
HOUSE

PO

BLACKTHORNE DR

OAKLEIGH DR

1

BELLA

WILLOW
HOLT

1 NOTTINGHAM RD
2 VICTORIA AVE
3 WORCESTER CL

Lowdham

A6097
B6386

PILGRIM SE

TRUSSEY CL

CRITCHLOW RD

46

65   A   66   B   67   C

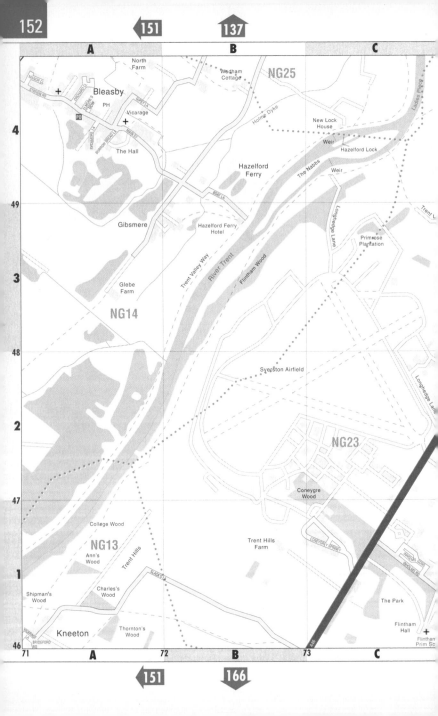

151
137

A **B** **C**

North Farm

Wedham Cottage

NG25

Manor La

Bleasby

STATION RD

Holme Dyke

New Lock House

4

PH

Vicarage

Hazelford Lock

Weir

The Hall

Hazelford Ferry

The Nabbs

Weir

49

Gibsmere

Hazelford Ferry Hotel

Longhedge Lane

Primrose Plantation

Trent L

3

Trent Valley Way

River Trent

Flintham Wood

Glebe Farm

NG14

48

Syerston Airfield

Longhedge Lane

2

NG23

47

College Wood

Coneygre Wood

NG13

Trent Hills Farm

CONEYGRE SPRING

1

Ann's Wood

Trent Hills

BLACK LA

The Park

Shipman's Wood

Charles's Wood

Flintham Hall

Flintham Prim Sc

46

Kneeton

Thornton's Wood

BRIDGFORD RD

A **B** **C**

71 72 73

151
166

153
139

A   B   C

4

Thorpe
Lodge

NG24

49

Honies Farm

The
Grange

Car Dyke

3

MOOR LA

River Devon

48

Fox Covert

Manor
Farm

Meadow Farm

NG23

Cotham

2

Carrgate Lane

The Old
Hall Farm

Devon Farm

47

Back Dyke

LANE

1

Grange Farm

BRECKS LA

Elston
Grange

Station
House

46

77   A   78   B   79   C

D
E
F

4

49

3

48

2

47

1

46

Staple Farm

NG24

Hundred Acres Lane

Balderton Grange

Cowtham House

A1

B6326

B6326

Shire
Bridge

GREAT NORTH RD

Holmes
Farm

Shirebridge
Farm

Shire Dyke

Bennington Fen

Fen Farm

Cotham
Thorns

ORANGE LA

Willow Tree
Farm

FEN LA

Fen Lane
Farms

NG23

Pasture Lodge
Farm

Cotham
Buildings

Askerton Hill

Red House
Farm

A1

Bennington Lodge
Farm

Valley Lane
Cottages

White House
Farm

Stonepit
Plantation

VALLEY LA

Middle
Farm

D
81
E
82
F

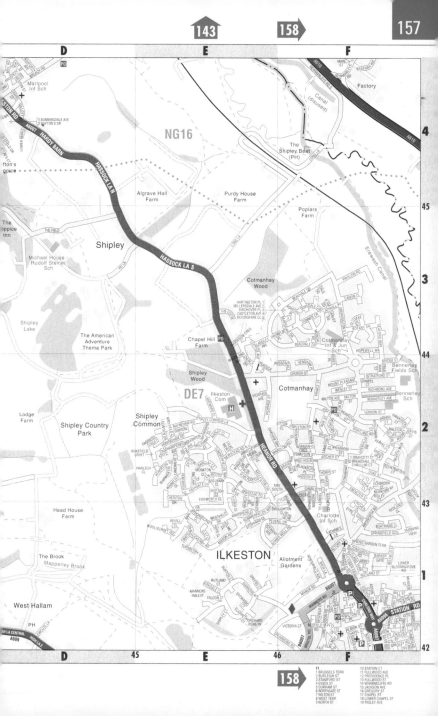

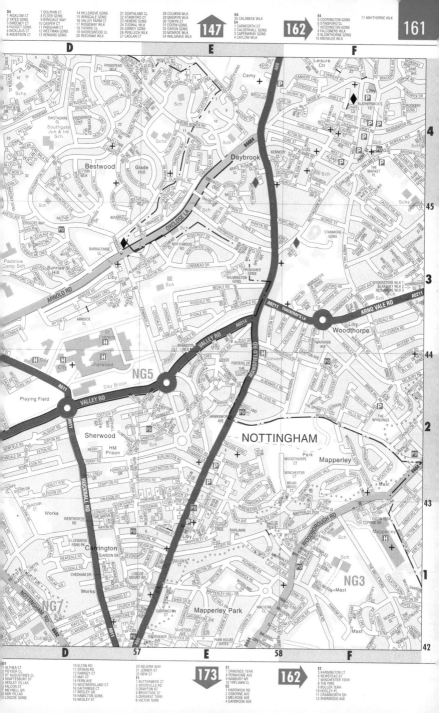

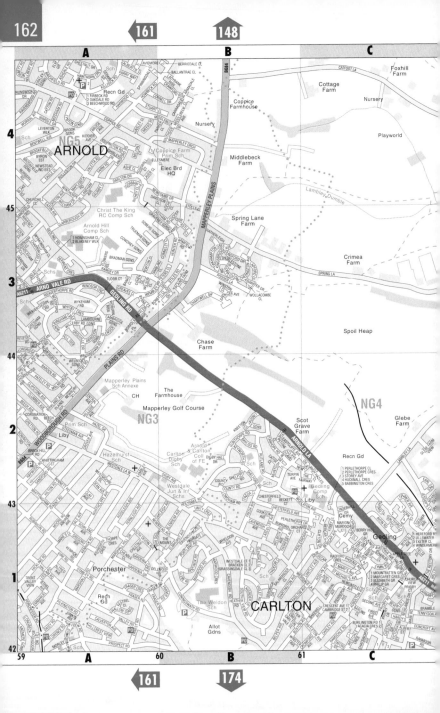

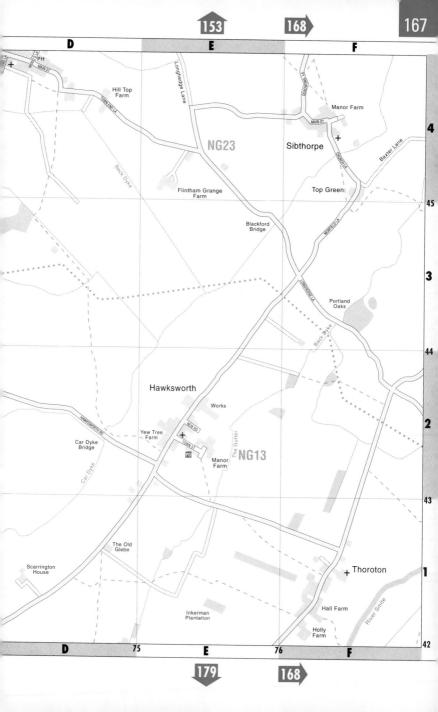

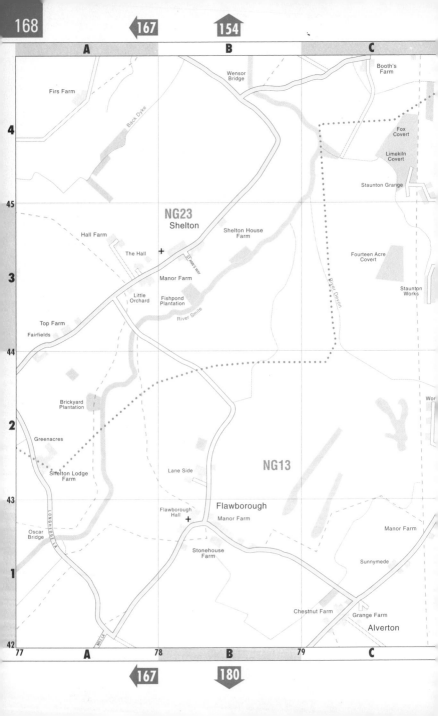

167
154

A

B

C

4

Firs Farm

Black Dyke

Wensor Bridge

Booth's Farm

Fox Covert

Limekiln Covert

Staunton Grange

45

NG23
Shelton

Hall Farm

The Hall

Shelton House Farm

Fourteen Acre Covert

3

Manor Farm

Little Orchard

Fishpond Plantation

River Smite

River Devon

Staunton Works

Top Farm

Fairfields

44

Brickyard Plantation

2

Greenacres

NG13

Lane Side

Wor

Shelton Lodge Farm

43

Flawborough Hall

Flawborough

Manor Farm

Manor Farm

Oscar Bridge

LONGHEDGE LA

Stonehouse Farm

Sunnymede

1

Chestnut Farm

Grange Farm

Alverton

42

77

A

78

B

79

C

167
180

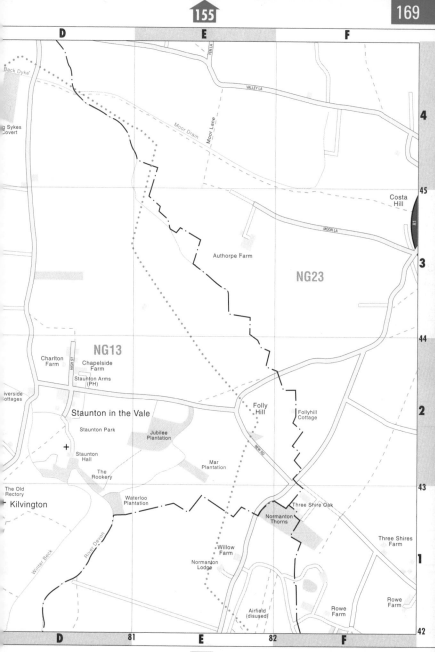

D **E** **F**

Back Dyke

g Sykes
Covert

VALLEY LA

Moor Drain

Moor Lane

FEN LA

4

45

Costa
Hill

A1

MOOR LA

Authorpe Farm

NG23

3

44

NG13

Charlton
Farm

HIGH ST

Chapelside
Farm

Staunton Arms
(PH)

iverside
ottages

Staunton in the Vale

2

Staunton Park

Jubilee
Plantation

Folly
Hill

Followhill
Cottage

Folly Hill

NEW RD

Staunton
Hall

The
Rookery

Mar
Plantation

The Old
Rectory

Kilvington

Waterloo
Plantation

43

Three Shire Oak

Normanton
Thorns

Three Shires
Farm

Winter Beck

River Devon

Willow
Farm

Normanton
Lodge

1

Rowe
Farm

Airfield
(disused)

Rowe
Farm

42

D 81 **E** 82 **F**

A   B   C

NG16

Oldmoor Wood

Shortwood Farm

ILKESTON

Larklands

Cemy

Field House

Robbinetts Arm (dis)

River Erewash

Meadow Farm

Gallows Inn

Robin Hood Way

Trowell Service Area

Trowell Moor

Grange Wood

Shortwood House

Moor Cottage

Trowell

Uplands Farm

Trowell Junction

Trowell Hall

Potter's Plantation

NG9

Trowell CE Sch

Hill Rise

Factories

Hallam Fields Lock

Nottingham Rd

Swancar Farm

Hallam Fields

Sewage Works

Nottingham Canal (disused)

Works

DE7

Stanton Works

Crompton Road Ind Est

Works

Stapleford Road

Field Farm

Junction Lock

Stapleford Hill

STAPLEFORD

Works

Ilkeston Rd

Trowell Rd

Stanton-by-Dale

Pasture Rd

Hickings La

Golf Course

Stanton Gate

Works

47   A   48   B   49   C

41 40 39 38

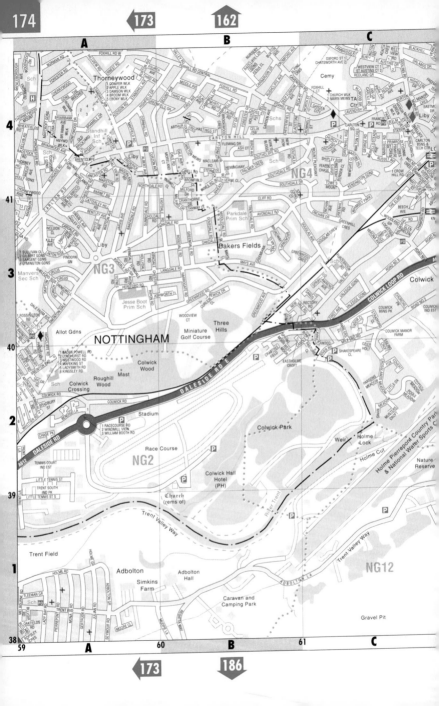

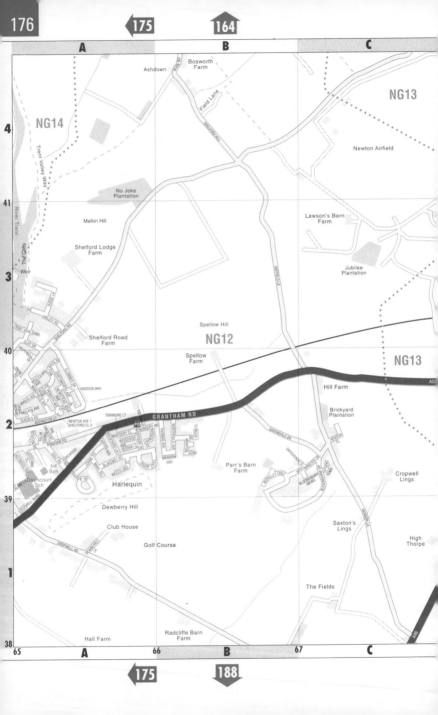

179
168

A
B
C

4

Lodge
Farm

LONGHEDGE LA

MILL LA

Orston Cty
Prim Sch

Orston

MILL LA

Sports
Ground

41

LONGHEDGE LA

River Devon

Winter Beck

LONGHEDGE LA

HILL RD

Manor
Farm

LONGHEDGE LA

Mushroom
Farm

3

Elton &
Orston

NG13

40

Occupation La

LC

Piggeries

ORSTON LA

2

Oldfield
Plantation

LONGHEDGE LA

Camp
Farm

39

Nursery

Highfield
Farm

NOTTINGHAM RD

Greenacres

A52

1

Orston
Grange

BARKESTONE E

38
77
A
78
B
79
C

179
192

D   E   F

River Devon

Piggery

Airfield
(disused)

Ease Drain

NG23

Normanton
Hall

Normanton
House

Peacock
Farm

Little Covert
Farm

Normanton

Elm Farm

Home Farm

NG13

Sewage
Works

Beacon Hill

LC

Rectory
Farm

The
Jook

Beckingthorpe

WINTERBECK
CL

LC

Bottesford

Bottesford

DEVON LA.

Ford

CHAPEL ST

WYGGESTON
AVE

O.S.STATION YD

FLEMING AVE

1 WEST END CL
2 NOTTINGHAM RD
3 BOWBRIDGE LA

ST MARY'S LA

HAND'S
WLK

RUTLAND LA.

ST MARY'S

PH

PO

WALNUT
RD

SILVERWOOD CL

Sch

BELVOIR AVE

JAY'S

Belvoir
High Sch

HOWITT'S RD

The
Elms

Manor
Farm

MANOR RD

GREEN LA

Easthorpe

South
View

River Devon

SHERRY LA

Castleview
Farm

CASTLE VIEW RD

MUSTON LA

Corner
Farm

A52

Winterbeck
Bridge

A52

CASTLE VIEW RD

EASTHORPE LA

Hospital
Farm

Muston

D   81   E   82   F

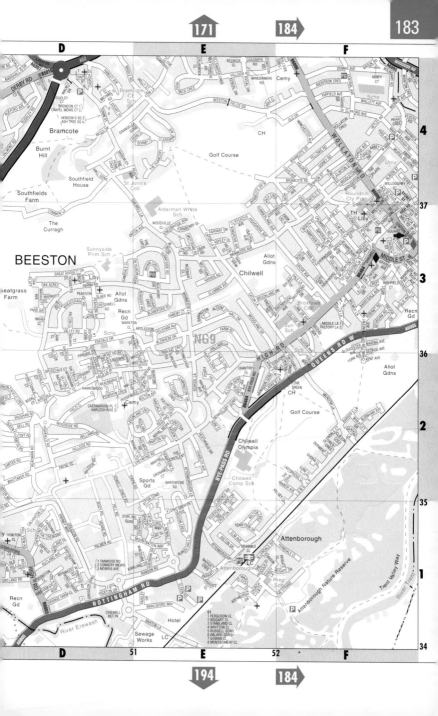

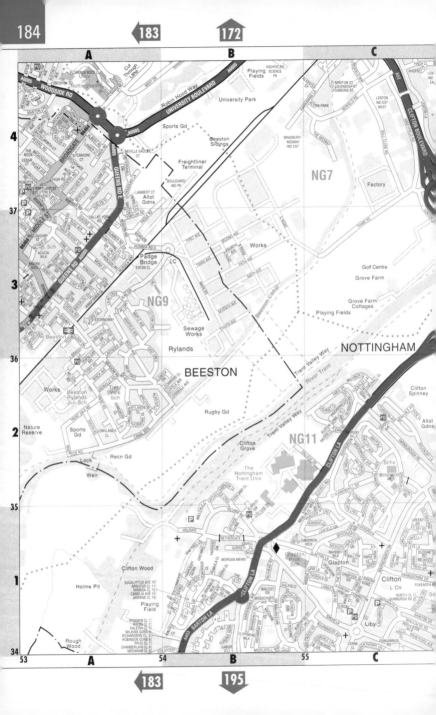

A B C

4

Tythby
Grange

Manor
Lodge

Crane's
Covert

37

Smite Hill Covert

Moat
Covert

River Smite

3

Wiverton
Hall

Smite Hill
Farm

NG13

36

Northfield
Farm

Wiverton
Smite
Bridge

BINGHAM RD

2

Walnuts
Farm

Church
Farm

MAIN RD

ORCHARD CL

Roadside
Farm

Barnstone

NG12

Stroom Dyke

Works

Works

35

Langar CE
Sch

Hall

Langar

P

PH

Works
Farm

1

Stroom Dyke

CROPWELL RD

Wild Flower
Farm

Ragnal
Farm

HARBY RD

COLSTON LA

Works

Stroomfields

LANGAR LA

34

71 A 72 B 73 C

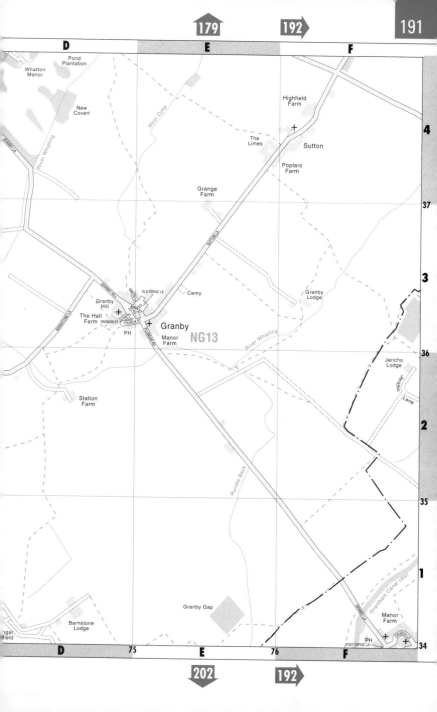

D E F

Pond
Plantation
Whatton
Manor

New
Covert

Moor Dyke

River Whipling

GRASMERE LA

Highfield
Farm

The
Limes

Sutton

Poplars
Farm

4

Grange
Farm

37

SUTTON LA

GRASMERE HILL

GREEN LA

OLD FORGE LA

Cemy

Granby
Lodge

3

Granby
Hill

CHAPEL LA

MAIN RD

The Hall
Farm

DRAGON ST

CHURCH ST

Granby

NG13

River Whipling

Jericho
Lodge

JERICHO
Lane

36

BARNSTONE LA

PH

Manor
Farm

ELSINGER RD

River Whipling

Station
Farm

Rundle Beck

2

35

1

Granby Gap

GRASMERE LA

Grantham Canal (dis)

Barnstone
Lodge

Manor
Farm

ngar
field

POST OFFICE LA

PH

CHURCH LA

34

D 75 E 76 F

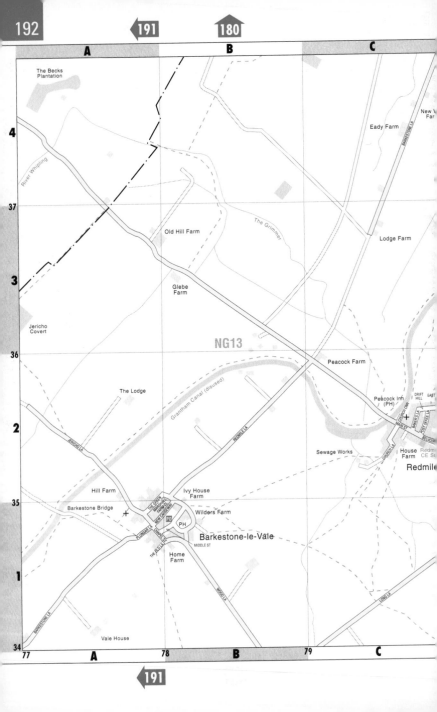

04
1 HARTSIDE GDNS
2 PORLOCK CL
3 MICKLEDON CL
4 COTSWOLD CL
5 MALVERN CL
6 BRECON CL
7 BREDON CL
8 INGLEBOROUGH GDNS
9 THE PLANTATIONS
10 COPSESIDE CL

182   194   193

Breaston
DE72

Wilsthorpe
West Park
LONG EATON

New Sawley

Long Eaton
Lower Sch

St Lawrence
CE Prim Sch

Factory
Wks

Sawley

NG10

Golf Course
Narrow Bridge

Trent
Rifle Lodge

South Junction

Cranfleet
Farm

Trent Farm

Sheetstores
Junction

Trent Junction
Trentlock

Church Farm
Grounds Farm
Trent Navigation
Inn (PH)

Harrington Bridge

River Trent
Club

Sailing
Club

Sawley Bridge
Marina

Sawley Cut

Midshires Way

Thrumpton
Park

Wood
Hill

Red
Hill

NG11

Ratcliffe on Soar
Power Station

Redhill Lock

DE74

Lockington Grounds
Farm

Redhill
Farm

Ratcliffe
Junction

193
183

A   **B**   **C**

NOTTINGHAM ROAD

HARLAXTON DR

Sewage Works

Attenborough Nature Reserve

Barton Island

SOMERSET CL

The Warren

Long Eaton Sailing Club

River Erewash

NG9

Trent Valley Way

River Trent

Grange Farm

4

Golden Brook

1 WARWICK RD
2 LITCHFIELD CL
3 RUGELEY AVE

Attenborough Junction

Old Farm

ST LUKE'S RD

NEW RD

LC

33

LC

1 THRUMPTON AVE
2 CHATSWORTH AVE

Trent Meadows (Picnic area)

Manor Farm

Barton in Fabis

MEADOW LA

JONES CL

Home Farm

Trent Valley Way

LITTLE LONDON

MANOR RD

3

JUNCTION RD

NG10

FASTDYKE LA

GREEN ST

32

NG11

Cranfleet Lock

Glebe Farm

2

Cranfleet Canal

Ferry Farm

Fields Farm

Thrumpton

Thrumpton Park

Thrumpton Hall

Manor Farm

Crowhole Wood

CHURCH LA

31

Church Farm

Wood Farm

Gotham Hill

Old Wood

Twenty Lands Plantation

Gotham Hill Wood

Wright's Hill

Wright's Hill Plantation

Hillside Cottage

1

Cottagers Hill

Power Station

M53

Cottagers Hill Spinney

Morley's Barn Farm

Stonepit Wood

30

50   **A**   51   **B**   52   **C**

193
204

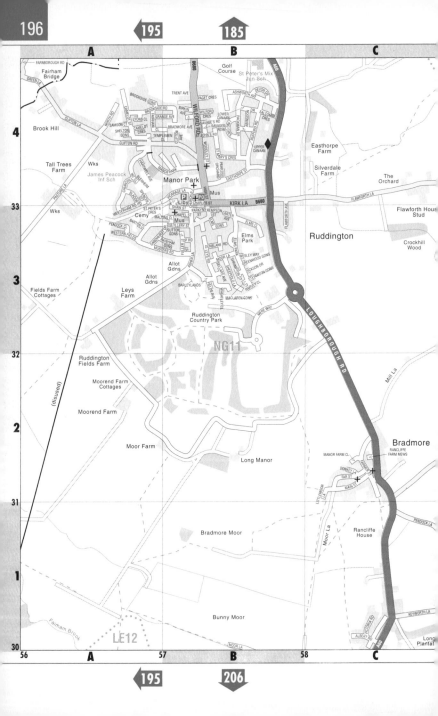

195
185

A   **B**   **C**

FARNBOROUGH RD

Fairham
Bridge

GREEN LA

Golf
Course

St Peter's Mix
Jun Sch

4

Brook Hill

CLIFTON LA

TRENT AVE

B680

PAGET CRES

ASHWORTH AVE

DEVON RD

WILFORD RD

A60

BROOKSIDE GDNS

BIRKIN AVE

BROOKSIDE RD

LYONS CL

GRANGE AVE

WILFORD CRES

LOWER CANAAN

SALCOMBE CRES

Tall Trees
Farm

SAMSON CT

SHELTON GDNS

CAMP LO

CAMEL CL

TEMPLEMAN CL

BRADMORE AVE

JAMES'S RD

SAVAGES RD

ROW'S RD

Wks

CLIFTON RD

James Peacock
Inf Sch

PASTURE LA

ST MARY'S CRES

Easthorpe
Farm

UPPER CANAAN

33

Wks

Manor Park

CARAGE LA

Mus

KIRK LA

B680

Silverdale
Farm

FLAWFORTH LA

The
Orchard

ST PETER'S CRES

Cemy

SHAW ST

CHAPEL ST

MALTING ST

DISTILLERY ST

CHARLES ST

PARKYNS ST

KEMPSON ST

CARTER AVE

ELMS RD

Ruddington

Flawforth House
Stud

Liby

Mus

SUTTON GDNS

NOTTINGHAM GDNS

MUSTERS RD

TOP RD

DUNBLANE RD

MOOR LA

ELMS GDNS

Elms
Park

WESLEY WAY

GREENWOOD GDNS

FLAWFORTH AVE

Crockhill
Wood

3

Fields Farm
Cottages

PEACOCK CL

WESTERN FIELDS

Leys
Farm

Allot
Gdns

Allot
Gdns

BARLEYLANDS

EASTHORPE ST

WHEATLEY CL

BARTON CL

ASHER LA

SHERWIN CL

WILFORD RD

WHEATLEY CL

HARLEY CL

BENSON DR

STEPHENSON GDNS

MACLAREN GDNS

Ruddington
Country Park

MERE WAY

LOUGHBOROUGH RD

32

(disused)

Ruddington
Fields Farm

Moorend Farm
Cottages

NG11

Mill La

2

Moorend Farm

Moor Farm

Long Manor

Bradmore

MANOR FARM CL

RANCLIFFE
FARM MEWS

DONKEY LA

TAR ST

LITTLEMOOR LA

MAIN ST

31

PENDOCK LA

Bradmore Moor

Moor La

Rancliffe
House

A60

KEYWORTH LA

1

Fairham Brook

LE12

Bunny Moor

VICTORIA RD

ALBERT RD

Long
Plantat

30

56   **A**   **57**   **B**   **58**   **C**

195
206

186
198

D   E   F

BENTINCK AVE

STELLA AVE

Flawford
House

MELTON RD

A606

4

Hall
Farm

FELLOWS

CHURCH LA

OLD MELTON

THE LEYS

CLIPSTON LA

PD

PH

SADDLERS YD

33

Plumtree

The
Poplars

Chestnut
Farm

BRAMMORE LA

3

Barn
Farm

Blackcliffe
Hill

NG11

NG12

Plumtree
Park

STATION RD

Crossdale Drive
Prim Sch

GREEN CL

32

POPLARS CL

PLATT LA

HILLCREST RD

Cotton's
Plantation

DEBDALE LA

SPINNEY RD

HAYES RD

PLANTATION RD

INTAKE RD

FAIRHAM RD

CROFT RD

PARK AVE W

PARK AVE

Greenhays
Farm

Keyworth
Prim Sch

ROSE HILL

BARNETT

FEIGNES
CT

ASHLEY CRES

WYNNDALE DR

ASH CL RD

CHURCH DR

LYNCOMBE
GDNS

WOLDS RISE

2

Liby

PO

South Wolds
Comp Sch

FAIRWAY

BEECLARS

ASH GR

31

Woodfields

Rancliffe Wood

WEST CL

EAST CL

HAWTHORN CL

WRIGHTS
ORCHARD

WEST AVE

BUNNY LA

Wheatcroft
Farm

Hillside
Farm

ELM CL

PH

THE SQUARE

SELBY LA

LINE TREE CL

Keyworth

PENDOCK LA

KEYWORTH LA

WIGHT RD

Long Plantation

Bunny Park

Woodfields

HOLGATE

BARROW SLADE

BRICK KILN LA

CEDAR DR

PH

LINGS LA

Holly
Farm

1

Sewage
Works

New Holme
Farm

Lings Lane
Farm

30

D   60   E   61   F

207
198

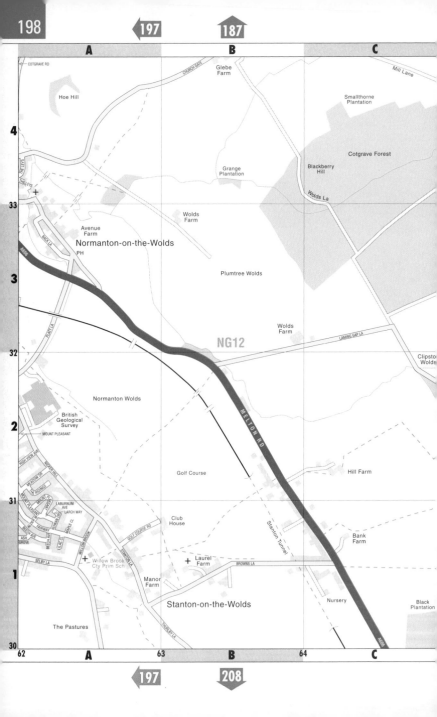

D E F

Wolds Hill
OWTHORPE RD
A46
Bells
Stud Farm

Taylors
Wolds
Fox
Holes
Nanny's
Plantation

Fishpond
Wood

STANK LA

Owthorpe
Hill

CHURCH ST

VILLAGE ST

Owthorpe

Fishpond
Cottage

4

Herrywell La

Borders
Wood

PARK LA

33

Cotgrave
Wolds

Woodman's
Cottage

Mackley's
Farm

Owthorpe
Wolds

Garston's
Hill

Newfield
Farm

Mackley's
Bridge

3

Wolds Farm

NG12

Wild's Bridge

32

KINGSTON LA

Barn
Farm

GAP LA

Devil's Elbow

Wynnstay
Wood

Owthorpe
Lodge

2

OWTHORPE LA

Lodge on the
Wolds

Kinoulton
Gorse

Vimy
Ridge

Grantham Canal
(disused)

GARDNER
DR

BROOK DR

Roundhill
Spinney

Woodlands

31

MEADOW WA

CHAPEL LA

TITHBY RD

+

LANGDALE GROVE

Blacks
Farm

MAIN ST

Kinoulton
Prim Sch

1

Kinoulton
Wolds

Ivy
Farm

KINOULTON LA

Needham Hill
Farm

Roehoe Wood

A46

30

D 66 E 67 F

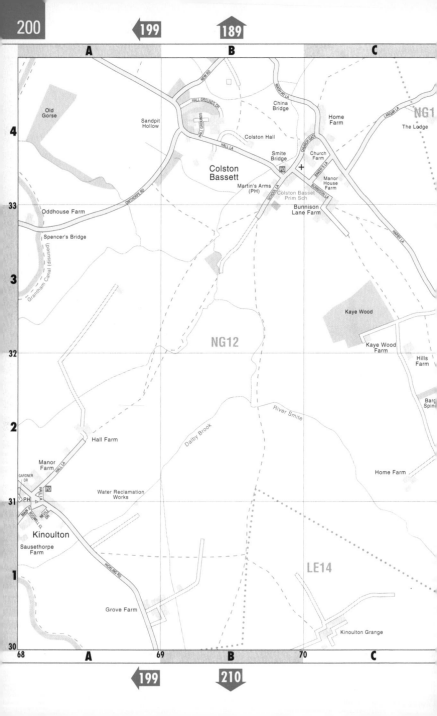

199
189

A   B   C

NG1

INDIA RD

HALL GROUNDS DR

HALL GROUNDS

China
Bridge

Home
Farm

NROTT PK LA

The Lodge

LANGAR LA

Sandpit
Hollow

Colston Hall

4

HALL LA

Smite
Bridge

Church
Farm

Church Farm

CHURCH GATE

Colston
Bassett

Martin's Arms
(PH)

Colston Bassett
Prim Sch

SCHOOL LA

Manor
House
Farm

BUNNISON LA

SMITE LA

33

Oddhouse Farm

OWTHORPE RD

Bunnison
Lane Farm

Spencer's Bridge

HARBY LA

Grantham Canal (disused)

3

Kaye Wood

Kaye Wood
Farm

Hills
Farm

32

NG12

Barc
Spin

River Smite

2

Hall Farm

Dalby Brook

Home Farm

Manor
Farm

GARDNER
DR

HALL LA

BOWNELL DR

MAIN ST

31

PH

Water Reclamation
Works

Kinoulton

Sausethorpe
Farm

LE14

1

HICKLING RD

Grove Farm

Kinoulton Grange

30

68   A   69   B   70   C

199
210

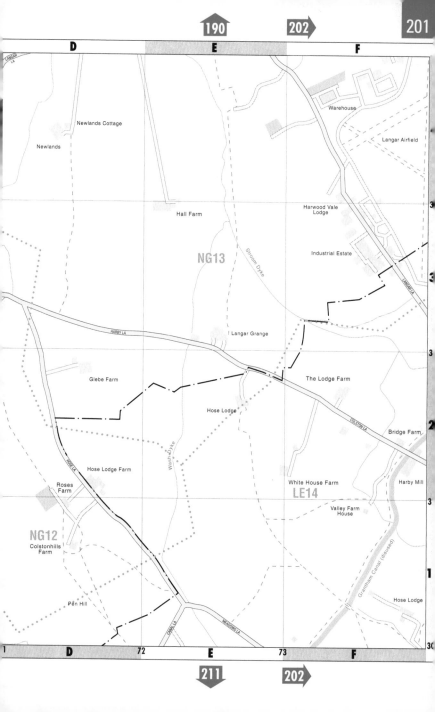

D   E   F

Warehouse

Langar Airfield

Newlands Cottage

Newlands

Harwood Vale
Lodge

Hall Farm

NG13

Industrial Estate

Stroom Dyke

LANGAR LA

Langar Grange

HARBY LA

Glebe Farm

The Lodge Farm

COLSTON LA

Hose Lodge

Bridge Farm

Wash Dyke

Hose Lodge Farm

White House Farm

LE14

Harby Mill

Roses
Farm

Valley Farm
House

NG12

Colstonhills
Farm

Grantham Canal (disused)

Pen Hill

Hose Lodge

CANAL LA

MEADOWS LA

D   72   E   73   F

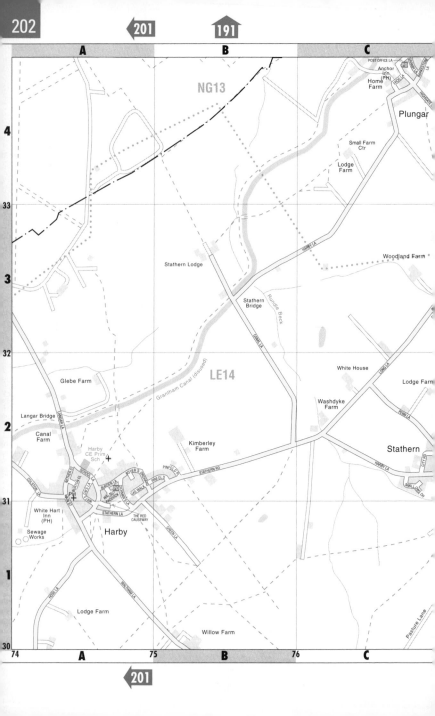

A   B   C

POST OFFICE LA
Anchor Inn (PH)
Home Farm
Plungar

NG13

Small Farm Ctr

4

Lodge Farm

Woodland Farm

33

HARBY LA

Stathern Lodge

3

Stathern Bridge

Rundle Beck

CANAL LA

32

White House

LE14

Lodge Farm

Glebe Farm

Grantham Canal (disused)

Washdyke Farm

Langar Bridge

Stathern

LONG LA

HARBY LA

FOSS LA

CITY LA

SHALLOW DR

2

Canal Farm

Kimberley Farm

STATHERN RD

Harby CE Prim Sch

DOVER'S DROVE

PINFOLD LA

HOSE OLD

GAS WALK

COLSTON LA

NETHER LA

SCHOOL LA

CHAPEL LA

MAIN ST

PO

STATHERN LA

31

White Hart Inn (PH)

THE RED CAUSEWAY

GREEN LA

Harby

Sewage Works

1

HOSE LA

WALTHAM LA

Lodge Farm

Willow Farm

Pasture Lane

30

74   A   75   B   76   C

203
194

A   **B**   **C**

Power Station

Winking Hill Farm

Fox Covert

Winking Hill

Stonepit Farm

Woodlands

4

Gotham Wood

Hillside Farm

Kingston Spinney

The Odells

Cuckoo Bush Farm

29

Hillside

Moor Wood

New Kingston

Kingston Works

NG11

Crownend Wood

Whitehills Farm

3

The Cottage

Kingston Park

Kingston Fields Farm

Lodge

KINGSTON CT

28

Kingston Hall

Lumbry Wood

Church Farm

Lodge

KEGWORTH RD

THE GREEN

LONG ROW

2

Kingston on Soar

The Pool

Station Plantation

Woodside

27

DE74

Scotland Farm

Cattle Breeding Centre

Scotland Wood

LE12

Moulter Hill

STATION RD

Kingston Brook

1

Midshires Way

Sewage Works

MILLHILL LA

COLLEGE RD

Froghole Farm

Domleo's Spinney

PH

BRICKYARD LA

26

Univ of Nottingham Sutton Bonington Campus

LANDCROFT

TROWELL LA

50   **A**   **51**   **B**   **52**   **C**

203
213

D　E　F

4

Fairholme
Farm

MOOR LA

Gotham Moor
Farm

Paradise

29

NG11

Works

Cuckoo
Bush

Cuckoo
Bush Farm

Court Hill
Shiddock's
Spinney

Ridgeway
Plantation

Golf Course

Highthorn
Farm

Kismet

Hotchley Hill
Farm

Hotchley
Bungalows

Hotchley
Hill

3

Leake New
Wood

West Leake
Hills

Works

28

Grange
Farm

Stone
House

Crow Wood
Hill

CH

STOCKING LA

Sports
Ground

Mine

Sharpley
Hill

2

The
Cottage

Crow
Wood

Rushcliffe
Lodge

RUSHCLIFFE DR

The
Heavens

ANGRAVE RD

Ash
Spinney

Fir Dale
Plantation

Midshires Way

LE12

Fox
Hill

Fox Hill
Farm

HOLLIS
MEADOW COTTAGE CL

SWEET
LEYS
DR

NORTHFIELDS RAI

TOWNSEND FIELD

27

Foxhill Wood

Harry Carlton
Comp Sch

Lantern Lane
Prim Sch

CARLTON CRES

STONEBRIDGE DR

Kingston Brook

West Leake

Masts

East Leake

MANOR FARM
MEADOW

SOUTHWELL RD
BATESMAN RD

WINCHESTER CL

P
Liby

THE KEEP

COSTOCK RD

1

Sewage
Works

WEST LEAKE RD

STATION RD

Allot
Gdns

TWENTYL
OAK CRES
BROOKSIDE
SYCAMORE

OLD RECTORY CL
BROOKSIDE
LEVERS CL
BURTON WLK

BRAMLEY

Sch

MAIN ST

26

D　54　E　55　F

197
208

D   E   F

Wolds Lane

Lodge Plantation

Brookfield

Wembley Lodge

Keyworth Wolds

Fairham Brook

4

NG11

Wysall Road Farm

Wembley Farm

29

Windmill Hill

Longcliffe Farm

3

Old Wood

NG12

Fairham Wood

Lodge Farm

28

Rough Plantation

Midshires Way

Vicarage

2

PH

Northfield Farm

Widmerpool Rd

Wysall Rough Plantation

Wysall Wood

Wysall

MANOR HOUSE DR

Long Rough Plantation

Southfields

27

Kingston Brook

Thorpe Lodge Farm

WYSALL RD

COTES RD

1

Scotland Hill Farm

Burnside

Brooklea Farm

Cinder Hill Plantation

Thorpe Lane

Windyridge Farm

WYMESWOLD RD

Thorpe in the Glebe

Woodside Farm

Annabell's Farm

26

D   60   E   61   F

216
208

207
198

A   B   C

Wolds Lane

Keyworth Wolds

4

Wolds Farm

Stanton Lodge
Farm

THURLBY LA

Roehoe Brook

Hill Farm

Roe Lod

The
Borders

School
In
(P)

MELTON RD

A606

29

North Lodge
Farm

Queensgate
Wood

STATION RD

The
Stonepits

Crow Hill

NG12

LE14

3

Widmerpool
Hall

Morris's
Plantation

Park
Farm

OLD HALL DR

Manor
Farm

The Grange

Flint
Hill

Fields Farm

KEYWORTH RD

28

Widmerpool

Fairham Brook

CRESCO LA

WIDMER LANE

PEN LA

WYSALL RD

WIDMERPOOL RD

2

Green Hill

Greenhill
Plantation

South
Lodge

WILLOUGHBY RD

Magpie
Plantation

27

Manor Farm

LE12

LE14

Willoughby
Lodge

Willoughby
Lodge

Lodge
Farm

1

Homeward

Midshires Way

Kingston Brook

The Grey
House

MELL LA

Fosse
Lodge

26

Thorpe
Plantation

62   A   63   B   64   C

207
217

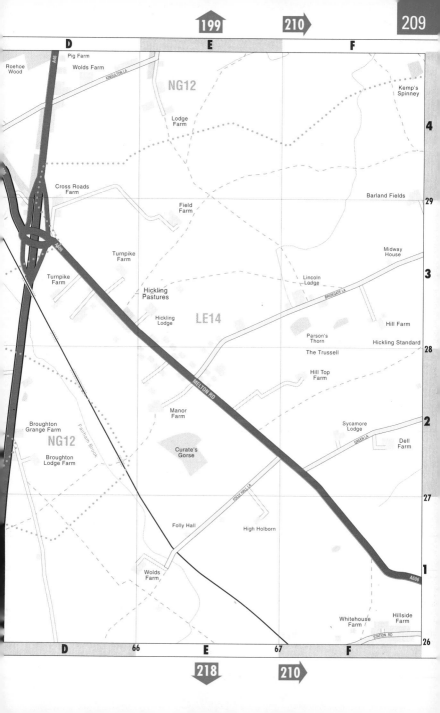

D
E
F

Roehoe Wood

Pig Farm
Wolds Farm

KINOULTON LA

NG12

Kemp's Spinney

Lodge Farm

4

Cross Roads Farm

Barland Fields

29

Field Farm

Midway House

Turnpike Farm

Lincoln Lodge

BRIDEGATE LA

3

Turnpike Farm

Hickling Pastures

LE14

Hill Farm

Hickling Lodge

Parson's Thorn

Hickling Standard

28

The Trussell

MELTON RD

Hill Top Farm

Manor Farm

2

Broughton Grange Farm

NG12

Sycamore Lodge

Dell Farm

GREEN LA

Fairham Brook

Broughton Lodge Farm

Curate's Gorse

27

JOLLY HILL LA

Folly Hall

High Holborn

Wolds Farm

1

A606

Whitehouse Farm

Hillside Farm

STATION RD

26

D
66
E
67
F

NG12

A   B   C

Clarke's
Bridge

Bridge
Farm

Canal
Farm

4   Bridge
Farm

Grantham Canal (disused)

The Plough Inn
(PH)
Church
Farm

Waterlane
Farm

Elms Farm

Hickling

29   Cricket
Ground

MARSH'S
PADDOCK

Burial
Ground

CLAWSON LA

Canal
Farm

BRIDEGATE LA

Manor
House

The Green

PH

CHARLES ACRES

LONG LA

PUDDING
LA

3   Oak
Farm

Castle
View

LE14

28   Hickling Standard

Dalby Brook

GREEN LA

Sherbrooke Fox
Covert

2   River Smite

27   Muxlow
Hill

Bridge
Farm

BROUGHTON LA

1   A606   Sulney
Fields

Upper
Broughton

The Golden Fleece
(PH)

CLAWSON LA

CHURCH LA

STA
RD   TOP GREEN

CHAPEL LA

BOTTOM GREEN

MELTON RD

Corner Farm

BOTTOM GREEN A606

26
68   A   69   B   70   C

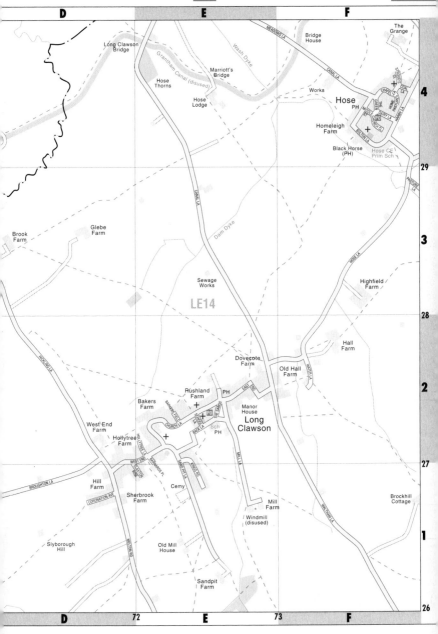

D   E   F

Long Clawson Bridge

MEADOWS LA

Bridge House

The Grange

CANAL LA

Granton Canal (disused)

Marriott's Bridge

Wash Dyke

Hose Thorns

Works

Hose
PH

4

Hose Lodge

Homeleigh Farm

Black Horse (PH)

Hose CE Prim Sch

29

PASTURE LA

Brook Farm

Glebe Farm

Dam Dyke

3

CANAL LA

HOSE LA

Sewage Works

Highfield Farm

LE14

28

Hall Farm

Dovecote Farm

BACK LA

Old Hall Farm

WATER LA

2

Rushland Farm

PH

Bakers Farm

BARKSTONE FIELDS

EAST END

Manor House

CHURCH LA

Sch PH

Long Clawson

SALMON LA

West End Farm

HALL CROFT LA

Hollytree Farm

WEST END

ST MARY'S PL

BACK LA

MILL LA

27

BROUGHTON LA

Hill Farm

CORONATION AVE

Cemy

Sherbrook Farm

Mill Farm

Brockhill Cottage

Windmill (disused)

1

Slyborough Hill

MELTON RD

Old Mill House

Sandpit Farm

MELTON LA

26

D   72   E   73   F

A   B   C

Springhouse
Farm

DE74

PH

Slade
Spinney

Slade
Farm

Devil's
Elbow

25

Windmill
Farm

His
Lordships

Intensive Dairy
Unit

Lodge

Woodyard
Plantation

Whatton
House

Home
Farm

Five Acre

Ash
Spinney

Gallow's
Wood

Marylea
Farm

Gorse
Covert

Lodge

24

Manor
House
Farm

WEST END

Long Whatton

Manor
Farm

MILL LA

Whatton
Fields
Farm

Long Whatton
Mill

Long Whatton Brook

2

PH

PH

LE12

Sewage
Works

PH

Rose Hill

HATHERN RD

WHATTON RD

Hathern
Turn

B5324

23

DRY POT LA

Works

WIDE LA

1

Piper
Farm

ASHBY RD

Mitchell's
Spring
Farm

Oakley Wood

Oakley Grange
Farm

SHEPSHED RD

22

B5324

47   A   48   B   49   C

D E F

4

Glebe
Farm

Univ

Valley
Farm

Cemy

SOAR LA

Univ of Nottingham
Department of
Ag Economics

LANDCROFT LA

EXETER RD

MAIN ST HILL

BRIDLEWAY

BRICKYARD LA

California
Farm

Sutton
Bonington

Hall Farm

St Anne's
Manor

THORNELL LA

HUNGARY LA

California
Plantation

Cold Harbour
Plantation

25

The
Hall

BELLAND ST

ST ANNE'S LA

THE ORCHARDS

PH

PH

Sutton Bonington
Prim Sch

Park Lane
Farm

WILLOW POOL LA

SHEPHERD'S CL

SUTTON CL
CHARNWOOD FIELDS

CHARNWOOD AVE

PARK LA

ORCHARD LA

PASTURE LA

Cold Harbour
Farm

A6006

REMPSTONE RD

The
Cedars

3

HATHERNWARE
IND EST

24

LE12

Zouch
Lock

Zouch Cut

PH

Zouch
Farm

MOOR LA

FAY LA

BUTT LA

Tebbutt's
Farm

2

MAIN ST

Zouch

Zouch
Bridge

ZOUCH RD

P

River Soar

MAIN ST

Normanton on Soar
Prim Sch

Butt
Lane
Bridge

SUMMERS LA

PH

Normanton on Soar

23

The
Stints

Ferry

VILLAGE RD

emy

GREEN HILL RISE

THE GREEN

HAWTHORNE AVE

Liby

WIDE LA

WESLEY CL

ST PETER'S AVE

GLADSTONE ST

NARROW LA

NUM CL

Sch

THE FARTHINGS
MEADS

OLD FORGE DR

ST JAMES RD

ANCHOR
LA

TANNER'S LA
ANCHOR LA

Hathern

Bowley's
Bridge

REMPSTONE RD

Bowley's
Barn
Farm

1

River Soar

LE11

22

D 51 E 52 F

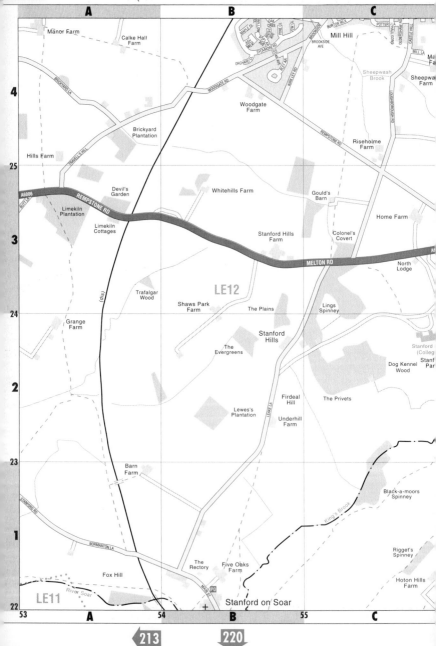

213
205
213
220

A **B** **C**

Manor Farm
Calke Hall Farm
Mill Hill

BROOKSIDE AVE

Sheepwash Brook

Sheepwa Fa

4

Woodgate Farm

Riseholme Farm

Brickyard Plantation

25

Hills Farm

Devil's Garden

Whitehills Farm

Gould's Barn

Home Farm

A6006

RUTLA

REMPSTONE RD

Limekiln Plantation

Limekiln Cottages

Stanford Hills Farm

Colonel's Covert

3

MELTON RD

North Lodge

A

(dis)

Trafalgar Wood

LE12

Shaws Park Farm

The Plains

Lings Spinney

24

Grange Farm

Stanford Hills

Stanford (Colleg

The Evergreens

Dog Kennel Wood

Stanf Par

2

Lewes's Plantation

Firdeal Hill

The Privets

LEAKE LA

Underhill Farm

23

Barn Farm

Black-a-moors Spinney

King's Brook

1

NORMANTON LA

Rigget's Spinney

STANFORD RD

The Rectory

Five Oaks Farm

Hoton Hills Farm

Fox Hill

River Soar

LE11

MAIN RD

Stanford on Soar

22

53 **A** 54 **B** 55 **C**

Canaan Farm

Hill Farm

Oaklands Farm

4

The Lings Farm

Sheepwash Brook

25

WYSALL RD

MELTON RD

LOUGHBOROUGH RD

3

SCHOOL LA

Lings Farm

Rempstone Hall
(Convent)

Rempstone Hall
Farm

PH

MAIN ST

Dales Farm

WYMESWOLD RD

THE OLD
ENGINE YARD

A6006

Damhead
Plantation

Rempstone

24

Sutcliffe
Plantation

LE12

Cherry
Hill

Sutcliffe
Hill

Floodgate
Plantation

2

King's Bridge

King's Brook

New
Covert

23

REMPSTONE RD

Gorse Farm

New Covert
Farm

WYMESWOLD RD

1

Sewage
Works

HOLLY TREE

PH

Hoton

Harts Farm

TOLL TER

LOUGHBOROUGH RD

OLD ASHBY RD

Peartree
Farm

Wymeswold Airfield
(disused)

A60

215
207

A B C

Hillcrest Farm

Woollerton's
Plantation

WYGILL RD

Church Site
Farm

4

Wolds Farm

NG12

Oak Tree
Farm

25

Mushill
Farm

Peaslands
Farm

Field Farm

Cripwell
Farm

3

Barn Farm
Cottage

Storkit Lane

MUSHILL LA

WYGILL LA

Mill Cottage

WYMESWOLD RD

LE12

A6006

24

Barn Farm

REMPSTONE RD

WIDE LA

A6006

Hillside
Farm

Wymeswold

EAST RD

Cemetery

FAR ST

ORCHARDS WAY

WIDOW ALCOCKS CL

2

LONDON LA

NETTLETON DR

HILL RISE

MARTS CL

LANDCROSS CL

RECTORY LA

CHURCH LA

BROOK ST

King's Brook

HOTON RD

TRINITY CRES

SIMPLY CL

River Mantle

THE STOCKWELL

Wymeswold
CE Sch

NARROW LA

23

WYMESWOLD RD

River Mantle

Airfield
(dis)

1

Dales
Spinney

Gamber's Hill
Lodge

WYMESWOLD
IND EST

22

59 A 60 B 61 C

D
E
F

NG12

4

Triangle
Plantation

Eelpool
Field

Willoughby-on
-the-Wolds

Field Farm

Bryans Lane

BELL LA

THORNPOOL LA

Broughton
Lodge

A46

Willoughby
Gorse

Old Hall
Farm

Willoughby-
on-the-Wolds
Prim Sch

VICA LA

MAIN ST

PH

Green Lane

WEST THORPE

MOB
LA

CHAPEL CT

UNION LA

25

Midshires Way

BACK LA

25

Barrack
Cottages

DEEPDALE LA

3

LE14

Turnpost
Farm

Kingston Brook

LE12

HARBY LA

24

A46

Dungehill
Farm

2

Hill Farm

Eller's
Gorse

WIDE LA

Ella's
Farm

Pasture
Lodge

Highthorn
Farm

23

NARROW LA

Common
Farm

Wymeswold
Lodge

Kingston Brook

Willoughby Fields
Farm

PADDY'S LA A6006

1

Kings
Farm

River Mantle

Wolds Farm

The Lodge

A46

22

D
63
E
64
F

A
B
C

4

Manor Barn
Farm

Manor Farm

STATION RD

Brookside
Cottage

The
Willoughby
Hotel

Top
Cottage

Farnham Brook

25

Longcliff Hill

Dalby Brook

3

Wad House

Spruce
Haven

Midshires Way

Dalby Lodges

LE14

North
Lodge

Beazley's
Farm

North Lodge
Farm

NOTTINGHAM LA

Old Dalby
CE. Sch

24

LONGCLIFF HILL

STATION LA

HAWTHORN

Old Dalby

CROFT

PH

PADDOCK LA

DEBDALE HILL

CHAPEL RD

Wood's Hill

Vale View
Farm

MAIN RD

2

CHURCH LA

Woodhill
Farm

WOOD HILL

Hall
Plantation

Fishpon
Plantatic

Hill Top
Farm

Thorney
Hollow

23

Yard Farm

Old Dalby Wood

Upper Grange
Farm

Grange
Cottages

Wavendon
Grange

LANE LA

Old Dalby Woo
House

Dalby Wolds

Old Dalby
Grange

Home Lodge
Farm

1

A6006

PADDY'S LA

Lower Grange
Farm

A6006

Bridgets
Covert

SIX HILLS LA

Lodge Farm

22

65

A

66

B

67

C

D | E | F

210

CHURCH END
HARGRAVES CT
CAUSECK LA
Moat Farm
CHURCH LA
MILLS LA
KING ST
BLACKSMITHS CL

Nether Broughton

Manor Farm

River Smite

PH
The Grange

NOTTINGHAM RD

A606

4

Sewage Works

Thompson Walk

25

GREAVES AVE
OLD DALBY LA
THE CRESCENT
OLD HIGHWAY
Hatton Lodge

Broughton Lodges

EARLS RD
PRINCE'S RD
MANOR RD
DUKES RD

Playing Field

Lodge Farm

3

Broughton Lodge

LE14

STATION LA
ION LA

24

Old Dalby Depot

Greenhill Farm

Crompton's Plantation

Stonepit Spinney

Stonepits Farm

2

Marriott's Spinney

Green Hill

Friars Well Farm

Grimston Tunnel

Saxelby Lodge Farm

Marriott's Wood

Wartnaby

23

Tunnel Farm

GREVILLE LA

Tunnel Farm

Barnes Hill Plantation

Friars Well

Ppg Sta

Old Dalby Wood

Air Shafts

Ten Acres Plantation

1

Tunnel Plantation

Midshires Way
TERNGELLS

Grimston Gorse

Barn Farm

Saxelby Pastures

22

Grimston

D | 69 | E | 70 | F

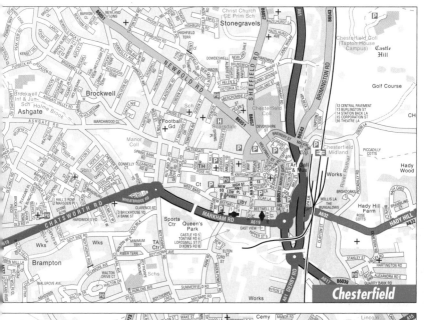

Chesterfield

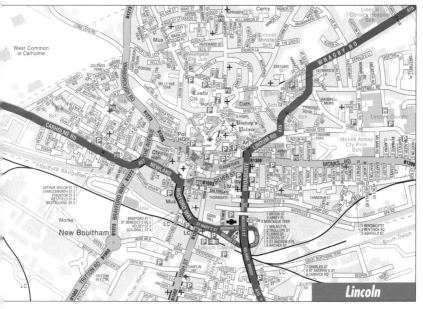

Lincoln

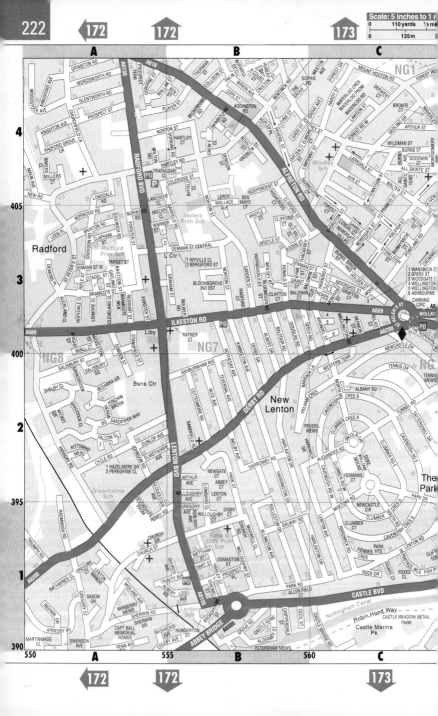

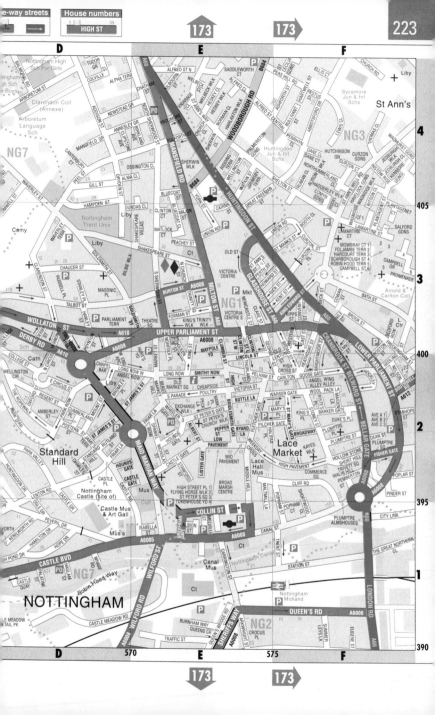

one-way streets

House numbers
HIGH ST

D   E   F

Nottingham High
Sch For Girls
BALMORAL RD
TUDOR GR
COLVILLE
ALFRED ST N
SADDLEWORTH
PEAS HILL RD
CECILIA
CHURCH RD
Liby

ingham
h Sch
h Boys
Clarendon Coll
(Annexe)
ARBORETUM ST
NEWSTEAD GR
ALPHA TERR
CHATHAM
WELBECK WLK
WELBECK CL
ASHFORTH ST
ELLIS CT
Sycamore
Jun & Int
Schs
St Ann's

Arboretum
Language
Sch
MANSFIELD GR
ADDISON ST
ANNESLEY GR
BIRKLAND
ROBIN HOOD CHASE
ST ANN'S WELL RD
ALBERT ST CENTRAL
WOODBOROUGH RD
ABBOTSFORD DR
HUTTON ST
PENRHYN
ABINGER
NG3
WADHURST GDNS
JEDBURGH CL
JEDBURGH WLK
KENMORE CL
4

NG7
CANTERBURY
PEEL ST
MANSFIELD GR
CLUMBER
RISE
OSSINGTON CL
MANSFIELD RD
PALMERSTON
WELLINGTON
HUNTINGDON ST
HUTTON ST
DANE CT
DANE CT WLK
NORTHUMBERLAND
CURZON
GDNS
CURZON CT
HUTTON ST
HUNGERHILL RD
ALMA CL
GILL ST
HAMPDEN ST
DUNDAS CL
BLUECOAT ST
CLINTON ST
MAJOR
YORK ST
CAIRNS
HUNTINGDON ST
UNION RD
BOOTH CL
ALLADDERLEY WLK
RITSON CL
PLANTAGENET
405

Cemy
RUSSELL PL
CLARENDON ST
STANLEY PL
GOLDSMITH ST
CHAUCER ST
BILBIE WLK
SHAKESPEARE ST
S SHERWOOD ST
MATLOCK CT
PEACHEY ST
OLD ST
ST MARKS ST
CURZON ST
MANSFIELD RD
ST ANN'S ST
KENT ST
BATH ST
MOWBRAY CT 1
FOLJAMBE TERR 2
HARCOURT TERR 3
SCARBOROUGH ST 4
ROBIN HOOD TERR 5
CAMPBELL ST 6
SALFORD
GDNS
CAMPBELL
GR
PROMENADE
3

TALBOT ST
PARLIAMENT
TERR
MASONIC
PL
BURTON ST
A6008
TRINITY WLK
FORMAN ST
N CHURCH ST
MILTON ST
Mkt
NEWCASTLE ST
GLASSHOUSE ST
ROCK ST
CLARE ST
KIPPIS ST
COWDEN ST
BROOK ST
Arnold &
Carlton Coll
BEDFORD
Ctr
L

WOLLATON
DERBY RD
A610
Sch
A610
TOLL HOUSE HILL
A6008
NORTHGATE
UPPER PARLIAMENT ST
A60
KING'S TRINITY
WLK
Victoria
Centre S
CLINTON ST W
ST
A6008
CLINTON ST E
LENTON ST
HIGH
CROSS ST
BRIGHTMOOR ST
CRANBROOK ST
BELWARD ST
LOWER PARLIAMENT ST
A60
STANHOPE
GEDLING ST
400

COLLEGE ST
WELLINGTON
CIR
Cath
CHAPEL
BAR
ANGEL ROW
MAYPOLE
YD
A6008
NORFOLK PL
LONG ROW W
LONG ROW
SMITHY ROW
CLUMBER ST
LINCOLN ST
THURLAND ST
PELHAM ST
CARLTON ST
GOOSE GATE
WOOL PACK LA
ANGEL WING
ALLEY ALLEY
MALIN ST
A612
AVE A 1
AVE B 2
AVE C 3
2

THE ROPEWALK
PARK ROW
REGENT ST
E CIRCUS ST
Liby
BROMLEY PL
MOUNT ST
ST JAMES ST
BEAST
MARKET
HILL
S PARADE
POULTRY
CHEAPSIDE
EXCHANGE
WLK
Victoria ST
BRIDLESMITH GATE
ST MARY'S
ST
ST MARY'S GATE
KING'S
PL
BARKER GATE
DUKE'S PL
WARSER GATE
BROADWAY
PLUMPTRE
HOLLOW STONE
STANHOPE
PLUMPTRE
FISHER GATE
POPLAR ST

AMBERLEY ST
PARK VALLEY
POSTERN ST
CUMBERLAND
PL
ST JAMES ST
STANDARD
HILL
CASTLE GATE
HOUNDS
GATE
FRIAR LA
SPANIEL
ROW
ALBERT ST
ST PETER'S GATE
ST PETER'S
CHURCH WLK
BOTTLE LA
BYARD
LA
PEPPER
ST
FLETCHER GATE
HALIFAX
PL
PILCHER GATE
KAYES
WLK
COMMERCE
SQ
RIVET ST
MALIN HILL
PEMBERTON
PINDER ST
395

Standard
Hill
HUNTINGDON DR
KENILWORTH RD
HAMILTON DR
HOPE DR
Nottingham
Castle (site of)
CASTLE PL
CASTLE GATE
Mus
Castle Mus
& Art Gall
Mus's
PEVERIL DR
LENTON RD
CASTLE GR
Coll
HIGH STREET PL 1
FLYING HORSE WLK 2
ST PETER S SQ 3
TOKENHOUSE YD 4
MID
PAVEMENT
LISTER GATE
STANFORD
CASTLE
GATE
LOW
PAVEMENT
Lace Hall
Mus
Lace
Market
HIGH PAVEMENT
SHORT HILL
CLIFF RD
BROAD
MARSH
CENTRE
MIDDLE HILL
MALTMILL LA
POPHAM
ST
POPHAM
PLUMPTRE
ALMSHOUSES
CITY LINK
A6008

SH POND DR
NG7
CASTLE
QUAY
PLANTINE
HASLAM ST
CASTLE BVD
WILFORD RD
WHARF ST
ISABELLA
Mus's
COLLIN ST
ALBION
GREYFRIAR GATE
A6006
CANAL ST
Canal Mus
CARRINGTON ST
TRENT ST
STATION ST
THE GREAT NORTHERN
CL
1

NOTTINGHAM
Robin Hood Way
A6005
CASTLE MEADOW RD
WILFORD RD
Ct
Ct
Nottingham Canal
Nottingham
Midland
LONDON RD
A60

LE MEADOW
tail PK
BURNHAM WAY
QUEENS GR
TRAFFIC GR
SHERIFFS WAY
ARKWRIGHT ST
TRENT BRIDGE WAY
NG2
CROCUS
PL
QUEEN'S RD
A6008
EUGENE ST
SUMMER
LEYS LA
A60

D   570   E   575   F   390

Index

Street names are listed alphabetically and show the locality, the Postcode District, the page number and
a reference to the square in which the name falls on the map page

Mount Pleasant 2 Mansfield NG18 ... 102 A4

Full street name
This may have been
abbreviated on the map

Location Number
If present, this indicates
the street's position on a
congested area of the
map instead of the name

Town, village or
locality in which the
street falls.

Postcode District for
the street name

Page number of the map
on which the street name
appears

Grid square in which the
centre of the street falls

Schools, hospitals, sports centres, railway stations, shopping centres,
industrial estates, public amenities and other places of interest are also
listed.

Abbreviations used in the index

App **Approach**	Comm **Common**	Est **Estate**	N **North**	Sq **Square**
Arc **Arcade**	Cnr **Corner**	Gdns **Gardens**	Orch **Orchard**	Strs **Stairs**
Ave **Avenue**	Cotts **Cottages**	Gn **Green**	Par **Parade**	Stps **Steps**
Bvd **Boulevard**	Ct **Court**	Gr **Grove**	Pk **Park**	St **Street, Saint**
Bldgs **Buildings**	Ctyd **Courtyard**	Hts **Heights**	Pas **Passage**	Terr **Terrace**
Bsns Pk **Business Park**	Cres **Crescent**	Ho **House**	Pl **Place**	Trad Est **Trading Estate**
Bsns Ctr **Business Centre**	Dr **Drive**	Ind Est **Industrial Estate**	Prec **Precinct**	Wlk **Walk**
Bglws **Bungalows**	Dro **Drove**	Intc **Interchange**	Prom **Promenade**	W **West**
Cswy **Causeway**	E **East**	Junc **Junction**	Ret Pk **Retail Park**	Yd **Yard**
Ctr **Centre**	Emb **Embankment**	La **Lane**	Rd **Road**	
Cir **Circus**	Ent **Enterprise**	Mans **Mansions**	Rdbt **Roundabout**	
Cl **Close**	Espl **Esplanade**	Mdw **Meadows**	S **South**	

Town and village index

Aldercar ... 143 D2	Cottam ... 43 D3	Holbeck ... 59 E3	North Leverton with
Annesley ... 130 A1	Creswell ... 58 B4	Holme ... 111 D2	Habblesthorpe ... 42 A4
Annesley Woodhouse ... 129 E4	Cromwell ... 110 B4	Hose ... 215 D1	North Muskham ... 110 B2
Arnold ... 162 A3	Cropwell Bishop ... 189 D1	Hoton ... 215 E1	North Scarle ... 83 D1
Askham ... 51 F1	Cropwell Butler ... 189 D3	Hoveringham ... 151 E1	North Wheatley ... 31 E4
Aslockton ... 179 D2	Cuckney ... 60 A1	Hucknall ... 145 E2	Norwell ... 110 A4
Astwith ... 85 D3	Darlton ... 67 D3	Huthwaite ... 99 F1	Nottingham ... 173 D2
Ault Hucknall ... 85 E2	Doddington ... 71 D1	Ilkeston ... 157 E1	Nuthall ... 159 D3
Austerfield ... 3 D2	Dry Doddington ... 156 B1	Ironville ... 128 A2	Old Dalby ... 218 A1
Averham ... 123 F1	Dunham on Trent ... 54 A1	Kegworth ... 203 D1	Old Clipstone ... 90 A3
Awsworth ... 158 A2	Eagle ... 84 A2	Kelham ... 124 A2	Oldcotes ... 17 D3
Babworth ... 39 D2	East Bridgford ... 165 D1	Kersall ... 94 A1	Ollerton ... 77 D1
Balderton ... 140 B1	East Drayton ... 53 D1	Keyworth ... 197 D1	Ompton ... 93 D4
Barkestone-le-Vale ... 192 B3	East Leake ... 205 E1	Kimberley ... 158 B2	Orston ... 180 A3
Barnby in the Willows ... 141 E3	East Markham ... 65 E4	Kingston-on-Soar ... 204 A2	Ossington ... 95 E3
Barnby Moor ... 28 B2	East Stockwith ... 7 E1	Kinoulton ... 200 A1	Owthorpe ... 199 F4
Barnstone ... 190 C2	East Stoke ... 153 D4	Kirkby in Ashfield ... 115 D1	Oxton ... 134 A1
Barton in Fabis ... 194 C3	Eastwood ... 143 E1	Kirklington ... 120 C4	Papplewick ... 131 F2
Bathley ... 110 A1	Eaton ... 40 A1	Kirton ... 78 A3	Pinxton ... 113 E1
Bawtry ... 10 A3	Edingley ... 120 A1	Kneesall ... 93 F3	Pleasley ... 87 D2
Beckingham (Lincs) ... 142 B4	Edwinstowe ... 76 A1	Kneeton ... 152 A1	Pleasleyhill ... 87 D2
Beckingham (Notts) ... 14 A1	Egmanton ... 79 E2	Lambley ... 163 D3	Plumtree ... 197 E3
Beeston ... 183 D1	Elkesley ... 50 A2	Laneham ... 54 A3	Plungar ... 202 C3
Besthorpe ... 97 F3	Elmton ... 58 A3	Langar ... 190 A2	Pye Bridge ... 128 A3
Bestwood Village ... 146 B2	Elston ... 153 E2	Langford ... 124 A4	Radcliffe on Trent ... 175 E1
Bilsthorpe ... 105 E1	Epperstone ... 150 A2	Langley Mill ... 143 D1	Radmanthwaite ... 87 E1
Bingham ... 177 D2	Everton ... 11 D1	Langold ... 16 B2	Ragnall ... 68 C4
Bircotes ... 9 D2	Farndon ... 139 D2	Langwith ... 72 C4	Rainworth ... 117 F4
Blaxton ... 1 A4	Farnsfield ... 119 D1	Laughterton ... 55 D2	Rampton ... 42 B1
Bleasby ... 152 A4	Fenton (nr Balderton) ... 142 B1	Laxton ... 79 D1	Ranby ... 38 A3
Blidworth ... 118 A1	Fenton (nr Saxilby) ... 55 D3	Lea ... 24 C1	Ranskill ... 19 D2
Blyth ... 18 A1	Finningley ... 1 A1	Letwell ... 16 A1	Ratcliffe on Soar ... 203 E4
Blyton ... 15 E4	Firbeck ... 16 A3	Linby ... 131 D2	Ravenshead ... 117 D1
Bole ... 23 E3	Fiskerton ... 137 E3	Little Carlton ... 124 A4	Redmile ... 192 C2
Bothamsall ... 63 F1	Flawborough ... 168 A1	Long Clawson ... 211 D1	Rempstone ... 215 E3
Bottesford ... 181 D1	Fledborough ... 68 B2	Long Eaton ... 193 D2	Retford ... 39 D3
Boughton ... 77 F3	Flintham ... 153 D1	Long Whatton ... 212 A1	Rhodesia ... 35 D2
Bradmore ... 196 C2	Gainsborough ... 24 A4	Loughborough ... 220 A1	Rockley ... 51 D1
Breaston ... 193 D4	Gamston ... 51 D2	Lound ... 29 E4	Rolleston ... 138 A3
Brinsley ... 143 E2	Girton ... 82 C1	Lowdham ... 150 A2	Ruddington ... 196 A3
Broadholme ... 57 D4	Glapwell ... 86 A4	Misson ... 4 B1	Sandiacre ... 182 A2
Brough ... 112 A2	Gotham ... 195 D1	Misterton ... 6 B1	Saundby ... 23 E3
Broxholme ... 57 F4	Granby ... 191 D3	Market Warsop ... 74 A1	Saxilby ... 56 C1
Bulcote ... 164 A4	Grassthorpe ... 81 F2	Marton ... 44 A4	Scarrington ... 178 C4
Bunny ... 206 B3	Greasley ... 144 A4	Mattersey ... 20 A3	Screveton ... 166 B3
Burton Joyce ... 163 E2	Gringley on the Hill ... 12 B1	Meden Vale ... 74 B4	Scrooby ... 10 A1
Calverton ... 149 D3	Grove ... 40 E3	Misson ... 4 B1	Selston ... 128 B1
Car Colston ... 166 A1	Gunthorpe ... 164 B4	Misterton ... 6 B1	Shelford ... 164 A1
Carlton ... 162 A1	Halam ... 120 C1	Morton (Lincs) ... 15 D2	Shelton ... 168 B3
Carlton in Lindrick ... 25 E4	Hallougton ... 136 B2	Morton (Notts) ... 137 E2	Shipley ... 157 D3
Carlton-on-Trent ... 96 C2	Harby (Leics) ... 202 A1	Muston ... 181 F1	Shirebrook ... 72 B1
Caunton ... 109 D2	Harby (Notts) ... 70 B1	Nether Broughton ... 219 D3	Shireoaks ... 34 A2
Caythorpe ... 165 E4	Hardstoft ... 85 D1	Nether Langwith ... 59 D1	Sibthorpe ... 167 F3
Church Warsop ... 74 A2	Harworth ... 8 C2	New Balderton ... 140 A2	Skellingthorpe ... 71 F1
Clarborough ... 30 B1	Hathern ... 213 D1	New Houghton ... 86 C4	South Clifton ... 68 A1
Claypole ... 156 A1	Hawksworth ... 167 D2	New Ollerton ... 77 D2	South Leverton ... 42 A3
Clayworth ... 21 E3	Hayton ... 30 B3	Newark-on-Trent ... 140 A2	South Muskham ... 124 A4
Clipstone ... 89 E1	Headon ... 52 F1	Newstead ... 130 A3	South Normanton ... 113 D2
Coddington ... 126 A1	Heanor ... 143 D1	Newton ... 99 D1	South Scarle ... 98 B2
Collingham ... 98 A1	Hickling ... 210 B3	Newton on Trent ... 55 D1	South Wheatley ... 31 E4
Colston Bassett ... 200 A4	High Marnham ... 68 C1	Normanton on Soar ... 214 A1	Southwell ... 121 E1
Cossall ... 158 A1	Hilcote ... 99 D1	Normanton on Trent ... 81 E3	Spalford ... 83 D3
Costock ... 206 A1	Hockerton ... 122 A3	Normanton-	Stainsby ... 85 D4
Cotes ... 220 B4	Hodsock ... 26 C4	on-the-Wolds ... 198 A4	Stanford on Soar ... 214 A1
Cotgrave ... 187 D3	Hodthorpe ... 45 E3	North Clifton ... 68 B2	Stanley ... 85 E1
Cotham ... 154 C2			Stanton Hill ... 100 A3
			Stanton-by-Dale ... 170
			Stanton-on-the-Wolds ... 198
			Stapleford (Lincs) ... 127
			Stapleford (Notts) ... 182
			Stathern ... 202
			Staunton in the Vale ... 169
			Staythorpe ... 138
			Stoke Bardolph ... 175
			Strelley ... 171
			Sturton le Steeple ... 32
			Styrrup ... 8
			Sutton ... 28
			Sutton Bonington ... 213
			Sutton in Ashfield ... 100
			Sutton on Trent ... 96
			Syerston ... 153
			Teversal ... 100
			Thorney ... 69
			Thorpe ... 138
			Thorpe Salvin ... 34
			Thrumpton ... 194
			Thurgarton ... 151
			Tibshelf ... 99
			Tickhill ... 8
			Tollerton ... 186
			Torksey ... 44
			Torworth ... 19
			Treswell ... 42
			Trowell ... 170
			Tuxford ... 66
			Upper Broughton ... 210
			Upper Langwith ... 72
			Upton ... 122
			Walesby ... 64
			Walkeringham ... 13
			Walkerith ... 14
			Wallingwells ... 25
			Wasop Vale ... 73
			Watnall ... 159
			Wellow ... 77
			West Bridgford ... 186
			West Drayton ... 51
			West Hallam ... 157
			West Leake ... 205
			West Markham ... 65
			West Stockwith ... 7
			Weston ... 81
			Westwood ... 128
			Westwoodside ... 2
			Whaley ... 58
			Whaley Thorns ... 59
			Whatton ... 179
			Whitwell ... 45
			Widmerpool ... 208
			Willoughby-
			on-the-Wolds ... 217
			Winkburn ... 108
			Winthorpe ... 125
			Woodbeck ... 53
			Woodborough ... 149
			Woodsetts ... 25
			Worksop ... 35
			Wroot ... 2
			Wymeswold ... 216
			Wysall ... 207
			Zouch ... 213

t Ave NG7 173 D4
d Ave NG7 173 D4
d Ave NG7 173 D4
i Ave NG7 173 D4
Road NG9 184 B3
ron Cl NG11 185 D4
ba Cl NG16 158 C4
bey Bridge NG7 172 C1
bey CE Jun Sch S80 35 F1
bey Cir NG2 186 A4
bey Cl Aslockton NG13 178 C3
ucknall NG15 145 F4
bey Ct Beeston NG9 183 F4
lansfield NG18 102 C4
ottingham NG7 222 B2
bey Dr NG9 183 F4
bey Gates Prim Sch
G15 117 D1
bey Gr NG3 173 F4
bey La NG13 178 C3
bey Rd Beeston NG9 183 F4
ingham NG13 178 A2
idworth NG21 118 A3
astwood NG16 144 A1
dwinstowe NG21 91 E4
irkby in A NG17 115 E3
lansfield NG18 102 C4
attersey DN10 20 B4
ewstead NG15 130 C3
est Bridgford NG2 186 A4
bey Road Prim Sch
G2 186 A3
bey St Ilkeston DE7 157 F1
ottingham NG7 172 C1
orksop S80 35 F1
beydale Dr NG18 102 B2
beyfield Rd NG7 184 C4
bot Cl NG12 197 F2
bot St NG16 158 B2
bots Cl NG5 161 E3
bots Dr NG15 145 F3
bots Rd NG15 145 F3
bots Wlk NG15 145 F3
botsbury Cl NG5 146 C1
botsford Dr NG3 223 F4
botsford Mews DE7 157 E2
bott Lea NG19 101 E4
bott St NG10 193 E3
bott's Way NG24 125 D1
botts Cres NG22 119 F4
botts Croft NG19 87 F1
botts Way NG8 172 B2
el Collin's Homes NG8 171 F1
ercarn Cl NG6 160 A4
erconway St NG21 118 A3
erdeen St 9 NG3 173 F3
erford Ave NG8 172 B4
ngdon Dr NG11 196 B4
ngdon Gdns
nold NG5 162 A3
eston NG9 183 E2
ngdon Rd NG2 186 A4
ngdon Sq NG8 160 A1
ngton Ave NG17 100 C3
ard Gdns 6 NG9 183 E1
acia Ave
nnesley Woodhouse NG17 130 A4
ainsborough DN21 15 E1
acia Cl NG15 146 A3
acia Cres NG4 162 C1
acia Ct NG19 88 C1
acia Gdns NG16 158 C4
acia Rd NG24 140 B3
acia Wlk NG9 183 F3
demy Cl NG6 160 C2
ster Cl NG9 184 A2
er Cl NG16 113 E2
ford Dr S80 35 E2
and St DN21 15 E1
e Gdns NG6 146 A1
orn Ave NG16 158 A4
orn Bank NG2 185 D2
orn Bsns Pk 11 NG18 102 A3
orn Cl NG24 140 B3
orn Dr NG4 163 D1
orn Pk NG7 184 C4
orn Ridge NG20 72 B3
orn Way NG18 103 D2
urt St NG7 222 B4
e Edge Rd NG22 78 C1
e The NG17 115 D2
eage La NG20 72 C1
on Ave
ng Eaton NG10 193 F3
ttingham NG6 160 B2
on Cl NG10 193 F3
on Gr NG10 193 F3
on Rd Arnold NG5 161 F4
ng Eaton NG10 193 F3
on Road Ind Est NG10 193 F3
on St NG10 193 F3
m St DE7 170 A3
ms Ct DE7 157 F2
ms Hill Keyworth NG12 197 F2
ttingham NG7 172 B1
ms Way DN21 44 B4
msway NG18 103 D2
olton Ave NG4 162 C1
olton Gr NG2 174 A1
olton La NG12 174 C1
erley Cl NG5 161 D3
ington Ct NG12 176 A2
ington Rd NG7 222 B4
ison Dr NG15 145 F4
ison Rd NG4 174 A4
ison St
ttingham NG1 223 D4
shelf DE55 99 D4

Addison Villas NG16 143 F1
Adel Dr NG4 162 C1
Adelaide Cl
Gainsborough DN21 24 C3
Stapleford NG9 170 C1
Adelaide Gr NG5 160 C4
Adenburgh Dr NG9 183 E1
Adrian Cl NG9 182 C1
Adrians Cl NG18 102 C3
Aegir Cl DN21 24 C3
Aeneas Ct 12 NG5 173 D4
Agnes Villas NG3 161 F1
Aiber Cres NG5 160 C3
Aidan Gdns NG5 147 D1
Ainsdale Cres NG8 160 A2
Ainsdale Gn DN22 39 E2
Ainsley Rd NG8 172 B3
Ainsworth Dr NG2 173 D1
Aintree Cl NG16 158 C4
Aira Cl NG2 186 B3
Airedale S81 36 A4
Airedale Ave DN11 8 A4
Airedale Cl NG10 193 D3
Airedale Ct NG9 183 D2
Airedale Wlk NG8 171 E2
Aisby Wlk DN21 24 C4
Aitchison Ave NG15 145 F4
Alandale NG22 105 F3
Alandale Ave NG20 72 C3
Alandene Ave NG16 159 D4
Albany Cl Arnold NG5 161 F4
Hucknall NG15 145 E3
Mansfield Woodhouse NG19 88 B1
Albany Ct NG9 170 C1
Albany Dr NG19 88 B1
Albany Inf Sch NG9 170 C1
Albany Jun & Inf Schs
NG9 182 C4
Albany Pl NG19 88 B1
Albany Rd NG7 173 D4
Albany Sq NG7 222 C2
Albany St
Gainsborough DN21 15 E1
Ilkeston DE7 170 A3
Albemarle Rd NG5 161 E2
Albert Ave Balderton NG24 140 B2
Carlton NG4 174 A4
Nottingham NG8 172 B4
Nuthall NG16 159 E3
Stapleford NG9 182 B4
Westwood NG16 128 A2
Albert Ball Cl NG5 160 C4
Albert Gr NG7 222 B3
Albert Pl LE11 220 A2
Albert Prom LE11 220 B2
Albert Rd Beeston NG9 184 A4
Bunny NG11 196 C1
Long Eaton NG10 193 E4
Nottingham, Alexander Park
NG3 173 E4
Nottingham, Old Lenton
NG7 222 A1
Retford DN22 39 F3
Sandiacre NG10 182 A3
West Bridgford NG2 185 F4
Albert Sq NG17 100 C1
Albert St Bottesford NG13 181 D2
Carlton NG4 162 C1
Eastwood NG16 143 F2
Hucknall NG15 146 A4
Loughborough LE11 220 A2
Mansfield NG18 102 A3
Mansfield Woodhouse NG19 88 B2
Market Warsop NG20 74 A3
Newark-on-T NG24 139 F4
Nottingham NG1 223 E2
Radcliffe on T NG12 175 F2
South Normanton DE55 113 D3
Stanton Hill NG17 100 B3
Stapleford NG9 182 B4
Worksop S80 35 F2
Alberta Ave NG16 129 D4
Alberta Terr NG7 173 D4
Albine Rd NG20 72 C3
Albion Cl S80 35 F2
Albion Ho (Univ of
Nottingham) NG9 183 F4
Albion Rd Long Eaton NG10 193 F4
Sutton in A NG17 100 C1
Albion Rise NG5 147 F1
Albion St Beeston NG9 183 F4
Ilkeston DE7 157 F1
Mansfield NG19 87 F1
Newark-on-T NG24 139 F4
Nottingham NG1 223 E1
Albion Terr DN10 7 D1
Albury Dr NG8 160 A1
Alcester St NG7 184 C4
Alcock Ave NG18 102 C4
Aldene Ct NG9 183 E3
Aldene Way NG14 149 E2
Alder Cl Mansfield NG19 88 C1
New Balderton NG24 140 B3
Shirebrook NG20 72 B3
Worksop S80 35 F1
Alder Ct NG19 101 E3
Alder Gdns NG6 160 A4
Alder Gr
Mansfield Woodhouse NG19 88 A3
New Ollerton NG22 77 E3
Alder Way Keyworth NG12 198 A1
Shirebrook NG20 72 B2
Sutton in A NG17 100 B2
Aldercar Inf Sch NG16 143 D2
Aldercar La NG16 143 D3
Aldercar Sch NG16 143 D2
Alderman Derbyshire
Comp Sch NG6 160 B4

Alderman Pounder
Inf Sch NG9 183 D3
Alderman White
Lower Sch NG9 183 F4
Aldermens Cl NG2 173 E1
Alderney St NG7 222 B1
Alderson Cl DN11 8 A4
Alderson Dr DN11 8 A4
Alderson Rd S80 35 F1
Alderton Rd NG5 161 E3
Aldgate Cl NG6 160 A4
Aldred's La DE75, NG16 143 D1
Aldridge Cl NG9 182 C1
Aldrin Cl NG6 159 F3
Aldworth Cl NG5 161 E3
Aldwych Cl
Nottingham NG5 147 D1
Nuthall NG16 159 E1
Alec Rose Gr DN21 24 C4
Alexander Ave
Newark-on-T NG24 125 D2
Selston NG16 128 B4
Alexander Cl NG15 131 D1
Alexander Rd
Farnsfield NG22 119 F3
Nottingham NG7 222 C2
Alexander St NG16 143 F1
Alexander Terr NG16 113 E1
Alexandra Ave
Mansfield NG18 102 A2
Mansfield Woodhouse NG19 88 A3
Sutton in A NG17 100 C2
Alexandra Cres NG9 184 A3
Alexandra Rd Bircotes DN11 9 D2
Long Eaton NG10 193 E4
Alexandra St
Kirkby in A NG17 115 D3
Market Warsop NG20 74 A3
Nottingham NG5 173 D4
Stapleford NG9 182 B3
Alexandra Terr NG17 100 B3
Alford Cl NG9 184 A3
Alford Rd NG2 186 A3
Alfred Ave NG3 162 A1
Alfred Cl NG3 223 E4
Alfred Ct 16 NG18 102 A4
Alfred St
Gainsborough DN21 15 E1
Kirkby in A NG17 115 D2
Loughborough LE11 220 A3
Pinxton NG16 113 E2
Sutton in A NG17 100 C2
Alfred St Central NG3 223 E4
Alfred St N NG3 223 E4
Alfred St S NG3 173 F3
Alfreton Rd
Huthwaite NG17 113 F4
Newton DE55 99 D2
Nottingham NG7 222 B4
Pinxton NG16 113 E2
Selston, Selston Green
DE55, NG16 128 B3
Selston, Underwood NG16 129 D2
South Normanton DE55 113 D3
Sutton in A NG17 100 B1
Alison Ave NG15 131 E1
Alison Wlk NG3 223 F4
All Hallows Cl DN22 39 F2
All Hallows Dr NG4 162 C1
All Hallows Prim Sch NG4 162 C1
All Hallows St DN22 39 F2
All Saints' RC Comp Sch
NG19 101 F4
All Saints' St NG7 222 C4
All Saints' Terr NG7 222 C4
Allcroft St NG19 88 B2
Allen Dr NG18 102 C3
Allen Field Ct NG7 222 B1
Allen St Hucknall NG15 146 A4
Worksop S80 35 F1
Allen's Green Ave NG16 128 C3
Allen's Wlk NG5 147 F1
Allenby Rd NG25 136 B4
Allendale Ave
Beeston NG9 183 E1
Nottingham NG8 160 A1
Allendale Rd NG21 118 A4
Allendale Way NG19 88 C1
Allesford La NG22 120 A2
Alliance St NG24 125 D1
Allington Ave NG7 222 B1
Allington Dr NG19 101 E4
Allison Ave DN22 40 A2
Allison Gdns NG9 183 E2
Allsopp Dr S81 35 F3
Allsopp's La LE11 220 B3
Allwood Dr NG4 174 C4
Allwood Gdns NG15 146 A3
Alma Cl Carlton NG4 163 D1
Nottingham NG1 223 E4
Alma Hill NG16 158 C4
Alma Rd Nottingham NG3 173 F3
Retford DN22 40 A4
Selston NG16 129 D3
Alma St NG7 173 D4
Almond Ave NG20 72 C3
Almond Cl Hucknall NG15 146 A3
Kimberley NG16 158 C4
Saxilby LN1 57 D2
Almond Gr Farndon NG24 139 D3
8 Kirkby in A NG17 114 C3
Worksop S80 35 F1
Almond Rise NG19 88 C1
Almond Wlk NG4 163 D2
Alnwick Cl NG6 160 B3
Alpha Terr NG1 223 D4
Alpine Cres NG4 174 B4
Alpine Ct S80 35 E1

Alpine St NG6 160 C1
Alport Pl NG18 103 D4
Althea Ct 1 NG7 161 D1
Althorpe St NG7 222 C3
Alton Ave NG11 185 D2
Alton Cl NG2 185 E2
Alum Ct NG5 160 C4
Alvenor St DE7 157 F1
Alverstone Rd NG3 161 E1
Alvey Rd NG24 140 C2
Alwood Gr NG11 184 B1
Alwyn Rd NG8 159 F1
Amanda Ave S81 25 F3
Amanda Rd DN11 8 C2
Amber Cl NG21 104 B1
Amber Dr NG16 143 D1
Amber Hill NG5 161 D4
Ambergate Rd NG8 172 A4
Amberley St NG1 223 D2
Ambleside
New Ollerton NG22 77 E3
West Bridgford NG2 186 B4
Ambleside Dr NG16 143 E2
Ambleside Grange S81 35 F4
Ambleside Jun & Inf Sch
NG8 160 A1
Ambleside Rd NG8 160 A1
Ambleside Way NG4 175 D4
Amcott Ave DN10 14 A4
Amcott Way DN22 39 F4
Amen Cnr NG23 109 D3
American Adventure
Theme Pk The DE75 157 D3
Amersham Rise NG8 160 A1
Amesbury Circ NG8 160 A2
Amethyst Cl NG21 104 B1
Amos La NG23 98 B2
Ampthill Rise NG5 161 D2
Anastasia Cl DN21 15 E2
Ancaster Gdns NG8 172 A2
Anchor Cl NG8 160 A1
Anchor La LE12 213 D1
Anchor Rd NG16 143 E1
Anders Dr NG6 159 F3
Anderson Cres NG9 183 F4
Anderson Ct 6 NG5 161 D4
Anderson Rd DN21 24 C1
Andover Cl 3 NG8 172 A3
Andover Rd
Mansfield NG19 101 E4
Nottingham NG5 160 C3
Andrew Ave Ilkeston DE7 170 A4
Nottingham NG3 162 A1
Andrew Dr NG21 118 A2
Andrews Dr NG16 143 D2
Anfield Cl NG9 183 D1
Anford Cl NG6 160 A3
Angel Alley NG1 223 F2
Angel Row NG1 223 E2
Angel Yd LE11 220 A2
Angela Ave NG17 115 D1
Angela Cl NG5 147 F1
Angell Gn NG11 195 E4
Anglia Way NG18 103 D2
Angrave Cl NG3 173 F4
Angus Cl Arnold NG5 148 A1
Kimberley NG16 159 D3
Anmer Cl 25 NG2 173 D1
Annan Ct NG8 172 A4
Anne's Cl NG3 162 A1
Annesley Cutting NG15 130 B4
Annesley Gr NG1 223 D4
Annesley La NG16 129 D3
Annesley Prim Sch NG15 130 A4
Annesley Rd
Hucknall NG15 145 F4
West Bridgford NG2 185 F4
Annesley Way NG19 101 E3
Annie Holgate Cty Jun
& Inf Schs The NG15 145 F3
Annies Wharf LE11 220 B3
Anslow Ave Beeston NG9 184 A4
Sutton in A NG17 100 C3
Anson Wlk DE7 157 F2
Anstee Rd NG10 193 E3
Anstey Rise NG3 173 F3
Anston Ave S81 35 F3
Anthony Bek Prim Sch
NG19 86 C3
Antill St NG9 182 B3
Apley Cl DN21 24 C4
Apollo Dr NG6 159 F3
Appin Rd NG19 101 E3
Apple Tree Cl NG12 186 A2
Apple Tree La NG4 162 C1
Apple Wlk NG4 174 A4
Appleby Cl NG24 140 B4
Appleby Ct S81 35 F4
Appleby Rd NG19 86 C3
Appledore Ave NG8 171 F1
Appledorne Way NG5 147 F1
Appleton Dr LE12 216 A2
Appleton Gate NG24 125 D1
Appleton Rd Beeston NG9 184 A2
Blidworth NG21 118 A3
Appleton St NG20 74 A2
Appletree Cl NG25 121 F1
Applewood Gr NG5 161 E2
Arboretum Language Sch
NG1 223 D4
Arboretum St NG1 223 D4
Arbrook Dr NG8 172 B3
Arbutus Cl NG11 184 B1
Arcade The NG24 139 F4
Arcadia Ave NG20 72 C3
Arch Hill NG5 147 F2
Archbishop Cranmer
CE Prim Sch NG13 179 D3

Archdale Rd NG5 161 E3
Archer Cres NG8 171 F3
Archer Rd NG9 182 C3
Archer St DE7 157 F2
Archers Dr NG22 106 A3
Archway Rd NG21 90 B4
Arden Cl Beeston NG9 184 A4
Hucknall NG15 146 B3
Arden Gr NG13 177 E3
Ardleigh Cl NG5 146 B1
Ardmore Cl NG2 173 F2
Ardsley Cl DE75 143 D1
Argosy Cl DN10 9 F4
Argyle Cl NG20 73 F2
Argyle Ct NG7 222 B3
Argyle St
Langley Mill NG16 143 E2
Mansfield NG18 102 B3
Nottingham NG7 222 B3
Ariel Cl NG6 160 C3
Arkers Cl NG6 160 B2
Arklow Cl NG8 160 A1
Arkwright Prim Sch NG2 173 E1
Arkwright St
Gainsborough DN21 15 E1
Nottingham NG2 173 E1
Arkwright Wlk NG2 173 E1
Arleston Dr NG8 171 E2
Arlington Ave NG19 88 C2
Arlington Cl NG15 146 A2
Arlington Dr NG3 161 E1
Arlington Way DN22 39 F4
Armadale Cl NG5 162 B4
Armfield Rd NG5 162 B3
Armitage Cl 3 LE11 220 A2
Armitage Dr NG10 194 A4
Armstrong Rd
Mansfield NG19 101 E4
Nottingham NG6 159 F3
Retford DN22 39 F4
Arncliff Cl NG8 171 E2
Arndale Rd NG5 161 E3
Arne Ct 12 NG2 173 E1
Arnesby Rd NG7 222 A1
Arno Ave 8 NG7 173 D4
Arno Vale Cty Jun Sch
NG5 161 F3
Arno Vale Gdns NG5 161 F3
Arno Vale Rd NG5 161 F3
Arnold Ave
Long Eaton NG10 193 D2
Retford DN22 40 A2
Southwell NG25 121 F1
Arnold & Carlton Coll
NG3 223 F3
Arnold & Carlton Coll
of F Ed NG4 162 B2
Arnold Church Drive
Prim Sch NG5 161 F4
Arnold Cres NG10 193 D2
Arnold Hill Comp Sch
NG5 162 A3
Arnold La NG3 162 B2
Arnold Rd NG5 161 D3
Arnos Gr NG16 159 E2
Arnot Hill Rd NG5 161 F3
Arnside NG9 182 C3
Arnside Cl NG5 161 D3
Arnside Rd NG5 161 D3
Arran Cl NG9 170 C1
Arran Sq NG19 101 E3
Arthur Ave
Nottingham NG7 222 B2
Stapleford NG9 182 C4
Arthur Cres NG4 174 B4
Arthur Green Ave NG17 114 C1
Arthur Mee Ctr
(Coll of F Ed) The NG9 182 B4
Arthur Mee Rd NG9 182 C3
Arthur Rd DN21 15 F1
Arthur Short Cl S80 45 D3
Arthur St Carlton NG4 175 D3
Mansfield NG18 102 B3
Nottingham NG7 222 C4
Pinxton NG16 113 E2
Artic Way NG16 158 B4
Arum Croft DN22 39 E2
Arun Dale NG19 88 B1
Arundel Cl
Gainsborough DN21 15 F1
Sandiacre NG10 182 A2
Arundel Dr Beeston NG9 171 D1
Carlton in L S81 25 F3
Mansfield NG19 101 F4
Ranskill DN22 19 D3
Arundel St NG7 222 C3
Arundel Way DN22 39 E4
Arundel Wlk DN11 9 D3
Ascot Ave NG16 158 C4
Ascot Cl NG17 115 E2
Ascot Dr Arnold NG5 161 E4
Hucknall NG15 145 E3
Mansfield NG18 102 C4
Ascot Park Est NG10 182 B4
Ascot Rd NG8 172 B4
Ascott Gdns NG2 185 D3
Ash Cl Bingham NG13 178 A2
Burton Joyce NG14 163 F2
Hucknall NG15 145 E3
Pinxton NG16 113 E1
Worksop S80 35 F1
Ash Cres
Kirkby in A NG17 114 B3
Nuthall NG16 159 D3
Ash Ct NG4 174 B4

Ash Gr Brinsley NG16 143 E4
Gainsborough DN21 15 E1
Hathern LE12 213 D1
Keyworth NG12 198 A1
Long Eaton NG10 193 E3
Sandiacre NG10 182 A4
Selston NG16 128 C4
Shirebrook NG20 72 B3
Stapleford NG9 182 B3
Sutton in A NG17 100 B4
Ash Grove NG14 149 E2
Ash Holt Dr S81 35 F4
Ash La LE12 206 B2
Ash Lea Cl NG12 187 F1
Ash Lea Sch NG12 187 F2
Ash Mount Rd NG16 143 D2
Ash Rd NG24 139 F2
Ash St DE7 157 F2
Ash Tree Ave DN10 9 F4
Ash Tree Cl NG25 136 B4
Ash Tree Cres NG19 88 B3
Ash Tree Sq NG9 183 D4
Ash Vale Rd NG22 64 A1
Ash Villas 8 NG7 161 D1
Ash Wlk LE12 214 B4
Ashbourne Cl NG9 171 D1
Ashbourne Ct NG6 159 F3
Ashbourne Rd NG16 129 D1
Ashbourne St
Nottingham NG7 222 C3
Shirebrook NG20 72 C2
Ashburnham Ave NG7 222 B2
Ashby Ave NG19 88 B3
Ashby Rd Kegworth DE74 203 D1
Long Whatton LE12 212 B1
Loughborough LE11 220 A2
Ashby Sq LE11 220 A2
Ashchurch Dr NG8 171 E1
Ashcroft DN22 39 E2
Ashcroft Rd DN21 24 B3
Ashdale Ave NG15 146 A3
Ashdale Rd Arnold NG5 162 A4
Ilkeston DE7 170 A3
Nottingham NG3 174 A3
Ashdown Cl NG11 185 D3
Ashdown Gr NG13 177 E2
Ashdown Way DN10 6 C1
Ashe Cl NG5 162 A4
Asher La NG11 196 B3
Ashes Park Ave S81 35 E4
Ashfield Ave
Beeston NG9 184 A3
Mansfield NG18 102 A4
Ashfield Com Hospl
NG17 115 D3
Ashfield Comp Sch NG17 114 B4
Ashfield Dr NG17 114 C3
Ashfield Prec NG17 115 D3
Ashfield Rd
Huthwaite NG17 100 A2
Nottingham NG2 173 F2
Ashfield St NG17 101 D3
Ashford Ct DN22 39 E2
Ashford Dr NG15 117 D2
Ashford Pl DE7 157 F3
Ashford Rise
Nottingham NG8 171 E1
Sutton in A NG17 100 B2
Ashforth Ave DE75 143 D1
Ashforth St NG3 223 F4
Ashgate NG17 100 B2
Ashgate Rd NG15 146 A3
Ashington Dr NG5 148 A1
Ashland Rd NG17 100 B2
Ashland Rd W NG17 100 A2
Ashlands Cl NG17 100 A2
Ashlea DN10 6 C1
Ashleigh Way NG19 89 D1
Ashley Cl NG9 183 E3
Ashley Cres NG12 197 F2
Ashley Ct S81 35 F3
Ashley Gr NG15 145 F4
Ashley La DN22 41 F1
Ashley Rd Keyworth NG12 197 F2
Worksop S81 35 F3
Ashley St 13 NG3 173 F3
Ashley Terr S80 35 F2
Ashling St NG2 173 E1
Ashmore Ave NG17 100 B1
Ashmount Sch LE11 220 A1
Ashness Cl NG2 186 B3
Ashover Cl
Nottingham NG3 173 F4
Ravenshead NG15 117 D2
Ashridge Way NG2 186 B2
Ashton Ave NG5 147 F1
Ashton Ct NG17 101 D3
Ashvale Rd NG22 66 A1
Ashview Cl NG10 193 D4
Ashville Cl NG2 173 D1
Ashwater Dr NG3 162 B3
Ashwell Ave NG19 88 C3
Ashwell Gdns NG7 172 C4
Ashwell St NG4 174 C3
Ashwick Cl NG11 185 D3
Ashwood Ave NG17 115 E3
Ashwood Cl NG19 88 C3
Ashworth Ave NG11 196 B4
Ashworth Cl
Newark-on-T NG24 140 B4
Nottingham NG3 174 B3
Ashworth Cres
North Leverton w H DN22 32 B1
Nottingham NG3 162 A1
Ashworth Dr NG19 88 C2
Askeby Dr NG8 159 E1
Askew La NG20 74 A2
Askham La DN22 52 A3
Askham Rd NG22 51 F1
Aslockton Dr NG8 160 B1
Aslockton Sta NG13 179 D2
Aspen Cl Bingham NG13 178 A2
Laughterton LN1 55 D2
Tuxford NG22 66 A1
Walesby NG22 64 A1
Aspen Ct
Gainsborough DN21 15 F1
Mansfield NG19 88 C1
Tuxford NG22 66 A1
Aspen Rd NG6 159 F4
Asper St NG4 175 D4
Aspinall Ct 3 NG8 172 B3
Aspley La NG8 172 B4
Aspley Park Dr NG8 172 A4
Aspley Pl NG7 222 B4
Aspley Rd NG17 100 B2
Aspley Wood Sch NG8 172 A4
Asquith Mews NG18 102 C3
Asquith St
Gainsborough DN21 15 D1
Mansfield NG18 102 C3
Assarts Rd NG16 159 F2
Astcote Cl DE75 143 D1
Aster Rd NG3 173 F4
Astle Ct NG5 162 B3
Astley Cl NG17 130 A4
Astley Dr NG3 161 F1
Aston Ave NG9 172 A1
Aston Ct DE7 157 F1
Aston Dr NG6 146 B1
Aston Gn NG9 182 C2
Astral Gr NG15 145 E2
Astrid Gdns NG5 160 C3
Astwith La S44, S45 85 D3
Astwood Cl NG8 171 F4
Athelstan Rd S80 35 F1
Atherfield Gdns NG16 143 F2
Atherton Rd Ilkeston DE7 157 E2
Shipley DE7 157 E2
Atherton Rise NG8 160 A2
Athorpe Gr NG6 160 C2
Atkin La NG18 102 A2
Attenborough La NG9 183 E2
Attenborough Nature
Reserve NG9 183 F1
Attenborough Prep Sch
NG9 183 E1
Attenborough Sta NG9 183 E1
Attercliffe Terr 15 NG2 173 E1
Attewell Rd NG16 158 A3
Attlee Ave NG19 89 D1
Aubrey Ave 15 NG2 173 F2
Aubrey Rd NG5 161 D1
Auckland Cl NG7 222 A3
Auckland Rd
Hucknall NG15 145 E3
Retford DN22 39 E4
Audley Cl DE7 157 E2
Audley Dr NG9 171 F1
Audon Ave NG9 183 F3
Audrey Cres NG19 88 B3
Augustine Gdns NG5 147 D1
Ault Hucknall La S44 86 A4
Aumberry Gap LE11 220 A2
Aurillac Way DN22 29 E1
Austen Ave
Long Eaton NG10 193 E3
Nottingham NG7 173 D4
Austin Cl NG18 102 C4
Austin St Nottingham NG6 160 B4
Shirebrook NG20 73 D2
Austins Dr NG10 182 A2
Austrey Ave NG9 184 A4
Avalon Cl NG6 160 C3
Ave A NG1 223 F2
Ave B NG1 223 F2
Ave C NG1 223 F2
Ave D NG1 173 F2
Ave E 10 NG1 173 F3
Avebury Cl NG11 195 E4
Avenue Cl NG5 160 C4
Avenue Rd DN22 39 F3
Avenue The
Calverton NG14 148 C4
Gainsborough DN21 15 F1
Gunthorpe NG14 164 C3
Mansfield NG18 102 C2
Newark-on-T NG24 140 A4
Sutton in A NG17 100 C1
Averham Cl NG19 101 E3
Averham Sch NG23 123 F1
Averton Sq NG8 172 B2
Aviemore Cl NG5 162 A4
Avocet Wharf 22 NG7 172 C1
Avon Ave NG15 145 F2
Avon Cl NG17 129 F4
Avon Gdns NG2 185 F4
Avon Pl NG9 184 A4
Avon Rd Carlton NG4 162 C1
Nottingham NG3 174 A3
Avon Rise DN22 40 A4
Avon Vale Rd LE11 220 B1
Avon Way
Mansfield NG18 103 D3
Worksop S81 35 F4
Avonbridge Cl NG5 148 B1
Avondale Cotgrave NG12 188 A2
Mansfield NG18 102 C4
Avondale Cl NG10 193 D3
Avondale Rd NG4 174 B3
Avonlea Cl DE7 170 A3
Awsworth Inf Sch NG16 158 B2
Awsworth Jun Sch NG16 158 B2
Awsworth La
Awsworth NG16 158 B3
Awsworth, Cossall Marsh
NG16 158 B2
Kimberley NG16 158 B3
Awsworth Rd DE7 157 F1
Axford Cl NG4 162 C1
Aylesham Ave NG5 161 F3
Aylestone Dr NG8 172 A4
Ayr St NG7 222 C4
Ayscough Ave NG16 159 E3
Ayton Cl NG2 173 D1
Ayton Gdns NG9 183 E1
Azalea Ct NG16 158 B4
Azimghur Rd NG13 179 D2

B Road NG9 184 B3
Babbacombe Cl NG5 161 D3
Babbacombe Way NG15 145 E3
Babbington Cres NG4 162 C1
Babbington La NG16 158 C2
Babbington St DE55 99 D3
Babington Ct NG9 183 E3
Babworth Cres DN22 39 E3
Babworth Ct NG18 102 B4
Babworth Rd DN22 39 D3
Back La Claypole NG23 156 B3
Cotes LE12 220 C3
Cropwell Butler NG12 189 D3
Eakring NG22 106 C4
East Markham NG22 66 A4
Halam NG22 120 C1
Huthwaite NG17 99 F2
Ilkeston DE7 157 F1
Keyworth NG12 198 A3
Long Clawson LE14 211 E2
Misson DN10 4 A1
Morton NG25 137 E2
Nuthall NG16 159 E3
Ollerton NG22 77 D2
Ranskill DN22 19 D2
Sutton in A NG17 100 C3
Thorpe Salvin S80 34 A3
Willoughby-on-t-W LE12 217 E3
Back St
Barnby in t W NG24 142 A3
East Stockwith DN21 7 F1
South Clifton NG23 68 C1
Back Terr DN22 39 F4
Bacon Cl NG16 158 A4
Bacon St DN21 24 B3
Bacton Ave NG6 160 A4
Bacton Gdns 2 NG6 160 A4
Baden Powell Rd NG2 174 A2
Bader NG11 185 D4
Bader Rise DN10 20 A4
Bader View DN10 20 A4
Badger Cl NG15 145 E3
Badger Way NG19 103 D4
Badgers Chase DN22 29 F1
Baggaley Cres NG19 88 A1
Bagnall Ave NG5 161 E4
Bagnall Rd NG6 160 B2
Bagshaw St NG19 87 D2
Bagthorpe Cl NG5 161 D2
Baildon Cl NG8 172 B2
Bailey Brook Cres NG16 143 D2
Bailey Brook Dr NG16 143 D2
Bailey Brook Ind Est
DE75, NG16 143 D1
Bailey Brook Wlk NG16 143 D2
Bailey Cl NG5 161 E4
Bailey Cres NG19 101 F4
Bailey Ct NG12 175 F1
Bailey Grove Rd NG16 143 E1
Bailey La NG12 175 F1
Bailey Rd NG24 139 F3
Bailey St Carlton NG4 175 D4
Nottingham NG6 160 C1
Stapleford NG9 182 B3
Bainbridge Rd
Loughborough LE11 220 B1
Market Warsop NG20 74 A2
Bainbridge Terr NG17 100 B3
Bainbridge The NG14 149 D4
Baines Ave NG24 140 B2
Baines Rd DN21 24 C4
Bainton Gr NG7 184 C1
Baker Ave NG5 148 A1
Baker Brook Ind Pk
NG15 146 B3
Baker La NG20 60 A1
Baker Rd Eastwood NG16 144 B1
Mansfield Woodhouse NG19 88 B3
Baker St Hucknall NG15 146 A4
Ilkeston DE7 157 F1
Nottingham NG1 173 D4
Baker's Hollow NG12 187 F2
Baker's La
Colston Bassett NG12 200 C4
Redmile NG13 192 C2
Bakerdale Rd NG3 174 A3
Bakers Cl NG7 222 A4
Bakewell Ave NG4 162 C1
Bakewell Cl NG24 140 B2
Bakewell Dr NG5 160 C4
Bakewell Rd NG10 193 F3
Bala Dr NG5 161 D4
Balderton Ct NG19 101 F4
Balderton Gate NG24 140 A4
Balderton La NG24 141 D4
Baldwin Cl NG19 89 D1
Baldwin Ct NG7 222 B3
Baldwin St Eastwood NG16 144 B1
Nottingham NG7 222 C3
Balfour Rd
Nottingham NG7 222 B3
Stapleford NG9 182 B3
Balfour St
Gainsborough DN21 15 E1
Kirkby in A NG17 115 E2
Balfron Gdns 13 NG2 173 D1
Ball Hill DE55 113 E3
Ball St NG3 173 F4
Ballantrae Cl NG5 162 A4
Ballater Cl NG19 87 F1
Ballerat Cres NG5 160 C4
Balloon Ho's NG9 171 D2
Balloon Wood Ind Est
NG8 171 D2
Balls La NG17 115 E1
Balmoral Ave NG2 185 F4
Balmoral Cl Carlton in L S81 25 F3
Mansfield Woodhouse NG19 88 C3
Sandiacre NG10 182 A2
Balmoral Cres NG8 171 E3
Balmoral Ct DN11 9 D3
Balmoral Dr Beeston NG9 171 E1
Mansfield NG19 87 F1
Balmoral Gr NG15 146 A4
Balmoral Rd
Bingham NG13 177 E2
Carlton NG4 174 C3
Nottingham NG1 223 D4
Bamburgh Cl 10 NG17 114 C4
Bamford Dr NG18 103 D3
Bamford St DE55 99 D2
Bamkin Cl NG15 146 A3
Bampton St 30 LE11 220 A2
Banbury Ave NG9 182 C2
Banbury Mount 9 NG5 161 E1
Banchory Cl NG19 87 F1
Bancroft La NG18 101 F4
Bancroft Rd NG24 140 A3
Bancroft St NG6 160 B4
Banes Rd NG13 178 A2
Bangor Wlk 8 NG3 173 E4
Bank Ave NG17 100 C1
Bank Cl Creswell S80 58 B4
Shirebrook NG20 72 C2
Bank End Rd DN10 1 B2
Bank Hill NG14 149 D2
Bank Pl NG1 223 E2
Bank Side DN22 39 F2
Bank St Langley Mill NG16 143 E2
Long Eaton NG10 193 F4
Bank Yd 24 NG6 160 A4
Bankfield Dr NG9 171 E1
Banks Ave NG17 114 C3
Banks Cl NG5 162 A3
Banks Cres NG13 177 F2
Banks Paddock NG13 177 F2
Banks Rd NG9 182 C1
Banks The NG13 177 F2
Bankwood Cl NG8 160 A1
Bannerman Rd
Kirkby in A NG17 114 C3
Nottingham NG6 160 B3
Baptist La NG23 111 F4
Bar Gate NG24 124 C1
Bar La NG6 160 B1
Bar Lane Ind Pk NG6 160 B1
Bar Rd Beckingham DN10 23 E4
Laxton NG22 79 E2
Bar Rd N DN10 23 E4
Bar Rd S DN10 23 E4
Barbara Sq NG15 130 C1
Barber Cl DE7 157 F2
Barber St NG16 144 A1
Barbers Wood Cl NG15 117 D1
Barbrook Cl NG8 172 A3
Barbury Dr NG11 195 E4
Barclay Ct DE7 157 E2
Barden Rd NG3 162 A2
Bardfield Gdns NG5 146 B1
Bardney Dr NG6 160 A4
Bardsey Gdns NG5 161 D4
Barent Cl NG5 160 C3
Barent Wlk NG5 160 C3
Barker Ave
Sutton in A NG17 100 B4
Westwood NG16 128 A2
Barker Ave E NG10 182 A3
Barker Ave N NG10 182 A3
Barker Gate
Hucknall NG15 145 F4
Ilkeston DE7 157 F1
Nottingham NG1 223 F2
Barker Hades Rd S81 16 A2
Barker Hill NG14 150 C1
Barker St NG17 99 F2
Barker's La NG9 183 F2
Barkers Field LE14 211 E2
Barkestone La
Barkestone-le-V NG13 192 A1
Bottesford NG13 181 D1
Barkla Cl NG11 195 E4
Barkston Cl NG24 140 B2
Barley Croft
South Normanton DE55 113 D2
West Bridgford NG2 185 E2
Barley Dale Dr NG9 170 B1
Barleylands NG11 196 B3
Barling Dr Ilkeston DE7 157 E1
Shipley DE7 157 E1
Barlock Rd NG6 160 C2
Barlow Dr N NG16 158 A2
Barlow Dr S NG16 158 A2
Barn Cl Cotgrave NG12 187 F1
Mansfield NG18 102 C3
Worksop S81 36 A4
Barn Croft NG9 183 D3
Barnards Pl LE14 211 E2
Barnby Gate NG24 140 A4
Barnby La NG23 156 C4
Barnby Rd NG24 140 B3
Barnby Road Prim Sch
NG24 140 A4
Barnby Wlk NG5 161 D2
Barndale Cl NG2 185 E2
Barnes Cres NG17 114 C4
Barnes Ct DN22 29 E1
Barnes Rd NG5 160 C4
Barnet Rd NG3 174 A4
Barnett Ct NG12 197 F2
Barnfield NG11 185 D2
Barnfield Cl LE12 212 A2
Barnfield Rd NG23 98 A1
Barnsley Terr 16 NG2 173 E1
Barnston Rd NG2 174 A3
Barnstone La NG13 191 D3
Barnstone Rd NG13 190 B1
Barnum Cl NG8 171 F3
Barons Cl NG4 162 C1
Barra Mews 20 NG2 173 D1
Barrack La NG7 222 B2
Barrack Row 11 LE11 220 A2
Barratt Cl Beeston NG9 183 E1
Cropwell Bishop NG12 189 D2
Barratt Cres NG9 183 E1
Barratt La NG9 183 E1
Barrel Hill Rd NG23 96 C4
Barrhead Cl NG5 146 C1
Barringer Rd NG19 88 B1
Barrington Cl NG12 175 F1
Barrique Rd NG7 172 C1
Barrow Rd LE12 220 C
Barrow Slade NG12 197 F
Barrow St LE11 220 A2
Barrowhill Wlk NG18 103 D
Barrows Hill La NG16 128 B
Barry St NG6 160 A
Barrydale Ave NG9 183 F
Bars Hill LE12 206 B
Bartlow Rd NG8 171 E
Barton Cl
Mansfield Woodhouse NG19 89 D
Ruddington NG11 196 A
Barton La
Barton in F NG11 195 D
Beeston NG9 183 E
Nottingham NG11 184 B
Barton Rd NG10 194 A
Barton St NG9 184 A
Bartons Cl NG16 144 B
Barwell Dr NG8 159 E
Basa Cres NG5 160 C
Basford Hall Coll Annexe
NG7 222 B
Basford Hall Coll
F Ed Annexe NG7 222 B
Basford Hall Coll of F Ed
NG6 160 B
Basford Hall Coll of F Ed
(The Hucknall Ctr)
NG15 146 A
Basford Rd NG6 160 B
Baskin La NG9 183 E
Baslow Ave NG4 162 C
Baslow Cl NG10 193 D
Baslow Dr NG9 172 A
Baslow Way NG18 103 D
Bassetlaw District
General Hospl S81 36 A
Bassett Cl NG16 158 C
Bassett Rd NG16 158 C
Bassett The NG20 72
Bassingfield La NG12 186 C
Bastion St NG7 222 A
Bateman Gdns 29 NG7 172 C
Bateman Rd LE12 205
Bateman's Yd NG17 114
Bath La Mansfield NG18 102
Market Warsop NG19 73
Bath St Ilkeston DE7 157
Mansfield NG18 102 A
Nottingham NG1 223
Sutton in A NG17 100
Bathley La
Little Carlton NG23 124
South Muskham NG23 110
Bathley St NG2 173
Baths La NG15 146
Bathurst Dr NG8 172
Bathurst Terr NG20 58
Bathwood Dr
Mansfield NG17, NG18 101
Sutton in A NG17, NG18 101
Batley La NG19 86
Baulk La Beeston NG9 183
Harworth DN11 8
Torworth DN22 19
Worksop S81 35
Baulk The
Clarborough DN22 40
Worksop S81 35
Baulker La
Blidworth NG21 118
Clipstone NG21 90
Farnsfield NG22 119
Baum's La NG18 102
Bawtry Cl DN11 8
Bawtry Rd Bawtry DN10 10
Blyth S81 18
Everton DN10 11
Harworth DN11 9
Misson DN10 4
Tickhill DN11 8
Bawtry Wlk NG3 17
Baxter Hill NG19 86
Baxter St LE11 220
Bayard Ct NG8 172
Bayard St DN21 15
Bayliss Rd NG4 162

yswater Rd NG16 ... 158 C4
ythorn Rd NG8 ... 171 E3
acon Dr
irkby in A NG17 ... 115 E3
oughborough LE11 ... 220 A1
acon Hill Dr NG15 ... 145 E3
acon Hill Rd
ringley on t H DN10 ... 13 D1
lewark-on-T NG24 ... 140 B4
acon Hill Rise NG3 ... 173 F3
acon Hts NG24 ... 140 B4
acon Rd Beeston NG9 ... 184 A3
oughborough LE11 ... 220 A1
acon View NG13 ... 181 D2
acon Way NG24 ... 140 B4
aconsfield St
ong Eaton NG10 ... 193 F4
lottingham NG7 ... 172 C4
an Ave S80 ... 36 A2
an Cl NG6 ... 159 F3
anford La
Calverton NG14 ... 133 F2
Oxton NG25 ... 134 A2
ardall St
Hucknall NG15 ... 146 A3
7 Mansfield NG18 ... 102 A4
ardall Street Prim Sch
NG15 ... 146 A3
ardsall's Row DN22 ... 39 F4
ardsley Gdns NG2 ... 173 D1
ardsley Rd NG21 ... 76 B1
ardsmore Gr NG15 ... 130 C1
ast Market Hill
Newark-on-T NG24 ... 124 C1
Nottingham NG1 ... 223 E2
atty Wlk DE7 ... 157 F2
auclerk Dr NG5 ... 160 C4
aufit La NG16 ... 113 F1
aufort Ct NG2 ... 185 E2
aufort Dr NG9 ... 183 E3
aufort Gdns DN10 ... 9 F4
aufort St DN21 ... 15 E2
aufort Way S81 ... 35 F4
aulieu Gdns NG2 ... 185 E3
auly Dr NG19 ... 101 E3
aumaris Dr
Beeston NG9 ... 183 D2
Carlton NG4 ... 163 D1
aumond Cross NG24 ... 139 F4
aumont Ave NG18 ... 102 C3
aumont Cl
Keyworth NG12 ... 197 F2
Stapleford NG9 ... 170 C1
aumont Ct LE11 ... 220 A3
aumont Gdns NG2 ... 185 E2
aumont Rd LE11 ... 220 A1
aumont Rise S80 ... 35 E2
aumont St
Gainsborough DN21 ... 24 B4
Nottingham NG2 ... 173 F2
aumont Wlk NG24 ... 125 D1
auvale NG16 ... 144 B1
auvale Cres NG15 ... 145 F3
auvale Dr DE7 ... 157 F3
auvale Rd
Annesley Woodhouse NG17 ... 114 C1
Hucknall NG15 ... 145 F3
Nottingham NG2 ... 173 E1
auvale Rise NG16 ... 144 A2
aver Pl S80 ... 35 F2
azley Ave NG18 ... 101 F4
ck Ave NG14 ... 148 C4
ck Cres
Blidworth NG21 ... 118 A2
Mansfield NG19 ... 101 F4
ck La Clayworth DN22 ... 21 F2
Farnsfield NG22 ... 119 F3
Sutton in A NG17, NG19 ... 101 D3
ck St Carlton NG4 ... 174 C4
Nottingham NG1 ... 223 F3
Thurgarton NG14 ... 151 E4
ckenham Rd NG7 ... 222 B4
ecket Main Sch The
NG11 ... 185 D3
ecket Sch The NG2 ... 185 E4
eckett Ave
Carlton in L S81 ... 25 F4
Gainsborough DN21 ... 15 F1
Mansfield NG19 ... 87 F1
eckett Ct NG4 ... 162 B2
eckford Rd 35 NG2 ... 173 F2
eckhampton Rd NG5 ... 161 D4
eckingham Ct NG19 ... 101 F4
eckingham Prim Sch
DN10 ... 23 D4
eckingham Rd DN10 ... 14 A2
eckingthorpe Dr NG13 ... 181 D2
eckland Hill NG22 ... 65 F3
eckley Rd NG8 ... 159 F1
eckon Mdw DN10 ... 23 E4
eckside Lowdham NG14 ... 150 C1
West Bridgford NG2 ... 186 B3
edale S81 ... 36 A4
edale Ct NG9 ... 183 D2
edale Rd NG5 ... 161 E3
edarra Gr NG7 ... 222 A2
ede House La NG24 ... 140 A4
ede Ling NG2 ... 185 E3
edford Ave NG18 ... 102 C4
edford Cl DE74 ... 203 E1
edford Ct Bawtry DN10 ... 9 F4
Stapleford NG9 ... 170 C1
edford Gr NG6 ... 160 B3
edford Row NG1 ... 223 F3
edford Sq 25 LE11 ... 220 A2
edford St LE11 ... 220 A2
edlington Gdns NG3 ... 161 F1
ee Hive La 26 LE11 ... 220 A2
Beech Ave Beeston NG9 ... 184 A3
Bingham NG13 ... 178 A2
Carlton NG4 ... 174 C3
East Leake LE12 ... 214 B4
Gainsborough DN21 ... 15 F1
Hucknall NG15 ... 146 A4
Huthwaite NG17 ... 100 A2
Keyworth NG12 ... 198 A1
Kirkby in A NG17 ... 114 C3
Long Eaton NG10 ... 182 C1
12 Mansfield NG18 ... 102 A3
New Ollerton NG22 ... 77 E2
Nottingham, Hyson Green
NG7 ... 173 D4
Nottingham, Mapperley
NG3 ... 162 A2
Nuthall NG16 ... 159 D3
Pinxton NG16 ... 113 F2
Ravenshead NG15 ... 116 C2
Sandiacre NG10 ... 182 A4
Tickhill DN11 ... 8 A4
Worksop S81 ... 35 F3
Beech Cl
Gringley on t H DN10 ... 12 C1
Nottingham NG6 ... 160 B2
Radcliffe on T NG12 ... 175 F1
West Bridgford NG12 ... 186 A2
Beech Cres S44 ... 86 A4
Beech Ct Nottingham NG3 ... 162 A2
Selston NG16 ... 129 D2
Beech Gr Blidworth NG21 ... 118 B3
Carlton in L S81 ... 25 F4
South Normanton DE55 ... 113 D3
Beech Hill Ave NG19 ... 87 F1
Beech Hill Cres NG19 ... 87 F1
Beech Hill Dr NG19 ... 87 F1
Beech Hill Sch NG19 ... 87 F1
Beech Rd Harworth DN11 ... 9 D3
Selston NG16 ... 129 D2
Beech St NG17 ... 100 B4
Beech Tree Ave NG19 ... 88 A3
Beech Wlk DN22 ... 50 A2
Beecham Ave NG3 ... 173 F4
Beechcroft S81 ... 36 A3
Beechdale Ave NG17 ... 100 C2
Beechdale Cres NG17 ... 100 C2
Beechdale Rd
Mansfield Woodhouse NG19 .. 89 D1
Nottingham NG8 ... 172 A4
Beecher La DN10 ... 14 A1
Beeches Rd LE11 ... 220 B1
Beeches The Carlton NG3 ... 174 A4
Sutton in A NG17 ... 100 B4
Tuxford NG22 ... 65 F1
Beechways DN22 ... 39 E2
Beechwood Cl
Mansfield Woodhouse NG19 .. 89 D1
Sutton in A NG17 ... 101 D3
Beechwood Cres DN22 ... 37 F3
Beechwood Ct NG17 ... 101 D3
Beechwood Dr DN22 ... 38 B3
Beechwood Gr NG17 ... 101 D3
Beechwood Rd
Arnold NG5 ... 162 A4
19 Kirkby in A NG17 ... 114 C4
Beehive La LN6 ... 84 C1
Beehive St DN22 ... 39 F3
Beeley Ave NG17 ... 100 C1
Beeley Cl NG18 ... 103 D3
Beeston Cl NG6 ... 146 C2
Beeston Ct NG6 ... 160 B3
Beeston Fields Dr NG9 ... 183 E4
Beeston Fields
Jun & Inf Schs NG9 ... 183 E3
Beeston La NG9 ... 184 A4
Beeston Rd
Newark-on-T NG24 ... 140 A3
Nottingham NG7 ... 172 B1
Beeston Rylands Jun Sch
NG9 ... 184 A2
Beeston Sta NG9 ... 184 A3
Beethan Cl NG13 ... 177 F2
Beggarlee Pk NG16 ... 144 A2
Behay Gdns NG23 ... 138 B4
Beighton Ct NG18 ... 103 D3
Beighton St NG17 ... 100 C2
Belconnen Rd NG5 ... 161 D3
Belfmoor Cl S80 ... 45 D3
Belford Cl NG6 ... 159 F4
Belfry Cl 1 NG17 ... 114 C4
Belfry Way NG2 ... 186 B2
Belgrave Ct DN10 ... 9 F4
Belgrave Rd NG6 ... 160 A4
Bell Foundry Mus LE11 ... 220 B2
Bell La Collingham NG23 ... 111 F4
Nottingham NG11 ... 185 D4
Weston NG23 ... 81 D3
Bell St NG4 ... 174 B4
Bellamy Rd NG18 ... 103 D1
Bellar Gate NG1 ... 223 F2
Belle Vue La NG21 ... 118 A3
Belle-isle Rd NG15 ... 146 A4
Belleville Dr NG5 ... 161 D4
Bellevue Ct NG3 ... 173 F3
Bellmore Gdns NG8 ... 171 E3
Bells La NG8 ... 160 A2
Bellsfield Cl S80 ... 45 D3
Belmond Cl NG24 ... 139 F3
Belmont Ave NG6 ... 160 B4
Belmont Cl Beeston NG9 ... 183 D2
Hucknall NG15 ... 146 A2
Mansfield Woodhouse NG19 .. 89 D1
Belmont Rd NG17 ... 115 D1
Belper Ave NG4 ... 162 B1
Belper Cres NG4 ... 162 B1
Belper Rd NG7 ... 172 C4
Belper St NG18 ... 102 B4
Belper Way NG18 ... 102 B4
Belsay Rd NG5 ... 161 D4
Belsford Ct NG16 ... 159 D4
Belt Rd The DN21 ... 15 F2
Belton Cl NG10 ... 182 A2
Belton Dr NG2 ... 185 D2
Belton Rd LE11 ... 220 A3
Belton Rd West Extension
LE11 ... 220 A3
Belton St 20 NG7 ... 172 C4
Belvedere Ave 23 NG7 ... 172 C4
Belvedere St NG18 ... 102 A3
Belvoir Ave NG13 ... 181 D1
Belvoir Cl Aslockton NG13 ... 178 C2
Long Eaton NG10 ... 193 F3
Belvoir Cres Langar NG13 ... 190 B1
Newark-on-T NG24 ... 140 A3
Belvoir High Sch NG13 ... 181 D1
Belvoir Hill NG2 ... 173 F2
Belvoir Pl NG24 ... 140 B2
Belvoir Rd Balderton NG24 .. 140 B2
Bottesford NG13 ... 181 D1
Carlton NG4 ... 175 D4
Redmile NG13 ... 192 C2
West Bridgford NG2 ... 174 A1
Belvoir St Hucknall NG15 ... 145 F4
Nottingham NG3 ... 161 F1
Belvoir Terr DN21 ... 15 D2
Belward St NG1 ... 223 F2
Belwood Cl NG7 ... 184 C1
Bembridge S81 ... 36 A3
Bembridge Ct NG9 ... 183 D4
Bembridge Dr NG5 ... 161 D3
Ben Mayo Ct NG7 ... 222 B4
Ben St NG7 ... 222 B4
Bendigo La NG2 ... 174 A2
Benedict Ct 3 NG5 ... 147 D1
Benet Dr NG22 ... 106 A3
Benington Dr NG8 ... 171 E2
Benner Ave DE7 ... 170 A3
Bennerley Ave DE7 ... 157 F2
Bennerley Ct NG6 ... 159 F4
Bennerley Fields Sch
DE7 ... 157 F2
Bennerley Rd NG6 ... 159 F4
Bennerley Sch DE7 ... 157 F2
Bennett Ave NG18 ... 102 C3
Bennett Rd NG3 ... 162 A2
Bennett St
Long Eaton NG10 ... 182 B1
Nottingham NG3 ... 161 F1
Sandiacre NG10 ... 182 A3
Benneworth Cl NG15 ... 145 F3
Bennington Wlk NG19 ... 88 C2
Bentick St NG18 ... 102 B4
Bentinck Ave NG12 ... 186 B1
Bentinck Cl
Annesley Woodhouse NG17 ... 114 C1
Boughton NG22 ... 77 F3
Bentinck Ct 8 NG2 ... 173 F2
Bentinck Prim Sch NG7 ... 222 B4
Bentinck Rd Carlton NG4 ... 162 B1
Newark-on-T NG24 ... 139 F3
Nottingham NG7 ... 222 B4
Bentinck St
Annesley Woodhouse NG17 . 129 F4
Hucknall NG15 ... 145 F4
Sutton in A NG17 ... 100 C2
Bentinck Terr NG20 ... 74 A2
Bentley Ave NG3 ... 174 A3
Bentwell Ave NG5 ... 162 A4
Beresford Dr DE7 ... 157 F3
Beresford Rd
Long Eaton NG10 ... 193 D3
Mansfield Woodhouse NG19 .. 88 B3
Beresford St
Mansfield NG18 ... 102 B3
Nottingham NG7 ... 222 A3
Berkeley Ave
Long Eaton NG10 ... 193 E3
Nottingham NG3 ... 173 E4
Berkeley Cres NG12 ... 176 B2
Bernard Ave
Hucknall NG15 ... 131 D1
Mansfield Woodhouse NG19 .. 88 A3
Bernard Rd NG19 ... 101 F4
Bernard St NG5 ... 161 D1
Bernisdale Cl NG5 ... 146 C1
Berridge Inf Sch NG7 ... 172 C4
Berridge Jun Sch NG7 ... 172 C4
Berridge Rd NG7 ... 173 D4
Berridge Rd W NG7 ... 172 C4
Berriedale Cl NG5 ... 162 B4
Berristow La DE55 ... 113 E4
Berry Ave NG17 ... 114 C3
Berry Hill Cl NG18 ... 102 B2
Berry Hill Fst Sch NG18 ... 102 C2
Berry Hill Gdns NG18 ... 102 C2
Berry Hill Gr NG4 ... 162 C1
Berry Hill La NG18 ... 102 B2
Berry Hill Mews NG18 ... 102 B2
Berry Hill Mid Sch NG18 ... 102 C2
Berry Hill Rd NG18 ... 102 B2
Berry Park Lea NG18 ... 102 B2
Berwick Ave NG19 ... 101 E4
Berwick Cl NG5 ... 161 E3
Berwin Cl NG10 ... 182 A1
Beryldene Ave NG16 ... 159 D4
Bescar La NG22 ... 77 D1
Bescoby St DN22 ... 39 F4
Besecar Ave NG4 ... 162 C1
Besecar Cl NG4 ... 162 C1
Bessell La NG9 ... 182 B3
Bessingham Dr NG2 ... 185 E2
Besthorpe Ct NG19 ... 101 F4
Besthorpe Prim Sch NG23 .. 97 F3
Besthorpe Rd
Collingham NG23 ... 98 A1
North Scarle LN6 ... 83 E1
Bestwick Ave DE75 ... 143 D1
Bestwood Ave NG5 ... 161 F4
Bestwood Cl NG5 ... 161 F4
Bestwood Ctry Pk NG6 ... 146 C2
Bestwood Lodge Dr NG5 ... 161 E4
Bestwood Park Dr NG5 ... 161 D4
Bestwood Park Dr W
NG5 ... 146 C1
Bestwood Park View NG5 . 147 F1
Bestwood Rd
Hucknall NG15 ... 146 B3
Nottingham NG6 ... 146 B1
Pinxton NG16 ... 113 F1
Bestwood Terr NG6 ... 160 B4
Bethel Gdns NG15 ... 145 E3
Bethel Terr S80 ... 34 C3
Bethnal Wlk 15 NG6 ... 160 A4
Betony Cl NG13 ... 177 E2
Betula Cl NG11 ... 184 B1
Beulah Rd NG17 ... 115 D2
Bevan Cl NG21 ... 118 A4
Bevel St NG7 ... 172 C4
Bevercotes Rd NG22 ... 65 E2
Beverley Cl
Nottingham NG8 ... 171 D2
Rainworth NG21 ... 104 B1
Beverley Dr
Coddington NG24 ... 125 F1
Kimberley NG16 ... 158 C4
Kirkby in A NG17 ... 115 E2
Mansfield NG18 ... 102 B1
Beverley Gdns NG4 ... 162 C1
Beverley Rd DN11 ... 9 D2
Beverley Sq NG3 ... 173 F3
Beverley Wlk S81 ... 25 F4
Beverleys Ave NG13 ... 178 C2
Bewcastle Rd NG5 ... 147 D1
Bewick Dr NG3 ... 174 B3
Bexhill Ct NG8 ... 171 F1
Bexwell Cl NG11 ... 195 F4
Biant Cl NG8 ... 160 A2
Bidford Rd NG8 ... 159 F1
Bidwell Cres NG11 ... 195 D1
Big Barn La NG18 ... 102 C3
Big La DN22 ... 30 B2
Big Wood Sch NG5 ... 147 D1
Biggart Cl 2 NG9 ... 183 E1
Biggin St LE11 ... 220 A2
Bigsby Rd DN22 ... 30 A1
Biko Sq 22 NG7 ... 172 C4
Bilberry Wlk NG3 ... 173 F4
Bilbie Wlk NG1 ... 223 D3
Bilborough Coll NG8 ... 171 E4
Bilborough Rd NG8 ... 171 E3
Bilby Gdns 20 NG3 ... 173 F3
Billesdon Dr NG5 ... 160 C2
Billingsley Ave NG16 ... 113 E2
Bilsthorpe Inf Sch NG22 ... 105 F3
Bilsthorpe Rd NG22 ... 92 B1
Bilton Cl NG24 ... 140 B1
Bingham Ave NG17 ... 101 D3
Bingham Ind Pk NG13 ... 177 F3
Bingham Inf Sch NG13 ... 177 F3
Bingham Rd
Cotgrave NG12 ... 187 F2
Langar NG13 ... 190 A2
Mansfield NG18 ... 103 D2
Nottingham NG5 ... 161 E1
Radcliffe on T NG12 ... 176 A2
Bingham Sta NG13 ... 177 F3
Bingley Cl 4 NG8 ... 172 A3
Birch Ave Beeston NG9 ... 184 A2
Carlton NG4 ... 174 B4
Farnsfield NG22 ... 119 F4
Ilkeston DE7 ... 170 A4
Nuthall NG16 ... 159 D3
Rainworth NG21 ... 104 B1
Birch Cl Nuthall NG16 ... 159 D3
Rampton DN22 ... 42 C1
Ravenshead NG15 ... 117 D1
Birch Croft Dr NG19 ... 89 D1
Birch Ct NG22 ... 65 F1
Birch Gr Gainsborough DN21 .. 15 E1
Mansfield NG18 ... 103 D2
Shirebrook NG20 ... 72 B3
Birch Lea Arnold NG5 ... 161 E4
East Leake LE12 ... 205 E1
Birch Pas NG7 ... 222 C3
Birch Rd Hodthorpe S80 ... 45 E3
New Balderton NG24 ... 140 B3
New Ollerton NG22 ... 77 E2
Birch Rise NG14 ... 149 E3
Birch St NG20 ... 73 F3
Birch Tree Cl NG19 ... 89 E2
Birch Tree Cres NG17 ... 114 C2
Birchdale Ave NG15 ... 146 A3
Birchen Holme DE55 ... 113 D2
Birchenhall Ct NG24 ... 139 D2
Birches The NG15 ... 117 D2
Birchfield Dr S80 ... 35 D1
Birchfield Rd NG5 ... 148 A1
Birchlands NG19 ... 88 C1
Birchover Pl DE7 ... 157 F3
Birchover Rd NG8 ... 171 E3
Birchwood Ave
Breaston NG10 ... 193 D4
Long Eaton NG10 ... 193 E3
Birchwood Cl
Ravenshead NG15 ... 117 D1
South Normanton DE55 ... 113 D2
Southwell NG25 ... 121 E1
Sutton in A NG17 ... 100 C3
Birchwood Dr
Ravenshead NG15 ... 117 D1
Sutton in A NG17 ... 100 B4
Birchwood Rd NG8 ... 171 E2
Bird Cl NG18 ... 102 B2
Bird's La NG17 ... 114 C1
Birdcroft La DN10 ... 14 A3
Birding St NG19 ... 88 A1
Birdsall Ave NG8 ... 171 F2
Birkdale S81 ... 36 A3
Birkdale Ave NG22 ... 77 E3
Birkdale Cl Ilkeston DE7 ... 157 E1
West Bridgford NG12 ... 186 A2
Birkdale Dr 5 NG17 ... 114 C3
Birkdale Gr DN22 ... 39 E2
Birkdale Way NG5 ... 160 C4
Birkin Ave Beeston NG9 ... 183 D1
Nottingham NG7 ... 172 C4
Radcliffe on T NG12 ... 176 A2
Ruddington NG11 ... 196 B4
Birkland Ave
Mansfield Woodhouse NG19 .. 88 B2
Market Warsop NG20 ... 74 A2
Nottingham, Mapperley
NG3 ... 162 A2
Nottingham, St Ann's NG1 ... 223 E4
Birkland Dr NG21 ... 76 A1
Birkland St NG18 ... 102 B4
Birklands Ave
New Ollerton NG22 ... 77 E3
Worksop S80 ... 36 B1
Birklands Cl NG20 ... 74 A3
Birklands Prim Sch NG20 ... 74 A2
Birks Cl S80 ... 45 E3
Birks Rd NG19 ... 101 E4
Birley St NG9 ... 182 B3
Birling Cl NG6 ... 159 F4
Birrel St DN21 ... 15 D1
Birrell Rd NG7 ... 173 D4
Bisham Dr NG2 ... 186 A4
Bishop Alexander
Prim Sch NG24 ... 125 D2
Bishop Alexandra Ct
NG24 ... 139 F4
Bishop St Eastwood NG16 ... 143 F1
Loughborough LE11 ... 220 B2
Mansfield NG18 ... 102 A3
Sutton in A NG17 ... 100 C2
Bishop's Dr NG25 ... 136 C4
Bishop's Wlk NG20 ... 74 A3
Bishopdale S81 ... 36 A4
Bishopdale Cl NG10 ... 193 D3
Bishopdale Dr NG16 ... 159 D4
Bishopfield La DN22 ... 19 D3
Bishops Cl NG12 ... 197 F2
Bishops Hill NG21 ... 103 F1
Bishops Rd NG13 ... 177 E3
Bishops Way NG15 ... 146 A4
Bispham Dr NG9 ... 182 C1
Black La LN6 ... 71 F1
Black Scotch La NG18 ... 102 C2
Blackacre NG14 ... 163 F3
Blackburn Cl NG23 ... 98 A1
Blackburn Pl DE7 ... 157 F2
Blackcliff Field Cl S80 ... 45 D3
Blacketts Wlk NG11 ... 195 E4
Blackfriars Cl NG16 ... 159 E2
Blackham Rd LE11 ... 220 A1
Blackhill Dr NG4 ... 174 C4
Blackrod Cl NG9 ... 183 D1
Blacksmith Ct NG12 ... 187 F2
Blacksmith La
Kelham NG23 ... 124 A2
Torworth DN22 ... 19 D1
Blacksmiths Cl LE14 ... 219 E4
Blacksmiths La LN6 ... 83 E1
Blackstone Wlk NG2 ... 173 E1
Blackstope La DN22 ... 40 A4
Blackthorn Cl NG13 ... 178 A2
Blackthorn Way NG17 ... 100 B1
Blackthorne Cl NG24 ... 140 A3
Blackthorne Dr
Lowdham NG14 ... 150 B1
Nottingham NG6 ... 160 A2
Blackwell Rd NG17 ... 99 F2
Bladon Cl NG3 ... 161 F1
Bladon Rd NG11 ... 196 A4
Blair Ct 11 NG2 ... 173 E1
Blair Gr NG10 ... 182 A2
Blaise Cl NG11 ... 195 F4
Blake Cl NG5 ... 162 A4
Blake Cres NG18 ... 102 C4
Blake Ct NG10 ... 193 D3
Blake Rd Stapleford NG9 ... 182 C3
West Bridgford NG2 ... 186 A4
Blake St Ilkeston DE7 ... 157 F1
Mansfield Woodhouse NG19 .. 88 A1
Blakeney Ct NG19 ... 88 C2
Blakeney Dr NG18 ... 102 B2
Blakeney Rd NG12 ... 176 A2
Blakeney Wlk NG5 ... 161 F3
Bland La NG14 ... 150 A3
Blandford Ave NG10 ... 193 D3
Blandford Dr DN22 ... 39 E2
Blandford Gdns NG2 ... 185 E3
Blandford Rd NG9 ... 183 E3
Blankney Cl LN1 ... 57 D2
Blankney St NG5 ... 160 C2
Blantyre Ave NG5 ... 146 C1
Blatherwick Rd NG24 ... 140 B4
Blatherwick's Yd NG5 ... 161 F4
Bleaberry Cl NG2 ... 186 B3
Bleachers Yd NG7 ... 160 C1
Bleak Hill Way NG18 ... 101 F2
Bleasby CE Sch NG14 ... 151 F4
Bleasby Cres NG17 ... 101 D1
Bleasby Rd NG14 ... 151 E4
Bleasby St NG2 ... 173 F2
Bleasby Sta NG14 ... 151 F4
Bleasdale Cl NG4 ... 163 D1
Blencathra Cl NG2 ... 186 B3

Blenheim Ave
Lowdham NG14 .... 150 C1
Nottingham NG3 .... 162 B1
Blenheim Cl
Mansfield NG18 .... 88 B1
Ruddington NG11 .... 196 A4
Blenheim Dr NG9 .... 183 E3
Blenheim Gdns NG18 .... 165 E1
Blenheim Ind Est NG6 ...... 159 F4
Blenheim La NG6,NG15 .... 145 F1
Blenheim Pl NG17 .... 99 F2
Blenheim Rise Bawtry DN10 .. 9 F3
Worksop S80 .... 35 F4
Blenheim St NG10 .... 182 A2
Blessed Robert Widmerpool
RC Prim Sch NG11 .... 195 F4
Bley Ave LE12 .... 214 B4
Blidworth Cl NG17 .... 159 F1
Blidworth Ind Pk NG21 .... 118 A3
Blidworth La
Blidworth NG21 .... 133 E4
Mansfield NG21 .... 103 E1
Rainworth NG21 .... 117 F4
Blidworth Rd
Farnsfield NG22 .... 119 F3
Kirkby in A NG15 .... 115 F2
Blidworth Waye NG15 .... 131 F4
Blind La NG25 .... 134 B2
Bloomgrove Rd NG7 .... 157 F1
Bloomsbury Dr NG16 .... 159 F2
Bloomsbury Mews NG12 ... 176 C2
Bloomsgrove Ind Est
NG7 .... 222 B3
Bloomsgrove St NG7 .... 222 B3
Blue Bell Hill Inf Sch
NG3 .... 173 F3
Blue Bell Hill Jun Sch
NG3 .... 173 F3
Blue Bell Hill Rd NG3 .... 173 F3
Blue Bell Rd Clipstone NG22 .. 65 F2
Bluebell Bank NG13 .... 177 E2
Bluebell Cl Hucknall NG15 .. 145 E3
Selston NG16 .... 128 C1
Stanton Hill NG17 .... 100 A3
Bluebell Gr █ NG22 .... 114 C4
Bluebell Wood Way NG17 .. 100 B1
Bluecoat Cl NG1 .... 223 E3
Bluecoat St NG1 .... 223 E4
Blundell Cl NG3 .... 173 F4
Blyth Cl NG19 .... 87 E1
Blyth Gdns NG3 .... 161 F1
Blyth Gr S81 .... 36 A3
Blyth Rd
Blyth, Bilby S81, DN22 .... 27 F3
Blyth, Nornay S81 .... 19 E4
Elkesley S80 .... 48 C2
Harworth DN11 .... 8 C2
New Ollerton NG22 .... 77 D3
Oldcotes S81 .... 16 C3
Ranskill DN22 .... 19 D2
Walesby NG22 .... 63 D2
Worksop, Kilton S81 .... 36 A3
Worksop, Perlethorpe
S80, NG20 .... 48 C2
Blyth St NG3 .... 161 F1
Blythe CE Prim Sch S81 ..... 18 A1
Blyton Rd DN21 .... 15 E2
Blyton Wlk NG5 .... 161 D4
Boar La NG24 .... 139 F4
Boat La Aldercar NG16 ...... 143 D4
Bleasby NG14 .... 152 B4
Hoveringham NG14 .... 151 F1
Boatmans Cl DE7 .... 157 F1
Bobbers Mill Bridge NG7 .. 172 B4
Bobbers Mill Rd NG7 .... 172 C4
Boden Dr NG16 .... 159 E3
Boden St NG7 .... 222 B3
Bodmin Ave NG15 .... 145 E3
Bodmin Ct NG18 .... 103 D1
Bodmin Dr NG8 .... 160 B1
Body Rd NG9 .... 183 D1
Boeing Cl NG10 .... 160 B2
Bohem Rd NG10 .... 182 B2
Bolero Cl NG8 .... 171 F3
Bolham La DN22 .... 29 F1
Bolingey Way NG15 .... 145 E3
Bollard's La LE12 .... 213 D4
Bolsover St Hucknall NG15 .. 146 A4
Mansfield NG18 .... 102 B3
Bolton Ave NG9 .... 183 E2
Bolton Cl NG2 .... 186 A4
Bolton La LE14 .... 211 F4
Bolton Terr NG12 .... 175 F2
Bond Cl LE11 .... 220 B1
Bond St Arnold NG5 .... 161 F4
Nottingham NG2 .... 173 F2
Bonemill La
Clarborough DN22 .... 30 B1
Worksop S81 .... 35 E3
Bonetti Cl NG5 .... 162 B3
Boniface Gdns █ NG5 ...... 147 F2
Bonington Dr NG5 .... 161 F4
Bonington Rd
Mansfield NG19 .... 101 F3
Nottingham NG3 .... 162 A2
Bonner Hill NG14 .... 148 C3
Bonner La NG14 .... 149 D3
Bonner's Rd NG16 .... 158 B2
Bonnington Cl NG6 .... 160 A3
Bonnington Cres NG16 ..... 161 E2
Bonnington Jun & Inf Sch
NG6 .... 160 A3
Bonny Mead NG12 .... 187 F1
Bonsal Ct NG18 .... 103 D3
Bonsall Rd NG10 .... 193 F4

Bonser Cl NG4 .... 174 C4
Bonser Cres NG17 .... 99 F1
Bonser Gdns NG17 .... 100 B1
Booth Ave NG19 .... 87 D3
Booth Cl NG3 .... 223 F3
Booth Cres NG19 .... 87 E1
Booth St NG19 .... 88 A2
Boots Yd NG17 .... 99 F2
Borders Ave NG17 .... 114 C4
Borlace Cres NG9 .... 182 C3
Borman Cl NG6 .... 159 F3
Borough St DE74 .... 203 E1
Borrow Bread La NG14 ..... 152 A4
Borrowdale Cl NG2 .... 186 B3
Borrowdale Dr NG10 .... 193 D3
Borrowell DE74 .... 203 E2
Borrowell Ct DE7 .... 157 F2
Bosden Cl NG8 .... 171 E3
Bosley Sq NG9 .... 184 A4
Bostock's La NG10 .... 182 A2
Boston St NG1 .... 223 F3
Boswell Cl Kinoulton NG12 .. 200 A1
Mansfield NG18 .... 102 B2
Bosworth Dr NG16 .... 144 A2
Bosworth Prim Sch NG2 .. 173 D1
Bosworth St NG19 .... 101 E4
Bosworth Way NG10 .... 193 F3
Bosworth Wlk █ NG2 ...... 173 D1
Botany Ave
Mansfield NG18 .... 101 F3
Nottingham NG3 .... 173 F4
Botany Cl NG12 .... 185 E1
Botany Dr DE7 .... 157 F3
Bothe Cl NG10 .... 193 E3
Bottesford CE Prim Sch
NG13 .... 181 D1
Bottesford Sta NG13 .... 181 E2
Bottle La NG1 .... 223 E2
Bottleacre La LE11 .... 220 A3
Bottom Gn LE14 .... 210 A1
Bottom Row NG17 .... 100 C3
Boughton Cl NG17 .... 100 C3
Boughton Ind Est NG22 ... 78 A3
Boughton Rd S80 .... 35 D3
Bould St NG19 .... 87 F1
Boulevard Ind Pk NG7 ..... 184 B4
Bovington Ct DN22 .... 29 F1
Bow St NG19 .... 88 C2
Bowbridge Gdns NG13 .... 181 D2
Bowbridge Inf Sch NG24 .. 140 A3
Bowbridge Jun Sch
NG24 .... 139 F3
Bowbridge La
Bottesford NG13 .... 180 C2
New Balderton NG24 .... 140 A2
Bowbridge Rd NG24 .... 140 A3
Bowden Dr NG9 .... 184 A3
Bowers Ave █ NG3 .... 173 E4
Bowes Well Rd DE7 .... 157 F1
Bowland Cl NG3 .... 174 A4
Bowland Rd NG13 .... 177 E2
Bowler Ct █ LE11 .... 220 B2
Bowling Green Rd DN21 .... 15 D1
Bowling St NG18 .... 102 B3
Bowmell Ave NG5 .... 160 C4
Bowne St NG17 .... 100 C2
Bowness Ave NG6 .... 160 B1
Bowness Cl NG2 .... 186 B4
Box Cres NG17 .... 114 C3
Boxley Dr NG2 .... 185 E2
Boxwell City Pk NG8 .... 159 F2
Boy La NG21 .... 76 A1
Boyce Gdns NG3 .... 161 F1
Boycroft Ave NG3 .... 173 F4
Boyd Cl NG5 .... 148 A1
Boyer St LE11 .... 220 B2
Boyer's Orch LE14 .... 202 A2
Boynton Dr NG3 .... 161 F1
Bracadale Rd NG5 .... 36 A2
Bracebridge S80 .... 36 A2
Bracebridge Ave S80 .... 36 A2
Bracebridge Ct S80 .... 36 A1
Bracebridge Dr NG8 .... 171 E4
Bracey Rise NG2 .... 185 F2
Bracken Ave NG22 .... 77 F3
Bracken Cl Carlton NG4 ... 162 B1
Gainsborough DN21 .... 15 D2
█ Kirkby in A NG17 .... 114 C3
Long Eaton NG10 .... 182 A1
Market Warsop NG20 .... 74 B2
Bracken Ct DN11 .... 8 C2
Bracken Hill NG18 .... 103 D3
Bracken Hill La DN10 .... 4 A3
Bracken Hill Sch NG17 .... 115 E3
Bracken La DN22 .... 24, 40 A3
Bracken Lane Prim Sch
DN22 .... 40 A3

Bracken Rd NG10 .... 182 A1
Bracken Way DN11 .... 8 C2
Brackendale Ave NG4 ...... 161 F4
Brackendale Dr NG22 ...... 64 A1
Brackenfield Ave NG10 .... 88 C2
Brackenfield Dr NG16 ..... 158 A4
Brackenfield Rise NG15 ... 117 D2
Brackenfield Specl Sch
NG10 .... 182 A1
Brackenhurst Coll NG25 .. 136 B3
Brackenwood Cl NG19 ..... 89 D1
Brackhills Cl NG19 .... 88 C1
Bracknell Cres NG8 .... 160 B1
Brackner La NG22 .... 106 A2
Bracton Dr NG3 .... 173 F3
Bradbourne Ave NG11 ..... 185 D3
Bradbury-Midway Ind Est
NG7 .... 184 B4
Bradbury St NG2 .... 174 A2
Bradden Ave NG9 .... 170 C1
Bradder Way NG18 .... 102 A3
Braddock Cl NG7 .... 222 A2
Bradfield Rd NG8 .... 159 F1
Bradforth Ave NG18 .... 103 D4
Bradgate Cl NG10 .... 182 A2
Bradgate Rd █ NG7 .... 173 D4
Bradley NG11 .... 195 F4
Bradley St NG10 .... 182 B3
Bradley Wlk NG11 .... 195 F4
Bradleys Orch NG14 .... 151 E1
Bradman Gdns NG5 .... 162 A3
Bradmore Ave NG11 .... 196 B4
Bradmore Ct NG18 .... 103 D2
Bradmore La NG12 .... 197 E3
Bradmore Rise NG5 .... 161 E2
Bradshaw St NG10 .... 193 D3
Bradwell Cl NG16 .... 158 B4
Bradwell Dr NG5 .... 161 D4
Braefell Cl NG2 .... 186 B3
Braemar Av NG16 .... 143 F1
Braemar Dr NG4 .... 163 D1
Braemar Rd Clipstone NG19 .. 89 F2
Nottingham NG6 .... 160 B4
Brailsford Cl NG18 .... 103 D3
Brailsford Way █ NG9 ...... 172 C1
Brailsford Way NG9 .... 183 E1
Brailwood Cl NG22 .... 66 A2
Brailwood Rd NG22 .... 106 A3
Brake La NG22 .... 77 F2
Brake Rd NG22 .... 63 F1
Brakes Way NG22 .... 77 F3
Bramber Gr NG11 .... 195 F4
Bramble Cl Beeston NG9 .. 183 F2
Long Eaton NG10 .... 193 D4
New Ollerton NG22 .... 77 E3
Nottingham NG6 .... 160 B2
Shirebrook NG20 .... 72 C3
Bramble Croft NG17 .... 100 B1
Bramble Cl NG4 .... 162 C1
Bramble Dr NG3 .... 174 A4
Bramble Gdns NG8 .... 172 A4
Bramble La NG18 .... 103 D4
Bramble Rd DN22 .... 40 A2
Bramble Way DN11 .... 8 C2
Brambles The NG22 .... 64 A1
Brambleway NG12 .... 188 A1
Brambling Cl NG18 .... 102 C4
Bramblings The NG7 .... 161 D4
Bramcote Ave NG9 .... 183 E3
Bramcote CE Sch NG9 ..... 183 D4
Bramcote Cr Sch NG18 ... 103 D2
Bramcote Dr Beeston NG9 .. 183 F4
Bramcote Dr W NG9 .... 183 E4
Bramcote Hills Comp Sch
NG9 .... 171 D1
Bramcote Hills Prim Sch
NG9 .... 171 D1
Bramcote L Ctr NG9 .... 171 D1
Bramcote La Beeston NG9 .. 183 F3
Nottingham NG8 .... 171 E2
Bramcote Lorne Sch
DN22 .... 51 D3
Bramcote Park Comp Sch
NG9 .... 171 D1
Bramcote Rd NG9 .... 183 F4
Bramcote St NG7 .... 222 A3
Bramcote Wlk NG7 .... 222 A3
Bramerton Rd NG8 .... 171 E3
Bramhall Rd NG8 .... 171 E3
Bramley Cl
East Leake LE12 .... 205 F1
Gunthorpe NG14 .... 165 D3
Southwell NG25 .... 136 C4
Bramley Ct
Gainsborough DN21 .... 15 F1
Kimberley NG16 .... 158 C3
Sutton in A NG17 .... 100 C2
Bramley Rd NG8 .... 159 F1
Bramley Wlk NG19 .... 101 E4
Brampton Ave DE75 .... 143 D1
Brampton Ct NG2 .... 186 B4
Brampton Dr NG9 .... 182 C2
Brancaster Cl NG6 .... 160 A2
Brancilffe La S81 .... 34 C4
Brand La NG17 .... 100 B3
Brandish Cres NG11 .... 184 B1
Brandon Cl NG24 .... 140 C2
Brandreth Ave
Nottingham NG3 .... 173 F4
Sutton in A NG17 .... 100 B2
Brandreth Dr NG16 .... 158 A4
Branklene Cl NG16 .... 158 C4
Branksome Wlk █ NG2 .... 173 E1
Bransdale S81 .... 36 A4

Bransdale Ave NG19 .... 88 C1
Bransdale Cl NG10 .... 193 D3
Bransdale Rd NG11 .... 184 B1
Branston Ave NG22 .... 119 F3
Branston Gdns NG2 .... 185 E2
Branston Wlk NG5 .... 161 E2
Brantford Ave NG7 .... 184 B1
Brassington Cl NG16 .... 158 A4
Brassington Ct NG19 .... 88 C2
Braunton Cl NG15 .... 145 E3
Brayton Cres NG6 .... 160 A3
Breach Rd DE75 .... 157 D4
Breach La NG16 .... 144 A2
Breadsall Ct DE7 .... 157 F2
Breamer Rd NG23 .... 112 A4
Brechin S81 .... 36 A3
Brechin Cl NG5 .... 148 A1
Breck Bank NG22 .... 77 E3
Breck Bank Cres NG22 ..... 77 E3
Breck Hill Rd NG3 .... 161 F2
Breck La DN10 .... 20 A4
Breckbank NG19 .... 88 C1
Brecks La Elston NG23 ..... 154 A1
Stapleford LN6 .... 127 F4
Brecon Cl █
█ Long Eaton NG10 .... 193 D4
Nottingham NG8 .... 160 A2
Ilkeston DE7 .... 157 F2
Nottingham NG7 .... 222 A3
Breckswood Dr NG11 ...... 195 F4
Brecon Cl
█ Long Eaton NG10 .... 193 D4
Nottingham NG8 .... 160 A2
Bredon Cl █ NG10 .... 193 D4
Breedon St NG10 .... 182 B3
Brendon Cl NG9 .... 183 D4
Brendon Dr
Kimberley NG16 .... 158 C4
Nottingham NG8 .... 172 A3
Brendon Gdns NG8 .... 172 A3
Brendon Gr NG13 .... 177 E3
Brendon Rd NG8 .... 172 A3
Brendon Way NG10 .... 182 A1
Brentcliffe Ave NG3 .... 174 A4
Bretby Cl NG18 .... 103 D3
Brett Cl NG15 .... 117 D2
Bretton Rd NG15 .... 117 D2
Brewer's Wharf NG24 ..... 124 C1
Brewery La Everton DN10 .. 11 E2
Retford DN22 .... 39 F3
Brewery St NG16 .... 158 C3
Brewsters Cl NG13 .... 177 F2
Brewsters Rd NG3 .... 173 F4
Brewsters Way DN22 .... 29 E1
Briar Ave NG10 .... 182 A2
Briar Cl Beeston NG9 ...... 171 F1
Hucknall NG15 .... 145 F3
Keyworth NG12 .... 197 F2
Rainworth NG21 .... 104 B3
Worksop S80 .... 35 E1
Briar Gate Cotgrave NG12 .. 188 A1
Long Eaton NG10 .... 182 A1
Briar La NG18 .... 103 D2
Briar Lea Retford DN22 ..... 39 E2
Worksop S80 .... 35 E1
Briar Rd Eastwood NG16 .. 158 A4
New Ollerton NG22 .... 77 E3
Briarbank Ave NG3 .... 174 A4
Briarbank Wlk NG3 .... 174 A4
Briars The DN10 .... 4 B2
Briarwood Ave NG3 .... 174 A4
Briarwood Cl NG19 .... 89 D1
Briarwood Ct NG3 .... 161 F2
Briber Hill S81 .... 18 A1
Briber Rd S81 .... 18 A1
Brick Kiln La NG18 .... 101 E4
Brick Yard Rd DN22 .... 50 B3
Brickcliffe Rd LE12 .... 205 F1
Brickenell Rd NG14 .... 148 C3
Brickenhole La LE12 .... 213 E1
Brickings Way DN22 .... 32 B3
Brickley Cres LE12 .... 205 F1
Brickyard NG15 .... 146 B3
Brickyard Dr NG15 .... 146 B3
Brickyard La
East Bridgford NG13 .... 165 E1
East Leake LE12 .... 214 A4
Farnsfield NG22 .... 120 A3
Misson DN10 .... 4 B2
Radcliffe on T NG12 .... 176 A2
South Normanton DE55 ... 113 D3
Sutton Bonington LE12 ... 213 F4
Walkeringham DN10 .... 13 D3
Bride Church La DN11 ...... 8 A4
Bridegate La LE14 .... 209 F3
Bridge Ave NG9 .... 183 F3
Bridge Cl S81 .... 45 D3
Bridge Ct NG15 .... 146 A3
Bridge End Ave NG16 ..... 128 C4
Bridge Farm La NG7 .... 184 C1
Bridge Gr NG2 .... 185 F3
Bridge Green Wlk █ NG8 .. 159 F1
Bridge Pl Saxilby LN1 ...... 57 F2
Worksop S80 .... 35 F2
Bridge Rd
Gainsborough DN21 .... 24 B4
Nottingham NG8 .... 171 E3
Bridge St
Gainsborough DN21 .... 24 B4
Ilkeston DE7 .... 157 F2
Langley Mill NG16 .... 143 E2
Long Eaton NG10 .... 182 B1
Loughborough LE11 .... 220 A2
Mansfield NG18 .... 102 B4
Newark-on-T NG24 .... 139 F4

Bridge St continued
Sandiacre NG10 182
Saxilby LN1 57
Worksop S80 35
Bridgegate DN22 39
Bridgend Cl NG9 182
Bridgeway CE NG2 173
Bridgeway Ctr NG2 173
Bridgford Rd
Kneeton NG13 166
West Bridgford NG2 185
Bridgnorth Dr NG7 184
Bridgnorth Dr NG7 184
Bridgnorth Way NG9 182
Bridgport Rd NG7 184
Bridle Cl NG17 100
Bridle Rd Beeston NG9 183
Burton Joyce NG14 164
Bridle Ways NG13 165
Bridlesmith Gate NG1 223
Bridleway The NG19 88
Bridlington St NG7 172
Bridport Ave █ NG8 172
Brierfield Ave NG11 185
Brierley Gn NG4 175
Brierly Cotts NG17 100
Brierly Rd NG17 100
Brigg Inf Sch DE55 113
Bright Sq NG19 87
Bright St
Gainsborough DN21 24
Ilkeston DE7 157
Nottingham NG7 222
South Normanton DE55 .. 113
Brightmoor St NG1 223
Brimington Ct NG19 88
Brindley Rd NG8 171
Brinkhill Cres NG11 184
Brinkhill Prim Sch NG11 .. 184
Brinkley Hill NG25 137
Brinsley Cl NG8 160
Brinsley Hill NG16 143
Brinsley Prim Sch NG16 .. 143
Brisbane Cl NG19 88
Brisbane Ct NG24 140
Brisbane Dr
Nottingham NG5 160
Stapleford NG9 170
Bristol Rd DE7 157
Britannia Ave NG6 160
Britannia Rd NG10 182
Britannia Terr DN21 24
Britch Fields NG22 65
British Horological
Institute NG23 122
Brittania Cl NG24 139
Britten Gdns NG3 173
Brixham Rd NG15 145
Brixton Rd NG7 222
Brixworth Way DN22 40
Broad Cl NG14 149
Broad Eadow Rd NG6 159
Broad Fen La NG23 156
Broad Gate NG22 66
Broad Gores DN22 30
Broad La Brinsley NG16 ... 143
Hodthorpe S80 45
South Leverton DN22 43
Broad Marsh Ctr NG1 ... 223
Broad Meer NG12 187
Broad Oak Cl NG3 173
Broad Oak Dr
Brinsley NG16 143
Stapleford NG9 182
Broad Pl S80 45
Broad St Long Eaton NG10 .. 193
Loughborough LE11 220
Nottingham NG1 223
Broad Valley Dr NG6 146
Broad Wlk NG6 160
Broadfields NG14 148
Broadgate NG9 184
Broadgate Ave Beeston NG9 .. 184
Kelham NG23 123
Broadholl Rd DE74 203
Broadholme St NG7 222
Broadhurst Ave NG6 146
Broadings La DN22 54
Broadlands
Sandiacre NG10 182
South Normanton DE55 ... 113
Broadleigh Cl NG2 185
Broadleigh Ct NG2 185
Broadmead NG14 163
Broadoak Pk NG17 114
Broadstairs Rd NG9 182
Broadway Carlton NG3 173
Ilkeston DE7 157
Nottingham NG3 223
Broadway E NG4 174
Broadway The NG18 102
Broadwood Cl NG6 160
Broadwood Rd NG5 161
Brockdale Gdns NG12 197
Brockenhurst NG19 101
Brockhall Rise DE75 143
Brockhole Cl NG2 186
Brockhurst Gdns NG3 173
Brocklebank Ct DN21 24
Brockwood Jun & Inf
Schs NG18 102
Brockley Rd NG2 186
Brockton Ave NG24 139
Brockwell The DE55 113

Brockwood Cres NG12 ..... 197 F2
Bromfield Cl NG3 .... 174 B4
Bromhead St LE11 .... 220 B2
Bromley Ave NG24 .... 140 A3
Bromley Cl NG5 .... 160 A3
Bromley Pl NG1 .... 223 D2
Bromley Rd NG2 .... 185 F3
Brompton Cl NG5 .... 147 D1
Brompton Way NG2 .... 185 E2
Bronte Cl NG10 .... 193 D4
Bronte Ct NG7 .... 222 C4
Brook Ave NG5 .... 162 A4
Brook Cl Eastwood NG16 .... 144 B1
  Long Eaton NG10 .... 193 F3
  Nottingham NG6 .... 160 A3
Brook Cotts DE7 .... 157 F2
Brook Ct NG16 .... 143 D1
Brook Dr NG12 .... 199 F1
Brook Gdns NG5 .... 162 A4
Brook Rd NG9 .... 183 F4
Brook Side ■ LE11 .... 220 A2
Brook St Hucknall NG15 .... 146 A4
  Nottingham NG1 .... 223 F3
  Sutton in A NG17 .... 100 C1
  Tibshelf DE55 .... 99 D3
  Wymeswold LE12 .... 216 B2
Brook Terr S80 .... 35 F1
Brook Vale Rd NG16 .... 143 E1
Brook View Cl NG12 .... 197 F1
Brook View Dr NG12 ...... 197 F1
Brookdale Ct NG5 .... 161 E3
Brookdale Rd NG12 .... 101 D2
Brooke Cl Balderton NG24 .. 140 B3
  Worksop S80 .... 36 B2
Brooke St Ilkeston DE7 ... 170 A3
  Sandiacre NG10 .... 182 A3
Brookfield Ave
  Hucknall NG15 .... 146 A3
  Sutton in A NG17 .... 100 B2
Brookfield Cres NG20 ..... 72 C3
Brookfield Ct ■ NG2 ..... 173 E1
Brookfield Dr NG14 .... 151 E2
Brookfield Gdns NG5 ...... 162 A4
Brookfield Prim Sch NG5 . 72 C3
Brookfield Rd NG5 .... 162 A4
Brookhill Cres NG8 .... 171 F2
Brookhill Dr NG8 .... 171 F2
Brookhill Ind Est NG16 .... 113 E1
Brookhill La NG16 .... 113 F3
Brookhill Leys Inf Sch
  NG16 .... 144 A1
Brookhill Leys Rd NG16 ... 143 F1
Brookhill Rd NG16 .... 113 E1
Brookhill St NG9 .... 182 B3
Brookland Ave NG18 ...... 101 F4
Brookland Cl NG14 .... 165 D2
Brookland Dr NG9 .... 183 E3
Brooklands NG12 .... 208 B2
Brooklands Cl NG23 .... 98 A1
Brooklands Cres NG4 ...... 163 D1
Brooklands Dr NG4 .... 163 D1
Brooklands Inf Sch NG10 . 193 E3
Brooklands Jun Sch
  NG10 .... 193 E4
Brooklands Rd NG3 .... 174 A4
Brooklyn Ave NG14 .... 163 F3
Brooklyn Cl NG6 .... 160 B3
Brooklyn Rd NG6 .... 160 B3
Brooks Cl NG13 .... 165 E2
Brooksby La NG11 .... 184 C2
Brookside East Leake LE12 . 214 C4
  Eastwood NG16 .... 143 F2
  Hucknall NG15 .... 146 A3
  Lowdham NG14 .... 150 B1
Brookside Ave
  East Leake LE12 .... 205 E1
  Mansfield Woodhouse NG19 .. 88 B3
  Nottingham NG8 .... 171 E1
Brookside Cl NG10 .... 193 D4
Brookside La NG16 .... 196 A4
Brookside Prim Sch LE12 . 205 F1
Brookside Rd NG11 .... 196 A4
Brookside Wlk DN11 ..... 9 D2
Brookthorpe Way NG11 .. 185 D2
Brookvale Cl NG18 .... 103 D3
Brookwood Cres NG4 ..... 174 B4
Broom Cl Calverton NG14 . 148 C4
  Tickhill DN11 .... 8 A4
Broom Rd NG14 .... 148 C4
Broom Wlk NG4 .... 174 A4
Broome Acre DE55 .... 113 E2
Broome Cl NG24 .... 124 C4
Broomfield Cl NG10 ..... 182 A3
Broomfield La
  Farnsfield NG22 .... 119 F3
  Mattersey NG10 .... 179 D4
Broomhill Ave
  Ilkeston DE7 .... 170 A3
  Worksop S80 .... 35 F4
Broomhill Fst Sch NG19 .. 101 F4
Broomhill La NG19 .... 101 F1
Broomhill Park View
  NG15 .... 146 B3
Broomhill Rd
  Hucknall NG15 .... 146 A3
  Kimberley NG16 .... 159 D3
  Nottingham NG6 .... 160 B3
Broomston La DN9 .... 2 C1
Brora Rd NG6 .... 160 B4
Brotts La NG23 .... 81 D4
Brotts Rd NG23 .... 81 F1
Brough La Brough NG23 .. 112 A2
Elkesley DN22 .... 50 A2
Brough Rd LN6 .... 127 D4

Brougham Ave NG19 .... 87 E1
Broughton Cl DE7 .... 157 E1
Broughton Dr NG8 .... 172 B2
Broughton Gdns NG24 .... 140 C2
Broughton La LE14 .... 211 D1
Broughton Rd LN6 .... 127 F4
Broughton St NG9 .... 183 F4
Broughton Way NG22 .... 78 A2
Brown Ave NG19 .... 88 A2
Brown Cres NG17 .... 101 D2
Brown La Barton in F NG11 . 194 C3
  Thorney NG23 .... 70 A3
Brown St Mansfield NG19 . 101 F4
  Nottingham NG7 .... 172 C4
Brown's Flats NG16 ..... 158 C3
Brown's La NG13 .... 165 E2
Brown's Rd NG10 .... 193 F4
Brownes Rd NG13 ...... 178 A3
Brownhill Cl NG12 ..... 189 D2
Browning Cl Arnold NG5 . 161 E4
  Worksop S80 .... 36 A3
Browning St ■ NG18 .... 102 A4
Browning St ■ NG18 ... 140 C3
Brownlow Cl NG21 ..... 153 E4
Brownlow Dr NG5 ...... 146 C1
Brownlow Rd NG19 .... 87 F1
Brownlow's Hill NG24 .. 126 A1
Browns Croft NG6 ..... 160 B2
Browns La
  Loughborough LE11 .... 220 A2
  Stanton-on-t-W NG12 .. 198 B1
Broxholme La LN1 ...... 57 E3
Broxton Rise NG8 ...... 160 A2
Broxtowe Ave
  Kimberley NG16 .... 158 B3
  Nottingham NG8 ...... 160 B1
Broxtowe Coll NG9 .... 183 F3
Broxtowe Dr
  Hucknall NG15 .... 131 D1
  Mansfield NG18 ...... 102 B3
Broxtowe Hall Cl NG8 . 160 A1
Broxtowe La NG8 ..... 160 A1
Broxtowe St ■ NG5 .. 161 E1
Bruce Cl NG2 .... 173 E1
Bruce Dr NG2 .... 185 E4
Brunel Ave NG16 .... 144 A2
Brunel Cl DN11 ...... 8 C1
Brunel Dr NG24 ...... 125 E1
Brunnen The DE55 ... 113 F3
Brunner Ave NG20 .... 72 C2
Brunswick Dr NG9 ... 182 C3
Brunt St NG18 .... 102 B3
Brunt's La NG13 ..... 165 E1
Brunts Sch The NG19 . 88 B1
Brushfield St NG7 ... 172 C4
Brussels Terr ■ DE7 . 157 F1
Brusty Pl NG14 ...... 163 F3
Bryans Close La DN10 .. 3 F2
Brynsmoor Rd NG16 .. 143 F4
Buck's La LE12 .... 213 D4
Buckfast Way NG2 ... 186 A4
Buckingham Ave NG15 . 146 A4
Buckingham Cl
  ■ Kirkby in A NG17 .. 114 C3
  Mansfield Woodhouse NG19 . 88 C3
Buckingham Dr NG12 . 182 A2
Buckingham Dr NG12 . 176 C2
Buckingham Rd
  Arnold NG5 .... 161 F3
  Sandiacre NG10 ...... 182 A2
Buckingham Rise S81 . 35 F4
Buckingham Way NG16 . 159 D4
Buckland Dr NG14 .... 149 E2
Bucklee Dr NG14 ..... 148 C4
Buckley Ct NG2 ...... 173 F4
Buckminster Rd NG13 . 165 F2
Buddy Cres NG20 .... 74 C4
Budby Rd NG20 ...... 60 A2
Budby Rise NG15 .... 146 A4
Bulcote Dr NG14 .... 164 A2
Bulcote Rd NG11 .... 184 C2
Bulgrave Mews NG2 . 185 E2
Bulham La NG23 ..... 81 F1
Bull Close Rd NG7 .. 184 C4
Bull Farm Fst & Mid Sch
  NG19 .... 87 E1
Bull Yd Southwell NG25 . 121 F1
  Worksop S80 .... 35 F1
Bullace Cl NG19 ..... 88 C1
Bullace Rd NG3 ..... 173 F4
Buller Cl NG23 ...... 98 A1
Buller St DE7 ...... 170 A3
Buller Terr ■ NG5 .. 161 E2
Bullfinch Rd NG6 ... 160 B4
Bullins Cl NG5 ..... 147 E1
Bullivant Ave S80 ... 36 B4
Bullivant St NG3 ... 223 F4
Bullock Cl NG19 ... 87 D2
Bullpit Rd NG24 ... 140 C3
Bulpit La LN6 ..... 84 C1
Bulstode Pl DE74 .. 203 E1
Bulwell Bsns Ctr NG6 . 160 A4
Bulwell High Rd NG6 . 160 A4
Bulwell La NG6 .... 160 B2
Bulwell St Mary's
  CE Prim Sch NG6 . 160 B4
Bulwell Sta NG6 ... 160 B3
Bulwer Rd
  Kirkby in A NG17 .. 114 C3
  Nottingham NG7 .. 222 B3
Bunbury St NG2 .... 173 E1
Bungalow La NG22 . 106 B3
Bunnison La NG12 . 187 F1
Bunny CE Prim Sch NG11 . 206 C4
Bunny Hill LE12, NG11 . 206 B3
Bunny La East Leake NG11 . 205 F3
  Keyworth NG12 .... 197 D1
Bunting St ■ NG7 . 172 C1

Buntings La NG4 .... 174 B4
Bunyan Green Rd NG16 . 128 B4
Burbage Cl NG18 .... 103 D3
Burcoats & Harworth
  Com Sch The DN11 ... 9 E3
Burden Cres DN22 ..... 53 D4
Burden La Harby LE14 . 202 A2
  Shelford NG12 .... 164 B1
Burder St LE11 .... 220 B3
Burfield Ave LE11 ..... 220 A2
Burford Prim Sch NG5 . 161 E3
Burford Rd NG7 ...... 172 C4
Burford St NG5 ..... 161 F4
Burgage NG25 ...... 121 F1
Burgage La NG25 ... 121 F1
Burgass Rd NG3 .... 174 A4
Burge Cl NG2 ...... 173 E1
Burgh Hall Cl NG9 . 183 E1
Burhill NG12 ..... 188 A1
Burke St NG7 .... 222 C3
Burleigh Cl NG4 . 174 C4
Burleigh Rd
  Loughborough LE11 . 220 A2
  West Bridgford NG2 . 186 A3
Burleigh Sq NG9 . 183 E2
Burleigh St ■ DE7 . 157 F1
Burley Rise DE74 . 203 E1
Burlington Ave
  Nottingham NG5 .. 161 D2
  Shirebrook NG20 . 72 C3
Burlington Dr NG19 . 87 F1
Burlington Rd Carlton NG4 . 174 C4
  Nottingham NG5 .. 161 E2
Burma Rd NG21 .. 118 A3
Burnaston Rd NG18 . 103 D3
Burn St NG17 .... 101 D2
Burnaby St NG6 . 160 B2
Burnaston Ct NG19 . 88 C2
Burnbank Cl NG2 . 186 B3
Burnbreck Gdns NG8 . 171 F2
Burndale Wlk NG5 . 160 C4
Burneham Cl NG13 . 165 E1
Burnham Ave NG9 . 183 F2
Burnham Ct NG18 . 102 B2
Burnham St NG5 . 161 E1
Burnham Way NG2 . 223 E1
Burnmoor La NG22 . 80 A4
Burnor Pool NG14 . 148 C4
Burns Ave
  Mansfield Woodhouse NG19 . 88 B1
  Nottingham NG7 .. 222 C4
Burns Cl NG5 .... 73 A3
Burns St Gainsborough DN21 . 15 D1
  Mansfield NG18 .. 102 A4
  Nottingham NG7 .. 222 C4
Burns The NG20 . 74 B3
Burnside Cl ■ NG12 . 114 C4
Burnside Dr Beeston NG9 . 171 E1
  Mansfield NG19 .. 87 F1
Burnside Gn NG8 . 171 E3
Burnside Gr NG12 . 186 B1
Burnside Rd
  Nottingham NG8 . 171 E3
  West Bridgford NG2 . 185 F4
Burnt Oak Cl NG16 . 159 E2
Burnt Oaks Cl NG17 . 88 B2
Burntleys Rd DN22 . 30 B4
Burntstump Ctry Pk NG5 . 132 B1
Burntstump Hill NG5 . 132 B1
Burnwood Ave NG18 . 103 D4
Burnwood Dr NG8 . 171 E3
Burr La DE7 ..... 157 F1
Burrow Wlk NG17 . 114 C3
Burrows Ave NG9 . 171 F1
Burrows Cres NG9 . 171 F1
Burrows Ct NG3 . 173 F3
Burtness Rd NG7 . 184 C1
Burton Ave NG4 . 174 A4
Burton Cl Carlton NG4 . 175 D4
  Sutton in A NG17 . 100 B2
Burton Rise NG22 . 64 A1
Burton St
  Gainsborough DN21 . 24 B4
  Loughborough LE11 . 220 A1
  Nottingham NG1 . 223 E3
Burton Wlk LE12 . 214 C4
Burton Wlks LE11 . 220 A1
Burwell Ct NG19 . 88 C2
Burwell St NG7 . 222 B4
Bush Cl NG5 .... 160 C4
Bushmead Mews ■ S80 . 35 F1
Bushy Cl NG10 . 193 D3
Buskeyfield La NG20 . 59 F2
Bute Ave NG7 . 222 B2
Butler Ave NG12 . 176 A2
Butler Cl NG12 . 189 D3
Butler Dr NG21 . 118 B3
Butler Dr NG21 . 117 F2
Butlers Cl NG15 . 146 A3
Butlers Hill Inf Sch NG15 . 146 B3
Butt Hill S80 . 45 D3
Butt La East Bridgford NG13 . 165 F2
  Mansfield Woodhouse NG19 . 88 B1
  Normanton on S LE12 . 213 F2
Butt Rd NG13 . 178 A2
Butt St NG10 . 182 A3
Butten Mdw DN10 . 10 B3
Buttercup Cl NG24 . 140 B3

Butterhall Cl S80 .... 45 D3
Buttermead Cl NG9 ..... 170 B1
Buttermere Cl
  Long Eaton NG10 ..... 182 A1
  West Bridgford NG2 .. 186 B4
Buttermere Ct ■ NG5 . 161 E1
Buttermere Dr NG9 .. 183 E4
Butterton Cl DE7 .... 170 A4
Buttery La NG17 ... 100 C4
Buxton Ave NG4 ... 162 C1
Buxton Ct DE7 .... 157 E1
Buxton Rd NG19 .. 87 E1
Byard La NG1 .... 223 E2
Bycroft Rd DN21 . 15 C1
Bye Path Rd DN22 . 39 E4
Bye-Pass Rd Beeston NG9 . 183 E2
  Gunthorpe NG14 .... 164 C3
Byfield Cl NG7 ..... 222 B4
Byford Cl NG3 .... 161 F1
Byley Rd NG8 .... 171 D3
Byrne Ct NG5 .... 162 A3
Byron Ave
  Kirkby in A NG17 .. 115 D4
  Long Eaton NG10 .. 182 A2
  Sutton in A NG17 .. 100 B3
Byron Cl Darlton NG22 . 67 D4
  Newark-on-T NG24 . 140 A3
Byron Cres
  Awsworth NG16 .... 158 B2
  Nottingham NG5 ... 116 C2
Byron Ct Balderton NG24 . 140 C2
  ■ Nottingham NG2 . 173 F2
  Stapleford NG9 .... 170 C1
Byron Est NG5 .... 162 A4
Byron Gdns NG25 . 121 F1
Byron Gr NG5 .... 161 E4
Byron Rd Annesley NG15 . 130 B3
  West Bridgford NG2 . 185 F4
Byron St Arnold NG5 .. 161 E3
  Mansfield Woodhouse NG19 . 88 B3
  Hucknall NG15 .... 146 A3
  Ilkeston DE7 ...... 157 F1
  Mansfield NG18 ... 102 A4
  Newark-on-T NG24 . 130 A3
  Shirebrook NG20 . 72 C2
  Byron Way S81 .. 36 A2
Bythorn Cl NG13 . 101 D3

C Road NG9 .... 184 B3
Cabin Leas ■ LE11 . 220 A3
Cad La NG23 ...... 83 F4
Caddaw Ave NG15 . 146 A3
Cadlan Cl NG5 ... 161 D4
Cadlan Ct ■ NG5 . 161 D4
Caenby Cl DN21 . 24 C4
Caernarvon Pl NG9 . 183 D2
Caincross Rd NG8 . 171 E4
Cairngorm Dr NG5 . 147 D1
Cairns Cl NG5 ... 161 D3
Cairns St NG1 .. 223 E3
Cairnsmore Cl NG10 . 182 A1
Cairo St NG7 ... 160 C1
Caister Rd NG11 . 195 F4
Caithness Ct ■ NG5 . 161 D1
Calcroft Cl NG8 . 160 B1
Caldbeck Cl NG2 . 186 B4
Caldbeck Ct NG9 . 183 D2
Caldbeck Wlk ■ NG5 . 161 D4
Calder Wlk ■ NG6 . 160 A4
Calderdale NG8 . 171 D2
Calderdale Dr NG10 . 193 D3
Calderhall Gdns ■ NG5 . 161 E4
Caldon Gn NG6 . 146 B1
Caldwell St ■ LE11 . 220 A2
Caledon Rd NG5 . 161 D2
Caledonian Rd DN22 . 40 A2
Calf Croft S80 ... 45 D3
California Rd NG24 . 139 D2
Calladine La NG17 . 114 B4
Callaway Cl NG8 . 171 F3
Calstock Rd NG5 . 161 F3
Calveley Rd NG8 . 171 F4
Calver Cl NG18 . 172 B2
Calver St NG19 . 88 C2
Calverton Ave NG4 . 162 A1
Calverton Cl NG9 . 183 D1
Calverton Cl NG18 . 103 D2
Calverton Dr NG16 . 159 E1
Calverton Rd Arnold NG5 . 148 A1
  Blidworth NG21 . 118 A1
Cambridge Cres NG9 . 170 B1
Cambridge Gdns NG5 . 162 A3
Cambridge Rd
  Harworth DN11 . 8 C2
  Nottingham NG8 . 172 A2
  Rainworth NG21 . 118 A3
  West Bridgford NG2 . 186 A3
Cambridge St
  Carlton NG4 . 174 C4
  Loughborough LE11 . 220 A3
  Mansfield NG18 . 102 A3
Camdale Cl NG9 . 183 D3
Camden Cl NG2 . 173 F3
Camelia Ave NG11 . 184 B1
Camelot Ave NG5 . 161 D1

Camelot Cres NG11 ...... 196 A4
Camelot St NG11 ...... 196 A4
Cameo Cl NG4 .... 174 C3
Cameron St NG5 .... 161 E1
Camerons The NG19 . 101 E3
Camomile Cl NG5 .. 160 C4
Camomile Gdns ■ NG7 . 172 C4
Campbell Cl S81 .. 36 A3
Campbell Dr NG4 . 174 B4
Campbell Gr NG3 . 223 F3
Campbell St
  Gainsborough DN21 . 15 D1
  Langley Mill NG16 . 143 E2
  Nottingham NG3 . 223 F3
Campden Gn NG7 . 184 C1
Campion St NG5 . 161 F4
Campion Way NG13 . 177 C1
Camrose Cl NG8 . 171 F4
Canal La Harby NG13 . 202 B3
  Hose LE14 . 211 F4
  Long Clawson LE14 . 211 E3
  Sutton in A NG17 . 7 E1
Canal Mus NG1 . 223 E1
Canal Rd S80 . 35 F2
Canal Side NG9 . 184 A3
Canal St Ilkeston DE7 . 158 A1
  Long Eaton NG10 . 182 B1
  Nottingham NG1 . 223 D1
  Retford DN22 . 39 F3
  Sandiacre NG10 . 182 B3
Canal Terr S80 . 36 A2
Canberra Cl NG9 . 170 C1
Canberra Cres NG2 . 185 E2
Canberra Gdns NG2 . 185 E2
Canberra Rd NG24 . 125 F1
Candle Mdw NG2 . 174 B3
Candleby Cl NG12 . 187 F2
Candleby Ct NG12 . 187 F2
Candleby La NG12 . 187 F2
Candlemass St NG16 . 88 B1
Canning Circ NG7 . 222 C3
Cannock Way NG10 . 194 A4
Cannon Cl NG24 . 125 F1
Cannon Sq DN22 . 39 F4
Cannon St NG5 . 161 E2
Canon Cl DE7 . 157 F3
Canon's Ct NG25 . 121 F1
Canonbie Cl NG5 . 148 A1
Cantabury Ave NG7 . 172 C4
Cantelupe Rd DE7 . 170 A4
Canterbury Cl
  Mansfield Woodhouse NG19 . 88 B3
  Worksop S81 . 36 A4
Canterbury Ct NG1 . 223 D4
Canterbury Rd NG8 . 172 B3
Canterbury Wlk S81 . 25 F4
Cantley Ave NG4 . 162 C1
Cantrell Prim Sch NG6 . 160 B4
Cantrell Rd NG6 . 160 B4
Canver Cl NG8 . 171 E3
Canwick Cl NG8 . 171 E3
Cape St NG18 . 101 F4
Capenwray Gdns ■ NG5 . 161 E4
Capes The NG13 . 178 C2
Capitol Ct ■ NG8 . 172 A3
Capri Ct NG9 . 160 B3
Capps Pl NG22 . 66 A1
Capt Ball Memorial
  Homes NG7 . 222 A1
Car La NG13 . 166 B1
Carburton Ave NG20 . 74 B4
Carburton Way NG17 . 115 E3
Cardale Rd
  Nottingham NG3 . 174 A3
  Radmanthwaite NG19 . 87 E2
Cardiff St ■ NG3 . 173 F3
Cardinal Cl NG3 . 223 F4
Cardinal Hinsley Cl NG24 . 139 F2
Cardington Cl NG5 . 146 B1
Cardwell St NG7 . 172 C4
Carew Rd NG7 . 184 C1
Carey Rd NG6 . 160 B4
Carisbrook Ave NG18 . 103 D4
Carisbrooke Ave
  Beeston NG9 . 184 A4
  Carlton NG4 . 163 D1
  Nottingham NG3 . 161 E1
Carisbrooke Dr NG3 . 161 E1
Carisbrooke Dr NG3 . 161 E1
Carlile Rd NG4 . 174 C4
Carlin St NG6 . 160 A4
Carling Ave S80 . 35 E2
Carlingford Rd NG15 . 146 A4
Carlisle Ave NG6 . 160 B4
Carlisle St DE55 . 113 E1
Carlisle St DN21 . 15 E1
Carlswark Gdns NG5 . 146 C1
Carlton Ave S81 . 36 A3
Carlton Bsns & Tech Ctr
  NG4 . 174 C4
Carlton Central Inf Sch
  NG4 . 174 B4
Carlton Central Jun Sch
  NG4 . 174 B4
Carlton Cl Clipstone NG19 . 89 E2
  Heanor DE75 . 143 D2
  Newark-on-T NG24 . 139 F3
  Worksop S81 . 35 F4
Carlton Cres LE12 . 205 F1
Carlton Digby Sch NG3 . 162 B2
Carlton Dr NG9 . 9 F3
Carlton Ferry La NG23 . 97 E1
Carlton Fold ■ NG2 . 173 F2
Carlton Hall La S81 . 25 F3

Carlton Hill NG4 174 B4
Carlton La Broxholme LN1 57 F4
Sutton on T NG23 97 D3
Carlton Mews NG4 174 B4
Carlton Netherfield Inf Sch NG4 174 C4
Carlton & Netherfield Sta NG4 174 C4
Carlton Park Inf Sch S81 25 F3
Carlton Phoenix Ind Est S80 36 A2
Carlton Rd
Long Eaton NG10 193 D3
Newark-on-T NG24 140 A3
Nottingham NG3 173 F3
Worksop S80, S81 35 F3
Carlton Sq NG4 174 C4
Carlton St
Mansfield Woodhouse NG19 88 B1
Nottingham NG1 223 F2
Carlton Vale Cl NG4 162 B1
Carlton-le-Willows Sch NG4 163 D1
Carlyle Rd NG2 185 F4
Carman Cl NG16 159 D4
Carmel Gdns NG5 161 F3
Carnarvon Cl NG13 177 F3
Carnarvon Dr NG14 164 A3
Carnarvon Gr
Carlton, Gedling NG4 162 C1
Carlton, Thorneywood NG4 174 B4
Sutton in A NG17 100 C3
Carnarvon Pl NG13 177 E2
Carnarvon Prim Sch NG13 178 A2
Carnarvon Rd
Huthwaite NG17 99 F1
West Bridgford NG2 185 F3
Carnarvon St Carlton NG4 175 D3
Teversal NG17 100 A4
Carnforth Cl NG9 182 B3
Carnforth Ct 1 NG5 161 E4
Carnoustie S81 36 A3
Carnoustie Cl 7 NG17 114 C4
Carnwood Rd NG5 161 D3
Carolgate DN22 39 F3
Caroline Cl NG15 117 D2
Caroline Ct DE7 170 A3
Caroline Wlk NG3 173 E4
Carpenter Ave NG19 87 E1
Carpenters Cl NG12 189 D3
Carr Cl DE55 113 D4
Carr Farm Rd NG17 114 C1
Carr Hill Prim Sch DN22 29 F1
Carr Hill Way DN22 29 F1
Carr La Blyton DN21 15 E4
Doddington LN6 71 D2
East Stockwith DN21 7 F1
Gainsborough DN21 24 B3
Market Warsop NG20 74 A2
Misterton DN10 6 C1
South Normanton DE55 113 D4
Carr Rd Bingham NG13 178 A3
Gringley on t H DN10 12 B3
Retford DN22 39 F3
Carr View DN10 11 E2
Carradale Cl NG5 162 B4
Carrfield Ave NG10 182 C1
Carrfield Cl NG17 100 B2
Carrgate La NG23 153 F3
Carrington Ct NG5 161 E1
Carrington La NG14 149 D4
Carrington Prim Sch NG5 161 D1
Carrington St NG1 223 E1
Carroll Gdns NG2 173 E1
Carsic Inf Sch NG17 100 B2
Carsic Jun Sch NG17 100 B2
Carsic La NG17 100 C2
Carsic Rd NG17 100 B2
Carside Ave NG17 100 B1
Carsington Ct NG19 88 C2
Carson Rd DN21 15 E1
Carswell Cl NG24 139 F3
Cartbridge NG12 187 F1
Carter Ave
Radcliffe on T NG12 176 A2
Ruddington NG11 196 B3
Carter Gate NG24 139 F4
Carter La Mansfield NG18 102 C3
Shirebrook NG20 72 C2
Warsop Vale NG20 73 E2
Carter La E DE55 113 E3
Carter La W
Shirebrook NG20 72 B2
South Normanton DE55 113 E3
Carter Lane Fst Sch NG18 102 C3
Carter Rd NG9 183 D2
Carters Wood Dr NG16 159 F2
Cartwright Cl NG22 54 A1
Cartwright St
Loughborough LE11 220 B3
Shireoaks S81 34 C4
Carver Cl NG21 76 A1
Carver St NG7 172 C4
Carver's Hollow NG22 120 A1
Carwood Rd NG9 171 E1
Caskgate St DN21 24 B4
Casper Ct 10 NG5 161 D4
Castellan Rise NG5 161 E4
Casterton Rd NG5 161 D4
Castle Brewery Ct NG24 139 F4
Castle Bridge Rd NG7 173 D1
Castle Bvd NG7 222 C1
Castle Cl Bottesford NG13 181 E1
Calverton NG14 148 C4
Castle Farm La S80 46 B3
Castle Gate
Newark-on-T NG24 139 F4
Nottingham NG1 223 E2
Tickhill DN11 8 A4
Castle Gdns NG7 222 B1
Castle Gr NG7 223 D1
Castle Hill LE12 205 F1
Castle Hill Sch DN21 15 E1
Castle Marina Pk NG7 173 D1
Castle Marina Rd NG7 173 D1
Castle Meadow Rd NG2 223 D1
Castle Meadow Ret Pk NG7 222 C1
Castle Mews NG19 88 A2
Castle Mus & Art Gall NG7 223 D1
Castle Pk NG2 173 D1
Castle Pl NG1 223 D2
Castle Quay NG7 223 D1
Castle Rd NG1 223 D2
Castle Rising NG24 139 F4
Castle St Eastwood NG16 144 A1
12 Mansfield NG18 102 A4
Mansfield Woodhouse NG19 88 A2
Nottingham NG2 173 F2
Worksop S80 35 F1
Castle View
Aldercar NG16 143 D2
West Bridgford NG2 185 E3
Castle View Rd NG13 181 E1
Castledine St LE11 220 A1
Castledine St Extension LE11 220 A1
Castlefields NG2 173 E1
Castlerigg Cl NG2 186 B3
Castleton Ave Arnold NG5 161 F3
Carlton NG4 162 C1
Ilkeston DE7 157 F3
Castleton Cl
Hucknall NG15 145 E3
Mansfield Woodhouse NG19 88 B2
24 Nottingham NG2 173 D1
Ravenshead NG15 117 D2
Castleton Ct NG6 159 F3
Caterham Cl NG8 171 E4
Catfoot La NG4 162 C4
Catherine Ave NG19 88 B2
Catherine Cl
24 Kirkby in A NG17 114 C4
Nottingham NG6 160 A4
Catkin Dr NG16 158 B4
Catkin Way NG24 140 A2
Catlow Wlk 4 NG5 161 E4
Caton Cl NG17 100 B2
Cator Cl NG4 162 B2
Cator La NG9 183 E3
Cator La N NG9 183 E3
Cator Rd NG19 87 E2
Catriona Cres NG5 148 A1
Catterley Hill Rd NG3 174 A3
Cattle Market 18 LE11 220 A2
Cattle Market Rd NG2 173 E1
Cattle Rd DN10 6 B1
Catton Rd NG5 162 A4
Caudwell Cl NG25 121 F1
Caudwell Dr NG18 102 B2
Cauldwell Rd NG17 101 F1
Caulton St NG7 222 B4
Caunt's Cres NG17 100 B2
Caunton Ave NG3 161 F1
Caunton Cl
Mansfield NG18 101 F3
Meden Vale NG20 74 B4
Caunton Rd Bathley NG23 109 F2
Hockerton NG25 122 A3
Causeway DN21 24 C2
Causeway La
Gamston DN22 51 D4
Morton NG25 137 E2
Causeway Mews 19 NG2 173 D1
Cavan Ct 10 NG2 173 E1
Cave's La DN10 13 E3
Cavell Cl Nottingham NG11 184 B1
Woodbeck DN22 53 D4
Cavell Ct NG7 172 B1
Cavendish Ave
Carlton NG4 162 B1
Edwinstowe NG21 75 F1
Newark-on-T NG24 140 A3
Nottingham NG5 161 E2
Sutton in A NG17 100 C2
Cavendish Cl Bawtry DN10 9 F3
Hucknall NG15 146 B3
Cavendish Cres
Annesley Woodhouse NG17 130 A4
Carlton NG4 162 B1
Stapleford NG9 170 B1
Cavendish Cres N NG7 222 C2
Cavendish Cres S NG7 222 C1
Cavendish Dr Carlton NG4 174 C4
Lea DN21 24 C1
Cavendish Pl NG9 183 F3
Cavendish Rd Carlton NG4 162 B1
Ilkeston DE7 170 A3
Long Eaton NG10 182 B1
Retford DN22 40 A2
Worksop S80 47 D4
Cavendish Rd E NG7 222 C2
Cavendish Rd W NG7 222 C2
Cavendish St Arnold NG5 161 F4
Langwith NG20 72 C4
Mansfield NG18 102 B3
Mansfield Woodhouse NG19 88 A3
Nottingham NG7 184 C4
Sutton in A NG17 101 D2
Cavendish Vale NG5 161 E2
Cawdron Wlk NG7 184 C1
Cawston Gdns 4 NG6 160 A4
Cawthorne Cl NG23 98 A1
Cawthorne Way NG18 102 C4
Caxmere Dr NG8 171 F3
Caxton Cl NG4 175 D4
Caythorpe Cres NG5 161 E2
Caythorpe Ct NG19 88 C2
Caythorpe Rd NG14 150 C1
Caythorpe Rise NG5 161 E2
Cecil Cl S80 35 D2
Cecil St
Gainsborough DN21 15 E1
Nottingham NG7 222 B1
Cedar Ave
Beeston NG9 184 A4
East Leake LE12 214 B4
Kirkby in A NG17 114 C2
Long Eaton NG10 193 E3
Mansfield Woodhouse NG19 88 B3
Newark-on-T NG24 125 D2
Nuthall NG16 159 F2
Cedar Cl Carlton in L S81 25 F4
Gainsborough DN21 15 D2
Sandiacre NG10 182 A4
Sutton in A NG17 100 B4
Cedar Ct NG9 184 A4
Cedar Dr Keyworth NG12 197 F1
Selston NG16 128 C4
Cedar Gr Arnold NG5 162 A4
Hucknall NG15 146 A3
Nottingham NG8 171 F2
South Normanton DE55 113 D2
Cedar La NG22 77 E3
Cedar Rd Beeston NG9 183 F3
Loughborough LE11 220 B1
Nottingham NG7 173 D4
Cedar St NG18 102 B3
Cedar Tree Rd
Elkesley DN22 50 A2
Nottingham NG5 147 D1
Cedarland Cres NG16 159 F2
Cedars The NG5 161 E2
Celandine Cl NG5 160 C4
Celandine Gdns NG13 177 E2
Celia Dr NG4 174 B4
Cemetery Rd
Stapleford NG9 182 C4
Worksop S80 36 A1
Centenary Cl NG24 140 B2
Central Ave Arnold NG5 161 F4
Beeston NG9 183 F4
Beeston, Chilwell NG9 183 E3
Blidworth NG21 118 A3
Creswell S80 58 B4
Hucknall NG15 146 A3
Kirkby in A NG17 115 D2
Mansfield NG18 102 B3
Nottingham, Mapperley NG3 162 A2
Nottingham, New Basford NG7, NG5 161 D1
Sandiacre NG10 182 A3
South Normanton DE55 113 D3
Stapleford NG9 182 C4
Walesby NG22 64 A1
West Bridgford NG2 185 F4
Worksop S80 35 F2
Central Ave S NG5 161 F4
Central Cl NG20 72 C2
Central Ct NG7 172 C1
Central Dr Bawtry DN10 10 A4
Clipstone NG21 89 F1
Elston NG23 153 F2
Shirebrook NG20 72 C2
Central St
5 Nottingham NG3 173 F3
Sutton in A NG17 101 D2
Central Wlk NG15 146 A4
Centre Way NG12 175 F2
Centurion Way NG11 185 D4
Century Ave NG18 101 F3
Century Rd DN22 39 F3
Century St NG24 140 A4
Cernan Ct NG6 159 F3
Cerne Cl NG7 184 C1
Chaceley Way NG11 185 D2
Chad Gdns NG5 147 D1
Chadborn Ave NG11 195 D1
Chadburn Rd NG18 102 C4
Chaddesden The NG3 173 E4
Chadwick Rd NG7 172 C4
Chadwick Way DN22 53 D4
Chaffinch Cl NG18 102 C4
Chaffinch Mews S81 35 E4
Chain Bridge Rd DN22 29 E4
Chain La
Newark-on-T NG24 139 F4
Nottingham NG7 172 C1
Chainbridge Cl LE11 220 A3
Chainbridge La DN22 29 E4
Chalfield Cl NG11 184 B1
Chalfont Dr NG8 172 B3
Chalons Cl DE7 157 F1
Chamberlain Cl NG11 184 B1
Chambers Ave DE7 170 A4
Champion Ave DE7 157 E2
Champion Cres NG19 101 F4
Chancery Cl NG17 101 D3
Chancery Ct NG11 185 D3
Chancery La DN22 39 F4
Chancery The NG9 183 E4
Chandos Ave NG4 175 D4
Chandos Ct NG22 65 F2
Chandos St Carlton NG4 175 D4
Nottingham NG3 173 F4
Chantrey Cl NG9 183 E2
Chantrey Rd NG2 185 F4
Chantry Cl
Kimberley NG16 159 D3
Long Eaton NG10 193 D2
Newark-on-T NG24 139 F3
Chantry The NG18 102 C3
Chantry Wlk NG22 65 F2
Chapel Bar NG1 223 D2
Chapel Cl Misterton DN10 6 C1
Walesby NG22 64 A1
Chapel Ct DE7 157 F2
Chapel Garth NG13 179 F3
Chapel Gate S81 26 A3
Chapel La Arnold NG5 161 F4
Aslockton NG13 179 D3
Bathley NG23 110 A2
Bingham NG13 177 F3
Caunton NG23 109 D3
Claypole NG23 156 B4
Coddington NG24 126 A1
Costock LE12 206 B1
Cotgrave NG12 187 F2
Epperstone NG14 150 A3
Everton DN10 11 E2
Farndon NG24 138 C2
Farnsfield NG22 119 F3
Granby NG13 191 D3
Hose LE14 211 F4
Lambley NG4 163 D4
Laxton NG22 79 E1
Misterton DN10 6 C1
Morton DN21 15 D2
Nether Broughton LE14 219 E4
North Scarle LN6 83 E2
Old Dalby LE14 218 C2
Oxton NG25 134 B2
Ravenshead NG15 117 D1
Scrooby DN10 10 A1
Upper Broughton LE14 210 A1
Walesby NG22 64 A1
Willoughby-on-t-W LE12 217 E4
Winthorpe NG24 125 E3
Chapel Mews Ct NG9 183 D4
Chapel Pl NG16 158 C3
Chapel Rd NG16 128 C3
Chapel St
Annesley Woodhouse NG17 115 D1
Barkestone-le-V NG13 192 A1
Beckingham LN5 142 B4
Beeston NG9 183 D4
Bottesford NG13 181 D2
Eastwood NG16 143 F1
Heanor DE75 157 D4
Hucknall NG15 146 A4
17 Ilkeston DE7 157 F1
Kimberley NG16 158 C3
Kirkby in A NG17 114 C3
Long Eaton NG10 193 F4
New Houghton NG19 87 D4
Orston NG13 179 F4
Ruddington NG11 196 B3
Selston NG16 129 D4
Whaley Thorns NG20 59 D2
Chapel Staith DN21 24 B4
Chapel Wlk S80 35 F1
Chapelgate DN22 39 F4
Chapman Ct NG8 172 A4
Chapman St LE11 220 B2
Chappel Gdns NG22 106 A2
Chapter Dr NG16 159 D3
Chard St NG7 160 C1
Charlbury Ct NG9 171 D2
Charlbury Rd NG8 172 A3
Charlecote Dr NG8 171 E2
Charlecote Park Dr NG2 185 E2
Charles Ave
Beeston NG9 172 A1
Beeston, Chilwell NG9 183 E2
Eastwood NG16 144 A1
Sandiacre NG10 182 A3
Stapleford NG9 182 C4
Charles Baines Cty Prim Sch DN21 24 C4
Charles Cl Carlton NG4 162 C1
Ilkeston DE7 170 A3
Charles Pk NG6 160 A3
Charles St Arnold NG5 161 F4
Gainsborough DN21 15 E1
Hucknall NG15 146 A4
Long Eaton NG10 193 E3
Loughborough LE11 220 A3
Mansfield NG19 88 A1
Mansfield Woodhouse NG19 88 B2
Newark-on-T NG24 140 A4
Ruddington NG11 196 B4
Sutton in A NG17 101 D2
Charlesworth Ave NG7 172 C4
Charlesworth Ct NG19 88 C2
Charlock Cl NG5 160 C4
Charlock Gdns NG13 177 E2
Charlotte Cl Arnold NG5 147 F1
Kirton NG22 78 A3
Newark-on-T NG24 140 A4
Charlotte Gr NG9 171 E1
Charlotte Inf Sch DE7 157 F1
Charlton Ave NG10 182 C1
Charlton Gr NG9 183 F3
Charlton Rd S81 26 A1
Charnock Ave NG8 172 B2
Charnwood Ave
Beeston NG9 183 F3
Keyworth NG12 197 F1
Long Eaton NG10 193 D2
Sandiacre NG10 182 A2
Sutton Bonington LE12 213 E3
Charnwood Cres DE55 99 D2
Charnwood Fields LE12 213 E3
Charnwood Gr
Bingham NG13 177 E2
Hucknall NG15 145 F4
Mansfield NG18 103 D4
Mansfield Woodhouse NG19 88 A3
West Bridgford NG2 185 F4
Charnwood La NG5 162 A3
Charnwood Rd LE11 220 A1
Charnwood St NG17 100 B1
Charnwood Way NG14 149 E2
Charter Pl NG22 66 A2
Charters Cl 18 NG17 114 C4
Chartwell Ave NG11 196 A4
Chartwell Gr NG3 162 B3
Chartwell Rd NG17 115 E3
Chase Pk NG2 174 A2
Chatham Ct NG24 139 F4
Chatham St
Nottingham NG1 223 E4
Southwell NG25 121 F1
Chatsworth Ave
Beeston NG9 183 E1
Carlton NG4 162 C1
Long Eaton NG10 194 A3
Nottingham NG7 160 C1
Radcliffe on T NG12 176 A2
Selston NG16 129 D4
Shirebrook NG20 72 C3
Southwell NG25 121 E1
Chatsworth Cl
Mansfield NG18 102 C1
Ravenshead NG15 117 D2
Sandiacre NG10 182 A2
Sutton in A NG17 100 C3
Chatsworth Ct
Harworth DN11 9 D3
Hucknall NG15 146 A3
Chatsworth Dr
Hucknall NG15 146 A3
Mansfield NG18 102 C1
Chatsworth Rd
Creswell S80 58 B4
Newark-on-T NG24 140 A3
West Bridgford NG2 186 A4
Worksop S81 35 F4
Chatsworth St
Sutton in A NG17 101 D2
Tibshelf DE55 99 D3
Chaucer Cres NG17 101 D2
Chaucer Jun Sch DE7 157 F1
Chaucer Rd NG24 140 C2
Chaucer St Ilkeston DE7 157 F1
Mansfield NG18 102 A4
Nottingham NG1 223 D3
Chaworth Ave NG16 145 D1
Chaworth Rd
Bingham NG13 177 E2
Carlton NG4 174 C3
West Bridgford NG2 185 F3
Chaworth St NG21 118 A3
Cheadle Cl
Nottingham, Bilborough NG8 171 E4
Nottingham, Portchester NG3 162 A1
Cheapside
Nottingham NG1 223 E2
Worksop S80 36 A1
Cheddar Cl NG21 104 B1
Cheddar Rd NG11 195 F4
Chedington Ave NG3 162 B3
Chediston Vale NG5 161 D4
Chedworth Cl 18 NG3 173 F
Chelmorton Cl NG19 88 C
Chelmsford Rd NG7 160 C
Chelmsford Terr NG7 160 C
Chelsea Cl NG16 159 F
Chelsea St NG7 160 C
Cheltenham Cl NG9 182 C
Cheltenham Ct NG18 102 C
Cheltenham St NG6 160 C
Chennel Nook NG12 188 A
Chepstow Rd NG11 195 F
Chepstow Wlk NG18 102 C
Chequers La NG22 54 A
Cherhill Cl NG11 195 E
Cheriton Cl NG19 87 F
Cheriton Dr
Ravenshead NG15 117 D
Shipley DE7 157 E
Chermside Cl NG15 117 D
Chernside NG15 117 D
Cherry Ave Hucknall NG15 146 A
Kirkby in A NG17 114 B
Cherry Cl Arnold NG5 161 F
Shirebrook NG20 72 C
South Normanton DE55 113 D
Cherry Gr Mansfield NG18 101 F
Market Warsop NG20 74 E
Cherry Hill NG12 197 F
Cherry Holt
Newark-on-T NG24 139 F
Retford DN22 29 E
Cherry La NG18 102 A
Cherry Orch NG12 187
Cherry Orchard Mount NG5 161 D
Cherry St NG13 177
Cherry Tree Ave S81 34
Cherry Tree Cl
Brinsley NG16 143
Mansfield Woodhouse NG19 88
Radcliffe on T NG12 175
Cherry Tree La NG12 186
Cherry Tree Rd DN21 15
Cherry Tree Wlk DN22 19
Cherry Wood Dr NG8 172
Cherryholt Cl NG13 165

herryholt La NG13 .... 165 E2
herrywood Gdns NG3 .... 174 A4
hertsey Cl NG3 .... 161 F1
herwell Ct NG9 .... 159 F3
hesham Dr
　Beeston NG9 .... 171 D1
　Nottingham NG5 .... 161 D1
heshire Way NG16 .... 128 B2
hesil Ave 4 NG8 .... 172 B3
hesil Cotts 5 NG8 .... 172 B3
heslyn Dr NG8 .... 172 B4
hess Burrow NG10 .... 88 B1
hester La 24 LE11 .... 220 A2
hester Gn NG9 .... 182 C1
hester Rd NG3 .... 174 A3
hester St NG3 .... 173 F2
hesterfield Ave
　Bingham NG13 .... 177 F3
　Carlton NG4 .... 162 B1
hesterfield Rd NG10 .... 193 F4
hesterfield Ct NG4 .... 162 B2
hesterfield Dr
　Burton Joyce NG14 .... 164 A3
　Retford DN22 .... 40 A4
hesterfield Rd
　Hardstoft DE55 .... 85 D1
　Huthwaite NG17 .... 99 F2
　New Houghton NG19 .... 86 C4
　Pleasley NG19 .... 87 D3
hesterfield Rd N NG19 .... 87 E2
hesterfield Rd S NG18 .... 102 A2
hesterfield St NG4 .... 174 B4
hesterman Ct NG16 .... 158 A2
hesterton Dr S81 .... 36 A3
hestnut Ave
　Beeston NG9 .... 183 F3
　Bingham NG13 .... 177 F2
　Gainsborough DN21 .... 15 E1
　Kirkby in A NG17 .... 114 C2
　Newark-on-T NG24 .... 125 D2
　Nottingham NG3 .... 162 A1
　Ravenshead NG15 .... 117 D1
　Retford DN22 .... 39 F2
hestnut Cl
　Bottesford NG13 .... 181 E2
　New Ollerton NG22 .... 77 E3
　Worksop S80 .... 35 F1
hestnut Copse NG12 .... 140 A3
hestnut Dr Bawtry DN10 .... 9 B4
　Mansfield NG18 .... 102 C1
　New Ollerton NG22 .... 77 E3
　Nuthall NG16 .... 159 D3
　Selston NG16 .... 128 C4
　Shirebrook NG20 .... 72 B2
　Selston NG16 .... 128 C4
　Shirebrook NG20 .... 72 B2
hestnut Gr Arnold NG5 .... 162 A4
　Burton Joyce NG14 .... 163 F2
　Carlton NG4 .... 162 C1
　Farndon NG24 .... 139 D2
　Hucknall NG15 .... 146 A2
　Kirkby in A NG17 .... 114 C3
　Mansfield Woodhouse NG19 .... 88 A3
　Nottingham NG3 .... 173 E4
　Radcliffe on T NG12 .... 175 F2
　Sandiacre NG10 .... 182 A4
　West Bridgford NG2 .... 185 E4
hestnut Hill NG18 .... 102 C1
hestnut La NG11 .... 194 C3
hestnut Mews NG18 .... 102 C1
hestnut Rd
　Langley Mill NG16 .... 143 D2
　Langold S81 .... 16 C2
hestnut St LE11 .... 220 A2
hestnut Way NG24 .... 66 A1
hestnuts The
　Carlton NG4 .... 163 D1
　Long Eaton NG10 .... 193 D4
　Nottingham NG3 .... 161 F1
　Radcliffe on T NG12 .... 175 F2
hettles Ind Est NG8 .... 172 B3
hetwynd Rd
　Beeston, Chilwell NG9 .... 183 E2
　Beeston, Toton NG9 .... 183 D1
heverton Ct 17 NG3 .... 173 F3
hevin Gdns 12 NG5 .... 147 D1
heviot Cl NG5 .... 147 D1
heviot Ct S81 .... 36 A4
heviot Dr NG6 .... 159 F4
hestnut Rd NG6 .... 182 A1
hewton Ave NG16 .... 144 A1
hewton Cl NG22 .... 105 F3
hewton St NG16 .... 144 A1
heyne Dr NG22 .... 106 A2
heyne Wlk Bawtry DN10 .... 9 B4
　Retford DN22 .... 39 E2
heyny Cl NG2 .... 173 E1
hichester Cl
　Ilkeston DE7 .... 170 A4
　Mansfield NG19 .... 101 E3
hichester Cl NG4 .... 160 C4
hichester Dr NG13 .... 187 F2
hichester Wlk S81 .... 25 F4
hidlow Rd NG8 .... 171 E4
higwell Cl NG16 .... 144 B4
hildrens Highway NG24 .... 140 C1
hilton Way NG15 .... 145 E3
hilton Cl NG17 .... 147 D1
hiltern Gdns NG10 .... 182 A1
hiltern Way
　Carlton in L S81 .... 25 F4
　Nottingham NG5 .... 161 D4
hilton Cres NG19 .... 88 B3
hilton Dr NG16 .... 159 D4
hilvers Cl NG5 .... 161 D4
hilwell College House
　Jun Sch NG9 .... 183 F3
hilwell Comp Sch NG9 .... 183 E2

Chilwell Ct NG6 .... 160 B4
Chilwell La NG9 .... 183 E3
Chilwell Olympia NG9 .... 183 E2
Chilwell Rd NG9 .... 183 F3
Chilwell Ret Pk NG9 .... 183 D1
Chilwell St NG7 .... 222 B1
Chimes Mdw NG25 .... 136 C4
Chine Gdns NG2 .... 185 E3
Chine The DE55 .... 113 D2
Chingford Rd NG8 .... 171 F4
Chiomere DN22 .... 39 F2
Chippendale St NG7 .... 222 B1
Chippenham Rd NG5 .... 161 E4
Chirnside NG19 .... 101 E3
Chisbury Gn NG11 .... 195 E4
Chisholm Way NG5 .... 161 D3
Chisworth Ct NG19 .... 88 C2
Christ Church CE Inf Sch
　NG24 .... 139 F4
Christ The King
　RC Comp Sch NG5 .... 162 A4
Christchurch Rd NG15 .... 145 E2
Christina Ave NG6 .... 160 B2
Christina Cres NG6 .... 160 B2
Christine Cl NG15 .... 131 E1
Christopher Cl NG8 .... 171 F3
Christopher Cres NG24 .... 140 B2
Chrysalis Way NG16 .... 143 E2
Church Ave Arnold NG5 .... 161 F4
　Long Eaton NG10 .... 193 D4
　Nottingham NG7 .... 222 B1
　Sutton in A NG17 .... 100 B1
Church Cl Arnold NG5 .... 161 F4
　Bingham NG13 .... 177 F3
　Church Warsop NG20 .... 74 A3
　East Leake LE12 .... 205 F1
　Hose LE14 .... 211 F4
　North Wheatley DN22 .... 31 F1
　Radcliffe on T NG12 .... 175 F2
　Trowell NG9 .... 170 B2
Church Cnr NG12 .... 192 C2
Church Cres Arnold NG5 .... 161 F4
　Beeston NG9 .... 183 D2
Church Croft NG2 .... 185 F4
Church Dr Arnold NG5 .... 161 F4
　Hucknall NG15 .... 146 A4
　Ilkeston DE7 .... 157 E2
　Keyworth NG12 .... 197 F2
　Misterton DN10 .... 6 C1
　Nottingham NG5 .... 161 D1
　Ravenshead NG15 .... 117 D1
　Sandiacre NG10 .... 182 A4
　Shirebrook NG20 .... 72 C2
　West Bridgford NG2 .... 185 F4
Church Dr E NG5 .... 161 F4
Church End LE14 .... 210 B1
Church Farm Gdns NG12 .... 197 F2
Church Field Cl S81 .... 26 A3
Church Gate
　Colston Bassett NG12 .... 200 C4
　Cotgrave NG12 .... 198 B4
　Kegworth DE74 .... 203 E1
　Loughborough LE11 .... 220 A2
Church Gr NG7 .... 222 A1
Church Hall Sch NG5 .... 161 F4
Church Hill
　Bilsthorpe NG22 .... 106 A3
　Keyworth NG12 .... 197 F4
　Kimberley NG16 .... 158 C3
　Kirkby in A NG17 .... 114 B2
　Mansfield Woodhouse NG19 .... 88 B2
　Newton DE55 .... 99 D1
　North Wheatley DN22 .... 31 F4
　Sutton in A NG17 .... 100 C1
Church Hill Ave NG19 .... 88 B2
Church Hill Ctr
　Broxtowe Coll of F Ed
　NG16 .... 158 C3
Church La Arnold NG5 .... 147 F1
　Averham NG23 .... 123 F1
　Balderton NG24 .... 140 C2
　Barton in F NG11 .... 194 C3
　Beeston NG9 .... 183 E1
　Besthorpe NG23 .... 98 A3
　Bingham NG13 .... 177 F3
　Bothamsall DN22 .... 63 F4
　Bottesford NG13 .... 181 D2
　Boughton NG22 .... 77 F3
　Brinsley NG16 .... 143 F4
　Car Colston NG13 .... 166 B2
　Carlton in L S81 .... 25 F2
　Clarborough DN22 .... 30 C2
　Clayworth DN22 .... 21 E3
　Collingham NG23 .... 98 A1
　Cossall NG16 .... 158 B1
　Costock LE12 .... 206 B1
　Cotgrave NG12 .... 187 F2
　Cromwell NG23 .... 110 C4
　Eagle LN6 .... 84 A2
　Eakring NG22 .... 92 C1
　East Drayton DN22 .... 53 D2
　East Stoke NG23 .... 138 A1
　Epperstone NG14 .... 150 A3
　Gamston DN22 .... 50 C4
　Halam NG22 .... 120 C1
　Harworth DN11 .... 8 C2
　Hayton DN22 .... 30 B3
　Hucknall NG15 .... 131 D1
　Letwell S81 .... 16 A1
　Long Clawson LE14 .... 211 E2
　Lowdham NG14 .... 150 B1
　Mansfield NG18 .... 102 A4
　Maplebeck NG22 .... 108 A3
　Misterton DN10 .... 6 C1
　Morton NG25 .... 137 E2
　North Clifton NG23 .... 68 B2
　North Scarle LN6 .... 83 E1

Church La continued
　Nottingham NG6 .... 160 B4
　Old Dalby LE14 .... 218 C2
　Owthorpe NG12 .... 199 F4
　Pleasley NG19 .... 87 D3
　Plumtree NG12 .... 197 F4
　Plungar NG13 .... 191 F1
　Redmile NG13 .... 192 C2
　Retford DN22 .... 39 F2
　Saxilby LN1 .... 56 C3
　Screveton NG13 .... 166 C2
　Scrooby DN10 .... 10 A1
　Selston, Selston Green
　NG16 .... 128 B4
　Selston, Underwood NG16 .... 129 D2
　Sibthorpe NG23 .... 167 F4
　South Muskham NG23 .... 124 C4
　Stapleford NG9 .... 182 B4
　Sutton in A NG17 .... 100 C1
　Thrumpton NG11 .... 194 B2
　Tibshelf DE55 .... 99 D3
　Tickhill DN11 .... 8 A4
　Upper Broughton LE14 .... 210 A1
　Upton NG23 .... 122 C1
　West Drayton DN22 .... 50 C1
　Widmerpool NG12 .... 208 C1
　Willoughby-on-t-W LE12 .... 217 E4
Church Lands 2 LE11 .... 220 A3
Church Mdw NG14 .... 148 C4
Church Mead NG17 .... 99 F2
Church Mews
　2 Nottingham NG7 .... 173 E1
　Sutton in A NG17 .... 100 C1
Church Rd
　Bestwood Village NG6 .... 146 C2
　Bircotes DN11 .... 9 B2
　Burton Joyce NG14 .... 163 F2
　Church Warsop NG20 .... 74 B3
　Clipstone NG21 .... 89 F2
　Greasley NG16 .... 144 C2
　Harby NG23 .... 70 B1
　Nottingham NG3 .... 223 F4
　Saxilby LN1 .... 57 D2
Church Side
　Farnsfield NG22 .... 119 F3
　Huthwaite NG17 .... 99 F2
　Mansfield NG18 .... 102 B3
Church Sq NG7 .... 222 B1
Church St Arnold NG5 .... 161 F4
　Bawtry DN10 .... 10 A3
　Beckingham DN10 .... 14 A1
　Beeston NG9 .... 183 F3
　Beeston, Bramcote NG9 .... 183 D4
　Bilsthorpe NG22 .... 105 F3
　Bingham NG13 .... 177 F2
　Bottesford NG13 .... 181 D1
　Bunny NG11 .... 206 C4
　Carlton NG4 .... 174 C4
　Collingham NG23 .... 111 F4
　Cropwell Bishop NG12 .... 189 D2
　East Markham NG22 .... 66 A3
　Eastwood NG16 .... 143 F1
　Edwinstowe NG21 .... 76 A1
　Everton DN10 .... 11 E2
　Farndon NG24 .... 138 C2
　Gainsborough DN21 .... 15 E1
　Gotham NG11 .... 195 D1
　Granby NG13 .... 191 D3
　Hathern LE12 .... 213 D1
　Ilkeston DE7 .... 157 F2
　Kirkby in A NG17 .... 114 B3
　Lambley NG4 .... 163 E4
　Langold S81 .... 16 C1
　Mansfield NG18 .... 102 A4
　Mansfield Woodhouse NG19 .... 88 B2
　Market Warsop NG20 .... 74 A3
　Newark-on-T NG24 .... 139 F4
　North Wheatley DN22 .... 31 F4
　Nottingham, Old Basford
　NG6 .... 160 C1
　Orston NG13 .... 179 F4
　Pleasleyhill NG19 .... 87 D2
　Ruddington NG11 .... 196 B4
　Sandiacre NG10 .... 182 A4
　Shelford NG12 .... 164 B1
　South Leverton DN22 .... 42 B4
　South Normanton DE55 .... 113 D3
　Southwell NG25 .... 136 C4
　Stapleford NG9 .... 182 B4
　Sturton le S DN22 .... 32 B2
　Sutton in A NG17 .... 100 C1
　Sutton on T NG23 .... 97 D4
　Whaley Thorns NG20 .... 59 D1
　Whatton NG13 .... 179 D2
　Wymeswold LE12 .... 216 B3
Church St E NG16 .... 113 E2
Church St W NG16 .... 113 E2
Church Vale Prim Sch
　NG20 .... 74 A4
Church View
　Balderton NG24 .... 140 B2
　Beckingham DN10 .... 14 A1
　Bottesford NG13 .... 181 D2
　Carlton NG4 .... 162 C1
　Glapwell S44 .... 86 A4
　New Houghton NG19 .... 86 C4
　Ollerton NG22 .... 77 D2
　Scrooby DN10 .... 10 A1
　Stanton Hill NG17 .... 100 B3
Church View Cl NG5 .... 147 F1
Church Way NG22 .... 29 D3
Church Wlk Bawtry DN10 .... 10 A4
　Brinsley NG16 .... 143 F4
　Carlton NG4 .... 174 C4
　Eastwood NG16 .... 143 F1

Church Wlk continued
　Harworth DN11 .... 8 C2
　Stapleford NG9 .... 182 C4
　Upton NG23 .... 122 C1
　Weston NG23 .... 81 D3
　Whatton NG13 .... 179 D2
　Worksop S80 .... 35 F2
Churchdale Ave NG9 .... 170 C1
Churchfield Ct NG5 .... 160 C4
Churchfield Dr NG21 .... 103 F1
Churchfield La NG7 .... 222 A4
Churchfield Terr NG7 .... 160 C1
Churchgate DN22 .... 39 F4
Churchill Cl NG5 .... 161 F4
Churchill Dr
　Newark-on-T NG24 .... 139 F3
　Ruddington NG11 .... 196 A4
　Stapleford NG9 .... 182 B4
Churchill Gdns NG19 .... 88 B2
Churchill Pk NG4 .... 174 C3
Churchill Way DN21 .... 24 C2
Churchmoor Ct NG5 .... 147 F1
Churchmoor La NG5 .... 147 F1
Churchside Gdns NG7 .... 172 C4
Churnet Cl NG11 .... 184 C2
Chutre Ede Prim Sch
　NG24 .... 140 C2
Cinder La NG22 .... 77 F3
Cinderhill Gr NG4 .... 162 C1
Cinderhill Rd NG6 .... 160 A3
Cinderhill Wlk NG6 .... 160 A3
Circle The NG19 .... 88 A2
Citadel St NG7 .... 222 A3
Citrus Gr DE74 .... 203 E2
City Ground The
　(Nottingham Forest FC)
　NG2 .... 173 F1
City Hospl NG5 .... 161 D2
City Link NG1,NG2 .... 173 F2
City Rd Beeston NG9 .... 184 A3
　Nottingham NG7 .... 172 B1
Stathern LE14 .... 202 C2
City The Beeston NG9 .... 184 A3
　Beeston NG9 .... 184 A4
Clandon Dr NG5 .... 161 D1
Clanfield Rd NG8 .... 171 F4
Clapham St NG7 .... 222 A3
Clapton La NG7 .... 184 B1
Clara Mount Rd DE75 .... 143 D1
Clarborough Dr NG5 .... 162 A3
Clarborough Hill DN22 .... 30 C2
Clarborough Jun &
　Inf Schs DN22 .... 30 C2
Clare Cl NG4 .... 160 C2
Clare Hill NG21 .... 118 A2
Clare Rd NG17 .... 114 C4
Clare St NG1 .... 223 E3
Clare Valley NG7 .... 223 D2
Clarehaven NG9 .... 182 C3
Claremont Ave 183 E4
Claremont La NG16 .... 146 A3
Claremont Dr NG2 .... 185 E2
Claremont Prim Sch
　NG5 .... 161 D1
Claremont Rd 24 C3
Claremont Cl NG19 .... 161 D1
Claremount Coll (Hamilton
　Annexe) NG5 .... 173 D4
Clarendon Coll
　Nottingham NG5 .... 173 D4
Clarendon Coll (Sherwood
　Annexe) NG5 .... 173 D4
Clarendon Ct 11 NG5 .... 173 D4
Clarendon Pk NG5 .... 173 D4
Clarendon Rd NG5 .... 101 F4
Clarendon St NG1 .... 223 D3
Clarewood Gr NG11 .... 195 F4
Clarges St NG6 .... 160 B3
Clark La NG22 .... 65 F1
Clarke Ave Arnold NG5 .... 161 F4
　Newark-on-T NG24 .... 139 F3
Clarke Cl NG12 .... 189 D2
Clarke Dr NG10 .... 193 D4
Clarke Rd NG2 .... 173 F1
Clarke's La NG9 .... 183 F2
Clarks La NG24 .... 125 D1
Clarkson Dr NG9 .... 184 A3
Clater's Ct DN22 .... 40 A4
Claude St NG7 .... 172 C1
Clawson La Hickling LE14 .... 210 B3
　Nether Broughton LE14 .... 210 C2
Claxton Rise LE14 .... 211 F1
Clay Ave NG3 .... 162 A2
Clay La NG24 .... 140 B4
Clay St LE12 .... 216 B2
Claye St NG10 .... 193 E4
Clayfield Cl NG6 .... 160 A3
Claygate NG3 .... 174 A4
Claylands Ave S81 .... 35 E3
Claylands Cl S81 .... 35 E3
Claylands La S81 .... 35 E3
Claypit La NG25 .... 137 F2

Che – Clo 231
Claypole CE Sch NG23 .... 156 C4
Claypole La NG23 .... 156 C4
Claypole Rd 17 NG7 .... 172 C4
Claythorne Dr DN21 .... 24 C4
Clayton Cl NG24 .... 140 A3
Clayton Ct NG7 .... 222 B3
Clayton's Wharf 11 NG7 .... 172 C2
Claytons Dr 11 NG7 .... 172 C1
Clayworth Comm DN22 .... 21 F2
Clayworth Ct NG18 .... 103 D2
Clayworth Rd DN10 .... 12 C1
Clegg Hill Dr NG17 .... 99 F2
Clement Ave NG24 .... 140 C2
Clensey La NG23 .... 156 C1
Clerkson St 4 NG18 .... 102 A3
Clerkson's Alley 11 NG18 .... 102 A4
Clether Rd NG8 .... 171 E3
Cleve Ave NG9 .... 182 C2
Cleveland Ave NG10 .... 182 C1
Cleveland Cl
　Carlton in L S81 .... 25 F4
　Nottingham NG7 .... 222 A3
Cleveland Sq NG24 .... 139 F3
Cleveland St DN21 .... 24 B4
Cleveleys Rd NG9 .... 183 D2
Clevely Way NG11 .... 184 C2
Cliff Bvd NG16 .... 158 C4
Cliff Cres NG12 .... 175 F2
Cliff Dr NG12 .... 176 A3
Cliff Gate NG22 .... 65 E4
Cliff La NG16 .... 113 F2
Cliff Nook DE55 .... 113 D2
Cliff Nook La NG24 .... 125 D1
Cliff Rd Carlton NG4 .... 174 B3
　Nottingham NG1 .... 223 F2
　Radcliffe on T NG12 .... 175 F2
Cliff St NG18 .... 102 A2
Cliff The NG6 .... 160 A2
Cliff Way NG12 .... 175 F2
Cliffe Hill Ave NG9 .... 182 B4
Cliffgrove Ave NG9 .... 183 E3
Cliffhill La NG13 .... 179 E3
Cliffmere Wlk NG11 .... 184 B1
Clifford Ave NG9 .... 183 F4
Clifford Cl
　Keyworth NG12 .... 197 F2
　Long Eaton NG10 .... 193 D2
Clifford Ct NG7 .... 222 B3
Clifford St
　Long Eaton NG10 .... 194 A4
　Mansfield NG18 .... 102 A2
　Nottingham NG7 .... 222 B3
Clifton Ave
　Long Eaton NG10 .... 194 A4
　Nottingham NG11 .... 196 B4
Clifton Cres
　Beeston NG9 .... 183 F2
　Newark-on-T NG24 .... 125 C2
Clifton Gr Carlton NG4 .... 162 C1
　Nottingham NG11 .... 102 C2
Clifton La
　Nottingham NG11 .... 184 C2
　Ruddington NG11 .... 196 A4
Clifton Pl 11 NG18 .... 102 A4
Clifton Rd NG11 .... 196 A4
Clifton St NG9 .... 184 A3
Clifton Terr NG7 .... 222 C1
Clifton Way DN22 .... 39 F4
Clinthill La S80 .... 45 D4
Clinton Ave
　Brinsley NG16 .... 143 E3
　Nottingham NG5 .... 173 D4
Clinton Ct NG1 .... 223 E3
Clinton Garden La NG22 .... 65 F1
Clinton St Arnold NG5 .... 161 F4
　Beeston NG9 .... 183 F4
　Newark-on-T NG24 .... 139 F4
　Worksop S80 .... 36 A1
Clinton St E NG1 .... 223 E3
Clinton St W NG1 .... 223 E3
Clinton Terr DN21 .... 24 B4
Clipsham Cl NG24 .... 140 C3
Clipstone Ave
　Mansfield NG18 .... 102 B4
　Nottingham NG1 .... 223 D4
　Nottingham, Mapperley
　NG3 .... 162 A2
　Sutton in A NG17 .... 101 D2
Clipstone Cl NG8 .... 159 E1
Clipstone Dr NG19 .... 89 E2
Clipstone Rd E NG19 .... 89 E1
Clipstone Rd W NG19 .... 89 D1
Clive Cres NG16 .... 159 D3
Cliveden Gn NG11 .... 184 B1
Cloister St NG7 .... 172 C1
Cloisters The NG9 .... 184 A4
Close Quarters NG9 .... 183 E4
Close The
　Averham NG23 .... 123 F1
　Beeston NG9 .... 183 E2
　Mansfield NG18 .... 103 D1
　Newark-on-T NG24 .... 140 A4
　Nottingham NG5 .... 161 C2
　Shirebrook NG20 .... 72 C2
　Upton NG23 .... 122 C1
Closes Side La NG13 .... 165 F2
Cloud Ave NG9 .... 182 C4
Clouds Hill NG11 .... 195 F4
Cloudside Cl NG10 .... 182 A4
Cloudside Jun Sch
　NG10 .... 182 A4
Cloudside Rd NG10 .... 182 A4
Clough Ct NG8 .... 172 A4

Clover Cl S81 36 A4
Clover Gn NG6 160 B2
Clover Rise NG16 158 A4
Clover St NG17 115 D3
Cloverdale NG12 188 A1
Cloverfields NG14 149 D4
Cloverlands NG2 185 E2
Cloverlands Dr NG16 159 D4
Club Ct NG24 140 B2
Clumber Ave
Beeston NG9 183 E3
Brinsley NG16 128 C1
Carlton NG4 175 D4
Edwinstowe NG21 75 F2
Mansfield NG21 103 F1
Newark-on-T NG24 140 A3
Nottingham, Hyson Green NG5 173 D4
Nottingham, Mapperley NG3 162 A2
Clumber Cres NG17 100 B3
Clumber Cres N NG7 222 C2
Clumber Cres S NG7 222 C1
Clumber Ct Ilkeston DE7 157 F3
Mansfield NG19 87 F1
Market Warsop NG20 74 A2
Nottingham NG7 222 C1
Clumber Dr
Mansfield NG19 87 F1
Radcliffe on T NG12 176 A2
Clumber Park (Ctry Pk) S80 48 A2
Clumber Pl S80 35 F2
Clumber Rd
West Bridgford NG2 185 F4
Worksop S80 47 D3
Clumber Rd E NG7 222 C2
Clumber Rd W NG7 222 C2
Clumber St
Hucknall NG15 146 B3
Kirkby in A NG17 115 E3
Long Eaton NG10 193 E4
Mansfield NG18 102 A4
Market Warsop NG20 74 A2
Nottingham NG1 223 E3
Retford DN22 39 F3
Sutton in A NG17 100 B1
Clumber Way NG22 106 A3
Clun Ct NG19 88 B1
Clyro Pl DN22 28 C3
Co-operative Ave NG15 146 A4
Co-operative St
Long Eaton NG10 193 F3
Stanton Hill NG17 100 B3
Coach Dr NG16 143 F2
Coach Gap La NG13 190 B1
Coach Rd NG20 74 B1
Coachmans Croft 9 NG8 172 A3
Coal La LE14 211 F4
Coal Yard La NG23 82 C4
Coalfields Cl NG17 100 B1
Coalpit La DN22 49 F2
Coates Ave NG15 130 C1
Coates Rd DN22 43 E4
Coatsby Rd NG16 158 C4
Cobden Pl NG19 87 F1
Cobden Prim Sch LE11 220 A2
Cobden St
Gainsborough DN21 24 B4
Kirkby in A NG17 115 D2
Long Eaton NG10 193 F4
1 Loughborough LE11 220 B2
Nottingham NG7 222 A3
Coburn St NG17 100 C1
Cobwell Rd DN22 39 F3
Cochrane Terr NG17 100 B3
Cock Hill La DN10 10 A3
Cockayne Cl NG10 182 A2
Cocker Beck NG4 163 E4
Cockerhouse Rd NG16 143 F2
Cockett La NG22 119 F4
Cockhill Cl DN10 10 A3
Cocking Hill NG22 78 B2
Cocking La DN22 42 B1
Cockington Rd NG8 171 E3
Cockleys NG10 193 E3
Cockshut La NG20 59 D2
Coddington CE Prim Sch NG24 126 A1
Coddington La LN6 127 D3
Coddington Rd NG24 140 C3
Codrington Gdns 5 NG5 161 E4
Cogenhoe Wlk NG5 147 F1
Coggin's La NG20 74 B3
Coghill Ct NG25 136 B4
Coging Cl NG24 140 B2
Cogley La NG13 178 A2
Cohen Cl NG5 162 A3
Cokefield Ave NG16 159 F2
Col Frank Seely Comp Sch NG14 148 C4
Colbeck St S80 35 F2
Colborn St NG3 173 F4
Colby Cl NG19 89 D1
Coleby Ave NG7 222 A1
Coleby Rd NG8 159 F1
Coledale NG2 186 B3
Coleman Ave NG24 140 A2
Coleridge Cres NG5 161 E4
Coleridge Rd
Balderton NG24 140 C3
Worksop S81 36 A3
Coleridge St NG7 222 B4
Colesbourne Rd NG7 184 C1
Colgrove Rd LE11 220 A1
Colin Broughton Ct NG6 160 B4
Colindale Gdns NG16 159 F2
Colinwood Ave NG5 146 C1
College Dr
Nottingham NG11 184 B1
Nottingham NG11 184 C2
College La
East Markham NG22 66 A4
Worksop S80 36 A1
College Rd Beeston NG9 183 F3
Sutton Bonington LE12 204 A1
College St
East Bridgford NG13 165 E2
Long Eaton NG10 182 B1
Nottingham NG1 223 D2
Colley La NG23 81 D2
Colleymoor Leys La NG7 184 C1
Collier Ave NG19 88 A3
Colliers Way NG6 160 A2
Colliery Cl NG2 173 D1
Colliery Rd DN11 9 D2
Collin Ave NG10 182 A2
Collin Gn NG5 161 E2
Collin St Beeston NG9 183 F3
Nottingham NG1 223 E1
Collingham Rd
Collingham LN6 98 C1
Mansfield NG19 87 E1
Collingham Sta NG23 112 A4
Collington St NG9 183 F3
Collington Way NG2 185 E3
Collingwood Cl NG11 184 C2
Collingwood Rd NG10 193 F3
Collins Ave
South Normanton DE55 113 D4
Sutton in A NG17 114 C4
Collins Cl NG6 159 F3
Collins Wlk DN22 39 F4
Collis Cl NG24 140 B4
Collison St NG7 222 B4
Colly Gate NG16 159 D3
Collyer Rd NG14 148 B4
Collygate Rd NG2 173 E1
Colmon Cl NG5 161 D4
Colmon Wlk 28 NG5 161 D4
Colne Ct NG19 88 B1
Colonel's La LE14 210 A1
Colonsay Cl NG9 170 B2
Colsterdale S81 36 A4
Colston Basset Prim Sch NG12 200 B4
Colston Cres NG2 185 E2
Colston Gate NG12 188 A2
Colston La LE14 201 F2
Colston Rd
Cropwell Bishop NG12 189 D1
Mansfield NG18 103 D2
Nottingham NG6 160 B4
Colton St DN10 6 C1
Columbia Ave
Mansfield NG18 102 C3
Sutton in A NG17 100 B1
Columbia Cl NG16 129 D4
Columbia St NG17 100 A1
Colville St NG1 173 D4
Colville Terr
Gainsborough DN21 24 B4
15 Nottingham NG1 173 D4
Colville Villas 14 NG1 173 D4
Colwick Bsns Pk NG4 174 C3
Colwick Cl NG19 87 F1
Colwick Ind Est NG4 174 C3
Colwick Loop Rd NG4 175 D4
Colwick Manor Farm NG4 174 C3
Colwick Park Cl NG4 174 C3
Colwick Rd
Nottingham NG2 174 A2
West Bridgford NG2 173 F1
Comery Ave NG3 174 A3
Comfrey Cl NG5 160 C4
Commerce Sq NG1 223 F2
Commercial Ave NG9 183 F3
Commercial Gate NG18 102 A3
Commercial Rd
Keyworth NG12 197 F1
19 Nottingham NG6 160 A4
Commercial St 5 NG18 102 A3
Commodore Gdns NG8 160 B1
Common La Beeston NG9 183 D3
Blyth S81 18 A2
Hucknall NG15 145 E3
Mansfield Woodhouse NG19 88 A2
Ranskill DN22 19 E2
Shirebrook NG20 72 B2
Sturton le S DN22 32 B2
Tickhill DN11 8 A4
Watnall NG16 159 D4
Common Rd Huthwaite NG17 99 F1
Retford DN22 39 F4
Common Rd S80 34 A3
Common Side NG16 128 C4
Common The
Hucknall NG15 145 E3
South Normanton DE55 113 D3
Commons Cl NG16 158 A4
Compton Acres NG2 185 D3
Compton Acres Sh Ctr NG2 185 E2
Compton Rd NG5 161 D2
Compton St NG20 72 C4
Comyn Gdns NG3 223 F4
Conduit Cl NG2 173 E1
Conery Gdns NG13 179 D2
Conery La NG13 178 C1
Coneygrey Spinney NG23 152 C1
Conifer Cres NG11 195 F4
Conifer Wlk NG3 174 A4
Coningsby Cl DN21 24 C4
Coningsby Gdns E NG5 161 F2
Coningsby Rd NG5 161 F3
Coningswath Rd NG4 162 B1
Conisborough Terr 17 NG2 173 E1
Conisbrough Ave NG4 163 D1
Coniston Ave NG6 160 B1
Coniston Cl
Mansfield Woodhouse NG19 88 C2
West Bridgford NG2 186 B4
Coniston Rd Beeston NG9 183 E4
Hucknall NG15 145 F4
Kirkby in A NG17 115 E3
Long Eaton NG10 182 A1
Worksop S81 35 F4
Connaught Rd DN21 15 E1
Connelly Cl NG5 162 B3
Connery Mews NG9 183 D1
Connery The NG15 146 A4
Conrad Cl S80 36 A2
Constance St NG7 161 D1
Convent Hospl NG5 161 E2
Convent St NG1 223 F3
Conway Ave NG4 175 D4
Conway Cl Mansfield NG19 101 E4
Nottingham NG3 173 E4
Conway Cres NG4 175 D4
Conway Dr S81 25 F3
Conway Gdns Arnold NG5 161 F3
Retford DN22 39 D4
Conway Rd Carlton NG4 175 D4
Hucknall NG15 145 E2
Conway St NG10 193 F4
Conway Wlk 9 NG3 173 E4
Cook Dr DE7 170 A3
Cooks La Fiskerton NG25 137 E1
Southwell NG25 136 A4
Cookson Ave NG4 162 B1
Cookson St NG17 114 C3
Coombe Cl NG8 172 B2
Cooper Cl Arnold NG5 162 B3
Cropwell Bishop NG12 189 D2
Nottingham NG6 159 F3
Cooper Ct LE11 220 B1
Cooper St NG4 175 D3
Coopers Gn NG8 171 F1
Coopers Rise NG21 104 A1
Coopers Yd NG24 139 F4
Cope St NG7 222 B4
Copeland Ave
1 Kirkby in A NG17 114 C3
Stapleford NG9 182 C4
Copeland Gr NG13 177 E3
Copeland Rd
Hucknall NG15 146 B4
Kirkby in A NG17 114 C3
Copenhagen Ct NG3 161 E1
Copper Hill NG23 81 F2
Coppice Ave DE7 157 E3
Coppice Cl NG15 145 F3
Coppice Croft NG17 100 B1
Coppice Dr NG16 143 E2
Coppice Farm Prim Sch NG5 162 A4
Coppice Gr NG3 161 F1
Coppice Rd Arnold NG5 162 A4
Clipstone NG19 89 E2
Worksop S81 35 F4
Coppice The
Barnby Moor DN22 28 B3
Shirebrook NG20 72 B2
Coppice View DE55 113 D2
Coppice Way S81 25 F4
Copplestone Dr NG3 162 B3
Copse Cl
Burton Joyce NG14 163 F3
Ravenshead NG15 116 B2
Copse The Beeston NG9 183 E3
Farndon NG24 139 D2
Hucknall NG15 146 B3
Ilkeston DE7 157 E3
Stanton Hill NG17 100 B3
Copseside Cl 10 NG10 193 D4
Copsewood DE55 113 D2
Corben Gdns NG6 159 F4
Corby Rd NG3 161 F1
Cordy La Brinsley NG16 143 F4
Selston NG16 143 F4
Corene Ave NG17 100 C1
Coriander Dr NG6 160 B2
Corinth Rd NG7 184 C1
Corkhill La NG22 121 E3
Corn Cl Cotgrave NG12 187 F1
South Normanton DE55 113 D3
Corncrake Ave NG6 160 B2
Cornell Dr NG5 162 B4
Corner The NG14 150 B1
Corneries The LE11 220 A2
Cornfield Ave DE55 113 D2
Cornfield Rd NG16 158 C4
Cornhill Rd NG4 174 A4
Cornley Rd DN10 6 B2
Cornwall Ave Beeston NG9 184 B2
Mansfield NG18 102 C3
Cornwall Cl NG16 128 B2
Cornwall Dr NG22 77 D2
Cornwall Rd Arnold NG5 161 E4
Retford DN22 30 A1
Shireoaks S81 34 C4
Cornwallis Cl NG10 193 E3
Coronation Ave
Long Clawson LE14 211 D1
Misson DN10 4 A2
New Houghton NG19 86 C4
Nottingham NG11 185 D4
Sandiacre NG10 182 A4
Coronation Dr
Mansfield NG19 103 D4
Shirebrook NG20 72 C1
South Normanton DE55 113 D3
Coronation Rd
Arnold NG3 161 F2
Bestwood Village NG6 146 C2
Cossall NG16 158 A1
Hucknall NG15 145 F4
Nuthall NG16 159 E3
Coronation St
Mansfield NG18 102 B3
New Balderton NG24 140 B3
Retford DN22 39 F3
Sutton in A NG17 100 C1
Whitwell S80 45 D3
Coronation Wlk NG4 163 D1
Corporation Oaks NG3 173 E4
Corporation Rd DE7 170 A3
Corporation St 8 NG18 102 A4
Corringham Rd DN21 15 F1
Corsham Gdns NG3 174 A4
Cosby Rd 29 NG2 173 F2
Cosgrove Ave NG17 101 D3
Cossall Ind Est NG16 158 A1
Cossall Rd Cossall NG9 170 B3
Trowell NG9 170 B3
Costhorpe Ind Est S81 16 C1
Costhorpe Villas S81 16 C1
Costock Ave NG5 161 D2
Costock CE Prim Sch LE12 206 B1
Costock Rd
East Leake LE12 206 A1
Wysall NG12 207 E1
Cotes Rd LE12 220 C3
Cotgrave Ave NG4 162 C1
Cotgrave CE Sch NG12 187 F2
Cotgrave Cl NG8 159 F1
Cotgrave Inf Sch NG12 187 F2
Cotgrave La NG12 187 D1
Cotgrave Manvers Sch NG12 187 F2
Cotgrave Rd
Cotgrave NG12 187 D1
Mansfield NG19 87 F1
Cotmanhay Inf & Jun Sch DE7 157 F3
Cotmanhay Rd DE7 157 F2
Coton Cl
Mansfield Woodhouse NG19 88 C2
Nottingham NG11 185 D2
Cotswold Cl 4 NG10 193 D4
Cotswold Ct Beeston NG9 171 E1
Carlton in L S81 25 F4
Cotswold Gr NG18 103 D3
Cotswold Rd NG8 159 F1
Cottage Ave NG13 178 C2
Cottage Cl
Balderton NG24 140 B1
Blidworth NG21 117 F2
East Leake LE12 205 F2
Ilkeston DE7 157 E2
Cottage La
Collingham NG23 111 F3
Market Warsop NG20 74 B1
North Clifton NG23 69 D2
Cottage Mdw NG4 174 C2
Cottage Pasture La NG14 164 C4
Cottage Terr NG1 222 C3
Cottam Dr NG5 161 D4
Cottam Gdns NG5 161 D4
Cottam Gr NG19 101 E3
Cottam Rd DN22 42 C4
Cottans Cl NG25 136 C4
Cottesmore Rd NG7 222 B2
Cotton Mill La NG22 120 A3
Coulby Cl NG23 156 C3
Coulton's Ave NG17 100 B2
Coulton's Cl NG17 100 B2
County Bsns Pk NG2 173 F1
County Cl NG9 184 A3
County Rd Carlton NG4 162 B2
Nottingham NG2 173 F1
Court Cres NG8 171 F2
Court Gdns NG2 185 D2
Court St 32 NG7 172 C4
Court Yd NG9 183 D4
Court-Field Rd NG17 101 D3
Courtenay Gdns NG3 173 E4
Courtlett Way NG6 160 A3
Courtney Cl NG8 171 F3
Cove Rd DN9 2 C3
Covedale Rd NG5 161 E3
Covent Gdns NG12 176 C2
Coventry Ct NG6 160 B3
Coventry Dr S81 36 A3
Coventry La NG9 171 D2
Coventry Rd
Beeston NG9 184 A4
Nottingham NG6 160 A3
Coverdale S81 36 A4
Covert Cl
Burton Joyce NG14 163 F3
Hucknall NG15 146 B3
Keyworth NG12 197 F2
Covert Rd NG2 186 A3
Cow La Beeston NG9 183 E4
Newark-on-T NG24 124 C1
Cow Pasture La NG17 114 B3
Cowan St NG1 223 F3
Cowdray Cl LE11 220 A1
Cowdrey Gdns NG5 162 A3
Cowlairs NG5 160 C4
Cowley St NG6 160 C2
Cowpasture La NG17 100 C1
Cowper Cl S81 36 A3
Cowper Rd Arnold NG5 161 F2
Eastwood NG16 158 A4
Cowpes Cl NG17 100 C2
Cox Dr NG13 180 C2
Cox's Hill DN21 15 E1
Cox's La NG19 88 A3
Coxmoor Cl NG2 186 B2
Coxmoor Ct 14 NG5 147 D1
Coxmoor Prim Sch NG17 115 E3
Coxmoor Rd NG17, NG15 115 F4
Crab La NG23 110 C1
Crab Nook La NG22 119 F3
Crabtree Field NG2 174 B2
Crabtree La
Beckingham DN10 23 D4
High Marnham NG23 67 E1
Crabtree Rd NG6 160 A3
Craddock St LE11 220 A2
Crafts Way NG25 121 F1
Cragdale Rd NG5 161 E3
Cragg La DE55 99 D1
Cragmoor Rd NG14 163 F2
Crags Rd S80 45 D1
Craig Moray NG12 176 A2
Craig St NG10 193 F4
Craigs Gn NG19 101 F3
Craigston Rd S81 25 F3
Crammond Cl 8 NG2 173 D1
Crampton Cl NG17 100 A2
Crampton Ct NG5 161 D4
Crampton Rd NG18 102 C4
Cramworth Dr 11 NG5 161 E2
Cranberry Cl NG2 185 D3
Cranborne Cl NG19 101 E4
Cranbourne Cl NG9 170 B1
Cranbourne Gr NG15 145 F4
Cranbrook Ct NG19 88 B3
Cranbrook St NG1 223 F3
Cranfleet Way NG10 193 D4
Cranford Gdns NG2 185 E2
Cranleigh Dr NG14 150 B1
Cranmer Ave NG13 178 C2
Cranmer Gr
13 Nottingham NG3 173 E4
Radmanthwaite NG19 87 E2
Cranmer Rd NG24 139 F3
Cranmer St Ilkeston DE7 157 F1
Long Eaton NG10 182 B1
Nottingham NG3 173 E4
Cranmore Cl NG5 148 A
Cranshaw Cl LE12 212 B
Cransley Ave NG8 171 E
Cranston Ave NG5 147 F
Cranston Rd NG9 171 E
Cranswick Cl NG19 89 D
Cranthorne Dr NG3 174 B
Crantock Gdns NG12 197 F
Cranwell Ct NG6 159 F
Cranwell Rd NG8 159 E
Craster Dr Arnold NG5 148 A
Nottingham NG6 159 F
Craster St NG17 100 C
Crathie Rd S81 25 F
Craven Rd NG7 172 C
Crawford Ave NG9 182 B
Crawford Cl NG8 171 F
Crawford Rise NG5 162 B
Crees La NG24 139 D
Crescent Ave NG4 162 C
Crescent Rd NG16 128 B
Crescent The Arnold NG5 161 F
Beckingham DN10 14 A
Beeston, Chilwell NG9 183 E
Beeston, Toton NG9 183 D
Bilsthorpe NG22 105 F
Bircotes DN11 9 E
Blidworth NG21 118 A
East Leake LE12 205 F
Eastwood NG16 144 A
Lea DN21 24 C
Mansfield NG18 102 B
Newark-on-T NG24 140 A
Nottingham NG3 173 E
Old Dalby LE14 219 D
Radcliffe on T NG12 176 A
Retford DN22 39 E
Shirebrook NG20 72 C
Stapleford NG9 170 C
Sutton in A NG17 100 B
Cresswell Rd
Beeston NG9 183 D
Worksop S80 35 F
Cresswell St S80 35 F
Cresta Gdns NG3 161 E
Creswell Crags Visitor Ctr S80 45 D
Creswell Ct NG19 88 C
Creswell Rd NG20 60 A
Crew La NG25 137 D
Crew Rd NG23 98 A
Crewe Cl Blidworth NG21 118 A
Nottingham NG7 222 B
Crewe Rd DN11 9 D
Cribb Cl NG11 185 D
Crich View Newton DE55 99 D
Nottingham NG5 161 E
Cricket Cl NG17 129 F
Cricket Field La DN22 39 F
Cricketers Ct NG2 173 F
Criftin Rd NG14 164 A
Crink La NG25 136 C
Cripps Hill NG7 172 B
Critch's Flats NG16 158 C
Critchley St DE7 157
Crocus Pl NG2 173
Crocus St
Kirkby in A NG17 115
Nottingham NG2 173

-oft Ave Hucknall NG15 ...... 146 A3
Mansfield NG18 .... 102 B1
-oft Cl Pinxton NG16 .... 113 E2
Rolleston NG23 .... 138 A3
-oft Cres NG16 .... 158 B3
-oft Ct NG17 .... 99 F2
-oft Dr DN11 .... 8 A4
-oft Farm Cl Everton DN10 .. 11 E2
Rolleston NG23 .... 138 A3
-oft Gdns LE14 .... 218 C2
-oft Prim Sch NG17 .... 100 C1
-oft Rd Arnold NG5 .... 161 F4
Finningley DN10 .... 1 A1
Keyworth NG12 .... 197 F2
West Bridgford NG2 .... 186 A2
-oft Rise NG13 .... 165 D3
-oft The Beckingham DN10 .. 23 E4
Kegworth DE74 .... 203 E1
Newark-on-T NG24 .... 140 A4
Retford DN22 .... 39 F4
South Normanton DE55 ...... 113 D3
Stanton Hill NG17 .... 100 B3
-oft Way DN10 .... 11 E2
-oft Wlk S80 .... 45 D3
-ofton Cl Beeston NG9 .... 183 E2
■ Nottingham NG8 .... 172 A3
-ofton Rd NG9 .... 183 E1
-The NG13 .... 177 F2
-omarty Cl NG11 .... 101 E3
-omarty Cl ■ NG2 .... 173 D1
-omdale Cl NG5 .... 148 B1
-omer Cl NG18 .... 102 B2
-omer Rd NG3 .... 173 F4
-omford Ave
Carlton NG4 .... 174 B4
Mansfield NG18 .... 102 A2
-omford Cl
Aldercar NG16 .... 143 D2
Long Eaton NG10 .... 193 D3
-omford Rd
Annesley Woodhouse NG17 .. 115 D1
Langley Mill NG16 .... 143 D2
West Bridgford NG2 .... 185 F3
Stanton DN21 .... 15 E1
-ompton Rd
Bilsthorpe NG22 .... 105 F3
Ilkeston DE7 .... 170 A2
Radmanthwaite NG19 .... 87 E2
-ompton St
New Houghton NG19 .... 86 C4
Teversal NG17 .... 100 A4
-omwell Ave DE7 .... 170 A3
-omwell Cres NG4 .... 163 D4
-omwell Dr LE12 .... 205 F1
-omwell Rd
Aslockton NG13 .... 178 C2
Beeston NG9 .... 183 F3
Newark-on-T NG24 .... 140 A4
-omwell St Carlton NG4 ..... 174 C4
Eastwood NG16 .... 158 B4
Gainsborough DN21 .... 24 B3
Mansfield NG18 .... 102 B3
Nottingham NG7 .... 222 C3
-omwell Way DN21 .... 24 C2
-ook's Ave NG19 .... 88 B2
-ookdale La NG14 .... 148 C4
-ooked Billet St DN11 .... 9 D2
-ookes Ave NG19 .... 87 D3
-oome Cl LE11 .... 220 B1
-opston Cl NG2 .... 185 F2
-opton Cres NG8 .... 172 A3
-opton Gr NG13 .... 177 F3
-opwell Bishop Prim Sch
NG12 .... 189 D2
-opwell Bishop Rd
NG12 .... 189 D3
-opwell Butler Rd NG12 .... 189 D2
-opwell Ct NG18 .... 102 B4
-opwell Gdns NG12 .... 176 A1
-opwell Gn NG3 .... 173 F3
-opwell Rd Langar NG13 ... 190 B1
Radcliffe on T NG12 .... 176 A1
-osby Cl NG10 .... 89 D1
-osby Rd NG2 .... 185 F4
-oss Dr Kirkby in A NG17 ... 115 D4
Rainworth NG21 .... 104 A1
-oss Hill DN10 .... 12 B1
-oss Hill Cl LE12 .... 216 B2
-oss La Austerfield DN10 ... 3 E3
Balderton NG24 .... 140 B1
Blidworth NG21 .... 117 E3
Collingham NG23 .... 112 B4
East Bridgford NG13 .... 165 E2
Elkesley DN22 .... 49 F2
Elston NG23 .... 154 A2
Farndon NG24 .... 138 C2
Gringley on t H DN10 .... 13 D1
Hardy NG23 .... 70 B1
Huthwaite NG17 .... 100 A1
North Leverton DN22 .... 100 B3
-oss St Arnold NG5 .... 161 F4
Barnby in t W NG24 .... 141 F3
Beeston NG9 .... 183 F4
Gainsborough DN21 .... 105 F3
Carlton, Netherfield NG4 .... 175 D4
Carlton, Thorneywood NG4 . 174 B4
Eastwood NG16 .... 144 A1
Gainsborough DN21 .... 24 B4
Long Eaton NG10 .... 193 F4
Loughborough LE11 .... 220 A4
Mansfield Woodhouse NG19 . 88 A1
Morton DN21 .... 15 D2
Newark-on-T NG24 .... 140 A4
Retford DN22 .... 40 A3
Sandiacre NG10 .... 182 A3
Sturton le S DN22 .... 32 B3

Cross The Carlton in L S81 .. 26 A3
Cotgrave NG12 .... 187 F2
Crossdale Dr N12 .... 197 F2
Crossdale Drive Prim Sch
NG12 .... 197 F2
Crossdale Wlk NG5 .... 160 C4
Crossfield Dr NG5 .... 161 D4
Crossgate Dr NG2 .... 173 D1
Crosshill NG12 .... 188 A2
Crosslands Mdw NG4 .... 174 C2
Crossley Ave NG17 .... 100 A2
Crossley Hill La S81 .... 26 B2
Crossley St NG5 .... 161 D1
Crossman St NG5 .... 161 E1
Crossways
East Markham NG22 .... 66 A4
Retford DN22 .... 39 F4
Crossways Dr NG13 .... 165 E2
Crow Ct NG13 .... 178 A2
Crow Hill NG19 .... 87 D3
Crow Hill Ct NG18 .... 102 A4
Crow Hill Dr NG18 .... 102 A4
Crow Hill La NG19 .... 88 A1
Crow Hill Rd NG4 .... 174 C4
Crow La NG23, NG24 .... 124 B4
Crow Park Ave NG23 .... 81 E1
Crow Park Dr NG14 .... 163 F2
Crowborough Ave NG8 ...... 171 F1
Crowcroft Way NG10 .... 182 A1
Crowley Cl NG8 .... 171 E5
Crown Ave NG19 .... 101 D4
Crown Cl Collingham NG23 . 98 A1
Long Eaton NG10 .... 193 D4
Rainworth NG21 .... 118 A4
Crown Ct NG22 .... 32 B3
Crown Farm Farm Way NG19 103 D4
Crown St Mansfield NG18 ... 102 C3
Newark-on-T NG24 .... 139 F4
Worksop S80 .... 35 F2
Crowthorne Cl NG5 .... 146 C1
Crowthorne Gdns NG5 ...... 146 C1
Crowtrees Dr NG17 .... 100 B1
Croxall Cl NG11 .... 184 C2
Croxley Gdns NG8 .... 159 E2
Croxton Ct NG19 .... 88 C2
Croydon Rd NG7 .... 222 A4
Crummock Cl NG9 .... 183 E4
Cuckney Hill NG20 .... 74 A4
Cuckoo Holt S81 .... 35 E4
Cuillin Cl NG10 .... 182 A1
Cul-de-sac NG22 .... 105 F3
Cullen Cl NG24 .... 124 C1
Cullen's Ct NG5 .... 161 E1
Cullin Cl NG5 .... 146 C1
Cumberland Ave
Beeston NG9 .... 183 E3
Market Warsop NG20 .... 74 A3
Cumberland Cl
Bircotes DN11 .... 9 E2
Carlton in L S81 .... 25 F4
Westwood NG16 .... 128 B2
Cumberland Dr NG10 .... 101 E4
Cumberland Pl NG1 .... 223 D2
Cumberlands Mid Sch
NG19 .... 101 E4
Cumbria Rd S81 .... 36 A3
Cundy Hill NG25 .... 136 A3
Cunningham Cl DN10 .... 19 F4
Cupar Cl NG20 .... 74 B3
Curie Ct NG7 .... 172 C1
Curlew Cl NG3 .... 174 B3
Curlew Wharf ■ NG7 .... 172 C1
Currie Rd NG24 .... 125 D1
Cursley Way NG9 .... 183 E1
Curtis Cl NG23 .... 98 A1
Curtis St NG15 .... 146 A3
Curzon Ave NG4 .... 174 B4
Curzon Cl NG21 .... 118 A4
Curzon Ct NG3 .... 223 F4
Curzon Dr S81 .... 35 F4
Curzon Gdns NG3 .... 223 F4
Curzon Pl NG3 .... 223 F3
Curzon St Carlton NG4 ..... 175 D4
Gotham NG11 .... 195 D1
Long Eaton NG10 .... 182 A1
Loughborough LE11 .... 220 A2
Nottingham NG3 .... 223 F3
Cusworth Way S80 .... 35 E2
Cuttings Ave NG17 .... 114 A4
Cuxton Cl NG8 .... 159 E1
Cycle Rd NG7 .... 222 A2
Cypress Ct NG15 .... 145 F4
Cyprus Ave NG9 .... 183 F4
Cyprus Dr NG9 .... 183 F4
Cyprus Rd NG3 .... 161 E1
Cyril Ave Beeston NG9 ..... 183 F4
Nottingham NG8 .... 172 B4
Stapleford NG9 .... 182 B4
Cyril Rd NG2 .... 186 A4

D H Lawrence Mus NG16 .. 143 F2
D'ayncourt Wlk NG22 ...... 120 A3
Dabek Rise NG17 .... 115 D1
Dabell Ave NG6 .... 159 F4
Dadley Rd S81 .... 25 F4
Dadsley Rd DN11 .... 8 A4
Dagfa House Sch NG9 ...... 184 A4
Dagmar Gr Beeston NG9 ... 184 A3
Nottingham NG3 .... 161 E1
Dahlia Ave DE55 .... 113 D4
Dairy La LE14 .... 211 F4
Daisy Cl NG12 .... 187 F1
Daisy Farm Rd NG16 .... 158 A4
Daisy Rd NG3 .... 162 A1
Dakeyne St NG3 .... 173 F3
Dalbeattie Cl NG5 .... 162 B2
Dalby Sq NG8 .... 172 B2

Dale Ave Carlton NG4 .... 174 B4
Long Eaton NG10 .... 182 B1
Newton DE55 .... 99 D2
Nottingham NG3 .... 162 A1
Dale Cl Hucknall NG15 ...... 145 E3
Langwith NG20 .... 72 C4
Retford DN22 .... 39 F2
Sutton in a NG17 .... 101 D3
West Bridgford NG2 .... 186 A4
Whatley Thorns NG20 .... 58 C1
Dale Cres NG24 .... 140 C1
Dale Farm Ave NG3 .... 174 A3
Dale Gr NG2 .... 173 F4
Dale La Ault Hucknall S44 .. 86 B4
Bonds NG5 .... 161 E1
Dale Rd Carlton NG4 .... 174 B4
Keyworth NG12 .... 197 F2
Kimberley NG16 .... 158 C3
Market Warsop NG20 .... 74 B3
Dale St Mansfield NG19 .... 88 A1
Nottingham NG2 .... 173 F2
Dale View S81 .... 36 A4
Dale View Rd NG3 .... 174 A4
Dalebrook Cres NG15 .... 145 E3
Dalehead Rd NG11 .... 184 B1
Dalemoor Gdns NG8 .... 172 A4
Dales Ave NG17 .... 100 C3
Dales La NG14 .... 4 C2
Daleside NG12 .... 187 F1
Daleside Cl NG12 .... 197 F2
Daleside Rd E NG2, NG3 .. 174 B2
Daleside Rd NG2, NG3 ..... 174 A2
Dalestorth Ave NG17 .... 87 E1
Dalestorth Cl NG17 .... 101 D3
Dalestorth Gdns NG17 ..... 101 D3
Dalestorth Prim Sch
NG17 .... 101 D2
Dalestorth Rd NG17 .... 101 D3
Dalestorth St NG17 .... 101 D2
Daleswood Cres DE55 ...... 113 D2
Dalkeith Terr ■ NG7 .... 172 C4
Dallas St NG18 .... 102 A3
Dallas York Rd NG9 .... 184 A3
Dalley Cl NG9 .... 182 C4
Dalton Cl NG9 .... 182 C3
Daltons Cl NG16 .... 143 D3
Dam Rd DN11 .... 8 A3
Dame Flogan St NG18 ...... 102 A3
Dame La DN10 .... 4 A1
Damson Wlk NG3 .... 174 A4
Danbury Mount NG5 .... 161 E1
Dane Cl NG3 .... 223 F4
Dane Ct NG3 .... 223 F4
Danes Cl NG5 .... 161 E4
Danes Rd NG5 .... 15 F1
Danesfield Rd S80 .... 35 F1
Daneshill Rd DN22 .... 29 F2
Daneswood Jun Sch
NG17 .... 100 C4
Danethorpe La NG4 .... 174 A4
Danethorpe Vale NG5 ...... 161 E2
Daniel Cres NG18 .... 101 F4
Daniels Way NG15 .... 145 F2
Danners Hill NG15 .... 131 F3
Darfield Ct DN11 .... 8 A4
Darfield Dr DE75 .... 143 D1
Dark La Aslockton NG13 .... 179 D2
Barnby in t W NG24 .... 141 F3
Bingham NG13 .... 178 A2
West Leake LE12 .... 204 C1
Darkey La NG9 .... 182 C3
Darley Ave Beeston NG9 ... 182 C2
Carlton NG4 .... 162 C1
Kirkby in a NG17 .... 115 C3
Nottingham NG7 .... 172 C4
Darley Dr NG10 .... 193 D3
Darley Rd NG7 .... 172 C4
Darley Sq DE7 .... 157 F3
Darleydale Cl NG18 .... 102 B2
Darlton Dr NG5 .... 162 A4
Darlton Rd
East Drayton DN22 .... 53 D1
Tuxford NG22 .... 66 B2
Darlton St NG19 .... 101 E3
Darnal Cl NG5 .... 160 C4
Darnhall Cres NG8 .... 171 E4
Daron Gdns ■ NG5 .... 161 D4
Darrel Rd DN22 .... 39 F3
Darricott Cl NG21 .... 118 A4
Darvel Cl ■ NG8 .... 172 A3
Darwin Cl Elston NG23 .... 153 F2
Mansfield NG18 .... 102 B2
Nottingham NG5 .... 160 C4
Darwin Dr NG20 .... 72 C4
Darwin Rd NG10 .... 193 D3
Darwin St DN21 .... 24 B3
Davey Rd NG5 .... 102 A4
David Gr NG9 .... 171 E1
David La NG6 .... 160 B2
David St NG17 .... 115 D4
Davids La NG14 .... 165 D3
Davidson Cl NG5 .... 162 B4
Davidson St ■ NG2 .... 173 F2
Davies Ave NG17 .... 100 C2
Davies Rd NG2 .... 186 A4
Davis Cl NG21 .... 90 A2
Davy Cl NG15 .... 131 D1
Dawber St NG1 .... 15 E1
Dawgates La NG19 .... 86 C1
Dawlish Cl NG15 .... 145 E3
Dawlish Ct NG16 .... 143 E2
Dawlish Dr NG5 .... 161 D3
Dawn Cl NG15 .... 131 D1
Dawn House Sch NG21 .... 103 F2
Dawn View NG9 .... 170 B1
Dawn's La NG13 .... 179 D3

Dawson Cl NG16 .... 144 A1
Dawver Rd NG16 .... 158 C3
Day St NG20 .... 74 A2
Daybell Cl NG13 .... 181 D2
Daybill Cl NG25 .... 121 E2
Daybrook Ave ■ NG5 ...... 161 E2
Daybrook St NG5 .... 161 E2
Dayncourt Sch NG12 ...... 176 A2
De Ferrers Cl LE12 .... 205 F1
De Lacy Ct NG22 .... 77 D2
De Morgan Cl NG16 .... 129 D1
De Vere Gdns NG5 .... 162 A3
Deabill St NG4 .... 175 D3
Dead La Cossall NG16 ..... 158 B1
■ Loughborough LE11 ..... 220 A2
Deadwong La NG23 .... 153 F1
Deakins Pl NG7 .... 222 A3
Deal Gdns NG6 .... 159 F4
Dean Ave NG3 .... 162 A2
Dean Cl Mansfield NG18 .. 102 B2
Nottingham NG8 .... 171 E3
Dean Hole CE Sch NG23 .. 109 D3
Dean Rd NG5 .... 161 F3
Dean St Langley Mill NG16 143 E2
Nottingham NG1 .... 223 F2
Deane's Cl NG23 .... 109 D3
Deane Cl NG23 .... 98 A1
Deane Rd DN10 .... 6 C1
Deans Croft NG9 .... 171 D1
Deanscourt NG12 .... 188 A2
Deansgate NG19 .... 87 D3
Death La DN22 .... 21 E3
Debdale Gate NG19 .... 88 A1
Debdale Hill LE14 .... 218 C2
Debdale La Keyworth NG12 197 F2
Mansfield NG19 .... 88 A1
Deddhill Rd DN10 .... 6 C1
Deddington La NG9 .... 171 E1
Deep Furrow Ave NG4 .... 174 B4
Deep La S45 .... 85 D2
Deepdale Ave NG9 .... 182 B3
Deepdale Cl NG2 .... 186 B4
Deepdale Gdns NG17 ..... 100 C2
Deepdale Pk NG17 .... 100 C2
Deepdale Rd
Long Eaton NG10 .... 193 D3
Mansfield NG19 .... 88 C1
Nottingham NG8 .... 171 E2
Deepdale St NG17 .... 100 C2
Deepdene Cl NG8 .... 160 A1
Deepdene Way NG8 ...... 160 A1
Deeps La DN10 .... 4 B2
Deer Park Dr Arnold NG5 . 147 E1
Nottingham NG5 .... 161 E4
Deer Pk NG8 .... 171 F2
Deerleap Dr NG5 .... 161 E4
Deers Acre LE11 .... 220 A3
Deetleton Cl NG16 .... 129 D4
Delamere Cl NG18 .... 102 B2
Delamere Dr NG18 .... 102 B2
Delia Ave NG15 .... 131 E1
Dell La DE NG18 .... 103 D2
Dell The NG17 .... 129 F4
Dell Way NG7 .... 184 C1
Dellwood Cl NG4 .... 162 B1
Delta St NG7 .... 160 C1
Delville Ave NG12 .... 197 F2
Denacre Ave NG10 .... 182 C1
Denbigh Cl NG21 .... 104 B1
Denbigh Ct NG23 .... 98 A1
Denbury Rd NG15 .... 117 D1
Denby Dr NG18 .... 102 B1
Dendy Dr DN22 .... 53 D4
Dene Cl DN10 .... 20 A4
Dene The S80 .... 35 E1
Denehurst Ave NG8 ...... 160 B1
Denewood Ave NG9 ...... 171 E1
Denewood Cres NG8 ..... 171 F3
Denholme Rd NG8 .... 171 E3
Denison Ave DN22 .... 40 A2
Denison St Beeston NG9 .. 183 F4
Nottingham NG7 .... 222 B4
Denman Cl DN22 .... 39 F4
Denman St Central NG7 .. 222 B3
Denman St E NG7 .... 222 B3
Denman Gr ■ NG1 .... 173 E4
Dennett Cl NG3 .... 173 F4
Dennis Ave NG9 .... 183 F4
Dennis St Carlton NG4 ... 175 D4
Worksop S80 .... 35 F1
Dennor Dr NG19 .... 88 C3
Denstone Rd NG3 .... 173 F3
Dentdale Dr NG8 .... 171 D2
Denton Ave NG10 .... 182 A3
Denton Cl
Balderton NG24 .... 140 B2
Mansfield NG19 .... 88 C1
Denton Dr NG2 .... 185 E2
Denton Gn NG8 .... 159 F1
Denver Ct NG9 .... 170 C1
Deptford Cres NG6 .... 160 B3
Derby Gr NG7 .... 222 B3
Derby Rd
Annesley Woodhouse
NG15, NG17 .... 130 A4
Beeston NG9 .... 171 E1
Eastwood NG16 .... 143 F1
Hathern LE12 .... 212 C1
Kegworth DE74 .... 203 E1
Kirkby in a NG17 .... 115 E2
Langley Mill NG16 .... 143 E2
Long Eaton NG10 .... 193 D4
Loughborough LE11 ...... 220 A3
Mansfield NG17, NG18 ... 101 F4
Nottingham NG7 .... 222 B2
Sandiacre NG10 .... 182 A3
Stapleford NG9 .... 182 B3

Cro – Don 233

Derby Rd Ind Est NG10 .... 182 A3
Derby Sq LE11 .... 220 A2
Derby St Arnold NG5 ...... 161 F4
Beeston NG9 .... 183 F4
Mansfield NG18 .... 102 B3
Nottingham NG1 .... 223 D3
Derbyshire Ave NG9 ...... 170 B2
Derbyshire Cres NG8 ..... 172 A3
Derbyshire Dr NG16 ...... 128 B2
Derbyshire La NG15 ...... 146 A4
Dereham Dr NG5 .... 162 A3
Derry Dr NG5 .... 147 F1
Derry Hill Rd NG5 .... 147 F1
Derry La NG13 .... 178 A2
Derrymount Sch NG5 ..... 147 F1
Derwent Ave Ilkeston DE7 157 F1
Mansfield NG18 .... 103 D3
Derwent Cl Beeston NG9 .. 183 F2
Mansfield NG18 .... 103 D3
Market Warsop NG20 ..... 74 B3
Rainworth NG21 .... 118 A4
West Bridgford NG2 ...... 186 B4
Worksop S81 .... 35 F3
Derwent Cres NG5 .... 162 A3
Derwent Ct
Balderton NG24 .... 140 B2
Nottingham NG7 .... 222 C4
Derwent Dr
Annesley Woodhouse NG17 130 A4
Hucknall NG15 .... 146 A2
Selston NG16 .... 129 D4
Derwent Street Ind Est
NG10 .... 193 E3
Derwent Terr ■ NG5 ..... 161 E2
Derwent Way NG5 .... 125 D1
Desborough Rd NG16 .... 128 B4
Desford Cl NG5 .... 161 D2
Devitt Dr NG15 .... 131 E1
Devon Circus NG5 .... 147 E1
Devon Cl Eastwood NG16 144 A1
Sandiacre NG10 .... 182 A3
Devon Dr Mansfield NG19 101 F4
Nottingham NG5 .... 161 E1
Ruddington NG11 .... 196 B4
Devon La NG13 .... 181 D2
Devon Rd NG24 .... 124 C3
Devon St Ilkeston DE7 ... 170 A3
Nottingham NG3 .... 173 F3
Devonshire Ave
Beeston NG9 .... 183 F3
Long Eaton NG10 .... 194 A4
Devonshire Cl
Huthwaite NG17 .... 100 A1
Worksop S81 .... 157 F3
Devonshire Cres NG5 .... 161 E2
Devonshire Dr
Eastwood NG16 .... 143 F1
Langwith NG20 .... 72 C4
Ollerton NG22 .... 77 D2
Stapleford NG9 .... 170 B1
Devonshire La LE11 ...... 220 A2
Devonshire Prom NG2 ... 222 A1
Devonshire Rd
Harworth DN11 .... 8 C2
Nottingham NG5 .... 161 D1
Retford DN22 .... 39 E3
West Bridgford NG2 ..... 185 F3
Devonshire Sq ■ LE11 ... 220 A2
Devonshire St
New Houghton NG19 .... 87 D4
Worksop S80 .... 35 F1
Dewberry La NG12 .... 176 A1
Dial The NG12 .... 187 F1
Diamond Ave
Kirkby in a NG17 .... 115 E2
Rainworth NG21 .... 104 B1
Dickens Ct NG16 .... 144 A2
Dickens Rd S81 .... 36 A2
Dickenson Terr DN21 .... 24 B4
Dickman's La LE14 ...... 202 A2
Dicks La NG16 .... 144 B2
Dickson Dr NG11 .... 196 B3
Didcot Dr NG8 .... 160 A1
Digby Ave NG3 .... 162 B2
Digby Ct NG7 .... 222 B1
Digby Hall Dr NG4 ...... 162 B2
Digby St Cossall DE7 ... 158 A1
Kimberley NG16 .... 158 B4
Dingley Cl NG19 .... 88 C3
Dirca Cl NG11 .... 195 E4
Diseworth Gr ■ NG2 .... 173 F1
Distillery St NG11 ...... 196 B3
Division Rd NG20 .... 72 C1
Dixie St NG16 .... 128 A2
Django Cty Tec Coll
NG1 .... 161 D1
Dobbin Cl NG12 .... 189 D2
Dock Rd S80 .... 35 F2
Dockholm Rd NG10 .... 182 B1
Doddington Hall LN6 ... 71 F1
Doddington La
Claypole NG23 .... 156 A1
Dry Doddington NG23 .. 156 C3
Dodford Ct DE75 .... 143 D1
Dog & Duck La DN21 ... 15 D2
Dog La DN10 .... 10 A1
Doghill La NG23 .... 153 D1
Dogwood Ave NG6 ...... 160 A4
Doles La Kirkby in A NG17 114 B3
Whitwell S80 .... 45 E5
Dolphin Cl ■ NG5 .... 161 D4
Dominie Cross Rd DN22 . 39 F3
Donbas Cl NG6 .... 160 A2
Doncaster Ave NG10 ... 182 A3

Doncaster Gr NG10 .... 182 C1
Doncaster Rd
Bawtry DN10 .... 10 A4
Carlton in L S81 .... 25 F4
Langold S81 .... 16 C2
Tickhill DN11 .... 8 A4
Westwoodside DN9 .... 2 C2
Doncaster Terr ■ NG2 .... 173 E1
Donington Rd NG7 .... 184 C1
Donkey La NG11 .... 196 C2
Donner Cres DE7 .... 157 F3
Dooland Dr NG3 .... 161 F1
Dorchester Cl NG18 .... 102 B1
Dorchester Dr NG18 .... 102 B1
Dorchester Gdns NG2 .... 185 F2
Dorchester Rd
Annesley Woodhouse NG17 .. 115 D1
Harworth DN11 .... 9 D3
Kimberley NG16 .... 158 C4
Doreen Dr NG17
Dorewood Ct NG24 .... 140 C2
Doris Rd DE7 .... 170 A4
Dorket Cl NG5 .... 148 A1
Dorket Dr NG8 .... 172 B2
Dorking Rd NG7 .... 222 B4
Dormy Cl Beeston NG9 .... 183 E4
Mansfield Woodhouse NG17 .. 88 C3
Radcliffe on T NG12 .... 176 A2
Dormy Ct NG6 .... 160 B4
Dorner Ave NG24 .... 139 E4
Dornoch Ave
Nottingham NG5 .... 161 E1
Southwell NG25 .... 121 F1
Dorothy Ave
Eastwood NG16 .... 144 A2
Hucknall NG15 .... 131 D1
Mansfield Woodhouse NG19 ... 88 B1
Sandiacre NG10 .... 182 A3
Dorothy Dr NG19 .... 88 C1
Dorothy Gr ■ NG8 .... 172 B3
Dorset Dr DN11 .... 8 C2
Dorset Gdns NG2 .... 185 E3
Dorset St NG8 .... 172 B3
Dorset Way NG18 .... 103 D2
Dorterry Cres DE7 .... 170 A3
Dorton Ave DN21 .... 24 C4
Douglas Ave
Awsworth NG16 .... 158 B3
Carlton NG4 .... 174 C3
Douglas Cl NG12 .... 175 F1
Douglas Cres NG4 .... 174 C3
Douglas Ct NG9 .... 183 D1
Douglas Prim Sch NG7 .... 222 B3
Douglas Rd
Bingham NG13 .... 178 A2
Long Eaton NG10 .... 182 A1
Mansfield Woodhouse NG19 ... 89 D1
Nottingham NG7 .... 222 B3
Sutton in A NG17 .... 100 B1
Douro Dr NG5 .... 148 A1
Dove Cl Ollerton NG22 .... 77 D2
Worksop S81 .... 35 F4
Dove Croft NG22 .... 77 D2
Dove Dr NG16 .... 129 D4
Dove La NG10 .... 193 E4
Dove St NG6 .... 160 A4
Dovecote St LE12 .... 213 D1
Dovecote Cl NG13 .... 165 E2
Dovecote Dr NG8 .... 171 F2
Dovecote La NG9 .... 184 A3
Dovecote Rd NG16 .... 144 A1
Dovedale Ave
Long Eaton NG10 .... 193 D3
Sutton in A NG17 .... 100 B1
Dovedale Cir DE7 .... 157 F3
Dovedale Cl
Edwinstowe NG21 .... 76 A1
Mansfield NG18 .... 102 B2
Dovedale Ct NG10 .... 193 D3
Dovedale Prim Sch
NG10 .... 193 D3
Dovedale Rd
Nottingham NG3 .... 174 B3
West Bridgford NG2 .... 186 A3
Dovenby Rd NG7 .... 184 C1
Dover Beck Cl
Calverton NG14 .... 149 D4
Ravenshead NG15 .... 116 C1
Dover Beck Dr NG14 .... 149 E2
Dover Bottom DN22 .... 50 B2
Dover St NG25 .... 121 F1
Doveridge Ave NG4 .... 175 D4
Doveridge Ct NG15 .... 117 D2
Doveridge Rd NG4 .... 175 D4
Doveys Orch NG14 .... 148 B4
Downes Cl NG6 .... 160 A4
Downham Cl NG5 .... 162 A3
Downham Gdns NG15 .... 117 D1
Downing Cl NG6 .... 160 A4
Downing Gdns ■ NG6 .... 160 A4
Downing St
Nottingham NG6 .... 160 A4
South Normanton DE55 .... 113 D3
Sutton in A NG17 .... 100 C2
Downs The NG11 .... 185 D2
Dowson St NG3 .... 173 F3
Doyne Ct ■ NG2 .... 173 E1
Dragon St NG13 .... 191 D3
Dragwell DE74 .... 203 E1
Drake Rd NG4 .... 175 D3
Drake St DN21 .... 24 B3
Drakemyre Cl NG5 .... 148 A1
Draycott Cl DE7 .... 157 F2
Draycott Rd NG10 .... 193 D2
Drayton Ave NG19 .... 87 E1

Drayton St ■ NG5 .... 161 E1
Drift Hill NG13 .... 192 C2
Drift The
Hucknall NG15 .... 131 D1
Nottingham NG5 .... 184 C2
Drinsey Nook La NG23 .... 70 B4
Drive The Beeston NG9 .... 183 F2
Clipstone NG21 .... 90 A2
Gainsborough DN21 .... 24 C4
Winthorpe NG24 .... 125 E3
Drive The, Park La DN22 .... 30 A1
Drmonde Terr ■ NG3 .... 161 E1
Dronfield Pl DE7 .... 157 F3
Dronley Dr NG20 .... 74 B4
Drove La NG24 .... 126 A2
Drovers Ct DN21 .... 24 C3
Droversdale Rd DN11 .... 9 E2
Drummond Ave NG4 .... 175 D4
Drummond Dr NG16 .... 159 F2
Drummond Rd DE7 .... 157 F1
Drury La DN11 .... 8 A4
Dry Pot La LE12 .... 212 A1
Dryden Ave NG24 .... 140 C2
Dryden Ct NG9 .... 170 C1
Dryden Dale S81 .... 36 A2
Dryden St NG1 .... 223 D4
Drysdale Cl NG6 .... 160 A3
Duchess Gdns ■ NG6 .... 160 A4
Duchess St Creswell S80 .... 58 C4
Whitwell S80 .... 45 D3
Ducie La DN22 .... 23 F2
Dudley Ct NG9 .... 183 D4
Duesbury The DE55 .... 113 D2
Duffield Cl NG10 .... 193 D3
Duffield Ct NG5 .... 160 C4
Duke Cl NG6 .... 160 A3
Duke Dr NG16 .... 181 E1
Duke La NG18 .... 35 F2
Duke St Arnold NG5 .... 161 F4
Hucknall NG15 .... 146 A4
Huthwaite NG17 .... 100 A2
Ilkeston DE7 .... 157 F2
Loughborough LE11 .... 220 A3
■ Nottingham NG7 .... 160 A4
Retford DN22 .... 39 F3
South Normanton DE55 .... 113 D3
Sutton in A NG17 .... 100 C1
Whitwell S80 .... 45 D3
Duke William Mount
NG7 .... 222 C2
Duke's Dr S44 .... 86 A4
Duke's Pl NG1 .... 223 F2
Duke's Terr DN10 .... 10 A4
Dukeries Cl S81 .... 35 E3
Dukeries Com Coll The
NG22 .... 77 E3
Dukeries Cres S80 .... 36 B1
Dukeries Ind Est The S81 .... 35 E3
Dukeries Way S81 .... 35 E3
Dukes Cl NG17 .... 101 E1
Dukes Pl DE7 .... 157 F2
Dukes Rd LE14 .... 219 D3
Dulverton Vale NG8 .... 160 A2
Dulwich Rd NG7 .... 222 A3
Dumb Hall La
Shireoaks S80 .... 34 A2
Thorpe Salvin S80 .... 34 A2
Dumbles The
Lambley NG4 .... 163 D4
Sutton in A NG17 .... 100 B1
Dunbar Cl DN21 .... 15 F1
Dunbar Dr NG19 .... 101 E3
Dunblane Rd NG11 .... 196 B3
Duncan Ave NG15 .... 117 D2
Duncombe Cl NG3 .... 173 F4
Duncroft Ave NG4 .... 162 C1
Dundas Cl NG1 .... 223 E3
Dundee Dr NG19 .... 88 A3
Dunelm Cl NG17 .... 100 B2
Dunelm Dr NG14 .... 149 D4
Dungannon Rd NG11 .... 195 F4
Dunham CE Prim Sch
NG22 .... 54 A1
Dunham Cl
Newton on T LN1 .... 55 D1
Southwell NG25 .... 136 B4
Dunham Rd
Laneham DN22 .... 54 A3
Newton on T DN22, LN1 .... 54 C1
Dunholme Ave NG24 .... 139 F4
Dunholme Cl
Gainsborough DN21 .... 24 C4
■ Nottingham NG6 .... 160 A4
Dunholme Rd NG11 .... 24 C4
Dunkery Rd NG11 .... 195 F4
Dunkirk Prim Sch NG7 .... 172 C1
Dunkirk Rd ■ NG7 .... 172 C1
Dunlin Wharf ■ NG7 .... 173 D1
Dunlop Ave NG7 .... 222 A2
Dunn Brigg NG19 .... 88 B1
Dunnett Rd NG19 .... 101 F3
Dunoon Cl NG5 .... 146 C1
Dunoon Rd NG19 .... 101 F3
Dunsby Cl NG7 .... 184 C1
Dunsford Dr NG3 .... 162 B3
Dunsil Dr NG11 .... 185 D4
Dunsil Rd NG16 .... 113 E1
Dunsmore Cl NG9 .... 184 A2
Dunstall Wlk DN21 .... 24 C4
Dunstan Cres S80 .... 35 F1
Dunstan St NG4 .... 175 D4
Dunster Rd
Eastwood NG16 .... 144 A1
Gainsborough DN21 .... 15 F1
West Bridgford NG2 .... 186 A3
Dunston Cl NG10 .... 193 F4
Dunvegan Dr NG5 .... 146 C1

Dunwoody Cl NG18 .... 102 C4
Durham Ave NG2 .... 173 F2
Durham Cl
Mansfield Woodhouse NG19 .. 88 B2
■ Nottingham NG2 .... 173 F2
Worksop S81 .... 36 A4
Durham Cres NG6 .... 160 B3
Durham Gr DN22 .... 30 A1
Durham St ■ DE7 .... 157 F1
Durlston Cl NG2 .... 185 D3
Durnford St NG7 .... 160 C3
Dursley Cl NG6 .... 160 A3
Dyce Cl NG6 .... 159 F4
Dykes End NG23 .... 112 A4
Dylan Thomas Rd NG5 .... 161 E4
Dyscarr Cl S81 .... 16 C2

Eagle Cl Arnold NG5 .... 162 A4
Beeston NG9 .... 183 E4
Eagle Ct NG6 .... 160 B4
Eagle Cty Prim Sch LN6 .... 84 B2
Eagle Moor LN6 .... 84 C2
Eagle Pl NG12 .... 176 A2
Eagle Rd Eagle LN6 .... 84 A2
North Scarle LN6 .... 83 F2
Eakring Cl NG18 .... 102 C4
Eakring Rd
Bilsthorpe NG22 .... 105 F4
Kneesall NG22 .... 93 F3
Mansfield
NG18, NG21, NG20 .... 103 E4
Wellow NG22 .... 92 B4
Ealing Ave NG6 .... 160 B2
Eardley Rd NG5 .... 160 C3
Earl Cres NG4 .... 162 C2
Earl Dr NG16 .... 144 B1
Earl Howe Cres NG13 .... 190 B1
Earls Cl NG9 .... 171 E3
Earls Rd LE14 .... 219 D3
Earlsfield Dr NG5 .... 146 C1
Earlswood Dr NG12 .... 186 A2
Earp Ave NG24 .... 140 A4
Easedale Cl NG2 .... 186 B4
Easegill Ct NG5 .... 160 C4
East Acres NG12 .... 187 F2
East Circus St NG1 .... 223 D2
East Cres NG9 .... 184 A3
East Cres NG12 .... 187 E1
East Dr NG7 .... 172 B1
East End LE14 .... 211 E2
East Gr Bingham NG13 .... 177 F2
■ Nottingham NG7 .... 173 D4
East Markham Prim Sch
NG22 .... 65 F4
East Midlands Television
Ctr NG7 .... 172 C1
East Moor NG12 .... 188 A1
East Rd LE12 .... 216 C2
East St Bingham NG13 .... 177 F2
Bole DN22 .... 23 F2
Gotham NG11 .... 195 D1
Harworth DN11 .... 9 D3
■ Heanor DE75 .... 157 D4
Long Eaton NG10 .... 193 E4
Nottingham NG1 .... 223 F3
Retford DN22 .... 39 F3
Sutton in A NG17 .... 101 D2
East View Bawtry DN10 ...... 10 A4
East Markham NG22 .... 65 F3
Shirebrook NG20 .... 72 C3
West Bridgford NG2 .... 185 E3
East Wlk DN22 .... 39 E4
Eastcliffe Ave NG4 .... 162 B2
Eastcote Ave NG9 .... 171 D1
Eastcroft LN1 .... 57 D3
Eastcroft La NG22 .... 52 A1
Eastdale Rd NG3 .... 174 B3
Eastern Ave DN21 .... 15 F1
Eastern Ct NG24 .... 140 A4
Eastern Dr NG24 .... 140 C1
Eastern Terrace La
NG24 .... 140 A4
Eastfield
North Muskham NG23 .... 110 C1
North Wheatley DN22 .... 31 F4
Eastfield Cl NG21 .... 89 F1
Eastfield Ct NG25 .... 136 B4
Eastfield Dr DE55 .... 113 D3
Eastfield Side NG17 .... 101 D2
Eastgate
Normanton on T NG23 .... 81 F4
Worksop S80 .... 35 F2
Eastglade Prim Sch
NG5 .... 161 D4
Eastglade Rd NG5 .... 161 D3
Eastham Cl NG3 .... 173 F3
Eastham Rd NG5 .... 162 B3
Eastholme Croft NG2 .... 174 B3
Easthorpe NG25 .... 136 C4
Easthorpe La NG13 .... 192 C2
Easthorpe St NG11 .... 196 B4
Easthorpe View NG13 .... 181 E1
Eastland Terr NG20 .... 74 C4
Eastlands Jun Sch NG20 .... 74 C4
Eastlands La NG20 .... 74 C4
Eastleigh Dr NG19 .... 88 A3
Eastmoor Dr NG4 .... 174 C4
Eastwell St NG15 .... 146 A4
Eastwold NG12 .... 188 A1
Eastwood Ave NG20 .... 74 A3
Eastwood Cl NG15 .... 145 F2
Eastwood Comp
Lower Sch NG16 .... 144 A2
Eastwood Comp Sch
NG16 .... 143 F2
Eel La NG22 .... 79 E1

Eel Pool Rd DN10 .... 11 F1
Eelwood Rd NG15 .... 145 E2
Egerton Cl NG18 .... 103 D4
Egerton Dr NG9 .... 170 B1
Egerton Rd NG16 .... 161 E2
Egerton St NG3 .... 173 E4
Egerton Wlk ■ NG3 .... 173 E4
Egham Cl NG21 .... 104 B1
Egling Croft NG4 .... 174 C2
Egmanton Rd
Mansfield NG18 .... 103 D2
Meden Vale NG20 .... 74 B4
Tuxford NG22 .... 65 F1
Egmont Ct ■ NG2 .... 173 E1
Eider Cl NG20 .... 72 B2
Eighth Ave Beeston NG9 .... 184 B3
Mansfield NG19 .... 103 D4
Eisele Cl NG6 .... 159 F3
Ekowe St NG7 .... 160 C1
Eland Rd NG20 .... 72 C3
Eland St NG7 .... 160 C1
Elder Cl NG5 .... 148 A1
Elder Gdns ■ NG5 .... 161 D4
Elder Rd NG3 .... 146 A2
Elder St
Kirkby in A NG17 .... 114 C3
Sutton in A NG17 .... 100 C4
Eldon Rd NG9 .... 183 E1
Eldon St
Newark-on-T NG24 .... 139 F4
Tuxford NG22 .... 65 F2
Eleanor Ave DE7 .... 170 A3
Eleanor Cres NG9 .... 182 C4
Electric Ave NG11 .... 185 D4
Elery Cl DE7 .... 157 E1
Elford Rise NG3 .... 173 F3
Elgar Dr NG10 .... 193 D3
Elgar Gdns NG3 .... 173 F4
Eliot Cl NG10 .... 193 D3
Eliot Wlk NG11 .... 195 E4
Elizabeth Cl
Gainsborough DN21 .... 15 E2
Hucknall NG15 .... 145 F3
Elizabeth Ct DE7 .... 157 E1
Elizabeth Gr NG4 .... 162 C1
Elizabeth Rd NG24 .... 139 F3
Elizabeth H Sch
(Lower Sch site) DN22 ...... 39 E4
Elizabeth H Sch
(Upper Sch site) DN22 ...... 39 F3
Elkesley Prim Sch DN22 .... 50 A2
Ella Bank Rd DE75 .... 143 D1
Ella Rd NG2 .... 173 F1
Ellastone Ave NG5 .... 161 D4
Ellerby Ave NG7 .... 184 C3
Ellerslie Cl NG24 .... 125 D1
Ellerslie Gr NG10 .... 182 A3
Ellesmere Bsns Pk NG5 .... 161 D1
Ellesmere Cl NG5 .... 162 A4
Ellesmere Dr NG9 .... 170 B3
Ellesmere Rd
Mansfield NG18 .... 102 C4
West Bridgford NG2 .... 185 F2
Ellington Rd NG5 .... 148 A1
Elliot Durham Sch NG3 .... 161 F3
Elliott St NG7 .... 222 C3
Ellis Ave NG15 .... 146 A3
Ellis Cl NG10 .... 193 E3
Ellis Gr NG9 .... 183 F3
Ellis Guildford Sch NG8 .... 160 B3
Ellis St NG17 .... 115 D2
Ellsworth Rise NG5 .... 160 C2
Ellwood Cres NG8 .... 172 A4
Elm Ave
Beeston, Attenborough
NG9 .... 183 E2
Beeston, Chilwell NG9 .... 183 F3
Bingham NG13 .... 178 A2
Carlton NG4 .... 174 C4
East Leake LE12 .... 205 F2
Keyworth NG12 .... 197 F1
Long Eaton NG10 .... 193 E4
Newark-on-T NG24 .... 140 A4
Nottingham NG3 .... 159 D1
Nuthall NG16 .... 182 A4
Sandiacre NG10 .... 182 A4
Elm Bank NG3 .... 173 E4
Elm Bank Dr NG3 .... 173 E4
Elm Cl Keyworth NG12 .... 197 F1
■ Newark-on-T NG24 .... 140 A4
Nottingham NG3 .... 173 E4
Pinxton NG16 .... 113 E3
Saxilby LN1 .... 57 D2
Elm Dr NG4 .... 174 C3
Elm Gr Arnold NG5 .... 148 A4
Church Warsop NG20 .... 74 A4
Elm Tree Ave
Mansfield Woodhouse NG19 .. 88 C4
Shirebrook NG20 .... 72 B3
West Bridgford NG2 .... 185 E3
Elm Tree Cl S81 .... 36 A2
Elm Tree Dr DN10 .... 9 F1
Elm Tree Pl DN22 .... 50 A4
Elm Tree Rd NG17 .... 99 F2
Elm Tree Rise NG22 .... 113 C2
Elm Tree St NG18 .... 102 B8
Elm Wlk DN22 .... 40 A4
Elma La NG20 .... 59 E
Elmbridge NG5 .... 161 D
Elmcroft NG25 .... 134 A3
Elmdale Gdns NG8 .... 172 A4
Elmhurst Ave
Nottingham NG3 .... 162 B1
South Normanton DE55 .... 113 D1

Imhurst Cl DE55 ... 113 D2
Imhurst Dr NG17 ... 100 A2
Imhurst Rd NG18 ... 88 C1
Imore Cl NG7 ... 222 B4
Imore's Mdw NG14 ... 152 A4
Ims Cl Rempstone LE12 ... 215 E3
Ruddington NG11 ... 196 B3
Ims Gdns NG11 ... 196 B3
Ims Gr LE11 ... 220 B2
Ims The
(Loughborough Univ of
Technology) LE11 ... 220 B2
Ims Pk NG11 ... 196 B3
Ims Prim Sch The NG3 ... 173 E4
Ims Rd S80 ... 35 F2
Ims The Carlton NG4 ... 174 C3
Watnall NG16 ... 158 C4
Imsfield Ave DE75 ... 143 D1
Imsham Ave NG5 ... 146 C1
Imsmere Dr S81 ... 17 D3
Imsthorpe Ave NG5 ... 161 E2
Imswood Gdns NG5 ... 161 E2
Imton Cl S80 ... 58 B4
Imton Rd S80 ... 35 E2
Imtree Ave NG16 ... 128 C4
Imtree Cl S81 ... 34 C4
Imtree Rd NG16 ... 148 B4
Imwood Cl DN22 ... 30 A1
Inor St NG16 ... 143 E2
Isham Wlk DN21 ... 24 C4
Ison St NG7 ... 172 C4
Iston All Saints Prim Sch
NG23 ... 153 E3
Iston Cl NG19 ... 88 B2
Iston Gdns NG12 ... 184 C2
Iston Hall NG23 ... 153 E2
Iston La NG23 ... 153 E3
Iswick Cl NG5 ... 161 D4
Iswick Dr NG9 ... 184 B2
Iterwater Dr NG2 ... 186 B3
Itham Cl NG8 ... 159 F2
Itham Dr NG8 ... 160 A1
Itham Rd NG2 ... 186 A4
Iton Cl Balderton NG24 ... 140 B2
Mansfield NG18 ... 103 D3
Stapleford NG9 ... 182 B4
Iton & Orston Sta
NG23 ... 180 A3
Iton Rd Mansfield NG18 ... 102 C3
Nottingham NG5 ... 161 D1
Iton Rd N NG5 ... 161 D1
Ivaston Ct NG18 ... 103 D3
Ivaston Dr NG10 ... 193 D2
Ivaston Rd NG8 ... 172 A3
Ivedon Dr DE7 ... 157 E2
ly Cl
Mansfield Woodhouse NG19 ... 88 B2
Worksop S80 ... 36 A1
merald Cl NG9 ... 87 F1
merald Ct NG17 ... 115 E2
merys Rd NG4 ... 175 D4
imma Bates Way NG21 ... 118 A3
immanuel Sch
Nottingham, Portchester
NG3 ... 162 A1
Nottingham, Rise Park
NG5 ... 147 D1
imneth Cl NG3 ... 173 E4
impingham Cl NG19 ... 183 D1
impire St NG18 ... 102 B3
impress Rd LE11 ... 220 B2
imsworth Ave DN22 ... 29 F1
imsworth Cl DE7 ... 157 E2
ina Ave NG2 ... 173 F3
inderby Cres
Gainsborough DN21 ... 24 C4
Mansfield NG18 ... 102 C3
inderby Gdns NG5 ... 147 F1
inderby Sq NG5 ... 183 F4
indsleigh Gdns
Beeston NG9 ... 183 D4
West Bridgford NG12 ... 186 A2
infield St NG19 ... 183 E4
ingine La NG4 ... 144 A2
ingland Cres DE75 ... 143 D1
inglish Martyrs RC Prim
Sch NG10 ... 182 A1
innerdale Cl NG22 ... 186 B4
innerdale Rd
Long Eaton NG10 ... 182 A1
Nottingham NG5 ... 161 E3
innismore Mews NG2 ... 185 E1
inright Cl NG24 ... 139 F3
inthorpe St 6 NG8 ... 172 A3
ipinal Way LE11 ... 220 A1
ipperstone By-Pass
NG14 ... 150 A2
ipperstone Ct NG18 ... 103 D1
ipperstone Rd
Lowdham NG14 ... 150 B4
Oxton NG25 ... 134 A1
West Bridgford NG2 ... 185 F4
ipping Way NG19 ... 103 D4
ipsom Rd NG9 ... 182 C2
ipsom St NG18 ... 102 C3
irdington Way NG9 ... 183 D1
irewash Cl DE7 ... 170 A3
irewash Dr DE7 ... 170 A3
irewash Gdns NG5 ... 161 D4
irewash Gr NG9 ... 182 C1
irewash Rd NG16 ... 113 F1
irewash Sq DE7 ... 170 A3
irewash St
Kirkby in Ashfield NG17 ... 115 D3
Long Eaton NG10 ... 193 F4
Pye Bridge DE55 ... 128 A3
iric Ave NG15 ... 130 C1
irewash Dr DE55 ... 113 D4

Erith Cl NG8 ... 159 E1
Ernehale Jun & Inf Sch
NG5 ... 162 A3
Ernest Rd NG4 ... 162 A1
Erskine Rd 11 NG5 ... 161 D1
Esher Gr NG3 ... 161 E1
Eskdale Cl NG10 ... 193 D3
Eskdale Ct NG2 ... 186 B4
Eskdale Dr Beeston NG9 ... 183 D3
Nottingham NG8 ... 172 A4
Worksop S81 ... 35 F4
Eskdale Jun Sch NG9 ... 183 D3
Eskhouse Cl NG2 ... 186 B2
Essex Cl NG16 ... 9 E2
Essex Rd DN11 ... 9 E2
Essex St 4 DE7 ... 157 F1
Estfeld Cl DN11 ... 8 A4
Estwic Ave NG16 ... 143 F2
Ethel Ave Hucknall NG15 ... 131 C1
Nottingham NG3 ... 162 A1
Ethel Rd NG2 ... 185 F4
Ethel Wainwright Fst Sch
NG19 ... 101 F4
Ethel Wainwright Mid Sch
NG19 ... 101 F4
Ethelbert Ave NG17 ... 115 E1
Etheldene NG12 ... 189 D2
Etherington St DN21 ... 24 B4
Eton Cl NG10 ... 193 F3
Eton Gr NG8 ... 172 A2
Eton Rd NG2 ... 185 F3
Eucalyptus Ave NG11 ... 184 B1
Eugene Gdns NG2 ... 173 E1
Eugene St NG2 ... 223 F1
Europa Way NG2 ... 185 E2
Evans Ave NG17 ... 100 B2
Evans Rd NG6 ... 160 B2
Evedon Wlk NG5 ... 147 D1
Evelyn St Beeston NG9 ... 184 A4
1 Nottingham NG2 ... 173 F2
Eversley Wlk NG5 ... 161 D4
Everton Cty Prim Sch
DN10 ... 11 D2
Everton Sluice La DN10 ... 11 E2
Everton St NG17 ... 87 F1
Evesham Ct NG9 ... 183 D1
Evesham Mews 7 S80 ... 35 F1
Ewart Rd NG7 ... 173 D4
Ewe Lamb Cl NG9 ... 170 C1
Ewe Lamb La NG9 ... 170 C1
Ewell Rd NG8 ... 171 F3
Exbourne Rd NG5 ... 159 F1
Exbury Gdns NG2 ... 185 D2
Exchange Rd NG2 ... 185 F4
Exchange Row 8 NG18 ... 102 A4
Exchange St DN22 ... 39 F4
Exe Fold NG19 ... 88 B1
Exeter Cl Carlton NG4 ... 162 C1
East Leake LE12 ... 205 E1
Exeter Rd
Nottingham NG7 ... 173 D4
West Bridgford NG2 ... 185 F3
Export Dr NG17 ... 113 F4
Exton Rd NG5 ... 161 D2
Eyam Cl Beeston NG9 ... 171 E1
Mansfield NG18 ... 103 D3
Eyre St NG2 ... 173 F2
Eyre's Gdns DE7 ... 157 F1
Eyre's La LE12 ... 205 D4
Fabis Dr NG11 ... 184 C2
Fackley Rd NG17 ... 100 B3
Fackley Way NG17 ... 100 B3
Factory La Beeston NG9 ... 183 F3
Ilkeston DE7 ... 157 F1
Factory St 8 LE11 ... 220 B2
Factory Yd NG17 ... 101 D2
Failsworth Cl NG11 ... 184 C2
Fair Lea Cl NG10 ... 193 E3
Fair Vale NG23 ... 110 A4
Fairbank Cres NG5 ... 161 E1
Fairburn Cl NG8 ... 171 E2
Faircroft Ave NG10 ... 182 C3
Fairdale Dr NG16 ... 144 A1
Fairfax Cl
Gainsborough DN21 ... 24 C3
Nottingham NG7 ... 160 C1
Fairfield DN22 ... 39 F2
Fairfield Ave
Farndon NG24 ... 139 D3
Hilcote DE55 ... 99 E1
New Balderton NG24 ... 140 B3
Fairfield Cl
Nether Langwith NG20 ... 59 D1
Nottingham NG11 ... 185 D3
Fairfield Cres NG10 ... 193 D2
Fairfield Dr
Mansfield NG18 ... 103 D4
Ravenshead NG15 ... 116 B2
Fairfield Prep Sch LE11 ... 220 A2
Fairfield Rd NG17 ... 101 D2
Fairfield St NG13 ... 177 F2
Fairham Cl NG11 ... 195 D1
Fairham Ave NG17 ... 101 E4
Fairham Com Coll NG11 ... 195 F4
Fairham Dr NG8 ... 172 B2
Fairham Rd NG12 ... 197 E2
Fairhaven NG17 ... 115 D2
Fairholme Cl NG21 ... 89 F1
Fairholme Dr NG19 ... 87 F1
Fairisle Cl NG11 ... 185 D1
Fairland Cres NG2 ... 185 F2
Fairlawn Pl NG5 ... 161 E1
Fairlie Ave NG19 ... 103 D4
Fairlie Ave NG14 ... 101 E3

Fairlight Way NG5 ... 161 D4
Fairmaid Gr NG7 ... 184 C1
Fairmead Cl NG3 ... 174 A4
Fairmead Rd NG8 ... 171 E4
Fairview Ave NG16 ... 128 C1
Fairview Ct NG2 ... 185 E1
Fairview Rd NG5 ... 161 F2
Fairway Kenyworth NG12 ... 198 A1
Fairway NG4 ... 139 E3
Fairway Ave DN21 ... 15 D2
Fairway Cres NG13 ... 177 D4
Fairway Dr Beeston NG9 ... 183 E3
Nottingham NG6 ... 160 B4
Fairway The NG4 ... 162 C2
Fairways Dr NG17 ... 114 C4
Fairways The NG19 ... 88 B3
Fairwinds Cl NG17 ... 114 C4
Fal Paddock NG19 ... 88 B1
Falcon Cl Eagle LN6 ... 84 B2
Nottingham NG7 ... 222 A2
Falcon Ct DE7 ... 157 E1
Falcon Gr NG7 ... 161 D1
Falcon St
Loughborough LE11 ... 220 B3
6 Nottingham NG6 ... 160 C2
Falconers Wlk 8 NG5 ... 161 E4
Falconwood Gdns NG11 ... 184 B1
Fallow Cl Nottingham NG7 ... 184 C1
Retford DN22 ... 29 F1
Fallow Ct S81 ... 36 A4
Falston Rd NG8 ... 172 A4
Falstone Ave NG24 ... 140 A3
Far Back La NG22 ... 119 F3
Far Croft Ave NG17 ... 100 B2
Far Holme La NG23 ... 97 D4
Far La LE12 ... 213 E2
Far New Cl NG10 ... 182 A3
Far Pasture Cl NG12 ... 197 F1
Far Rd NG22 ... 67 E2
Far Rye NG8 ... 171 F3
Far St Bradmore NG11 ... 196 C3
Wymeswold LE12 ... 216 B2
Faraday Ave NG22 ... 66 A2
Faraday Ct NG7 ... 170 C1
Faraday Rd
Mansfield NG18 ... 102 C3
Nottingham NG7 ... 222 A2
Farfield Ave NG9 ... 183 F4
Farfield Gr NG9 ... 183 F4
Farfield Rd DE7 ... 170 A4
Farley Rd NG6 ... 160 A4
Farley St NG15 ... 146 A3
Farm Ave NG15 ... 145 E2
Farm Cl
East Bridgford NG13 ... 165 E2
Ilkeston DE7 ... 170 A4
Long Eaton NG10 ... 193 F3
Nottingham NG11 ... 184 C1
Farm Croft Rd NG19 ... 88 B4
Farm Gr S81 ... 36 A4
Farm La NG22 ... 65 F4
Farm Rd Arnold NG5 ... 162 A4
Beeston NG9 ... 183 E3
Farm View NG22 ... 77 D3
Farm View Rd NG17 ... 115 E3
Farmer St NG11 ... 196 C2
Farmhouse Cl NG13 ... 181 D2
Farmilo Cres NG19 ... 87 F1
Farmilo Fst Sch NG19 ... 87 E2
Farmway NG19 ... 88 C3
Farnborough Comp Sch
NG11 ... 185 D1
Farnborough Rd NG11 ... 185 D1
Farndale S81 ... 36 A3
Farndale Cl
Long Eaton NG10 ... 193 D3
Sutton in A NG17 ... 100 C1
Farndale Dr NG8 ... 171 D2
Farndale Rd NG17 ... 100 C3
Farndon Dr NG9 ... 182 C2
Farndon Gn NG8 ... 172 B2
Farndon Rd
Newark-on-T NG24, NG23 ... 139 E3
Nottingham NG11 ... 101 E1
Farndon St Peter's
CE Prim Sch NG24 ... 139 D3
Farndon Way NG19 ... 101 F4
Farnes Ct S81 ... 36 A3
Farnham 6 LE11 ... 220 A1
Farnham Rd NG16 ... 164 A3
Farnsfield CE Sch NG22 ... 103 D2
Farnsfield Endowed CE
Sch NG22 ... 119 F3
Farnsfield Rd NG22 ... 105 F2
Farnsfield Walter
D'aynecourt Prim Sch
NG22 ... 119 F3
Farnsworth Ave NG21 ... 103 F1
Farnsworth Cl NG16 ... 145 D1
Farrar Cl NG24 ... 125 D1
Farrendale Cl NG19 ... 88 B1
Farriers Croft DE7 ... 157 E2
Farriers Gn NG11 ... 184 C1
Farrington Cl NG16 ... 159 E2
Farthing Ct NG10 ... 193 D4
Farthingate NG25 ... 136 C4
Farthingate Cl NG25 ... 136 C4
Farthings The LE12 ... 213 D1
Farwells Cl NG6 ... 160 B3
Faulconbridge Cl NG6 ... 160 A3
Fawcett St DN21 ... 15 E1
Fearn Chase NG4 ... 174 C4
Fearn Cl DE72 ... 193 D4
Fearnleigh Dr NG6 ... 160 B1
Fearon Cl NG14 ... 164 C3

Featherbed La S80 ... 34 C1
Featherston Ave S80 ... 36 A1
Featherstone Cl
Carlton NG4 ... 162 B2
Mansfield NG18 ... 101 E2
Feignes Ct NG12 ... 197 F2
Felen Cl NG5 ... 161 D4
Fell Croft NG24 ... 139 D4
Fell Side NG5 ... 162 A3
Fell Wilson St NG20 ... 74 B2
Felley Ave NG17 ... 114 C1
Felley Mill La N NG16 ... 129 E1
Fellows Rd NG9 ... 183 F4
Fellows Yd NG12 ... 197 F4
Fellside Cl NG2 ... 186 B3
Felly Cl NG15 ... 145 F3
Felly Mill La S NG16 ... 129 D1
Felstead Cl NG9 ... 171 E1
Felton Ave NG19 ... 88 B3
Felton Cl NG9 ... 183 D3
Felton Rd NG2 ... 173 E1
Fen La Balderton NG24 ... 141 D2
Balderton NG23 ... 155 E2
Fenchurch Cl NG5 ... 147 D1
Fenimore Ct NG12 ... 176 A2
Fennel St LE11 ... 220 A2
Fenroth Cl NG6 ... 159 F4
Fenton Cl Radcliffe NG12 ... 125 D1
Fenton Dr NG6 ... 146 B1
Fenton Rd Fenton NG23 ... 142 B1
Nottingham NG5 ... 160 C2
Fenwick Cl NG8 ... 159 F1
Fenwick Rd NG8 ... 159 F1
Fenwick St NG20 ... 74 A2
Ferguson Ave NG19 ... 88 A2
Ferguson Cl 11 NG9 ... 183 E1
Fern Ave 14 NG5 ... 161 D1
Fern Bank Ave NG22 ... 64 A1
Fern Cl Beeston NG9 ... 183 E4
Bilsthorpe NG22 ... 106 A3
Ravenshead NG15 ... 117 D1
Shirebrook NG20 ... 72 C3
Southwell NG25 ... 121 E1
Fern Cres NG16 ... 143 E2
Fern Lea Ave NG12 ... 187 F1
Fern Rd NG12 ... 189 D2
Fern St NG17 ... 100 B2
Ferndale Cl NG9 ... 183 F1
New Ollerton NG22 ... 77 F3
Ferndale Gr NG3 ... 174 A4
Ferndale Rd NG3 ... 174 A4
Ferndene Dr NG10 ... 193 D4
Ferngill Cl 17 NG2 ... 173 E1
Fernleigh Ave NG3 ... 162 A1
Fernleigh Rise NG19 ... 88 B1
Fernwood Cl NG19 ... 89 D1
Fernwood Comp Sch
NG8 ... 171 E2
Fernwood Cres NG8 ... 171 E2
Fernwood Dr NG12 ... 175 F2
Fernwood Inf Sch
(Russell Annexe) NG8 ... 171 F2
Fernwood Jun & Inf Sch
NG8 ... 171 E2
Ferny Hollow Cl NG5 ... 160 C4
Ferous Cl NG11 ... 195 F4
Ferrers Wlk NG3 ... 173 E1
Ferryside Gdns NG17 ... 114 C4
Ferry La Everton DN10 ... 11 E2
North Muskham NG23 ... 110 C1
Festival Ave DN11 ... 9 D2
Festival Dr LE11 ... 220 A3
Festus Cl NG3 ... 223 F4
Festus St Carlton NG4 ... 175 D4
Kirkby in A NG17 ... 115 D2
Field Ave NG15 ... 145 E2
Field Cl Beeston NG9 ... 183 D2
Carlton NG4 ... 162 C1
Mansfield Woodhouse NG19 ... 88 B3
Worksop S80 ... 36 A4
Field Dr Balderton NG24 ... 140 C1
Shirebrook NG20 ... 72 C1
Field End Cl LE12 ... 205 E1
Field House Cl NG8 ... 171 E3
Field La
Ault Hucknall NG19, S44 ... 86 B3
Blidworth NG21 ... 118 A2
Cropwell Bishop NG12 ... 189 D2
Morton DN21 ... 15 D2
Woodborough NG14 ... 149 E2
Fieldfare Dr NG7 ... 114 B4
Fields Ave NG11 ... 196 B2
Fields Farm Rd NG10 ... 193 F3
Fields The DE75 ... 157 D3
Field View
South Normanton DE55 ... 113 D1
Sutton in A NG17 ... 100 C3
Fieldway NG11 ... 185 D2
Fieldfare Dr S81 ... 35 E4
Fifth Ave Beeston NG9 ... 184 B3
Clipstone NG21 ... 89 F2
Edwinstowe NG21 ... 75 F1
Mansfield NG19 ... 102 B1
Fiftyeights Rd DN10 ... 1 B2
Filey St NG6 ... 160 B4
Finch Cl NG7 ... 184 C4
Finchley Cl NG11 ... 184 B1
Findern Ct NG18 ... 103 D4
Findern Gn NG3 ... 174 A3
Fingal Cl NG7 ... 184 C1
Fingle St DN22 ... 32 B1
Fingleton S81 ... 36 A3
Finkell St DN10 ... 12 C2
Finley Way DE55 ... 113 D2

Finningley Rd NG18 ... 103 D2
Finsbury Ave
8 Loughborough LE11 ... 220 B2
Nottingham NG2 ... 173 F2
Finsbury Park Cl NG2 ... 185 E3
Finsbury Rd Beeston NG9 ... 171 E2
Nottingham NG5 ... 147 D1
Fir Cl Nottingham NG6 ... 159 F4
Shirebrook NG20 ... 72 B3
Fir Dale NG12 ... 188 A2
Fir Tree Cl NG19 ... 89 E1
Fir View NG22 ... 77 E3
Firbank Ct NG9 ... 183 D3
Firbeck Ave NG18 ... 102 C3
Firbeck Cres S81 ... 16 C2
Firbeck Prim Sch NG8 ... 171 D2
Firbeck Rd Arnold NG5 ... 162 A4
Nottingham NG8 ... 171 D2
Fircroft Ave NG8 ... 171 F4
Fircroft Dr NG15 ... 145 E3
Firecrest Way NG6 ... 160 B2
Firemen's Row NG17 ... 100 C1
Firs Ave NG9 ... 183 F4
Firs Rd NG12 ... 186 A2
Firs St NG10 ... 193 D2
Firs The 11 NG5 ... 161 E2
Firsby Rd NG8 ... 159 F1
First Ave Beeston NG9 ... 184 B3
Carlton, Colwick NG4 ... 174 C3
Carlton, Gedling NG4 ... 162 C1
Carlton, Thorneywood NG4 ... 174 B4
Clipstone NG21 ... 90 A2
Edwinstowe NG21 ... 76 A1
Mansfield NG21 ... 103 F1
Mansfield Woodhouse NG19 ... 89 D1
Nottingham NG4 ... 174 B4
First Holme La NG23 ... 97 D4
Firth Cl NG5 ... 148 B1
Firth Dr NG9 ... 183 E1
Firth Rd DN22 ... 39 E4
Firth Way NG6 ... 160 A4
Fish Pond Dr NG7 ... 223 D1
Fisher Ave NG5 ... 161 F3
Fisher Cl Collingham NG23 ... 98 A1
East Leake LE12 ... 205 F1
Fisher Ct DE7 ... 157 F2
Fisher Gate NG1 ... 223 F2
Fisher La Bingham NG13 ... 177 F2
Mansfield NG18 ... 102 B3
Fisher St 17 NG7 ... 172 C4
Fishers St NG17 ... 115 D1
Fishpool Rd NG21 ... 117 E2
Fiskerton Cl NG18 ... 103 D2
Fiskerton Rd
Rolleston NG23 ... 138 A3
Southwell NG23 ... 137 D3
Fiskerton Sta NG25 ... 137 F2
Fitzherbert St NG20 ... 74 B2
Five Acres NG11 ... 185 D2
Five Fields Cl DN22 ... 40 A2
Five Fields La DN22 ... 40 A2
Flagholme NG12 ... 187 F1
Flamingo Ct 11 NG7 ... 173 D1
Flamstead Ave NG4 ... 163 D4
Flamstead Rd DE7 ... 157 F1
Flaxen Way NG5 ... 160 C4
Flatts La Calverton NG14 ... 133 F1
Westwood NG16 ... 128 B2
Flatts The NG9 ... 183 D3
Flawforth Ave NG11 ... 196 C4
Flawforth La NG11 ... 196 C4
Flaxendale NG12 ... 188 A1
Flaxton Way NG5 ... 160 C4
Fleam Cl NG5 ... 184 C2
Fleeman Gr NG2 ... 174 A1
Fleet Cl NG7 ... 172 C4
Fleetway S81 ... 35 F4
Fleetwith Cl NG2 ... 186 B3
Fleming Ave
Newark-on-T NG24 ... 125 D2
Tuxford NG22 ... 65 F2
Fleming Dr Carlton NG4 ... 174 B4
Newark-on-T NG24 ... 125 D2
Woodbeck DN22 ... 53 D4
Fleming Gdns NG11 ... 184 B1
Fletcher Ct NG22 ... 119 F4
Fletcher Gate NG1 ... 223 E2
Fletcher Rd NG9 ... 184 A4
Fletcher St NG10 ... 193 E4
Fletcher Terr NG3 ... 161 F1
Fletcher Way NG19 ... 103 D4
Flewitt Gdns NG3 ... 173 F3
Flint Ave NG19 ... 88 C1
Flintham Dr NG5 ... 161 E2
Flintham La NG23 ... 96 C2
Flintham Prim Sch
NG23 ... 152 C1
Flixton Rd NG16 ... 158 C4
Flood Rd The DN21 ... 24 A4
Floral Villas NG23 ... 98 A1
Florence Ave NG10 ... 182 C1
Florence Boot Cl NG9 ... 184 A4
Florence Cres NG4 ... 175 D4
Florence Ct DE7 ... 157 F1
Florence Gr NG3 ... 174 A3
Florence Rd Carlton NG4 ... 175 D4
Nottingham NG3 ... 162 A1
West Bridgford NG2 ... 186 A4
Florence St NG15 ... 146 A3
Florence Terr DN21 ... 24 B4
Florey Ct NG7 ... 172 C1

Florey Wlk NG11 .... 195 E4
Florin Gdns NG10 .... 193 D4
Floss La DN22 .... 43 E2
Flowers Cl NG5 .... 162 A3
Flying Horse Wlk NG1 ...... 223 E2
Foljambe Terr NG3 .... 223 F3
Folkton Gdns NG3 .... 161 F1
Folly Hall La LE12 .... 209 E2
Folly La Besthorpe NG23 ..... 98 A4
  Stapleford NG9 .... 112 C3
Folly Nook La DN22 .... 19 D3
Fonton Hall Dr NG17 .... 114 A4
Forbes Cl NG10 .... 193 E3
Ford La NG23 .... 109 D3
Ford St NG7 .... 161 D1
Ford St N NG7 .... 161 D1
Fordbridge La DE55 .... 113 D4
Fordham Gn NG11 .... 195 E4
Foredrift Cl NG11 .... 195 D1
Forest Ave NG18 .... 102 B3
Forest Cl
  Annesley Woodhouse NG17 . 130 A4
  Cotgrave NG12 .... 187 F2
  Rainworth NG21 .... 104 B1
  Selston NG16 .... 129 D4
Forest Ct Mansfield NG18 .. 103 D4
  Nottingham NG7 .... 222 C3
Forest Fields Prim Sch
  NG7 .... 173 D4
Forest Gdns NG15 .... 130 A4
Forest Glade Prim Sch
  NG17 .... 101 D2
Forest Gr Nottingham NG1 . 173 D4
  Nottingham NG7 .... 222 C4
Forest Hill Hill NG18 .... 102 B1
Forest Hill Rd S81 .... 36 A4
Forest Hospl NG18 .... 102 C3
Forest La Papplewick NG15 . 131 F4
  Walesby S80 .... 53 F2
  Worksop S80 .... 36 B1
Forest Link NG22 .... 106 A3
Forest Rd
  Annesley Woodhouse NG17 . 130 A4
  Bingham NG13 .... 177 E2
  Blidworth NG21 .... 118 A3
  Calverton NG14 .... 148 B4
  Clipstone NG21 .... 89 F2
  Loughborough LE11 .... 220 A2
  Mansfield NG18 .... 102 B3
  Market Warsop NG20 ...... 74 B1
  New Ollerton NG22 .... 77 E2
  Oxton NG25 .... 134 A3
  Sutton in A NG17 .... 101 D3
Forest Rd E NG1 .... 173 D4
Forest Rd W NG7 .... 222 C4
Forest Rise NG20 .... 74 B1
Forest Sch NG7 .... 173 D4
Forest St
  Annesley Woodhouse NG17 . 130 A4
  Kirkby in A NG17 .... 115 D2
  Sutton in A NG17 .... 100 C1
Forest Town Jun Sch
  NG19 .... 89 D1
Forest View
  New Ollerton NG22 .... 77 D2
  Retford DN22 .... 39 E2
Forest View Dr NG15 .... 145 F4
Forest View Jun Sch NG22 . 77 D3
Forester Cl NG9 .... 183 E2
Forester Gr NG4 .... 174 B4
Forester Rd NG3 .... 174 A4
Forester St NG4 .... 175 D4
Forewood La DN22 .... 42 A2
Forge Ave NG14 .... 148 C4
Forge Cl
  South Muskham NG23 ..... 124 C4
  Sutton on T NG23 .... 96 C4
Forge Hill NG9 .... 183 E2
Forge Mill Gr NG15 .... 146 B3
Forge The NG9 .... 170 A3
Forman St NG1 .... 223 E3
Forrests Yd S80 .... 35 F2
Forster Ave NG24 .... 139 F3
Forster St
  Gainsborough DN21 .... 15 E1
  Kirkby in A NG17 .... 114 C3
  Nottingham NG7 .... 222 A3
Forsythia Gdns NG7 .... 172 C1
Fosbrooke Dr NG10 .... 193 E3
Fossdyke Gdns LN1 .... 57 D2
Fosse Cl 57 D2
Fosse Rd NG24, NG23 ..... 139 D2
Fosse Wlk NG12 .... 188 A1
Fossett's Ave NG16 .... 128 C4
Foster Ave NG9 .... 183 F3
Foster Rd NG23 .... 98 A1
Foster St NG18 .... 102 B3
Fosters Dr NG5 .... 161 E2
Fosters La NG13 .... 177 F2
Foston Cl NG18 .... 103 D3
Fothergill Ct NG3 .... 173 E4
Foundry Cl NG24 .... 140 B2
Fountain Dale Ct NG3 ...... 173 E4
Fountain Hill DN10 .... 13 E4
Fountain Hill Rd DN10 ..... 13 E4
Fountaindale Sch NG18 .... 116 B3
Fountains Cl
  Kirkby in A NG17 .... 115 E3
  West Bridgford NG2 ...... 186 A3
Fourth Ave Beeston NG9 .. 184 B3
  Carlton NG4 .... 174 B4
  Clipstone NG21 .... 89 F2
  Edwinstowe NG21 .... 76 A1
  Mansfield NG18 .... 103 D4
  Rainworth NG21 .... 103 F1

Fowler St NG3 .... 173 E4
Fox Cl NG10 .... 193 E3
Fox Covert Carlton NG4 ... 174 C2
  Collingham LE11 .... 220 A3
Fox Covert Cl NG17 .... 100 B1
Fox Covert La
  Misterton DN10 .... 14 A4
  Nottingham NG11 .... 184 B1
Fox Covert Way NG19 ...... 103 D4
Fox Gr NG6 .... 160 C2
Fox Grove Ct NG6 .... 160 C2
Fox Hill NG12 .... 187 F1
Fox Mdw NG15 .... 145 F3
Fox Rd Nottingham NG2 ... 173 F1
Whitwell S80 .... 45 D3
Fox St
  Annesley Woodhouse NG17 . 130 A4
  Sutton in A NG17 .... 100 C2
Foxby Hill DN21 .... 24 C3
Foxby La DN21 .... 24 C3
Foxearth Ave NG11 .... 185 D1
Foxes Cl NG7 .... 222 C1
Foxglove Cl
  New Balderton NG24 ...... 140 B2
  Worksop S80 .... 36 A1
Foxglove Rd NG16 .... 158 A4
Foxgloves The NG13 .... 177 E2
Foxhall Rd NG7 .... 173 D4
Foxhill Cl NG17 .... 100 A2
Foxhill Ct NG4 .... 174 C4
Foxhill Rd
  Burton Joyce NG14 .... 163 F3
  Carlton NG4 .... 174 B4
Foxhill Rd Central NG4 .... 174 B4
Foxhill Rd E NG4 .... 174 B4
Foxhill Rd W NG4 .... 174 A4
Foxhills DE74 .... 203 E1
Foxhollies NG5 .... 161 D2
Foxton Cl NG6 .... 159 F4
Foxwood Gr NG14 .... 148 C4
Foxwood La NG14 .... 149 D3
Foxwood Spec Sch NG9 ... 171 D1
Fradley Cl NG6 .... 146 B1
Frampton Rd NG8 .... 172 A4
Frances Gr NG15 .... 131 D1
Frances St NG16 .... 128 B1
Francis Chichester Wlk
  DN21 .... 24 C4
Francis Gr NG6 .... 160 C2
Francis Rd NG4 .... 174 C4
Francis St
  Mansfield NG18 .... 102 C4
  Nottingham NG7 .... 222 C4
Francklin Rd NG14 .... 150 B1
Franderground Dr NG17 .. 114 C3
Frank Ave NG18 .... 101 F3
Franklin Cl NG5 .... 161 F4
Franklin Dr NG12 .... 186 B1
Franklin Rd NG16 .... 128 A2
Franklyn Gdns
  Keyworth NG12 .... 197 F2
  Nottingham NG8 .... 172 B3
Fraser Cres NG4 .... 162 A1
Fraser Rd Carlton NG4 .... 162 A1
  Nottingham NG2 .... 173 E1
Fraser Sq NG4 .... 162 A1
Fraser St NG15 .... 130 B3
Fearson Farm Ct NG16 .... 143 F1
Freckingham St NG1 .... 223 F2
Freda Ave NG4 .... 162 B1
Freda Cl NG4 .... 162 B2
Frederick Ave
  Carlton NG4 .... 174 A4
  Ilkeston DE7 .... 170 A3
  Kegworth DE74 .... 203 E2
  Kirkby in A NG17 .... 114 B3
Frederick Gent Sch
  DE55 .... 113 D3
Freeby Ave NG19 .... 88 B3
Freehold St LE11 .... 220 B2
Freeland Cl NG9 .... 182 C2
Freeman's La DN22 .... 32 B3
Freemans Rd NG4 .... 175 D4
Freemans Terr NG4 .... 175 D4
Freemantle Wlk NG5 ...... 160 C4
Freeston Dr NG6 .... 159 F4
Freeth St NG2 .... 173 F1
Freiston St NG7 .... 222 B4
Fremount Dr NG8 .... 172 A4
French St DE7 .... 157 E3
French Terr NG20 .... 59 D1
Fretwell St NG7 .... 172 C4
Friar La
  Market Warsop NG20 ...... 74 B1
  Nottingham NG1 .... 223 D2
Friar St Long Eaton NG10 . 193 E4
  Nottingham NG7 .... 172 C1
Friar Wlk NG13 .... 177 E4
Friars Cl NG16 .... 144 C4
Friars Cres NG24 .... 139 F3
Friars Ct NG7 .... 222 C1
Friary Cl NG4 .... 174 C4
Friary Rd NG24 .... 140 A4
Friary The NG7 .... 162 C1
Friday La NG4 .... 163 D1
Friend La NG21 .... 76 A1
Frinton Rd NG8 .... 159 F1
Frisby Ave NG10 .... 193 F3

Fritchley Ct NG18 .... 103 D3
Frith Gr NG19 .... 101 F4
Frithwood La S80 .... 58 B4
Frobisher Gdns NG5 .... 161 E3
Frog La NG13 .... 202 C4
Frogmore St NG1 .... 223 E4
Front St
  Barnby in t W NG24 .... 141 F3
  East Stockwith DN21 ...... 7 F4
  Morton DN21 .... 15 D2
  South Clifton NG23 .... 68 C1
Frost Ave NG16 .... 143 D2
Fryar Rd NG16 .... 143 F2
Fulford Ave DN22 .... 39 F4
Fulforth St NG1 .... 223 E4
Fuller Cl NG18 .... 102 A2
Fuller St NG11 .... 196 B3
Fullwood Ave ID DE7 ...... 157 F1
Fullwood Cl NG9 .... 183 E2
Fullwood St ID DE7 .... 157 F1
Fulmar Way S81 .... 35 E4
Fulwood Cres NG8 .... 160 A1
Fulwood Dr NG10 .... 193 D4
Fulwood Rd N 99 F1
  Sutton in A NG17 .... 114 A4
Fulwood Rd S NG17 .... 114 A4
Fulwood Rise NG17 .... 114 A4
Furlong Ave NG5 .... 161 F4
Furlong Cl NG9 .... 182 B4
Furlong St NG5 .... 161 F4
Furnace Rd DE7 .... 170 A3
Furness Cl NG2 .... 186 A4
Furness Rd NG6 .... 160 B2
Furnival St S80 .... 36 A1
Furze Gdns NG3 .... 173 E4
Furze The NG22 .... 78 B3
Furzebrook Rd NG4 .... 174 C3
Fylde Cl NG9 .... 182 C1
Fylingdale Way NG8 .... 171 E2

Gable's Lea LE12 .... 213 D3
Gables Farm Dr LE12 ...... 206 B1
Gabor Cl NG11 .... 195 E4
Gabrielle Cl NG6 .... 160 B2
Gadd St NG7 .... 222 B4
Gaddick View NG22 .... 79 F3
Gainas Ave DN21 .... 15 E1
Gainsborough Central Sta
  DN21 .... 24 B4
Gainsborough Cl
  Kinoulton NG12 .... 199 F1
  Long Eaton NG10 .... 193 F3
  Stapleford NG9 .... 182 C3
Gainsborough Rd NG24 ... 125 D2
Gainsborough Rd
  Bawtry DN10 .... 10 A3
  Everton DN10 .... 11 E1
  Girton NG23 .... 82 C2
  Gringley on t H DN10 .... 12 B1
  Lea DN21 .... 24 C1
  North Wheatley DN22 ...... 31 D4
  Saundby DN22 .... 23 E3
  Saxilby LN1 .... 56 C1
  Sturton le S DN22 .... 32 B3
  Winthorpe NG24 .... 125 E3
  Gainsford Cl NG5 .... 160 C3
Gainsford Cres NG5 .... 160 C3
Gaitskell Cres NG21 .... 76 B1
Gaitskell Way NG24 .... 140 C2
Gala Way NG5 .... 160 C3
Gale Cl NG9 .... 184 A3
Galen Ave DN22 .... 27 D2
Galen Ct ID NG7 .... 172 C1
Galena Dr NG3 .... 174 A4
Galley Hill Rd NG25 .... 122 A1
Gallows Inn Cl DE7 .... 170 A3
Galway Ave DN11 .... 9 E3
Galway Cres DN22 .... 39 E4
Galway Dr NG5 .... 147 F1
Galway Rd Arnold NG5 .... 161 F4
  Bircotes DN11 .... 9 E3
  Nottingham NG7 .... 222 B1
Gamage Cl NG24 .... 140 C2
Gamble St NG7 .... 222 C4
Gamston CE Prim Sch
  DN22 .... 50 C3
Gamston Cres NG5 .... 161 E2
Gamston Lings Bar Rd
  NG12 .... 186 B2
Gamston Rd NG18 .... 103 D2
Gant Ct DN11 .... 8 A4
Ganton Cl NG3 .... 161 F1
Garden Ave Carlton NG4 . 174 B4
  New Houghton NG19 ...... 86 C4
  Rainworth NG21 .... 104 A1
  Shirebrook NG20 .... 72 C2
Garden City NG4 .... 174 C4
Garden La NG17 .... 101 D2
Garden Rd
  Bingham NG13 .... 177 E2
  Eastwood NG16 .... 144 A2
  Hucknall NG15 .... 145 F4
  ID Mansfield NG18 .... 102 B4
Garden Row DE74 .... 203 E2
Garden St NG7 .... 222 B3
Gardendale Ave NG11 .... 184 B1
Gardenia Cres NG3 .... 162 A1
Gardenia Gr NG3 .... 162 A1
Gardens Ct NG2 .... 186 A4
Gardiner Terr NG17 .... 100 B3
Gardinia Cl NG9 .... 183 D1
Gardner Dr NG12 .... 199 F2
Garfield Cl NG8 .... 170 C1
Garfield Rd NG7 .... 222 B3
Garfield St DN21 .... 15 E1
Garforth Cl NG8 .... 172 B4
Garibaldi Rd NG18 .... 89 E1

Garibaldi Sch NG19 .... 89 E1
Garnet Ct NG3 .... 173 F3
Garnet St NG4 .... 174 C4
Garnon St NG18 .... 101 F3
Garratt Ave NG18 .... 102 B4
Garrett Gr NG11 .... 184 B1
Garsdale Cl 186 B3
Garsdale Dr NG11 .... 185 D2
Garside St S80 .... 36 A2
Garth Ave NG17 .... 114 C4
Garth Rd NG18 .... 102 A2
Garton Cl Beeston NG9 ... 183 D3
  Nottingham NG6 .... 160 A3
Garton Rd NG11 .... 196 B1
Garwick Cl NG19 .... 89 D1
Gas St NG10 .... 182 B3
Gas Wlk LE14 .... 202 A2
Gatcombe Cl NG12 .... 176 A2
Gatcombe Gr NG10 .... 182 A2
Gateford Ave S81 .... 35 E3
Gateford Cl Beeston NG9 . 171 E1
  Worksop S81 .... 35 E4
Gateford Dr S81 .... 35 E3
Gateford Glade S81 .... 35 E3
Gateford Rd S81, S80 .... 35 E3
Gateford Rise S81 .... 35 E4
Gateside Rd NG2 .... 173 D1
Gatling St NG7 .... 222 C3
Gattlys La NG22 .... 77 D2
Gaul St NG6 .... 160 A4
Gauntley Ct NG7 .... 172 C4
Gauntley St NG7 .... 172 C4
Gautries Cl NG5 .... 161 D1
Gawthorne St NG7 .... 160 C1
Gayhurst Gn NG6 .... 160 C3
Gayhurst Rd NG6 .... 160 C3
Gaynor Ct NG8 .... 172 A3
Gayrigg Cl NG9 .... 182 C3
Gayton Cl NG8 .... 171 E4
Gaywood Cl NG11 .... 195 F4
Gedling Comp Sch NG4 .. 162 C2
Gedling Gr NG7 .... 222 C4
Gedling Rd Arnold NG5 ... 162 A3
  Carlton NG4 .... 174 C4
Gedling St
  Mansfield NG18 .... 102 A3
  Nottingham NG1 .... 223 F2
Gedney Ave NG3 .... 173 F4
Gelding Gr NG5 .... 161 F4
Gell Rd NG9 .... 183 D2
George Ave
  Beeston NG9 .... 183 F3
  Long Eaton NG10 .... 182 C1
George Dere Cl NG22 .... 77 E2
George Rd Carlton NG4 .. 174 C4
  West Bridgford NG2 ..... 185 F4
George Spencer
  Comp Sch NG9 .... 182 C3
George St Arnold NG5 .... 161 F3
  Gainsborough DN21 .... 15 E1
  Hucknall NG15 .... 146 A4
  Langley Mill NG16 .... 143 D2
  Mansfield NG19 .... 101 F4
  Whaley Thorns NG20 ..... 59 D1
  Worksop S80 .... 35 F2
George St ID NG1 .... 223 E4
George's La NG14 .... 148 B3
Georgia Dr NG5 .... 147 F1
Georgina Rd NG9 .... 183 F3
Gerard Cl NG5 .... 147 D1
Gerrard Cres DE74 .... 203 E1
Gertrude Rd NG2 .... 174 A1
Gervase Gdns NG11 ...... 184 B1
Ghest Villas S81 .... 16 C1
Ghost House La NG9 ...... 183 D2
Gibb St NG10 .... 193 E4
Gibbet Hill La DN10 .... 9 F2
Gibbons Ave NG9 .... 182 B3
Gibbons Rd NG18 .... 101 F3
Gibbons St NG7 .... 172 C1
Gibdyke DN10 .... 4 A2
Gibson Cres NG24 .... 140 B2
Gibson Rd NG7 .... 173 D4
Gibson's La LE14 .... 218 B1
Gifford Gdns NG2 .... 173 D1
Gilbert Ave Gotham NG11 . 195 D1
Gilbert Boulevard NG5 ... 162 A2
Gilbert Gdns NG3 .... 174 A3
Gilbert St NG15 .... 9 D2
Gilcroft St
  Mansfield NG18 .... 102 B3
  Sutton in A NG17 .... 100 C3
Gilead St NG6 .... 160 A4
Giles Ave NG2 .... 185 E3
Gill Green Wlk DN22 .... 30 B2
Gill St Nottingham NG1 .. 223 D4
  Selston NG16 .... 129 D3
  Sutton in A NG17 .... 100 B1
Gillercomb Cl NG2 .... 186 B3
Gillies The NG19 .... 101 E4
Gilliver La NG12 .... 187 E1
Gillot St DE75 .... 157 D4
Gillotts Cl NG13 .... 177 E4
Gilpet Ave NG3 .... 173 F4
Gilstrap Cl NG24 .... 140 A4
Gilt Hill NG16 .... 158 B4

Gilt Hill Prim Sch NG16 .. 158 B4
Giltbrook Cres NG16 ...... 158 B4
Giltway NG16 .... 158 B4
Gimson Cl DE7 .... 157 E2
Gin Close Way
  Awsworth NG16 .... 158 B3
  Kimberley NG16 .... 158 B3
Gipsy La NG14 .... 152 A4
Girton Cl NG18 .... 103 D1
Girton La NG6 .... 83 D1
Girton Rd NG5 .... 161 D2
Gisburn Cl NG11 .... 185 D2
Gisburn Gr NG19 .... 103 D4
Glade Ave NG8 .... 172 B3
Glade Hill Prim Sch
  NG5 .... 161 E4
Glade The NG11 .... 195 F4
Gladehill Rd NG5 .... 161 E4
Gladstone Ave
  Gotham NG11 .... 195 D1
  Loughborough LE11 ...... 220 A3
Gladstone Dr NG16 .... 143 F4
Gladstone St
  Beeston NG9 .... 183 F3
  Carlton NG4 .... 174 B4
  Gainsborough DN21 .... 15 E1
  Hathern LE12 .... 213 D1
  Kirkby in A NG17 .... 115 D3
  Langley Mill NG16 .... 143 E2
  Long Eaton NG10 .... 193 E3
  Loughborough LE11 ...... 220 A3
  Mansfield NG18 .... 102 A4
  Mansfield Woodhouse NG19 . 88 B1
  Nottingham NG7 .... 173 D4
  South Normanton DE55 .. 113 D3
  Worksop S80 .... 35 F2
Gladstone Terr
  ID Kirkby in A NG17 ...... 114 C3
  Mansfield Woodhouse NG19 . 88 B1
Gladys St NG7 .... 161 D1
Glaisdale S81 .... 36 A4
Glaisdale Comp Sch
  NG8 .... 171 F4
Glaisdale Dr E NG8 .... 171 F3
Glaisdale Dr W NG8 ...... 171 E3
Glaisdale Park Ind Est
  NG8 .... 171 E3
Glaisdale Parkway NG8 .. 171 E3
Glamis Rd
  Carlton in L S81 .... 25 F3
  Nottingham NG5 .... 161 D1
Glannis Seg NG20 .... 74 B3
Glanton Way NG5 .... 148 B1
Glapton Prim Sch NG11 .. 184 B3
Glapton Rd NG2 .... 173 E1
Glaramara Cl ID NG2 ..... 173 D1
Glasby Cl NG2 .... 77 D2
Glasshouse St NG1 .... 223 E2
Glastonbury Cl NG19 ...... 88 B2
Glaven Cl NG19 .... 88 B3
Glebe Ave
  Market Warsop NG20 ..... 74 B2
  Pinxton NG16 .... 113 E2
Glebe Cl
  North Wheatley DN22 ..... 31 F4
  South Normanton DE55 .. 113 D3
  Worksop S80 .... 35 E2
Glebe Cres DE7 .... 170 A4
Glebe Dr NG14 .... 163 E1
Glebe Farm Cl NG2 ...... 185 E2
Glebe Farm View NG4 ... 162 C2
Glebe Jun Sch DE55 ...... 113 D3
Glebe Pk NG24 .... 140 B3
Glebe Rd Carlton NG4 ... 162 B1
  Kirkby in A NG17 .... 115 D3
  Nuthall NG16 .... 159 E2
  West Bridgford NG2 ..... 185 F4
Glebe St
  Annesley Woodhouse NG17 . 129 F4
  Beeston NG9 .... 183 F2
  Hucknall NG15 .... 146 A4
  Loughborough LE11 ...... 220 B3
Glebe The
  Awsworth NG16 .... 158 A2
  Retford DN22 .... 39 E2
Glebe View NG18 .... 102 C4
Glen Ave NG16 .... 144 A2
Glen Cl DE55 .... 99 D3
Glen Eagles Way DN22 .... 39 E4
Glen Helen NG4 .... 174 C4
Glen Mooar Cl NG19 ...... 88 B3
Glen Parva Ave NG5 ...... 147 F3
Glen Rd NG14 .... 163 F4
Glen St NG17 .... 100 C4
Glen The DE74 .... 184 C4
Glenbrook NG12 .... 188 A4
Glenbrook Cres NG8 ..... 172 A4
Glenbrook Prim Sch
  NG8 .... 171 F4
Glencairn Dr NG8 .... 172 A4
Glencoe Rd NG11 .... 185 D1
Glencoyne Rd NG11 ...... 184 C2
Glendale Cl NG4 .... 174 C3
Glendale Ct NG9 .... 183 F3
Glendale Gdns NG5 ...... 161 F4
Glendoe Gr NG13 .... 177 E2
Glendon Dr
  Hucknall NG15 .... 146 A3
  Nottingham NG5 .... 161 D2
Gleneagles Cl NG2 .... 186 B3
Gleneagles Dr
  Arnold NG5 .... 148 A2
  Kirkby in A NG17 .... 114 C2
Glenfield Ave NG16 .... 158 B3
Glenfield Rd NG10 .... 193 E2
Glenlivet Gdns NG7 ...... 184 C1
Glenloch Dr NG11 .... 195 F4
Glenmore Rd NG2 .... 186 A3

lenorchy Cres NG5 .... 160 C4
lenridding Cl NG2 .... 186 B3
lensford Gdns NG5 .... 146 C1
lenside Arnold NG5 .... 162 A3
Kirkby in A NG17 .... 115 E3
llenside Rd NG9 .... 171 E1
lenstone Ct 22 NG7 .... 172 C4
lenthorn Cl S81 .... 34 C4
lentworth Rd NG7 .... 222 A4
lenwood Ave NG8 .... 171 E2
llenus Rd NG5 .... 160 C4
lossop Ave NG18 .... 103 D3

loucester Ave
Beeston NG9 .... 183 F3
Nottingham NG7 .... 222 A2
lnuthall NG16 .... 159 F2
Sandiacre NG10 .... 182 A2
loucester Rd S81 .... 36 A4
lover Ave NG18 .... 171 E2
lover Cl DN22 .... 42 B3
lovers Cl NG20 .... 60 A2
lovers La NG24 .... 140 B2
loatchurch Ct 8 NG5 .... 161 D4
loathland Cl 21 NG5 .... 161 D4
lodber Rd NG15 .... 145 F3
lodfrey St NG4 .... 175 D3
lodfrey's Ct S80 .... 35 F2
lodkin Dr NG16 .... 143 D2
loldcrest Rd NG6 .... 160 A2
loldcrest Rise S81 .... 35 E4
loldendolme La DN22 .... 43 D1
loldfinch Cl NG18 .... 102 C4
loldham Rd NG4 .... 171 E4
loldsmith Rd
Balderton NG24 .... 140 B3
Worksop S81 .... 36 A3
loldsmith St
Mansfield NG18 .... 102 A4
Nottingham NG1 .... 223 D3
loldswong Terr NG3 .... 173 E4
loldthorpe Cl S81 .... 16 C2
loldthorpe Cl S81 .... 16 C2
lolf Club Rd DE7 .... 170 A4
lolf Course Rd NG12 .... 198 A1
lolf Rd NG12 .... 176 A2
lomersall Cl DN22 .... 40 A3
lonalston La
Epperstone NG14 .... 150 B2
Hoveringham NG14 .... 151 E1
lood Shepherd Prim Sch
NG5 .... 161 D3
loodacre St NG10 .... 182 B4
loodall Cres NG15 .... 146 B3
loodall St 8 NG7 .... 172 C4
loodhand Cres NG18 .... 101 F3
loodliffe St 10 NG7 .... 172 C4
loodman La NG16 .... 158 B4
loodwin Cl
Newark-on-T NG24 .... 140 B4
Sandiacre NG10 .... 182 A3
loodwin Ct NG22 .... 119 F4
loodwin Dr NG16 .... 158 C3
loodwin St NG7 .... 222 C4
loodwood Ave NG5 .... 161 F4
loodwood Dr NG9 .... 182 C1
loodwood Rd NG16 .... 171 E2
loodwood Way NG18 .... 102 C4
loose Gate
Cotgrave NG12 .... 187 F2
Nottingham NG1 .... 223 F2
loosedale La NG6 .... 147 D4
loossemoor La DN22 .... 39 F2
lopher Rd NG24 .... 139 F3
lordon Ave NG18 .... 102 C3
lordon Brae NG18 .... 102 B2
lordon Cl Beeston NG9 .... 183 E1
Farnsfield NG22 .... 119 F3
Worksop S80 .... 36 A2
lordon Cres DE55 .... 113 D2
lordon Rd
Burton Joyce NG14 .... 164 A3
Loughborough LE11 .... 220 A2
West Bridgford NG2 .... 185 F4
lordon Rise NG3 .... 161 F1
lordon Sq NG2 .... 185 F4
lorse Cl
Calverton NG14 .... 148 B4
Eastwood NG16 .... 158 A4
Long Eaton NG10 .... 182 A1
lorse Ct NG6 .... 160 C3
lorse Hill NG15 .... 117 D1
lorse Rd Keyworth NG12 .... 197 E2
Newark-on-T NG24 .... 139 F3
lorselands Ave S80 .... 36 A1
lorseway NG21 .... 90 A2
lorsey Rd NG3 .... 173 E4
lorsy La NG25 .... 137 E1
losforth Cl NG2 .... 173 E1
lotham La NG11 .... 206 B4
lotham Prim Sch NG11 .... 195 D1
lotham Rd
East Leake LE12 .... 205 F2
Kingston-on-S NG11 .... 204 B3
lothic La NG6 .... 160 C2
loverton Hill NG14 .... 136 C1
loverton Sq NG8 .... 160 B3
lowan Cl 7 NG9 .... 183 E1
loyden Cl NG3 .... 161 D4
lrace Ave NG9 .... 184 A3
lrace Dr NG9 .... 172 B4

Gracefield La NG23 .... 81 F4
Grafton Ave NG5 .... 161 F3
Grafton Cl NG17 .... 101 D3
Grafton Ct NG7 .... 222 C3
Grafton St S80 .... 35 F2
Graham Ave NG24 .... 140 A2
Graham St NG7 .... 222 B3
Grainger Ave
Annesley Woodhouse NG17 .... 115 D1
West Bridgford NG2 .... 185 F2
Graingers Terr NG15 .... 146 A3
Grampian Dr NG5 .... 147 D1
Grampian Way NG10 .... 193 D4
Granary Cl DN21 .... 15 D2
Granary St NG21 .... 26 A3
Granby Ave
Mansfield NG18 .... 102 A4
Newark-on-T NG24 .... 140 A3
Granby Cl NG13 .... 177 E2
Granby Dr
Balderton NG24 .... 140 B2
Bottesford NG13 .... 181 D1
Granby Hill NG13 .... 191 D3
Granby Jun Sch DE7 .... 157 F2
Granby La Plungar NG13 .... 191 F1
Whatton NG13 .... 178 B1
Granby St Ilkeston DE7 .... 157 F1
Loughborough LE11 .... 220 A2
Grandfield Ave NG12 .... 175 F2
Grandfield Cres NG12 .... 175 F2
Grange Ave
Bawtry DN10 .... 9 F4
Beeston NG9 .... 183 F3
Mansfield NG18 .... 101 F3
Misterton DN10 .... 14 A4
Newark-on-T NG24 .... 139 F2
Ollerton NG22 .... 77 D2
Ruddington NG11 .... 196 B4
Grange Cl
Carlton in L S81 .... 26 A3
Lambley NG4 .... 163 E4
Misterton DN10 .... 14 A4
Nottingham NG1 .... 185 D4
Grange Cres NG4 .... 162 C2
Grange Ct
Kirkby in A NG17 .... 115 E3
West Bridgford NG2 .... 185 E1
Grange Dr
Harworth DN11 .... 9 D3
Long Eaton NG10 .... 193 F4
Misterton DN10 .... 14 A4
Grange Farm Cl NG9 .... 183 D1
Grange La NG24 .... 155 D2
Grange Pk
Cropwell Butler NG12 .... 189 D4
West Bridgford NG2 .... 186 B3
Grange Prim Sch NG2 .... 185 F2
Grange Rd Arnold NG5 .... 161 F2
Bildworth NG21 .... 118 A3
Long Eaton NG10 .... 193 F4
Nottingham NG6 .... 160 B2
Retford DN22 .... 39 F2
West Bridgford NG2 .... 186 A2
Grange St 10 LE11 .... 220 A3
Grange The
North Muskham NG23 .... 110 C2
Retford DN22 .... 39 F2
South Normanton DE55 .... 113 D2
Grange View
Eastwood NG16 .... 143 F2
Harworth DN11 .... 9 D3
Grange View Rd NG4 .... 163 D1
Grange Wlk DN10 .... 7 D1
Grangelea Gdns NG9 .... 183 E4
Granger Ct 4 LE11 .... 220 A2
Grangewood Cl NG8 .... 171 E2
Grangewood Rd
NG8 Kirkby in A NG17 .... 114 C4
Nottingham NG8 .... 171 E2
Grannis Dr NG8 .... 172 A4
Grant St NG7 .... 222 B3
Grantham Cl NG16 .... 158 B4
Grantham Rd
Bingham NG13 .... 178 B2
Bottesford NG13 .... 181 E1
Radcliffe on T NG4 .... 175 F1
Grantleigh Cl NG8 .... 171 E4
Granton Ave NG11 .... 195 F4
Granton Rise NG19 .... 101 E3
Granville Ave NG10 .... 182 B1
Granville Cres NG12 .... 175 F1
Granville Cr 22 NG3 .... 173 F3
Granville Ct NG3 .... 173 F3
Granville St 11 NG3 .... 220 A2
Grasmere Cl
Gainsborough DN21 .... 15 F1
Hucknall NG15 .... 145 F4
Grasmere Rd
Beeston NG9 .... 183 E4
Long Eaton NG10 .... 182 A1
Worksop S81 .... 35 F4
Grasmere St NG10 .... 182 A3
Grass St DE7 .... 157 F2
Grassingdale Cl NG4 .... 162 B1
Grassington Rd NG8 .... 172 B4
Grassmere NG12 .... 188 A2
Grassthorpe Rd NG23 .... 81 F1
Grassy La NG9 .... 184 A3
Gratton Ct 9 NG17 .... 114 C4
Gravel La NG22 .... 79 E4
Gravel Pit La DN22 .... 50 C1
Gravelholes La DN10 .... 6 C1
Gravelly Hollow NG14 .... 133 D1
Gravelly La NG25 .... 124 C4
Graveney Gdns NG5 .... 162 B3
Graves Moor La S81 .... 18 C1
Gray Fallow DE55 .... 113 D2

Gray La NG22 .... 120 C1
Gray St LE11 .... 220 A1
Graylands NG18 .... 171 F3
Grays Dr NG15 .... 132 A3
Graystones Cl NG12 .... 186 B3
Grazingfield NG11 .... 185 D2
Greasley Ave NG16 .... 144 A1
Greasley Beauvale
Inf Sch NG16 .... 144 A1
Greasley Beauvale
Jun Sch NG16 .... 144 A1
Greasley Cl NG18 .... 103 D2
Greasley St NG6 .... 160 A4
Great Central Rd
Loughborough LE11 .... 220 B2
Mansfield NG18 .... 102 B3
Great Central Rly LE11 .... 220 B1
Great Freeman St NG3 .... 223 E4
Great Hoggett Dr NG9 .... 183 D3
Great La NG22 .... 65 F4
Great North Rd
Balderton NG23, NG24 .... 155 F3
Barnby Moor DN22 .... 28 B3
Carlton-on-T NG23 .... 96 C3
Eaton DN22 .... 40 A1
Gamston DN22 .... 51 D2
North Muskham NG23 .... 110 C3
Ranskill DN10 .... 19 D2
Scrooby DN10 .... 10 A1
South Muskham
NG23, NG24 .... 124 B3
West Markham NG22 .... 65 E3
Weston NG23 .... 81 E2
Great Northern Cl The
NG2 .... 223 F1
Great Northern Rd NG16 .... 143 E1
Great Northern Way
NG4 .... 175 D4
Greave Ave LE14 .... 219 D3
Greaves Cl Arnold NG5 .... 162 A3
Newark-on-T NG24 .... 140 B4
Nottingham NG8 .... 159 E1
Greaves La NG22 .... 120 A2
Grebe Cl NG12 .... 140 B3
Greek St NG7 .... 222 C3
Green Acre
Nottingham NG8 .... 171 D3
West Bridgford NG2 .... 186 A2
Green Ave NG4 .... 175 D4
Green Bank NG12 .... 118 B4
Green Cl Blidworth NG21 .... 118 A2
Hucknall NG15 .... 146 B3
Keyworth NG12 .... 197 F2
Newton DN10 .... 99 D2
Green Farm Rd NG16 .... 128 B3
Green Hill LE12 .... 213 D1
Green Hill Rise LE12 .... 213 D1
Green Inf Sch The DE55 .... 113 D3
Green La Babworth DN22 .... 38 C3
Bathley NG23 .... 110 A1
Bottesford NG13 .... 181 E1
Collingham NG23 .... 112 A4
Darlton NG22 .... 67 E2
Dry Doddington NG23 .... 156 C1
Eagle LN6 .... 84 C2
Granby NG13 .... 191 D3
Harby LE14 .... 202 B1
Hodthorpe S80 .... 45 E3
Ilkeston DE7 .... 170 A4
Lambley NG4 .... 149 D1
Laxton NG22 .... 79 F4
Laxton, Moorhouse NG23 .... 80 A1
Lea DN21 .... 24 C2
Mansfield NG18 .... 102 B2
Mansfield, Moorhaigh NG19 .... 87 F1
Nottingham NG7 .... 184 C1
Pleasley S44 .... 86 B4
Green Leys NG2 .... 185 E2
Green Mile La DN22 .... 38 C4
Green Platt NG12 .... 187 F2
Green Rd DN10 .... 13 D1
Green St Barton in F NG11 .... 195 D4
Nottingham NG2 .... 173 E1
Green The
Barkestone-le-V NG13 .... 192 A1
Beeston NG9 .... 183 F2
Bilsthorpe NG22 .... 105 F4
Car Colston NG13 .... 165 F4
Carlton in L S81 .... 26 A3
Coddington NG24 .... 126 A1
Collingham NG23 .... 111 F4
East Leake LE12 .... 205 F1
Elston NG23 .... 153 E2
Gainsborough DN21 .... 24 C4
Glapwell S44 .... 86 A4
Hardstoft S45 .... 85 D2
Harworth DN11 .... 8 C2
Hathern LE12 .... 213 D1
Hose LE14 .... 211 F4
Kingston-on-S LE12 .... 204 A2
Kirklington NG22 .... 120 C4
Long Whatton LE12 .... 212 B2
Lowdham NG14 .... 149 F1
Mansfield Woodhouse NG19 .... 88 B3
Orston NG13 .... 179 F4
Radcliffe on T NG12 .... 175 F2
Green Wlk NG3 .... 178 C2
Green's Farm La NG4 .... 163 E1
Greenacre
Burton Joyce NG14 .... 163 F3
Mansfield NG18 .... 102 C3
Stanton Hill NG17 .... 100 B3

Greenacre Ave DE75 .... 143 D2
Greenacre Rd S81 .... 36 A3
Greenacres NG17 .... 115 D1
Greenacres Cl NG16 .... 144 B1
Greenacres Dr DE55 .... 113 D3
Greenbank NG4 .... 174 B3
Greenbank Dr NG17 .... 100 C3
Greenburn Cl NG2 .... 186 B3
Greenclose La 15 LE11 .... 220 A2
Greencroft NG11 .... 184 C2
Greencroft Prim Sch
NG11 .... 184 C2
Greendale Ave NG21 .... 76 A2
Greendale Cl NG20 .... 74 A2
Greendale Cres NG21 .... 76 A1
Greendale Gdns NG8 .... 172 A4
Greendale Rd
Arnold NG5 .... 161 F3
Nottingham NG3 .... 174 B3
Greenfield Ave S80 .... 45 E3
Greenfield Cl
Edwinstowe NG21 .... 91 D4
Mansfield Woodhouse NG19 .... 89 D1
Greenfield Gr NG4 .... 174 B4
Greenfield St NG7 .... 172 B1
Greenfield Way NG22 .... 106 B1
Greenfields NG12 .... 177 D2
Greenfields Cres NG22 .... 66 A2
Greenfinch Dale S81 .... 35 E4
Greenford Cl NG16 .... 159 F2
Greengate NG23 .... 153 D2
Greengate Rd DN22 .... 53 D2
Greengates Ave NG3 .... 161 F2
Greenhill Cres NG4 .... 174 C3
Greenhill La NG17 .... 129 F4
Greenhill Rd NG4 .... 174 C4
Greenhill Rise NG4 .... 174 C4
Greenhills Ave NG16 .... 144 A2
Greenhills Rd NG16 .... 143 F2
Greenholme Sch NG7 .... 222 A1
Greenland Cres NG9 .... 183 E2
Greenland Rd NG17 .... 100 C4
Greenland St NG7 .... 157 E1
Greens Ct NG9 .... 159 D3
Greens Windmill
Science Mus NG2 .... 173 F2
Greensfields NG17 .... 101 D3
Greenside Ave DN22 .... 42 C1
Greenside Cl NG10 .... 193 F4
Greensquare Rd NG16 .... 113 E1
Greenview Cl NG22 .... 120 A3
Greenview Cl NG19 .... 89 D1
Greenway
Carlton in L S81 .... 26 A3
Clipstone NG19 .... 89 E2
Newark-on-T NG24 .... 139 F3
Retford DN22 .... 39 E2
Greenway Cl NG12 .... 175 E3
Greenway The NG10 .... 182 A3
Greenwich Ave NG6 .... 160 B2
Greenwich Park Cl NG2 .... 185 E3
Greenwood Ave
Edwinstowe NG21 .... 76 A1
Harworth DN11 .... 8 C3
Hucknall NG15 .... 145 F4
Huthwaite NG17 .... 99 F1
Ilkeston DE7 .... 170 A4
Mansfield Woodhouse NG19 .... 88 A2
Nottingham NG3 .... 174 B3
Retford DN22 .... 39 F4
Greenwood Cl NG22 .... 120 A3
Greenwood Cotts NG18 .... 102 C4
Greenwood Cres
Boughton NG22 .... 77 D3
Carlton NG4 .... 174 C3
Greenwood Dale
Comp Sch NG2 .... 174 A2
Greenwood Dr NG17 .... 114 C3
Greenwood Gdns NG11 .... 196 B3
Greenwood Inf Sch NG3 .... 174 A3
Greenwood Jun Sch
NG2 .... 174 A2
Greenwood Prim Sch
NG17 .... 114 C3
Greenwood Rd NG3 .... 174 B3
Greenwood Vale NG15 .... 145 F4
Greer La S44 .... 86 B4
Greers Ct NG24 .... 125 F1
Greetwell Cl NG8 .... 171 D2
Gregg's Mill Fst Sch
NG18 .... 102 C3
Gregory Ave
Aldercar NG16 .... 143 D2
Langley Mill NG16 .... 143 D2
Nottingham, New Lenton
NG7 .... 222 B1
Nottingham, Portchester
NG3 .... 162 A1
Gregory Bvd NG7 .... 173 D4
Gregory Cl NG9 .... 183 E2
Gregory Cres DN11 .... 8 C2
Gregory Ct Beeston NG9 .... 183 D2
Nottingham NG7 .... 222 A1
Gregory Gdns NG22 .... 119 F3
Gregory St
20 Loughborough LE11 .... 220 A2
Nottingham NG7 .... 172 C1
Gregson Gdns NG9 .... 183 D1
Gregson Rd NG9 .... 183 D1
Grendon Way NG17 .... 101 D3
Grenville Dr Ilkeston DE7 .... 157 F1
Stapleford NG9 .... 182 C4
Grenville Rd NG4 .... 174 B4
Grenville Rise NG5 .... 147 F1
Gresham Cl
Newark-on-T NG24 .... 140 C4
West Bridgford NG2 .... 185 E4

Gresham Gdns
Arnold NG5 .... 162 A3
West Bridgford NG2 .... 185 E4
Gresley Ave DN10 .... 10 A4
Gresley Dr NG2 .... 173 F2
Gresley Rd Ilkeston DE7 .... 157 F1
Retford DN22 .... 39 E3
Gressy Rd NG7 .... 184 C1
Gretton Cl NG23 .... 156 B3
Gretton Rd NG3 .... 162 A3
Grey St Eastwood NG16 .... 144 A1
Gainsborough DN21 .... 15 D1
Kirkby in A NG17 .... 114 B3
Greyfriar Gate NG1 .... 223 E1
Greys La NG25 .... 136 B4
Greystone Dr NG8 .... 171 E4
Greystones Rd DN21 .... 15 D2
Greythorn Dr NG2 .... 185 E2
Greythorn Prim Sch NG2 .... 185 E3
Griceson Cl NG22 .... 77 D1
Grierson Ave NG5 .... 161 D4
Griffs Hollow NG4 .... 174 C4
Grimesmoor Rd NG14 .... 149 D4
Grimsby Terr NG3 .... 223 E4
Grimston Rd NG7 .... 222 A4
Grindon Cres NG6 .... 146 B1
Gringley Rd
Clayworth DN22 .... 21 F3
Misterton DN10 .... 6 C1
Walkeringham DN10 .... 13 F2
Grinsbrook NG7 .... 222 A2
Gripps Comm NG12 .... 187 F1
Grisedale Ct NG9 .... 183 D2
Gritley Mews NG2 .... 173 D1
Grives La NG17 .... 115 D1
Grizedale Cl NG13 .... 103 D4
Grizedale Gr NG13 .... 177 D2
Grosvenor Ave
Long Eaton NG10 .... 193 D2
Nottingham NG3 .... 161 E1
Sutton in A NG17 .... 100 B1
Grosvenor Cl NG12 .... 176 C2
Grosvenor Rd
Bircotes DN11 .... 9 D2
Eastwood NG16 .... 143 F1
New Balderton NG24 .... 140 A2
Grouville Dr NG5 .... 162 A3
Grove Ave Beeston NG9 .... 183 F3
Nottingham NG7 .... 222 C4
Grove Cl NG14 .... 163 F3
Grove Coach Rd DN22 .... 40 A2
Grove La DN22 .... 40 A3
Grove Mews NG16 .... 143 F1
Grove Pk DN10 .... 6 C1
Grove Rd
Church Warsop NG20 .... 74 A3
Nottingham NG7 .... 222 B1
Retford DN22 .... 40 B2
Sutton in A NG17 .... 101 D2
Grove Sch The NG24 .... 140 B3
Grove Sports Ctr NG24 .... 140 B3
6 Mansfield NG18 .... 102 A3
Mansfield Woodhouse NG19 .... 88 A2
New Balderton NG24 .... 140 B3
Retford DN22 .... 39 F4
Grove The
Beckingham DN10 .... 14 A1
Calverton NG14 .... 149 D4
Newton on T LN1 .... 55 D1
Nottingham NG2 .... 222 B4
Nottingham, Carrington
NG5 .... 161 D1
Grove Way NG19 .... 88 A2
Grove Wood Rd DN10 .... 6 C1
Grove Wood Terr DN10 .... 6 C1
Grover Ave NG3 .... 162 A2
Groveside Cres NG11 .... 184 B2
Groveview Rd NG24 .... 140 B3
Grundy Ave NG16 .... 128 B4
Grundy Nook S80 .... 45 D3
Grundy St NG7 .... 172 C4
Guildford Ave NG19 .... 88 B3
Guildhall St NG24 .... 140 A4
Guinea Cl NG10 .... 193 D4
Gum Cl NG6 .... 160 A4
Gunnersbury Way NG16 .... 159 F2
Gunthorpe Cl NG18 .... 103 D2
Gunthorpe Ct NG18 .... 103 D2
Gunthorpe Dr NG5 .... 161 E2
Gunthorpe Prim Sch
NG14 .... 165 D3
Gunthorpe Rd
Carlton NG4 .... 162 B2
Lowdham NG14 .... 164 C4
West Stockwith DN9 .... 7 F4
Gutersloh Ct NG9 .... 182 C3
Guy Cl NG9 .... 182 C3
Gwenbrook Ave NG9 .... 183 E3
Gwenbrook Rd NG9 .... 183 E3
Gwndy Gdns 22 NG5 .... 161 D4
Gypsum Way NG11 .... 205 D4

Habblesthorpe Cl DN22 .... 32 C1
Habblesthorpe Rd DN22 .... 32 C1
Hackers Cl NG13 .... 165 E2
Hackworth Cl NG16 .... 144 A2
Hadbury Rd NG5 .... 160 C2
Hadden Ct NG8 .... 171 E3
Hadderley Wlk NG3 .... 223 F4
Haddon Cl Carlton NG4 .... 162 B1
Hucknall NG15 .... 146 A3
Selston NG16 .... 129 D4

Haddon Cres NG9 .... 183 E1
Haddon Dr NG24 .... 140 B2
Haddon Nurseries DE7 .... 157 F2
Haddon Pl NG20 .... 72 B3
Haddon Prim Sch NG4 .... 162 B1
Haddon Rd
Mansfield NG18 .... 102 A4
Ravenshead NG15 .... 117 D2
Retford DN22 .... 40 A2
West Bridgford NG2 .... 185 F3
Haddon St Ilkeston DE7 .... 157 F2
Nottingham NG5 .... 161 A1
Sutton in A NG17 .... 100 C2
Tibshelf DE55 .... 99 D3
Haddon Way NG12 .... 176 A2
Hades La LE12 .... 217 E3
Hadfield Wlk NG18 .... 103 D3
Hadleigh Cl NG9 .... 182 C1
Hadley St DE7 .... 170 A3
Hadrian Gdns NG5 .... 147 D1
Hadstock Cl NG10 .... 182 A2
Hagg La Bawtry DN10 .... 10 C4
Egmanton NG22 .... 80 A3
Epperstone NG14 .... 150 A3
Haggonfields Prim Sch
S80 .... 35 D2
Hagley Cl NG3 .... 174 A3
Haileybury Cres NG2 .... 185 F3
Haileybury Rd NG2 .... 185 F3
Hainton Cl DN21 .... 24 C4
Haise Ct NG6 .... 159 F3
Halam Cl NG22 .... 120 C1
Halam CE Sch NG22 .... 120 C1
Halam Ct NG6 .... 161 A4
Halam Hill NG22 .... 121 D1
Halberton Dr NG2 .... 185 E2
Haldane St DE7 .... 15 D1
Hales Cl NG12 .... 187 F2
Haley Cl NG16 .... 158 B3
Halfmoon Dr NG17 .... 114 C2
Halifax Cl NG8 .... 159 E1
Halifax Dr S81 .... 35 F4
Halifax Pl NG1 .... 223 E2
Hall Barn La NG19 .... 101 E4
Hall Cl
Rainworth on T NG12 .... 175 F2
Rainworth NG21 .... 118 A4
Hall Cl The NG22 .... 66 A4
Hall Croft NG9 .... 183 F3
Hall Dr Beeston NG9 .... 183 E3
Clayworth DN22 .... 21 E3
Cropwell Bishop NG12 .... 189 D2
Gotham NG11 .... 195 D1
Nottingham NG8 .... 171 F2
Sandiacre NG10 .... 182 A3
Hall Gdns Beeston NG9 .... 183 D4
East Leake LE12 .... 214 C4
Hall Grounds NG12 .... 200 B4
Hall Grounds Dr NG12 .... 200 B4
Hall La Brinsley NG16 .... 143 E3
Colston Bassett NG12 .... 200 B4
East Markham NG22 .... 66 A4
Kinoulton NG12 .... 200 A2
Newton DE55 .... 99 D2
Hall Rd NG16 .... 143 E2
Hall St Mansfield NG18 .... 102 C3
Nottingham NG5 .... 161 C2
Sutton in A NG17 .... 100 C3
Hall The NG12 .... 175 D2
Hall View Dn10 .... 20 A4
Hall View Dr NG8 .... 171 E3
Hall's Rd DN10 .... 13 D2
Hallam Fields Rd DE7 .... 170 A2
Hallam Rd Beeston NG9 .... 183 F3
Nottingham NG3 .... 162 A1
Hallam's La NG5 .... 161 F4
Hallams La NG9 .... 183 E3
Hallamway NG19 .... 88 B1
Hallcroft Ave DN22 .... 39 F4
Hallcroft Ind Est DN22 .... 29 E1
Hallcroft Inf Sch DN22 .... 29 E1
Hallcroft Rd DN22 .... 29 E1
Hallfield Rd DE55 .... 99 D2
Hallfields NG2 .... 186 A2
Halliday Cl S80 .... 35 E2
Halifax Ave NG20 .... 74 A4
Halliwell Cl NG24 .... 125 D2
Halloughton Rd NG25 .... 136 B4
Hallowell Dr NG8 .... 171 F2
Halls La NG16 .... 158 A4
Halls Rd NG9 .... 182 B3
Hallum Ct DE7 .... 157 F2
Halstead Cl Beeston NG9 .... 183 E2
Nottingham NG8 .... 160 A2
Haltham Gn DN21 .... 24 C4
Haltham Wlk NG11 .... 195 E4
Hamble Cl NG9 .... 88 B2
Hambledon Dr NG8 .... 172 A3
Hambleton Cl NG10 .... 182 A1
Hambleton Ct S81 .... 25 F4
Hambling La NG6 .... 160 A4
Hamilton Cl Arnold NG5 .... 148 B1
Beeston NG9 .... 182 C1
Hamilton Dr
Market Warsop NG20 .... 74 A2
Nottingham NG7 .... 223 D1
Radcliffe on T NG12 .... 175 F2
Hamilton Gdns NG5 .... 161 D1
Hamilton Rd
Long Eaton NG10 .... 182 B1
Nottingham NG5 .... 173 D4
Sutton in A NG17 .... 101 E1
Hamilton St
Mansfield NG18 .... 102 C3
Worksop S81 .... 35 F3
Hamlet La DE55 .... 113 D3

Hamlet The DE55 .... 113 D3
Hammersmith Cl NG16 .... 159 F2
Hammerwater Dr NG20 .... 74 A2
Hammond Gr NG17 .... 115 D1
Hampden Gr NG9 .... 183 E3
Hampden St
Eastwood NG16 .... 158 B4
Kirkby in A NG17 .... 114 C3
Nottingham NG1 .... 223 D3
Hampshire Ct NG16 .... 128 A2
Hampshire Dr NG10 .... 182 A3
Hampstead Rd NG3 .... 161 F1
Hampton Cl NG9 .... 182 C2
Hampton Rd NG2 .... 185 F3
Hanbury Ct NG18 .... 103 D3
Hand's Rd DE7 .... 143 D1
Hand's Wlk NG13 .... 181 D1
Handel House Sch DN21 .... 15 E1
Handel St NG3 .... 173 F3
Handley Arc NG18 .... 102 A4
Handley Ct NG24 .... 124 C1
Hanford Way LE11 .... 220 A3
Hangar Hill S80 .... 45 D3
Hankin Ave NG16 .... 129 D1
Hankin St NG15 .... 146 B3
Hanley Ave NG9 .... 183 D4
Hanley St NG1 .... 223 D3
Hannah Cres NG11 .... 185 D4
Hannam's Yd DN22 .... 39 E4
Hanover Ct NG8 .... 171 E3
Hanslope Cres NG8 .... 171 E4
Hanson Cres NG15 .... 146 A4
Hanstubbin Rd NG16 .... 128 C3
Hanworth Gdns NG5 .... 161 E4
Harberton Cl NG5 .... 147 F1
Harby Ave
Mansfield Woodhouse NG19 .... 88 B3
Sutton in A NG17 .... 101 D1
Harby CE Prim Sch LE14 .... 202 A2
Harby Cl NG24 .... 140 B2
Harby Dr NG8 .... 172 B2
Harby La
Colston Bassett NG12 .... 200 C3
Hose LE14 .... 211 F4
Plungar LE14 .... 202 C3
Stathern NG13 .... 202 C2
Harby Rd NG13 .... 190 B1
Harcourt Cres NG16 .... 159 F2
Harcourt Pl DN22 .... 40 A2
Harcourt Rd NG7 .... 173 D4
Harcourt St Beeston NG9 .... 183 F3
Kirkby in A NG17 .... 101 D3
Mansfield NG18 .... 102 B3
Newark-on-T NG24 .... 140 A4
Harcourt Terr NG3 .... 223 F3
Harden Ct NG11 .... 195 E4
Hardigate Rd NG12 .... 189 D4
Hardstaff Cl
Annesley Woodhouse NG17 .... 114 C1
Retford DN22 .... 29 E1
Hardstaff Rd NG2 .... 174 A2
Hardwick Ave
Mansfield NG21 .... 103 F1
Newark-on-T NG24 .... 139 F4
Shirebrook NG20 .... 72 C2
Sutton in A NG17 .... 101 D3
Hardwick Cl NG17 .... 101 D3
Hardwick Cres NG18 .... 36 A1
Hardwick Ct DN11 .... 9 D3
Hardwick Dr
Ollerton NG22 .... 77 D2
Selston NG16 .... 129 D4
Hardwick Gr
Nottingham NG2 .... 222 B2
West Bridgford NG2 .... 173 F1
Hardwick Hall S44 .... 85 F3
Hardwick La NG17 .... 100 C1
Hardwick Old Hall S44 .... 85 F3
Hardwick Park Nature Wlk S44 .... 85 E2
Hardwick Rd
[21] Nottingham, Carrington NG5 .... 161 C2
Nottingham, The Park NG7 .... 222 C1
Hardwick Rd E S80 .... 36 A1
Hardwick Rd W S80 .... 35 F1
Hardwick Sch NG17 .... 171 F4
Hardwick St
Langwith NG20 .... 72 C4
Mansfield NG18 .... 102 B4
Shirebrook NG20 .... 73 D2
Sutton in A NG17 .... 100 C1
Tibshelf DE55 .... 99 D4
Hardwick View DN11 .... 9 D3
Hardwood Cl NG6 .... 159 F4
Hardy Barn DE75 .... 157 D4
Hardy Cl Kimberley NG16 .... 158 C4
Long Eaton NG10 .... 193 F4
Hardy Pl NG18 .... 101 F4
Hardy St Kimberley NG16 .... 158 C4
Nottingham NG7 .... 222 C4
Worksop S80 .... 35 F1
Hardy's Dr NG4 .... 162 C1
Hardys Cl NG12 .... 189 D2
Harebell St NG18 .... 102 A4
Harewood Ave
Newark-on-T NG24 .... 139 F4
Nottingham NG6 .... 160 B3
Retford DN22 .... 39 E3
Harewood Cl NG12 .... 176 A2
Harewood Ct
Harworth DN11 .... 9 D3
Sandiacre NG10 .... 182 A2

Harewood Rd S81 .... 35 F4
Hargon La NG24 .... 125 E3
Harkstead Rd NG5 .... 147 D1
Harlaxton Dr
Long Eaton NG10 .... 194 A4
Nottingham NG7 .... 222 B2
Harlaxton Wlk NG3 .... 223 E4
Harlech Cl DE7 .... 157 F2
Harlech Rise NG9 .... 183 D2
Harlequin Cl NG12 .... 176 A2
Harlequin Ct NG16 .... 143 E2
Harles Acres LE14 .... 210 B3
Harley St NG7 .... 222 B1
Harlow Ave NG18 .... 102 B2
Harlow Cl
Mansfield Woodhouse NG19 .... 88 B3
Sutton in A NG17 .... 100 C3
Harlow Gr NG4 .... 162 C1
Harlow St NG18 .... 118 A2
Harmston Rise NG5 .... 160 C2
Harold Ave NG16 .... 143 D2
Harold St NG2 .... 173 F2
Harpenden Sq NG8 .... 160 A2
Harpole Wlk NG5 .... 147 F1
Harrier Gr NG15 .... 145 F2
Harriett St NG9 .... 182 B4
Harrimans La NG7 .... 184 C4
Harrington Cl NG4 .... 163 D1
Harrington Dr NG7 .... 222 B2
Harrington Jun Sch
NG10 .... 182 A1
Harrington St
Long Eaton NG10 .... 193 A3
Mansfield NG18 .... 103 D3
Worksop S80 .... 35 E1
Harris Cl NG8 .... 171 F3
Harris Rd NG9 .... 183 E3
Harrison Ct NG13 .... 177 E2
Harrison Dr S81 .... 16 C2
Harrison Rd
Mansfield NG18 .... 101 F3
Stapleford NG9 .... 182 B4
Harrison Way NG25 .... 121 F1
Harrogate Rd NG3 .... 174 B3
Harrogate St NG4 .... 174 C4
Harrop White Rd NG18 .... 101 F4
Harrow Cl
Gainsborough NG21 .... 15 F1
Rainworth NG21 .... 118 A4
Harrow Gdns NG8 .... 172 B2
Harrow La NG22 .... 119 F3
Harrow Rd Hucknall NG15 .... 145 E3
Nottingham NG8 .... 172 A2
West Bridgford NG2 .... 185 F3
Harrowby Rd NG7 .... 222 B2
Harry Carlton Comp Sch
LE12 .... 205 F1
Harstoft Ave S81 .... 35 F3
Hart Ave NG10 .... 182 A3
Hart St NG7 .... 222 B1
Hartcroft Rd NG5 .... 161 D3
Hartford Cl [20] NG2 .... 173 E1
Hartill Dr NG19 .... 101 E3
Hartington Ave
Carlton NG4 .... 162 B1
Hucknall NG15 .... 145 E3
Hartington Ct NG18 .... 103 D3
Hartington Dr
Selston NG16 .... 129 D4
Sutton in A NG17 .... 101 D2
Hartington Pl DE7 .... 157 F3
Hartington Rd NG5 .... 161 C2
Hartington St NG20 .... 73 E1
Hartland Comp Sch S80 .... 46 C4
Hartland Rd S80 .... 35 F1
Hartley Cl NG7 .... 222 B4
Hartley Dr NG9 .... 184 A3
Hartley Rd
Kirkby in A NG17 .... 114 C3
Nottingham NG7 .... 222 B4
Old Dalby LE14 .... 218 C2
West Bridgford NG2 .... 186 A2
Hartness Rd NG11 .... 184 B4
Hartside Cl LE11 .... 220 A4
Hartside Gdns [1] NG10 .... 193 D4
Hartwell St NG3 .... 223 F4
Hartwood Dr NG9 .... 170 B1
Harvest Cl Bingham NG13 .... 177 E2
Carlton in L S81 .... 25 F4
Nottingham NG5 .... 160 C4
Worksop S81 .... 36 A4
Harvey Ave NG24 .... 125 F1
Harvey Cl NG11 .... 196 B3
Harvey Croft NG9 .... 170 B2
Harvey Ct NG7 .... 222 B2
Harvey Hadden Sports Ctr
NG8 .... 171 F4
Harvey Rd
Mansfield NG18 .... 102 C3
Nottingham, Bilborough NG8 .... 171 F4
Nottingham, Dunkirk NG7 .... 172 C1
Harvey's Field NG25 .... 136 C4
Harwall La DN10 .... 11 D2
Harwell Sluice La DN10 .... 11 D3
Harwich Cl NG6 .... 160 A4
Harwill Cres NG8 .... 160 A1
Harwood Cl Arnold NG5 .... 162 A4
Sutton in A NG17 .... 100 C3
Harwood Pl NG17 .... 101 D2
Harworth Ave S81 .... 18 A3
Harworth CE Prim Sch
DN11 .... 8 C2
Harworth Cl NG19 .... 101 E3
Haslam St NG7 .... 223 D1
Haslehurst Gdns S81 .... 35 F1
Haslemere Gdns NG15 .... 116 C3
Haslemere Rd
Long Eaton NG10 .... 193 D4
Nottingham NG8 .... 172 B4

Hassock La N DE75 .... 157 D4
Hassock La S DE75 .... 157 E3
Hassocks La NG9 .... 184 A4
Hassop Wlk NG18 .... 103 D3
Hastings St Carlton NG4 .... 174 B4
[6] Loughborough LE11 .... 220 A2
Haswell Rd NG6 .... 160 A3
Hatchet's La NG24 .... 125 D2
Hatfield Ave
Meden Vale NG20 .... 74 C4
Sandiacre NG10 .... 182 A2
Hatfield Cl NG21 .... 104 A1
Hatfield Dr NG2 .... 185 E2
Hatfield Rd NG3 .... 161 E1
Hatfield St DN22 .... 40 A3
Hather Cl DN22 .... 51 D3
Hatherleigh Cl NG3 .... 163 D3
Hathern Cl NG10 .... 193 E3
Hathern Gn NG9 .... 184 A4
Hathern Rd LE12 .... 212 B1
Hathernware Ind Est
LE12 .... 213 E3
Hathersage Rise NG15 .... 117 D2
Hathersage Way NG17 .... 100 C2
Hathersage Wlk NG18 .... 103 D3
Hatherton CE Prim Sch
LE12 .... 213 D1
Hatley Cl [21] NG2 .... 173 D1
Hatton Cl NG5 .... 147 D1
Hatton Crofts NG10 .... 193 E3
Hatton Ct NG18 .... 103 D3
Hatton Gdns
Newark-on-T NG24 .... 140 A4
Nuthall NG16 .... 159 F2
Haughgate Hill DN22 .... 22 A1
Havelock Gdns NG3 .... 223 F4
Haven Cl Clipstone NG21 .... 89 F2
Sutton in A NG17 .... 100 B2
West Bridgford NG2 .... 185 E2
Haven Hill S81 .... 16 B3
Havenden Gdns [7] NG2 .... 173 D1
Havenwood Rise NG11 .... 195 E4
Haverhill Cres NG5 .... 146 C1
Haversage Ave NG10 .... 193 D3
Haversham Cl NG6 .... 160 B1
Hawarden Terr [10] NG7 .... 172 C4
Hawbush Rd NG1 .... 81 D3
Hawk Ridge Gdns [7]
NG3 .... 173 F3
Hawkesworth Ave NG5 .... 89 D1
Hawkhill Cl NG22 .... 77 D2
Hawkhurst Dr NG8 .... 171 E1
Hawking La S44 .... 85 D4
Hawkins Ct NG7 .... 222 B2
Hawkshead Cl NG2 .... 186 B3
Hawksley Gdns NG11 .... 184 B1
Hawksley Rd [22] NG7 .... 172 C4
Hawkswood Cl NG9 .... 183 D2
Hawksworth Ave NG5 .... 161 E2
Hawksworth Rd
Hawksworth NG13 .... 167 D2
Scarrington NG13 .... 178 C4
Syerston NG23 .... 153 D2
West Bridgford NG2 .... 173 F1
Hawksworth St
Gainsborough DN21 .... 24 B4
[7] Nottingham NG3 .... 173 F3
Hawley Cl LE12 .... 205 F1
Hawson Way S81 .... 35 E4
Hawthorn Ave
Gainsborough DN21 .... 15 E1
Glapwell S44 .... 86 A4
Hucknall NG15 .... 145 F4
Stapleford NG9 .... 182 B3
Hawthorn Cl
Beckingham DN10 .... 23 D4
Keyworth NG12 .... 197 F1
New Ollerton NG22 .... 77 E3
[21] Nottingham NG2 .... 173 D1
Old Dalby LE14 .... 218 C2
West Bridgford NG2 .... 186 A2
Hawthorn Cres
Arnold NG5 .... 148 A1
Kirkby in A NG17 .... 115 D3
[22] Nottingham NG2 .... 173 D1
Hawthorn Dr NG22 .... 15 E1
Hawthorn Rd DN21 .... 15 E1
Hawthorn Way S81 .... 25 F4
Hawthorne Ave
Hathern LE12 .... 213 D1
Long Eaton NG10 .... 193 E3
Shirebrook NG20 .... 72 B2
Tibshelf DE55 .... 99 D4
Hawthorne Cl
Stanton Hill NG17 .... 100 A3
Woodborough NG14 .... 149 E2
Hawthorne Cres NG22 .... 139 D2
Hawthorne Gr NG9 .... 184 A3
Hawthorne Rd NG18 .... 113 E2
Hawthorne Rise NG16 .... 158 A2
Hawthorne Way NG21 .... 91 E4
Hawthorns Prim Sch The NG6 .... 146 C2
Hawthorns The
Market Warsop NG20 .... 74 A2
Walesby NG22 .... 64 A1
Hawthorn Cl
Gainsborough DN21 .... 15 F1
Mansfield NG19 .... 88 A1
Hawton Cres NG8 .... 172 B2
Hawton La NG24 .... 139 F3
Hawton Rd NG24 .... 139 F3
Hawton Spinney NG8 .... 172 B2
Hawtonville & Eastwood
Day Hospl NG24 .... 140 A3
Hawtonville Hospl NG24 .... 140 A3
Hawtonville Jun Sch
NG24 .... 139 F3

aton St DN21 .... 24 B4
avytrees Ave NG15 .... 117 D1
cadeck La LE14 .... 219 E4
ckdyke La DN10 .... 7 F3
ckington Dr NG8 .... 172 A3
ddington Gdns 🔲 NG5 .... 161 E4
ddon Bar NG10 .... 88 C2
dgerow Cl NG17 .... 100 B1
dley St Ng7 .... 173 D4
dley Villas 🔲 Ng7 .... 161 D1
len Cl NG9 .... 183 E3
lenship La DN22 .... 54 A4
llebore Cl NG15 .... 160 C4
'm Cl NG6 .... 159 F4
lmsdale Cl
  rnold NG5 .... 148 A1
  nansfield NG19 .... 101 F3
lmsdale Gdns NG5 .... 146 C1
lmsley Rd Ng21 .... 103 F2
lston Dr NG8 .... 159 F1
lvellyn Cl 🔲 NG2 .... 173 E1
lvellyn Way NG10 .... 182 A1
lmingway Cl
  narlton NG4 .... 174 B4
  lastwood NG16 .... 144 B1
nlock Ave
  long Eaton NG10 .... 182 B1
  tapleford Ng9 .... 182 C4
ndlock Gdns NG6 .... 159 F3
lmmingfield Cl S81 .... 35 F4
lmmingfield Cres S81 .... 35 F4
lmmingfield Rd S81 .... 36 A4
lmmingfield Way S81 .... 36 A4
lmplands La NG23 .... 96 C4
lmplands The NG23 .... 98 A1
lmpshill Hall Prim Sch
  NG6 .... 159 F3
lmpshill La NG6 .... 160 A2
lmsby Gdns 🔲 NG6 .... 160 A4
lmscott Cl NG6 .... 159 F4
lmsley Dr NG16 .... 143 E2
lnswell Cl NG3 .... 174 A3
lndon Rise NG3 .... 173 F4
ndre Gdns 🔲 NG5 .... 161 D4
nley Cl NG4 .... 175 D4
nley Ct DN21 .... 15 E1
nley Cres NG9 .... 170 C1
nley Rise NG5 .... 161 D4
nning Gdns 🔲 NG5 .... 161 D4
nning La NG17 .... 100 A1
nnymoor Cl S80 .... 45 D3
nnymoor La S80 .... 45 E1
nrietta St NG6 .... 160 B3
nry Ave NG19 .... 88 A3
nry Ct NG2 .... 173 E1
nry Mellish Sch The
  NG6 .... 160 B3
nry Rd Beeston NG9 .... 184 A3
  lottingham NG7 .... 222 A1
  West Bridgford NG2 .... 185 F4
nry St Arnold NG5 .... 147 F1
  lucknall NG15 .... 146 A3
  🔲 Nottingham Ng7 .... 173 F2
  utton in a NG17 .... 100 C1
nry Whipple
  lun & Inf Sch NG5 .... 160 C3
nshaw Pl DE7 .... 157 F2
nson Cl Ng12 .... 176 C2
nson La NG12 .... 176 C1
nson's Sq NG9 .... 183 E4
nton Rd NG11 .... 76 B1
pple Dr NG6 .... 159 F4
rald Cl NG9 .... 184 A4
rbert Rd
  lonesley Woodhouse NG17 .... 115 D1
  lottingham NG5 .... 161 D1
rbert St
  loughborough LE11 .... 220 A3
  lllerton NG22 .... 77 D2
reford Ave
  lansfield Woodhouse NG19 .... 88 B3
  lllerton NG22 .... 77 D2
reford Cl S81 .... 36 A3
reford Rd
  lrnold NG5 .... 161 F3
  larlton NG4 .... 162 C1
  lottingham NG3 .... 174 A3
  lavenshead NG15 .... 117 D2
rewood Cl NG20 .... 72 C2
res Cl DN10 .... 9 F4
rmitage Ave NG18 .... 101 F3
rmitage La NG18 .... 101 F2
rmitage Sq 🔲 NG2 .... 173 F2
rmitage Way NG18 .... 101 F2
rmitage Wlk NG7 .... 222 C1
rmon St NG7 .... 222 C3
ne St NG17 .... 101 D2
ron Dr NG7 .... 222 A2
ron Glade S81 .... 35 E4
ron Way NG24 .... 140 B3
ron Wharf 🔲 NG7 .... 172 C1
rons Ct NG12 .... 186 B2
rrick Rd LE11 .... 220 A1
rril Ings DN11 .... 8 A4
rriot Dr DN11 .... 9 D2
rvey Gn NG7 .... 184 C1
skey Cl NG3 .... 223 E4
skey Wlk NG3 .... 223 E4
slington Ave NG8 .... 172 C4
slop Ct S80 .... 35 D2
thbeth Cl 🔲 NG2 .... 173 E1
thersett Gdns 🔲 NG6 .... 160 A4
tley Rd Ng9 .... 183 F4
t's La NG20 .... 74 A3
ts Lane Inf Sch NG20 .... 74 A3
wett St NG20 .... 73 E3
wson's La NG23 .... 112 A3
xham Ave DE7 .... 170 A2

Hexham Cl
  Mansfield NG18 .... 102 C3
  West Bridgford NG2 .... 185 F4
Hexham Gdns 🔲 NG5 .... 147 D1
Hey St NG10 .... 193 E2
Heyes The NG15 .... 117 D1
Heyford Ct DE75 .... 143 D1
Heymann Sch NG2 .... 185 E2
Heyward St NG18 .... 102 B4
Heywood Cl NG25 .... 121 F1
Heywood St NG18 .... 102 B4
Hibbert Cres NG17 .... 101 D2
Hibbert Rd NG18 .... 102 B4
Hickings La NG9 .... 182 C4
Hickling Ct NG18 .... 102 B4
Hickling La LE14 .... 211 D2
Hickling Rd
  Kinoulton NG12 .... 200 A1
  Nottingham NG3 .... 162 A1
Hickling Way NG12 .... 188 A1
Hickman Cres DN21 .... 15 E2
Hickman Ct DN21 .... 24 C4
Hickman St DN21 .... 24 B4
Hickory Cl 🔲 NG17 .... 114 C4
Hickton Dr Ng9 .... 183 D1
Hide Hill View NG12 .... 186 B1
High Church St Ng7 .... 161 D1
High Cl NG17 .... 115 D1
High Common La
  Austerfield DN10 .... 3 D2
  Tickhill DN11 .... 9 D4
High Cres NG17 .... 115 D1
High Cross NG14 .... 136 C1
High Cross St NG1 .... 223 F3
High Field La DN10 .... 3 C3
High Grounds Rd S80 .... 35 E2
High Grounds Way S80 .... 35 D2
High Hazles Cl NG4 .... 162 C2
High Hazles Dr NG17 .... 100 A1
High Hoe Ct S80 .... 36 A2
High Hoe Dr S80 .... 36 A2
High Hoe Rd S80 .... 36 A2
High Holborn DE7 .... 157 F3
High Hurst NG14 .... 148 C4
High La Central DE7 .... 157 D1
High La E DE7 .... 157 D1
High Leys Dr Ng15 .... 116 B2
High Leys Rd Ng15 .... 145 F3
High Mdw Bawtry DN10 .... 9 F4
  Hathern LE12 .... 213 D1
  Tollerton NG12 .... 186 B1
High Oakham Dr NG18 .... 102 A2
High Oakham Hill NG18 .... 102 A2
High Oakham Mid Sch
  NG18 .... 102 A2
High Oakham Rd NG18 .... 102 A2
High Park Cotts NG16 .... 144 B3
High Pavement
  Nottingham NG1 .... 223 F2
  Sutton in a NG17 .... 100 C1
High Pavement
  Sixth Form Coll NG5 .... 160 C2
High Rd Beeston Ng9 .... 184 A4
  Beeston, Chilwell NG9 .... 183 E2
  Beeston, Toton NG9 .... 183 D1
  Carlton in L S81 .... 26 A3
High Ridge NG19 .... 88 C1
High Spania NG16 .... 158 C4
High St Arnold NG5 .... 161 F4
  Bawtry DN10 .... 10 A4
  Beckingham DN10 .... 23 D4
  Blyth S81 .... 18 A1
  Bottesford NG13 .... 181 D1
  Brinsley NG16 .... 128 B1
  Collingham NG23 .... 112 A4
  Eagle LN6 .... 84 B2
  East Markham NG22 .... 65 F3
  Edwinstowe NG21 .... 76 A1
  Elkesley DN22 .... 50 A2
  Everton DN10 .... 12 B2
  Gainsborough DN21 .... 24 B4
  Girton NG23 .... 82 C1
  Gringley on t h DN10 .... 12 C1
  Harby NG23 .... 70 C1
  Hucknall NG15 .... 146 A4
  Huthwaite NG17 .... 100 A2
  Kegworth DE74 .... 203 E1
  Kimberley NG16 .... 158 C3
  Long Eaton NG10 .... 193 F4
  Loughborough LE11 .... 220 A2
  🔲 Mansfield NG18 .... 102 A3
  Mansfield Woodhouse NG19 .... 88 B2
  Market Warsop NG20 .... 74 A2
  Marton DN21 .... 44 B4
  Misson DN10 .... 4 B1
  Misterton DN10 .... 6 C1
  Newton on T LN1 .... 55 D1
  North Scarle LN6 .... 83 E1
  Nottingham NG1 .... 223 E2
  Orston NG13 .... 179 F4
  Pleasleyhill NG19 .... 87 D3
  Retford DN22 .... 39 F2
  Ruddington NG11 .... 196 B4
  Saxilby LN1 .... 57 D2
  South Leverton DN22 .... 42 B3
  South Normanton DE55 .... 113 D3
  Stanton Hill NG17 .... 100 B3
  Stapleford NG9 .... 182 C4
  Staunton in t V NG13 .... 169 D2
  Sutton in a NG17 .... 100 C1
  Sutton on T NG23 .... 96 C4
  Tibshelf DE55 .... 99 D4
  Walkeringham DN10 .... 13 F3
High Street Ave NG5 .... 161 F4
High Street Pl NG1 .... 223 E2
High Tor NG17 .... 100 C4
High View Ave NG12 .... 198 A2
High View Rd DE55 .... 113 E4

Highbank Dr NG11 .... 195 F4
Highbank Prim Sch
  NG11 .... 195 E4
Highbury Ave NG6 .... 160 B3
Highbury Cl NG16 .... 159 F2
Highbury Hospl NG6 .... 160 B3
Highbury Rd
  Keyworth NG12 .... 197 F2
  Nottingham NG6 .... 160 B3
Highbury Wlk NG6 .... 160 B3
Highclere Dr NG4 .... 174 C4
Highcliffe Ave NG20 .... 72 B2
Highcliffe Rd NG12 .... 174 C4
Highcroft NG3 .... 161 F2
Highcroft Cl NG10 .... 193 F3
Highcroft Dr NG8 .... 171 D3
Highcross Ct Ng7 .... 222 B4
Highcross Hill
  NG25, NG14 .... 136 B2
Highfield DN22 .... 24 B4
Highfield Ave
  Kirkby in a NG17 .... 114 C3
  Mansfield NG13 .... 88 A1
  Shirebrook NG20 .... 72 B3
Highfield Cl
  Gainsborough DN21 .... 15 F1
  Mansfield NG19 .... 88 A1
  Ravenshead NG15 .... 117 D1
Highfield Ct NG9 .... 183 F3
Highfield Dr
  Bilsthorpe NG22 .... 105 F2
  Carlton NG4 .... 174 A4
  Nuthall NG16 .... 159 F2
  South Normanton DE55 .... 113 D3
  Stapleford LN6 .... 127 D2
Highfield Gr
  Carlton in L S81 .... 26 A3
  West Bridgford NG2 .... 185 F4
Highfield La S80 .... 36 B1
Highfield Prim Sch
  Cotgrave NG12 .... 187 F2
  Long Eaton NG10 .... 182 B1
Highfield Rd
  Bawtry DN10 .... 10 A4
  Beeston NG9 .... 183 D2
  Clipstone NG21 .... 90 A2
  Keyworth NG12 .... 197 F2
  Nottingham NG7 .... 172 B1
  Nuthall NG16 .... 159 F2
  Saxilby LN1 .... 57 D2
  Sutton in a NG17 .... 100 B2
  West Bridgford NG2 .... 185 F4
Highfield St NG10 .... 182 B1
Highfield Villas S81 .... 25 F4
Highfield Way NG18 .... 102 A3
Highfields Sch NG24 .... 140 B3
Highfields Science Pk
  NG7 .... 172 B1
Highgate Cl NG4 .... 162 B1
Highgate Dr DE7 .... 157 E2
Highgate La NG13 .... 202 C4
Highgrove Ave NG9 .... 183 E3
Highgrove Gdns NG12 .... 186 A2
Highland Cl NG19 .... 88 B2
Highland Gr S81 .... 36 A3
Highland Rd NG18 .... 102 C1
Highurst St NG7 .... 222 C3
Highwood Ave NG8 .... 171 F4
Highwood Player Jun &
Inf Sch
  Bestwood Village NG6 .... 146 C2
Highwood Player Jun &
Inf Sch Nottingham NG8 .... 171 F4
Highwray Gr NG11 .... 184 B1
Hilary Cl NG8 .... 171 E2
Hilcot Dr NG8 .... 160 B1
Hilcote La DE55 .... 99 D1
Hilcote St DE55 .... 113 D3
Hill Cl Eastwood NG16 .... 144 B1
  West Bridgford NG2 .... 186 A3
Hill Crest
  Gainsborough DN21 .... 15 F1
  Sutton in a NG17 .... 101 D2
Hill Crest Rd NG20 .... 72 B2
Hill Crest Gr NG5 .... 161 D2
Hill Dr NG13 .... 177 E3
Hill Farm Cl NG12 .... 186 B1
Hill Farm Ct NG12 .... 186 B1
Hill Fields DE55 .... 113 D2
Hill Rd Beeston NG9 .... 183 E1
  Bestwood Village NG6 .... 146 C2
  Gotham NG11 .... 205 D4
  Harworth DN11 .... 8 C2
  Orston NG13 .... 180 A3
Hill Rise NG9 .... 170 B2
Hill Rise Infants Sch NG5 .... 161 F4
Hill Side NG7 .... 172 B2
Hill St Pleasleyhill NG19 .... 87 D3
  Retford DN22 .... 39 F2
  Worksop S80 .... 35 F1
Hill Syke NG14 .... 150 A4
Hill The NG17 .... 114 C3
Hill Top NG13 .... 180 A3
Hill Top Ave NG20 .... 72 C2
Hill Top Ct NG11 .... 9 D2
Hill Top View NG17 .... 100 B1
Hill View Rd Beeston NG9 .... 183 D1
  Kirkby in a NG17 .... 115 E3
Hill Vue Ave NG24 .... 140 A4
Hill Vue Gdns NG24 .... 140 A4
Hillary Way NG24 .... 140 C3
Hillbeck Cres NG8 .... 171 E2
Hillcrest NG25 .... 136 B4
Hillcrest Ave DE55 .... 113 D2
Hillcrest Cl NG16 .... 159 D4
Hillcrest Dr NG15 .... 145 E3
Hillcrest Gdns NG14 .... 163 F3

Hillcrest Mews DN22 .... 40 A4
Hillcrest Rd NG12 .... 197 F2
Hillcrest View NG4 .... 162 A1
Hillfield Gdns NG5 .... 146 C1
Hillfield Rd NG9 .... 170 C1
Hillgrove Gdns 🔲 NG5 .... 161 D4
Hilliers Ct NG5 .... 160 C4
Hillington Rise NG5 .... 161 E4
Hillmoor St NG19 .... 87 E2
Hillocks Prim Sch NG17 .... 101 D2
Hills Rd NG5 .... 161 F2
Hillsborough Ave NG17 .... 114 B4
Hillsborough Way NG17 .... 114 B4
Hillsford Cl NG8 .... 172 A3
Hillside Beckingham LN5 .... 142 B4
  Kegworth DE74 .... 203 E1
  Langley Mill NG16 .... 143 D2
  Marton DN21 .... 44 B4
  Tuxford NG22 .... 66 A2
Hillside Ave
  Misterton DN10 .... 7 D1
  Nottingham NG3 .... 162 A2
Hillside Cres
  Beeston NG9 .... 183 F4
  Worksop S81 .... 35 F3
Hillside Dr
  Burton Joyce NG14 .... 163 F3
  Long Eaton NG10 .... 193 D4
  Southwell NG25 .... 136 B4
Hillside Gr NG10 .... 182 A3
Hillside Rd
  Beeston, Bramcote NG9 .... 183 E4
  Beeston, Chilwell NG9 .... 183 D2
  Blidworth NG21 .... 118 A2
  Radcliffe on T NG12 .... 176 A2
Hillside Wlk NG21 .... 118 A2
Hillsway NG20 .... 72 B2
Hillsway Cres NG18 .... 102 A2
Hilltop Cl LN6 .... 84 B2
Hilltop Rd NG16 .... 113 E2
Hillview Ave NG3 .... 161 E1
Hillview Cres DN22 .... 30 C2
Hillview Ct NG19 .... 88 B2
Hillview Rd Carlton NG4 .... 162 A1
  West Bridgford NG2 .... 185 F3
Hillwood Cl S80 .... 35 D1
Hilton Cres NG2 .... 186 A3
Hilton Ct NG2 .... 186 A3
Hilton Rd NG3 .... 162 A2
Hinchin Brook NG7 .... 222 A2
Hind St DN22 .... 40 A3
Hindlow Ct NG18 .... 103 D3
Hine Ave NG24 .... 140 C4
Hinsley Cl NG5 .... 162 A4
Hirst Cres NG8 .... 171 F2
Hirst Rd DN22 .... 40 A4
Hives La LN6 .... 83 E2
Hoare Rd NG9 .... 183 D1
Hobart Cl NG2 .... 173 E1
Hobart Dr NG9 .... 170 C1
Hobhouse Rd NG19 .... 87 E1
Hobsic Cl NG16 .... 143 E4
Hobsic La NG16 .... 128 C4
Hobson's Acre NG14 .... 165 D3
Hockerton Hts NG23 .... 122 A3
Hockerton Rd
  Southwell NG25, NG23 .... 122 C1
  Upton NG25 .... 122 C1
Hockerwood Cl NG23 .... 122 B1
Hockerwood La NG23 .... 122 B1
Hockley NG1 .... 223 F2
Hockley Pl NG17 .... 114 C2
Hodgkin Cl NG11 .... 184 B1
Hodgkinson Rd NG17 .... 115 D2
Hodgkinson St NG4 .... 175 D3
Hodmire La S44 .... 85 F4
Hodsock La S81 .... 26 A4
Hodsock Priory Gdns
  S81 .... 26 A3
Hodthorpe Prim Sch
  S80 .... 45 E3
Hoe La NG12 .... 189 D3
Hoe Nook NG12 .... 189 D2
Hoe View Rd NG12 .... 189 D2
Hoefield Cres NG6 .... 160 A3
Hoewood Rd NG6 .... 160 A4
Hogan Gdns NG5 .... 147 D1
Hogarth Cl NG9 .... 182 C3
Hogarth Prim Sch NG3 .... 174 A4
Hogarth St NG3 .... 173 F3
Hogg La NG12 .... 175 F2
Hoggetts Cl NG9 .... 183 D3
Hoggs Field NG16 .... 143 F1
Holbeck La S80 .... 59 E4
Holbeck Rd
  Hucknall NG15 .... 131 D1
  Nottingham NG8 .... 172 B3
Holbeck Way NG21 .... 104 A1
Holbein Cl LE11 .... 220 B2
Holborn Ave NG2 .... 173 F2
Holborn Cl NG16 .... 159 E2
Holborn Pl NG6 .... 160 B4
Holbrook Cl NG19 .... 103 D3
Holbrook Ct
  Mansfield NG18 .... 103 D3
  Nottingham NG11 .... 195 F4
Holbrook St DE75 .... 143 D1
Holby Cl NG5 .... 160 C4
Holcombe Cl NG8 .... 160 A1
Holdale Rd NG3 .... 174 A3
Holden Cres
  Newark-on-T NG24 .... 139 F3
  Nuthall NG16 .... 159 E3
Holden Gdns NG9 .... 182 C2
Holden Rd NG9 .... 183 F4
Holden St
  Mansfield NG18 .... 102 A3
  Nottingham NG7 .... 222 C3

Holdenby Cl DN22 .... 40 A4
Holderness Cl DN11 .... 9 D2
Holding S81 .... 36 A3
Holgate La NG11 .... 195 D1
Holgate NG22 .... 77 E2
Holgate Cl NG22 .... 184 B1
Holgate Comp Sch The
  NG15 .... 145 F3
Holgate Rd NG2 .... 173 E1
Holgate Wlk NG15 .... 145 F3
Holkham Ave NG9 .... 183 E3
Holkham Cl Arnold NG5 .... 162 A3
  Shipley DE7 .... 157 E2
Holland Cl NG11 .... 195 D1
Holland Cres NG16 .... 129 D4
Holland Mdw NG10 .... 193 E3
Holland St NG7 .... 172 C4
Holles Cl NG22 .... 66 A2
Holles St S80 .... 35 F1
Hollies Ave NG24 .... 125 D2
Hollies Cres NG7 .... 222 C1
Hollies Dr NG12 .... 186 A2
Hollies The
  Eastwood NG16 .... 143 F1
  Rainworth NG21 .... 104 A1
  Ravenshead NG15 .... 116 C1
  Sandiacre NG10 .... 182 A3
Hollington Rd NG8 .... 172 A3
Hollington Way NG18 .... 103 D4
Hollingwood La NG14 .... 163 F3
Hollingworth Ave NG10 .... 182 A2
Hollins The NG14 .... 149 D4
Hollinwell Ave NG8 .... 172 B3
Hollinwell Cl 🔲 NG17 .... 114 C4
Hollinwell Ct NG12 .... 186 A2
Hollis Mdw LE12 .... 205 F2
Hollis St NG7 .... 161 D1
Hollow Stone NG1 .... 223 F2
Holloway Cl NG13 .... 165 E2
Hollowdyke La
  Balderton NG24 .... 140 C1
  Newark-on-T NG24 .... 140 C2
Hollowgate La NG23 .... 68 A1
Hollows The
  Long Eaton NG10 .... 194 A4
  Maplebeck NG22 .... 108 A4
  Nottingham NG11 .... 185 D2
  Thurgarton NG14 .... 151 E4
Holly Ave Carlton NG4 .... 174 A4
  Nottingham, Thorneywood
  NG3 .... 174 A4
  Nottingham, Wilford NG11 .... 185 D4
Holly Bush Cl DN22 .... 50 A2
Holly Cl Bingham NG13 .... 178 A2
  Hucknall NG15 .... 146 A3
Holly Ct Beeston NG9 .... 183 E4
  Harworth DN11 .... 8 C2
  Mansfield NG19 .... 88 B1
  Retford DN22 .... 39 F2
  Rolleston NG23 .... 138 A3
Holly Dr NG19 .... 89 D1
Holly Farm Ct NG16 .... 144 B1
Holly Gdns NG3 .... 174 A4
Holly Gr NG17 .... 114 C3
Holly Hill Rd NG16 .... 129 D3
Holly La NG9 .... 183 F3
Holly Prim Sch NG19 .... 89 D1
Holly Rd
  Mansfield Woodhouse NG19 .... 89 D1
  Retford DN22 .... 40 A3
  Watnall NG16 .... 159 D4
Holly Rise NG22 .... 77 E3
Hollybrook Gr NG16 .... 159 D4
Hollycroft NG2 .... 186 A2
Hollydale Rd NG3 .... 174 A3
Hollydene Cl NG15 .... 145 E3
Hollydene Cres NG6 .... 160 A2
Hollygate Ind Pk NG12 .... 188 A2
Hollygate La NG12 .... 188 A3
Hollygate Sch NG23 .... 138 A3
Hollyhouse Dr DE55 .... 113 D3
Hollythorpe Pl NG15 .... 145 E3
Hollytree Cl LE12 .... 215 E1
Hollytree La LE14 .... 211 E2
Hollywell Prim Sch
  NG16 .... 158 C4
Holme Ave LE12 .... 205 F2
Holme Cl Ilkeston DE7 .... 157 F1
  Whatton NG13 .... 179 F2
  Woodborough NG14 .... 149 E2
Holme Gr NG2 .... 174 A1
Holme La
  Egmanton NG22 .... 79 F3
  Halam NG22 .... 120 C2
  Langford NG23 .... 111 F2
  Normanton on T NG23 .... 82 A4
  Normanton on T,
  Low Marnham NG23 .... 82 A3
  Radcliffe on T NG12 .... 175 E2
  Rockley DN22 .... 52 A1
  Normanton NG23 .... 125 E4
Holme Pierrepont Ctry Pk
  NG12 .... 174 C1
Holme Rd Bingham NG13 .... 178 A2
  West Bridgford NG2 .... 174 A1
Holme The NG25 .... 121 F1
Holme The NG25 .... 136 A4
Holme Wlk DN21 .... 15 E1
Holmecroft Ave NG17 .... 100 C3
Holmefield NG24 .... 139 D2
Holmefield Cres DE7 .... 170 A4
Holmefield Rd S80 .... 45 D3
Holmes Cl NG16 .... 143 D2
Holmes Rd DN22 .... 30 C1
Holmesfield Dr DE75 .... 157 D4
Holmewood Cres NG5 .... 161 D3

Holmewood Dr NG16 ... 158 A4
Holmfield Cl S81 ... 36 A3
Holmfield Rd NG9 ... 183 E2
Holmhurst Cl S81 ... 35 F3
Holmsfield NG12 ... 197 F1
Holmwood Rd NG21 ... 104 B1
Holroyd Ave NG2 ... 173 F2
Holt Dr 5 LE11 ... 220 A1
Holt Gr NG14 ... 148 C4
Holt The NG24 ... 139 E3
Holwood Ct NG6 ... 160 A3
Holy Cross RC Prim Sch NG15 ... 131 D1
Holy Family RC Prim Sch S80 ... 47 D4
Holy Trinity Inf Sch NG25 ... 136 B4
Holy Trinity RC Prim Sch NG24 ... 139 F4
Holyoake Rd NG3 ... 162 B2
Holyrood Ct NG9 ... 171 E1
Holywell Rd DE7 ... 157 E2
Home Cl NG5 ... 161 E4
Home Croft The NG9 ... 183 D4
Home Farm Cl NG11 ... 195 D1
Home Fm Ct NG16 ... 128 B3
Home Mdws DN11 ... 8 A3
Home Pastures LE14 ... 211 F4
Homecroft Dr NG16 ... 128 C4
Homefarm La NG23 ... 70 A3
Homefield Ave NG5 ... 148 A1
Homefield Croft DN10 ... 10 A1
Homefield Rd NG8 ... 172 B4
Homelands The NG11 ... 100 C1
Homestead NG9 ... 143 D2
Homesteads The NG20 ... 74 A2
Homewood Dr NG17 ... 114 C4
Honeycroft Ct DE55 ... 113 D2
Honeyknab La NG25 ... 134 B3
Honeys La NG11 ... 139 D1
Honeysuckle Cl
  New Balderton NG24 ... 140 B2
  4 Nottingham NG8 ... 159 F1
Honeysuckle Gr
  Bingham NG13 ... 177 E2
  Nottingham NG6 ... 160 A2
Honeywood Dr NG3 ... 174 A4
Honeywood Wlk NG3 ... 174 A4
Honing Dr NG25 ... 136 B4
Honingham Cl NG3 ... 162 A3
Honingham Rd DE7 ... 157 E2
Honister Cl
  Mansfield NG18 ... 102 B2
  Nottingham NG11 ... 195 E4
  West Bridgford NG2 ... 186 B4
Honister Ct NG18 ... 102 B2
Honiton Cl NG9 ... 183 D1
Honiton Rd NG8 ... 159 F1
Hood St NG5 ... 161 E1
Hooley Cl NG10 ... 193 D3
Hooley Pl NG5 ... 161 E2
Hooley St NG16 ... 128 C3
Hoopers Wlk 6 NG2 ... 173 E1
Hooton Rd NG4 ... 174 B4
Hooton St NG3 ... 173 F3
Hope Cl NG2 ... 173 D1
Hope Dr NG7 ... 223 D1
Hope St Beeston NG9 ... 183 F4
  Mansfield NG18 ... 102 B3
Hopedale Cl NG7 ... 222 A3
Hopewell Cl NG12 ... 176 A2
Hopewell Wlk DE7 ... 157 F3
Hopkin La NG25 ... 121 E1
Hopkins Cl NG16 ... 143 F2
Hopyard La
  Egmanton NG22 ... 79 F4
  Normanton on T NG23 ... 82 A3
Horace Ave NG9 ... 182 B3
Hornbeam Cl DE7 ... 170 A4
Hornbeam Gdns NG6 ... 159 F4
Hornbuckle St NG7 ... 222 B3
Hornchurch Rd NG8 ... 171 E4
Hornsby Wlk NG5 ... 160 C4
Horridge St DE7 ... 157 F2
Horsecroft Cl DE7 ... 157 E1
Horsendale Ave NG16 ... 159 F2
Horsendale Prim Sch NG16 ... 159 F2
Horsewells St DN10 ... 12 C1
Horsham Dr NG5 ... 160 C4
Horsley Cres NG16 ... 143 D2
Hose CE Prim Sch LE14 ... 211 F4
Hose La
  Colston Bassett LE14 ... 201 D2
  Harby LE14 ... 202 A1
  Hose LE14 ... 211 F3
Hoselett Field Rd NG10 ... 193 F3
Hosiery St NG17 ... 115 D3
Hospital Rd DN22 ... 39 F3
Hoton Rd 5 NG2 ... 173 F2
Hoton Rd LE12 ... 216 A2
Hotspur Cl NG6 ... 160 C3
Hotspur Rd DN21 ... 15 E1
Houfton Rd NG18 ... 102 C4
Hougham Rd NG23 ... 156 C1
Houghton Ave DE7 ... 157 E2
Houghton Cl NG16 ... 159 F2
Houldsworth Rise NG5 ... 147 F1
Hound Rd NG2 ... 185 F4
Hounds Gate
  Nottingham NG1 ... 223 D2
  Nottingham NG1 ... 223 E2
Hounsfield Cl NG24 ... 140 C4
Hounsfield Way NG23 ... 96 C4
Houseman Gdns NG2 ... 173 E1

Houston Cl NG5 ... 146 C1
Hove Rd NG5 ... 160 C3
Hoveringham Rd NG14 ... 165 E4
Howard Cl NG10 ... 182 C1
Howard Rd Bircotes DN11 ... 9 E2
  Mansfield NG19 ... 101 F4
Howard St
  Loughborough LE11 ... 220 A3
  Nottingham NG1 ... 223 E3
  Sutton in A NG17 ... 100 C2
  Worksop S80 ... 35 F2
Howbeck La DN22 ... 30 C2
Howbeck Rd NG5 ... 162 A4
Howden Rd NG6 ... 146 B1
Howe Rd LE11 ... 220 A1
Howell-Jones Rd NG9 ... 183 D2
Howells Cl NG5 ... 161 E4
Howes Ct NG24 ... 140 A4
Howick Dr NG6 ... 159 F4
Howitt St Heanor DE75 ... 143 D1
  Long Eaton NG10 ... 193 F4
Howitts Rd NG13 ... 181 D1
Hoylake Cl NG19 ... 88 C3
Hoylake Cres NG8 ... 171 E4
Hoyland Ave NG7 ... 172 C1
Hubert St NG7 ... 222 B4
Huckerby Rd DE7 ... 157 E1
Hucklow Cl NG18 ... 103 D3
Hucknall Cl NG8 ... 159 E1
Hucknall Cres NG4 ... 162 C1
Hucknall Ind Pk NG15 ... 145 F2
Hucknall La NG6 ... 146 B1
Hucknall Rd
  Newstead NG15 ... 130 B3
  Nottingham NG5 ... 160 C3
  Nottingham NG6 ... 146 B4
Huddlestones Wharf NG24 ... 139 F4
Hudson St
  Loughborough LE11 ... 220 B2
  Nottingham NG3 ... 173 F3
Hufton's Ct DE75 ... 157 D4
Hufton's Dr DE75 ... 157 D4
Hugessen Ave NG15 ... 146 B4
Hugget Gdns 4 NG5 ... 161 D4
Humber Cl NG2 ... 173 E1
Humber La NG23 ... 153 D4
Humber Rd Beeston NG9 ... 184 A4
  Long Eaton NG10 ... 182 B1
Humber Rd S NG9 ... 184 A3
Humber St Retford DN22 ... 40 A3
  Worksop S80 ... 35 F2
Humberston Rd NG8 ... 171 E2
Humberstone Rd LE11 ... 220 B2
Humphries Gdns S81 ... 35 F1
Hundred Acre La S81 ... 26 B2
Hundred Acres La NG24 ... 140 B1
Hundreds La DN10 ... 5 D2
Hungary La LE12 ... 213 E4
Hungerhill Rd NG3 ... 173 E4
Hungerton St NG7 ... 222 B1
Hunston Cl NG8 ... 172 A4
Hunt's Hill NG16 ... 144 B3
Hunter Rd NG5 ... 162 B3
Hunter's Dr NG12 ... 12 C1
Hunters Cl NG11 ... 185 D3
Hunters Ct NG17 ... 114 C3
Huntingdon Dr NG7 ... 223 D2
Huntingdon Jun Sch NG3 ... 223 F4
Huntingdon St NG1 ... 223 E3
Huntingdon Way NG9 ... 182 C1
Huntingdon Wlk NG10 ... 182 A3
Huntly Cl Mansfield NG19 ... 101 E3
  Nottingham NG11 ... 184 C1
Huntsman Pl DN22 ... 19 D1
Hurcomb St NG3 ... 173 F4
Hurst Cl NG21 ... 103 F1
Hurt's Yd NG1 ... 223 E2
Hurts Croft NG9 ... 183 E2
Huss's La NG10 ... 193 F4
Hutchinson Gn NG3 ... 223 F4
Huthwaite CE Inf Sch ... 99 F1
Huthwaite La DE55 ... 99 E1
Huthwaite Rd NG17 ... 100 B1
Hutton Cl NG9 ... 171 E1
Hutton St NG2 ... 173 F3
Huxley Cl NG8 ... 171 E4
Hyde Cl NG11 ... 184 C2
Hyde Park Cl NG2 ... 185 E3
Hyson Cl 24 NG7 ... 172 C4
Hyson Green St Mary's RC Sch The NG7 ... 172 C4
Hyson St 8 NG7 ... 172 C4

Ian Gr NG4 ... 174 C4
Idle Bank DN9 ... 3 D3
Idle Ct DN10 ... 10 A4
Idle View DN22 ... 29 F1
Idlewells Sh Ctr NG17 ... 100 C1
Ilam Sq DE7 ... 157 F3
Ilford Cl DE7 ... 157 F3
Ilion St NG19 ... 87 F1
Ilkeston Com Hospl DE7 ... 157 E2
Ilkeston Rd
  Sandiacre NG10 ... 182 B4
  Stapleford NG9 ... 170 C1
  Trowell NG9 ... 170 B3
Imperial Ave
  Beeston NG9 ... 183 F3
  Carlton NG4 ... 162 C1
Imperial Rd Beeston NG9 ... 183 F3
  Nottingham NG6 ... 160 B3
Inchwood Cl NG9 ... 182 C1
Incinerator Rd NG2 ... 173 F1

Independent St NG7 ... 222 B4
Infield La Cuckney NG20 ... 60 A3
  North Leverton w H DN22 ... 32 C1
  Weston NG3 ... 81 D2
Ingham Gr NG7 ... 222 A1
Ingham Rd Bawtry DN10 ... 9 F4
  Long Eaton NG10 ... 182 B1
Ingleborough Gdns 6 NG10 ... 193 D4
Ingleby Cl
  Cotgrave NG12 ... 187 F1
  Nottingham NG8 ... 171 D2
Inglefield Cl DE7 ... 170 A3
Inglemere Cl S81 ... 36 A3
Inglewood Cl NG24 ... 140 A3
Inglewood Rd NG7 ... 184 C1
Ingram La NG23 ... 82 A2
Ingram Rd NG6 ... 160 B3
Ingram Terr NG6 ... 160 B3
Ings Rd DN10 ... 12 C3
Inham Cir NG9 ... 183 E3
Inham Cl NG9 ... 183 D3
Inham Fields LE14 ... 165 D3
Inham Rd NG9 ... 183 D3
Inholms Gdns NG23 ... 152 C1
Inholms Rd NG23 ... 152 C1
Inkerman Rd NG16 ... 128 C3
Inkerman St NG16 ... 128 C3
Innes Rd NG4 ... 174 B4
Institute St NG17 ... 100 B3
Intake Rise NG3 ... 223 F4
Intake Ave NG18 ... 101 F3
Intake Farm Fst Sch NG19 ... 101 F4
Intake Rd Clipstone NG21 ... 90 A2
  Keyworth NG12 ... 197 E2
Iona Cl DN21 ... 15 F1
Iona Dr NG9 ... 170 B1
Iona Gdns NG5 ... 147 D1
Ipswich Cir NG3 ... 174 A3
Ireland Ave NG9 ... 184 A3
Ireland Cl NG9 ... 184 A3
Iremonger Rd NG2 ... 173 E1
Irene Terr NG7 ... 160 C1
Ireton Gr NG9 ... 183 E1
Ireton St Beeston NG9 ... 183 E1
  Nottingham NG7 ... 222 C3
Irwin Dr NG6 ... 160 A3
Isaac's La NG9 ... 182 B4
Isabella St NG7 ... 223 E1
Islay Cl Arnold NG5 ... 147 F1
  Stapleford NG9 ... 170 B1
Ivatt Cl DN10 ... 10 A4
Ivatt Dr NG2 ... 173 F2
Iveagh Cl NG20 ... 74 B3
Ives Cl NG2 ... 185 E2
Ivies The NG5 ... 161 E2
Ivy Cl NG16 ... 144 C1
Ivy Gr Carlton NG4 ... 174 B4
  Kirkby in A NG17 ... 114 C3
  Nottingham NG7 ... 173 D4
Ivy La NG16 ... 143 F1
Ivy Lodge La S81 ... 16 A2
Ivy Row NG13 ... 179 D2

Jacklin Gdns NG5 ... 147 D1
Jacksdale Prim Sch NG16 ... 128 A2
Jackson Ave NG10 ... 182 A3
Jackson Terr NG20 ... 74 C4
James' Murray Mews NG18 ... 102 C2
James Peacock Inf Sch NG11 ... 196 A4
James St
  Annesley Woodhouse NG17 ... 115 D1
  Arnold NG5 ... 161 F4
  Kimberley NG16 ... 158 C3
  Worksop S80 ... 35 F3
James William Turner Ave NG17 ... 100 C1
Japan Rd DN21 ... 15 D1
Japonica Dr NG6 ... 160 A2
Jardine Cl NG16 ... 143 E3
Jarrow Gdns NG5 ... 146 C1
Jarvis Ave NG3 ... 174 A3
Jasmin Cl NG20 ... 72 B3
Jasmine Cl Bawtry NG16 ... 171 E1
  2 Nottingham, Broxtowe NG8 ... 159 F1
  Nottingham, Glapton NG11 ... 184 B1
Jasmine Rd NG5 ... 160 C2
Jasper Cl NG12 ... 175 F1
Jay's Cl NG21 ... 181 D1
Jayne Cl Carlton NG4 ... 163 D1
  Nottingham NG8 ... 171 F3
Jedburgh Cl NG3 ... 223 F4
Jedburgh Wlk NG3 ... 223 F4
Jeffares Cl DE74 ... 203 C2
Jellicoe St NG20 ... 59 D1
Jenford St NG18 ... 101 F3
Jenkins Ave NG19 ... 101 E4
Jenned Rd NG5 ... 148 A1
Jenner St 8 NG5 ... 161 E3
Jenness Ave NG5 ... 146 C1
Jennison St
  Mansfield NG19 ... 88 A1
  Nottingham NG6 ... 160 B4
Jenny Beckett's La NG18 ... 102 C2
Jenny Burton Way NG15 ... 146 B3
Jephson Rd NG17 ... 114 C4
Jericho La NG13 ... 192 A2
Jericho Rd NG4 ... 162 C4
Jermyn Dr NG5 ... 147 D1
Jersey Gdns NG3 ... 173 F3
Jersey St NG24 ... 139 F3

Jerusalem NG7 ... 71 F1
Jerusalem Rd LN6 ... 71 F2
Jervis Ct DE7 ... 157 F2
Jesmond Rd NG6 ... 160 B3
Jesse Boot Prim Sch NG3 ... 174 A3
Jesse Gray Sch NG2 ... 185 F3
Jessop Cl NG24 ... 125 E1
Jessop Way NG24 ... 125 E1
Jessop's La NG4 ... 162 C1
Job La DN10 ... 20 A4
Job's La LN6 ... 84 C1
Jockey La DN22 ... 50 A3
John Barrow Cl NG21 ... 118 B4
John Blow Prim Sch NG23 ... 112 A4
John Carroll Ct 2 NG3 ... 173 F3
John Clifford Sch NG9 ... 184 A3
John Coupland Hospl DN21 ... 15 D2
John Davies Prim Sch NG17 ... 99 F2
John Hunt Inf Sch NG21 ... 140 B2
John Hunt Jun Sch NG21 ... 140 B2
John King Inf Sch NG16 ... 113 E2
John Pope Way NG24 ... 125 D2
John St Ilkeston DE7 ... 157 F1
  Nottingham NG1 ... 160 C1
  Sutton in A NG17 ... 100 C2
  Worksop S80 ... 35 F2
John T Rice Sch NG19 ... 89 F2
Johns Rd NG12 ... 176 A2
Johnson Ave NG15 ... 146 A3
Johnson Dr NG18 ... 102 B2
Johnson Rd NG7 ... 222 A2
Joseph Whitaker Sch The NG21 ... 117 F4
Joyce Ave Beeston NG9 ... 182 C2
  Nottingham NG5 ... 161 E3
Joyce Cl NG5 ... 161 E2
Jubilee Cl DN10 ... 4 A2
Jubilee Dr LE11 ... 220 A3
Jubilee Rd Arnold NG5 ... 161 F3
  Retford DN22 ... 39 E3
  Sutton in A NG17 ... 100 B2
Jubilee St
  Kimberley NG16 ... 158 C4
  Newark-on-T NG24 ... 140 A4
  2 Nottingham NG2 ... 173 F2
Jubilee Way S NG18 ... 103 E3
Jubilee Way N NG18 ... 103 D3
Judges St LE11 ... 220 B2
Judson Ave NG9 ... 182 C3
Julian Cl DE7 ... 170 A3
Julian La NG23 ... 164 B1
Julian Rd NG2 ... 174 A1
Julie Ave DE75 ... 143 D1
Jumelles Dr NG14 ... 148 B4
Junction Rd
  Long Eaton NG10 ... 194 A3
  Sutton in A NG17 ... 184 B1
Juniper Cl NG11 ... 184 B1
Juniper Ct NG16 ... 158 B4
Juniper Gdns NG13 ... 178 A2

Kelvedon Gdns NG3 ... 173 F3
Kelvin Cl NG9 ... 182 B3
Kelvin Rd Eastwood NG19 ... 89 E2
  Nottingham NG3 ... 174 A4
Kemmel Rd NG6 ... 160 B3
Kempsey Cl NG5 ... 160 C4
Kempson St NG11 ... 196 B3
Kempton Cl NG16 ... 158 B3
Kempton Dr NG5 ... 148 A1
Kempton Rd NG18 ... 102 C4
Kendal Cl
  Annesley Woodhouse NG17 ... 130 A4
  Hucknall NG15 ... 145 E3
  Worksop S81 ... 35 F4
Kendal Ct NG2 ... 186 A4
Kendal Dr NG9 ... 183 E4
Kendal Rd NG12 ... 189 D2
Kendale Ct NG3 ... 161 F4
Kendale La NG4 ... 174 B4
Kenilworth Ave NG17 ... 101 D2
Kenilworth Cl S80 ... 36 A1
Kenilworth Ct
  Beeston NG9 ... 184 A4
  Nottingham NG7 ... 223 D1
Kenilworth Rd
  Beeston NG9 ... 184 A4
  Nottingham NG7 ... 223 D1
Kenmare Cres NG21 ... 104 C3
Kenmore Cl NG17 ... 101 F3
Kenmore Gdns NG3 ... 223 F4
Kennack Cl DE55 ... 113 E3
Kennedy Ave
  Long Eaton NG10 ... 193 E3
  Mansfield Woodhouse NG19 ... 88 B2
Kennedy Cl NG5 ... 161 F4
Kennedy Ct
  Walesby NG22 ... 64 A1
  Worksop S80 ... 35 F4
Kennedy Dr NG9 ... 170 C1
Kennedy Rise NG22 ... 64 A1
Kennedy Wlk NG24 ... 140 C2
Kennel Dr DN22 ... 28 B3
Kennel La NG6 ... 71 E1
Kennet Paddock NG19 ... 88 B2
Kenneth Rd NG5 ... 147 F1
Kennington Rd NG8 ... 172 B3
Kenrick Rd NG3 ... 162 A1
Kenrick St NG4 ... 175 D4
Kensington Cl
  Beeston NG9 ... 183 D1
  Mansfield Woodhouse NG19 ... 88 C3
  Sutton in A NG17 ... 100 C1
Kensington Ct NG24 ... 161 E2
Kensington Gdns
  Carlton NG4 ... 174 C4
  Ilkeston DE7 ... 170 A4
Kensington Jun Sch DE7 ... 170 A4
Kensington Park Cl NG2 ... 185 E3
Kensington Rd NG10 ... 182 A3
Kenslow Ave NG7 ... 172 C4
Kent Ave Beeston NG9 ... 183 F2
  Westwood NG16 ... 128 A2
Kent Cl S81 ... 36 A3
Kent Rd Eastwood NG16 ... 158 B4
  Nottingham NG3 ... 162 A2
Kent St NG1 ... 223 F3
Kentmere Cl NG2 ... 186 B4
Kenton Ave NG16 ... 159 E2
Kenton Ct NG2 ... 173 E1
Kentwood Rd NG2 ... 173 F2
Kenyon Rd NG7 ... 222 B1
Keppel Ct DE7 ... 157 F2
Kersall Ct NG6 ... 160 B3
Kersall Dr NG6 ... 160 B3
Kersall Gdns NG15 ... 146 A4
Kestral Rd NG18 ... 101 F2
Kestrel Cl NG24 ... 162 A1
Kestrel Mews S81 ... 35 E4
Kestrel Rise LN6 ... 84 B3
Keswick Cl Beeston NG9 ... 183 E4
  West Bridgford NG2 ... 186 B4
Keswick Ct
  Long Eaton NG10 ... 182 A1
  3 Nottingham NG2 ... 173 F3
Keswick Rd S81 ... 35 E4
Keswick St NG2 ... 173 F3
Ketlock Hill La DN22 ... 32 B
Kett St NG6 ... 160 A4
Kettlethorpe Rd LN1 ... 55 E
Keverne Cl NG8 ... 160 B4
Kevin Rd NG8 ... 171 E
Kew Cl NG2 ... 185 E
Kew Cres DE75 ... 143 D
Kew Gdns
  New Balderton NG24 ... 140 A
  Nuthall NG16 ... 159 F
Kexby Wlk DN21 ... 24 C
Key St NG3 ... 173 F
Keyes Cl DN10 ... 19 F
Keyes Ct DN10 ... 19 F
Keyes Rise DN10 ... 19 F
Keys Cl NG6 ... 160 A
Keyworth Cl NG19 ... 101 F
Keyworth Dr NG19 ... 89 E
Keyworth Prim Sch NG12 ... 197 F
Keyworth Rd
  Carlton NG4 ... 162 B
  Widmerpool NG12 ... 208 B
  Wysall NG12 ... 207 F
Kibworth Cl NG5 ... 160 C
Kid La S81 ... 16 A
Kiddier Ave NG5 ... 162 A
Kighill La NG15 ... 132 A
Kilbourn St NG3 ... 223 E
Kilbourne Rd NG5 ... 148 A

Kilburn Cl NG9 .... 171 D1
Kilby Ave NG3 .... 174 A3
Kildare Rd NG3 .... 173 F4
Kildonan Cl NG8 .... 159 E1
Killerton Gn NG11 .... 195 F4
Killerton Park Dr NG2 ... 185 D2
Killisick Jun Sch NG5 ... 148 A1
Killisick Rd NG5 .... 148 A1
Kilnbrook Ave NG5 .... 148 A1
Kilnwood Cl NG3 .... 174 A4
Kilsby Rd NG7 .... 184 C1
Kilton Cl S81 .... 36 A2
Kilton Cres S81 .... 36 A2
Kilton Glade S81 .... 36 A2
Kilton Hill S81 .... 36 A3
Kilton Rd S80 .... 36 A2
Kilton Terr S80 .... 36 A2
Kilton Terrace Ind Est
S80 .... 36 A2
Kilverton Cl NG8 .... 172 B2
Kilvington Rd NG5 .... 162 A4
Kimber Cl NG8 .... 171 E3
Kimberley Cl NG16 ...... 158 C3
Kimberley Comp Sch
NG16 .... 159 D3
Kimberley Prim Sch
NG16 .... 159 D3
Kimberley Rd
Nottingham NG1 .... 174 A3
Nuthall NG16 .... 159 E3
Kimbolton Ave NG7 ..... 222 B2
Kindlewood Dr NG9 ..... 183 D1
King Charles St NG1 .... 223 D2
King Edward Ave NG18 .. 102 A2
King Edward Fst Sch
NG18 .... 102 B3
King Edward Gdns NG10 182 A3
King Edward Rd LE11 ... 220 B2
King Edward St
Hucknall NG1 .... 146 A3
Nottingham NG1 .... 223 F3
Sandiacre NG10 .... 182 A4
Shirebrook NG20 .... 72 C2
King Edward VI Sch
(Lower) DN22 .... 40 A3
King Edward VI Sch
(Upper) DN22 .... 39 F3
King Edward's Terr DN22 39 F3
King Edwin Prim Sch
NG21 .... 75 F1
King George Ave LE11 .. 220 B1
King George Rd LE11 ... 220 B1
King George V Ave
NG18 .... 102 C3
King John's Rd NG21 .... 90 A2
King Rd NG20 .... 74 A2
King St Beeston NG9 .... 183 F1
Eastwood NG16 .... 143 F1
Gainsborough DN21 ..... 24 B4
Hodthorpe S80 .... 45 E3
Huthwaite NG17 .... 100 A2
Ilkeston DE7 .... 157 F1
Kirkby in A NG17 .... 115 D2
Long Eaton NG10 .... 193 E4
Loughborough LE11 ..... 220 B2
Mansfield NG18 .... 102 B4
Mansfield Woodhouse NG19 88 B1
Nether Broughton LE14 . 219 E4
Newark-on-T NG24 ...... 139 F4
Nottingham NG1 .... 223 E3
Pinxton NG16 .... 113 E2
South Normanton DE55 . 113 D3
Southwell NG25 .... 121 F1
Sutton in A NG17 .... 100 C1
Tibshelf DE55 .... 99 A4
Warsop Vale NG20 ...... 73 E3
Worksop S80 .... 35 F1
King St E DN21 .... 24 B4
King's Meadow Rd NG2 . 173 D1
King's Pl NG1 .... 223 F2
King's Rd NG24 .... 124 C1
King's Sch The NG2 ..... 173 E3
King's Wlk NG1 .... 223 E3
Kingerby Cl DN21 .... 24 C4
Kingfield Cl NG21 .... 118 A4
Kingfisher Cl
New Balderton NG24 .... 140 B3
Nottingham NG6 .... 160 B2
Kingfisher Cl
Beeston NG9 .... 184 A3
Loughborough LE11 ..... 220 A1
Kingfisher Wlk LE11 .... 220 A1
Kingfisher Wlk S81 ...... 35 E4
Kingfishers Ct NG2 ..... 186 B2
Kinglake Pl NG2 .... 173 E1
Kingrove Ave NG9 ...... 183 E3
Kings Ave NG4 .... 162 C1
Kings Ct NG25 .... 121 F1
Kings Dr NG16 .... 143 F4
Kings Lodge Dr NG18 ... 101 F2
Kings Rd
Long Clawson LE14 ..... 211 E1
Sandiacre NG10 .... 182 A3
Kings Way S80 .... 45 E3
Kings Wood Cl DN10 .... 10 A4
Kingsbridge Ave NG3 ... 162 A2
Kingsbridge Rd NG3 .... 162 A2
Kingsbridge Way NG9 .. 183 D3
Kingsbury Dr NG8 ...... 172 A4
Kingsdale S81 .... 36 A4

Kingsdale Cl NG10 ...... 193 D3
Kingsdown Mount NG8 .. 171 F1
Kingsford Ave NG7 ..... 222 A4
Kingsley Ave NG19 ...... 88 B3
Kingsley Cl NG19 .... 88 B2
Kingsley Cres NG10 .... 193 D2
Kingsley Ct NG19 .... 88 B3
Kingsley Dr NG4 .... 175 D4
Kingsley Rd NG2 .... 174 A2
Kingsley St NG17 .... 115 D2
Kingsmead DN22 .... 39 E2
Kingsmead Ave NG9 .... 170 B1
Kingsmeadow NG21 .... 118 A4
Kingsnorth Cl NG24 .... 140 A4
Kingsthorpe Cl
Mansfield NG19 .... 88 C1
Nottingham NG3 .... 161 F1
Kingston Ave DE7 ...... 170 A2
Kingston Cl S80 .... 47 E4
Kingston Ct
Kingston-on-S NG11 .... 204 B3
Ollerton NG22 .... 77 D2
Kingston Dr
Cotgrave NG12 .... 187 F1
Ollerton NG22 .... 77 D2
Kingston Jun Sch S81 ... 25 F3
Kingston La DE74 .... 203 F2
Kingston Rd
Carlton in L S81 .... 25 F3
Mansfield NG18 .... 102 B4
West Bridgford NG2 .... 185 F3
Worksop S80 .... 47 E4
Kingsvay Ilkeston DE7 . 170 A3
Kirkby in A NG17 .... 115 D2
Mansfield Woodhouse NG19 89 D1
New Balderton NG24 ... 140 B2
Radcliffe on T NG12 .... 175 F1
Worksop S81 .... 36 A2
Kingsway Ave NG22 .... 77 E3
Kingsway Gdns NG15 .. 145 F2
Kingsway Prim Sch
NG15 .... 130 C1
Kingsway Rd NG15 .... 145 F2
Kingswell Jun Sch NG5 . 161 F4
Kingswell Rd NG5 ...... 161 F3
Kingswood Cl Firbeck S81 16 A3
West Bridgford NG2 .... 185 E3
Kingswood Dr NG17 .... 114 C3
Kingswood Rd NG8 .... 172 A3
Kinlet Rd NG3 .... 161 D3
Kinoulton La
Kinoulton, Owthorpe NG12 199 F2
Kinoulton NG12 .... 209 D4
Kinoulton Prim Sch
NG12 .... 199 F1
Kinoulton Rd NG12 ..... 188 C1
Kinsdale Wlk NG11 .... 184 C2
Kipling Cl
Nottingham NG1 .... 195 E4
Kipling St NG18 .... 102 A4
Kipps St NG1 .... 223 F3
Kirby Cl Bildworth NG21 118 A2
Keyworth NG12 .... 198 A1
Kirby Ctr Comp Sch
NG17 .... 115 D2
Kirby Dr DE74 .... 203 E1
Kirby Rd NG16 .... 144 A2
Kirk Ave DE74 .... 203 E1
Kirk Cl NG9 .... 183 E2
Kirk Dr NG22 .... 77 F3
Kirk Gate NG24 .... 124 C1
Kirk Hill NG13 .... 165 D1
Kirk La NG11 .... 196 B4
Kirk Ley Rd LE12 ...... 214 B4
Kirk Rd NG3 .... 162 A1
Kirk White Ct NG2 .... 173 E1
Kirk's Bldgs NG4 ...... 174 B4
Kirkbride Ct NG9 ...... 183 D2
Kirkby Folly Rd NG17 .. 101 D1
Kirkby Gdns NG2 ...... 173 E1
Kirkby House Dr NG17 . 114 C3
Kirkby in Ashfield Sta
NG17 .... 115 D3
Kirkby La NG16 .... 114 A2
Kirkby Mill View NG17 .. 114 C3
Kirkby Rd
Ravenshead NG15 ...... 116 B2
Sutton in A NG17 ...... 100 C1
Kirkby Woodhouse
Prim Sch NG17 .... 114 C1
Kirkdale Cl NG8 .... 171 D2
Kirkdale Gdns NG10 ... 193 D3
Kirkdale Rd
Long Eaton NG10 ...... 193 D3
Nottingham NG3 .... 174 A3
Kirke St DN22 .... 39 F4
Kirke White Ave NG10 .. 193 E4
Kirkfell Cl NG2 .... 186 B3
Kirkham Dr NG9 .... 182 C1
Kirkhill NG13 .... 177 F3
Kirkland Ave NG18 .... 101 F3
Kirkland Cl NG17 ...... 114 B1
Kirkland Dr NG9 .... 183 E1
Kirklands Rd NG5 ..... 162 A4
Kirklington Cty Prim Sch
NG22 .... 120 C4
Kirklington Rd
Bilsthorpe NG22 .... 105 E1
Eakring NG22 .... 106 C4
Rainworth NG21, NG22 . 104 B1
Southwell NG25 .... 121 E1
Kirkpatrick Dr S81 ..... 35 E4
Kirkstead Cl NG16 ..... 113 E2
Kirkstead Gdns NG3 ... 172 C4
Kirkstead Jun Sch NG16 113 E2

Kirkstead Rd NG16 .... 113 E2
Kirkstead St NG7 ...... 172 C4
Kirkstone Ct NG10 ..... 182 A1
Kirkstone Dr NG2 ...... 186 B4
Kirtle Cl NG8 .... 172 A4
Kirtley Dr NG7 .... 173 D1
Kirton Ave NG10 .... 193 E4
Kirton Cl Mansfield NG19 101 E4
Meden Vale NG20 ...... 74 C4
Kirton Rd NG22 .... 78 A3
Kirton Pk NG22 .... 78 B3
Kirton Rd NG22 .... 79 E3
Kissingate L Ctr NG20 . 72 C2
Kitchener Dr NG18 .... 102 B3
Kitchener Terr NG11 ... 59 D1
Kitson Ave NG16 .... 128 B2
Kittiwake Mews NG7 ... 222 A2
Kiwi Cl NG15 .... 145 E3
Knapp Ave NG16 .... 143 F1
Knaton Rd S81 .... 25 F4
Kneesall CE Prim Sch
NG22 .... 93 F3
Kneesall Gr NG15 ...... 146 A4
Kneesall Rd NG18 ..... 103 D3
Kneeton Cl Carlton NG4 162 B2
Nottingham NG5 .... 161 E2
Kneeton Rd NG13 ...... 165 F3
Kneeton Vale NG5 ..... 161 E2
Knight St NG4 .... 175 D3
Knight's Cl NG13 ...... 166 C2
Knight's Ct NG24 ...... 140 A4
Knighton Ave NG7 .... 222 A4
Knighton Rd NG5 ..... 161 E3
Knights Cl
West Bridgford NG2 .... 185 E2
Knightsbridge Dr
Nuthall NG16 .... 159 F2
West Bridgford NG2 .... 185 E2
Knightsbridge Gdns
NG15 .... 130 C1
Knipton Cl NG24 ...... 140 B2
Knitton Rd NG17 ...... 114 A3
Knoll Ave NG15 .... 146 A4
Knoll The
Mansfield NG18 .... 101 F3
Shirebrook NG20 .... 72 B2
Knott End S81 .... 16 C2
Knowle Hill NG16 ..... 159 D3
Knowle Pk NG16 ...... 159 D3
Knowles Wlk NG5 ...... 161 E4
Krebs Cl NG11 .... 184 B1
Kyle View NG5 .... 147 D1
Kyme St NG7 .... 222 B3
Kynance Cl DE55 ..... 113 E3
Kynance Gdns NG11 .. 185 D3

Labray Rd NG14 .... 148 C4
Laburnum Cl NG24 .... 140 B3
Laburnum Ave
Gainsborough DN21 .... 15 E1
Kirkby in A NG17 ...... 114 B2
Shirebrook NG20 .... 72 C3
Laburnum Cl
Hathern LE12 .... 213 D1
South Normanton DE55 . 113 D4
Worksop S80 .... 35 E1
Laburnum Gr
Beeston NG9 .... 184 A3
Carlton NG4 .... 174 C1
Mansfield Woodhouse NG19 88 A2
Laburnum Rd NG16 ... 16 C2
Sandiacre NG10 .... 173 A4
Lace Hall Museums NG1 223 E2
Lace Rd NG9 .... 183 F4
Lace St NG7 .... 172 B1
Laceby Ct NG19 .... 88 C2
Lacey Ave NG15 .... 146 A3
Lacey Cl DE7 .... 157 E2
Lacer Fields Rd DE75 . 143 D1
Lacer Gn NG24 .... 140 C2
Ladbrooke Cres NG6 .. 160 B2
Lady Bay Ave NG2 .... 173 F1
Lady Bay Bridge NG2 . 173 F1
Lady Bay Prim Sch NG2 174 A1
Lady Bay Rd NG2 ...... 174 A1
Lady Well La DN22 .... 52 A4
Ladybank Rise NG5 ... 162 B4
Ladybridge Cl NG9 ... 183 F2
Ladybrook Fst Sch NG19 101 E4
Ladybrook La NG18 .. 101 F4
Ladybrook Pl NG19 ... 101 F4
Ladycroft Ave NG15 .. 146 A4
Ladycross Inf Sch NG10 182 A3
Ladylea Rd NG10 ..... 193 D2
Ladysmith Rd NG2 ... 174 A2
Ladysmock Gdns NG2 173 E1
Ladywood La NG23 ... 80 C3
Lake Ave NG19 .... 101 F4
Lake Farm Rd NG21 .. 103 F1
Lake St NG7 .... 222 B4
Lake View Prim Sch
NG22 .... 77 D2
Lakeland Ave NG15 .. 146 B3
Lakeside Ave NG10 .. 193 D1
Lakeside Cres NG10 . 193 D1
Lakeside Inf Sch NG10 193 D3
Lamartine St NG3 ..... 223 F3
Lamartine St NG3 ..... 223 F3
Lamb Cl NG24 .... 139 E4
Lamb Close Dr NG16 . 144 A2
Lamb La S81 .... 16 B3
Lambcroft Rd NG16 .. 113 E2

Lambert Ave NG22 ... 184 A4
Lambert Gdns NG8 .... 172 B4
Lambert St NG7 ...... 172 C4
Lambeth Rd NG5 ..... 147 D1
Lambie Cl NG8 .... 172 B3
Lambley Ave
Nottingham NG3 .... 102 C3
Nottingham NG3 .... 162 A2
Lambley Bridle Rd NG14 163 E3
Lambley La
Burton Joyce NG14 .... 163 F3
Carlton NG4 .... 162 C2
Lambley Prim Sch NG4 163 D4
Lambley Rd NG14 ..... 150 A1
Lambourne Cres NG14 . 150 C1
Lambourne Gdns NG5 . 162 A3
Lamcote Cl DE7 .... 157 F2
Lamcote Gdns NG12 .. 175 F2
Lamcote Gr NG2 ..... 173 E1
Lamcote Mews NG4 ... 175 F2
Lamcote St NG2 ...... 173 E1
Laming Gap La NG12 . 198 C3
Lamins La NG5 .... 147 E2
Lammas Cl NG17 ..... 100 C1
Lammas Gdns
East Bridgford NG13 .. 165 E2
Nottingham NG2 ...... 173 E1
Lammas La NG13 ..... 165 E2
Lammas Rd NG17 .... 100 C1
Lammas Sch The NG17 100 C1
Lamond Cl NG19 ..... 101 F3
Lamorna Gr NG11 .... 185 D3
Lamp Wood Cl NG14 . 148 C4
Lamplands NG12 ..... 187 F2
Lanark Cl NG8 .... 172 B2
Lancaster Ave
Sandiacre NG10 .... 182 A2
Stapleford NG9 .... 182 C4
Lancaster Dr DN10 ... 9 F4
Lancaster Rd
Bestwood Village NG6 . 146 C2
Gringley on t H DN10 .. 22 A4
Hucknall NG15 .... 145 E2
Nottingham NG3 ...... 174 A4
Lancaster Way NG8 ... 159 E1
Lancaster Wlk S81 .... 35 F4
Lancastrian Way S81 . 36 A3
Lancelot Dr NG16 .... 145 D1
Lancelyn Gdns NG2 ... 185 F2
Lancaster Cres DN11 . 8 A4
Landa Gr NG22 ...... 66 A2
Landcroft La NG14 ... 165 E2
Landcroft La LE12 .... 204 B1
Landmere Cl DE7 .... 157 E2
Landmere Gdns NG3 . 161 F1
Landmere La
West Bridgford NG2 .. 185 E2
Landmere Rd NG7 .... 221 F3
Landsdown Gr NG10 . 182 C1
Landsdowne Ct DN22 . 39 E2
Landsdowne Rd NG5 . 160 C2
Landseer Cl
Nottingham NG2 ...... 222 A4
Southwell NG25 ...... 136 B4
Lane End NG17 ...... 115 D3
Laneham Ave NG5 ... 162 A4
Laneham Rd NG22 .. 54 A1
Lanercost Mews S81 . 35 F1
Lanesborough Ct LE11 220 A1
Laneside Ave NG12 .. 182 C1
Laneward Cl DE7 .... 157 E2
Langar CE Sch NG13 . 190 B1
Langar Cl NG5 ...... 161 E2
Langar La
Colston Bassett NG12 . 200 C4
Harby LE14 .... 202 B2
Langar Pl NG19 ..... 103 D4
Langar La NG11 ..... 196 C2
Langdale Cl NG24 ... 139 F2
Langdale Dr
Long Eaton NG10 ..... 193 D3
Tickhill DN11 .... 8 A4
Langdale Gr NG13 ... 177 D2
Langdale Rd
Nottingham NG3 ..... 174 B3
Worksop S81 .... 35 F4
Langdon Cl NG10 ... 182 A1
Langdown Cl NG6 ... 160 A4
Langford La NG23 .. 111 D2
Langford Rd Arnold NG5 162 A4
Mansfield NG18 ..... 101 E3
Langford St NG17 ... 100 C2
Langham Ave NG3 .. 174 A3
Langham Dr NG14 .. 163 F3
Langley Ave Arnold NG5 161 F3
Ilkeston DE7 .... 157 F3
Langley Cl NG19 ... 87 F1
Langley Dr DE74 ... 203 F1
Langley Mill CE Inf Sch
NG16 .... 143 D2
Langley Mill Inf Sch
NG16 .... 143 D2
Langley Mill Jun Sch
NG16 .... 143 D2
Langley Mill Sta NG16 143 D2
Langley Pk NG16 .... 143 D3
Langold Cl S81 ...... 35 F1
Langold Cty Prim Sch
Jun & Inf Sch S81 .... 16 B2
Langstrath Dr NG2 .. 186 B2

Langstrath Rd NG7 ... 184 C1
Langton Ave NG17 ... 114 B3
Langton Hollow NG16 128 B3
Langton Rd NG17 .... 100 C1
Langtree Gdns NG13 . 177 F3
Lanity Gr NG7 .... 161 D1
Langwell Dr NG19 ... 89 E1
Langwith Bassett Prim Sch
NG20 .... 72 C4
Langwith Ctry Pk NG20 58 C1
Langwith Dr NG20 ... 58 C1
Langwith Maltings NG20 72 C4
Langwith Rd Cuckney NG20 60 A1
Shirebrook NG20 ...... 72 C3
Lansbury Ave NG22 .. 77 F3
Lansbury Dr
Bilsthorpe NG22 ...... 105 F4
South Normanton DE55 113 D3
Lansbury Gdns NG18 . 102 C4
Lansbury Rd
Bilsthorpe NG22 ...... 105 F4
Edwinstowe NG21 ... 76 A1
New Balderton NG24 . 140 B2
Sutton in A NG17 .... 100 C1
Lansdall Ave DN21 ... 24 C2
Lansdown Cl NG9 ... 183 D2
Lansdowne Ave NG18 102 B1
Lansdowne Dr
Loughborough LE11 .. 220 A1
West Bridgford NG2 .. 185 E2
Lansic La NG14 ...... 151 E1
Lansing Cl NG11 ..... 195 F4
Lantern La
Lantern Lane Prim Sch
LE12 .... 205 F1
Lanthwaite Cl NG7 .. 184 C1
Lanthwaite Rd NG7 . 184 C1
Lapford Cl NG3 ...... 162 B3
Larch Ave
Mansfield Woodhouse NG19 88 A3
Shirebrook NG20 .... 72 B2
Larch Cl Bingham NG13 178 A2
Hucknall NG15 ...... 146 A3
Nottingham NG5 .... 161 E4
Larch Cres Beeston NG9 183 E4
Eastwood NG16 .... 143 F1
Larch Ct DN21 ...... 15 F1
Larch Dr NG10 ..... 182 A4
Larch Gdns NG6 .... 160 A4
Larch Rd NG17 .... 115 D3
Larch Way NG12 ... 198 A1
Larchdale Cl DE55 . 113 D2
Larchene Ave NG16 171 E2
Largs Cl NG5 .... 146 C1
Lark Cl NG9 .... 183 D3
Lark Spinney S81 ... 35 E3
Larkdale St NG7 .... 222 C4
Larkfield Ave NG17 . 114 C1
Larkfield Rd NG16 .. 159 D3
Larkfields Jun & Inf Sch
NG16 .... 159 D3
Larkhall Pl NG19 ... 101 F3
Larklands Ave NG10 170 A4
Larklands Inf Sch DE7 170 A4
Larkspur Ave NG5 .. 147 F1
Larkspur Cl
Mansfield NG19 ..... 88 B1
South Normanton DE55 113 D4
Larpit Gn S80 ...... 45 D3
Larwood S81 .... 36 A3
Larwood Cres NG17 114 C1
Larwood Gr NG5 ... 161 E2
Lascelles Ave NG4 . 162 B1
Latham St NG6 ..... 160 A4
Lathkill Ave DE7 ... 157 F3
Lathkill Cl NG6 .... 160 A4
Lathkill Dr NG16 .. 128 C4
Lathkilldale Cres NG10 193 D3
Latimer Cl NG6 .... 160 B3
Latimer Dr NG9 ... 171 D2
Launceston Cres NG11 185 D2
Launder St DN21 .. 15 E4
Launds Ave NG16 .. 128 B4

Laurel Ave
Church Warsop NG20 . 74 A4
Keyworth NG12 ...... 197 F2
Mansfield NG18 ..... 102 B3
Mansfield Woodhouse NG19 89 D1
Mastreton DE11 ..... 6 C2
Laurel Cl
Gainsborough DN21 . 15 F1
Shirebrook NG20 ... 72 B3
Wysall NG12 .... 207 E2
Laurel Cres
Long Eaton NG10 ... 193 E2
Nuthall NG16 .... 159 D3
Laurel Gr
Kirkby in A NG17 .... 115 D3
South Normanton DE55 113 D2
Laurel Rd NG4 ..... 174 B4
Laurie Ave NG7 .... 173 D4
Laurie Cl NG7 ..... 173 D4
Lauriston Dr NG6 .. 160 B2
Lavender Cl NG8 ... 159 F1
Lavender Cres NG4 . 162 B1
Lavender Gr NG9 .. 184 A3
Lavender Wlk NG3 . 173 E4
Lavenham Mews S80 . 35 F1
Laver Cl NG5 ...... 162 A4
Laverick Rd NG16 . 128 A2

Lawdon Rd NG5 .... 148 A1
Lawley Ave NG7 .... 172 A1
Lawn Ave NG17 .... 100 C1
Lawn La Old Dalby LE14 .... 218 C1
 Sutton in A NG17 .... 100 C1
Lawn Mill Rd NG16 .... 158 C4
Lawn Rd Carlton in S S81 .... 25 F4
 Sutton in A NG17 .... 101 D2
Lawns Rd NG17 .... 129 F4
Lawns The
 Collingham NG23 .... 98 A1
 Whatton NG13 .... 179 D2
Lawnwood Ave DN22 .... 50 A2
Lawnwood La DN22 .... 50 A2
Lawrence Ave
 Awsworth NG16 .... 158 B2
 Carlton NG4 .... 174 C3
 Eastwood NG16 .... 143 F1
 Kirkby in A NG17 .... 114 C3
 Mansfield Woodhouse NG19 .. 88 A2
Lawrence Cl NG12 .... 187 F2
Lawrence Cres NG17 .... 101 D2
Lawrence Dr NG16 .... 143 E4
Lawrence Pk NG16 .... 129 D2
Lawrence Pl NG24 .... 125 D1
Lawrence St
 Long Eaton NG10 .... 193 E4
 Newark-on-T NG24 .... 125 D1
 Sandiacre NG10 .... 182 B3
 Stapleford NG9 .... 182 B3
Lawson Ave NG10 .... 193 F4
Lawson Cl NG23 .... 50 C1
Lawson Sq S81 .... 18 A1
Lawson St W NG7 .... 222 C4
Lawton Dr NG6 .... 146 B1
Laxton Ave
 Nottingham NG6 .... 160 B3
 Sutton in A NG17 .... 101 E1
Laxton Dr Hucknall NG15 ...... 145 F3
 Meden Vale NG20 .... 74 B4
Laxton Heritage Mus
 NG22 .... 79 E2
Laxton Rd NG22 .... 79 E2
Laxton Visitors Ctr NG22 ... 79 E2
Laycock Ave DN10 .... 12 C1
Layton Ave NG18 .... 102 A4
Layton Burroughs
 13 NG18 .... 102 A4
Le Brun Sq S81 .... 25 F4
Le Page Ct NG8 .... 172 A4
Lea Cl NG15 .... 117 D1
Lea Ct S80 .... 35 E1
Lea La NG16 .... 128 C3
Lea Rd
 Gainsborough DN21 .... 24 C3
 Market Warsop NG20 .... 74 B2
 Ravenshead NG15 .... 117 D1
Lea Rd W DN21 .... 24 B3
Lea Road Sta DN22 .... 113 D2
Leabrook Cl NG11 .... 184 B2
Leabrook Gdns NG15 .... 146 B4
Leabrooks Ave
 Mansfield Woodhouse NG19 .. 88 B3
 Sutton in A NG17 .... 101 E1
Leach Cl NG22 .... 54 B1
Leachcroft Hill NG25 .... 136 A4
Leacroft Rd NG8 .... 172 B4
Lead Hill S80 .... 35 F1
Leadale Ave NG15 .... 146 B4
Leadale Cres NG19 .... 88 C3
Leafe Cl NG11 .... 131 D1
Leafe Cl NG9 .... 183 E1
Leafield DN22 .... 39 E4
Leafield Gn NG7 .... 184 B1
Leahurst Gdns NG2 .... 186 A3
Leahurst Rd NG2 .... 186 A3
Leake La LE12 .... 214 B2
Leake Rd Costock LE12 .... 206 A1
 Gotham NG11 .... 205 E3
Leam Glen NG19 .... 88 B1
Leamington Dr
 Beeston NG9 .... 183 E2
 South Normanton DE55 .... 113 D3
 Sutton in A NG17 .... 114 C4
Leamington Hall NG17 .... 100 C1
Leamington Jun &
 Mix Inf Sch NG17 .... 114 C4
Leander Cl NG11 .... 185 D3
Leas Ave NG19 .... 87 D3
Leas Park Jun Sch NG18 ...... 88 B2
Leas Rd NG19 .... 88 B2
Leas The NG14 .... 164 A3
Leatherlands DE74 .... 203 E2
Leaway The NG20 .... 72 B2
Lechlade Rd NG5 .... 161 D3
Ledbury Vale NG8 .... 172 A4
Lee Cres DE7 .... 170 A4
Lee La DE75 .... 143 D1
Lee Rd
 Burton Joyce NG14 .... 164 A3
 Calverton NG14 .... 148 B4
Leech Ct NG16 .... 158 A4
Leeds Cl NG18 .... 34 C4
Leeks Rd NG15 .... 121 F1
Leeming Cl NG18 .... 74 B3
Leeming La N NG19, NG20 ... 88 C4
Leeming La N NG19 .... 88 C3
Leeming La S NG19 .... 88 B1
Leeming Pk NG18 .... 88 B2
Leeming St NG18 .... 102 A4
Leen Cl
 Bestwood Village NG6 .... 146 C2
 Hucknall NG15 .... 146 B4

Leen Ct NG22 .... 78 A2
Leen Dr Hucknall NG15 .... 131 D1
 Nottingham NG6 .... 146 B1
Leen Gate NG7 .... 172 C1
Leen Mills La NG15 .... 131 D1
Leen Mills Sch NG15 .... 146 A4
Leen Pl NG7 .... 222 A3
Leen Valley Dr NG20 .... 72 C2
Leen Valley Way NG15 .... 146 B3
Lees Ave NG19 .... 101 E4
Lees Barn Rd NG12 .... 175 E1
Lees Hill St NG2 .... 173 F2
Lees La DE55 .... 113 D3
Lees Rd NG3 .... 162 A1
Leeway Cl NG21 .... 103 F1
Leeway Rd
 Mansfield NG1 .... 103 F1
 Southwell NG25 .... 121 E1
Legion Dr NG17 .... 100 B3
Leicester Rd LE11 .... 220 B1
Leicester St NG10 .... 193 F3
Leigh Cl NG2 .... 185 E3
Leigh Rd NG9 .... 182 C2
Leighton St NG3 .... 173 F3
Leiston Gdns NG5 .... 161 D4
Leivers Ave NG5 .... 161 E4
Leivers Cl LE12 .... 205 F1
Lema Cl NG6 .... 160 B4
Lemont Rd NG19 .... 89 D1
Lemyngton St LE11 .... 220 A2
Lendrum Ct NG14 .... 163 F2
Lennox St NG1 .... 223 F3
Lenton Ave
 Nottingham NG7 .... 222 C1
 Tollerton NG12 .... 186 B1
Lenton Bvd NG7 .... 222 B2
Lenton Cir NG12 .... 186 A1
Lenton Ct NG7 .... 222 B2
Lenton Hall Dr NG7 .... 172 B1
Lenton Ind Est E NG7 .... 184 C4
Lenton Ind Est W NG7 .... 184 C4
Lenton La
 Nottingham NG7 .... 184 C3
 Nottingham NG7 .... 184 C4
Lenton Manor NG7 .... 222 A1
Lenton Rd NG7 .... 223 D2
Lenton St NG10 .... 182 B3
Lenton St NG16 .... 182 B4
Leonard Ave NG5 .... 161 D1
Leonard St NG6 .... 160 B3
Leopold St
 Long Eaton NG10 .... 193 E4
 Loughborough LE11 .... 220 A3
 Sutton in A NG17 .... 100 C1
Leroy Wallace Ave NG2 ..... 222 B4
Lerwick Cl NG11 .... 185 D1
Leslie Ave
 Beeston NG9 .... 183 F3
 Kimberley NG16 .... 158 C3
 6 Nottingham NG7 .... 173 D4
Leslie Gr NG14 .... 148 C4
Leslie Rd NG7 .... 173 D4
Letchworth Cres NG9 .... 183 E2
Letcombe Rd NG11 .... 184 C2
Letwell Ave S81 .... 16 A1
Levels La Blaxton DN9 .... 1 A4
 Misson DN10 .... 4 C4
Levens Cl NG2 .... 186 B3
Leverton Gn NG7 .... 184 C1
Leverton Rd
 Mansfield NG19 .... 101 F4
 Retford DN22 .... 40 B4
 Sturton le S DN22 .... 32 B2
Leverton Wlk NG5 .... 162 A4
Levick Ct 3 NG2 .... 173 E1
Lewcote La DE7 .... 157 D1
Lewindon Ct NG5 .... 161 F2
Lewis Cl NG3 .... 223 F4
Lewis St DN21 .... 24 B4
Lexington Ct NG22 .... 65 F1
Lexington Gdns
 Nottingham NG5 .... 161 E2
 Tuxford NG22 .... 65 F1
Ley Croft NG19 .... 88 B3
Ley La
 East Drayton DN22 .... 53 E2
 Mansfield Woodhouse NG19 .. 88 B2
Ley St NG4 .... 175 D4
Leybourne Dr NG5 .... 160 C3
Leyland Cl NG9 .... 182 C1
Leys La DN10 .... 12 C1
Leys Rd NG11 .... 196 B3
Leys The
 Lowdham NG14 .... 150 B1
 Normanton-on-t-W NG12 ... 197 F4
 Nottingham NG11 .... 184 B1
Leyton Ave NG17 .... 101 D3
Leyton Cres NG9 .... 184 A3
Liber Cl NG18 .... 102 C4
Library Rd NG7 .... 172 B1
Lichfield Ave NG18 .... 102 B1
Lichfield Cl
 Beeston NG9 .... 182 C2
 Mansfield NG18 .... 102 B1
 Worksop S81 .... 36 A3
Lichfield La NG18 .... 102 B2
Lichfield Rd NG2 .... 174 A2
Lichfield Wlk S81 .... 25 F4
Liddell Gr NG8 .... 171 F2
Liddington St NG7 .... 160 C1
Lido Cl NG6 .... 160 A4
Lifton Ave DN22 .... 29 F1
Lightfoot Cl NG24 .... 140 C4
Lilac Ave NG4 .... 174 B4
Lilac Cl Keyworth NG12 ..... 198 A1
 Newark-on-T NG24 .... 139 F2
 7 Nottingham NG8 .... 159 F1
Lilac Cres NG9 .... 184 A3

Lilac Gr Bawtry DN10 .... 9 F4
 Beeston NG9 .... 184 A3
 Carlton NG4 .... 163 D1
 Kirkby in A NG17 .... 114 B3
 Shirebrook NG20 .... 72 B3
 South Normanton DE55 .... 113 D2
 Stapleford NG9 .... 182 C3
Lilac Mews DE7 .... 157 E2
Lilac Rd NG15 .... 146 A3
Lilee Cl S81 .... 36 A3
Lilleker Rise NG5 .... 147 F1
Lillington Rd NG6 .... 160 A4
Lily Ave NG4 .... 175 D4
Lily Gr NG9 .... 184 A3
Limb Cres NG17 .... 100 C1
Lime Ave Firbeck S81 .... 16 A3
 Hythwaite NG17 .... 100 A2
 Langley Mill NG16 .... 143 E1
 Loughborough LE11 .... 220 B2
 Sutton in A NG17 .... 100 C2
Lime Cl Nuthall NG16 .... 159 D3
 Pinxton NG16 .... 113 E2
 Radcliffe on T NG12 .... 175 F2
Lime Cres NG20 .... 73 F4
 Long Eaton NG10 .... 193 E4
 Mansfield Woodhouse NG19 ... 89 E1
 Newark-on-T NG24 .... 139 F4
 Retford DN22 .... 39 E4
 Sandiacre NG10 .... 182 C3
 South Normanton DE55 .... 113 D3
 Stapleford NG9 .... 182 B3
Lime Gr Ave NG9 .... 183 F3
Lime La NG5 .... 147 F2
Lime St Kirkby in A NG17 .. 115 D3
 Nottingham NG6 .... 160 A4
 Sutton in A NG17 .... 101 D2
Lime Terr NG10 .... 193 E4
Lime Tree Ave
 Carlton in S S81 .... 25 F4
 Gainsborough DN21 .... 15 E1
 Glapwell S44 .... 86 A4
 Kirkby in A NG17 .... 114 C3
 Mansfield Woodhouse NG19 ... 88 A3
 Nottingham NG8 .... 160 B2
 Retford DN22 .... 39 E4
 Sutton in A NG17 .... 100 B3
Lime Tree Cl
 Collingham NG23 .... 112 A4
 New Ollerton NG22 .... 77 E3
Lime Tree Cres NG10 .... 193 E4
Lime Tree Ct NG9 .... 172 A1
Lime Tree Gdns NG14 ...... 150 C1
Lime Tree Pl
 Mansfield NG18 .... 102 B3
 Ranworth NG21 .... 104 B1
Lime Tree Rd
 Elkesley DN22 .... 50 A2
 Hucknall NG15 .... 146 A2
 New Ollerton NG22 .... 77 E3
Limehurst Ave LE11 .... 220 A3
Limehurst High Sch
 (Annexe) LE11 .... 220 A2
Limekiln Ct NG6 .... 160 A4
Limekilns NG18 .... 103 D3
Limes Ave NG20 .... 59 D1
Limes Cres NG20 .... 72 B3
Limes Ct NG17 .... 101 E1
Limes The DN10 .... 14 A1
Limestone Terr NG19 .... 88 A2
Limetree Ave S80 .... 48 B3
Limetree Cl NG12 .... 197 F1
Limmen Gdns NG3 .... 173 F3
Limpenny St NG7 .... 222 C4
Linby Ave Hucknall NG15 ... 146 A4
 Mansfield NG18 .... 101 E3
Linby Cl Carlton NG4 .... 162 C1
 Nottingham NG5 .... 161 E3
Linby Gdns Papplewick
 Prim Sch NG15 .... 131 D2
Linby Dr NG8 .... 159 E1
Linby Gr NG15 .... 146 A4
Linby La NG15 .... 132 A2
Linby Rd NG15 .... 146 A4
Linby Wlk NG15 .... 146 A4
Lincoln Ave NG10 .... 182 A2
Lincoln Cir NG7 .... 222 C2
Lincoln Cl
 Stapleford NG9 .... 170 C1
 Tibshelf DE55 .... 99 D3
Lincoln Ct NG8 .... 171 F4
Lincoln Dr NG19 .... 88 B2
Lincoln Gr NG12 .... 175 F2
Lincoln Rd
 East Markham NG22 .... 66 A4
 Fenton LN1 .... 55 E3
 Newark-on-T NG24 .... 125 D2
 Saxilby LN1 .... 57 E2
 Tuxford NG22 .... 66 A2
Lincoln Road Bridge
 NG24 .... 125 D1
Lincoln St
 Gainsborough DN21 .... 15 E1
 Newark-on-T NG24 .... 125 D1
 Nottingham NG1 .... 223 E2
 Nottingham, Old Basford
 NG6 .... 160 C2
 Tibshelf DE55 .... 99 D3
Lincoln View S80 .... 36 A1
Lincolnshire TEC DN21 .... 15 E2
Lind Cl NG21 .... 103 F1
Lindale Cl NG10 .... 186 B3
Lindbridge Rd NG8 .... 159 F1
Linden Ave
 New Balderton NG24 .... 140 A3
 Nottingham NG11 .... 184 B1
 Tuxford NG22 .... 66 A1

Linden Gr Beeston NG9 .... 184 A3
 Carlton NG4 .... 163 D1
 Kirkby in A NG17 .... 114 B3
 Sandiacre NG10 .... 182 A4
 Shirebrook NG20 .... 72 C2
 Stapleford NG9 .... 182 C3
Linden Rd
 Loughborough LE11 .... 220 A3
 Mansfield NG18 .... 102 C4
Linden St Mansfield NG18 ... 88 A1
 Nottingham NG3 .... 173 E4
 Shirebrook NG20 .... 72 C2
Linden Terr DN21 .... 24 B4
Lindfield Cl NG8 .... 160 A1
Lindfield Rd NG8 .... 159 F1
Lindholme Way NG17 .... 100 C3
Lindhurst La NG18 .... 102 C2
Lindisfarne Gdns 6 NG5 ... 147 D1
Lindley St
 Eastwood NG16 .... 144 A2
 Mansfield NG18 .... 102 A4
 Selston NG16 .... 128 B3
Lindley Terr 2 NG7 .... 172 C4
Lindleys La NG17 .... 115 D2
Lindleys Ct NG17 .... 115 D2
Lindrick Cl
 Ilkeston DE7 .... 8 A3
Lindrick Cl Carlton in S S81 ... 25 F4
 Mansfield Woodhouse NG19 ... 88 B3
 West Bridgford NG2 .... 186 B2
 Worksop S81 .... 36 A3
Lindrick Ct NG22 .... 39 E1
Lindrick La DN11 .... 8 A3
Lindrick Rd NG17 .... 114 C4
Lindsay Ave
 Annesley Woodhouse NG17 115 D1
 Newark-on-T NG24 .... 139 F2
Lindsay Cl NG18 .... 102 A3
Lindsay Dr NG18 .... 103 D2
Lindsey Rd DN11 .... 9 D3
Lindum Gr 23 NG2 .... 173 F2
Lindum Mews NG14 .... 148 A4
Lindum Rd NG6 .... 160 B2
Lindum St NG24 .... 140 A4
Lindwall Ct S81 .... 36 A3
Lindy Cl NG12 .... 199 F1
Linecroft La DN10 .... 14 B4
Linette Cl NG5 .... 161 D1
Linford NG9 .... 171 D2
Ling Beeches DN22 .... 39 E2
Ling Cres NG11 .... 196 B4
Ling Rd LE11 .... 220 A1
Lingfield Cl NG18 .... 103 C3
Lingfield Cl LE11 .... 220 A1
Lingfield Ct NG8 .... 171 E2
Lingford NG12 .... 188 A2
Lingford St NG15 .... 146 A3
Lingforest Cl NG18 .... 103 D3
Lingforest Rd NG18 .... 103 D3
Lings La NG12 .... 207 F4
Lings View NG20 .... 74 B2
Lingwood Gr NG18 .... 103 D3
Lingwood La NG14 .... 149 D2
Link Rd NG19 .... 88 A3
Linkmel Cl NG2 .... 173 D1
Linkmel Rd NG16 .... 143 E2
Linkmell Cl NG2 .... 186 B3
Links The NG18 .... 103 D3
Linkfield Cl NG2 .... 185 E1
Linley Cl NG23 .... 112 A4
Linnell St NG3 .... 173 F3
Linnet Dr NG18 .... 102 C4
Linnets The S81 .... 35 E4
Linsdale Cl NG8 .... 171 D3
Linsdale Gdns NG4 .... 162 B2
Lintin Ave NG21 .... 75 F1
Linton Cl Farndon NG24 ... 139 D3
 Mansfield NG18 .... 103 D2
Linton Dr NG22 .... 77 F3
Linton Rise NG3 .... 174 A3
Linwood Cl DN21 .... 24 C4
Linwood Cres
 Eastwood NG16 .... 144 A3
 Ravenshead NG15 .... 116 C2
Linwood Ct NG19 .... 88 C2
Lion Cl NG8 .... 160 B1
Liquorice La S81 .... 26 A2
Lisle St LE11 .... 220 A3
Lismore Cl NG2 .... 222 A3
Lismore Cl NG19 .... 101 E3
Lissington Rd DN21 .... 24 C4
Lister Ct 8 NG7 .... 172 C1
Lister Gate NG1 .... 223 E2
Lister Rd NG7 .... 172 C1
Listerwell Cres NG11 ...... 195 F4
Litchen Cl DE7 .... 157 F1
Litchfield Cl NG10 .... 194 A4
Litchfield Rise NG5 .... 147 F1
Little Barn Ct NG18 .... 102 C3
Little Barn Gdns NG18 ..... 102 C3
Little Barn La NG18 .... 102 C3
Little Belt The DN21 .... 15 E2
Little Debdale La NG18 .... 102 A2
Little Debdale La NG17 .... 87 F1
Little Hallam La DE7 .... 170 A3
Little Hayes NG2 .... 185 E2
Little Hollies NG19 .... 89 D1
Little John Ave NG20 .... 72 B3
Little John Cl NG22 .... 77 E3
Little John Dr NG21 .... 104 A1
Little John Wlk 14 NG3 .... 173 E4
Little La Blyth S81 .... 18 A2
 Calverton NG14 .... 148 B4
 Collingham NG23 .... 111 F4
 Edingley NG22 .... 120 B2
 Gringley on t H DN10 .... 12 C1
 Hythwaite NG17 .... 99 F1

Little La continued
 Kimberley NG16 .... 158 C3
 Pleasleyhill NG19 .... 87 D3
 Shirebrook NG20 .... 72 B2
 Thorpe Salvin S80 .... 34 A3
 Tollerton NG12 .... 186 C2
Little Lunnon NG11 .... 194 C3
Little Mdw NG12 .... 188 A1
Little Moor La LE11 .... 220 B2
Little Oak Ave NG17 .... 130 A4
Little Oak Dr NG17 .... 129 F4
Little Oakwood Dr NG5 .... 146 B1
Little Ox NG4 .... 174 C2
Little Ricket La NG15 ...... 116 B2
Little Tennis St NG2 .... 174 A2
Little Tennis St S NG2 ..... 174 A1
Little Top La NG20 .... 20 B1
Littleborough Rd DN22 ...... 33 D2
Littlegreen Rd NG5 .... 161 F3
Littlemoor La NG11 .... 196 C2
Littleover Ave NG18 .... 103 D3
Littlewood Gdns NG8 ...... 171 E3
Littlewood La NG19 .... 88 A3
Littleworth NG18 .... 102 B3
Litton Ave NG17 .... 101 D3
Litton Cl Arnold NG5 ...... 161 F2
 Ilkeston DE7 .... 157 F2
 Ravenshead NG15 .... 117 D2
Litton Rd NG19 .... 88 C2
Littondale S81 .... 36 A4
Liverpool St NG3 .... 173 F3
Livingstone St NG15 .... 130 C3
Llanberis Gr NG8 .... 160 A3
Lloyd St NG5 .... 161 E1
Loach Ct NG8 .... 172 B3
Lobelia Cl NG3 .... 173 E4
Lock La
 Long Eaton NG10 .... 193 E2
 Sandiacre NG10 .... 182 B2
Lockerbie St NG4 .... 174 C3
Locksley La NG11 .... 184 C2
Lockwood Cl
 Beeston NG9 .... 184 B2
 10 Nottingham NG5 .... 147 D1
Lockwood Dr DN22 .... 39 E2
Lodge Cl Arnold NG5 ...... 147 F1
 Nottingham NG8 .... 172 B4
Lodge Farm La NG5 .... 147 F1
Lodge La Elston NG23 ..... 153 E2
 Kirkby in A NG17 .... 115 E2
 Screveton NG13 .... 166 B3
 Tuxford NG22 .... 66 A1
Lodge Rd
 Eastwood NG16 .... 158 A4
 Long Eaton NG10 .... 193 E3
Lodgefield La NG14 .... 151 F1
Lodgewood Cl NG6 .... 160 A3
Lodore Cl NG2 .... 186 B3
Lodore Rd S81 .... 36 A3
Logan Sq NG6 .... 160 B3
Lois Ave NG7 .... 222 B1
Lombard Cl NG7 .... 222 B2
Lombard St
 Newark-on-T NG24 .... 139 F4
 Orston NG13 .... 180 A3
Lonan Cl NG19 .... 89 D1
London La
 Willoughby-on-t-W LE12 .. 217 E4
 Wymeswold LE12 .... 216 A2
London Rd
 Kegworth DE74 .... 203 E1
 Newark-on-T NG24 .... 140 B3
 Nottingham NG2 .... 173 E1
 Retford DN22 .... 40 A2
Long Acre NG15 .... 145 E4
Long Brecks La S81 .... 18 B1
Long Chaworth
 CE Prim Sch LE14 .... 211 E2
Long Eaton Lower Sch
 NG10 .... 193 E3
Long Eaton Sta NG10 ...... 193 D3
Long Hill Rise NG15 .... 145 F3
Long La
 Barkestone-le-V NG13 .... 192 C1
 Barnby in t W NG24 .... 141 F4
 Beeston NG9 .... 183 F2
 Carlton in L S81 .... 25 F3
 East Drayton DN22 .... 53 E2
 Farndon NG24 .... 139 D3
 Hardstoft DE4 .... 210 B3
 Hickling LE14 .... 210 B3
 Kegworth DE74 .... 203 E3
 Shipley DE75 .... 157 E3
 Shirebrook NG20 .... 72 C2
 Stathern LE14 .... 202 C2
 Watnall NG16 .... 145 D1
Long Mdw
 Farnsfield NG22 .... 120 A3
 Mansfield Woodhouse NG19 ... 88 B3
Long Mdws DN10 .... 11 D2
Long Meadow Hill NG14 .. 150 A1
Long Row
 Kingston-on-S LE12 .... 204 A2
 Newark-on-T NG24 .... 140 A4
 Nottingham NG1 .... 223 E2
Long Row W NG1 .... 223 E2
Long Stoop Way NG19 ..... 103 D4
Longacre NG5 .... 161 F2
Longbeck Ave NG3 .... 162 A3
Longcliff Cl LE14 .... 218 C2
Longcliff Hill LE14 .... 218 C2
Longcroft View S80 .... 45 D3
Longdale NG19 .... 88 C3
Longdale Ave NG15 .... 117 D3
Longdale Craft Ctr & Mus
 NG15 .... 132 B3

ongdale La
Calverton NG21 133 D3
Ravenshead NG15 132 B4
ongdale Rd NG5 161 E3
ongden Cl NG9 170 C1
ongden St 11 NG3 173 F3
ongden Terr
Market Warsop NG20 74 A2
Stanton Hill NG17 100 B3
ongfellow Dr
Balderton NG24 140 B3
Worksop S81 36 A2
ongfellows Cl NG5 161 D4
ongfield La DE7 170 A3
ongford Cres NG6 146 B1
ongford Wlk NG18 103 D3
onghedge La
Bottesford NG13 180 C2
Flawborough NG13, NG23 168 A1
Orston NG13 180 C4
Pleasley NG19 86 C3
Sibthorpe NG13 167 F3
onghill Rise NG17 114 C1
ongholme Rd DN22 40 A4
onghurst S81 36 A3
onghurst View S80 45 D3
ongland La NG22 119 E2
onglands Cl NG9 184 A2
onglands Dr NG2 186 B3
onglands Rd NG9 184 A2
ongleat Cres NG9 183 E3
ongmead Cl NG5 161 E3
ongmead Dr
Fiskerton NG25 137 F2
Nottingham NG5 161 E3
ongmoor Ave NG14 164 C4
ongmoor Gdns NG10 182 A1
ongmoor La
Long Eaton NG10 182 A1
Sandiacre NG10 182 A2
Scarrington NG13 179 D4
ongmoor Prim Sch
NG10 182 B2
ongmoor Rd NG10 182 A1
ongnor Wlk NG18 103 D3
ongore Sq NG8 172 B2
ongridge Rd NG5 161 F3
ongshaw Rd NG18 103 D3
ongster La NG20 73 E2
ongstone Way NG19 101 E3
ongue Dr NG14 148 B4
ongwall Ave NG2 173 D1
ongwest Croft NG14 148 B4
ongwood Ct NG5 160 C4
ongwood Inf Sch NG16 113 E1
ongwood Rd NG16 113 F1
onsdale Dr NG9 182 C1
onsdale Rd NG7 222 A4
ord Haddon Rd DE7 157 F1
ord Nelson St NG2 173 F2
ord St
Gainsborough DN21 24 B4
Mansfield NG18 102 A3
Nottingham NG2 173 F2
ordship La NG13 180 A3
orimer Ave NG4 162 C1
orne Cl 10 NG3 173 E4
orne Gr NG12 175 F2
orne House Sch DN22 40 A3
orne Wlk 11 NG3 173 E4
ortas Rd NG5 160 C1
oscoe Gdns 9 NG5 161 D1
oscoe Mount Rd NG5 161 E1
oscoe Rd NG5 161 E1
othian Rd NG12 186 B1
othmore Ct 7 NG2 173 D1
otus Cl NG3 173 F4
oughbon NG13 180 A4
oughborough Ave NG2 173 F2
oughborough Carillon
Twr & War Meml LE11 220 A2
oughborough Endowed
Schs LE11 220 A2
oughborough General
Hospl LE11 220 A2
oughborough
Grammar Sch LE11 220 B1
oughborough
High Sch LE11 220 A1
oughborough Limehurst
High Sch Annexe)
LE11 220 A3
oughborough Rd
Bradmore NG11 196 C3
Bunny NG11 206 C4
East Leake LE12 214 C4
Hathern LE12 213 D1
Hoton LE12 215 E1
Loughborough LE11 220 B1
Rempstone LE12 215 E3
West Bridgford NG12 185 F3
oughborough Shelthorpe
Prim Sch LE11 220 B1
oughborough St Mary's
RC Prim Sch LE11 220 A2
oughborough Sta LE11 220 B3
oughborough Univ Sch
of Art & Design LE11 220 A2
oughborugh Rd LE12 220 C3
oughrigg Cl 18 NG2 173 D1
ouis Ave NG9 183 F4
ouise Ave NG4 175 D4
ound House Cl NG17 100 C3
ound House Rd NG17 100 C3
ound Low Rd DN22 29 E4
ouwil Ave NG19 88 C3
ove La DN21 15 E1
oveden Cl NG24 140 B2

Lovell Cl NG6 159 F3
Lover's La NG24 125 D1
Lovers Lane Prim Sch
NG24 125 D1
Low Field La DN10 3 E1
Low Holland La DN22 32 C2
Low Moor Rd NG17 115 D3
Low Pavement NG1 223 E2
Low Rd Besthorpe NG23 97 F3
Scrooby DN10 10 A1
Sutton in A NG17 100 C4
Low St Beckingham DN10 14 B1
Carlton in L S81 26 A3
Collingham NG23 111 F4
East Drayton DN22 53 D2
East Markham NG22 66 A3
Elston NG23 153 E3
Gringley on t H DN10 12 C1
Harby NG23 70 B1
North Wheatley DN22 31 E4
Sutton in A NG17 100 C1
Torworth DN22 19 D1
Low Wood La LN6 98 C4
Low Wood Rd NG6 159 F3
Low's La DE7 170 A1
Lowater St NG4 174 A4
Lowcroft NG5 161 F2
Lowdam Rd NG14 150 A3
Lowdham CE Sch NG14 150 B1
Lowdham La NG14 149 F2
Lowdham Rd Carlton NG4 162 B2
Gunthorpe NG14 164 C4
Lowdham St 14 NG3 173 F3
Lowdham Sta NG14 164 C4
Lower Bagthorpe NG16 128 C2
Lower Beauvale NG16 144 A2
Lower Bloomsgrove Rd
DE7 157 F1
Lower Brook St NG10 193 F4
Lower Cambridge St
LE11 220 A3
Lower Canaan NG11 196 B4
Lower Chapel St 18 DE7 157 F1
Lower Clara Mount Rd
DE75 143 D1
Lower Ct NG9 184 A4
Lower Dunstead Rd
Aldercar NG16 143 D2
Langley Mill NG16 143 D2
Lower Eldon St 12 NG2 173 F2
Lower Gladstone St 8
LE11 220 A3
Lower Granby St DE7 157 F1
Lower Kirklington Rd
NG25 121 E1
Lower Maples DE75 157 D4
Lower Middleton St DE7 158 A1
Lower Oakham Way
NG18 101 F2
Lower Orchard St NG9 182 B4
Lower Park St NG9 182 B3
Lower Parliament St
NG1 223 F2
Lower Pasture La DN22 31 F4
Lower Rd NG9 184 A4
Lower Regent St NG9 184 A3
Lowes Wong NG25 136 B4
Lowes Wong Anglican
Methodist Jun Sch
NG25 121 E1
Loweswater Ct NG2 186 B4
Lowfield DN22 29 E1
Lowfield La NG24 140 B1
Lowlands Dr NG12 197 F2
Lowmoor Road Ind Est
NG17 115 D4
Lowther Sq S81 25 F4
Lowther Way LE11 220 A1
Lowtown Cl S80 36 A1
Lowtown St S80 36 A1
Lowtown View S80 36 A1
Loxley Dr NG18 103 D2
Lucerne Cl NG11 185 D3
Lucknow Ave NG3 161 E1
Lucknow Ct NG3 173 E4
Lucknow Dr
Mansfield NG17, NG18 101 F3
Nottingham NG3 161 E1
Sutton in A NG17, NG18 101 D2
Lucknow Rd NG3 173 E4
Ludborough Wlk NG19 88 C2
Ludford Cres DN21 24 C4
Ludford Rd NG6 160 B4
Ludgate Cl NG5 147 D1
Ludgate Dr NG13 165 E1
Ludham Ave NG6 160 A4
Ludlam Ave NG16 158 A4
Ludlow Cl NG9 171 E1
Ludlow Hill Rd NG2 185 F3
Lulworth Cl NG2 185 E3
Lulworth Ct NG16 158 C4
Lumley Dr DN11 8 A4
Lune Cl NG9 183 F2
Lune Mdw NG19 88 C2
Lunn La NG23 111 F4
Lupin Cl NG3 173 E4
Luther Ave NG17 100 C1
Luther Cl NG3 173 F4
Luton Cl NG8 160 B1
Lutterell Ct NG2 185 E3
Lutterell Way NG2 186 B3
Lybster Mews 12 NG2 173 D1
Lydia Gdns NG16 143 F1
Lydney Pk NG2 185 E3
Lyle Cl NG16 158 C4
Lyme Pk NG2 185 D3
Lymington Gdns NG3 174 A3
Lymington Rd NG19 101 E3

Lymn Ave NG4 162 C1
Lyncombe Ct DN22 39 E2
Lyncombe Gdns NG12 197 F2
Lyncroft Prim Sch NG16 144 A2
Lynd Cl NG16 129 D4
Lyndale Rd NG9 183 D4
Lynden Ave NG10 193 E3
Lyndhurst Ave NG21 118 A3
Lyndhurst Gdns NG2 185 E2
Lyndhurst Rd NG2 173 F2
Lynds Cl NG21 76 A1
Lyngs The NG13 165 E1
Lynmouth Cres NG7 172 C4
Lynmouth Dr DE7 157 E2
Lynncroft NG16 144 A2
Lynnes Cl NG21 118 A2
Lynstead Dr NG15 145 E3
Lynton Gdns NG5 162 A4
Lynton Rd NG9 183 E3
Lyons Cl NG11 196 A4
Lytham Dr NG12 186 B2
Lytham Gdns NG5 147 D1
Lytham Rd NG17 114 C4
Lythe Cl NG11 185 D3
Lytton Cl NG3 173 F3

Mabel Ave NG17 101 D1
Mabel Gr NG2 186 A4
Mabel St NG2 173 E1
Mable St S80 35 D2
Macaulay Cl
Balderton NG24 140 B3
Worksop S81 36 B2
Macaulay Dr NG24 140 B3
Macaulay Gr NG16 159 D3
Machin Gr S81 35 E4
Machins La NG12 186 A2
Mackinley Ave NG9 170 C1
Mackleys La NG23 110 C1
Mackworth Ct NG18 103 D3
Maclaren Gdns NG11 196 B3
Maclean Rd NG4 174 B4
Macmillan Cl NG3 161 F1
Madison Dr DN10 9 F3
Madryn Wlk 20 NG5 161 D4
Mafeking St NG2 174 A2
Mag La NG20 58 B3
Magdala Rd NG3 173 E4
Magdalen Dr NG13 165 E2
Magdalene View NG24 140 A4
Magdalene Way NG15 146 A4
Magna Cl NG14 150 C1
Magnolia Cl 3 NG8 159 F1
Magnolia Ct NG9 171 E1
Magnolia Gr NG15 146 A2
Magnus Comp Sch The
NG24 140 A3
Magnus Rd NG5 161 E2
Magnus St NG24 140 A4
Magpie Cl S81 35 E4
Magpie La DN22 32 C1
Magson St NG3 173 F3
Maid Marian Ave NG16 129 D4
Maid Marian Way NG1 223 E2
Maid Marion Ave NG22 106 A2
Maid Marion Way NG22 77 E3
Maid Marrion Dr NG21 76 B1
Maida La NG22 77 D2
Maiden La NG1 223 F2
Maidens Dale NG5 161 E4
Maidstone Dr NG8 171 E1
Main Ave NG19 103 D4
Main La NG12 164 B1
Main Rd
Annesley Woodhouse NG17 114 C1
Barnstone NG13 190 C2
Beeston NG9 184 B3
Boughton NG22 77 F3
Carlton NG4 163 D1
Cotgrave NG12 187 F2
Kelham NG23 124 A2
Nether Langwith NG20 59 D1
Nottingham NG11 185 D4
Old Dalby LE14 218 C2
Plumtree NG12 197 F4
Pye Bridge DE55 128 A3
Radcliffe on T NG12 175 F2
Radcliffe on T, Shelford
NG12 176 B4
Ravenshead NG15 117 D2
Selston NG16 128 C1
Upton NG23 122 C1
Watnall NG16 159 D4
Westwood NG16 128 A2
Main St
Annesley Woodhouse NG17 129 F4
Aslockton NG13 179 D3
Awsworth NG16 158 B3
Balderton NG24 140 C2
Bathley NG23 110 A2
Bleasby NG14 152 A4
Blidworth NG21 117 F2
Bothamsall DN22 63 F4
Bradmore NG11 196 C2
Brinsley NG16 128 B1
Bunny NG11 206 C4
Burton Joyce NG14 163 F2
Calverton NG14 148 B4
Caunton NG23 109 D3
Clarborough DN22 30 B3
Coddington NG24 126 A1
Costock LE12 206 B1
Cromwell NG23 110 C4
Cropwell Butler NG12 189 D4
Doddington LN6 71 E1
Dry Doddington NG23 156 C1
Eakring NG22 92 C1
East Bridgford NG13 165 E1

Main St continued
East Leake LE12 205 F1
Eastwood NG16 143 F1
Eastwood, Beauvale NG16 144 B1
Edingley NG22 120 B2
Egmanton NG22 79 F3
Farndon NG24 139 D2
Farnsfield NG22 119 F3
Fenton NG23 142 B1
Fiskerton NG25 137 F2
Flintham NG13 167 D4
Granby NG13 191 E2
Gunthorpe NG14 165 D3
Harby LE14 202 A2
Harworth DN11 8 C2
Hickling LE14 210 B3
Hoveringham NG14 151 E1
Huthwaite NG17 99 F2
Keyworth NG12 197 F1
Kimberley NG16 158 C3
Kinoulton NG12 199 F1
Kirton NG22 78 A3
Lambley NG4 163 E4
Laneham DN22 54 A3
Langar NG13 190 B1
Laxton NG22 79 E2
Linby NG15 131 D2
Long Eaton NG10 193 F4
Long Whatton LE12 212 A2
Lowdham NG14 150 B1
Mattersey DN10 20 A4
Morton NG25 137 E2
Newton DE55 99 D2
Normanton on S LE12 213 E2
North Leverton w H DN22 32 B1
North Muskham NG23 110 C1
Nottingham NG6 160 B4
Oldcotes S81 16 C3
Ollerton NG22 77 D2
Ossington NG23 95 E3
Oxton NG25 134 A2
Papplewick NG15 131 F3
Redmile NG13 192 C2
Scarrington NG13 178 C4
Shirebrook NG20 72 B2
Sibthorpe NG23 167 F4
South Muskham NG23 124 B4
South Normanton DE55 113 D3
Stanford on S LE12 214 B1
Strelley NG16 159 D1
Sutton Bonington LE12 213 D4
Sutton on T NG23 96 C4
Torksey LN1 44 A1
Walesby NG22 64 A1
West Bridgford NG2 186 B4
West Leake LE12 204 C1
West Stockwith DN10 7 F1
Weston NG23 81 D2
Whaley Thorns S44 59 D1
Whatton NG13 179 D2
Willoughby-on-t-W LE12 217 E4
Woodborough NG14 149 E2
Wysall NG12 207 E2
Zouch LE12 213 D2
Mainside Cres NG16 129 D1
Maitland Ave NG5 161 F2
Maitland Rd NG5 161 F2
Major St NG1 223 E3
Malbon Cl NG3 173 F4
Malcolm Cl NG3 173 E4
Maldon Cl NG9 183 E2
Malham Cl DN10 9 F4
Malin Hill NG1 223 F2
Malkin Ave NG12 176 A2
Mallam Rd NG22 77 E3
Mallard Cl
Nottingham NG6 160 C2
Shirebrook NG20 72 C2
Mallard Ct NG9 184 A3
Mallard Gn NG24 140 A3
Mallard Rd NG4 175 D3
Mallards The S81 35 E4
Mallatratt Pl NG19 88 A3
Mallow Way NG13 177 E2
Malmesbury Rd NG3 162 A2
Malpas Ave DN21 15 E1
Malt Cotts NG7 160 C1
Malt St NG11 195 D1
Maltby Cl NG8 160 A1
Maltby Rd
Mansfield NG18 102 C3
Nottingham NG3 162 A2
Oldcotes S81 16 C3
Malthouse Cl NG16 143 F1
Malthouse Rd S80 45 D3
Malting Cl NG11 196 B3
Maltings The Blyth S81 18 A2
Cropwell Bishop NG12 189 D2
Maltkiln Cl NG22 77 E1
Maltkiln La NG24 125 D1
Maltkiln Rd LN1 55 E3
Maltkins The DN22 42 B4
Maltmill La NG1 223 E2
Malton Rd NG5 160 C1
Maltsters The NG24 139 E3
Malvern Cl NG3 161 F1
Malvern Cres NG2 185 F3
Malvern Gdns 5 NG10 193 D4
Malvern Rd
Nottingham NG3 161 F1
West Bridgford NG2 185 F3
Manby Ct NG20 74 B4
Manchester St NG10 193 E3
Mandalay St NG6 160 B2
Mandeen Gr NG18 103 D2
Manesty Cres NG11 195 F4
Mangham La DN11 8 A4
Manifold Dr NG16 129 D4

Manifold Gdns NG2 173 E1
Manitoba Way NG16 128 C4
Manly Cl NG5 160 C4
Mann St 18 NG7 172 C4
Manners Ave DE7 157 E1
Manners Ind Est DE7 157 F1
Manners Rd
Balderton NG24 140 B2
Ilkeston DE7 157 F1
Newark-on-T NG24 124 C1
Manners St DE7 170 A3
Manning Sch for Girls
NG8 172 A4
Manning St NG3 173 E4
Manning View DE7 157 F1
Mannion Cres NG10 193 D3
Manns Leys NG12 187 F1
Manor Ave Beeston NG9 183 F3
Beeston, Attenborough
NG9 183 F2
17 Nottingham NG2 173 F2
Stapleford NG9 182 B4
Manor Cl Bleasby NG14 152 A4
Boughton NG22 77 F3
Costock LE12 206 B1
Eagle LN6 84 B2
Gamston DN22 50 C3
Long Whatton LE12 212 A2
Misson DN10 4 B2
Newton DE55 99 D2
Southwell NG25 121 F1
Walesby NG22 64 A1
West Bridgford NG12 186 A2
Worksop S80 35 E1
Manor Comp Lower Sch
NG19 88 A1
Manor Comp Mid Sch
NG19 88 B3
Manor Comp Upper Sch
NG19 88 B3
Manor Cres Carlton NG4 174 C4
Kirkby in A NG17 115 D2
Manor Croft NG6 160 C2
Manor Ct Beeston NG9 183 D4
Carlton NG4 174 C4
Church Warsop NG20 74 B3
Manor Dr NG25 137 E2
Manor Farm Cl
Bradmore NG11 196 C2
Rolleston NG23 138 A3
Manor Farm La NG7 184 C1
Manor Farm Mdw LE12 205 F1
Manor Farm Rise DN22 32 B1
Manor Gr S80 35 E1
Manor Green Wlk NG4 174 C4
Manor House Cl NG14 150 B1
Manor House Ct NG17 114 B2
Manor House Dr NG12 207 E2
Manor House La NG23 156 B1
Manor House Rd NG10 193 F3
Manor La Broadholme LN6 71 D4
Shelford NG12 164 B1
Whatton NG13 179 D1
Manor Park Inf Sch
NG14 148 C4
Manor Pk NG11 196 B4
Manor Rd
Barton in F NG11 194 C3
Bingham NG13 177 F2
Bottesford NG13 181 E1
Calverton NG14 148 C4
Carlton NG4 174 C4
Caunton NG23 109 D2
Church Warsop NG20 74 B3
Collingham NG23 112 A4
East Leake LE12 205 F2
Eastwood NG16 143 F1
Ilkeston DE7 157 F1
Keyworth NG12 197 F2
Mansfield Woodhouse NG19 88 A2
Morton DN21 15 D2
Saxilby LN1 57 D2
Scrooby DN10 10 A1
Sutton in A NG17 100 C4
Manor Rise NG13 165 E2
Manor St Nottingham NG2 173 F2
Sutton in A NG17 100 C1
Manorwood Rd NG12 187 F1
Manse Ave S80 58 B4
Manse Cl S80 58 B4
Mansell Cl NG16 144 A1
Mansfield Com Hospl
NG18 102 A3
Mansfield Ct 13 NG5 173 D4
Mansfield Gr NG1 223 D4
Mansfield La
Calverton NG14 148 C4
Sutton in A NG17 101 D3
Mansfield Rd
Annesley NG15 130 A3
Arnold NG5, NG15 147 E3
Babworth DN22 38 B2
Blidworth NG21 118 A3
Brinsley NG16 143 F2
Clipstone NG21 90 A3
Cuckney NG20 60 A2
Eastwood NG16 143 F2
Edingley NG22 120 B3
Edwinstowe NG21 75 F1
Farnsfield NG22 119 E4
Glapwell S44 86 B4
Heanor DE75 143 D1
Mansfield Woodhouse NG19 88 B1
Market Warsop NG20 73 F1
Nottingham NG5 161 E2

Mansfield Rd continued
Ollerton NG22 .... 76 C2
Ravenshead NG15 .... 116 C1
Selston NG16 .... 128 C4
Selston, Friezeland NG16 .... 129 E2
South Normanton DE55 .... 113 E3
Sutton in A, Skegby NG17 .... 100 C3
Sutton in A,
  Sutton Forest Side NG17 .... 101 D2
Tibshelf DE55 .... 99 D4
Worksop S80 .... 46 A4
Mansfield St NG5 .... 161 E1
Mansfield Sta NG18 .... 102 A3
Mansfield Woodhouse Sta
NG19 .... 88 A2
Manthorpe Cres NG5 .... 161 F2
Manthorpe Ho NG24 .... 140 C2
Manthorpe Way NG24 .... 140 C2
Manton Cl NG21 .... 118 A4
Manton Cres
Beeston NG9 .... 184 A4
Worksop S80 .... 36 A1
Manton Dale S80 .... 36 A1
Manton Inf Sch S80 .... 36 B1
Manton Jun Sch S80 .... 36 B1
Manton Villas S80 .... 36 B1
Manvers Cres NG21 .... 75 F1
Manvers Ct
Market Warsop NG20 .... 73 D2
  8 Nottingham NG6 .... 173 F2
Manvers Gr NG12 .... 175 F2
Manvers Rd Retford DN22 ... 39 E3
West Bridgford NG2 .... 185 F3
Manvers Sec Sch NG3 .... 174 A3
Manvers St Carlton NG4 ...... 175 D3
Mansfield NG18 .... 102 A4
Mansfield Woodhouse NG19 .. 88 A2
Market Warsop NG20 .... 74 A2
Nottingham NG2 .... 173 F2
Shirebrook NG20 .... 73 D2
Worksop S80 .... 35 F2
Manvers View NG22 .... 77 F3
Manville Cl Beeston NG9 ..... 171 D2
Nottingham NG8 .... 172 B3
Maori Ave NG15 .... 145 E3
Maple Ave Beeston NG9 ...... 184 A3
Sandiacre NG10 .... 182 A4
Maple Cl East Leake LE12 .... 214 B4
Gainsborough DN21 .... 15 D2
Keyworth NG12 .... 198 A1
Mansfield NG19 .... 88 C1
Radcliffe on T NG12 .... 175 F1
Tuxford NG22 .... 66 A1
Maple Cres NG17 .... 114 C3
Maple Dr Carlton NG4 .... 163 D1
Elkesley DN22 .... 50 A2
Hucknall NG15 .... 145 F3
Nuthall NG16 .... 159 E3
South Normanton DE55 .... 113 D2
Worksop S81 .... 36 A4
Maple Gr Bawtry DN10 ...... 9 F4
Glapwell S44 .... 86 A4
Newark-on-T NG24 .... 139 F2
Maplebeck Ave NG20 .... 74 B4
Maplebeck Rd
Arnold NG5 .... 162 A4
Caunton NG23 .... 108 C3
Mapledene Cres NG8 .... 171 E2
Maples St **16** NG7 .... 172 C4
Maplestead Ave NG11 .... 185 D3
Mapletoft Ave NG19 .... 88 A3
Mapleton Way NG17 .... 101 D2
Mapletree Cl NG5 .... 161 D4
Mapperley Cres NG3 .... 161 E1
Mapperley Hall Dr NG3 .... 161 E1
Mapperley Hospl NG3 .... 161 F1
Mapperley Orch NG5 .... 162 B4
Mapperley Park Dr 3
NG3 .... 173 E4
Mapperley Plains NG3 .... 162 B3
Mapperley Plains
  Prim Sch NG3 .... 162 A2
Mapperley Plains Sch
  (Annexe) NG3 .... 162 A2
Mapperley Rd NG3 .... 173 E4
Mapperley Rise NG3 .... 161 F1
Mapperley St NG5 .... 161 E1
Mapperton Dr NG18 .... 103 D3
Mapplewells Cres NG17 ...... 100 A1
Mapplewells Rd NG17 .... 100 A1
Mapplewells Sch NG17 .... 100 A1
March Cl NG5 .... 160 C4
Marches Cl NG15 .... 145 F2
Marchwood Cl NG8 .... 172 B3
Mardale Cl NG2 .... 186 B3
Margaret Ave
Long Eaton NG10 .... 182 C1
Sandiacre NG10 .... 182 A2
Margaret Cres NG4 .... 162 C1
Margaret Glen-Bott
  Comp Sch NG8 .... 172 A2
Margaret Pl NG13 .... 177 E3
Margaret's Ct NG9 .... 183 D4
Marham Cl NG2 .... 173 F2
Marhill Rd NG4 .... 174 C4
Marie Gdns NG15 .... 146 A3
Marina Ave NG9 .... 183 F3
Mariner Ct NG6 .... 160 A3
Marion Ave
Hucknall NG15 .... 131 E1
Kirkby in A NG17 .... 115 D1
Marion Murdoch Ct NG4 ..... 162 C1
Maris Cl NG11 .... 184 B1
Maris Dr NG14 .... 163 F2
Marjorie St NG20 .... 35 D2

Mark La NG22 .... 65 F3
Mark St NG10 .... 182 B3
Market Cl Shirebrook NG20 .. 72 C2
South Normanton DE55 .... 113 D3
Market House Pl 24
NG18 .... 102 A4
Market Pl Bingham NG13 ..... 177 F2
Gainsborough DN21 .... 24 B4
Hucknall NG15 .... 146 A4
Huthwaite NG17 .... 99 F2
Kegworth DE74 .... 203 E1
Long Eaton NG10 .... 193 F4
Loughborough LE11 .... 220 A2
  2 Mansfield NG18 .... 102 A4
Mansfield Woodhouse NG19 .. 88 A2
Nottingham NG6 .... 160 A4
Ollerton NG22 .... 77 D2
Retford DN22 .... 39 E4
South Normanton DE55 .... 113 D3
Southwell NG25 .... 136 C4
Stanton Hill NG17 .... 100 C1
Tickhill DN11 .... 8 A4
Tuxford NG22 .... 65 F2
Worksop S80 .... 35 F1
Market Pl The NG5 .... 161 F4
Market Side **22** NG6 .... 160 A4
Market St Bingham NG13 ..... 177 F2
Bottesford NG13 .... 181 D2
Gainsborough DN21 .... 24 B4
Huthwaite NG17 .... 99 F2
Loughborough LE11 .... 220 A2
  27 Mansfield NG18 .... 102 A4
Nottingham NG1 .... 223 E2
Shirebrook NG20 .... 72 C2
South Normanton DE55 .... 113 D3
Sutton in A NG17 .... 100 C1
Worksop S80 .... 35 F2
Markham Ave NG24 .... 125 D2
Markham Cl NG22 .... 77 D2
Markham Cres NG5 .... 161 E2
Markham Pl NG19 .... 101 E4
Markham Rd Beeston NG9 ... 171 F1
Langold S81 .... 16 C2
Retford DN22 .... 39 F2
Markham St NG15 .... 130 B3
Markhams The NG22 .... 77 D2
Markland La NG20 .... 58 A4
Marklew Cl NG21 .... 118 A3
Markwick Cl NG24 .... 140 B4
Marl Rd NG12 .... 176 A2
Marlborough Cl NG24 .... 139 E3
Marlborough Ct NG24 .... 139 E3
Marlborough Rd
Arnold NG5 .... 161 F3
Beeston NG9 .... 183 F4
Kirkby in A NG17 .... 115 D3
Long Eaton NG10 .... 182 C1
Mansfield NG18 .... 87 F1
Marlborough St
Gainsborough DN21 .... 24 B4
  2 Nottingham NG7 .... 172 C1
Marldon Cl NG8 .... 171 E3
Marle Pit Hill LE12 .... 213 D4
Marlock Cl NG25 .... 137 F2
Marlow Ave NG6 .... 160 C1
Marlow Rd DN22 .... 15 F1
Marlowe Dr NG24 .... 140 B2
Marlowe Gdns S81 .... 36 A2
Marlpool Inf Sch DE75 .... 157 D4
Marlpool Jun Sch DE75 ...... 143 D1
Marlwood NG12 .... 188 A1
Marmion Rd NG3 .... 174 A3
Marnham Dr NG3 .... 161 F1
Marnham Rd NG22 .... 66 B1
Marple Sq NG3 .... 173 E4
Marples Ave NG19 .... 88 C3
Marquis Ave NG24 .... 140 B2
Marquis Gdns DN22 .... 40 A2
Marquis Rd LE14 .... 219 D3
Marriots La NG21 .... 117 F2
Marriott Ave
Beeston NG9 .... 183 D3
Mansfield NG18 .... 101 F4
Marriott Cl NG9 .... 183 D3
Marsant Cl **2** NG8 .... 172 B3
Marsh La Farndon NG24 ...... 139 D3
Misterton DN10 .... 7 D1
North Leverton w H DN22 ..... 33 E1
North Muskham DN22 .... 110 C1
Saundby DN22 .... 23 E3
Marsh Rd DN10 .... 14 B3
Marsh's Paddock LE14 .... 210 B3
Marshall Ave NG17 .... 115 E2
Marshall Ct NG24 .... 140 C2
Marshall Dr NG9 .... 183 D4
Marshall Farm Cl NG13 ...... 192 A1
Marshall Hill Dr NG3 .... 162 A1
Marshall Rd
Cropwell Bishop NG12 .... 189 D2
Nottingham NG3 .... 162 A1
Marshall St Heanor DE75 .... 143 D1
Nottingham NG5 .... 161 E1
Marshall Terr NG17 .... 100 B3
Marston Ave NG20 .... 74 B4
Marston Cl NG24 .... 140 B2
Marston Rd NG3 .... 174 A4
Martin Cl NG6 .... 160 A4
Martin Ct NG6 .... 160 A4
Martin La DN10 .... 9 F4
Martin Roe Jun Sch
NG15 .... 117 D2
Martindale Cl NG2 .... 186 B3
Martinmass Cl NG7 .... 222 A1
Martins Hill NG4 .... 174 C4
Martlet Way S80 .... 47 D4
Martlett Sch The S80 .... 35 F1
Marton Cty Prim Sch
DN21 .... 44 B4

Marton Rd Beeston NG9 ...... 183 E2
Newark-on-T NG24 .... 140 A3
Nottingham NG6 .... 159 E4
Martyn Ave NG17 .... 100 C1
Marvin Rd NG9 .... 183 F3
Marwood Cres NG4 .... 162 B1
Marwood Rd NG4 .... 162 B1
Mary Rd NG16 .... 143 E3
Mary St Kirkby in A NG17 .... 115 D3
Rhodesia S80 .... 35 D2
Whaley Thorns NG20 .... 59 D1
Maryfield Cl DN22 .... 29 F1
Maryland Cl NG9 .... 170 C1
Marys Cl LE12 .... 216 B2
Masefield Cres NG24 .... 140 B2
Masefield Pl S81 .... 36 A2
Mason Rd DN7 .... 157 E1
Mason St NG17 .... 101 D2
Masonic Pl NG1 .... 223 D3
Massey Cl NG14 .... 163 F2
Massey Gdns **3** NG3 .... 173 F3
Massey St NG24 .... 140 A4
Masson Ct **7** NG5 .... 147 D1
Mather Rd NG24 .... 124 C1
Matlock Ave NG18 .... 102 A3
Matlock Ct NG1 .... 223 E3
Matlock St NG4 .... 175 D4
Mattersey Ct NG19 .... 88 A1
Mattersey Cty Prim Sch
DN10 .... 20 C4
Mattersey Priory DN10 ..... 20 C4
Mattersey Rd
Everton DN10 .... 11 E1
Lound DN22 .... 20 A1
Ranskill DN22 .... 19 E3
Sutton DN22 .... 29 D4
Matthew Holland
  Comp Sch NG16 .... 128 C4
Matthews Ct NG9 .... 170 C1
Mattingly Rd NG6 .... 160 A3
Mattley Ave NG17 .... 115 D1
Maud St NG7 .... 161 D1
Maun Ave
Kirkby in A NG17 .... 115 D4
Nottingham NG7 .... 172 B3
Maun Cl Mansfield NG18 ..... 101 F2
Retford DN22 .... 39 F3
Maun Cres NG22 .... 77 E3
Maun Lea NG24 .... 125 D1
Maun Inf Sch NG22 .... 77 D3
Maun Valley Ind Pk
NG17 .... 101 E1
Maun Way
Mansfield NG18 .... 101 F2
Wellow NG22 .... 78 A2
Maundale Ave NG17 .... 101 D2
Maunleigh NG19 .... 88 C1
Maunside NG18 .... 101 F2
Maunside Ave NG17 .... 101 D1
Maurice Dr NG3 .... 161 F2
Mavis Ave NG15 .... 117 D1
Mawkin La NG16 .... 113 F3
Maws La NG16 .... 158 C4
Maxtoke Rd NG7 .... 222 C1
Maxwell Cl NG7 .... 222 B1
May Ave NG8 .... 171 F2
May Ct **15** NG5 .... 161 D1
May Fair Pl NG22 .... 66 A1
May Lodge Dr NG22 .... 91 F3
May South DE7 .... 157 F2
May St DE7 .... 157 F2
Maycroft Gdns NG3 .... 174 A4
Maydene Cl NG11 .... 184 B1
Mayes Rise NG6 .... 146 C2
Mayfair Ave NG18 .... 102 B3
Mayfair Cl DN11 .... 8 A2
Mayfair Ct NG7 .... 160 C1
Mayfair Gdns NG5 .... 160 C3
Mayfield Ave
Burton Joyce NG14 .... 163 F3
Gainsborough DN21 .... 15 D2
Mayfield Cl NG18 .... 103 D3
Mayfield Ct NG2 .... 173 E1
Mayfield Dr
Loughborough LE11 .... 220 A1
Stapleford NG9 .... 170 C1
Mayfield Gr NG10 .... 182 C1
Mayfield Pl NG17 .... 100 B1
Mayfield Rd NG4 .... 174 A4
Mayfield St NG17 .... 114 B2
Mayfield Terr NG20 .... 74 A2
Mayflower Ave DN10 .... 10 A4
Mayflower Cl Bawtry DN10 .. 10 A4
Gainsborough DN21 .... 24 C2
West Bridgford NG2 .... 186 A4
Mayflower Ct NG20 .... 72 C2
Mayflower Jun & Inf Sch
DN10 .... 10 A4
Mayflower Rd NG16 .... 158 A4
Mayhall Ave NG19 .... 88 A2
Mayland Cl NG8 .... 171 E3
Maylo Rd NG5 .... 161 D1
Maypole NG11 .... 184 C2
Maypole Cl NG22 .... 92 C4
Maypole Rd NG22 .... 92 C4
Maypole Yd NG1 .... 223 E3
Mays Ave NG4 .... 174 B3
Mays Cl NG4 .... 174 B3
Mays La LN1 .... 57 E2
Maythorn Cl NG12 .... 185 E2
Maythorn Gr NG21 .... 76 A2
Maythorne Cl NG24 .... 140 B3
Maythorne Wlk **11** NG5 .... 161 E4
McIntosh Rd NG4 .... 162 B2
Meade Dr S81 .... 36 A4
Meadow Ave
Loughborough LE11 .... 220 A3
Mansfield NG18 .... 102 B3

Meadow Bank
Mansfield Woodhouse NG19 .. 88 C3
South Normanton DE55 .... 113 D4
Meadow Cl
Aslockton NG13 .... 179 D3
Eastwood NG16 .... 143 F2
Farnsfield NG22 .... 120 A3
Hucknall NG15 .... 145 E3
  2 Kirkby in A NG17 .... 114 C3
North Muskham NG23 .... 110 C1
Nottingham NG2 .... 173 F1
Retford DN22 .... 29 F1
Tibshelf DE55 .... 99 D4
Meadow Cotts
Carlton NG4 .... 174 C4
Mansfield Woodhouse NG19 .. 88 B2
Meadow Ct
Nottingham NG2 .... 173 F1
South Normanton DE55 .... 113 D2
Meadow Dr
Keyworth NG12 .... 198 A2
Misterton DN10 .... 6 C1
Sutton in A NG17 .... 100 B2
Tickhill DN11 .... 8 A4
Worksop S80 .... 35 E1
Meadow End
Gotham NG11 .... 195 D1
Radcliffe on T NG12 .... 176 B2
Meadow Farm View
NG17 .... 114 C3
Meadow Gdns NG3 .... 183 F2
Meadow Gr Newton DE55 .. 99 D2
Nottingham NG2 .... 173 F1
Meadow La Beeston NG9 ... 183 F2
Bothamsall DN22 .... 63 F4
Burton Joyce NG14 .... 163 F2
Girton NG23 .... 82 C2
Long Eaton NG10 .... 193 F4
Loughborough LE11 .... 220 A4
North Scarle LN6 .... 83 F1
Nottingham NG2 .... 173 F1
  27 Nottingham NG2 .... 173 F2
South Normanton DE55 .... 113 D4
Wilford NG2 .... 81 D2
Meadow Lane Ind Est
LE11 .... 220 A3
Meadow Lane Inf Sch
NG9 .... 183 F2
Meadow Lane (Notts
  County FC) NG2 .... 173 F1
Meadow Pl NG20 .... 74 A2
Meadow Rd
Awsworth NG16 .... 158 B3
Beeston NG9 .... 184 A3
Blidworth NG21 .... 118 A3
Carlton NG4 .... 174 C4
New Balderton NG24 .... 140 B2
Worksop S80 .... 35 E1
Meadow Rise
Nottingham NG6 .... 159 F3
Saxilby LN1 .... 57 D2
Meadow St DE7 .... 157 F1
Meadow The DN22 .... 39 F4
Meadow View NG25 .... 121 F1
Meadow Way
Harworth DN11 .... 8 C3
Kinoulton NG12 .... 199 F2
Meadowbank Day Hospl
NG2 .... 173 D1
Meadowbank Way NG16 ..... 143 E2
Meadows La LE14 .... 201 E1
Meadows Prim Sch NG2 ..... 173 E1
Meadows The
Beckingham DN10 .... 23 D4
Clifton NG11 .... 239 D3
South Wheatley DN22 .... 31 E4
Woodborough NG14 .... 149 D2
Meadows Way NG2 .... 173 E1
Meadowsweet Hill NG13 ..... 177 E2
Meadowvale Cres NG7 .... 184 C1
Medawar Cl NG11 .... 184 B1
Meden Ave
Market Warsop NG20 .... 74 B3
New Houghton NG19 .... 86 C4
Meden Bank
Bothamsall DN22 .... 63 F4
Pleasleyhill NG19 .... 87 D3
Stanton Hill NG17 .... 100 B3
Meden Cl
Nottingham NG11 .... 184 C2
Pleasleyhill NG19 .... 87 D3
Meden Comp Sch NG20 .... 74 A3
Meden Cres NG17 .... 100 B2
Meden Gdns NG7 .... 172 B4
Meden Glen NG20 .... 74 B3
Meden Rd
Mansfield Woodhouse NG19 .. 88 B2
Wellow NG22 .... 78 A2
Meden Sq NG19 .... 87 D4
Meden Way NG22 .... 39 F3
Medina Dr NG12 .... 186 C1
Medway DN22 .... 29 F1
Medway Cl NG9 .... 183 E3
Meeks Rd NG5 .... 162 A4
Meer Rd NG9 .... 183 D3
Meering Ave NG24 .... 125 D2
Meering Cl NG23 .... 98 A1
Meerings The NG23 .... 81 F1
Meeting House Cl LE12 ...... 213 D1
Meetinghouse La DN22 ...... 42 A3
Melbourne Cl
Mansfield NG18 .... 103 D3
Nottingham NG8 .... 160 B1
Melbourne Gr DN11 .... 8 C2
Melbourne Rd
Nottingham NG8 .... 160 B1
Stapleford NG9 .... 170 C1
West Bridgford NG2 .... 174 A1

Melbourne St
Mansfield Woodhouse NG19 .. 88 B4
Selston NG16 .... 129 D3
Melbury Prim Sch NG8 .... 171 E4
Melbury Rd
Nottingham, Bilborough
NG8 .... 171 E4
Nottingham, Woodthorpe
NG3 .... 162 A4
Meldreth Rd NG8 .... 171 F4
Meldrum Cres NG24 .... 139 F2
Melford Hall Dr NG2 .... 185 E2
Melford Rd NG8 .... 171 E4
Melksham Rd NG5 .... 161 E3
Mellers Prim Sch NG7 .... 222 B4
Mellish Rd S81 .... 16 C
Mellors Rd Arnold NG5 ...... 147 F
Mansfield NG19 .... 101 E
West Bridgford NG2 .... 185 F
Melrose Ave
Beeston NG9 .... 184 A
Mansfield NG18 .... 102 B
  3 Nottingham NG5 .... 161 E
Melrose Gdns NG2 .... 185 E
Melrose Rd DN21 .... 15 E
Melrose St NG5 .... 161 E
Melrose Wlk **2** S80 .... 35 F
Melton Ct NG10 .... 182 A
Melton Gdns NG12 .... 186 A
Melton Gr NG2 .... 185 F
Melton La LE12 .... 204 B
Melton Rd
East Leake LE12 .... 214 C
Long Clawson LE14 .... 211 D
Plumtree NG12 .... 197 F
Rempstone LE12 .... 215 E
Stanton-on-t-W NG12 .... 198 B
Tollerton NG12 .... 187 F
Upper Broughton LE14 .... 210 A
West Bridgford NG2, 186 A
Widmerpool NG12, LE12 ..... 209 E
Melton Way NG18 .... 101 F
Melville Cl **6** NG3 .... 173 E
Melville Ct NG3 .... 173 E
Melville Gdns NG3 .... 173 E
Melville St NG1 .... 223 E
Melvyn Dr NG13 .... 177 F
Memorial Ave S80 .... 35 F
Mendip Cl NG10 .... 182 A
Mendip Ct
Carlton in L S81 .... 25 F
Nottingham NG5 .... 160 C
Mensing Ave NG12 .... 187 F
Mercer Rd DN21 .... 15 D
Merchant St
Nottingham NG6 .... 160 A
Shirebrook NG20 .... 73 D
Mercia Ave NG12 .... 189 D
Mercia Cl S81 .... 36 A
Mercia Rd NG24 .... 139 F
Mercury Cl NG6 .... 160 C
Mere Ave NG14 .... 148 C
Mere Cl NG14 .... 148 C
Mere Way NG14 .... 196 B
Meredith Cl NG7 .... 173 D
Meredith Ct NG9 .... 170 C
Meregill Cl NG5 .... 146 C
Merevale Ave NG11 .... 184 C
Merevale Cl NG14 .... 150 C
Meriac Cl NG5 .... 160 C
Meriden Ave NG9 .... 184 A
Meridian Cl DE7 .... 157 F
Meridian Ct NG5 .... 161 D
Merlin Cl NG11 .... 184 C
Merlin Dr NG15 .... 145 F
Merrick Dr S81 .... 36 B
Merrivale Ct NG3 .... 173 E
Merryvale Dr NG19 .... 101 E
Merryweather Cl
Edwinstowe NG21 .... 91 E
Southwell NG25 .... 121 F
Mersey St NG6 .... 160 A
Merton Ave DN22 .... 29 F
Merton Cl NG5 .... 148 A
Merton Ct NG9 .... 170 C
Metcalf Cl NG22 .... 105 F
Metcalf Rd NG16 .... 144 A
Metcalfe Cl NG25 .... 136 C
Methuen St NG18 .... 102 C
Metro Ave DE55 .... 99 D
Mettham St NG7 .... 222 B
Mews La NG14 .... 148 C
Mews The S81 .... 18 A
Meynell Gr **7** NG7 .... 161 D
Meynell Rd NG10 .... 193 E
Meyrick Rd NG24 .... 125 D
Miall Ct NG7 .... 222 A
Michael House-Rudolf
  Steiner Sch DE75 .... 157 D
Micklebarrow Cl NG25 ...... 136 B
Mickleborough Ave NG3 .... 174 A
Mickleborough Way NG2 .... 185 E
Mickledale Cl NG22 .... 105 F
Mickledale La NG22 .... 105 F
Mickleden Cl **15** NG10 .... 193 D
Mickledon Cl **3** NG10 ..... 193 D
Middle Furlong Gdns 11
NG2 .... 173 D
Middle Furlong Mews 10
NG2 .... 173 D
Middle Gate NG24 .... 139 F
Middle Hill NG1 .... 223 E
Middle Holme La NG23 ..... 97 D
Middle La
Beeston NG9 .... 183 F
Morton NG25 .... 137 E
Nether Broughton LE14 ...... 219 E
Middle Pavement NG1 .... 223 E

Middle St
Barkestone-le-V NG13 ...... 192 B1
Beeston NG9 .... 184 A3
Hose LE14 .... 211 F4
Misson DN10 .... 4 B1
Middle Wood La DN10 .... 4 B3
Middlebeck Ave NG5 .... 162 B4
Middlebeck Dr NG5 .... 162 B4
Middlebridge Rd DN10 .... 12 C2
Middlebrook Rd NG16 ...... 129 D2
Middledale Rd NG4 .... 174 B3
Middlefield Way NG11 ...... 184 B1
Middlefield La DN21 .... 24 C4
Middlefield Rd DN22 .... 31 F4
Middlefield Sch The DN21 .. 24 C4
Middlegate Field Dr S80 ..... 45 D3
Middleton Bvd NG8 .... 172 B2
Middleton Cl NG16 .... 159 E3
Middleton Cres NG9 .... 171 F1
Middleton Ct
    Mansfield NG18 .... 103 D3
    Nottingham NG5 .... 77 E3
Middleton Pl LE11 .... 220 A1
Middleton Prim Sch NG8 .. 172 B2
Middleton Rd
    Ilkeston DE7 .... 170 A3
    Mansfield Woodhouse NG19 . 88 B3
    Newark-on-T NG24 .... 125 E2
Middleton St
    Awsworth NG16 .... 158 B2
    Beeston NG9 .... 183 F4
    Cossall DE7 .... 158 A1
    Nottingham NG7 .... 222 A3
Midfield Rd NG17 .... 115 D1
Midhurst Cl NG9 .... 183 D2
Midhurst Way NG7 .... 184 C1
Midlame Gdns NG16 .... 159 F4
Midland Ave Carlton NG4 .. 175 D4
    Nottingham NG7 .... 222 A1
    Stapleford NG9 .... 182 B3
Midland Cres NG4 .... 174 C4
Midland Ct NG7 .... 172 B3
Midland Gr NG4 .... 175 D4
Midland Rd Carlton NG4 ... 174 C4
    Eastwood NG16 .... 143 F1
    Sutton in A NG17 .... 101 D1
Midland St NG10 .... 193 F4
Midway The NG7 .... 184 C4
Midworth St NG18 .... 102 A3
Mikado Rd NG10 .... 193 E3
Milburn Gr NG13 .... 177 E2
Mildenhall Cres NG5 .... 161 E4
Mile End Rd NG4 .... 174 C3
Miles Yd LE11 .... 220 A2
Milford Ave NG10 .... 182 A2
Milford Cl NG6 .... 160 A4
Milford Cres NG19 .... 101 E4
Milford Ct NG5 .... 161 E3
Milford Dr Ilkeston DE7 .... 157 E2
    Nottingham NG3 .... 174 B4
Mill Baulk Rd DN10 .... 14 A3
Mill Cl Huthwaite NG17 .... 100 A2
    North Leverton w H DN22 ... 32 B1
    Sutton on T NG23 .... 96 C4
Mill Cl The NG8 .... 160 C2
Mill Cres Arnold NG5 .... 161 F4
    Whitwell S80 .... 45 D3
Mill Croft NG17 .... 100 C1
Mill Field Cl
    Burton Joyce NG14 .... 163 F2
    Harby NG23 .... 70 B1
Mill Gate
    East Bridgford NG13 .... 165 E2
    Newark-on-T NG24 .... 139 F4
Mill Gdns S80 .... 35 E1
Mill Gn NG24 .... 140 A4
Mill Heyes NG13 .... 165 E2
Mill Hill DN10 .... 12 B1
Mill Hill Rd NG13 .... 177 E2
Mill Holme DE55 .... 113 D2
Mill La
    Annesley Woodhouse NG17 . 114 C1
    Arnold NG5 .... 161 F4
    Caunton NG23 .... 109 D3
    Cossall NG16 .... 158 B1
    Colgrave NG12 .... 187 F2
    Eagle LN6 .... 84 C2
    East Leake LE12 .... 214 C4
    Edwinstowe NG21 .... 76 A1
    Hickling LE14 .... 210 B4
    Huthwaite NG17 .... 100 A1
    Kegworth DE74 .... 203 E1
    Lambley NG4 .... 163 D4
    Long Clawson LE14 .... 211 F2
    Long Whatton LE12 .... 212 B2
    Loughborough LE11 .... 220 B3
    Morton DN21 .... 15 E3
    Newark-on-T NG24 .... 139 F4
    Normanton on T NG23 ..... 81 E4
    North Leverton w H DN22 .. 68 C3
    North Leverton w H DN22 .. 42 A4
    North Muskham NG23 ...... 110 C1
    Orston NG13 .... 180 A4
    Pinxton NG16 .... 113 E1
    Rockley DN22 .... 51 D1
    Sandiacre NG10 .... 182 B3
    Saxilby LN1 .... 57 D2
    Scarrington NG13 .... 178 C4
    Scrooby DN10 .... 10 A2
    South Leverton DN22 .... 42 B4
    Stainsby S44 .... 85 E4
    Upton NG23 .... 137 F4
    Walesby NG22 .... 63 F1
    Walkeringham DN10 .... 13 F2
    Whitwell S80 .... 45 D3
    Willoughby-on-t-W LE12 ... 217 E4
Mill Lakes Ctry Pk NG6 .... 146 B2

Mill Meadow View S81 ...... 18 A2
Mill Pk NG25 .... 121 F1
Mill Rd Beeston NG9 .... 144 A2
    Elston NG23 .... 153 F2
    Heanor DE75 .... 157 D4
    Stapleford NG9 .... 182 B4
Mill St Ilkeston DE7 .... 157 F1
    Mansfield NG18 .... 102 B3
    Nottingham NG6 .... 160 B2
    Retford DN22 .... 39 F3
    Sutton in A NG17 .... 100 C1
    Worksop S80 .... 35 F2
Mill Wlk S80 .... 45 D3
Mill Yd Beeston NG9 .... 183 F3
    Hucknall NG15 .... 146 A4
Millash La S80 .... 45 D2
Millbank DE75 .... 143 D1
Millbank Cl DE7 .... 157 E2
Millbaulk La NG22 .... 93 F4
Millbeck Ave NG8 .... 171 E2
Millbeck Cl NG2 .... 186 B3
Milldale Cl NG11 .... 184 B1
Milldale Ct NG11 .... 103 D3
Milldale Rd
    Farnsfield NG22 .... 120 A3
    Long Eaton NG10 .... 193 D3
Milldale Wlk NG17 .... 100 B2
Millennium Way E NG6 .... 160 A2
Millennium Way NG6 .... 160 A2
Miller Hives Cl NG12 .... 187 F2
Miller's La LE12 .... 206 B1
Millers Bridge NG12 .... 187 F1
Millers Cl Retford DN22 ..... 39 F3
    Shelford NG12 .... 164 B1
Millers Ct NG7 .... 222 A4
Millers Way DN22 .... 39 E4
Millersdale Ave
    Ilkeston DE7 .... 157 F3
    Mansfield NG18 .... 101 F2
Millfield Ave LN1 .... 57 D2
Millfield Cl Ilkeston DE7 ... 157 E2
    Retford DN22 .... 39 F2
Millfield Rd Ilkeston DE7 .. 170 A4
    Kimberley NG16 .... 158 C4
    South Leverton DN22 .... 42 A3
Millfield View S80 .... 35 E1
Millicent Gr NG2 .... 185 F4
Millicent Rd NG2 .... 185 F4
Millington Ave NG16 .... 159 E2
Millman Way DN22 .... 29 E1
Mills Dr NG24 .... 139 E3
Millview Cl S81 .... 173 F2
Millview Ct S81 .... 173 F2
Millway NG19 .... 88 B1
Milne Ave DN11 .... 9 E2
Milne Dr DN11 .... 9 E2
Milne Gr DN11 .... 9 E2
Milne Rd DN11 .... 9 E2
Milner Rd
    Long Eaton NG10 .... 193 E4
    Nottingham NG5 .... 161 D1
Milner St
    Newark-on-T NG24 .... 140 A4
    Sutton in A NG17 .... 101 D3
Milncroft DN22 .... 29 E1
Milncroft Gn DN22 .... 29 E1
Milnhay Rd Heanor NG16 . 143 E1
    Langley Mill NG16 .... 143 E1
Milton Ave DE7 .... 157 F2
Milton Cl S81 .... 25 F2
    Nottingham NG8 .... 172 A4
Milton Cres Beeston NG9 . 183 E1
    Ravenshead NG15 .... 117 D1
Milton Ct NG5 .... 162 A4
Milton Dr
    Ravenshead NG15 .... 117 D1
    Worksop S81 .... 36 A2
Milton Rd
    Gainsborough DN21 .... 15 F1
    Ilkeston DE7 .... 157 F2
    West Markham NG22 .... 65 D3
Milton Rise NG15 .... 145 E3
Milton St Ilkeston DE7 ..... 157 F2
    Kirkby in A NG17 .... 115 D3
    Long Eaton NG10 .... 193 E4
    Mansfield NG18 .... 102 A4
    New Balderton NG24 .... 140 B3
    Nottingham NG1 .... 223 E3
Milton Wlk S81 .... 36 A2
Milverton Rd NG5 .... 161 E4
Mimosa Cl NG11 .... 184 B1
Minerva St NG6 .... 160 B4
Minster Cl Hucknall NG15 . 146 A4
    Kirkby in A NG17 .... 114 C3
Minster Gdns NG16 .... 144 A1
Minster Rd NG24 .... 6 C1
Minster Sch The NG23 .... 136 B4
Mint Cl NG10 .... 193 D4
Minver Cres NG8 .... 160 A1
Mirberry Mews NG7 .... 222 A1
Mire La DN22 .... 28 C3
Misk Hollows NG15 .... 145 F4
Misk View NG16 .... 144 A1
Mission St NG3 .... 161 F1
Misson Prim Sch DN10 ...... 4 A2
Misterton Cres NG15 ...... 116 C1
Misterton Ct NG19 .... 88 A1
Misterton Prim Sch DN10 .. 13 F4
Mitchel Ave NG24 .... 125 F1
Mitchell Ave NG16 .... 143 D2
Mitchell Cl
    Nottingham NG6 .... 160 A3
    Worksop S81 .... 35 F4
Mitchell St NG10 .... 193 F4
Mitchell Terr DE7 .... 170 A3
Mob La LE12 .... 217 E4
Model Village S80 .... 58 C4
Model Village Prim Sch
    NG20 .... 72 C2

Moffat Cl NG3 .... 173 F4
Moira St LE11 .... 220 A2
Mollington Sq NG6 .... 160 A2
Mona Rd NG2 .... 174 A1
Mona St NG9 .... 184 A3
Monarch Way LE11 .... 220 A3
Monckton Rd
    Bircotes DN11 .... 9 E2
    Retford DN22 .... 39 E4
Monk's La NG11 .... 195 D1
Monks Cl DE7 .... 170 A4
Monks Mdw LE12 .... 205 F1
Monks Way S81 .... 34 C4
Monksway NG11 .... 185 D2
Monkton Cl DE7 .... 157 E2
Monkton Dr
    Nottingham NG8 .... 171 F4
    Southwell NG25 .... 121 F1
Monkwood Cl NG23 .... 98 A1
Monmouth Cl NG8 .... 171 D2
Monmouth Rd S81 .... 36 A3
Monroe Wlk NG5 .... 161 D4
Monsaldale Cl NG10 .... 193 D3
Monsall Ave DE7 .... 157 F3
Monsall St NG7 .... 160 C1
Monsell Dr NG5 .... 147 F1
Montague Rd NG15 .... 146 A4
Montague St Beeston NG9 . 183 F4
    Mansfield NG18 .... 102 C3
    Nottingham NG6 .... 160 B4
Montfort Cres NG5 .... 161 E2
Montfort St NG7 .... 222 C3
Montgomery Cl ⬛ NG9 .... 183 E4
Montgomery Rd NG24 ..... 140 A3
Montgomery St NG7 .... 222 C4
Montpelier Rd NG7 .... 172 C1
Montrose NG12 .... 36 A3
Montrose Ct NG9 .... 170 C1
Montrose Sq NG19 .... 88 A3
Montys Mdw S81 .... 35 E4
Monyash Cl DE7 .... 157 F2
Moor Bridge NG6 .... 146 B1
Moor Farm Inn La NG9 ... 171 D1
Moor La Aslockton NG13 . 179 D3
    Beeston NG9 .... 171 D2
    Besthorpe NG23 .... 98 B3
    Bingham NG13 .... 177 F3
    Blyth S81 .... 18 B1
    Bunny LE12 .... 206 B4
    Calverton NG14 .... 149 E3
    Elston NG23 .... 154 A3
    Gotham NG11 .... 205 E4
    Dry Doddington NG23 ..... 169 F3
    Loughborough LE11 .... 220 B1
    Mansfield NG18 .... 101 F3
    Morton NG25 .... 137 E2
    Normanton on S LE12 .... 213 E2
    North Clifton NG23 .... 69 D2
    Ruddington NG11 .... 196 B3
    South Clifton NG23 .... 69 E2
    Stathern NG13 .... 202 C3
    Syerston NG23 .... 153 E2
    Upper Langwith S44 .... 72 A4
    Moor La East Leake LE12 . 205 F1
Moor Rd
    Bestwood Village NG6 ..... 146 C3
    Brinsley NG16 .... 143 F4
    Calverton NG14 .... 149 D4
    Collingham NG23 .... 98 A1
    Nottingham NG8 .... 159 E3
Moor St Carlton NG4 .... 175 D4
    Mansfield NG18 .... 102 A3
Moor The NG16 .... 143 E4
Moor Top Rd DN11 .... 8 C3
Moorbridge Cotts NG6 .... 146 B1
Moorbridge La NG9 .... 177 F3
Moorbridge La NG9 .... 182 A4
Moorbridge Rd NG6 .... 170 B1
Moorbridge Rd NG13 ...... 177 F3
Moorbridge Rd E NG13 ... 177 F3
Moore Ave DE74 .... 203 E2
Moore Cl East Leake LE12 . 205 F1
    West Bridgford NG2 .... 174 A1
Moore Gate NG9 .... 184 A3
Moore Rd NG3 .... 162 A1
Moores Ave NG10 .... 182 B4
Moorfield Cres NG10 ...... 182 A4
Moorfield Ct NG5 .... 147 E1
Moorfield La NG20 .... 58 C2
Moorfield PI NG20 .... 74 B3
Moorfields Ave NG16 ...... 143 F2
Moorgate Ave NG19 .... 86 C1
Moorgate PI NG2 .... 39 F4
Moorgate St NG7 .... 222 C3
Moorgreen NG16 .... 144 B2
Moorgreen Dr NG8 .... 159 E1
Moorhaugh La NG19 .... 87 D2
Moorhouse Rd
    Egmanton NG22 .... 80 B2
    Nottingham NG8 .... 171 F3
Moorings The ⬛ NG7 ..... 172 C1
Moorland Ave
    Stapleford NG9 .... 182 B3
    Walkeringham DN10 .... 13 F3
Moorland Cl
    Sutton in A NG17 .... 101 D3
Moorland Way NG18 .... 103 D3
Moorland Wlk DN10 .... 13 F3
Moorlands Cl NG10 .... 182 A1
Moorsholm Dr NG8 .... 171 E2
Moray Ct NG16 .... 159 D4
Moray Sq NG19 .... 101 F4
Morden Cl NG8 .... 171 E4
Morden Rd NG16 .... 158 B4
Moreland Ct Carlton NG4 . 174 B4
    ⬛ Nottingham NG2 .... 173 E2
Moreland PI ⬛ NG2 .... 173 F2
Moreland St NG2 .... 173 F2

Moreley Jun Sch NG3 ...... 173 F4
Morello Ave NG4 .... 174 C4
Moreton Rd NG11 .... 195 F4
Morgan Mews NG7 .... 184 C1
Morgans Cl NG24 .... 126 A1
Morkinshire Cres NG12 .. 187 F2
Morkinshire La NG12 ...... 187 F2
Morley Ave
    Nottingham NG3 .... 161 F1
    Retford DN22 .... 29 E1
Morley Cl NG18 .... 103 D3
Morley Ct ⬛ DE7 .... 157 F2
Morley Dr DE7 .... 157 E2
Morley Rd NG3 .... 162 A1
Morley St Arnold NG5 ..... 161 F3
    Gainsborough DN21 .... 24 B4
    Kirkby in A NG17 .... 115 E4
    Loughborough LE11 .... 220 B3
    Stanton Hill NG17 .... 100 B3
    Sutton in A NG17 .... 100 C2
Morley's Cl NG14 .... 150 C1
Mornington Cl NG10 .... 182 B3
Mornington Cres NG16 ... 159 E2
Mornington Prim Sch
    NG16 .... 159 E2
Morrell Bank NG5 .... 160 C3
Morris Ave NG9 .... 183 D1
Morris Cl LE11 .... 220 B2
Morris Rd NG8 .... 159 E1
Morris St NG4 .... 175 D4
Morton Cl Mansfield NG18 . 103 D3
    Morton DN21 .... 15 D2
    Radcliffe on T NG12 .... 176 B2
Morton Gdns NG12 .... 176 B2
Morton Gr S81 .... 35 F4
Morton Hall Gdns NG23 ... 38 A3
Morton Rd DN21 .... 15 E2
Morton St NG19 .... 87 F1
Morton Terr DN21 .... 15 E1
Morton Trentside
    Cty Prim Sch DN21 .... 15 D2
Morval Rd NG8 .... 171 F4
Morven Ave
    Hucknall NG15 .... 146 A3
    Mansfield Woodhouse NG19 . 88 A1
    Sutton in A NG17 .... 100 C1
Morven Park Prim Sch
    NG17 .... 115 D3
Morven Rd NG17 .... 115 D5
Morven St S80 .... 58 C4
Morven Terr NG20 .... 74 A2
Mosborough Rd NG17 .... 100 A1
Moseley Rd NG15 .... 130 B4
Mosgrove Cl S81 .... 35 E4
Mosley St Hucknall NG15 . 146 A3
    Nottingham NG7 .... 172 C4
Moss Cl Arnold NG5 .... 147 E1
    East Bridgford NG13 .... 165 D2
Moss Dr NG9 .... 183 D4
Moss Rd NG15 .... 145 F4
Moss Rise NG3 .... 162 A1
Moss Side NG11 .... 185 D2
Mosscroft Ave NG11 ...... 184 B1
Mossdale NG19 .... 36 A4
Mossdale Rd
    Mansfield NG18 .... 102 C4
    Nottingham NG5 .... 161 E3
Mosswood Cres NG5 ...... 161 D4
Mottram Rd NG9 .... 183 E3
Moulton Cres NG24 .... 140 A3
Mount Ave S81 .... 35 F3
Mount CE Prim Sch
    NG24 .... 125 D1
Mount Cl DN11 .... 8 C3
Mount Cres
    Market Warsop NG20 .... 74 B2
    South Normanton DE55 .. 113 D2
Mount Ct NG24 .... 140 B2
Mount Hooton Rd NG7 ... 222 C4
Mount La NG24 .... 140 A4
Mount Milner NG18 .... 102 B3
Mount Pleasant
    Carlton NG4 .... 174 C4
    Ilkeston DE7 .... 157 F2
    Keyworth NG12 .... 198 A2
    Lowdham NG14 .... 150 B1
    ⬛ Mansfield NG18 .... 102 A4
    Nottingham NG6 .... 160 C1
    Radcliffe on T NG12 .... 175 F2
    Retford DN22 .... 39 F4
    Sutton in A NG17 .... 100 C2
Mount Pleasant Cl DN21 .. 44 B4
Mount Rd NG24 .... 140 B2
Mount St
    Nottingham, New Basford
    NG7 .... 160 C1
    Nottingham, Standard Hill
    NG1 .... 223 D2
    Stapleford NG9 .... 182 C4
Mount The NG5 .... 147 E1
    Bestwood Village NG6 ..... 146 C2
    Clipstone NG19 .... 89 F2
    Nottingham, Broxtowe NG8 . 159 F2
    Nottingham, Portchester
    NG3 .... 162 B1
    Stapleford NG9 .... 182 C4
Mount View Cl NG18 ...... 102 B3
Mountbatten Ct DE7 ...... 157 F2
Mountbatten Gr NG4 ...... 162 C1
Mountbatten Way NG9 ... 183 E1
Mountfield Ave NG10 ...... 182 A1
Mountfield Dr NG5 .... 161 D4
Mountsorrel Dr NG2 .... 186 A3
Mowbray Ct NG3 .... 223 F3
Mowbray Gdns NG2 .... 185 F3
Mowbray Rise NG5 .... 161 F4
Mowbray Str DN21 .... 15 E1

Mowlands Cl NG17 .... 101 D1
Moyra Dr NG5 .... 161 E4
Mozart Cl NG7 .... 222 A3
Muir Ave NG12 .... 197 E4
Muirfield S81 .... 36 A3
Muirfield Cl ⬛ NG17 ...... 114 C4
Muirfield Rd NG5 .... 147 D1
Muirfield Way NG19 .... 88 C3
Mulberry Cl NG12 .... 185 D3
Mulberry Cres S81 .... 25 F4
Mulberry Gdns ⬛ NG6 .. 160 A4
Mulberry Gr NG15 .... 146 A2
Mumby Cl NG24 .... 125 D1
Mundella Rd NG2 .... 173 E1
Mundy St DE7 .... 157 F1
Munford Circ NG6 .... 160 A2
Munks Ave NG15 .... 145 F4
Murby Cres NG6 .... 160 A4
Murden Way NG9 .... 184 A3
Muriel Rd NG9 .... 184 A4
Muriel St NG6 .... 160 A4
Murray St NG18 .... 102 A3
Muschamp Terr NG20 ..... 74 A2
Mushill La LE12 .... 216 B3
Muskham Ave DE7 .... 157 F2
Muskham Ct NG19 .... 88 A1
Muskham La NG23 .... 110 B1
Muskham Prim Sch
    NG23 .... 110 C1
Muskham St NG2 .... 173 E2
Musters Cres NG2 .... 185 F3
Musters Croft NG4 .... 174 C2
Musters Rd
    Bingham NG13 .... 177 E2
    Langar NG13 .... 190 B1
    Newstead NG15 .... 130 B3
    Ruddington NG11 .... 196 B3
    West Bridgford NG2 .... 185 F3
Musters St NG20 .... 73 D2
Musters Wlk ⬛ NG6 .... 160 A4
Muston Cl NG3 .... 161 F1
Muston La NG13 .... 181 E1
Mutton La DN10 .... 23 D4
Muttonshire Hill DN22 ..... 50 C3
Mynd The NG19 .... 88 C3
Myrtle Ave
    Long Eaton NG10 .... 193 E3
    ⬛ Nottingham NG7 .... 173 D4
    Stapleford NG9 .... 182 C3
Myrtle Cl NG20 .... 72 B3
Myrtle Gr NG9 .... 184 A4
Myrtle Rd NG4 .... 174 B4
Myrtle St NG22 .... 39 E3
Myrtus Cl NG11 .... 184 B1

Nabbs La NG15 .... 145 F3
Naburn Ct ⬛ NG8 .... 172 B4
Nairn Cl Arnold NG5 ...... 148 A1
    Farnsfield NG22 .... 119 F3
Nairn Mews NG4 .... 174 C4
Nan Sampson Bank DN9 ... 1 B4
Nansen St NG6 .... 160 B3
Naomi Cres NG6 .... 146 B1
Naomi Ct NG6 .... 146 B1
Narrow La Bawtry DN10 ... 10 A4
    Greasley NG16 .... 145 D2
    Hathern LE12 .... 212 C1
    Wymeswold LE12 .... 217 D2
Naseby Cl NG5 .... 160 C2
Naseby Dr NG10 .... 193 F2
Nash Cl S81 .... 36 B2
Nathaniel Rd NG10 .... 193 F3
Nathans La NG12 .... 187 D4
National CE Jun &
    Inf Sch The NG15 .... 146 A4
National Sch The NG11 .. 130 C1
National Water Sports Ctr
    NG12 .... 174 C2
Navenby Wlk NG7 .... 184 C1
Navigation Way LE11 ...... 220 A3
Navigation Yd NG24 .... 139 F4
Naworth Cl NG6 .... 160 C3
Naylor Ave Gotham NG11 . 195 D1
    Loughborough LE11 .... 220 B1
Neal Ct NG16 .... 143 D2
Neale St NG10 .... 193 F4
Near Mdw NG10 .... 193 F3
Nearsby Dr NG2 .... 186 B4
Needham Rd NG5 .... 162 A4
Needham St NG13 .... 177 F2
Needwood Ave NG9 ...... 170 B1
Neeps Croft NG4 .... 150 A3
Neep La NG21 .... 163 D3
Neighwood Cl NG9 .... 182 C1
Nell Gwyn Cres NG5 ...... 147 E1
Nelper Cres DE7 .... 170 A3
Nelson La NG23 .... 110 C1
Nelson Rd Arnold NG5 ... 161 F4
    Beeston NG9 .... 184 A2
    New Balderton NG24 ..... 140 A2
    Nottingham NG6 .... 160 B4
Nelson St
    Gainsborough DN21 .... 15 E1
    Ilkeston DE7 .... 157 F2
    Long Eaton NG10 .... 193 E3
    Nottingham NG1 .... 223 F2
    Retford DN22 .... 39 F3
Nene Cl NG15 .... 146 B4
Nene Wlk S81 .... 35 F4
Nesbitt St NG17 .... 100 C1
Nesfield Ct DE7 .... 157 F2
Nesfield Rd DE7 .... 157 F1
Neston Dr NG6 .... 160 A4
Nether Cl Eastwood NG16 . 143 F2
    Nottingham NG3 .... 174 A3

Nether Ct NG22 .... 120 A3
Nether Pasture NG4 .... 175 D3
Nether St Beeston NG9 .... 184 A3
  Harby LE14 .... 202 A2
Nether Thorpe Rd S80 .... 34 A3
Nethercross Dr NG20 .... 74 B3
Netherfield & Colwick Sta
  NG4 .... 174 C3
Netherfield Inf Sch NG20 ... 74 B4
Netherfield Jun Sch
  NG4 .... 175 D4
Netherfield La
  Church Warsop NG20 .... 74 B4
  Market Warsop NG20 .... 61 E1
Netherfield Rd
  Long Eaton NG10 .... 193 E2
  Sandiacre NG10 .... 182 A2
Nethergate NG11 .... 184 B1
Nethergate Sch NG7 .... 184 C1
Netherton Pl S80 .... 36 A1
Netherton Rd S80 .... 47 D4
Nettle Croft DN11 .... 8 B4
Nettlecliff Wlk NG5 .... 160 C4
Nettleworth Inf Sch
  NG19 .... 88 B2
Nevile Dr NG12 .... 200 A1
Neville Rd NG14 .... 148 C3
Neville Sadler Ct NG9 .... 184 A4
New Brickyard La DE74 ..... 203 E1
  Kirkby in A NG17 .... 115 D3
New CI Bildworth NG21 ..... 118 A3
  Kirkby in A NG17 .... 115 D3
New Cotts NG20 .... 59 F2
New Cross St NG17 .... 100 C2
New Derby Rd NG16 .... 143 E1
New Eaton Rd NG9 .... 182 C3
New England Way NG19 .... 87 E2
New Fall St NG17 .... 99 F2
New Farm La NG16 .... 159 E3
New Hill Farnsfield NG22 ... 119 F3
  Walesby NG22 .... 64 A1
New Holles CI S80 .... 35 F1
New Inn Wlk DN7 .... 39 F3
New King St LE11 .... 220 B2
New La Aslockton NG13 .... 178 C3
  Firbeck S81 .... 16 A3
  Greasley NG16 .... 144 C3
  Hawksworth NG13 .... 167 E2
  Morton NG25 .... 137 E3
  Nottingham NG7 .... 172 B3
  Oxton NG25 .... 134 A2
  Radcliffe on T NG12 .... 175 F4
  Stapleford NG9 .... 170 B1
  Staunton in t V NG13 .... 169 E2
  Tickhill DN11 .... 8 A4
  Treswell DN22 .... 42 A4
New Row Carlton NG4 .... 174 B4
  Westwood NG16 .... 128 A3
New St
  Gainsborough DN21 .... 15 E1
  Hilcote DE55 .... 113 E4
  Huthwaite NG17 .... 100 A2
  Kegworth DE74 .... 203 F2
  Kirkby in A NG17 .... 115 D2
  Long Eaton NG10 .... 193 F4
  Loughborough LE11 .... 220 A2
  Newcastle-u-T LE12 .... 140 a4
  Newton DE55 .... 99 F2
  22 Nottingham NG5 .... 161 D1
  Retford DN22 .... 39 F3
  South Normanton DE55 ..... 113 D3
  Sutton in A NG17 .... 100 C1
New Terr Pleasley NG19 ..... 86 C3
  Sandiacre NG10 .... 182 A3
New Tythe St NG10 .... 193 F4
New Vale Rd NG4 .... 174 C3
Newall Dr Beeston NG9 ..... 183 E1
  Everton DN10 .... 11 D1
Newark Air Mus NG24 ...... 126 A3
Newark Ave 16 NG2 .... 173 F2
Newark CI NG18 .... 102 C1
Newark Cres NG2 .... 173 F2
Newark Ct NG15 .... 160 C3
Newark Dr NG18 .... 102 C1
Newark High
  Comp Sch The NG24 .... 139 F4
Newark Northgate Sta
  NG24 .... 125 D1
Newark Orchard Sch
  New Balderton NG24 .... 140 B3
  Newark-on-T NG24 .... 125 D1
Newark Rd
  Barnby in t W NG24 .... 141 E3
  Caunton NG23 .... 109 D2
  Coddington NG24 .... 125 F1
  Collingham LN6 .... 112 C2
  Eakring NG22 .... 92 C1
  Kirklington NG22 .... 120 C4
  Laughterton LN1 .... 55 D4
  Ollerton NG22 .... 77 D2
  Southwell NG25 .... 121 F1
  Stapleford LN6 .... 127 E4

Newark Rd continued
  Sutton in A NG17 .... 101 E1
  Tuxford NG22 .... 65 F1
  Wellow NG22 .... 77 E1
Newark & Sherwood
  Tech Coll NG24 .... 140 A4
Newark St NG2 .... 173 F2
Newark Tech Coll The
  Grange Centre NG24 .... 139 E3
Newark Way NG18 .... 103 D1
Newburn CI NG20 .... 72 B1
Newberry CI NG12 .... 189 D2
Newbery Ave NG10 .... 193 F3
Newbery CI NG21 .... 76 A1
Newbold Way NG12 .... 199 F1
Newbound La NG17 .... 86 B1
Newboundmill La NG19 .... 87 D2
Newbury CI NG3 .... 162 A2
Newbury Ct 13 NG5 .... 173 E4
Newbury Dr NG16 .... 159 D3
Newbury Mews 15 S80 ..... 35 F1
Newcastle Ave
  Beeston NG9 .... 183 F3
  Carlton NG4 .... 162 C1
  Newark-on-T NG24 .... 140 A3
  Worksop S80 .... 35 F1
Newcastle Cir NG7 .... 222 C2
Newcastle Dr NG7 .... 222 C3
Newcastle Farm Dr NG8 ... 160 B1
Newcastle St
  Huthwaite NG17 .... 100 A2
  4 Mansfield NG18 .... 102 A4
  Mansfield Woodhouse NG19 .. 88 A2
  Market Warsop NG20 .... 74 B3
  Nottingham NG1 .... 223 D3
  Nottingham, Bulwell NG6 ... 160 B4
  Tuxford NG22 .... 65 F1
  Worksop S80 .... 35 F1
Newcombe Dr NG5 .... 162 B4
Newdigate Rd NG16 .... 159 D4
Newdigate St
  Ilkeston DE7 .... 170 A3
  Kimberley NG16 .... 159 D3
  Nottingham NG7 .... 222 C3
  West Hallam DE7 .... 157 F4
Newfield La NG23 .... 167 F3
Newfield Rd NG5 .... 161 D2
Newgate Ct NG4 .... 174 C4
Newgate Ct NG7 .... 222 B2
Newgate Fst Sch NG18 .... 102 B4
Newgate La NG18 .... 102 B4
Newgate St
  Bingham NG13 .... 177 F3
  Worksop S80 .... 35 F1
Newhall Gr NG2 .... 173 E1
Newhall La NG18 .... 102 B1
Newham CI DE75 .... 143 D1
Newhaven Ave NG2 .... 88 A2
Newholm Dr NG11 .... 185 D2
Newings La DN22 .... 42 C4
Newington Rd DN10 .... 10 B4
Newland CI
  Beeston NG9 .... 183 D1
  Nottingham NG8 .... 172 B3
Newlands
  Gainsborough DN21 .... 15 F1
  Retford DN22 .... 39 E2
Newlands Ave NG22 .... 77 F3
Newlands CI NG12 .... 186 B2
Newlands Cres DE55 .... 99 D2
Newlands Dr
  Carlton NG4 .... 162 C1
  Clipstone NG19 .... 89 E1
Newlands Jun Sch NG19 ... 89 F2
Newlands Rd
  Clipstone NG19 .... 89 E1
  Mansfield NG19 .... 103 D4
Newlyn Dr
  Nottingham NG8 .... 172 B4
  South Normanton DE55 ... 113 E3
Newlyn Gdns NG8 .... 172 B4
Newmanleys Rd NG16 ..... 157 F4
Newmanleys Rd S NG16 .. 157 F4
Newmarket St NG18 .... 102 C3
Newmarket Way NG9 ...... 183 D3
Newnham Rd NG24 .... 125 D1
Newport Cres NG19 .... 87 F1
Newport Dr NG8 .... 160 B1
Newquay Ave 11 NG7 .... 172 C4
Newstead Abbey NG15 ... 131 E4

Newstead Ave
  Newark-on-T NG24 .... 125 D1
  Sutton in A NG17 .... 101 D1
Newstead Dr NG12 .... 186 B1
Newstead Gr
  Bingham NG13 .... 177 E2
  Nottingham NG1 .... 223 D4
Newstead Ind Est NG5 .... 162 A4
Newstead Prim Sch
  NG15 .... 130 B3
Newstead Rd
  Long Eaton NG10 .... 182 B2
  Newstead NG15 .... 130 B4
Newstead Rd S DE7 .... 157 E2
Newstead St
  Mansfield NG18 .... 101 E4
  6 Nottingham NG5 .... 161 E2
Newstead Sta NG15 .... 130 C3
Newstead Terr NG15 .... 146 A4
Newstead Way NG8 .... 159 E1
Newthorpe Comm NG16 .. 144 A1
Newthorpe St NG2 .... 173 E1

Newton Ave
  Bingham NG13 .... 177 E2
  Radcliffe on T NG12 .... 176 A2
Newton CI Arnold NG5 ..... 162 A3
  Gainsborough DN21 .... 24 C4
  Lowdham NG14 .... 150 C1
  Worksop S81 .... 35 E4
Newton Dr
  Stapleford NG9 .... 182 C3
  West Bridgford NG2 .... 185 E2
Newton Gdns NG13 .... 177 E3
Newton Prim Sch DE55 ..... 99 D2
Newton Rd Carlton NG4 ... 162 C2
  Newton DE55 .... 99 D2
Newton St Beeston NG9 ... 183 F3
  Mansfield NG18 .... 102 B3
  Newark-on-T NG24 .... 140 A4
  Nottingham NG7 .... 172 C1
  Retford DN22 .... 39 F2
Newton's La NG16 .... 158 A2
Newton-on-Trent
  CE Prim Sch LN1 .... 55 D1
Newtondale Ave NG19 ...... 88 C1
Newtondale CI NG8 .... 160 B1
Newtonwood La DE55 .... 99 D3
Nicholas PI NG22 .... 66 A2
Nicholas Rd NG9 .... 171 E1
Nicholson St NG24 .... 140 A4
Nicholson's Row NG20 ...... 72 C2
Nicker Hill NG12 .... 198 A2
Nicklaus Ct 5 NG5 .... 161 D4
Nidderdale NG8 .... 171 E2
Nidderdale CI NG8 .... 171 E2
Nightingale Ave
  Hathern LE12 .... 213 D1
  Pleasley NG19 .... 87 D2
Nightingale CI
  Balderton NG24 .... 140 C2
  Hucknall NG16 .... 159 E3
Nightingale Cres NG16 .... 159 D3
Nightingale Dr NG19 .... 87 F1
Nightingale Gr S81 .... 35 E4
Nightingale Way NG22 .... 53 D4
Nile St NG1 .... 223 F3
Nilsson Rd NG9 .... 183 D2
Nine Acre Gdns NG6 ...... 159 F4
Nine Acres DE74 .... 203 E1
Nine Scores La DN9 .... 1 C4
Ninth Ave NG19 .... 103 D4
Nixon Rise NG15 .... 145 E3
Noble La NG13 .... 179 D3
Noburn Cres NG6 .... 160 C2
Noel St
  Gainsborough DN21 .... 15 E1
  Kimberley NG16 .... 159 D3
  Mansfield NG18 .... 102 A4
  Nottingham NG7 .... 172 C4
Nook The Beeston NG9 .... 184 A4
  Beeston, Chilwell NG9 ..... 183 F2
  Calverton NG14 .... 148 C4
  East Leake LE12 .... 205 F1
  Nottingham NG8 .... 171 F2
  Shireorbrook NG20 .... 72 B2
Nookin NG22 .... 66 A3
Norbett CI NG9 .... 183 E2
Norbett Rd NG5 .... 148 A1
Norbett Rd NG5 .... 148 A1
Norbreck CI NG8 .... 160 A2
Norbury Dr NG18 .... 102 C2
Norbury Way NG10 .... 182 A3
Norbury Way NG10 .... 182 A3
Norfolk Ave Beeston NG9 .. 183 D1
  Bircotes DN11 .... 9 E2
Norfolk CI Hucknall NG15 . 145 E3
  Market Warsop NG20 .... 74 A2
Norfolk Dr NG18 .... 102 B4
Norfolk Dr Bircotes DN11 ... 9 E2
  Mansfield NG18 .... 102 A4
Norfolk PI Arnold NG5 ..... 162 A3
  Nottingham NG1 .... 223 E3
Norfolk Rd Bircotes DN11 ... 9 E2
  Long Eaton NG10 .... 182 C1
Norfolk St S80 .... 35 F1
Norfolk Wlk NG10 .... 182 A3
Norland CI NG3 .... 173 F4

Norman Ave
  Newark-on-T NG24 .... 125 D2
  Sutton in A NG17 .... 101 D1
Norman CI Beeston NG9 ... 183 E3
  Nottingham NG3 .... 223 E4
Norman Cres DE7 .... 157 F2
Norman Dr
  Eastwood NG16 .... 144 A1
  Hucknall NG15 .... 145 F2
Norman Rd NG3 .... 174 A4
Norman St Carlton NG4 ... 175 D3
  Ilkeston DE7 .... 157 F2
  Kimberley NG16 .... 158 C4
Normanby Rd NG8 .... 171 E2
Normanton CI NG21 .... 75 F2
Normanton Dr NG18 .... 102 C4
Normanton La
  Bottesford NG13 .... 181 D3
  Keyworth NG12 .... 197 F2
  Stanford on S LE12 .... 214 A1
Normanton on Soar
  Prim Sch LE12 .... 213 E2
Normanton Rd NG25 ...... 121 F1
Nornay CI S81 .... 18 A2
North Ave Bawtry DN10 .... 10 A4
  Rainworth NG21 .... 104 A1
  Sandiacre NG10 .... 182 A3
North Border Jun &
  Inf Schs DN11 .... 9 D2
North Carr Rd DN10 .... 7 E2
North Church St NG1 ...... 223 E3
North Circus St NG1 .... 223 D2

North Clifton Sch NG23 .... 68 C2
North Cr NG21 .... 90 A2
North Cres NG13 .... 181 D1
North Dr Balderton NG24 . 140 C1
  Beeston NG9 .... 183 F3
  Bilsthorpe NG22 .... 105 F4
North End NG24 .... 138 C3
North Gate
  Newark-on-T NG24 .... 125 D1
  Nottingham NG7 .... 160 C1
  Tickhill DN11 .... 8 A4
North Gate Pl NG7 .... 160 C1
North On Calverton NG14 . 133 E1
  East Drayton DN22 .... 53 D2
North Hill Ave NG15 .... 145 F4
North Hill Cres NG15 ...... 145 F4
North Leverton
  CE Prim Sch DN22 .... 32 B1
North Leys Rd DN22 .... 43 E4
North Marsh Rd DN21 ...... 15 E1
North Midlands Ind Mus
  NG8 .... 172 A2
North Moor Dr DN10 .... 13 F3
North Moor Rd DN10 .... 13 F3
North Nottinghamshire
  Coll S81 .... 35 F3
North Par DN21 .... 24 C4
North Pk NG18 .... 102 C2
North Rd
  Long Eaton NG10 .... 193 E3
  Loughborough LE11 .... 220 B3
  Nottingham NG7 .... 222 C2
  Retford DN22 .... 29 D1
  Ruddington NG11 .... 196 A4
  West Bridgford NG2 .... 185 F4
North Scarle Cty Prim Sch
  LN6 .... 83 E1
North Scarle Rd NG23 ..... 98 C4
North Sherwood St NG1 .. 223 E4
North St Beeston NG9 ..... 183 F3
  Eastwood NG16 .... 144 B1
  Gainsborough DN21 .... 15 E1
  Huthwaite NG17 .... 100 A2
  9 Kimberley NG16 .... 159 D3
  Kirkby in A NG17 .... 115 D1
  Langley Mill NG16 .... 143 D2
  Morton DN21 .... 15 D2
  4 Nottingham NG2 .... 173 F2
  Pinxton NG16 .... 113 E2
  South Normanton DE55 ... 113 D3
  Sturton le S DN22 .... 32 B3
  Sutton in A NG17 .... 100 C2
  Warsop Vale NG20 .... 73 E2
  Whaley Thorns NG20 .... 59 D1
North Warren Rd DN21 ..... 15 D1
North Way S81 .... 25 F4
North Wheatley
  CE Prim Sch DN22 .... 31 F4
North Wlk DN22 .... 39 E4
Northall Ave NG6 .... 160 A3
Northampton St 4 NG3 ... 173 F3
Northcliffe Ave NG3 .... 162 A1
Northcote St NG10 .... 193 F4
Northcote Way NG6 .... 160 B3
Northcroft LN1 .... 57 D3
Northdale Rd NG3 .... 174 A4
Northdown Dr NG9 .... 183 E2
Northdown Rd NG8 .... 172 B3
Northern Ct NG6 .... 160 B2
Northern Dr NG9 .... 170 B2
Northern Rd NG24 .... 125 D1
Northern View NG17 .... 100 C2
Northfield Ave
  Ilkeston DE7 .... 157 F1
  Long Eaton NG10 .... 193 E2
  Mansfield Woodhouse NG19 .. 88 A2
  Radcliffe on T NG12 .... 176 B2
Northfield Cres NG9 .... 183 D2
Northfield Dr NG18 .... 102 C3
Northfield Way LE12 .... 205 F2
Northfield La
  Mansfield Woodhouse NG19 .. 88 A3
  Treswell DN22 .... 42 A2
Northfield Pk NG19 .... 88 A3
Northfield Rd
  Beeston NG9 .... 183 D2
  North Leverton w H DN22 . 33 D1
Northfield Way NG19 .... 39 E4
Northfields NG10 .... 193 D2
Northfields CI NG17 .... 100 C2
Northfields Way LE12 ..... 205 F2
Northgate Prim Sch
  NG7 .... 160 C1
Northgate St 8 DE7 .... 157 F1
Northolme DN21 .... 15 F1
Northolme Ave NG6 .... 160 B4
Northolt Dr NG16 .... 159 E2
Northrowe NG17 .... 129 F4
Northside La DN22 .... 42 A4
Northside Wlk NG5 .... 147 F1
Northumberland Ave S81 .. 35 E4
Northumberland CI 23 NG3 .. 173 F3
Northumberland St S81 .... 36 A3
Northumbria Dr DN22 .... 39 E3
Northwold Ave NG2 .... 185 E3
Northwood Ct NG5 .... 162 A2
Northwood Rd NG5 .... 162 A2
Northwood Cres NG5 ...... 161 E3
Northwood Rd NG5 .... 161 E3
Northwood St NG9 .... 182 B4
Norton La NG20 .... 60 A2
Norton Rd LN6 .... 127 F4
Norton St NG7 .... 222 B3
Norwell CE Prim Sch
  NG23 .... 110 A3
Norwell Ct NG19 .... 88 A1

Norwell La Brough NG23 .. 112 B1
  Cromwell NG23 .... 110 B4
Norwell Rd NG23 .... 109 E3
Norwich CI NG19 .... 88 B3
Norwich Gdns NG6 .... 146 A1
Norwood CI NG17 .... 100 A2
Norwood Gdns NG5 .... 121 F1
Norwood Rd NG7 .... 222 A3
Nostell Mews 19 S80 .... 35 F1
Notintone St NG2 .... 173 F2
Nottingham Airport
  NG12 .... 186 C3
Nottingham Bluecoat Sch
  NG8 .... 172 B4
Nottingham Castle
  (site of) NG1 .... 223 D2
Nottingham Cath NG1 ..... 223 D2
Nottingham High Sch
  For Boys NG7 .... 223 D4
Nottingham High Sch
  For Girls NG1 .... 223 D4
Nottingham La LE14 .... 218 B3
Nottingham Midland Sta
  NG2 .... 223 F1
Nottingham Rd
  Arnold NG5 .... 161 F3
  Beeston NG9 .... 183 D1
  Bingham NG13 .... 177 E2
  Bottesford NG13 .... 181 A2
  Burton Joyce NG14 .... 163 E2
  Costock LE12 .... 206 B1
  Cropwell Bishop NG12 ... 188 C2
  Eastwood NG16 .... 144 A1
  Eastwood, Giltbrook NG16 ... 158 B4
  Gotham NG11 .... 195 D2
  Gunthorpe NG14 .... 164 A4
  Hucknall NG15 .... 146 B2
  Ilkeston DE7 .... 170 A3
  Kegworth DE74 .... 203 E1
  Keyworth NG12 .... 197 F2
  Kimberley NG16 .... 159 D3
  Kirkby in A NG17 .... 115 D1
  Long Eaton NG10 .... 193 F4
  Loughborough LE11 .... 220 B3
  Mansfield NG18 .... 102 B2
  Nether Broughton LE14 .. 219 F4
  Nottingham, New Basford
    NG7 .... 160 C1
  Nottingham, Old Basford
    NG6 .... 160 C2
  Oxton NG25 .... 134 A1
  Radcliffe on T NG12 .... 175 E1
  Ravenshead NG15 .... 116 C2
  Selston NG16 .... 129 D3
  Southwell NG25 .... 136 B3
  Stapleford NG9 .... 182 C4
  Thurgarton NG14 .... 151 E3
  Trowell NG9 .... 170 C3
  Woodborough NG14 .... 148 C1
Nottingham Rd E NG16 ... 144 A1
Nottingham South &
  Wilford Ind Est NG2 ...... 185 D2
Nottingham Trent Univ
  The NG11 .... 184 B2
Nuart Rd NG9 .... 183 F4
Nugent Gdns 6 NG3 ...... 173 F3
Nuncar Ct NG17 .... 115 D1
Nuncargate Rd NG17 ...... 115 D1
Nunn Brook Rd NG17 ...... 99 F1
Nunn Brook Rise NG17 .... 99 F1
Nunn CI NG17 .... 99 F1
Nurseries The NG16 .... 144 A1
Nursery Ave Beeston NG9 . 183 E3
  Farndon NG24 .... 139 D3
  Sutton in A NG17 .... 100 B1
Nursery CI Hucknall NG15 . 146 A2
  Radcliffe on T NG12 .... 176 A2
  Sutton in L NG17 .... 57 D2
Nursery La
  Nottingham NG6 .... 160 C2
  Sutton on T NG23 .... 96 C4
Nursery Rd Arnold NG5 ... 162 A4
  Bingham NG13 .... 178 A3
  Radcliffe on T NG12 .... 176 A2
Nursery St NG18 .... 102 B4
Nursury Gdns NG14 .... 150 B1
Nuthall Gdns NG8 .... 172 B4
Nuthall Rd NG8 .... 160 B1
Nutkin CI 4 LE11 .... 220 A1

Oak Acres NG9 .... 183 D3
Oak Ave Aldercar NG16 ... 143 D3
  Bingham NG13 .... 178 A2
  Bildworth NG21 .... 118 A2
  Farndon NG24 .... 139 D2
  Mansfield NG18 .... 102 B4
  New Ollerton NG22 .... 77 E2
  Radcliffe on T NG12 .... 175 F2
  Rainworth NG21 .... 104 A1
  Sandiacre NG10 .... 182 A4
  Shireorbrook NG20 .... 72 B2
Oak Bank CI NG18 .... 102 A4
Oak CI Pinxton NG16 ...... 113 E2
  Worksop S80 .... 35 F2
Oak Cres LE12 .... 214 B4
Oak Dr Eastwood NG16 ... 143 F1
  New Balderton NG24 ...... 140 B2
  Selston NG16 .... 159 D1
Oak Flatt NG9 .... 183 D3

Oak Gr NG15 .... 146 A2
Oak Lodge Dr NG16 .... 158 C4
Oak Rise NG22 .... 105 F4
Oak St Kirkby in A NG17 .... 115 D3
  Nottingham NG5 .... 161 D1
  Sutton in A NG17 .... 100 B4
Oak Tree Ave
  Edwinstowe NG21 .... 76 A1
  Glapwell S44 .... 86 A4
  Radcliffe on T NG4 .... 175 F2
Oak Tree Bsns Pk NG18 .... 103 D2
Oak Tree Cl Hucknall NG15 ... 145 E2
  Mansfield NG18 .... 103 D2
  West Bridgford NG2 .... 186 A4
Oak Tree Cres NG19 .... 88 A2
Oak Tree Dr NG4 .... 163 D1
Oak Tree La NG18 .... 103 D3
Oak Tree Lane Fst Sch
 NG18 .... 103 D3
Oak Tree Rd Bawtry DN10 .... 9 F4
  Sutton in A NG17 .... 101 D2
Oak Tree Rise S81 .... 25 F4
Oakdale Dr NG9 .... 183 E2
Oakdale Rd Arnold NG5 .... 162 A4
  Carlton NG3 .... 174 B3
  South Normanton DE55 .... 113 D2
Oakdale Sch NG19 .... 87 F1
Oakenhall Ave NG15 .... 146 B4
Oakfield LN1 .... 57 D2
Oakfield Ave
  Market Warsop NG20 .... 74 A2
  Sutton in A NG17 .... 114 C4
Oakfield Cl
  Mansfield NG18 .... 102 C1
  Nottingham NG8 .... 171 E2
Oakfield Dr NG10 .... 182 A2
Oakfield La NG20 .... 74 A1
Oakfield Rd
  Hucknall NG15 .... 146 A3
  Nottingham NG8 .... 171 E2
  Stapleford NG9 .... 182 B4
Oakfields Rd NG2 .... 174 A3
Oakford Cl NG8 .... 160 A1
Oakham Bsns Pk NG18 .... 101 F2
Oakham Cl
  Mansfield NG18 .... 102 A2
  Nottingham NG5 .... 160 C4
Oakham Rd NG11 .... 185 E1
Oakham Way DE7 .... 157 F2
Oakhampton Cres NG3 .... 162 B3
Oakholme Ave S81 .... 35 F3
Oakholme Rise S81 .... 35 F3
Oakington Cl NG5 .... 161 D3
Oakland Ave
  Huthwaite NG17 .... 99 F1
  Long Eaton NG10 .... 193 E3
Oakland Ct NG9 .... 171 D1
Oakland Gr NG14 .... 148 C4
Oakland Rd NG14 .... 148 C4
Oakland St ⊠ NG7 .... 172 C4
Oakland Terr NG10 .... 193 E3
Oaklands NG23 .... 112 A4
Oaklands Ave DE75 .... 143 D1
Oaklands Dr DN11 .... 8 B1
Oaklands La DN22 .... 40 A3
Oaklands The DE55 .... 113 D2
Oakleaf Cres NG17 .... 100 B1
Oakleigh Ave
  Mansfield Woodhouse NG19 .. 88 C2
  Nottingham NG3 .... 162 B1
Oakleigh St NG6 .... 160 B2
Oakley Dr LE12 .... 212 B1
Oakley Mews NG5 .... 159 F3
Oakley's Rd NG10 .... 193 F4
Oakley's Rd W NG10 .... 193 E3
Oakmead Ave NG18 .... 171 F4
Oakmere Cl NG2 .... 186 B2
Oakridge Cl NG19 .... 88 C1
Oaks Ave S80 .... 58 B4
Oaks Cl DN22 .... 19 D3
Oaks Ind Est LE11 .... 220 A3
Oaks La Oxton NG25 .... 133 F4
  Walkeringham DN10 .... 13 F2
Oaktree Ave DN21 .... 15 F1
Oaktree Dr NG22 .... 106 A2
Oaktree Rd DE55 .... 99 C3
Oakwood Dr
  Nottingham NG8 .... 172 B4
  Ravenshead NG15 .... 117 D1
Oakwood Gr NG21 .... 91 E4
Oakwood Rd NG18 .... 103 D2
Oardale Rd NG18 .... 101 F4
Oatfield La NG12 .... 176 B3
Oban Rd NG9 .... 183 E3
Occupation La
  Kirkby in A NG17 .... 114 C3
  Rolleston NG25 .... 137 C3
  Willoughby-on-t-W LE12 ...... 217 F3
Occupation Rd
  Hucknall NG15 .... 146 A3
  New Houghton NG19 .... 86 C4
Ochbrook Ct DE7 .... 157 F2
Ockerby St NG6 .... 160 B3
Oddicroft La NG17 .... 101 D1
Odesa Dr NG6 .... 160 A2
Ogdon Ct NG3 .... 173 F3
Ogle Dr NG7 .... 223 D1
Ogle St NG15 .... 146 A4
Old Basford Prim Sch
 NG6 .... 160 B2
Old Bell La NG23 .... 96 C2
Old Blyth Rd DN22 .... 38 B3
Old Brickyard NG3 .... 174 A4
Old Chapel Cl NG17 .... 114 C3
Old Chapel La
  Elston NG23 .... 153 F3
  Selston NG16 .... 129 D2

Old Church St ⓭ NG7 .... 172 C1
Old Coach Rd
  Nottingham NG8 .... 171 F3
  Nottingham NG8 .... 172 A3
  Worksop S80 .... 47 F4
Old Courtyard The DN21 .... 44 B4
Old Dalby CE Sch LE14 .... 218 C2
Old Dalby La LE14 .... 219 E3
Old Derby Rd NG16 .... 143 E2
Old Dr NG9 .... 183 F4
Old Engine Yard The
 LE12 .... 215 F3
Old Epperstone Rd NG14 .... 150 A2
Old Farm Rd NG5 .... 160 C4
Old Forge Cl LE12 .... 213 D1
Old Forge La NG13 .... 191 E3
Old Forge Rd NG13 .... 6 C1
Old Grantham Rd NG13 .... 179 D2
Old Great North Rd NG23 ... 96 C4
Old Hall Cl
  Calverton NG14 .... 148 C4
  Farndon NG24 .... 138 C2
  Market Warsop NG20 .... 74 B3
Old Hall Dr
  Nottingham NG3 .... 161 E1
  Widmerpool NG12 .... 208 B3
Old Hall Gdns NG24 .... 125 F1
Old Hall La
  East Markham NG22 .... 65 F4
  Norwell NG23 .... 110 A4
Old Hall The DN21 .... 15 E1
Old La NG10 .... 185 E1
Old La The NG13 .... 192 A1
Old Lenton Cl NG12 .... 189 D2
Old Lenton St NG1 .... 223 F2
Old London Rd
  Babworth DN22 .... 49 F4
  Barnby Moor DN22 .... 28 B2
  West Drayton DN22 .... 50 C1
Old Main Rd
  Bulcote NG14 .... 164 A3
  Costock LE12 .... 206 B1
Old Manor Cl NG14 .... 149 E2
Old Manor Rd NG19 .... 88 B2
Old Market Pl
  Mansfield NG18 .... 102 A4
  South Normanton DE55 ...... 113 D3
Old Market Sq NG1 .... 223 D2
Old Melton Rd NG12 .... 197 F4
Old Mill Cl Beeston NG9 ...... 183 D1
  Bestwood Village NG6 .... 146 B2
  Nottingham NG7 .... 222 B3
Old Mill Cres NG24 .... 140 A4
Old Mill Ct NG13 .... 177 F3
Old Mill La Cuckney NG20 ..... 60 A2
  Mansfield NG18 .... 88 C1
Old Newark Rd NG18 .... 102 C1
Old Park Cl NG11 .... 203 F3
Old Park The NG12 .... 187 F1
Old Parsonage La LE12 .... 215 E1
Old Pond The DE75 .... 157 D4
Old Post Office St DN10 ...... 11 E2
Old Rd NG17 .... 100 C3
Old Rectory Cl LE12 .... 205 F1
Old Rufford Rd
  Bilsthorpe NG22 .... 105 E2
  Calverton NG14 .... 133 E3
  Farnsfield NG22 .... 119 D3
  Ollerton NG22 .... 77 D2
  Edwinstowe NG22 .... 91 E2
Old School Cl NG11 .... 195 F4
Old School House Cl
 NG12 .... 189 D4
Old School La NG19 .... 87 F3
Old Showfields DN21 .... 15 E1
Old Sookholme La NG20 .... 74 A2
Old St NG1 .... 223 E3
Old Station Yd NG13 .... 181 E2
Old Storth La DE55 .... 113 D2
Old Terr NG19 .... 86 C2
Old Tollerton Rd NG12 .... 186 B4
Old Trent Rd DN10 .... 14 C1
Old Way LE12 .... 213 D1
Oldacres NG14 .... 149 E2
Oldbury Cl NG11 .... 195 E4
Oldershaw Ave DE74 .... 203 E1
Oldershaw Rd LE12 .... 205 F1
Oldknow St NG7 .... 172 C4
Oldoak Rd NG11 .... 185 D1
Olga Rd NG3 .... 173 F3
Olive Ave
  Long Eaton NG10 .... 182 C1
  Shirebrook NG20 .... 72 C3
Olive Ct NG17 .... 100 C2
Olive Gr
  Burton Joyce NG14 .... 163 F3
  Mansfield NG19 .... 103 D4
Oliver Cl Heanor DE75 .... 143 F1
  Nottingham NG7 .... 222 C4
  Oliver Cl NG24 .... 140 A4
Oliver Quibell
  Cty Inf Sch NG24 .... 140 A4
Oliver Rd LE11 .... 220 A1
Oliver St NG7 .... 222 C4
Ollerton Jun & Inf Schs
 NG22 .... 77 E3
Ollerton Rd Arnold NG5 ...... 147 F3
  Calverton NG14 .... 132 C1
  Edwinstowe NG21 .... 76 B2
  Farnsfield NG22 .... 119 D1
  Gamston DN22 .... 50 C2
  Kelham NG23 .... 124 A3
  Kirton NG22 .... 78 C4
  Ollerton NG22 .... 77 D2
  Retford DN22 .... 39 F2
  South Muskham NG23 .... 124 A4
  Tuxford NG22 .... 65 E1
  Worksop S80 .... 47 D2

Olton Ave NG9 .... 171 F1
Olympus Ct NG15 .... 145 E2
Omberley Ave NG17 .... 101 D3
Onchan Ave NG4 .... 174 C3
Ontario Dr NG6 .... 146 C1
Opal Cl NG21 .... 104 B1
Orange Cl NG20 .... 72 C3
Orange Croft DN11 .... 8 A4
Orange Gdns NG2 .... 173 F2
Orby Cl NG3 .... 173 F3
Orby Wlk NG3 .... 173 F3
Orchard Ave
  Bingham NG13 .... 177 E2
  Carlton NG4 .... 174 C4
  North Leverton w H DN22 ... 42 B4
Orchard Cl
  Barnstone NG13 .... 190 C2
  Bleasby NG14 .... 152 A4
  Burton Joyce NG14 .... 163 F3
  East Bridgford NG13 .... 165 E2
  East Leake LE12 .... 214 B4
  Gunthorpe NG14 .... 165 D3
  Morton DN21 .... 15 D3
  North Leverton w H DN22 ... 42 B4
  Radcliffe on T NG12 .... 175 F2
  Rampton DN22 .... 43 D1
  Shirebrook NG20 .... 72 C3
  Southwell NG25 .... 121 E1
  Sutton Bonington LE12 ...... 213 E3
  Tollerton NG12 .... 186 B1
Orchard Cres
  Beeston NG9 .... 183 E3
  Glapwell S44 .... 86 A4
  Tuxford NG22 .... 65 F1
Orchard Ct Carlton NG4 .... 162 B1
  Hucknall NG15 .... 146 A3
  Langley Mill NG16 .... 143 D2
  Nottingham NG6 .... 160 C4
Orchard Dr NG14 .... 149 D4
Orchard Gr NG5 .... 161 F3
Orchard Rise NG4 .... 163 E4
Orchard St
  Eastwood NG16 .... 144 A1
  Gotham NG11 .... 195 D1
  Hucknall NG15 .... 146 A3
  Kimberley NG16 .... 158 C3
  Langley Mill NG16 .... 143 D2
  Long Eaton NG10 .... 193 F4
  ⊠ Loughborough LE11 ...... 220 A2
  Mansfield NG18 .... 88 A1
  Stapleford NG9 .... 182 B4
Orchard The
  Elston NG23 .... 153 F2
  Sutton in A NG17 .... 101 D3
Orchard View NG18 .... 88 A2
Orchard Way
  Bawtry DN10 .... 10 A4
  Sandiacre NG10 .... 182 A2
  Sutton in A NG17 .... 114 B4
  Wymeswold LE12 .... 216 B2
Orchard Wlk NG17 .... 114 B4
Orchards The
  Carlton NG4 .... 163 D1
  Lowdham NG14 .... 164 C4
  Oxton NG25 .... 134 A1
  Westwood NG16 .... 128 A2
Orchid Cl
  ⊠ Kirkby in A NG17 .... 114 C4
  New Balderton NG24 .... 140 A3
  West Bridgford NG2 .... 185 E2
Orchid Dr NG24 .... 139 D3
Ordsall Cty Jun & Inf Schs
 DN22 .... 39 E2
Ordsall Hall Comp Sch
 DN22 .... 39 E3
Ordsall Park Cl DN22 .... 39 E3
Ordsall Park Dr DN22 .... 39 E3
Ordsall Park Rd DN22 .... 39 E3
Ordsall Rd DN22 .... 39 E3
Orford Ave
  Nottingham NG11 .... 184 C2
  Radcliffe on T NG12 .... 175 F1
Orion Cl NG8 .... 171 F4
Orion Dr NG8 .... 171 F4
Orlando Dr NG4 .... 174 C4
Orlock Wlk NG5 .... 161 D3
Ormonde St NG16 .... 143 D2
Ormonde Terr
  Aldercar NG16 .... 143 D2
  Nottingham NG5 .... 161 D1
Ornsay Cl NG5 .... 146 C1
Orpean Way NG9 .... 182 C1
Orston Ave Arnold NG5 ..... 162 A4
  Newark-on-T NG24 .... 140 C2
Orston Cty Prim Sch
 NG13 .... 180 A4
Orston Dr NG8 .... 172 B4
Orston Gn NG8 .... 172 B2
Orston La NG13 .... 180 A2
Orston Rd E NG2 .... 173 F1
Orston Rd W NG2 .... 173 F1
Orston Rd NG3 .... 183 E3
Ortzen St NG7 .... 222 B4
Orville Rd NG5 .... 160 C4
Osberton Rd DN22 .... 39 F3
Osberton View S81 .... 36 A3
Osborne Ave ⊠ NG5 .... 161 E2
Osborne Cl NG10 .... 182 A2
Osborne Gr NG5 .... 161 E2
Osborne St NG7 .... 222 A4
Osborne Cl NG16 .... 159 D4

Osbourne St NG17 .... 129 F4
Osgood Rd NG5 .... 162 B3
Osier Dr NG15 .... 130 A3
Osier Rd NG2 .... 173 E1
Osiers The DE74 .... 203 E1
Osman Cl NG2 .... 173 D1
Osmanton St
  Nottingham NG7 .... 222 B1
  Sandiacre NG10 .... 182 B3
Osprey Cl NG11 .... 184 B1
Ossington Cl
  Meden Vale NG20 .... 74 B4
  Nottingham NG1 .... 223 E4
Ossington Rd NG22 .... 93 F3
Ossington St NG7 .... 222 B4
Ossington Way NG24 .... 124 C1
Oster Fen La NG23 .... 156 C4
Osterley Gr NG16 .... 159 E1
Otter Ave LN1 .... 57 D2
Oulton Cl NG5 .... 161 F3
Oundle Dr Ilkeston DE7 ..... 170 A4
  Mansfield NG19 .... 87 E1
  Nottingham NG8 .... 172 B2
Our Lady of Perpetual
  Succour RC Sch NG6 ...... 160 B3
Our Lady's Convent Sch
 LE11 .... 220 A1
Ousmanton St NG17 .... 100 C1
Ouse Bridge Dr NG4 .... 175 D4
Ousebridge Cres NG4 .... 175 D4

Outgang La
  Mansfield Woodhouse NG19 .. 88 B2
  Pleasley NG19 .... 87 D3
  Treswell DN22 .... 42 C2
Outgang Rd DN22 .... 43 E2
Outram St NG17 .... 100 C2
Oval Gdns ⊠ NG8 .... 172 B4
Oval The Retford DN22 ...... 39 F2
  Tickhill DN11 .... 8 A4
Overdale Ave NG17 .... 100 C4
Overdale Cl NG10 .... 193 D3
Overdale Rd NG6 .... 160 B2
Overend Rd S80 .... 35 F2
Overstone Cl NG17 .... 100 C3
Overstrand Cl NG5 .... 161 F3
Owday La S81 .... 25 E2
Owen Ave NG10 .... 194 A3
Owlston Cl NG16 .... 143 F2
Owsthorpe Cl NG5 .... 161 D4
Owston Ferry Rd DN9 .... 7 E4
Owston Rd DN10 .... 7 E2
Owthorpe Gr NG5 .... 161 D1
Owthorpe La NG12 .... 199 F2
Owthorpe Rd
  Colston Bassett NG12 ...... 200 A3
  Cotgrave NG12 .... 187 F1
Oxborough Rd NG5 .... 161 E4
Oxbow Cl NG2 .... 173 E1
Oxbury Rd NG16 .... 158 C4
Oxclose La
  Mansfield Woodhouse NG19 .. 88 A2
  Nottingham NG5 .... 161 E3
  Radmanthwaite NG19 .... 87 E2
Oxcroft La NG20 .... 58 A4
Oxendale Cl NG2 .... 186 B3
Oxengate NG5 .... 161 E3
Oxford Cl NG21 .... 118 A4
Oxford Dr DN11 .... 8 A3
Oxford Rd
  Carlton in L S81 .... 25 F3
  West Bridgford NG2 .... 186 A4
Oxford St Carlton NG4 ...... 174 C4
  Eastwood NG16 .... 143 F1
  Kirkby in A NG17 .... 115 D2
  Long Eaton NG10 .... 193 E4
  Loughborough LE11 .... 220 A2
  Mansfield Woodhouse NG19 .. 88 B1
  Nottingham NG1 .... 223 D2
  Sutton in A NG17 .... 100 C2
Oxpasture La NG20 .... 58 A3
Oxton Ave NG5 .... 161 E2
Oxton By-Pass NG25 .... 134 A2
Oxton Cl Mansfield NG19 ... 101 F4
  Retford DN22 .... 39 F2
Oxton Hill NG25 .... 134 C2
Oxton Rd Calverton NG14 .. 133 E1
  Southwell NG25 .... 121 D3
Ozier Holt Carlton NG4 ..... 174 C2
  Long Eaton NG10 .... 193 D3

Pacey Cl LE12 .... 220 A2
Packe St LE11 .... 220 A2
Packington Hill DE74 .... 203 E1
Packman Dr NG11 .... 196 B4
Paddock Cl
  Calverton NG14 .... 148 C4
  Edwinstowe NG21 .... 76 A2
  Nottingham NG6 .... 160 A3
  Radcliffe on T NG12 .... 175 F1
Paddock The
  Beeston NG9 .... 183 E1
  Bingham NG13 .... 177 F2
  Collingham NG23 .... 112 A4
  Gunthorpe NG13, NG14 .... 164 C3
  Kirkby in A NG17 .... 114 C2
  Retford DN22 .... 40 A2
  Stanton Hill NG17 .... 100 B3
  Tickhill DN11 .... 8 A4
Paddocks Cl Elston NG23 ... 153 F2
  Pinxton NG16 .... 113 E2
Paddocks The
  Beckingham DN10 .... 14 A1
  Bottesford NG13 .... 181 D1
  Elston NG23 .... 153 F2
  Hockerton NG25 .... 122 A3
  Lound DN22 .... 20 B1
  Mansfield Woodhouse NG19 .. 88 C3

Paddocks The continued
  Marton DN21 .... 44 B4
  Newark-on-T NG24 .... 140 A4
  Newton on T LN1 .... 55 D1
  Sandiacre NG10 .... 182 A3
  Stapleford LN6 .... 127 F4
  Sutton Bonington LE12 ..... 213 D3
  West Bridgford NG12 .... 186 A2
  Worksop S81 .... 36 A4
Paddocks View NG10 .... 193 E2
Padley's La LE14 .... 218 A1
Padge Rd NG9 .... 184 A3
Padgham Ct ⓫ NG5 .... 161 D4
Padley Hill NG18 .... 102 A3
Padleys La NG14 .... 163 F3
Padstow Comp Sch
 NG5 .... 161 D3
Padstow Rd NG5 .... 160 C3
Padstow Sec Sch NG5 ...... 160 C3
Pagdin Dr DN11 .... 8 C1
Paget Cres NG11 .... 196 B4
Paget St ⓫ LE11 .... 220 A3
Paignton Cl NG8 .... 160 A1
Paisley Gr NG9 .... 183 E1
Palace View NG25 .... 136 C4
Palatine St NG2 .... 223 D1
Palin Gdns NG12 .... 176 A2
Palin St NG7 .... 222 B4
Paling Cres NG17 .... 100 C2
Palm Court Ind Ctr NG7 ... 160 C1
Palm St NG7 .... 160 C1
Palm Wood Ct NG6 .... 160 B3
Palmer Ave NG15 .... 146 A4
Palmer Cres NG4 .... 174 B4
Palmer Dr NG9 .... 182 B3
Palmer Rd Beeston NG9 ... 183 D1
  Retford DN22 .... 30 A1
  Sutton on T NG23 .... 96 C4
Palmerston Gdns NG3 ...... 223 E4
Palmerston St
  Selston NG16 .... 128 C1
  Westwood NG16 .... 128 B2
Palmwood Ct NG6 .... 160 B3
Paper Mill La DN11 .... 8 B4
Papplewick Grange
 NG15 .... 131 E1
Papplewick La NG15 .... 146 B4
Paradise La LE14 .... 218 C2
Parish Church
  CE Prim Sch The DN21 ..... 15 E1
Park Ave
  Annesley Woodhouse NG17 130 A4
  Arnold NG5 .... 161 F3
  Awsworth NG16 .... 158 A3
  Blidworth NG21 .... 118 A3
  Burton Joyce NG14 .... 163 F2
  Carlton NG4 .... 174 C4
  Eastwood NG16 .... 143 F2
  Hucknall NG15 .... 145 F4
  Keyworth NG12 .... 197 F2
  Kimberley NG16 .... 159 D2
  Loughborough LE11 .... 220 A1
  Mansfield NG18 .... 102 B4
  Mansfield Woodhouse NG19 .. 88 B2
  Misterton DN10 .... 6 C2
  Nottingham NG3 .... 173 E4
  Shirebrook NG20 .... 72 C2
  West Bridgford NG2 .... 185 F4
  Woodborough NG14 .... 149 D2
Park Ave E NG12 .... 197 F2
Park Ave W NG12 .... 197 F2
Park Chase NG6 .... 160 A3
Park Cl Ilkeston DE7 .... 157 F1
  Nottingham NG3 .... 161 F1
  Pinxton NG16 .... 113 E1
Park Cres
  Eastwood NG16 .... 143 F2
  Ilkeston DE7 .... 170 A4
  Newark-on-T NG24 .... 125 D2
  Nottingham NG8 .... 171 E2
  Retford DN22 .... 40 A4
Park Ct
  Loughborough LE11 .... 220 A1
  Mansfield NG18 .... 102 B4
Park Dr Blyth S81 .... 18 A2
  Hucknall NG15 .... 146 A4
  Nottingham NG7 .... 222 C2
  Sandiacre NG10 .... 182 A2
Park Farm Cotts LN1 .... 55 F1
Park Gate NG15 .... 131 D1
Park Hall Rd NG18 .... 88 B3
Park Hall Rd NG18 .... 88 B3
Park Hill NG16 .... 158 A3
Park Hill Dr S81 .... 16 A3
Park Hospl NG5 .... 132 B1
Park House Gates NG3 ...... 161 E1
Park Hts NG7 .... 222 C1
Park Jun & Inf Schs The
 NG20 .... 72 C3
Park La Elkesley DN22 .... 50 B2
  Holbeck NG20 .... 59 E3
  Kirkby in A NG17 .... 114 B1
  Lambley NG4 .... 163 A4
  Mansfield NG18 .... 102 B3
  Nottingham NG6 .... 160 C2
  Nottingham NG6 .... 199 F4
  Pinxton NG16 .... 113 E1
  Retford DN22 .... 40 A4
  Southwell NG25 .... 121 E3
Park Mews
  Mansfield Woodhouse NG19 .. 88 B2
  Nottingham NG3 .... 173 E4
Park Pl S80 .... 35 F1
Park Ravine NG7 .... 222 C1

Park Rd Arnold NG5 .... 161 F3
Barnstone NG13 .... 190 C2
Bawtry DN10 .... 9 F4
Beeston, Bramcote NG9 .... 183 D4
Beeston, Chilwell NG9 .... 183 F3
Bestwood Village NG6 .... 146 C2
Calverton NG14 .... 148 C4
Carlton NG4 .... 174 C4
Hucknall NG15 .... 145 F4
Ilkeston DE7 .... 170 A4
Keyworth NG12 .... 197 F3
Loughborough LE11 .... 220 A1
Mansfield Woodhouse NG19 .. 88 A2
Nottingham NG7 .... 222 B1
Radcliffe on T NG12 .... 175 F2
Shirebrook NG20 .... 72 C3
Park Rd E NG14 .... 149 D4
Park Rd N NG9 .... 183 F3
Park Row NG1 .... 223 D2
Park Springs Rd DN21 .... 24 C3
Park St Beeston NG9 .... 183 F3
Kirkby in A NG17 .... 114 C3
Long Eaton NG10 .... 182 B1
Loughborough LE11 .... 220 A2
Mansfield Woodhouse NG19 .. 88 A2
Nottingham NG7 .... 222 B2
Stapleford NG9 .... 182 B3
Sutton in A NG17 .... 100 C2
Park Terr
Keyworth NG12 .... 197 F3
Nottingham NG1 .... 223 D2
Park The Cotgrave NG12 .... 187 F2
Mansfield NG18 .... 102 B4
Newark-on-T NG24 .... 140 A4
North Muskham NG23 .... 110 C2
Park Valley NG7 .... 223 D2
Park View Beeston NG9 .... 183 E3
Nottingham NG3 .... 161 F1
Park View Way NG18 .... 102 B3
Parkcroft Rd NG2 .... 185 F3
Parkdale Prim Sch NG3 .. 174 B3
Parkdale Rd NG3 .... 174 B3
Parker Cl NG5 .... 162 B4
Parker St
Hucknall NG15 .... 146 A4
Newark-on-T NG24 .... 140 A4
Parker's La NG19 .... 88 B1
Parkes Cl NG24 .... 126 A1
Parkham Rd NG16 .... 158 C4
Parkin Cl NG12 .... 189 D2
Parkland Cl
Mansfield NG18 .... 102 C1
Nottingham NG11 .... 184 B2
Parklands Cl
Coddington NG24 .... 125 F1
Nottingham NG5 .... 147 D1
Parklands Dr 7 LE11 .... 220 A1
Parklands Inf Sch NG10 .. 182 A1
Parkside
Huthwaite NG17 .... 100 A2
Keyworth NG12 .... 197 F2
Nottingham NG8 .... 171 F1
Parkside Ave NG10 .... 193 D4
Parkside Dr NG10 .... 193 D4
Parkside Gdns NG8 .... 171 F1
Parkside Rd NG21 .... 75 F1
Parkside Rise NG8 .... 171 F1
Parkside Sch NG16 .... 144 A1
Parkstone Ave NG21 .... 103 F1
Parkstone Cl NG2 .... 185 E3
Parkview Rd NG5 .... 161 D4
Parkway
Clipstone NG19 .... 89 E2
Newark-on-T NG24 .... 139 F3
Sutton in A NG17 .... 100 A2
Whitwell S80 .... 45 D3
Parkway Ct NG8 .... 171 E3
Parkwood Cres NG5 .... 161 F2
Parkwood Ct NG6 .... 160 C3
Parkyn Rd NG5 .... 161 E3
Parkyns St NG11 .... 196 B3
Parliament Ct NG24 .... 139 F4
Parliament Rd NG19 .... 101 F4
Parliament St
Newark-on-T NG24 .... 139 F4
Sutton in A NG17 .... 100 C1
Parliament Terr NG1 .... 223 D3
Parliament Wlk NG24 .... 139 F4
Parnell Cl DN21 .... 24 B4
Parnham's Cl LE14 .... 219 E4
Parr Gate NG9 .... 183 D3
Parr La NG14 .... 150 A3
Parrs The NG9 .... 184 A3
Parry Way NG5 .... 162 A4
Parsons Mdw NG4 .... 174 C2
Paschall Rd NG7 .... 115 D1
Pasteur Ct 9 NG7 .... 172 C1
Pasture Cl Carlton NG2 .. 174 C2
Carlton in S81 .... 26 A4
Stanton Hill NG17 .... 100 B3
Worksop S80 .... 35 E1
Pasture Rd
Gainsborough DN21 .... 24 C4
Stapleford NG9 .... 170 B1
Pasture View NG14 .... 165 D3
Pastures Ave NG11 .... 195 E4

Pastures The
Bawtry DN10 .... 10 A3
Calverton NG14 .... 148 B4
Eastwood NG16 .... 158 A4
Mansfield Woodhouse NG19 .. 88 C3
Rampton DN22 .... 43 D1
Tuxford NG22 .... 65 F1
Patchills The NG18 .... 102 C4
Pateley Rd NG3 .... 162 A2
Paton Rd NG5 .... 160 C3
Patricia Dr NG5 .... 148 A1
Patrick Rd NG2 .... 185 F4
Patterdale Cl NG2 .... 186 B3
Patterdale Rd NG5 .... 161 F3
Patterson Pl NG18 .... 102 B4
Patterson Rd 34 NG7 .. 172 C4
Paul Ave NG18 .... 103 D3
Paulson's Dr NG18 .... 102 A4
Pavilion Cl
Market Warsop NG20 .... 74 A2
22 Nottingham NG2 .... 173 E1
Pavilion Ct NG14 .... 164 C4
Pavilion Gdns NG19 .... 86 C4
Pavilion Rd Ilkeston DE7 .. 157 F3
Nottingham NG5 .... 147 D1
West Bridgford NG2 .... 173 F1
Paxton Gdns NG3 .... 173 F3
Paxtons Ct NG24 .... 124 C1
Payne Rd NG9 .... 183 D2
Peach Ave Selston NG16 .. 128 C3
South Normanton DE55 .... 113 D4
Peache Way NG9 .... 183 E4
Peachey St NG1 .... 223 E3
Peacock Cl
Gunthorpe NG14 .... 165 D2
Ruddington NG11 .... 196 A3
Peacock Cres NG7 .... 184 C1
Peacock Dr NG21 .... 118 B4
Peacock Pl DE7 .... 157 E2
Peacock St 8 NG18 .... 102 A3
Peafield La NG19 .... 88 C2
Peafield Lane Prim Sch
NG19 .... 88 C2
Peak The NG20 .... 72 C2
Peakdale Cl NG10 .... 193 D3
Peake's Croft NG10 .... 10 A4
Pear Tree Cl DN22 .... 30 B2
Pear Tree La NG20 .... 60 C2
Pear Tree Dr NG20 .... 72 C3
Pearce Dr NG8 .... 160 A2
Pearl Ave NG17 .... 115 D2
Pearl Cl NG21 .... 104 B1
Pearmain Dr NG3 .... 173 F4
Pearson Ave NG9 .... 183 D3
Pearson Cl NG9 .... 183 D3
Pearson St Carlton NG4 .. 175 D3
Nottingham NG7 .... 160 C1
Peartree La NG17 .... 86 A1
Peartree Orch NG11 .... 196 B4
Peary Cl NG5 .... 160 C4
Peas Hill Rd NG3 .... 223 F4
Peatfield Rd NG9 .... 170 B1
Peck La NG1 .... 223 E2
Pecks Hill NG18 .... 102 C4
Pedmore Valley NG5 .... 161 D4
Peebles Rd NG24 .... 125 E1
Peel Ave Retford DN22 .... 40 A2
Tuxford NG22 .... 65 F1
Peel Cres NG19 .... 87 E1
Peel Dr LE11 .... 220 B2
Peel Rd NG19 .... 101 F4
Peel St Langley Mill NG16 .. 143 D2
Long Eaton NG10 .... 193 F4
Nottingham NG1 .... 223 D4
South Normanton DE55 .. 113 D3
Sutton in A NG17 .... 101 D2
Peets Dr NG23 .... 110 C1
Pelham Ave Ilkeston DE7 .. 157 F1
Nottingham NG5 .... 173 D4
Pelham Cl NG24 .... 139 F4
Pelham Cres
Beeston NG9 .... 184 A4
Nottingham NG7 .... 222 B2
Pelham Ct 10 NG5 .... 173 D4
Pelham Gdns NG24 .... 139 F4
Pelham Rd
Kirkby in A NG17 .... 115 D3
Nottingham NG5 .... 173 D4
Retford DN22 .... 39 E3
Pelham St
Mansfield NG18 .... 102 B4
Newark-on-T NG24 .... 139 F4
Nottingham NG1 .... 223 E2
Sutton in A NG17 .... 100 B1
Worksop S80 .... 36 A1
Pelham Way NG18 .... 89 E2
Pemberton St NG1 .... 223 F2
Pemberton The DE55 .... 113 D2
Pembleton Dr NG19 .... 87 E1
Pembrey Cl NG9 .... 170 B1
Pembridge Cl NG6 .... 160 B1
Pembroke Cres NG24 .. 125 E2
Pembroke Dr
Carlton in S81 .... 25 F3
Nottingham NG3 .... 161 E1
Pembury Rd NG8 .... 171 F2
Pen Cl NG5 .... 99 D2
Pen La NG12 .... 208 B2
Penarth Gdns NG5 .... 161 F2
Penarth Rise NG5 .... 161 F2
Pendean Cl LE12 .... 15 F1
Pendennis Cl NG4 .... 163 D1
Pendine Cl Arnold NG5 .. 147 E1
South Normanton DE55 .. 113 D3
Pendle Cres NG3 .... 161 F1
Pendock La NG12 .... 197 D1
Penfold Cl LE12 .... 213 D1

Penhale Dr NG15 .... 145 E3
Penhurst Cl NG11 .... 185 D2
Penllech Cl NG5 .... 161 D4
Penllech Wlk 20 NG5 .... 161 D4
Penn Ave NG7 .... 222 A1
Penn La LE14 .... 202 C2
Penn St NG17 .... 100 C2
Pennant Rd NG6 .... 160 B1
Pennard Wlk NG11 .... 195 E4
Pennhome Ave 5 NG5 .. 161 E1
Penniment La
Mansfield NG19 .... 87 D1
Mansfield NG19 .... 101 E4
Pennine Cl
Huthwaite NG17 .... 99 F2
Long Eaton, Breaston
NG10 .... 182 A1
Long Eaton, New Sawley
NG10 .... 193 E2
Mansfield Woodhouse NG19 .. 88 B2
Newton DE55 .... 99 D2
Nottingham NG5 .... 147 D1
Pennine Dr
Kirkby in A NG17 .... 114 B2
Selston NG16 .... 128 C4
Pennington Wlk DN22 .. 40 A3
Penny Gn S80 .... 45 D3
Pennyfields Bvd NG10 .. 193 D4
Pennyfoot St NG1 .... 173 F2
Penrhyn Cl NG3 .... 223 F4
Penrhyn Cres NG9 .... 183 D2
Penrith Ave NG12 .... 176 A2
Penrith Cres NG8 .... 160 B1
Penrith Pl NG19 .... 101 E4
Penshore Cl NG11 .... 184 B1
Penswick Gr NG24 .... 125 F1
Pentland Ct NG19 .... 101 E3
Pentland Dr
Carlton in S81 .... 25 F4
Nottingham NG5 .... 147 D1
Pentland Gdns NG10 .. 182 A1
Pentrich Wlk NG18 .... 103 D3
Pentwood Ave NG5 .... 147 F1
Penzance Pl NG18 .... 103 D4
People's Coll of
Tertiary Ed NG1 .... 223 E1
Peoples Coll (Annexe)
NG7 .... 222 B4
Peoples Coll The NG3 .. 173 F3
Pepper Rd NG14 .... 148 C4
Pepper St
Nottingham NG1 .... 223 E2
Sutton in A NG17 .... 101 D1
Peppercorn Gdns NG8 .. 172 B3
Peppers Dr DE74 .... 203 D1
Percival Cl NG17 .... 100 C2
Percival Cres NG17 .... 100 C2
Percival Rd NG5 .... 161 E1
Percival St S81 .... 35 F3
Percy St Eastwood NG16 .. 144 A3
Nottingham NG6 .... 160 B2
Sutton in A NG17 .... 100 B1
Peregrine Cl NG7 .... 222 A2
Peregrine Ct S81 .... 35 E4
Perivale Cl NG16 .... 159 E2
Perkin's La LE14 .... 219 D1
Perlethorpe Ave
Carlton NG4 .... 162 C1
Mansfield NG19 .... 88 A1
18 Nottingham NG1 .... 173 F2
Perlethorpe Cl
Carlton NG4 .... 162 C1
Edwinstowe NG21 .... 75 F2
Perlethorpe Cres NG4 .. 162 C1
Perlethorpe Dr
Carlton NG4 .... 162 C1
Hucknall NG15 .... 146 A4
Perry Gdns NG5 .... 161 D2
Perry Gr Bingham LE12 .. 177 F2
Loughborough LE11 .... 220 B1
Perry Rd NG5 .... 161 D2
Perth Cl NG19 .... 88 B3
Perth Dr NG9 .... 170 C1
Perth St NG1 .... 223 E3
Peterborough Rd NG3 .. 98 A4
Peters Cl Arnold NG5 .. 162 B3
Eastwood NG16 .... 144 B1
Petersfield Cl
Mansfield NG19 .... 101 E4
Nottingham NG5 .... 160 C4
Petersgate NG10 .... 182 A1
Petersgate Cl NG10 .... 182 A1
Petersham Mews NG7 .. 222 C2
Petersham Rd NG10 .... 182 A1
Petersmiths Cl NG22 .... 77 E3
Petersmiths Cres NG22 .. 77 E3
Petersmiths Dr NG22 .... 77 E3
Petworth Ave NG9 .... 182 C2
Petworth Dr NG5 .... 160 C2
Peveril Cres NG10 .... 193 D3
Peveril Dr Ilkeston DE7 .. 157 F1
Nottingham NG7 .... 223 D1
Sutton in A NG17 .... 100 B1
West Bridgford NG2 .... 185 F2
Peveril Mews NG7 .... 222 C2
Peveril Rd NG9 .... 184 A3
Peveril St Hucknall NG15 .. 146 A4
Nottingham NG7 .... 222 C4
Pheasant Hill NG19 .... 88 A1
Philip Ave
Eastwood NG16 .... 144 A1
Kirkby in A NG17 .... 115 D1
Nuthall NG16 .... 159 E4
Philip Cl NG11 .... 118 B4
Philip Gr NG4 .... 162 C1
Philip Rd NG24 .... 139 F3
Phoenix Ave NG4 .... 162 C1

Phoenix Cl NG2 .... 173 D1
Phoenix Ct
Eastwood NG16 .... 144 A1
Nottingham NG7 .... 184 C4
Phoenix Ctr NG6 .... 160 A2
Phoenix Inf Sch NG4 .. 162 C1
Phoenix St NG17 .... 101 D2
Phyllis Cl NG15 .... 130 C1
Phyllis Gr NG10 .... 193 F4
Piccadilly NG6 .... 160 B3
Pickard St NG18 .... 102 C4
Pickering Ave NG16 .... 143 F1
Pieris Dr NG11 .... 184 B1
Pierrepont Ave NG4 .... 162 C1
Pierrepont Rd NG2 .... 174 A1
Pierson St NG24 .... 139 F3
Pilcher Gate NG1 .... 223 E2
Pilgrim Cl Ranby DN22 .. 28 C1
Ravenshead NG15 .... 116 C3
Pilgrim Ct S81 .... 34 C4
Pilgrim Oaks Inf Sch
NG15 .... 117 D2
Pilgrim Rise DN10 .... 3 E1
Pilgrim Way S80 .... 35 F1
Pilkington Rd NG3 .... 162 A1
Pilkington St 21 NG6 .. 160 A4
Pillared House La DN21 .. 24 B4
Pimlico Ave NG9 .... 171 D2
Pinder St NG1 .... 223 F2
Pine Ave
Langley Mill NG16 .... 143 D2
New Ollerton NG22 .... 77 E2
Pine Cl East Leake LE12 .. 214 B4
Everton DN10 .... 11 E2
Kirkby in A NG17 .... 114 C3
Mansfield NG21 .... 103 F1
Mansfield Woodhouse NG19 .. 88 B3
Newark-on-T NG24 .... 125 D2
Shirebrook NG20 .... 72 C3
Pine Hill Cl NG5 .... 146 C1
Pine Tree Cl S80 .... 35 F1
Pine Tree Wlk NG16 .... 143 E1
Pinehurst Ave NG15 .... 145 E3
Pines The DN21 .... 24 C3
Pineview Cl NG18 .... 102 C1
Pinewood Ave
Arnold NG5 .... 148 A1
Edwinstowe NG21 .... 91 E4
Pinewood Cl
Kirkby in A NG17 .... 115 E3
Southwell NG25 .... 121 E1
Pinewood Dr NG18 .... 102 C2
Pinewood Gdns NG11 .. 195 E4
Pinewood Inf Sch NG5 .. 148 A1
Pinfold NG13 .... 177 F2
Pinfold Cl
Bottesford NG13 .... 181 D2
Collingham NG23 .... 98 A1
Cotgrave NG12 .... 187 F2
Kinoulton NG12 .... 199 F1
Lound DN22 .... 20 B1
Tickhill DN11 .... 8 A4
Woodborough NG14 .... 149 E2
Pinfold Cres NG14 .... 149 E2
Pinfold Dr S81 .... 35 E4
Pinfold Gate LE11 .... 220 A2
Pinfold Gdns 12 LE11 .. 220 A2
Pinfold Jetty LE11 .... 220 B2
Pinfold La
Averham NG23 .... 123 F1
Balderton NG24 .... 140 B2
Bottesford NG13 .... 181 D2
Clarborough DN22 .... 40 C4
Elston NG23 .... 153 E3
Harby LE14 .... 202 B2
Kinoulton NG12 .... 199 F1
Nottingham NG11 .... 185 D3
Shelford NG12 .... 164 B1
Stapleford NG9 .... 182 C4
Styrrup DN11 .... 8 B1
Pinfold Place LE14 .... 202 B2
Pinfold Rd NG16 .... 144 B1
Pinfold The DN10 .... 4 A1
Pingle Cl DN22 .... 24 C4
Pingle Cres NG5 .... 160 C4
Pingle The NG10 .... 193 E4
Pingley Cl NG23 .... 138 B4
Pingley Ct NG23 .... 138 B4
Pingley La NG23 .... 138 B4
Pintail Cl NG4 .... 175 D3
Pinxton Ct NG18 .... 103 D3
Pinxton Gn NG16 .... 113 F2
Pinxton La
Kirkby in A, Fulwood NG17 .. 114 A4
Kirkby in A, Tichfield Park
NG17 .... 114 B2
South Normanton DE55 .. 113 E3
Pinxton Rd NG17 .... 114 C4
Piper Cl Hucknall NG15 .. 131 D1
Long Whatton LE12 .... 212 B1
Piper Dr LE12 .... 212 B1
Piper La S80 .... 61 E4
Pippin Cl
Newark-on-T NG24 .... 125 D1
Nottingham NG3 .... 173 F4
Pit La DE75 .... 157 D3
Pitcairn Cl NG2 .... 173 E1
Pithouse La LE12 .... 204 C1
Pitt Hill NG20 .... 58 C1
Pitt La DN10 .... 12 C2
Plains Farm Cl NG3 .... 162 B3
Plains Gr NG3 .... 162 A2
Plains Rd NG3 .... 162 A2
Plainspot Rd NG16 .... 128 C1
Plane Cl NG6 .... 159 F4
Plant La NG10 .... 193 D2
Plantagenet Ct NG3 .... 223 F3
Plantagenet St NG3 .... 223 F3
Plantation Ave NG22 .... 66 A4

Plantation Cl NG5 .... 147 D1
Plantation Dr DN10 .... 11 D
Plantation Hill S81 .... 36 A
Plantation La S81 .... 27 D
Plantation Rd
East Markham NG22 .... 66 A
Keyworth NG12 .... 197 E
Nottingham NG8 .... 171 F
Plantation Side NG7 .... 172 C
Plantations The 9 NG10 .. 193 D
Plants Yd S80 .... 35 F
Platt La NG12 .... 198 A
Platts The NG24 .... 139 F
Player St NG7 .... 222 B6
Playworld NG4 .... 162 C
Plaza Gdns NG6 .... 160 C
Pleasant Cl 11 LE11 .... 220 A
Pleasant Pl DE74 .... 203 E
Pleasant Row NG7 .... 172 C
Pleasley Rd NG17 .... 101 D
Plot La NG23 .... 98 C
Plough La NG2 .... 25 F
Lowdham NG14 .... 150 B
Nottingham NG2 .... 173 F
Ploughman Ave NG14 .. 149 D
Plover Dene S81 .... 35 E
Plover Wharf 8 NG7 .. 173 D
Plowman Ct NG9 .... 182 B6
Plowright Ct 10 NG3 .. 173 E
Plowright St 17 NG3 .. 173 E
Plum Tree Ave NG19 .... 89 D
Plumb Rd NG15 .... 145 F
Plummer La DE74 .... 203 E
Plumptre NG16 .... 143 D
Plumptre Almshouses
NG1 .... 223 F
Plumptre Cl LE11 .... 143 F
Plumptre Pl NG1 .... 223 F
Plumptre Sq NG1 .... 223 F
Plumptre St NG1 .... 223 F
Plumptre Way NG16 .. 143 F
Plumtree Gdns NG14 .. 148 C
Plumtree Rd
Bircotes DN11 .... 9 E
Cotgrave NG12 .... 187 F
Plungar Cl NG8 .... 172 A
Plungar La NG13 .... 192 A
Plungar Rd NG13 .... 191 E
Plymouth Ave NG16 .... 113 F
Poacher's La DN22 .... 31 E
Pocklington Cres NG24 .. 125 E
Pocklington Rd NG23 .... 98 A
Podder La NG3 .... 162 B
Point The NG3 .... 173 E
Pollard Dr NG18 .... 102 B
Pollard's La NG25 .... 136 C
Polly Taylor's Rd NG23 .. 67 F
Polperro Way NG15 .... 145 F
Pond Hills La NG5 .... 147 F
Pond St NG17 .... 115 D
Pool Cl NG16 .... 113 E
Poole Mdw NG12 .... 174 C
Popham Ct NG1 .... 223 F
Popham St NG1 .... 223 F
Poplar Ave
East Leake LE12 .... 214 B
Kirkby in A NG17 .... 115 E
Nottingham NG5 .... 161 D
Sandiacre NG10 .... 182 A
Poplar Cl Bingham NG13 .. 178 A
Carlton NG3 .... 174 B
Sutton on T NG23 .... 96 C
Worksop S80 .... 35 E
Poplar Cres NG16 .... 159 D
Poplar Dr Glapwell S44 .. 86 A
Pleasleyhill NG19 .... 87 D
Poplar Gr
Church Warsop NG20 .... 74 A
Mansfield Woodhouse NG19 .. 89 E
Radcliffe Ind DE55 .... 113 D
Poplar St
Mansfield Woodhouse NG19 .. 88 B
New Ollerton NG22 .... 77 E
Nottingham NG1 .... 173 E
Retford DN22 .... 39 F
Poplars Ave NG14 .... 164 A
Poplars Cl NG12 .... 197 F
Poplars The Beeston NG9 .. 183 F
Sutton in A NG17 .... 101 D
West Bridgford NG2 .... 185 F
Whitwell S80 .... 45 D
Porchester Cl NG15 .... 146 B
Porchester Jun Sch
NG4 .... 162 A
Porchester Rd
Bingham NG13 .... 177 E
Nottingham NG3 .... 162 A
Porlock Cl 2 NG10 .... 193 C
Port Arthur Rd NG2 .... 174 A
Portage Cl NG12 .... 175 F
Porter Cl NG11 .... 195 E
Portinscale Cl NG2 .... 186 B
Portland College for
People with Disabilities
NG18 .... 116 C
Portland Court Mews
NG19 .... 88 A
Portland Cres
Mansfield Woodhouse NG19 .. 88 B
Stapleford NG9 .... 182 C
Portland Ct NG5 .... 161 D
Portland Gdns NG15 .... 145 E
Portland Grange NG15 .. 145 E
Portland Hill NG7 .... 172 B
Portland Ind Est NG17 .. 115 D
Portland Mdws DN22 .... 29 C

ortland Park Cl NG15 .... 145 F4
ortland Pl Sutton DN22 ...... 29 D3
ortland St
  Worksop S80 .... 35 F2
  ortland Rd Beeston NG9 .. 182 C1
  Carlton NG4 .... 162 B1
  Eastwood NG16 .... 158 A4
  Hucknall NG15 .... 146 A3
  Ilkeston DE7 .... 157 F2
  Long Eaton NG10 .... 193 D2
  Nottingham NG7 .... 222 A2
  Retford DN22 .... 39 E3
  Shirebrook NG20 .... 72 C2
ortland Terr
  Gainsborough DN21 .... 24 B4
  Meden Vale NG20 .... 60 C1
  Whaley Thorns NG20 .... 59 D1
ortland Row NG1 .... 91 E4
ortland Sq NG17 .... 100 C1
ortland St Arnold NG5 .... 161 F3
  Beeston NG9 .... 184 A4
  Kirkby in A NG17 .... 115 D3
  Mansfield NG18 .... 102 A3
  Mansfield Woodhouse NG19 .. 88 B2
  Market Warsop NG20 .... 74 A2
  New Houghton NG19 .... 87 D4
  Newark-on-T NG24 .... 139 F4
  Sutton in A NG17 .... 100 C1
  Worksop S80 .... 35 F2
ost Office La
  Bilsthorpe NG22 .... 105 F4
  Plumtree NG13 .... 202 C4
  Redmile NG13 .... 192 C2
ost Office Rd NG17 .... 115 D3
ost Office Yd NG14 .... 151 E1
ostern St NG1 .... 223 D2
osts The NG12 .... 189 D3
ot Yard The NG22 .... 119 F3
otter La NG22 .... 92 B4
otter St
  Sutton in A NG17 .... 101 D2
  Worksop S80 .... 35 F1
otters Cl NG5 .... 161 D4
otters Ct NG9 .... 171 E1
otters La LE12 .... 214 C4
otters Nook S81 .... 34 C4
otters Way DE7 .... 170 A4
oulter Cl NG24 .... 182 B4
oulter St NG9 .... 58 C1
oulter View DN22 .... 39 F3
oulton Dr NG2 .... 173 F1
oultry NG1 .... 223 E2
owtrell Pl DE7 .... 170 A3
oynton St NG3 .... 223 D3
oyser Cl 🢂 NG2 .... 161 D1
ratt Cl NG19 .... 87 E1
rebends Cl NG24 .... 138 C2
recinct Rd NG17 .... 115 D3
recinct The NG12 .... 187 F2
remier Rd NG7 .... 173 D4
rendwick Gdns NG5 .... 161 D4
rest Ave NG16 .... 74 C4
reston Rd NG21 .... 118 A4
restwick Ct NG8 .... 159 E1
restwold Ave
  Mansfield NG18 .... 102 B3
  Mansfield Woodhouse NG19 .. 89 D1
restwold La LE12 .... 215 E1
restwood Dr NG8 .... 172 A4
revin Gdns NG3 .... 173 F3
riestgate NG22 .... 65 F3
riestsic Prim Sch NG17 ... 100 C2
riestsic Rd NG17 .... 100 C2
rim Sch of St Mary &
  St Martin, Blyth S81 .... 18 A1
rimrose Ave
  Farndon NG24 .... 139 D3
  Newark-on-T NG24 .... 140 A2
  Selston NG16 .... 128 C1
rimrose Bank NG13 .... 177 E2
rimrose Cl 🢂
  🢂 Kirkby in A NG17 .... 114 C3
  Nottingham NG3 .... 173 E4
  South Normanton DE55 ... 113 D4
rimrose Cres NG4 .... 174 C4
rimrose La NG22 .... 78 B3
rimrose Rise NG16 .... 158 A4
rimrose St Carlton NG4 ... 174 C4
  Gainsborough DN21 .... 24 B4
  Ilkeston DE7 .... 157 F2
rimrose Way
  Sutton in A NG17 .... 100 B1
  Worksop S81 .... 36 A3
rimula Cl NG21 .... 184 B1
rince Charles Rd S81 .... 35 E3
rince Edward Cres
  NG12 .... 175 F1
rince Of Wales St DN22 .. 39 F3
rince St Ilkeston DE7 ...... 157 F2
  Long Eaton NG10 .... 193 E4
rince William Rd LE11 .. 220 A3
rince William Way
  LE11 .... 220 A1
rince's St NG24 .... 139 F4
rince's Rd LE11 .... 219 D3
rinces St NG3 .... 102 A3
rinces Anne Rd S81 ...... 35 F3
rincess Ave
  Beeston NG9 .... 184 A3
  Hucknall NG15 .... 146 B4
  Market Warsop NG20 .... 74 B2
  South Normanton DE55 ... 113 D3
rincess Cl NG4 .... 162 C1
rincess Diana Ct DN21 .. 15 E2

Princess Dr NG10 .... 182 A2
Princess St
  Eastwood NG16 .... 143 F2
  Kirkby in A NG17 .... 114 B2
  Long Eaton NG10 .... 193 E4
Princess Wlk DN21 .... 15 F1
Prior Cl NG17 .... 101 D2
Prior Rd NG5 .... 161 E3
Prioridge NG12 .... 188 A1
Priors Cl NG13 .... 178 A3
Priors The NG14 .... 150 B1
Priorswell Rd S80 .... 35 F1
Priory Ave
  Annesley Woodhouse NG17 .. 130 A4
  Ravenshead NG15 .... 117 D1
  Tollerton NG12 .... 186 B1
Priory Cir NG12 .... 186 B1
Priory Cl Balderton NG24 . 140 C2
  Blyth S81 .... 18 A2
  Gainsborough DN21 .... 24 C4
  Mattersey DN10 .... 20 A3
Priory Cres NG4 .... 162 C1
Priory Ct NG4 .... 162 C1
Priory Ctr The S80 .... 35 F2
Priory Cty Jun Sch NG4 . 162 C1
Priory Gr NG17 .... 115 E3
Priory La NG14 .... 151 E4
Priory Mews 🔟 NG7 .... 172 C1
Priory Pk NG14 .... 151 E4
Priory RC Prim Sch
  NG16 .... 144 A1
Priory Rd Blidworth NG21 .. 118 A3
  Carlton NG4 .... 162 C1
  Eastwood NG16 .... 143 F1
  Hucknall NG15 .... 145 F4
  Mansfield Woodhouse NG19 .. 88 A2
  West Bridgford NG2 .... 186 A4
Priory Sq NG19 .... 88 A2
Priory St NG7 .... 172 C1
Pritchard Dr NG9 .... 182 C3
Private Rd Hucknall NG15 .. 145 F4
  Nottingham NG5, NG3 .... 161 E1
  Southwell NG25 .... 121 F1
  Woodborough NG14 .... 149 E3
Private St NG24 .... 140 A4
Privet Ave NG17 .... 115 D3
Prize Cl NG11 .... 184 B1
Procters Dr NG23 .... 82 C1
Promenade NG3 .... 223 F3
Promenade The NG1 .... 115 E3
Prospect Cl NG17 .... 115 D4
Prospect Dr 🔢 NG17 ...... 99 F1
Prospect Dr
  Shirebrook NG20 .... 72 C2
  Worksop S81 .... 35 F3
Prospect Hill Jun Sch
  S81 .... 36 A4
Prospect Pl
  Nottingham NG2 .... 222 B1
  Sutton in A NG17 .... 100 C1
Prospect Prec S81 .... 36 A3
Prospect Rd Carlton NG4 . 162 A1
  Heanor DE75 .... 157 D4
Prospect St
  Mansfield NG18 .... 102 B3
  Nottingham NG7 .... 222 A4
Prospect Terr
  Gainsborough DN21 .... 24 B4
  Nottingham NG2 .... 222 B1
Providence Pl 🔢 DE7 ..... 157 F1
Providence Rd NG16 .... 128 A2
Prudhoe Ct 🔢 NG2 .... 173 E1
Pudding La LE14 .... 210 B3
Pulborough Cl NG5 .... 160 C2
Pullman Rd 🔢 NG2 ...... 173 F2
Pump Hollow La NG18 . 103 D4
Pump Hollow Rd NG19 . 103 D4
Pump La Fenton NG23 .. 142 C1
  Walesby NG22 .... 64 A1
Purbeck Cl
  Long Eaton NG10 .... 193 D4
  Mansfield Woodhouse NG19 .. 88 B3
Purbeck Dr NG2 .... 185 D4
Purdy Mdw NG10 .... 193 D3
Pyatt St NG2 .... 173 E1
Pye Ave NG19 .... 101 E4
Pye Hill Rd NG16 .... 128 A2
Pygall Ave NG11 .... 195 D1
Pym St NG3 .... 173 F3
Pym Wlk NG3 .... 173 F3
Python Hill Jun & Inf Sch
  NG21 .... 104 A1
Python Hill Rd NG21 ... 104 A1

Quadrangle The
  Blidworth NG21 .... 118 A3
  Newstead NG15 .... 130 B3
Quakefield Rd NG22 .... 66 A3
Quaker La
  Farnsfield NG22 .... 119 F3
  🔢 Mansfield NG18 .... 102 A4
Quaker Way NG18 .... 102 A4
Quantock Cl NG5 .... 147 D1
Quantock Gr NG13 .... 177 E2
Quantock Rd NG10 ...... 182 A1
Quarries Way NG17 .... 114 B3
Quarry Ave NG6 .... 160 A3
Quarry Cl NG15 .... 132 A4
Quarry Dr NG17 .... 115 D2
Quarry Gr S81 .... 35 E4
Quarry Hill NG10 .... 182 A4
Quarry Hill Rd NG17 .. 115 D2
Quarry Rd NG15 .... 132 A4
Quarrydale Ave NG17 . 100 C3
Quarrydale Dr NG17 ... 100 C3

Quarrydale Rd NG17 .... 100 C2
Quarrydale Sch NG17 .. 100 C3
Quayside NG2 .... 173 F1
Queen Eleanor
  Cty Prim Sch NG23 ...... 70 B2
Queen Elizabeth Cres
  S80 .... 35 D2
Queen Elizabeth High Sch
  DN21 .... 15 E2
Queen Elizabeth Rd NG9 . 183 D2
Queen Elizabeth's Sch The
  NG19 .... 88 A1
Queen St Arnold NG5 .... 148 A1
  Balderton NG24 .... 140 C2
  Bottesford NG13 .... 181 D1
  Collingham NG23 .... 98 A1
  Gainsborough DN21 .... 24 B4
  Hucknall NG15 .... 146 A4
  Kirkby in A NG17 .... 115 D2
  Langley Mill NG16 .... 143 E2
  Long Eaton NG10 .... 193 F4
  Loughborough LE11 .... 220 B2
  🔢 Mansfield NG18 .... 102 A4
  Market Warsop NG20 .... 74 A3
  Newark-on-T NG24 .... 139 F4
  Nottingham NG1 .... 223 E3
  Pinxton NG16 .... 113 D3
  🔢 Whaley Terr LE11 ...... 220 B3
  South Normanton DE55 . 113 D3
  Southwell NG25 .... 121 E1
  Sutton in A NG17 .... 100 C2
  Worksop S80 .... 35 F1
Queen's Ave NG4 .... 162 C2
Queen's Bridge Rd NG2 . 223 E1
Queen's Cres NG5 .... 147 D4
Queen's Cl Bingham NG13 . 177 E3
  Clipstone NG19 .... 89 E2
  Newark-on-T NG24 .... 125 D1
  Long Eaton NG10 .... 193 E4
Queen's Head Ct NG24 . 139 F4
Queen's Medical Ctr
  (Univ Hospl) NG7 .... 172 B1
Queen's Rd
  Loughborough LE11 ..... 220 B2
  Newark-on-T NG24 .... 125 D1
  Radcliffe on T NG12 .... 176 A2
Queen's Sq NG16 .... 143 F1
Queen's Wlk
  Nether Langwith NG20 .. 59 D1
  Nottingham NG2 .... 173 D1
Queens Ave DE7 .... 170 A3
Queens Bower Rd NG5 . 161 E4
Queens Cl S80 .... 45 E3
Queens Dr Beeston NG9 . 184 A3
  Brinsley NG16 .... 143 F4
  Nottingham NG7, NG2 . 185 D4
  Sandiacre NG10 .... 182 A2
Queens Gr NG2 .... 223 E1
Queens Rd Beeston NG9 . 184 A3
  Carlton in L NG4 .... 25 E4
  Hodthorpe S80 .... 45 E3
  Keyworth DE74 .... 208 B3
Queens Rd E NG9 .... 184 A4
Queens Rd N NG16 .... 143 F1
Queens Rd S NG16 .... 143 F1
Queens Rd W NG9 .... 183 F2
Queens Wlk 🔢 NG18 .. 102 A4
Queensberry St NG6 .. 160 C2
Queensbury Ave NG2 . 185 E2
Queensway
  Gainsborough DN21 .... 24 C4
  Kirkby in A NG17 .... 115 D1
  Mansfield NG18 .... 102 A3
  Nether Broughton LE14 . 219 D1
  Saxilby LN1 .... 57 D2
  Skellingthorpe LN6 ..... 71 F2
  Worksop S80 .... 35 F2
Quernby Ave NG3 .... 161 F1
Quernby Rd NG3 .... 161 F1
Quibell Rd NG24 .... 140 A3
Quibell's La NG24 ...... 125 D2
Quines Hill Rd NG19 .. 89 D1
Quinton Cl NG11 .... 185 D3
Quorn Cl Beeston NG9 . 183 F2
  Loughborough LE11 .... 220 B1
Quorn Gr NG5 .... 161 D2
Quorn Rd NG5 .... 161 D1
Quorndon Cres NG10 . 193 E3

Rabbitball La NG23 .... 83 D3
Racecourse Rd
  Mansfield NG18 .... 102 C3
  Nottingham NG2 .... 174 A2
Rad Mdws NG10 .... 193 E3
Radbourne Rd 🔢 NG2 . 173 E1
Radbourne St NG19 ... 88 C2
Radburn Ct NG9 .... 170 C1
Radcliffe Mount NG2 . 173 F1
Radcliffe on Trent
  Inf Sch NG12 .... 176 A2
Radcliffe on Trent
  Jun Sch NG12 .... 175 F1
Radcliffe on Trent Sta
  NG12 .... 175 F2
Radcliffe Rd
  Carlton NG12 .... 175 D1
  Cropwell Butler NG12 . 189 D4
  West Bridgford NG2 ... 186 B4
Radcliffe St NG2 .... 173 F1
Radford Bridge Rd NG8 . 172 B3
Radford Bvd NG7 ...... 222 A4
Radford Cres NG4 ..... 162 C1
Radford Ct NG7 .... 222 B3
Radford Grove La NG7 . 222 A4
Radford Prim Sch NG7 . 222 A3

Radford Rd NG7 .... 172 C4
Radford St
  🔢 Mansfield NG18 .... 102 A3
  Worksop S80 .... 36 A1
Radley Rd NG22 .... 135 E4
Radley Sq NG6 .... 160 B3
Radmanthwaite Rd
  NG19 .... 87 E2
Radmarsh Rd NG7 ...... 222 A1
Radmoor Rd 🟥 LE11 . 220 A2
Radnor Gr NG13 .... 177 E2
Radnor Pl NG19 .... 87 E2
Radstock Rd NG3 .... 174 A4
Radway Dr NG11 .... 185 D3
Raeburn Dr NG9 .... 182 C1
Ragdale Rd NG6 .... 160 A3
Raglan Cl NG3 .... 173 E4
Raglan Ct Beeston NG9 . 172 A1
  Newark-on-T NG24 ..... 140 A4
Raglan Dr NG4 .... 163 D1
Raglan Gdns NG3 ...... 140 A4
Raglan Rd NG3 .... 144 A1
Raibank Gdns NG5 .... 161 F3
Railway Ave S80 .... 58 B3
Railway Cotts NG5 .... 158 C3
Railway Cl NG1 .... 57 D2
  🔢 Whaley Terr LE11 .. 220 B3
Raines Ave NG22 ...... 40 A4
Raines Park Rd S81 .. 35 F4
Rainham Gdns NG11 . 196 B3
Rainworth Water Rd
  NG21 .... 103 F1
Raithby Cl NG5 .... 161 D3
Raleigh Cl Ilkeston DE7 . 157 F2
  Nottingham NG1 .... 184 B1
Raleigh Rd NG19 .... 101 F4
Raleigh St NG7 .... 222 C3
Ralf Cl NG2 .... 185 F2
Ramblers Cl NG4 ...... 174 C3
Ramper Rd Letwell S81 . 16 A2
  Saundby DN22 .... 23 E2
Rampton Cty Prim Sch
  DN22 .... 42 B1
Rampton Green Rd DN22 . 42 C1
Rampton Hospl DN22 .. 53 D4
Rampton La DN22 .... 42 B3
Rampton Rd
  Laneham DN22 .... 54 A3
  Rampton DN22 .... 42 B1
Ramsdale Ave NG14 .. 148 B4
Ramsdale Cres NG5 .. 161 E2
Ramsdale Rd NG4 ..... 163 D1
Ramsden Ave S81 ...... 16 C1
Ramsden Cres S81 ... 25 F4
Ramsden Croft NG21 . 104 A1
Ramsey Cl
  Mansfield Woodhouse NG19 .. 89 D1
  Stapleford NG9 .... 170 C1
Ramsey Dr NG5 .... 161 D1
Ramsey Dr NG5 .... 161 D1
Ranby CE Jun & Inf Sch
  DN22 .... 38 A4
Ranby House Prep Sch
  DN22 .... 38 A4
Ranby Wlk NG3 .... 173 F3
Rancliffe Ave NG12 ... 197 E2
Rancliffe Cres Mews
  NG11 .... 196 C2
Randal Gdns 🔢 NG7 . 172 C4
Randal St NG7 .... 172 C4
Randall Cl NG24 .... 140 B4
Randall Way DN22 ... 29 E2
Randall Gr NG10 .... 182 A1
Ranelagh Gr NG8 ...... 172 A3
Ranmere Rd NG8 ...... 172 A3
Ranmoor Rd NG4 ...... 162 C1
Ranmore Cl NG9 .... 171 D1
Rannoch Cl NG19 ..... 101 F3
Rannoch Rise NG5 ... 147 F1
Rannock Gdns NG12 . 197 F3
Ranskill Gdns NG5 ... 161 D4
Ranskill Prim Sch DN22 . 19 D3
Ranskill Rd DN22 ..... 19 E2
Ransom Dr NG3 .... 161 E1
Ransom Rd
  Mansfield NG21 .... 103 E3
  Nottingham NG3 .... 173 F4
Ransome Cl NG24 .... 140 B4
Ransom Rd NG3 .... 161 E1
Ratcher Way NG19 ... 103 D4
Ratcliffe Gate NG18 . 102 B3
Ratcliffe La LE74 .... 203 E4
Ratcliffe Rd LE11 ...... 220 B3
Ratcliffe St NG16 ...... 143 F1
Rathgar Cl NG8 .... 171 E2
Rathmines Cl NG7 .... 222 A1
Rathvale Cl NG8 .... 171 D3
Raven Ave NG5 .... 161 D2
Ravencroft La DN10 .. 14 A1
Ravendale Rd DN21 .. 24 C3
Ravenhill Cl NG9 .... 183 D2
Ravens Ct NG5 .... 161 D3
Ravenscourt S81 .... 36 A3
Ravensdale Ave
  Long Eaton NG10 ...... 193 E4
  Mansfield NG18 .... 102 B4
Ravensdale Rd NG18 . 102 B4
Ravensdale Mid Sch
  NG18 .... 102 C4
Ravensdene Ct 🔢 NG3 . 173 E4
Ravensfleet Rd DN21 . 7 F2
Ravenshead L Ctr
  NG15 .... 132 A4
Ravenshill Cl DN22 .. 19 D2
Ravensmore Rd NG5 . 161 D1

Ravenswood Rd NG5 .. 162 A4
Ravensworth Rd NG6 .. 160 A4
Rawson St
  Nottingham NG7 .... 160 C1
  Selston NG16 .... 129 D3
Raylawn St NG18 .... 103 D3
Raymede Cl NG5 .... 160 C3
Raymede Dr NG5 .... 160 C3
Raymond Cl NG17 ..... 114 C4
Raymond Dr NG21 .... 178 A2
Raymoth La S81 .... 35 F4
Rayneham Rd DE7 .... 157 E2
Rayner Ct NG7 .... 222 B3
Raynford Ave NG9 .... 183 E2
Raysmith Cl NG25 .... 121 F1
Rayton Cl DN11 .... 9 D2
Rayton La S81 .... 36 B2
Rayton Spur S81 .... 36 B2
Read Ave NG9 .... 184 A3
Read Way NG16 .... 158 C4
Rearsby Cl NG8 .... 171 E3
Recreation Dr NG20 . 72 C1
Recreation Rd
  Annesley NG15 .... 130 B4
  New Houghton NG19 . 86 C4
  Sandiacre NG10 .... 182 A3
  Shirebrook NG20 .... 72 C2
Recreation St
  Long Eaton NG10 ...... 193 F4
  Mansfield NG18 .... 102 B4
  Selston NG16 .... 129 D3
Recreation Terr NG9 . 182 B3
Recreation View NG20 . 72 C3
Rectory Ave
  Gainsborough DN21 ... 15 E1
  Nottingham NG8 .... 171 F2
Rectory Dr The NG4 .. 162 C1
Rectory Gdns
  Beckingham DN10 .... 14 A1
  Kirton NG22 .... 78 A3
  Nottingham NG8 .... 171 F2
Rectory La
  Bottesford NG13 ...... 181 D2
  Claypole NG23 .... 156 C4
  Gamston DN22 .... 50 C3
  Lea DN21 .... 24 C1
Rectory Pl
  Barton in F NG11 .... 194 C3
  🔢 Loughborough LE11 . 220 A2
  Wymeswold LE12 .... 216 B2
Rectory Rd Carlton NG4 . 174 C4
  Church Warsop NG20 . 74 B4
  Cotgrave NG12 .... 187 F2
  Loughborough LE11 . 220 A2
  Retford DN22 .... 39 F4
  Treswell DN22 .... 42 A2
  West Bridgford NG2 . 185 F4
Rectory St LN5 .... 142 B4
Red Barn Cl DE55 .... 99 D2
Red Causeway The LE14 . 202 A1
Red Hall La NG22 ... 92 C2
Red La Brinsley NG16 . 128 C1
  Carlton in L S81 ...... 25 E4
  Lowdham NG14 .... 150 B1
Red Lodge La NG15 . 166 A4
Redbarn La DE55 .... 99 D2
Redbarn Way NG17 . 100 B3
Redbridge Dr NG16 . 159 E2
Redcar Cl Carlton NG4 . 162 C1
  Mansfield NG18 .... 102 C3
Redcliffe Gdns NG3 . 173 E4
Redcliffe Rd
  Mansfield NG18 .... 102 B3
  Nottingham NG3 .... 173 E4
Redcliffe St NG17 ... 101 D2
Redcroft Cl NG21 .... 75 F1
Redfield Rd NG7 ...... 184 C4
Redfield Way NG7 ... 184 C4
Redford Park Ave DN22 . 29 E1
Redford Cl NG8 .... 171 E4
Redford Park Rd DN22 . 29 E1
Redgate Cl NG19 ... 101 E4
Redgate St
  Nottingham NG6 ..... 101 F4
  Pinxton NG16 .... 113 E1
Redgates Ct NG14 . 148 B4
Redhill Comp Sch NG5 . 147 F1
Redhill La DN22 ..... 63 F4
Redhill Lodge Dr NG5 . 147 E1
Redhill Rd NG5 ...... 147 F1
Redland Ave NG4 ... 174 C4
Redland Cl Beeston NG9 . 183 E2
  Ilkeston DE7 .... 157 F2
Redland Dr NG9 ..... 183 E2
Redland Gr NG4 ..... 174 C4
Redmile La NG13 .. 192 C2
Redmile CE Sch NG13 . 192 C2
Redmile Rd NG8 .... 172 B3
Redoubt St NG7 ..... 222 A3
Redruth Cl NG8 ..... 171 E3
Redruth Dr NG18 ... 103 D1
Redthorn Way NG23 . 156 C3
Redwood NG2 .... 185 E3
Redwood Ave NG8 . 171 E2
Redwood Cres NG9 . 183 E3
Redwood Ct NG15 . 145 F4
Reedham Wlk 🔢 NG5 . 161 D4
Reedman Rd NG10 . 193 D2
Rees Gdns NG5 ..... 147 D1
Rees Row DN22 .... 42 A1

Reform St
Annesley Woodhouse NG17 .... 129 F4
Sutton in A NG17 .... 100 C1
Regatta Way NG2 .... 186 B4
Regency Ct NG9 .... 184 A4
Regent St Beeston NG9 .... 184 A4
  Kimberley NG16 .... 158 C3
  Kirkby in A NG17 .... 114 C2
  Langley Mill NG16 .... 143 D2
  Long Eaton NG10 .... 193 E4
  Loughborough LE11 .... 220 A2
  Mansfield NG18 .... 102 A4
  Nottingham, New Basford NG7 ... 172 F8
  Nottingham, Standard Hill NG1 ... 223 D2
  Stapleford NG10 .... 182 B3
  Sutton in A NG17 .... 100 B1
Regents Ct NG23 .... 112 A4
Regents Park Cl NG2 .... 185 E3
Regina Cl NG12 .... 175 F1
Regina Cres NG15 .... 116 C1
Reid Gdns NG16 .... 159 D4
Reigate Cl NG8 .... 183 F1
Reigate Dr NG9 .... 183 F1
Reigate Rd NG7 .... 160 C1
Reindeer St NG18 .... 102 C3
Rempstone Dr NG6 .... 160 B3
Rempstone Rd
  East Leake LE12 .... 214 C4
  East Leake, Stanford Hills LE12 ... 214 A3
  Hoton LE12 .... 215 E1
  Wymeswold LE12 .... 216 A2
Renals Way NG14 .... 148 C4
Rendell Prim Sch LE11 .... 220 A3
Renfrew Ct NG19 .... 101 F3
Renfrew Dr NG8 .... 171 F2
Repton Ct NG19 .... 88 C2
Repton Dr DE7 .... 170 A4
Repton Rd
  Nottingham NG6 .... 160 B3
  West Bridgford NG2 .... 185 F3
Retford Gate DN22 .... 41 F4
Retford Hospl DN22 .... 39 E4
Retford Rd
  Askham DN22 .... 52 C2
  Blyth S81 .... 18 A1
  Boughton NG22 .... 77 F4
  Mattersey DN10 .... 20 B3
  North Leverton w H DN22 ..... 41 F4
  North Wheatley DN22 .... 31 E4
  Nottingham NG5 .... 161 D2
  Rampton DN22 .... 42 B1
  Ranby S81 .... 37 E2
  South Leverton DN22 .... 42 A4
  Worksop S80 .... 35 F1
Retford Sta DN22 .... 39 F3
Revelstoke Ave NG5 .... 146 B1
Revelstoke Way NG5 .... 146 C1
Revesby Gdns NG8 .... 172 B4
Revesby Rd NG5 .... 161 F3
Revill Cl DE7 .... 157 E1
Revill Cres NG9 .... 182 C4
Revill Ct **15** NG17 .... 114 C4
Reydon Dr NG8 .... 160 B1
Reynolds Dr NG8 .... 171 F4
Rhodes Wlk NG18 .... 101 F3
Rhyl Cres NG4 .... 162 C1
Ribblesdale S81 .... 36 A4
Ribblesdale Ct NG9 .... 183 D2
Ribblesdale Rd
  Long Eaton NG10 .... 193 D3
  Nottingham NG5 .... 161 E3
Rider Cl
  Annesley Woodhouse NG17 .... 115 D3
  Long Eaton NG10 .... 193 E3
Richard Bonnington Prim Sch NG5 ... 147 F1
Richard St DN22 .... 40 A3
Richards Cl NG12 .... 189 D2
Richardson Cl NG11 .... 184 B1
Richborough Pl NG8 .... 171 F1
Richey Cl NG5 .... 162 A4
Richmond Ave
  Breaston DE72 .... 193 D4
  Calverton NG14 .... 149 D4
  Eastwood NG16 .... 144 A1
  Ilkeston DE7 .... 157 F2
  Nottingham NG3 .... 173 H4
  Sandiacre NG10 .... 182 A2
Richmond Cl NG24 .... 140 A2
Richmond Dr
  Beeston NG9 .... 183 F3
  Mansfield Woodhouse NG19 ... 88 B1
  Nottingham NG3 .... 161 G1
  Radcliffe on T NG12 .... 175 F2
Richmond Gdns NG5 .... 147 F1
Richmond La DN10 .... 9 F3
Richmond Rd
  Carlton in L S81 .... 25 F3
  Gainsborough DN21 .... 24 C4
  Kirkby in A NG17 .... 115 E3
  Retford DN22 .... 40 A1
  West Bridgford NG2 .... 173 H1
  Worksop S80 .... 36 A1
Richmond St NG18 .... 102 C3
Richmond Terr NG12 .... 175 F2
Rick St NG1 .... 223 F3
Ricket La
  Blidworth NG21 .... 117 E3
  Ravenshead NG15 .... 116 C2
Ricklow Ct NG5 .... 161 D4
Riddell Ave S81 .... 16 C2
Ridding Terr NG3 .... 223 E4

Ridge Cl NG17 .... 100 B2
Ridge Hill NG14 .... 150 B1
Ridge La NG12 .... 176 A3
Ridgeway
  Nottingham NG5 .... 161 D4
  Shipley DE75 .... 157 D4
  Southwell NG25 .... 121 C1
  Worksop S81 .... 36 A3
Ridgeway Cl NG22 .... 119 F3
Ridgeway La NG20 .... 74 A2
Ridgeway St NG3 .... 173 F3
Ridgeway Terr NG20 .... 74 A2
Ridgeway The NG22 .... 120 A3
Ridgeway Wlk **1** NG5 ..... 161 D4
Ridgewood Dr NG9 .... 183 E2
Ridgewood Gr NG15 .... 117 D1
Ridgmont Walk NG11 .... 195 E4
Ridgway Cl NG2 .... 186 B3
Riding or Ridinge La
  DN10 .... 3 D2
Ridings The
  Bulcote NG14 .... 164 A3
  East Bridgford NG13 .... 165 E2
  Keyworth NG12 .... 198 A2
  Mansfield Woodhouse NG19 ... 88 C1
Ridsdale Rd NG5 .... 161 E3
Rifle St NG7 .... 222 A3
Rigg La NG21 .... 132 C4
Rigley Ave **15** DE7 .... 157 F1
Rigley Dr NG5 .... 160 C4
Riley Ave NG17 .... 100 B2
Riley Cl NG17 .... 100 B2
Ring Leas NG12 .... 188 A1
Ringrose Cl NG24 .... 140 B4
Ringstead Cl NG2 .... 185 E3
Ringstead Wlk NG5 .... 161 D4
Ringwood S81 .... 36 A3
Ringwood Ave NG18 .... 102 B2
Ringwood Cres NG8 .... 172 B3
Ringwood Rd NG13 .... 177 E2
Ripon Rd NG3 .... 174 A3
Rise Park Jun & Inf Sch
  NG5 .... 146 C1
Rise Park Rd NG5 .... 146 C1
Rise The NG5 .... 161 E2
Riseborough Wlk NG6 .... 146 B1
Risegate NG12 .... 187 F2
Riseholme Ave NG8 .... 171 E2
Riseholme Rd DN21 .... 24 C4
Risley Ct DE7 .... 157 F2
Risley Dr NG2 .... 173 D1
Riste's Pl NG2 .... 223 F2
Ritchie Cl NG12 .... 188 A1
Ritson Cl NG3 .... 223 F4
River Cl DN22 .... 29 F3
River La Misson DN10 ...... 4 B1
  Retford DN22 .... 39 F4
River Rd NG4 .... 174 C2
River View
  Market Warsop NG20 .... 74 A3
  Nottingham NG2 .... 173 E1
  Pye Bridge DE55 .... 128 A3
  Retford DN22 .... 39 F2
Riverdale Rd NG9 .... 183 E1
Rivergreen NG11 .... 184 C2
Rivergreen Cl NG9 .... 171 E1
Rivergreen Cres NG9 .... 171 E1
Rivermead
  Cotgrave NG12 .... 188 A2
  Newark-on-T NG24 .... 139 F3
Riverside NG7 .... 172 C1
  Riverside Southwell NG25 ... 121 F1
  Whatton NG13 .... 179 D2
Riverside Cl
  Bottesford NG13 .... 181 D2
  Cuckney NG20 .... 60 A2
Riverside Rd
  Beeston NG9 .... 184 A2
  Newark-on-T NG24 .... 139 E3
Riverside Ret Pk NG11 ...... 185 D4
Riverside Way
  Mansfield Woodhouse NG19 ... 88 B3
Riverside Wlk NG13 .... 181 D2
Riverview Cotts DN10 .... 4 B1
Riverway Gdns NG2 .... 173 E1
Rivington Rd NG9 .... 182 C2
Road No 1 NG4 .... 174 C3
Road No 2 NG4 .... 174 C3
Road No 3 NG4 .... 174 C3
Road No 4 NG4 .... 175 E3
Road No 5 NG4 .... 175 D3
Road No 6 NG4 .... 174 C3
Road No 7 NG4 .... 174 C3
Road No 8 NG4 .... 174 C3
Roadwood La NG23 .... 69 F4
Rob Roy Ave NG7 .... 222 B1
Robbie Burns Rd NG5 .... 161 E4
Robert Ave NG18 .... 101 F3
Robert Dukeson Ave NG24 ... 125 D2
Robert Jones Jun Sch NG21 ... 118 A3
Robert Mellors Prim Sch NG5 ... 161 F4
Robert Miles Jun Sch NG13 ... 177 F2
Robert Shaw Prim Sch NG8 ... 172 B3
Robert's La NG15 .... 145 F4
Roberts Ave NG17 .... 99 F1
Roberts Cl
  Dunham on T NG22 .... 54 A1
  Kegworth DE74 .... 203 E2
Roberts St Ilkeston DE7 ..... 170 A3
  Nottingham NG2 .... 173 F3
Roberts Yd NG9 .... 184 A4
Robey Cl Hucknall NG15 .... 131 D1
  Mansfield Woodhouse NG19 ... 89 D1
Robey Dr NG16 .... 143 F2

Robin Down Cl NG18 .... 102 B1
Robin Down La NG18 .... 102 B1
Robin Gr NG15 .... 117 D1
Robin Hood Ave
  Edwinstowe NG21 .... 91 E4
  Market Warsop NG20 .... 74 B1
Robin Hood Cl NG16 .... 143 F1
Robin Hood Dr NG15 .... 145 F3
Robin Hood Ind Est **B** NG3 ... 173 F3
Robin Hood Inf & Jun Sch
  Mansfield Woodhouse NG19 ... 88 A2
  Nottingham NG5 .... 161 D3
Robin Hood Rd
  Annesley Woodhouse NG17 ... 130 A4
  Arnold NG5 .... 147 E1
  Blidworth NG21 .... 118 A3
  Nottingham NG3 .... 173 F3
Robin Hood Terr
  Nottingham NG3 .... 223 F3
  Ravenshead NG15 .... 117 D2
Robin Hood Way NG2 .... 173 E1
Robin's Wood Rd NG8 .... 172 A4
Robina Dr NG16 .... 158 B4
Robinet Rd NG9 .... 183 F3
Robinettes La NG16 .... 158 B1
Robinia Ct NG2 .... 186 A3
Robins Ct NG24 .... 140 A4
Robinson Cl NG24 .... 140 C4
Robinson Dr S80 .... 35 F1
Robinson Gdns NG11 .... 184 B1
Robinson Rd NG3 .... 162 A1
Rochdale Ct NG18 .... 103 D3
Roche Cl NG5 .... 162 B4
Rochester Ave NG4 .... 175 D4
Rochester Cl
  Long Eaton NG10 .... 193 D4
  Worksop S81 .... 36 A4
Rochester Ct NG6 .... 159 F3
Rochester Rd NG21 .... 118 A4
Rochester Wlk NG7 .... 184 C1
Rochford Cl NG12 .... 186 B4
Rock Ct Mansfield NG18 .... 102 B4
  Nottingham NG6 .... 160 B4
Rock Dr NG7 .... 222 C1
Rock Hill NG18 .... 102 B3
Rock St Mansfield NG18 .... 102 B4
  Nottingham NG6 .... 160 A4
Rock Valley NG18 .... 102 B3
Rockford Ave NG21 .... 118 A4
Rockford Cl NG12 .... 170 C1
Rockford Rd NG5 .... 160 C2
Rockingham Gr NG13 ...... 177 E2
Rocklands The NG2 .... 72 C2
Rockley Ave
  Eastwood NG16 .... 144 A1
  Radcliffe on T NG12 .... 175 F3
Rockley Cl NG15 .... 145 E3
Rockley Way NG20 .... 72 C2
Rockleys View NG14 .... 150 A1
Rockwood Cl NG21 .... 118 A3
Rockwood Wlk NG15 ...... 145 F3
Rodel Ct NG3 .... 223 F4
Roden St NG3 .... 173 F3
Roderick Ave NG17 .... 115 D1
Roderick St NG6 .... 160 B2
Rodney Rd NG2 .... 186 A3
Rodney St NG21 .... 121 D4
Rodney Way DE7 .... 157 F2
Rodwell Cl NG8 .... 172 B3
Roe Hill NG14 .... 149 E3
Roebuck Cl NG5 .... 161 D4
Roebuck Dr NG18 .... 102 A2
Roebuck Way S80 .... 48 A4
Roecliffe NG2 .... 185 F2
Roehampton Dr NG9 ..... 170 B1
Roes La NG14 .... 149 D4
Roewood Cl NG17 .... 114 C4
Roewood La NG22 .... 107 F1
Roger Cl NG17 .... 100 C3
Roker Cl NG8 .... 160 A1
Rolaine Cl NG19 .... 88 B2
Roland Ave
  Nottingham NG11 .... 185 D4
  Nuthall NG16 .... 159 F2
Rolleston Cl NG15 .... 145 E3
Rolleston Cres NG16 .... 144 C1
Rolleston Dr
  Arnold NG5 .... 162 A4
  Eastwood NG16 .... 158 A4
  Nottingham NG7 .... 222 B1
Rolleston Sta NG25 ..... 137 F3
Roman Bank NG19 ...... 88 B2
Roman Bank La DN10 ... 18 C2
Roman Dr NG6 .... 160 C2
Romans Ct NG6 .... 160 C1
Romilay Cl NG9 .... 172 A1
Romney Ave NG8 ...... 171 F1
Romsey Pl NG19 .... 101 E3
Rona Cl NG19 .... 101 F3
Rona Ct NG6 .... 160 C3
Ronald St NG7 .... 222 B3
Rook's La DN10 .... 6 C1
Rookery Gdns NG5 .... 161 F4
Rookery La NG17 ..... 114 A4
Rookery The
  Collingham NG23 .... 98 A1
  1 Mansfield NG18 ..... 102 A4
Rookwood Cl NG9 ...... 183 F3
Rookwood Cres NG15 .. 145 E3
Rooley Ave NG17 ...... 100 B2
Rooley Dr NG17 .... 100 B2
Roosa Cl NG6 .... 159 F3
Roosevelt Ave NG10 .. 193 E3
Roosevelt Rd NG17 ... 101 D2
Rooth St NG18 .... 102 A3
Rope Wlk LE12 .... 205 E1
Ropery Rd DN21 ...... 15 E1
Ropewalk DE74 .... 203 E1

Ropewalk Ind Ctr DE7 .... 158 A1
Ropewalk The
  Ilkeston DE7 .... 158 A1
  Newark-on-T NG24 .... 140 A4
  Nottingham NG1 .... 223 D2
  Southwell NG25 .... 121 F1
Ropsley Cres NG2 .... 186 A4
Roscoe Ave NG5 .... 147 F1
Rose Ash La NG5 .... 161 D4
Rose Ave Ilkeston DE7 ..... 157 F1
  Retford DN22 .... 40 A2
Rose Cl NG3 .... 173 E4
Rose Cottage Dr NG17 ..... 99 F1
Rose Cotts NG14 .... 163 F3
Rose Ct NG10 .... 182 A1
Rose Farm Dr NG23 .... 96 C4
Rose Gr Beeston NG9 ..... 184 A3
  Keyworth NG12 .... 197 F2
Rose Hill NG12 .... 197 F2
Rose La DN22 .... 39 E2
Rose Lea DN22 .... 39 E2
Roseacre NG9 .... 184 A3
Rosebank Dr NG5 .... 148 A1
Roseberry Ave NG2 ...... 173 F1
Roseberry Gdns NG15 ... 146 B3
Roseberry St NG17 ...... 115 E2
Rosebery Hill NG18 ..... 102 B3
Rosebery St NG6 .... 160 C2
Rosecroft Dr NG5 .... 161 E3
Rosedale S81 .... 36 A4
Rosedale Cl NG10 ...... 193 D3
Rosedale Dr NG8 .... 171 D2
Rosedale La NG15 ..... 116 C2
Rosedale Rd NG3 ...... 174 A3
Rosedale Way NG19 ... 88 C1
Rosegarth Wlk NG6 ... 160 B2
Rosegrove Ave NG5 ... 147 F1
Rosehill Cl LN1 .... 57 D2
Rosehill Sch NG3 ..... 173 F3
Roseleigh Ave NG3 ... 162 A1
Rosemary Ave NG18 .. 102 A4
Rosemary Cl **1** NG8 . 159 F1
Rosemary St NG18 ... 102 A4
Rosemont Ct NG17 ... 100 C3
Roseneath Ave NG5 .. 146 C1
Rosetta Rd NG7 ...... 160 C1
Rosewall Ct NG5 .... 162 A4
Roseway NG21 ...... 15 E1
Rosewood Ct
  Newark-on-T NG24 ...... 125 D1
  South Normanton DE55 ... 113 D4
Rosewood Cres DE75 ... 143 D2
Rosewood Dr NG17 .... 115 E3
Rosewood Gdns
  Nottingham NG6 .... 159 F4
  West Bridgford NG2 .... 185 E2
Roslyn Ave NG4 .... 162 C1
Ross Cl
  Coddington NG24 ...... 126 A1
  Lowdham NG14 .... 150 C1
Ross La NG4 .... 163 E4
Rossell Dr NG9 ...... 182 C3
Rossendale DE7 ..... 157 F2
Rossett Cl NG2 ..... 186 B3
Rossetti Gdns S81 .. 36 B2
Rossington Rd NG2 . 173 F3
Rosslyn Dr
  Hucknall NG15 ...... 146 B4
  Nottingham NG6 .... 160 A1
Rosslyn Jun & Inf Sch
  NG8 .... 160 A1
Rosthwaite Cl NG2 . 186 B3
Roston Cl NG18 .... 103 D3
Rothbury Ave NG9 . 170 B1
Rothbury Gr NG13 . 177 E3
Rotherham Baulk S81 . 25 E4
Rotherham Rd NG19 . 101 E3
Rothesay Ave NG7 .. 222 B2
Rothley Ave NG3 ... 173 F3
Rothwell Cl
  Gainsborough DN21 . 24 C4
  Nottingham NG11 ... 185 D2
Roughs Wood La NG15 . 145 E2
Roulstone Cres LE12 .. 205 F2
Roundhill Cl NG17 ... 101 E1
Roundhill Cty Prim Sch
  NG9 .... 183 F4
Roundwood Jun Sch
  NG5 .... 161 E4
Roundwood Rd NG5 . 161 E4
Row The NG11 ..... 179 F3
Rowan Ave
  Hathern LE12 ...... 213 D1
  Stapleford NG9 .... 170 C1
Rowan Cl Calverton NG14 . 148 B4
  Kirkby in A NG17 .. 114 C3
  Mansfield NG19 ... 88 B1
Rowan Cres S80 ... 35 F1
Rowan Croft NG17 . 99 F2
Rowan Ct NG16 ... 159 D3
Rowan Dr
  Keyworth NG12 ... 198 A1
  Kirkby in A NG17 . 114 C3
  Nottingham NG15 . 185 D2
  Ravenshead NG15 . 117 D1
  Selston NG16 ..... 128 B4
  Shirebrook NG20 . 72 B3
Rowan Gdns NG6 . 159 F4
Rowan Way NG24 . 140 A3
Rowan Wlk NG4 ... 174 A4
Rowe Gdns NG6 .. 160 B3
Rowland Ave NG3 . 162 A1
Rowland Mews NG3 . 173 E4
Rowsley Ave NG10 . 193 D3
Rowston Cl DN21 . 15 E1
Rowthorne La
  Ault Hucknall S44 . 86 A4
  Glapwell S44 ..... 86 A4

Roxton Ct NG16 .... 158 C3
Roy Ave NG9 .... 184 A3
Royal Ave NG10 .... 182 B3
Royal Cres S81 .... 35 F3
Royal Mews NG9 .... 183 E3
Royal Oak Ct NG21 ...... 76 A2
Royal Oak Dr NG16 ...... 129 C2
Royal Way LE11 .... 220 A2
Royce Ave NG15 .... 145 F4
Royds Cres S80 .... 35 C2
Royland Rd LE11 .... 220 A2
Royston Cl NG2 .... 173 E1
Rrith Way NG6 .... 160 A4
Ruby Paddocks NG16 .. 158 C3
Ruddington St NG18 ... 103 D3
Ruddington Ctry Pk
  NG11 .... 196 B3
Ruddington La NG11 ... 195 E4
Ruddington Mus NG11 . 196 B3
Ruddington Rd NG18 .. 103 D3
Ruddington Village Mus
  NG11 .... 196 B3
Rudge Cl NG8 .... 171 F3
Ruffles Ave NG5 ..... 162 A4
Rufford Ave
  Beeston NG9 .... 183 D3
  Carlton NG4 .... 162 F4
  Mansfield NG18 ...... 102 B2
  Meden Vale NG20 ... 74 C2
  New Ollerton NG22 .. 77 E2
  Newark-on-T NG24 . 139 F4
  Rainworth NG21 .... 104 B3
  Retford DN22 .... 39 E4
Rufford Cl
  Bilsthorpe NG22 .... 106 A4
  Hucknall NG15 ...... 146 B3
  Sutton in A NG17 ... 100 C2
Rufford Ct NG21 ..... 104 B3
Rufford Ctry Pk NG22 . 91 F1
Rufford Dr NG19 ..... 88 B3
Rufford Gr NG13 .... 177 E2
Rufford Jun & Inf Sch
  NG6 .... 160 A4
Rufford La
  Edwinstowe NG22 ... 91 A3
  Wellow NG22 .... 92 A1
Rufford Rd
  Edwinstowe NG21 ... 91 B3
  Long Eaton NG10 ... 193 C2
  Nottingham NG5 ... 161 E1
  Ruddington NG11 .. 196 B3
Rufford Sch The NG21 . 75 F4
Rufford St S80 ...... 47 D2
Rufford Way NG2 ... 186 A3
Rufford Wlk **14** NG6 . 160 A4
Ruffs Dr NG15 ..... 145 F3
Rugby Cl NG5 ...... 160 C2
Rugby Rd NG21 ... 118 A4
Rugeley Ave NG10 . 194 A3
Ruislip Cl NG16 ... 158 C3
Runcie Cl NG12 ... 187 F2
Runnymede Rd NG7 . 222 C3
Runswick Dr Arnold NG5 . 161 F2
  Nottingham NG8 .. 172 A4
Runton Dr NG6 ... 160 B3
Rupert Cres NG24 . 124 C2
Rupert Rd NG13 .. 177 E3
Rupert St DE7 .... 158 A2
Rush Leys NG10 . 193 E4
Rushcliffe Ave
  Carlton NG4 ...... 174 B4
  Radcliffe on T NG12 . 175 F3
Rushcliffe Ct NG6 . 160 B3
Rushcliffe Gr LE12 . 205 F2
Rushcliffe Rd NG15 . 145 F4
Rushcliffe Rise NG5 . 161 E1
Rushcliffe Sch NG12 . 185 D2
Rushes The
  Gotham NG11 ..... 195 C4
  Loughborough LE11 . 220 A2
  Mansfield Woodhouse NG19 . 88 C4
Rushey Cl S80 ... 36 A4
Rushford Dr NG8 . 171 F3
Rushley View NG17 . 100 C1
Rushmere Wlk NG5 . 161 F4
Rushpool Ave NG19 . 88 B3
Rushton Gdns NG3 . 173 F4
Rushworth Ave NG2 . 185 F3
Rushworth Cl NG3 . 173 F4
Rushy Cl NG8 .... 171 E1
Ruskin Ave
  Beeston NG9 ..... 183 D3
  Long Eaton NG10 . 193 C2
Ruskin Cl NG5 ... 161 F4
Ruskin Rd NG19 . 87 F1
Ruskin St DN21 .. 24 B4
Russell Ave
  Harworth DN11 .. 8 C4
  New Balderton NG24 . 140 A4
  Nottingham NG8 . 171 E1
Russell Cres NG8 . 171 E1
Russell Dr NG8 .. 171 E1
Russell Gdns **8** NG9 . 183 C2
Russell Pl NG1 .. 223 D2
Russell Rd NG7 . 172 C4
Russell St
  Long Eaton NG10 . 182 F4
  Loughborough LE11 . 220 A2
  Nottingham NG7 . 222 A4
  Sutton in A NG17 . 100 C1
Russet Ave NG4 . 174 C4
Russet Dr DN11 . 10
Russley Rd NG9 . 183 D4
Ruth Dr NG5 .... 148 B2
Rutherford Ave NG18 . 102
Ruthwell Gdns NG5 . 147
Rutland NG17 115

Rutland Ave
Beeston NG9 .... 183 D1
Newark-on-Tr NG24 .... 140 A3
Rutland Cl NG10 .... 74 A2
Rutland Cres DN11 .... 8 C3
Rutland Ct DE7 .... 157 E1
Rutland Dr DN11 .... 8 C3
Rutland Gr NG10 .... 182 B3
Rutland House Sch NG3 .... 173 E4
Rutland La NG13 .... 181 D1
Rutland Rd
Bingham NG13 .... 177 F3
Carlton NG4 .... 162 B2
Retford DN22 .... 40 A2
West Bridgford NG2 .... 186 A4
Woodthorpe NG6 .... 128 B2
Rutland St Ilkeston DE7 .... 157 F1
[5] Loughborough LE11 .... 220 B2
Mansfield NG18 .... 102 B3
Nottingham NG1 .... 223 D2
Rutland Terr DE7 .... 157 F1
Rydal Ave NG10 .... 182 A1
Rydal Dr Beeston NG9 .... 183 E4
Hucknall NG15 .... 145 F4
Worksop S81 .... 35 F4
Rydal Gdns NG2 .... 186 A3
Rydal Gr NG6 .... 160 C2
Rydal Rd NG5 .... 161 E3
Ryder St NG6 .... 160 B2
Rye Croft DN11 .... 8 A4
Rye St NG7 .... 160 C1
Ryecroft St NG9 .... 182 C4
Ryedale Ave NG18 .... 103 D3
Ryehill Cl NG2 .... 173 E1
Ryehill St NG2 .... 173 E1
Ryeholme Cl LE12 .... 205 F2
Ryeland Gdns NG2 .... 173 E1
Ryemere Cl NG16 .... 143 F1
Rylands Cl NG9 .... 184 A2
Ryton Cl S81 .... 18 A1
Ryton Ct [23] NG2 .... 173 E1
Ryton Fields S81 .... 18 A1
Ryton Pl S80 .... 35 F2
Ryton Sq NG8 .... 160 A1
Ryton St S80 .... 35 F2

Sacheverall Ave NG16 .... 113 E2
Sacred Heart Prim Sch NG4 .... 174 B4
Sacred Heart Sch LE11 .... 220 A1
Saddlers Cl NG19 .... 88 C1
Saddlers Yd NG12 .... 197 F4
Saddleworth Ct NG3 .... 223 E4
Sadler St NG19 .... 101 F4
Saffron Gdns NG2 .... 173 D1
St Agnes Cl NG8 .... 171 E4
St Aidan's Ct NG6 .... 160 C2
St Albans Cl NG15 .... 147 D1
St Albans Cty Prim Sch NG5 .... 161 E3
St Albans Mews NG6 .... 160 B3
St Albans Rd Arnold NG5 .... 161 F4
Bestwood Village NG6 .... 160 B4
St Albans St NG5 .... 161 E3
St Andrew Cl NG11 .... 195 D1
St Andrew St NG18 .... 102 B3
St Andrew's CE Prim Sch NG17 .... 100 C3
St Andrew's Cl NG15 .... 146 A4
St Andrew's Rd NG3 .... 173 E4
St Andrew's Rise DE74 .... 203 E1
St Andrews Cl NG6 .... 160 B4
St Andrews Cres NG17 .... 100 C3
St Andrews Ct NG6 .... 160 B4
St Andrews Dr LN1 .... 56 C2
St Andrews
Kirkby in A NG17 .... 115 D3
Sutton in A NG17 .... 100 C3
St Ann's Gdns NG3 .... 173 F3
St Ann's Hill NG3 .... 173 E4
St Ann's Hill Rd NG3 .... 173 E4
St Ann's Hospital Sch NG3 .... 174 A4
St Ann's Hospl NG3 .... 174 A4
St Ann's St NG1 .... 223 E3
St Ann's Valley NG3 .... 173 F4
St Ann's Way
Nottingham NG3 .... 223 E4
Shelton NG23 .... 168 B3
St Ann's Well Inf Sch NG3 .... 173 F3
St Ann's Well Rd NG3 .... 173 F3
St Anne's La LE12 .... 213 D3
St Annes Cl S80 .... 35 E2
St Annes Ct S80 .... 35 E2
St Annes Mews S80 .... 35 E2
St Annes View S80 .... 35 E2
St Anthony Ct NG7 .... 172 C1
St Augustine's
Jun & Inf Schs S81 .... 36 A2
St Augustine's
RC Prim Sch NG3 .... 173 E4
St Augustines Cl [8] NG7 .... 161 D1
St Austell Dr NG11 .... 185 D3
St Austins Ct NG4 .... 174 C4
St Austins Dr NG4 .... 174 C4
St Bartholomew's Rd NG3 .... 173 F3
St Botolphs Cl DN11 .... 57 D3
St Catherine St NG18 .... 102 B5
St Catherines Cl NG24 .... 139 F4
St Catherines St NG12 .... 175 F1
St Cecilia Gdns NG3 .... 223 E3
St Chad's Cl NG18 .... 102 B2
St Chad's Rd NG3 .... 173 F3

St Christopher St [31] NG2 .... 173 F2
St Clare's Gate NG24 .... 140 A3
St Cuthbert St S80 .... 35 F1
St Cuthbert's Rd [17] NG3 .... 173 F3
St David's Cl S81 .... 36 A3
St Edmund Campion
RC Prim Sch NG2 .... 186 A3
St Edmund's Ave NG19 .... 88 B2
St Edmund's CE Prim Sch
NG12 .... 187 D4
St Edmund's CE Prim Sch
NG12 .... 88 B2
St Edward's RC Prim Sch
NG3 .... 173 F4
St Edwin's Dr NG21 .... 76 A1
St Ervan Rd NG11 .... 185 D3
St Francis Hospl NG5 .... 161 D3
St George's CE Prim Sch
DN21 .... 24 C3
St George's Ct NG15 .... 146 A4
St George's Dr NG2 .... 173 E1
St Giles Sch DN22 .... 39 E4
St Giles' Way NG24 .... 140 C2
St Giles Way NG14 .... 189 D2
St Helen's Cres
Burton Joyce NG14 .... 163 F2
Trowell NG9 .... 170 B2
St Helen's Dr NG16 .... 128 B4
St Helen's Gr NG14 .... 163 F2
St Helen's La NG22 .... 120 C1
St Helen's Rd
Retford DN22 .... 40 A2
West Bridgford NG2 .... 185 F3
St Helen's St NG7 .... 222 C3
St Helens Ave NG16 .... 113 E2
St Jame's Terr NG1 .... 223 D2
St James Ave DE7 .... 170 A4
St James Ct NG10 .... 182 A2
St James' Dr NG16 .... 143 E4
St James's Ct NG15 .... 146 A4
St James's St
Nottingham NG1 .... 223 D2
Stapleford NG9 .... 182 B3
St James's Terr NG9 .... 182 B3
St John
Mansfield NG18 .... 102 A4
Retford DN22 .... 39 F4
St John the Baptist
Prim Sch NG4 .... 174 C3
St John's Ave NG17 .... 115 D2
St John's CE Mid Sch
NG18 .... 102 A4
St John's CE Prim Sch
NG18 .... 102 C4
St John's Cl NG16 .... 128 B1
St John's Coll NG9 .... 183 D4
St John's Cres NG15 .... 146 B3
St John's Dr DN22 .... 30 B2
St John's Pl [8] NG18 .... 102 A4
St John's Prim Sch S81 .... 35 F4
St John's Rd
Ilkeston DE7 .... 170 A4
Ruddington NG11 .... 196 B4
St John's St NG10 .... 193 E4
St John's Terr DN21 .... 24 B4
St Johns Ct NG7 .... 161 D1
St Joseph's Prim Sch
DN22 .... 39 E4
St Joseph's RC Prim Sch
Boughton NG22 .... 77 F3
Shirebrook NG20 .... 72 C3
St Joseph's Sch NG1 .... 223 D3
St Jude's Ave NG3 .... 161 F1
St Judes Way NG21 .... 104 A1
St Laurence Cl NG13 .... 193 F3
St Lawrence Blvd NG12 .... 175 F1
St Lawrence CE Prim Sch
NG13 .... 193 F3
St Leonard's DN11 .... 8 A4
St Leonard's Ct NG24 .... 124 C1
St Leonard's Dr NG8 .... 171 F2
St Leonards Way NG19 .... 103 D4
St Leven Cl NG8 .... 171 E4
St Luke's CE Sch NG24 .... 186 A3
St Luke's Sch S81 .... 34 C4
St Luke's St [2] NG3 .... 173 F3
St Luke's Way NG14 .... 175 F4
St Lukes Way S81 .... 53 D4
St Margaret Clitherow
Prim Sch NG5 .... 161 E4
St Margaret St NG18 .... 102 B3
St Margarets Ave NG8 .... 172 A4
St Mark's La NG24 .... 139 F4
St Mark's Pl NG24 .... 139 F4
St Marks St NG3 .... 223 E3
St Martin's Ave DN10 .... 9 F4
St Martin's Cl Firbeck S81 .... 16 A3
Nottingham NG8 .... 171 F4
St Martin's Rd NG8 .... 171 F4
St Martin's Wlk S80 .... 45 E3
St Martins Ct S81 .... 18 A1
St Martins Rd DN22 .... 42 B4
St Mary's Ave NG4 .... 162 C1
St Mary's CE Sch NG21 .... 76 B2
St Mary's Cl Arnold NG5 .... 147 F1
Bottesford NG13 .... 181 D2
[4] Loughborough LE11 .... 220 A2
Lowdham NG14 .... 150 B1
St Mary's Cres
East Leake LE12 .... 205 F2
Ruddington NG11 .... 196 B4
Tickhill DN11 .... 8 A4
St Mary's Ct NG17 .... 100 B2
St Mary's Dr NG21 .... 76 A1
St Mary's Gate
Nottingham NG1 .... 223 F2
Tickhill DN11 .... 8 A4

St Mary's Gdns NG24 .... 139 F3
St Mary's La NG13 .... 181 D1
St Mary's Mews DN11 .... 8 A4
St Mary's Pl NG1 .... 223 F2
St Mary's Prim Sch
NG17 .... 100 B2
St Mary's Rd
Sutton in A NG17 .... 100 B2
Tickhill DN11 .... 8 A4
St Mary's Way NG15 .... 146 A4
St Marys Dr NG15 .... 128 A2
St Marys Cl NG9 .... 183 E1
St Marys Rd NG13 .... 177 F3
St Matthew's CE Prim Sch
NG23 .... 81 F4
St Matthias Rd NG3 .... 173 F3
St Mawes Ave NG11 .... 185 D3
St Mellion Way [8] NG17 .... 114 C4
St Michael's Ave NG4 .... 162 C1
St Michael's Cl NG22 .... 120 C1
St Michael's Dr DE55 .... 113 D4
St Michael's Gn DN22 .... 39 E4
St Michael's Sq NG9 .... 183 D4
St Michael's St NG17 .... 101 D2
St Michael's View NG15 .... 131 D1
St Michaels Ave NG8 .... 171 E4
St Nicholas Cl NG5 .... 161 F4
St Nicholas St NG1 .... 223 E2
St Patrick's RC Prim Sch
Bircotes DN11 .... 9 D2
Mansfield NG18 .... 103 D3
Nottingham NG11 .... 185 D4
St Patrick's Rd
Hucknall NG15 .... 145 F4
Nuthall NG16 .... 159 E3
St Paul's Ave NG7 .... 172 C4
St Paul's Rd
Gainsborough DN21 .... 15 D2
Worksop S80 .... 36 A1
St Paul's St [1] NG8 .... 172 B3
St Paul's Terr NG7 .... 172 C4
St Peter's Ave NG20 .... 74 A3
St Peter's CE Fst Sch
NG18 .... 103 D1
St Peter's CE Prim Sch
East Bridgford NG13 .... 165 E2
Gringley on t H DN10 .... 12 C1
St Peter's Church Wlk
NG11 .... 223 E2
St Peter's Cres NG11 .... 196 B4
St Peter's Gate NG1 .... 223 E2
St Peter's Gate NG1 .... 223 E2
St Peter's La DN22 .... 21 E3
St Peter's Mix Jun Sch
NG11 .... 196 B4
St Peter's Sch NG18 .... 102 B3
St Peter's Sq NG1 .... 223 E2
St Peter's St NG7 .... 222 A3
St Peter's Way NG18 .... 102 B3
St Peters La LE12 .... 213 D1
St Peters Cl
East Stockwith DN21 .... 7 F1
Farndon NG24 .... 138 C2
New Ollerton NG22 .... 77 D2
St Peters Dr NG21 .... 104 A1
St Saviour's Cl DN22 .... 40 A4
St Saviour's Gdns NG2 .... 173 E1
St Stephen's Ave [8] NG2 .... 173 F2
St Stephen's Rd
Nottingham NG2 .... 173 F2
Retford DN22 .... 40 A2
St Swithun's CE Prim Sch
DN22 .... 39 F4
St Teresa's RC Prim Sch
NG8 .... 172 A4
St Thomas' Ave NG17 .... 115 D2
St Thomas Dr NG13 .... 179 D3
St Vincent Cl NG10 .... 193 E4
St Wilfreds Cl NG23 .... 110 C1
St Wilfrid's CE Sch NG14 .... 148 C4
St Wilfrids Dr NG17 .... 114 B3
Salamander Cl NG4 .... 162 B1
Salcey Dr NG9 .... 170 B3
Salcombe Circus NG5 .... 147 E1
Salcombe Cl NG16 .... 144 B1
Salcombe Cres NG11 .... 196 B4
Salcombe Dr NG5 .... 147 E1
Salcombe Gr DN10 .... 9 F4
Salcombe Rd NG5 .... 160 C2
Salford Gdns NG3 .... 223 F3
Salisbury Dr NG19 .... 88 C2
Salisbury Ave LE12 .... 205 F1
Salisbury Cl NG19 .... 88 C2
Salisbury Rd
Mansfield NG19 .... 101 F4
Newark-on-T NG24 .... 124 C1
Salisbury Sq NG7 .... 222 A2
Salisbury St
Beeston NG9 .... 184 A4
Gainsborough DN21 .... 15 E1
Long Eaton NG10 .... 193 F4
Nottingham NG7 .... 222 A2
Sallie Bank La LN1 .... 55 D2
Salmon Cl NG6 .... 159 F4
Salmon La NG17 .... 129 E4
Salop St NG5 .... 161 E4
Salt Hill S81 .... 16 A4
Saltburn Rd NG8 .... 172 A3
Salterford Ave NG14 .... 148 C4
Salterford House Sch
Calverton NG14 .... 133 E3
Oxton NG25 .... 134 B4
Salterford La NG14 .... 133 E3
Salterford Rd NG15 .... 145 E3
Saltford Cl NG4 .... 162 C1
Salthouse Cl NG9 .... 184 A4
Salthouse La NG9 .... 184 A4

Saltney Way NG11 .... 185 D2
Salvin Cl NG12 .... 189 D2
Sampson St NG17 .... 130 A4
Sampson's La NG19 .... 87 D2
Samson Cl NG11 .... 195 D1
Samuel Barlow Jun Sch
NG21 .... 96 A4
Samuel Cl NG11 .... 101 F4
Sand La Besthorpe NG23 .... 97 F4
Broadholme NG23 .... 70 C4
Spalford NG23 .... 83 D4
Torksey LN1 .... 44 B1
Sand Pit La LE14 .... 211 E2
Sandale Cl NG2 .... 186 B3
Sandalwood Cl NG18 .... 103 D2
Sandalwood Dr NG17 .... 115 E3
Sandays Cl NG2 .... 173 E1
Sandby St NG9 .... 183 E3
Sanders Ave NG18 .... 102 C4
Sanderson Dr NG23 .... 97 F4
Sanderson's Bank DN9 .... 2 A2
Sandfield Ave NG15 .... 132 A4
Sandfield Cl NG18 .... 103 D2
Sandfield La NG22 .... 78 A3
Sandfield Rd
Annesley Woodhouse NG17 .... 129 F4
Arnold NG5 .... 161 F3
Beeston NG9 .... 182 C1
Nottingham NG7 .... 222 B2
Sandfield Way NG24 .... 139 E3
Sandford Ave NG10 .... 193 F4
Sandford Rd NG3 .... 162 A2
Sandgate NG9 .... 171 E1
Sandgate Ave NG19 .... 88 B2
Sandgate Rd NG19 .... 88 B2
Sandhill Rd Farndon NG24 .... 139 D3
Selston NG16 .... 129 D2
Sandhill St S80 .... 35 F2
Sandholes The NG22 .... 119 F3
Sandhurst Ave NG18 .... 102 B2
Sandhurst Dr
Beeston NG9 .... 183 E1
Ruddington NG11 .... 196 A3
Sandiacre Rd NG9 .... 182 B3
Sandmartins S81 .... 35 E4
Sandon St NG7 .... 161 D1
Sandown Rd
Beeston NG9 .... 182 C1
Mansfield NG18 .... 103 D2
Sutton in A NG17 .... 101 D2
Sandpiper Way NG7 .... 222 A2
Sandringham Ave NG2 .... 185 F4
Sandringham Cres NG8 .... 171 E3
Sandringham Ct NG19 .... 35 F3
Sandringham Dr
Harworth DN11 .... 9 D3
Mansfield Woodhouse NG19 .... 88 A3
Sandringham Pl NG15 .... 146 A4
Sandringham Rd
Mansfield Woodhouse NG19 .... 88 C3
[2] Nottingham NG2 .... 173 F2
Retford DN22 .... 29 E1
Sandiacre NG10 .... 182 A2
Sandrock Rd DN11 .... 8 C3
Sands The LE14 .... 211 E2
Sandsfield La DN22 .... 24 B3
Sandside NG12 .... 187 F1
Sandwich Cl [8] NG17 .... 114 C4
Sandwood Cl DE55 .... 99 D2
Sandy La Beeston NG9 .... 171 E1
Carlton NG12 .... 91 D4
Edwinstowe NG21 .... 91 D4
Gamston DN22 .... 50 C2
Hucknall NG15 .... 146 A4
Market Warsop NG20 .... 74 A3
Oxton NG25 .... 134 B2
Ravenshead NG15 .... 117 D2
Worksop S80 .... 35 E2
Sandycliffe Cl NG19 .... 88 C1
Sandyford Cl NG6 .... 160 B2
Sandymount DN11 .... 9 D3
Sandymount E DN11 .... 9 D2
Sandymount W DN11 .... 9 D2
Sanger Cl NG11 .... 195 E4
Sanger Gdns NG11 .... 195 E4
Sankey Dr NG6 .... 160 A4
Santon Rd NG19 .... 89 D1
Sapele Cl NG4 .... 163 D1
Sapling Cl NG24 .... 140 B3
Sapphire Cl NG21 .... 104 B1
Sapphire Dr NG17 .... 115 E2
Saracen Cl DN21 .... 24 C3
Saracen La DN10 .... 4 A3
Saracen's Head Yd
NG24 .... 139 F4
Sargent Gdns [8] NG3 .... 173 F3
Sartfield Rd NG19 .... 88 C1
Saskatoon Cl NG12 .... 175 F1
Saucers The NG13 .... 177 F4
Saunby Cl NG5 .... 162 A4
Saundby Ave NG19 .... 87 E1
Saundby Rd DN22 .... 23 E1
Savage's Rd NG11 .... 196 B4
Savages Row NG11 .... 196 B4
Saversick La NG25 .... 136 B4
Savile Rd NG22 .... 105 F3
Savile St NG22 .... 105 F3
Saville Cl NG9 .... 182 C4
Saville House Sch NG19 .... 88 A2

Saville Rd Arnold NG5 .... 161 F3
Sutton in A NG17 .... 100 C3
Saville St NG21 .... 118 A3
Saville Way NG20 .... 74 A2
Saw Pit Ind Est DE55 .... 99 E3
Saw Pit La DE55 .... 99 D3
Sawley Dr NG18 .... 103 D2
Sawley Jun & Inf Schs
NG10 .... 193 D3
Sawyers Cl NG24 .... 140 A4
Saxby Dr NG18 .... 103 D2
Saxelby Gdns NG6 .... 160 A4
Saxilby CE Prim Sch LN1 .... 57 D2
Saxilby Rd LN6 .... 71 F4
Saxilby Sta LN1 .... 57 D2
Saxon Gn NG7 .... 222 A1
Saxon Way Cotgrave NG12 .... 188 A1
Harworth DN11 .... 8 C3
Saxondale Dr Nottingham NG6 .... 160 C3
Radcliffe on T NG12 .... 176 B2
Saxton Cl Beeston NG9 .... 184 A3
Worksop S80 .... 35 E1
Scafell Way NG11 .... 195 E4
Scalby Cl NG16 .... 143 E1
Scalford Dr NG8 .... 172 B2
Scampton Way DN21 .... 24 C4
Scarborough Rd NG22 .... 105 F3
Scarborough St NG3 .... 223 F3
Scarbrough Ct DN10 .... 8 A4
Scarcliffe Cl NG17 .... 100 C2
Scarcliffe La NG20 .... 72 B4
Scarcliffe St NG18 .... 102 B4
Scarcliffe Terr NG20 .... 59 D1
Scarf Wlk NG2 .... 185 D4
Scarfell Cl NG2 .... 186 B3
Scargill Ave NG16 .... 144 A1
Scargill Cl NG16 .... 144 A1
Scargill Wlk NG16 .... 143 F2
Scarle La LN6 .... 84 B2
Scarrington Ct NG18 .... 103 D1
Scarrington Rd NG2 .... 173 F1
Sceptre St NG5 .... 161 E1
School Ave NG15 .... 145 E2
School Cl Newton DE55 .... 99 D2
Nottingham NG2 .... 173 E1
School Gn LE12 .... 205 F1
School House La DN10 .... 13 F3
School La
Beckingham LN5 .... 142 B4
Beeston NG9 .... 183 E2
Bingham NG13 .... 177 F2
Caunton NG23 .... 109 D2
Claypole NG23 .... 156 C4
Colston Bassett NG12 .... 200 B4
Cuckney NG20 .... 60 A2
Eakring NG22 .... 92 C1
East Stoke NG23 .... 153 E4
Farndon NG24 .... 139 D2
Halam NG22 .... 121 D2
Harby LE14 .... 202 A2
Kingston-on-S NG2 .... 120 C4
Kneesall NG22 .... 93 F3
Long Clawson LE14 .... 211 E2
Mansfield Woodhouse NG19 .... 88 B2
North Scarle LN6 .... 83 E1
Norwell NG23 .... 110 A4
Ollerton NG22 .... 77 D2
Rempstone LE12 .... 215 E3
South Normanton DE55 .... 113 D2
Whatton NG13 .... 179 D2
School Rd Langold S81 .... 16 C2
Selston NG16 .... 129 D4
Selston, New Bagthorpe NG16 .... 129 D2
School St
Kirkby in A NG17 .... 115 D3
Loughborough LE11 .... 220 A3
Lound NG22 .... 181 D1
School View NG13 .... 181 D1
School Wlk Bawtry DN10 .... 10 A4
Bestwood Village NG6 .... 146 C2
Schrimshire's Rd DN22 .... 32 A1
Science Rd NG7 .... 172 B1
Scotholme Ave [2] NG7 .... 172 C4
Scotholme Prim Sch
NG7 .... 172 C4
Scotland Bank NG17 .... 187 F2
Scotland Rd NG5 .... 160 C2
Scotswood Rd NG19 .... 88 A3
Scott Ave NG9 .... 184 A3
Scott Cl Nottingham NG6 .... 159 F3
Worksop S80 .... 36 B2
Scott St
Gainsborough DN21 .... 15 E1
Whaley Thorns NG20 .... 59 D1
Scotton Sq DN22 .... 29 E1
Scotts Way NG17 .... 115 D1
Scratta La S80 .... 34 B1
Scrimshire La NG12 .... 187 F2
Script Dr NG6 .... 160 C2
Scrooby Rd Bircotes DN11 .... 9 E2
Scrowby Gdns NG5 .... 147 D1
Seaburn Rd NG9 .... 182 C1
Seaford Ave NG8 .... 172 A3
Seaford Way DE7 .... 157 F3
Seaforth Sq NG19 .... 101 E3
Seagrave Ave NG17 .... 115 D1
Seagrave Prim Sch NG8 .... 159 E1
Seagrave Rd NG8 .... 159 E1
Seagrave Sch NG8 .... 159 E1
Seamer Rd NG16 .... 158 C4
Searby Rd NG17 .... 101 E1

Searwood Ave NG17 .... 114 C4
Seathwaite Cl NG2 .... 186 B2
Seatoller Cl NG2 .... 186 B3
Seaton Cres NG8 .... 160 A1
Second Ave Beeston NG9 .... 184 B3
  Carlton, Gedling NG4 .... 162 C1
  Carlton, Thorneywood NG4 .. 174 B4
  Clipstone NG21 .... 90 A2
  Edwinstowe NG21 .... 76 A1
  Mansfield NG21 .... 103 F1
  Mansfield Woodhouse NG19 .. 89 D1
  Nottingham NG6 .... 160 A4
Sedgebrook Cl NG6 .... 160 B2
Sedgebrook St NG19 .... 88 C2
Sedgeley Rd NG13 .... 186 B1
Sedgewood Gr NG11 .... 184 C2
Sedgley Ave NG2 .... 173 F3
Sedgmere DN22 .... 39 E2
Sedgwick St
  Langley Mill NG16 .... 143 D2
  Westwood NG16 .... 128 A2
Sedley Ave NG16 .... 159 E3
Seely Ave NG14 .... 148 C4
Seely Church Sch NG5 .... 132 C1
Seely Jun & Inf Sch NG5 .... 161 E2
Seely Rd NG7 .... 222 C3
Sefton Ave NG9 .... 182 C4
Sefton Dr NG3 .... 161 E1
Selbourne St ☐ LE11 .... 220 B2
Selbourne St LE11 .... 220 B2
Selby Cl NG9 .... 182 C2
Selby La NG12 .... 197 F1
Selby Rd Styrrup DN11 .... 8 C1
  West Bridgford NG2 .... 185 F3
Selhurst Ct NG7 .... 172 C4
Selhurst St ☒ NG7 .... 172 C4
Selkirk Way ☒ NG5 .... 161 D1
Sellars Ave NG11 .... 196 B3
Seller's Wood Dr NG6 .... 160 A4
Seller's Wood Dr W NG6 .... 159 F4
Selsey Cl DN22 .... 29 F1
Selside Ct NG9 .... 183 D2
Selston Bagthorpe
  Prim Sch NG16 .... 129 D2
Selston CE Inf Sch
  NG16 .... 128 C3
Selston Dr NG8 .... 172 B2
Selston Holly Hill Sch
  NG16 .... 129 D4
Selston Rd NG16 .... 129 D4
Selwyn Cl NG6 .... 160 C3
Selwyn St NG18 .... 102 C3
Sennen Ct DN22 .... 29 F1
Serlby Rd NG16 .... 144 A2
Serlby Rise NG3 .... 173 F3
Seven Hills NG24 .... 125 D2
Seven Oaks Cres NG9 .... 171 E1
Seven Oaks Rd DE7 .... 170 A1
Seventh Ave
  Beeston NG9 .... 184 B3
  Clipstone NG21 .... 89 F1
  Mansfield NG19 .... 103 D4
Severals NG9 .... 182 C4
Severn St NG6 .... 160 A4
Seward St ☒ LE11 .... 220 A2
Seymour Rd
  Eastwood NG16 .... 143 F1
  Hucknall NG15 .... 145 F3
  West Bridgford NG2 .... 186 A4
Seymour St NG3 .... 173 F3
Shackleton Cl NG8 .... 159 E1
Shacklock Cl NG5 .... 147 D1
Shadwell Gr NG12 .... 175 F2
Shady La NG9 .... 183 E1
Shaftesbury Ave
  Burton Joyce NG14 .... 164 A3
  Long Eaton NG10 .... 193 D2
  Mansfield NG19 .... 87 F1
  Sandiacre NG10 .... 182 A3
Shaftesbury St ☐ NG7 .... 161 D1
Shakespeare Ave NG16 .... 88 A2
Shakespeare Cl NG4 .... 174 C3
Shakespeare Rd NG16 .... 158 B3
Shakespeare St
  Gainsborough DN21 .... 24 B3
  Long Eaton NG10 .... 182 B1
  Loughborough LE11 .... 220 A2
  New Balderton NG24 .... 140 A3
  Nottingham NG1 .... 223 E3
  Worksop S81 .... 36 A2
Shakespeare Villas NG1 .. 223 E3
Shaldon Cl NG5 .... 146 C1
Shandwick Cl NG5 .... 148 A1
Shanklin Dr NG9 .... 182 B4
Shanwell Cl NG8 .... 159 E1
Shardlow Way NG18 .... 103 D2
Sharnford Way NG9 .... 171 D2
Sharp Cl NG10 .... 193 E3
Sharphill Rd NG12 .... 186 A2
Sharpley Dr LE12 .... 205 F2
Sharrard Cl NG16 .... 129 D1
Sharrat Ct NG18 .... 103 D1
Shaw Cres NG15 .... 145 F2
Shaw Rd DN10 .... 12 C2
Shaw St Mansfield NG18 .. 102 C4
  Ruddington NG11 .... 196 B3
  Worksop S80 .... 35 F1
Shaw St E DE7 .... 170 A3
Shaw St W DE7 .... 170 A3
Sheaf Pl S81 .... 35 F4
Shearing Cl NG4 .... 163 D1
Shearing Hill NG4 .... 163 D1
Sheepbridge La NG18 .... 101 F3
Sheepfold La NG11 .... 196 B3
Sheepwalk La NG15 .... 116 C1

Sheepwash La
  Sutton in A NG17 .... 101 D1
  Tickhill DN11 .... 8 C4
Sheet Stores Ind Est
  NG10 .... 193 E3
Sheffield Rd S81 .... 18 A2
Shelby Cl NG7 .... 222 A2
Sheldon Cl NG10 .... 182 A2
Sheldrake Rd NG24 .... 140 B4
Shelford Ave NG17 .... 114 B3
Shelford Cl Beeston NG9 .. 183 E2
  Radcliffe on T NG12 .... 176 A2
Shelford Cres NG14 .... 164 A3
Shelford Dr NG13 .... 177 E2
Shelford Hill
  Mansfield NG19 .... 101 F3
  Radcliffe on T NG12 .... 176 B4
Shelford Rd Carlton NG4 .. 162 B2
  Radcliffe on T NG12 .... 176 A3
Shelford Rise NG3 .... 174 A3
Shellburne Cl NG5 .... 160 C4
Shelley Ave
  Mansfield Woodhouse NG19 .. 88 A2
  Nottingham NG11 .... 184 C2
Shelley Cl
  Balderton NG24 .... 140 B2
  Hucknall NG15 .... 145 E3
  Nuthall NG16 .... 159 D3
Shelley Rd NG5 .... 161 E4
Shelley St S80 .... 36 A2
Shelthorpe Ave LE11 .... 220 A1
Shelthorpe Rd LE11 .... 220 A1
Shelthorpe Sch LE11 .... 220 A1
Shelton Ave
  Hucknall NG15 .... 146 B2
  Newark-on-T NG24 .... 139 F3
Shelton Gdns NG11 .... 196 A4
Shelton Rd NG18 .... 103 D1
Shelton St NG3 .... 223 F4
Shenfield Gdns NG5 .... 146 C1
Shepard Cl NG8 .... 159 F3
Shepherd Sch NG8 .... 171 F4
Shepherd Wlk DE74 .... 203 E1
Shepherd's Ave NG8 .... 36 A3
Shepherd's Cl LE12 .... 213 E3
Shepherds Cl NG8 .... 172 A4
Shepherds Oak NG17 .... 100 C3
Shepherds Way NG17 .... 101 D1
Shepherds Wood Dr
  NG8 .... 172 B4
Shepshed LE12 .... 212 C1
Shepton Cl DE7 .... 157 E2
Shepton Cres NG8 .... 160 A1
Sheraton Dr NG8 .... 171 F2
Sherborne Rd
  Nottingham NG8 .... 160 A1
  West Bridgford NG2 .... 185 F3
Sherbrook Ave NG5 .... 161 E3
Sherbrook Cl NG14 .... 148 C4
Sherbrook Rd NG5 .... 161 E3
Sherbrook Terr NG5 .... 161 E3
Sherbrooke Rd NG5 .... 161 D3
Sheridan Cl NG24 .... 140 B3
Sheridan Ct NG9 .... 170 C1
Sheriffs Way NG2 .... 173 E1
Sheringham Cl NG5 .... 161 F3
Sheringham Dr NG18 .... 102 B3
Sherman Dr NG9 .... 183 E1
Sherriff's La NG17 .... 182 C1
Sherrington Cl NG11 .... 195 E4
Sherview Ave NG18 .... 103 D4
Sherwin Cl NG3 .... 223 E4
Sherwin Gr NG7 .... 222 A1
Sherwin Rd
  Nottingham NG7 .... 222 A1
  Stapleford NG9 .... 170 C1
Sherwin Wlk NG3 .... 223 E4
Sherwood Ave
  Bildworth NG21 .... 118 B3
  Calverton NG14 .... 148 B4
  Edwinstowe NG21 .... 76 A1
  Newark-on-T NG24 .... 140 A4
  ☐ Nottingham NG5 .... 161 E2
  Pinxton NG16 .... 113 E2
  Shirebrook NG20 .... 72 C2
Sherwood Cl NG18 .... 102 C4
Sherwood Cres S81 .... 18 A1
Sherwood Dr
  New Ollerton NG22 .... 77 E2
  Shirebrook NG20 .... 72 C2
Sherwood Forest Ctry Pk
  NG22 .... 76 A2
Sherwood Forest Farm Pk
  NG21 .... 89 F4
Sherwood Gr
  Bingham NG13 .... 177 E2
  Calverton NG14 .... 148 C4
Sherwood Hall Gdns
  NG18 .... 102 C4
Sherwood Hall Rd
  NG18 .... 102 C4
Sherwood Hall Upper Sch
  NG18 .... 102 C4
Sherwood Hospl NG5 .... 161 D2
Sherwood Jun Sch NG20 .. 74 A2
Sherwood Lodge Dr NG5 .. 132 B1
Sherwood Pines Forest Pk
  NG21 ....
Sherwood Pl
  Annesley Woodhouse NG17 115 D1
  Clipstone NG21 .... 90 A2
Sherwood Rd
  Harworth DN11 .... 9 D2
  Rainworth NG21 .... 104 B1
  Retford DN22 .... 39 F2
  Sutton in A NG17 .... 100 C1
  Worksop S80 .... 35 F2

Sherwood Rise
  Annesley Woodhouse NG17 115 D1
  Eastwood NG16 .... 143 F1
  Mansfield Woodhouse NG19 . 88 C2
  Nottingham NG7 .... 173 D4
Sherwood St
  Annesley Woodhouse NG17 130 A4
  Hucknall NG15 .... 146 B3
  Huthwaite NG17 .... 99 F2
  Kirkby in A NG17 .... 115 D3
  ☒ Mansfield NG18 .... 102 A3
  Mansfield Woodhouse NG19 . 88 A1
  Market Warsop NG20 .... 74 A2
  Newton DE55 .... 99 D2
Sherwood Vale NG5 .... 161 F2
Sherwood Way NG16 .... 129 D4
Sherwood Wlk NG15 .... 131 D1
Shetland Cl NG19 .... 88 C1
Shilling Way NG10 .... 193 D4
Shining Cliff Ct DN10 .... 9 E4
Shipley Ct NG7 .... 157 E1
Shipley Ctry Pk DE75 .... 157 D3
Shipley Rd NG8 .... 159 F1
Shipley Rise NG4 .... 174 C4
Shipstone St
  Ilkeston DE7 .... 170 A3
  ☒ Nottingham NG7 .... 172 C4
Shipstones Yd NG6 .... 160 B4
Shirburn Ave NG18 .... 102 B4
Shire La NG23, NG24 .... 156 A4
Shirebrook Com Sch
  NG20 .... 72 B3
Shirebrook Sta NG20 .... 73 D2
Shirebrooke Cl NG6 .... 160 B2
Shireoaks Comm
  Shireoaks S81 .... 34 C4
  Shireoaks, Gateford Common
  S81 .... 35 D4
Shireoaks Ct NG18 .... 103 D1
Shireoaks Rd S80 .... 35 D3
Shireoaks Row S81 .... 34 C4
Shireoaks Sta S81 .... 34 C4
Shires The NG17 .... 88 C1
Shirland Dr NG18 .... 103 D2
Shirley Dr NG3 .... 162 A4
Shirley Rd NG3 .... 173 E4
Shirley St NG10 .... 193 D2
Shorewood Cl ☒ NG5 .... 161 D4
Short Hill NG1 .... 223 F2
Short St
  Market Warsop NG20 .... 74 A2
  Sutton in A NG17 .... 101 D2
Short Wheatley La
  NG23 .... 112 A3
Shortcross Ave NG3 .... 161 F2
Shortwood Ave NG15 .... 145 F2
Shortwood Cl NG1 .... 223 F1
Shortwood La NG22 .... 93 E4
Shorwell Rd NG3 .... 174 B4
Shotton Dr NG5 .... 148 A1
Shoulder Of Mutton Hill
  NG17 .... 115 D1
Shrewsbury Rd
  Bircotes DN11 .... 9 D2
  Nottingham NG2 .... 174 A2
  Worksop S80 .... 36 A1
Shrewsbury View DN22 .. 29 F1
Shrimpton Cl NG11 .... 196 B3
Shropshire Ave NG16 .... 128 B2
Sibcy La NG24 .... 140 B2
Sibson Wlk NG5 .... 148 A1
Sibthorpe St NG18 .... 102 A3
Siddalls Dr NG17 .... 100 A2
Side La NG20 .... 106 C4
Side Ley DE74 .... 203 E2
Side Row NG24 .... 140 A4
Sidings Rd NG17 .... 115 E4
Sidings The
  Aslockton NG13 .... 179 D3
  Saxilby LN1 .... 57 D2
  Sidlaw Rise NG5 .... 147 D1
  Sidmouth Cl NG12 .... 197 F2
Sidney Rd NG9 .... 183 F4
Sidney St
  Kimberley NG16 .... 158 C3
  Long Eaton NG10 .... 193 E3
Sidsaph Hill DN10 .... 14 A3
Sikorski Cl NG24 .... 124 C1
Silbury Cl NG11 .... 195 E4
Silk St NG17 .... 100 C1
Silken Holme DE55 .... 113 D2
Silver Birch Cl NG6 .... 160 A2
Silver Hill Cl NG8 .... 159 E1
Silver St
  Gainsborough DN21 .... 24 B4
  Grassthorpe NG23 .... 81 F2
  North Clifton NG23 .... 68 C4
  Retford DN22 .... 39 E3
Silverdale NG9 .... 182 C3
Silverdale Ave NG19 .... 88 A2
Silverdale Cl DN22 .... 29 E1
Silverdale Rd NG7 .... 160 C1
Silverhill Cotts NG17 .... 100 A4
Silverhill La NG17 .... 99 F4
Silverwood Ave NG15 .. 117 D1
Silverwood Rd
  Beeston NG9 .... 183 F3
  Bottesford NG13 .... 181 D1
Silvey Ave NG25 .... 121 E1
Sime St S80 .... 35 F2
Simkin Ave NG3 .... 162 A1
Simon Cl DN22 .... 42 A1
Simone Gdns NG7 .... 184 C1
Simons Cl NG17 .... 114 C3
Simpson Cl NG24 .... 140 C2
Simpson Rd NG19 .... 88 A3
Singleton Ave NG18 .... 102 C4

Sir Edmund Hillary
  Cty Prim Sch S81 .... 36 A2
Sir John Sherbrooke
  Jun Sch NG14 .... 148 C4
Sir Philip Neri with
  St Bede's RC Prim Sch
  NG18 .... 102 A4
Siskin Ct S81 .... 35 E4
Sisley Ave NG9 .... 182 C3
Sitwell Cl S81 .... 36 A2
Sitwell Rd S81 .... 36 B2
Six Hills La LE14 .... 219 D1
Sixth Ave Beeston NG9 .. 184 B3
  Clipstone NG21 .... 89 F2
  Edwinstowe NG21 .... 76 A1
  Mansfield NG19 .... 103 D4
Skeavington's La DE7 .... 157 F3
Skegby La NG17, NG19 .... 101 E3
Skegby Mount NG19 .... 101 E3
Skegby Rd
  Annesley Woodhouse NG17 . 129 F4
  Huthwaite NG17 .... 100 A2
  Normanton on T NG23 .... 81 E4
  Sutton in A NG17 .... 100 C3
Skelwith Cl NG2 .... 186 B3
Skerry Hill NG18 .... 102 C4
Skerry La NG13 .... 181 F1
Sketchley Ct ☐ NG6 .... 160 A4
Sketchley St NG3 .... 173 F3
Ski 2000 Ilkeston NG16 .. 170 C3
Skiddaw Cl NG2 .... 186 B3
Skipton Cir NG3 .... 174 A3
Skipton Cl DE7 .... 157 E2
Skirbeck Dr LN1 .... 57 D2
Skithorne Rise NG14 .... 164 B4
Skylark Dr NG6 .... 160 B2
Slack Wlk S80 .... 35 F1
Slack's La NG13 .... 152 A1
Slade Cl DE55 .... 113 D2
Slade La NG18 .... 103 D3
Slaidburn Ave NG11 .... 185 D3
Slake La NG24 .... 124 C3
Slant La NG19 .... 88 A2
Slant The NG20 .... 72 B2
Slater St NG17 .... 100 C2
Slaughter House La
  NG24 .... 124 C1
Sleaford Rd
  Beckingham LN5 .... 142 B4
  Coddington NG24 .... 126 B1
  Newark-on-T NG24 .... 125 D1
Sleights La NG16 .... 113 E1
Sloan Dr NG9 .... 171 D2
Sloane Ct NG2 .... 185 E2
Slowthorne Gdns ☒
  NG5 .... 161 E4
Small Farm Ctr NG11 .... 202 C4
Small Gate NG19 .... 88 C3
Small's Croft NG14 .... 149 E2
Smalley Cl NG16 .... 129 D1
Smeath La DN22 .... 20 A3
Smeath Rd Retford DN22 .. 30 A2
  Selston NG16 .... 129 D1
Smedley Ave DE7 .... 170 A4
Smedley Cl NG8 .... 160 A1
Smedley's Ave NG10 .... 182 B3
Smeeton St DE75 .... 143 D1
Smite Cl NG13 .... 179 D2
Smite La NG13 .... 179 F4
Smith Dr NG16 .... 143 D2
Smith Sq DN11 .... 9 D2
Smith St Mansfield NG18 .. 102 C3
  Newark-on-T NG24 .... 140 A4
  Newark-on-T, New Balderton
  NG24 .... 140 B3
Smithfield Ave NG9 .... 170 C3
Smithson Cl NG21 .... 89 D2
Smithson Cl NG24 .... 140 C1
Smithson Dr NG8 .... 171 F2
Smithurst Rd NG16 .... 158 A4
Smithy Cl NG11 .... 184 C1
Smithy Cres NG5 .... 161 F4
Smithy La LE12 .... 212 A1
Smithy Row NG1 .... 223 E2
Smithy View NG14 .... 148 C4
Snaefell Ave NG19 .... 89 D1
Snape La DN11 .... 9 D1
Snape Nook Ct NG6 .... 159 F4
Snape Wood Prim Sch
  NG6 .... 160 A4
Snape Wood Rd NG6 .... 159 F4
Snead Ct NG5 .... 147 D1
Sneinton Bdd NG2 .... 174 A2
Sneinton Dale NG2 .... 174 A3
Sneinton Hermitage
  NG2 .... 173 F2
Sneinton Hollows NG2 .. 173 F3
Sneinton Rd NG2 .... 173 F3
Sneinton CE Prim Sch The
  NG2 .... 173 F2
Snell Cl NG23 .... 81 F1
Snipe Park Rd DN11 .... 9 D2
Snowdon Cl NG5 .... 147 D1
Snowdon Rd NG23 .... 112 A4
Soar La
  Normanton on S LE12 .. 213 E2
  Sutton Bonington LE12 .. 213 E4
Soarbank Cl NG16 .... 158 C4
Sobers Gdns NG5 .... 162 A3
Softwood Cl NG6 .... 159 F4
Soloman Pk NG16 .... 158 A1
Soloman Rd NG16 .... 158 A1
Solway Cl NG9 .... 183 E3
Somerby Ct NG9 .... 171 D4
Somerby Rd DN21 .... 15 E1
Somersall St NG19 .... 101 F4
Somersby Rd NG3, NG5 .. 161 F3
Somersby Rd NG18 .... 103 D3
Somerset Cl NG3 .... 162 A3

Somerset Cl NG10 .... 194 A4
Somerton Ave NG11 .... 185 D2
Songthrush Ave NG6 .... 160 B2
Sookholme Cl NG20 .... 72 C2
Sookholme Dr NG20 .... 74 A2
Sookholme La NG20 .... 73 F3
Sookholme Rd
  Shirebrook NG20 .... 73 F1
  Shirebrook NG20 .... 72 C2
Sophie Rd NG7 .... 222 B4
Sorrel Dr NG13 .... 177 E2
Soss La DN10 .... 7 F1
Sotheby Ave NG17 .... 101 E1
Soudan Dr NG2 .... 173 D1
Sough Rd DE55 .... 113 D4
South Ave Bawtry DN10 .. 10 A4
  Radcliffe on T NG12 .... 176 A2
  Rainworth NG21 .... 104 B1
  Shirebrook NG20 .... 72 C2
  Worksop S80 .... 36 A1
South Cres
  Bottesford NG13 .... 181 D1
  Clipstone NG21 .... 90 A2
South Croft NG17 .... 51 F1
South City Inf Sch DN21 .. 24 B3
South Devon Ave NG3 .. 162 A1
South Dr NG14 Balderton NG24 140 C1
  Bilsthorpe NG22 .... 105 F3
South East Derbyshire Coll
  DE7 .... 170 A3
South End NG23 .... 111 F4
South Gn NG23 .... 81 F3
South Moor Rd DN10 .... 13 F3
South Nottingham Coll
  Nottingham NG11 .... 185 D1
  West Bridgford NG2 .... 185 E3
South Nottingham
  Coll of F Ed NG2 .... 185 F4
South Par Bawtry DN10 .. 10 A3
  Gainsborough DN21 .... 24 C4
  Nottingham NG1 .... 223 E2
  Saxilby LN1 .... 57 D2
  Worksop S80 .... 36 A2
South Rd Beeston NG9 .. 184 A2
  Eastwood, Giltbrook NG16 . 158 B4
  Hucknall NG15 .... 146 A4
  Long Eaton NG10 .... 193 E4
  Loughborough LE11 .... 220 A3
  Morton DN21 .... 15 D2
  Normanton on T NG23 .... 81 F3
  Retford DN22 .... 39 F3
  South Normanton DE55 ...... 113 D2
South View
  Austerfield DN10 .... 3 E4
  Worksop S81 .... 35 F1
South View Dr DN22 .... 30 B2
South View Rd NG4 .... 162 B3
South Wilford
  CE Prim Sch NG2 .... 185 D4
South Wolds Comp Sch
  NG12 .... 197 F1
Southampton St NG3 .... 173 F4
Southbeck Rise S80 .... 36 A4
Southchurch Dr NG7 .... 184 C1
Southcliffe Rd NG4 .... 174 B4
Southdale Dr NG4 .... 174 B4
Southdale Rd NG4 .... 174 B4
Southdene S81 .... 36 A4
Southend Ave NG24 .... 139 F4
Southern Wood S80 .... 35 F2
Southey St NG7 .... 222 C4
Southfall Cl DN22 .... 19 D1
Southfield Cl DN22 .... 40 A3
Southfield Dr DE55 .... 113 E3
Southfield Ind Site S80 .. 45 D2
Southfield La S80 .... 45 D3
Southfield Rd NG8 .... 172 B3
Southfields 193 D3
Southfields Cl NG17 .... 114 C3
Southfields Rise NG22 .. 42 B4
Southgate Rd NG20 .... 74 B4
Southglade Jun & Inf Sch
  NG6 .... 160 C3
Southglade Rd NG5 .... 160 C4
Southgore La DN22 .... 27 F2
Southgreen Cl NG18 .... 102 C2
Southgreen Hill NG18 .... 102 C2
Southlands Dr LE12 .... 205 E1
Southlands Gdns DN21 .. 15 E1
Southlea Rd NG4 .... 174 B4
Southmoor Rd S80 .... 36 A4
Southmoor La NG23 .... 69 D2
Southpark Ave NG18 .... 102 C2
Southport Terr ☒ NG7 .. 172 C4
Southside NG5 .... 162 A3
Southview Gdns Kett Sch NG5 160 C4
Southwark Jun Sch NG6 .. 160 C4
Southwark St NG6 .... 160 C4
Southwell
  East Leake LE12 .... 205 ...
  Kirkby in A NG17 .... 115 ...
  Worksop S80 .... 36 ...

hwell La NG17 .... 114 C3
hwell Lane Ind Est
7 .... 115 D4
hwell Rd
nsfield NG22 .... 120 A3
ilington NG22 .... 120 C4
dham NG14 .... 150 C1
ttingham NG1 .... 223 F2
on NG25 .... 134 B2
urgarton NG14 .... 151 E4
nsfield NG21 .... 103 F1
nsfield NG21 .... 118 A4
thwell Rd W NG18 ...... 102 C3
thwell Rise NG15 .... 158 A4
thwold Dr NG6 .... 172 B3
hwolds Prim Sch
.... 172 B3
chwood Ave NG17 .... 100 B2
ereigh Gr NG10 .... 193 D4
ter Ave NG17 .... 100 C2
CI NG17 .... 114 C4
La NG13 .... 180 A4
Rd DN22 .... 39 F3
ford CI DN21 .... 44 B4
ding Rd NG3 .... 173 F3
lford La LN6 .... 83 E2
lford Rd LN6 .... 83 F3
ford Warren (Nature
serve) NG23 .... 83 D3
lgy La NG12 .... 99 F2
niel Row NG1 .... 223 E2
cken CI S80 .... 46 C4
rken Dale S80 .... 46 C4
rrow Hill **1** LE11 ...... 220 A2
rron La NG3 .... 68 A1
an Ct **1** NG3 .... 172 A3
an Dr NG8 .... 172 A4
eds Pingle **1** LE11 .... 220 A2
edwell La NG16 .... 158 C3
edwell PI S80 .... 35 D2
ncer Ave Arnold NG3 .. 162 B3
idiacre NG10 .... 182 A3
ncer CI NG11 .... 196 A4
ncer Cres NG9 .... 182 C4
ncer Dr NG9 .... 159 E3
ncer St NG18 .... 102 A3
ry CI NG16 .... 128 C3
y CI NG15 .... 145 E2
ndie St NG16 .... 183 E1
ndie Gdns NG6 .... 160 A4
ndie View NG14 .... 148 C3
ney CI
rgrave NG12 .... 187 F1
kby in A NG17 .... 114 C3
nsfield Woodhouse NG19 ... 88 C3
warn-on-T NG24 .... 139 F3
est Bridgford NG2 .... 186 B2
aney Cres NG3 .... 182 C2
aney Rd NG1 .... 182 B1
aney Rd
gham NG13 .... 177 E2
worth NG12 .... 197 F2
ng Eaton NG10 .... 182 B1
aney Rise NG9 .... 182 C2
aney The 161 F2
stwood Village Rd NG4 ... 146 C3
rside NG14 .... 164 A3
nton NG23 .... 153 E3
irebrook NG20 .... 72 B2
thorpe NG24 .... 125 C2
aney Way NG11 .... 185 D2
aneymead DN22 .... 19 D3
nningdale NG3 .... 162 A4
re View NG13 .... 181 D2
al Hill
insborough DN21 .... 15 F1
tford DN22 .... 39 F4
al Rd S81 .... 18 A1
al Terr DN21 .... 15 E1
talfields S81 .... 18 A1
ndon St NG5 .... 161 E1
rton CI DE55 .... 113 D4
rton La DE55 .... 113 D4
uth View S80 .... 45 D3
ay CI NG4 .... 174 C3
dgeon Ct NG10 .... 182 B1
ight CI NG24 .... 125 E3
ing CI NG16 .... 159 D4
ing Ct NG22 .... 119 F4
ing Dale Gdns NG9 ... 170 B2
ing Dr NG22 .... 140 C1
ing Garden Terr DE7 ... 157 F1
ing Gdns
wtry DN10 .... 10 A4
insborough DN21 .... 24 B4
ewark-on-T NG24 .... 139 F4
orksop S81 .... 195 F4
ing Hill
nberley NG16 .... 158 C3
nsfield Woodhouse NG19 ... 88 A2
uthwell NG25 .... 136 C4
nsfield S80 .... 35 D2
ing La Arnold NG3 ...... 162 C3
lderton NG24 .... 140 C1
nington NG20 .... 58 A4
ornsfield NG22 .... 119 F4
nsham NG13 .... 166 C4
nbley NG4 .... 163 D3
ang Whatton LE12 .... 212 B1
eireoaks S80 .... 34 C3
ie S DN22 .... 32 B2
ing Mdw NG12 .... 188 A2
ing Rd
ttingham NG6 .... 160 B4
rton in A NG17 .... 100 C1

Spring St
Hucknall NG15 .... 146 A4
Whitwell S80 .... 45 D3
Spring Street Prim Sch
NG15 .... 146 A4
Spring Terr NG16 .... 159 E3
Spring The NG10 .... 193 E3
Spring Wlk S80 .... 35 F1
Springdale La NG15 ...... 165 F1
Springfield DE74 .... 203 D1
Springfield Ave
Eastwood NG16 .... 144 A1
Long Eaton NG10 .... 193 F4
Sandiacre NG10 .... 182 A2
Shirebrook NG20 .... 72 C3
Springfield CI
Cropwell Bishop NG12 ... 189 D2
Gainsborough DN21 ...... 24 C4
Mansfield NG18 .... 103 D3
Springfield Dr NG15 ...... 170 C1
Springfield Dr NG6 .... 159 F3
Springfield Gdn DE7 ...... 157 F1
Springfield Prim Sch
NG6 .... 146 B1
Springfield Rd
Arnold NG5 .... 147 F1
Hucknall NG15 .... 145 E3
Retford DN22 .... 39 F4
Southwell NG25 .... 121 C1
Springfield Ret Pk
NG6 .... 160 B4
Springfield St NG7 .... 160 C1
Springfield Way NG17 ... 115 E3
Springfields 185 E3
Springhead Ct NG6 ...... 160 B4
Springhill CI NG6 .... 146 A1
Springland Farm Cotts
NG16 .... 159 E3
Springs Rd DN10 .... 4 B3
Springthorpe Rd DN21 ... 24 C4
Springwater Way **1** NG17 ... 99 F1
Springwood Gdns NG5 ... 161 F2
Springwood View CI
NG17 .... 100 B2
Spruce Ave NG16 .... 128 B3
Spruce Ct S80 .... 35 D1
Spruce Gdns NG6 .... 160 A4
Spruce Gr Hucknall NG15 ... 146 A3
Kirkby in A NG17 .... 115 E3
Sprydon Wlk NG11 .... 195 F4
Spur Cres S80 .... 47 D4
Square The Beeston NG9 ... 183 F3
Bestwood Village NG6 ... 146 C2
Bottesford NG13 .... 181 D2
Costock LE12 .... 206 B1
Gotham NG11 .... 195 D1
Keyworth NG12 .... 197 F3
Nottingham NG8 .... 171 F2
Rainworth NG21 .... 104 A1
Retford DN22 .... 39 F4
Squires Ave NG6 .... 160 A4
Squires La NG22 .... 189 D2
Squires Croft NG21 .... 90 B3
Squires La NG9 .... 90 A3
Squires Way NG2 .... 185 E3
Squirrel Way **3** LE11 ... 220 A1
Stable CI
East Bridgford NG13 ...... 165 E2
Worksop S81 .... 36 A4
Stacey Ave NG6 .... 160 C4
Stacey Rd NG19 .... 87 E1
Stadium CI NG6 .... 160 A3
Stadium Ind Pk NG10 ... 193 F4
Stafford Ave
New Balderton NG24 ..... 140 B2
Nottingham NG6 .... 160 A3
Stafford Ct NG6 .... 159 F3
Stafford St
Long Eaton NG10 .... 193 F4
Mansfield NG19 .... 101 F4
Staffords Acre DE74 ...... 203 E1
Stagsden Cres NG8 ...... 171 E3
Staindale Dr NG8 .... 160 B1
Stainforth St NG19 .... 101 F1
Stainmore Gr NG13 ...... 177 E2
Stainsborough Rd NG15 ... 145 E3
Stainsby Dr NG18 .... 103 D4
Stamford CI NG10 .... 193 F2
Stamford Ct **28** NG5 ... 161 D4
Stamford Rd NG2 .... 186 A3
Stamford St
Awsworth NG16 .... 158 B2
Eastwood NG16 .... 144 B1
3 Ilkeston DE7 .... 157 F1
Stamper Cres NG17 ...... 100 C3
Stanage Ct NG18 .... 103 D3
Stancliffe Ave NG6 .... 160 B4
Standard Hill NG1 .... 223 D2
Standhill Ave NG4 .... 174 A4
Standhill Inf Sch NG4 ... 174 A4
Standhill Rd NG4 .... 174 A4
Stanesby Rise NG7 ...... 184 C1
Stanford Gdns NG12 ... 175 F2
Stanford Hall (Coll)
LE12 .... 214 C2
Stanford Hill LE11 .... 220 A3
Stanford La LE12 .... 220 B4
Stanford Rd LE12 .... 213 F1
Stanford St NG1 .... 223 E2
Stanhome Dr NG2 .... 185 E2
Stanhome Sq NG2 .... 185 E2
Stanhope Ave Newark NG24 ... 125 E2
Stanhope CI NG22 .... 64 A1
Stanhope Cres
Arnold NG5 .... 161 F4
Stoke Bardolph NG14 ... 175 F4
Stanhope Cty Inf Sch
NG4 .... 162 B2

Stanhope Prim Sch NG4 ... 162 B2
Stanhope Rd Arnold NG5 ... 161 F4
Carlton NG4 .... 162 B2
Stanhope St
Ilkeston DE7 .... 170 A3
Long Eaton NG10 .... 193 E4
Nottingham NG1 .... 223 F2
Stanhope Way NG13 ...... 177 F2
Staniland CI **3** NG9 ... 183 E1
Stanley Ave **4** NG7 ... 173 D4
Stanley CI NG15 .... 117 D2
Stanley Dr NG9 .... 171 D1
Stanley La NG17 .... 85 E1
Stanley PI NG1 .... 223 D3
Stanley Rd
Mansfield NG18 .... 102 A2
Mansfield Woodhouse
NG19 .... 89 D1
Nottingham, Hyson Green
NG7 .... 173 D4
Nottingham, Portchester
NG3 .... 162 A1
West Bridgford NG2 ...... 185 F3
Stanley St
Gainsborough DN21 ...... 24 B3
Long Eaton NG10 .... 193 F4
Loughborough LE11 ...... 220 A1
Newark-on-T NG24 .... 125 D1
Retford DN22 .... 40 A2
Worksop S81 .... 35 F3
Stanley Terr NG1 .... 223 D2
Stanmore CI NG16 .... 159 F2
Stanmore Gdns NG5 .... 161 F3
Stansfield St NG7 .... 222 A3
Stanstead Ave
Nottingham NG5 .... 146 B1
Tollerton NG12 .... 186 B1
Stanstead Prim Sch NG6 ... 146 B1
Stanthorne CI NG11 ..... 185 D2
Stanton Cres NG17 ...... 100 C3
Stanton Gate DE7 .... 170 B1
Stanton La NG12 .... 198 A1
Stanton PI
Mansfield NG18 .... 102 A4
New Houghton NG19 ..... 86 C4
Stanton Rd NG10 .... 182 A4
Stanwall CI NG8 .... 86 C4
Stanway CI NG3 .... 174 B3
Stanwick CI NG8 .... 171 F4
Staple La NG24 .... 140 B1
Stapleford La
Beeston NG9 .... 182 C2
Brough NG23 .... 112 B1
Coddington NG24 .... 126 B2
Stapleford Rd
Stapleford NG9 .... 170 B2
Trowell NG9 .... 170 B2
Staplehurst Dr NG5 ..... 161 D2
Staples St NG3 .... 161 F1
Stapleton Rd DE7 .... 157 F2
Starch CI LE12 .... 205 F1
Starch La NG10 .... 182 B4
Starr Ave NG17 .... 100 B2
Starth Wood Rd NG15 ... 145 E2
Statham CI S81 .... 36 A3
Stathern La LE14 .... 202 B2
Stathern Wlk NG5 .... 161 D4
Station Ave Carlton NG4 ... 163 D1
Ranskill DN22 .... 19 D3
Station CI NG23 .... 112 A4
Station Ct **6** DE7 .... 157 F1
Station Hill NG19 .... 88 A2
Station La
Edwinstowe NG21 .... 76 A1
Farnsfield NG22 .... 119 F4
Ironville NG16 .... 170 A4
Old Dalby LE14 .... 218 C2
Station Rd
Awsworth NG16 .... 158 B3
Barnby Moor DN22 ...... 28 C3
Bawtry DN10 .... 10 A4
Beckingham DN10 .... 23 E4
Beeston NG9 .... 184 A3
Bleasby NG14 .... 151 F4
Bottesford NG13 .... 181 F2
Burton Joyce NG14 ..... 163 F2
Carlton NG4 .... 174 C4
Clipstone NG21 .... 89 F1
Collingham NG23 .... 112 A4
East Leake LE12 .... 205 E1
Edingley NG22 .... 120 C3
Fiskerton NG25, NG23 ... 137 F2
Harby NG23 .... 70 C2
Heanor NG16 .... 143 D1
Hucknall NG15 .... 146 A4
Ilkeston DE7 .... 157 F1
Kegworth DE74 .... 203 F1
Keyworth NG12 .... 197 F3
Kimberley NG16 .... 158 C3
Kingston-on-S LE12 ..... 204 A2
Langley Mill NG16 .... 143 D1
Long Eaton NG10 .... 193 E4
Lowdham NG14 .... 150 C1
Mansfield NG18 .... 102 A3
Misson DN10 .... 4 A2
Newstead NG15 .... 130 C3
Nottingham NG6 .... 160 B3
Ollerton NG22 .... 77 D2
Rainworth NG21 .... 118 A4
Ranskill DN22 .... 19 D2
Retford DN22 .... 39 F3
Rolleston NG23 .... 138 A3
Sandiacre NG10 .... 182 B3
Scrooby DN10 .... 10 A3
Selston NG16 .... 113 F1

Station Rd continued
Shirebrook NG20 .... 72 C3
South Leverton DN22 ..... 42 B4
Southwell NG21 .... 121 F1
Sturton le S DN22 .... 32 B3
Sutton in A NG17 .... 101 D1
Sutton on T NG23 .... 96 C4
Thurgarton NG14 .... 151 E3
Torksey LN1 .... 44 A2
Upper Broughton LE14 ... 218 B4
Walkeringham DN10 .... 14 A3
Whitwell S80 .... 45 D3
Widmerpool NG12 .... 208 C3
Station St Bingham NG13 ... 177 F3
Cossall DE7 .... 158 A1
Kirkby in A NG17 .... 115 D3
Long Eaton NG10 .... 193 F4
Mansfield NG18 .... 102 A3
Mansfield Woodhouse NG19 ... 88 A2
Misterton DN10 .... 7 D1
Nottingham NG2 .... 223 F1
Sutton in A NG17 .... 100 C1
Station Terr
Hucknall NG15 .... 146 A4
Radcliffe on T NG12 ..... 175 F2
Station View NG4 .... 175 D4
Station Yd NG12 .... 100 C4
Staunton Dr NG5 .... 161 E2
Staunton Rd NG24 ...... 139 F3
Staveley CI
Farndon NG24 .... 139 D2
4 Loughborough LE11 ... 220 A3
Staverton Rd NG8 .... 171 F4
Staythorpe Rd
Averham NG23 .... 123 F1
Rolleston NG23 .... 138 B4
Steadfold CI NG6 .... 146 C2
Steads CI NG4 .... 174 C4
Steedman Ave NG3 ...... 162 A2
Steeles Way NG4 .... 163 D4
Steeple Row **1** LE11 ... 220 A2
Steetley La Rhodesia S80 ... 35 D2
Whitwell S80 .... 34 C2
Worksop S80 .... 34 C2
Steinbeck Rd NG4 .... 174 B4
Stella Ave NG12 .... 197 E4
Stella Cres NG12 .... 197 E4
Stella St NG18 .... 102 A3
Stenton CI NG25 .... 121 F1
Stepnall Hts NG22 .... 77 F3
Stepney St NG8 .... 159 F1
Sterndale Rd NG10 ..... 193 D3
Sternthorpe CI NG23 ... 81 F1
Steven CI NG9 .... 182 C2
Stevenholme Cres NG5 ... 161 D3
Stevens Rd NG10 .... 182 A3
Stevenson Cres NG17 ... 100 C2
Stevenson Gdns NG11 ... 196 B3
Stevenson Jun Sch
NG9 .... 182 C4
Stevenson Rd S81 .... 36 A2
Stewart CI S81 .... 25 F3
Stewart Rd S81 .... 25 F3
Stewarton CI NG5 .... 148 A1
Stiles Rd NG5 .... 162 B3
Stinsford CI **1** NG5 ... 161 D4
Stinting La
Mansfield Woodhouse NG19 ... 88 C1
Shirebrook NG20 .... 72 C3
Stirling Ave Bawtry DN10 ... 10 A4
Mansfield NG19 .... 101 F3
Stirling CI DN21 .... 15 F1
Stirling Dr S81 .... 25 F3
Stirling Gdns NG9 .... 183 D1
Stirling Gr
Kimberley NG16 .... 158 C3
Nottingham NG11 .... 195 F4
Stirling Rd NG22 .... 77 F3
Stock Well NG6 .... 160 A3
Stockdale CI NG5 .... 147 D1
Stockgill CI NG2 .... 186 B3
Stockhill Cir NG8 .... 160 B1
Stockhill La NG6 .... 160 B2
Stocking La
Askham DN22 .... 51 F2
East Leake LE12 .... 205 E2
Stocks Rd NG5 .... 158 C4
Stockton St **16** NG6 ... 160 A4
Stockwell Gate NG18 ... 102 A4
Stockwell La NG12 ...... 189 D2
Stockwell The LE12 ..... 216 B2
Stockwith Rd
Misterton DN10 .... 14 A4
Walkerith DN10, DN21 ... 14 B4
Stodman Mews NG24 ... 139 F4
Stodman St NG24 .... 139 F4
Stoke Ave NG24 .... 139 F2
Stoke Ferry La NG12 ... 164 A1
Stoke La
Burton Joyce NG14 ..... 163 F1
Stoke Bardolph NG14 ... 175 E4
Stokes Trad Est NG18 ... 101 F2
Stolle CI NG5 .... 162 A4
Stone Bridge Rd NG3 ... 173 F3
Stone Cres NG19 .... 101 E4
Stone Cross La NG18 ... 102 A4
Stone La DN10 .... 3 E3
Stone Mdws NG10 .... 193 F3
Stonacre NG5 .... 161 D4
Stonebridge Court
Ind Est **18** NG3 .... 173 F3
Stonebridge Dr LE12 ... 205 F1
Stonebridge La NG20 ... 74 A2
Stonebridge Rd NG3 ... 173 F3
Stonechurch View NG5 ... 130 A4
Stonehaven CI NG5 ..... 148 A1
Stonehill CI DN22 .... 19 D3

Stonehills DE74 .... 203 E1
Stonehurst La LE12 ...... 213 E2
Stoneleigh CI NG9 .... 183 E3
Stoneleigh St NG7 .... 222 C3
Stonemasons Mews
NG7 .... 115 D3
Stoney CI NG3 .... 115 D3
Stoney Bank NG14 ...... 150 B1
Stoney Houghton Gdns
NG6 .... 159 F4
Stoney La Brinsley NG16 ... 143 E3
Selston NG16 .... 128 C4
Trowell NG9 .... 170 A3
Stoney St Beeston NG9 ... 183 F4
Nottingham NG1 .... 223 F2
Sutton in A NG17 .... 101 D2
Stoneycroft Rd NG6 ..... 160 C3
Stoneyford Rd NG17 .... 100 C2
Stonish Hill NG22 .... 92 B1
Stoppard Ct DE7 .... 157 E1
Storcroft Rd DN22 .... 40 A3
Storey Ave NG4 .... 162 C1
Stormont CI DE55 .... 113 D2
Stornoway CI NG9 ...... 184 A3
Stort Sq NG19 .... 88 B1
Storth Ave NG15 .... 146 A3
Storth La DE55 .... 113 D2
Storthfield Way DE55 ... 113 D2
Story Gdns NG15 .... 146 B3
Stotfield Rd NG8 .... 171 D3
Stourdale CI NG10 .... 193 D3
Stow Ct NG19 .... 88 C2
Stow Park Rd DN21 ..... 44 B4
Stowe Ave NG2 .... 185 E3
Strafford St DN21 .... 24 B3
Straight Mile LN6 .... 38 B3
Strand The NG9 .... 183 F1
Stranrear CI NG19 .... 88 B3
Stratford CI NG4 .... 174 C3
Stratford Cres DN22 ...... 39 E3
Stratford Rd NG2 .... 185 F4
Stratford St DE7 .... 157 F2
Strathavon Rd S81 .... 25 F3
Strathglen CI NG16 ..... 158 C3
Strathmore CI NG15 ... 145 F3
Strathmore Dr S81 .... 25 F3
Strathmore Rd NG5 ..... 148 A1
Straw's La NG13 .... 165 E2
Strawberry Bank NG17 ... 99 F2
Strawberry Hall La
NG24 .... 125 D1
Strawberry Rd DN22 ...... 40 A3
Strawberry Way NG19 ... 103 D4
Street Lane Rd DN22 ... 42 C4
Strelley La NG8 .... 171 D4
Strelley Rd NG8 .... 159 F1
Striding Edge CI NG10 ... 182 A1
Stripe Rd DN11 .... 8 B4
Stripes View NG14 ...... 148 C3
Strome CI **14** NG2 ... 173 D1
Strome Ct **1** NG2 ..... 173 D1
Stroud Ct NG13 .... 181 D2
Stroud's CI LE14 .... 211 F4
Stuart Ave
Mansfield NG18 .... 102 A4
New Ollerton NG22 .... 77 E3
Stuart CI NG5 .... 162 A4
Stuart St Mansfield NG18 ... 102 C4
Sutton in A NG17 .... 100 C1
Stubbin Wood Sch NG20 ... 72 C3
Stubbin's La NG22 ...... 136 B3
Stubbing La S80 .... 35 E2
Stubbins Wood NG20 ... 72 C3
Stubbins Wood La NG20 ... 72 C3
Stubton Rd NG23 .... 156 C3
Studland CI NG23 .... 88 B3
Studland Way NG2 ..... 185 E3
Sturgate White DN21 ... 24 C4
Sturgeon Ave NG11 .... 184 C2
Sturton CE Prim Sch
DN22 .... 32 B2
Sturton Rd Boie DN22 ... 32 B1
North Leverton w H DN22 ... 32 B1
Saxilby LN1 .... 57 D4
South Wheatley DN22 ... 31 F4
Sturton St NG7 .... 173 D4
Styring St NG9 .... 183 F3
Styrrup La DN11 .... 8 A1
Sudbury Ave
Ilkeston DE7 .... 170 A4
Sandiacre NG10 .... 182 A3
Sudbury Ct NG18 .... 103 D3
Sudbury Mews NG16 ... 143 F1
Suez St NG7 .... 172 C4
Suff La NG16 .... 113 E2
Suffolk Ave
Beeston NG9 .... 184 B2
Bircotes DN11 .... 9 E2
Hucknall NG15 .... 145 E3
Suffolk Gr DN11 .... 9 E2
Suffolk Rd DN11 .... 9 E2
Sulby CI NG19 .... 89 D1
Sullivan CI NG3 .... 174 A3
Sumburgh Rd NG11 .... 185 D3
Summer Hill DN21 .... 15 F1
Summer Leys La NG2 ... 223 F1
Summer Way NG12 ...... 175 F2
Summer's Rd NG24 ...... 125 D1
Summercourt Dr NG15 ... 116 C2
Summerfield Rd **11**
NG17 .... 114 C4
Summerfields Way DE7 ... 157 E2

Summerfields Way S DE7 ... 157 E1
Summergangs La DN21 ... 24 B3
Summerwood La NG11 ... 195 F4
Summit Cl NG17 ... 115 D3
Summit Dr NG20 ... 72 C2
Sunbeam St NG13 ... 179 D2
Sunbourne Ct NG7 ... 222 C4
Sunbury Gdns NG3 ... 148 A1
Sunderland Gr NG8 ... 159 E1
Sunderland Pl DN11 ... 8 A4
Sunderland St DN11 ... 8 A4
Sundown Pets Gdn DN22 ... 42 C2
Sundridge Park La NG2 ... 185 E3
Sunfield Ave S81 ... 36 A2
Sunlea Cres NG3 ... 182 C3
Sunningdale Dr NG12 ... 186 C1
Sunningdale DN22 ... 39 E1
Sunningdale Ave DE75 ... 157 D4
Sunningdale Cl 4 NG17 ... 114 C4
Sunningdale Dr NG12 ... 149 E3
Sunningdale Rd NG6 ... 160 C3
Sunningdill Dr NG11 ... 184 C2
Sunninghill Rise NG5 ... 148 A1
Sunny Bank
  Mansfield NG18 ... 102 B2
  Newton DE55 ... 99 D3
  Worksop S81 ... 36 A2
Sunnydale Rd NG3 ... 174 A3
Sunnymede S81 ... 36 A3
Sunnyside
  Farnsfield NG22 ... 119 F3
  Whitwell S80 ... 45 D3
  Worksop S81 ... 35 F3
Sunnyside Prim Sch NG9 ... 183 D3
Sunnyside Rd NG9 ... 183 E3
Sunridge Ct NG3 ... 173 E4
Sunrise Ave NG5 ... 160 C3
Surbiton Sq NG8 ... 160 A2
Surfleet Cl NG8 ... 171 E2
Surgery La NG21 ... 118 A2
Surgey's La NG5 ... 148 A1
Surrey Dr NG19 ... 101 F4
Susan Cl NG15 ... 131 D1
Susan Dr NG6 ... 160 B2
Sussex Way NG10 ... 182 A3
Sutherland Cl S81 ... 25 E4
Sutherland Dr NG2 ... 186 A2
Sutherland Rd NG3 ... 174 A4
Suthers Rd DE74 ... 203 E1
Sutton Ave NG24 ... 139 F3
Sutton Bonington Prim Sch LE12 ... 213 D3
Sutton Cl
  Sutton Bonington LE12 ... 213 E3
  Sutton in A NG17 ... 101 D3
Sutton Cl NG16 ... 143 E4
Sutton Gdns NG11 ... 196 B3
Sutton La Granby NG13 ... 191 E3
  Retford DN22 ... 29 D1
Sutton Middle La NG17 ... 114 C3
Sutton Parkway Sta NG17 ... 115 D4
Sutton Passeys Cres NG8 ... 172 A2
Sutton Rd Arnold NG5 ... 147 F1
  Beckingham LN5 ... 142 C3
  Huthwaite NG17 ... 99 F2
  Kegworth DE74 ... 203 E1
  Kirkby in A NG17 ... 114 C3
  Mansfield NG18 ... 101 F3
  Sutton in A NG17 ... 100 C3
Sutton Rd Fst Sch NG18 ... 101 F3
Sutton-cum-Lound CE Prim Sch DN22 ... 29 D3
Swab's La
  Cropwell Bishop NG12 ... 188 C1
  Owthorpe NG12 ... 199 F4
Swain's Ave NG3 ... 174 A3
Swaledale S81 ... 36 A4
Swaledale Cl NG8 ... 160 B1
Swales Cl DN22 ... 39 E4
Swallow Cl
  Mansfield NG18 ... 103 D2
  Nottingham NG6 ... 160 B2
Swallow Ct DN10 ... 7 D1
Swallow Gdns NG4 ... 162 A1
Swallow Gr S81 ... 35 E4
Swallow Wlk LE12 ... 213 D1
Swallows Dr LE14 ... 202 C2
Swan Cl
  Sutton Bonington LE12 ... 213 D3
  Worksop S81 ... 35 E4
Swan La NG19 ... 88 A2
Swan Mdw NG4 ... 174 C2
Swan St Bawtry DN10 ... 10 A3
  Loughborough LE11 ... 220 A2
Swann Yd NG17 ... 99 F2
Swans Quay DN22 ... 40 A2
Swansdowne Dr NG7 ... 184 C1
Swanson Ave NG17 ... 99 F2
Swanwick Ave NG20 ... 72 C2
Sweeny Ct 3 NG5 ... 161 D4
Sweet Leys Dr LE12 ... 205 F2
Sweet Leys Rd 4 NG2 ... 173 E1
Swenson Ave NG7 ... 222 A1
Swift Cl NG16 ... 158 C4
Swift's Cl LE12 ... 216 B2
Swigert Cl NG6 ... 159 F3
Swildon Wlk NG5 ... 160 C4
Swinburne Cl NG24 ... 140 B3
Swinburne St 22 NG3 ... 173 F3

Swinburne Way NG5 ... 161 E4
Swinderby Rd
  Collingham NG23 ... 112 A4
  Eagle LN6 ... 84 B1
  North Scarle LN6 ... 83 F1
Swindon Cl NG18 ... 158 B4
Swinecote Rd NG21 ... 76 A2
Swiney Way NG9 ... 183 D1
Swinfen Brown NG18 ... 102 B2
Swingate NG16 ... 159 D3
Swinnow Rd DN11 ... 9 E2
Swinscoe Gdns NG5 ... 160 C4
Swinstead Ct NG8 ... 171 F3
Swinton Copse NG22 ... 77 F3
Swinton Rise NG15 ... 117 D1
Swish La NG22 ... 105 F4
Swithland Dr NG2 ... 185 F2
Swynford Cl LN1 ... 55 D2
Sycamore Ave
  Glapwell S44 ... 86 A4
  Kirkby in A NG17 ... 114 C3
Sycamore Cl
  Bingham NG13 ... 178 A2
  Hucknall NG15 ... 145 F3
  Newark-on-T NG24 ... 139 E2
  Pinxton NG16 ... 113 E2
  Radcliffe on T NG12 ... 175 F1
  Rainworth NG21 ... 104 A1
  Selston NG16 ... 128 B4
  Worksop S80 ... 35 F1
Sycamore Cres
  Bawtry DN10 ... 9 F4
  Sandiacre NG10 ... 182 A4
Sycamore Ct NG9 ... 184 A4
Sycamore Dr
  Coddington NG24 ... 125 F1
  Gainsborough DN21 ... 15 F1
  Ilkeston DE7 ... 170 A4
Sycamore Gr NG18 ... 102 C3
Sycamore Inf Sch NG17 ... 223 F4
Sycamore Jun Sch NG17 ... 223 F4
Sycamore La NG14 ... 152 A4
Sycamore Pl 4 NG3 ... 173 E4
Sycamore Rd
  Awsworth NG16 ... 158 B3
  Carlton in L S81 ... 25 F4
  East Leake LE12 ... 214 B4
  Long Eaton NG10 ... 193 E3
  Mansfield Woodhouse NG19 ... 88 B3
  New Ollerton NG22 ... 77 C2
Sycamore Rise NG6 ... 160 B1
Sycamore St NG20 ... 74 A3
Sycamores The
  Eastwood NG16 ... 143 F1
  South Normanton DE55 ... 113 D3
Sydenham Ct 18 NG2 ... 173 C4
Syderstone Wlk NG5 ... 161 F3
Sydney Cl NG19 ... 88 B3
Sydney Gr NG12 ... 175 F2
Sydney Rd NG8 ... 172 A3
Sydney St NG24 ... 125 D1
Sydney Terr NG24 ... 140 A4
Syerston Rd NG18 ... 103 D1
Syke Rd NG5 ... 160 C4
Sykes La Balderton NG24 ... 140 B2
  Saxilby LN1 ... 56 C3
Sylvan Cres NG17 ... 101 D3
Sylvester St NG18 ... 101 F3
Synge Cl NG11 ... 195 E4
Sywell Cl NG17 ... 100 C3

T

Taft Ave NG10 ... 182 A3
Taft Leys Rd LE12 ... 205 F1
Talbot Cl NG12 ... 175 F2
Talbot Dr NG9 ... 170 B1
Talbot Rd Bircotes DN11 ... 9 D2
  Worksop S80 ... 36 A1
Talbot St
  Mansfield NG18 ... 102 A2
  Nottingham NG1 ... 223 D3
  Pinxton NG16 ... 113 E2
Tall Gables NG17 ... 114 C4
Tamarix Cl NG4 ... 163 D1
Tambling Cl NG3 ... 162 A3
Tame Cl NG11 ... 184 C2
Tamworth Gr NG7 ... 184 C1
Tamworth Rd NG10 ... 193 E3
  Tanglewood LN6 ... 84 B2
Tangmere Cres NG8 ... 159 F1
Tanner's La LE12 ... 213 D1
Tannery Wharf NG24 ... 139 F4
Tanwood Rd NG9 ... 183 D1
Tanyard NG22 ... 79 F3
Tarbert Cl NG2 ... 173 D1
Target St NG7 ... 222 A3
Tatham's La DE7 ... 157 F1
Tatmarsh LE11 ... 220 A3
Tattersall Wlk NG11 ... 88 C2
Tattershall Dr
  Beeston NG9 ... 184 A4
  Nottingham NG7 ... 222 C2
Taunton Rd NG2 ... 185 F3
Taupo Dr NG15 ... 145 E3
Tavern Ave NG8 ... 160 B1
Tavistock Ave NG3 ... 161 F1
Tavistock Cl NG15 ... 145 E3
Tavistock Ct NG5 ... 161 E1
Tavistock Rd NG2 ... 185 F3
Taylor Cl NG2 ... 174 A2
Taylor Cres
  Stapleford NG9 ... 182 C4
  Sutton in A NG17 ... 100 C1
Taylor St DE7 ... 157 F1
Taylor's Cl NG18 ... 102 C4
Taylor's Croft NG14 ... 149 E2
Teague Pl S80 ... 35 E2
Teak Cl NG3 ... 173 E4
Teal Ave NG18 ... 103 D2

Teal Cl Carlton NG4 ... 175 D3
  Shirebrook NG20 ... 72 B2
Teal Ct S81 ... 35 E4
Teal Wharf 4 NG7 ... 173 D1
Tealby Cl NG16 ... 159 F4
Tealby Wlk NG19 ... 88 C2
Teasels The NG13 ... 177 D2
Technology Dr NG9 ... 184 A3
Tedburn Dr NG18 ... 103 D1
Teddy's Farm Pk LN5 ... 142 C4
Teesbrook Dr NG8 ... 171 D2
Teesdale Ct NG9 ... 183 D2
Teesdale Rd
  Long Eaton NG10 ... 193 D3
  Nottingham NG5 ... 161 D1
Teignmouth Ave NG18 ... 102 C3
Telford Dr
  Eastwood NG16 ... 144 A2
  Newark-on-T NG24 ... 125 E2
Temperance La NG23 ... 111 F4
Templar Rd NG9 ... 184 A3
Temple Cres NG16 ... 159 F2
Temple Dr NG16 ... 159 F2
Templemans Way NG25 ... 136 C4
Templemen Cl NG11 ... 196 A4
Templeoak Dr NG8 ... 171 E2
Tenbury Cres NG8 ... 160 B1
Tenby Gr S80 ... 36 A1
Tene Cl NG5 ... 147 F1
Tenman La NG13 ... 166 A1
Tennis Court Ind Est NG2 ... 174 A2
Tennis Dr NG7 ... 222 C2
Tennis Mews NG7 ... 222 C2
Tennyson Ave
  Carlton NG4 ... 162 C1
  Mansfield Woodhouse NG19 ... 88 B1
Tennyson Ct NG15 ... 145 E3
Tennyson Dr
  Beeston NG9 ... 183 E1
  Worksop S81 ... 36 B2
Tennyson Rd Arnold NG5 ... 161 F2
  Balderton NG24 ... 140 B2
Tennyson Sq NG16 ... 158 B2
Tennyson St
  Gainsborough DN21 ... 15 E1
  Ilkeston DE7 ... 157 F2
  Kirkby in A NG17 ... 115 D2
  10 Mansfield NG18 ... 102 A4
  Nottingham NG7 ... 222 C4
Tenter Cl
  Long Eaton NG10 ... 193 E3
  Nottingham NG5 ... 160 C4
Tenter La NG18 ... 102 A3
Tenters La NG22 ... 92 C1
Tenzing Wlk NG24 ... 140 C2
Terrace La NG19 ... 86 C3
Terrace Rd NG18 ... 102 B4
Terrace St NG7 ... 172 C4
Terrian Cres NG12 ... 185 F4
Terry Ave NG24 ... 125 D2
Terton Rd NG5 ... 160 C4
Tetford Wlk NG19 ... 88 C2
Tetney Wlk NG8 ... 172 A3
Tettenbury Rd NG5 ... 160 C2
Teversal Ave
  Nottingham NG7 ... 222 B2
  Pleasleyhill NG19 ... 87 D3
Teversal Visitor Ctr NG17 ... 100 A4
Tevery Cl NG9 ... 182 C4
Teviot Rd NG5 ... 160 C3
Tewkesbury Ave NG19 ... 88 B2
Tewkesbury Cl NG2 ... 186 A3
Tewkesbury Dr
  Kimberley NG16 ... 158 C4
  Nottingham NG6 ... 160 C2
Tewkesbury Rd NG10 ... 193 F3
Thackeray Cl S81 ... 36 A3
Thackeray's La NG5 ... 161 F3
Thackeray St NG7 ... 222 B3
Thames St NG6 ... 160 A4
Thane Rd NG9 ... 184 C3
Thaxted Cl NG8 ... 171 E3
Theaker Ave DN21 ... 10 B3
Theaker La DN10 ... 10 B1
Theatre Sq NG1 ... 223 D3
Thelda Ave NG12 ... 197 F2
Theresa Ct NG24 ... 140 B2
Thetford Cl NG5 ... 162 A3
Thickley Cl NG20 ... 72 C2
Thievesdale Ave S81 ... 35 F4
Thievesdale Cl S81 ... 36 A4
Thievesdale La S81 ... 36 A4
Third Ave Beeston NG9 ... 184 B3
  Carlton, Gedling NG4 ... 162 C1
  Carlton, Thorneywood NG4 ... 174 A4
  Clipstone NG21 ... 89 F2
  Edwinstowe NG21 ... 76 A1
  Mansfield NG21 ... 103 F3
  Mansfield Woodhouse NG19 ... 89 D1
  Nottingham NG6 ... 160 A4
Thirlbeck NG12 ... 188 A1
Thirlmere NG2 ... 186 B3
Thirlmere Cl
  Long Eaton NG10 ... 182 A1
  Nottingham NG3 ... 173 F4
Thirlmere Rd NG10 ... 182 A1
Thirston Cl NG6 ... 159 F4
Thistle Cl NG16 ... 158 A4
Thistle Green Cl DE75 ... 143 D1
Thistledown Rd NG11 ... 195 F4
Thomas Ave NG12 ... 176 B2
Thomas Cl NG3 ... 223 F4
Thomas Parkyn Cl NG11 ... 206 C4
Thomas Rd DE74 ... 203 E1
Thomas St NG17 ... 39 F3

Thompson Ave DN11 ... 8 C2
Thompson Gr 3 NG9 ... 183 E2
Thompson Cres NG17 ... 100 C1
Thompson Gdns NG5 ... 147 D1
Thompson St NG21 ... 143 D2
Thonock Cl DN11 ... 56 C2
Thonock Hill DN21 ... 15 E2
Thonock Rd DN21 ... 15 F3
Thor Gdns NG5 ... 146 C1
Thoresby Ave Carlton NG4 ... 162 B1
  Edwinstowe NG21 ... 76 A1
  Kirkby in A NG17 ... 115 E2
  Newark-on-T NG24 ... 140 A3
  Nottingham NG2 ... 173 F2
  Shirebrook NG20 ... 72 C2
Thoresby Cl
  Harworth DN11 ... 9 D3
  Meden Vale NG20 ... 74 B4
  Radcliffe on T NG12 ... 176 A2
Thoresby Cres NG17 ... 100 B3
Thoresby Ct NG3 ... 173 E4
Thoresby Dale NG15 ... 146 A4
Thoresby Glade NG22 ... 106 A3
Thoresby Rd
  Beeston NG9 ... 171 E1
  Bingham NG13 ... 177 E2
  Long Eaton NG10 ... 193 E1
  Mansfield NG21 ... 103 F1
  Mansfield Woodhouse NG19 ... 88 A2
Thoresby St
  3 Mansfield NG18 ... 102 A4
  10 Nottingham NG2 ... 173 F2
Thoresby Way DN22 ... 39 F2
Thorn Ave NG19 ... 87 F1
Thorn Bank DN9 ... 2 B4
Thorn Dr NG16 ... 158 B4
Thorn Gr NG15 ... 146 A2
Thorn Tree Gdns NG16 ... 143 F2
Thornbury Dr NG19 ... 101 E4
Thornbury Hill La S81 ... 16 B4
Thornbury Way NG5 ... 160 C4
Thorncliffe Rd NG3 ... 173 E4
Thorncliffe Rise NG3 ... 173 E4
Thorndale Rd
  Calverton NG14 ... 148 C4
  Nottingham NG6 ... 160 B1
Thorndike Cl NG9 ... 184 A2
Thorndike Way NG21 ... 24 C4
Thorne Rd DN10 ... 10 A4
Thorner Cl NG6 ... 160 C3
Thorney Abbey Rd NG21 ... 118 A3
Thorney Cl NG18 ... 103 D1
Thorney Hill NG3 ... 173 F4
Thorneywood Ave NG17 ... 129 F4
Thorneywood Mount NG3 ... 173 F4
Thorneywood Rd NG10 ... 193 F4
Thornham Cres NG17 ... 129 F4
Thornhill Cl NG9 ... 171 D1
Thornhill Dr NG22 ... 77 F3
Thornhill La DN22 ... 33 E1
Thornhill Rd DN11 ... 8 C3
Thornley St NG7 ... 172 C4
Thornthwaite Cl NG2 ... 186 B3
Thornton Ave NG5 ... 147 F1
Thornton Cl
  Mansfield NG18 ... 103 D2
  Nottingham NG8 ... 171 F2
Thornton Dale S81 ... 36 A4
Thornton Rd NG23 ... 112 A4
Thornton St
  Gainsborough DN21 ... 15 F1
  Sutton in A NG17 ... 100 C1
Thorntons Cl NG12 ... 188 A1
Thorold Cl NG7 ... 184 C1
Thoroton Ave NG24 ... 140 B2
Thoroton St NG7 ... 222 C3
Thoroughfare La NG23 ... 125 E4
Thorpe Cl
  Coddington NG24 ... 126 A1
  Newark-on-T NG24 ... 139 F2
  10 Nottingham NG5 ... 161 D4
  Stapleford NG9 ... 182 A1
Thorpe La Eagle LN6 ... 84 C1
  Shireoaks S80 ... 34 B3
Thorpe Lea NG14 ... 165 D3
Thorpe Leys NG10 ... 193 E3
Thorpe Rd
  Eastwood NG16 ... 143 F2
  Mansfield NG18 ... 103 D1
  Mattersey DN10 ... 20 A4
Thorpe St Askham DN22 ... 52 B4
  Ilkeston DE7 ... 157 F2
Thorpelands Ave NG19 ... 88 C1
Thrapston Ave NG5 ... 147 F1
Three Leys La DN22 ... 32 C3
Three Tuns Rd NG16 ... 144 A1
Threlkeld Cl NG2 ... 186 B3
Thrumpton Ave NG10 ... 194 A4
Thrumpton Cl DN22 ... 39 F2
Thrumpton Dr NG2 ... 173 E1
Thrumpton Hall NG11 ... 194 A3
Thrumpton La DN22 ... 39 F2
Thrumpton Prim Sch DN22 ... 39 F2
Thurcaston Way DE55 ... 99 D2
Thurgarton Ave 50 NG2 ... 173 E2
Thurgarton La NG14 ... 151 F2
Thurgarton Rd NG14 ... 173 F2
Thurgarton Sta NG14 ... 151 E3
Thurland St NG1 ... 223 E2
Thurlby Cl NG23 ... 189 D2
Thurlby Rd NG19 ... 88 C2
Thurlby La
  Stanton-on-t-W NG12 ... 198 B1
  Widmerpool NG12 ... 208 B4

Thurlby Rd DN21 ... 24 C
Thurlestone Dr NG3 ... 162 B
Thurley Wlk NG18 ... 103 D
Thurloe Ct NG2 ... 185 E
Thurman Dr NG12 ... 187 F
Thurman St Ilkeston DE7 ... 170 A
  Nottingham NG7 ... 222 B
Thursby Rd NG11 ... 184 C
Thymus Wlk NG11 ... 184 B
Thyra Ct NG3 ... 161 F
Thyra Gr Beeston NG9 ... 184 A
  Nottingham NG3 ... 161 F
Tibshelf Inf Sch DE55 ... 99 D
Tibshelf Rd NG17 ... 100 A
Tibshelf Sch DE55 ... 99 D
Tickhill CE Mid Sch DN11 ... 8 A
Tickhill Cry Fst Sch DN11 ... 8 A
Tickhill Estfeld Prim Sch DN11 ... 9 E
Tickhill Rd Bawtry DN10 ... 9 E
  Harworth DN11 ... 8 B
Tideswell Cl NG15 ... 117 C
Tideswell Ct NG18 ... 102 B
Tidworth Cl NG8 ... 172 A
Tilberthwaite Cl NG2 ... 186 B
Tilbury Rise NG8 ... 160 A
Tilford Gdns NG9 ... 182 C
Till Bridge La DN21 ... 44 C
Tiln Ct DN22 ... 29 E
Tiln La DN22 ... 29 E
Tilstock Cl NG16 ... 159 E
Timothy Rd NG22 ... 79 F
Tindale Bank Rd DN10 ... 6 B
Tinker La DN22 ... 27
Tinker's La NG23 ... 97
Tinsley Cl NG23 ... 156
Tinsley Rd NG16 ... 143
Tintagel Gn NG7 ... 184
Tintern Dr NG8 ... 160
Tip Tree Cl NG16 ... 158
Tippett Cl NG3 ... 173
Tippings La NG22 ... 119
Tiree Cl NG9 ... 170
Tishbite St 20 NG6 ... 160
Tissington Ave NG20 ... 74
Tissington Cl 3 NG7 ... 173
Tissington Rd NG7 ... 173
Titchfield Ave
  Mansfield Woodhouse NG19 ... 88
  Sutton in A NG17 ... 100
Titchfield St
  Hucknall NG15 ... 146
  Mansfield NG18 ... 102
  Market Warsop NG20 ... 74
Titchfield Terr NG15 ... 146
Tithby Ct NG18 ... 103
Tithby Dr NG5 ... 161
Tithby Rd Bingham NG13 ... 177
  Cropwell Butler NG12 ... 189
Tithe Barn Ct NG7 ... 224
Tithe Gdns 2 NG5 ... 147
Tithe La NG14 ... 148
Tithes La DN11 ... 1
Tiverton Cl
  Hucknall NG15 ... 145
  Nottingham NG8 ... 160
Toad La Elston NG23 ... 153
  Epperstone NG14 ... 150
  Laxton NG22 ... 79
Tobias Cl NG5 ... 160
Todd Cl NG11 ... 195
Todd Ct NG11 ... 195
Toft Cl NG12 ... 187
Toft Rd NG9 ... 183
Tokenhouse Yd NG1 ... 223
Toll Bar Ave NG13 ... 181
Tollerton Gn NG6 ... 160
Tollerton Prim Sch NG12 ... 186
Tollerton Rd NG12 ... 186
Tollhouse Hill NG1 ... 223
Tolney La NG24 ... 139
Tom Otter's La NG23 ... 70
Tom Wass Rd NG17 ... 114
Tomlinson Ave NG11 ... 195
Tonbridge Mount NG8 ... 171
Tonnlie Dr DN22 ... 24
Tool Hill Comp Sch NG3 ... 172
Toothill La NG18 ... 102
Toothill Rd
  Loughborough LE11 ... 220
  10 Mansfield NG18 ... 102
Top Gn LE14 ... 210
Top La NG19 ... 87
Top Pasture La DN22 ... 31
Top Rd Blidworth NG21 ... 118
  Misson DN10 ...
  Ruddington NG11 ... 196
  Thorne NG23 ... 69
Top Row
  Newark-on-T NG24 ... 140
  Westwood NG16 ... 128
Top Sandy La NG20 ... 72
Top St Askham NG22 ... 51
  Bawtry DN10 ... 10
  North Wheatley DN22 ... 31
Top Valley Comp Sch NG5 ... 160
Top Valley Dr NG5 ... 160
Top Valley Way NG5 ... 160
Toppard La DN22 ...
Tor La NG22 ... 72
Torbay Cres NG5 ... 161

orkard Dr NG5 .... 160 C4
arksey Ave LN1 .... 56 C2
arksey Ferry Rd DN22 .... 49 E1
orksey Dr NG9 .... 43 D1
arksey St NG22 .... 43 D1
orksey St Walk NG19 ...... 88 C2
orr St DN21 .... 24 B4
orridon House Sch
DN24 .... 124 C2
arvill Dr NG8 .... 171 E3
aston Dr NG8 .... 172 B2
island Dr NG8 .... 160 B1
aston Rd NG8 .... 171 E2
etley Cl NG6 .... 146 B1
atnes Cl NG15 .... 145 E3
otnes Rd NG3 .... 174 A3
aton Banks Road Inf Sch
NG9 .... 182 C1
aton & Chetwynd Road
Prim Sch NG9 .... 183 D1
aton Cl NG6 .... 160 B3
aton Cty Jun Sch NG9 .. 182 C2
aton La NG9 .... 182 C3
ottle Gdns NG27 ...... 172 B3
attle Rd NG1 .... 185 D4
aw Ct NG24 .... 139 D2
awe's Mount NG4 ...... 174 C4
ower Cres NG11 .... 159 D2
ower St DN21 .... 15 E1
awle St NG10 .... 193 D2
wilsons Croft NG6 ...... 160 B2
wwn End La NG23 ...... 167 D4
own La NG5 .... 99 D2
own St Askham NG22 .. 52 A2
Beeston NG9 .... 183 D4
Claypole NG23 .... 156 B4
Clayworth DN22 .... 21 E3
Cottam DN22 .... 43 E3
Grassthorpe NG23 ...... 81 F2
Hawksworth NG13 ...... 167 E2
Lound DN22 .... 20 B1
Pinxton NG16 .... 113 F2
Sandiacre NG10 .... 182 A3
South Leverton DN22 .. 42 B4
Sutton DN22 .... 28 C3
Tresswell DN22 .... 42 A2
awn View NG11 .... 158 C4
ownroe Dr NG19 ...... 101 E4
ownsend Ct NG5 ...... 147 D1
ownside Cl NG10 ...... 193 D2
ownside La DN22 ...... 42 B2
ownside Rd DN22 ...... 32 B1
owpath Cl LE11 .... 220 B3
owson Ave NG16 ...... 143 E1
owson Field LE12 ...... 205 F1
owyn Ct NG5 .... 161 D4
racy Cl NG9 .... 171 F1
afalgar Cl NG7 .... 222 B4
afalgar Rd
Beeston NG9 .... 184 A2
Long Eaton NG10 ...... 193 E3
afalgar Sq
Long Eaton NG10 ...... 193 F4
Sutton on T NG23 ...... 97 D4
affic St NG2 .... 173 F2
afford Gdns NG8 .... 172 B4
andy Gdns NG6 ...... 171 F2
efan Gdns NG5 ...... 161 D4
elawn Cl NG5 ...... 161 E1
emayne Rd NG8 ...... 171 E3
enchard Ave NG24 .. 125 F1
enchard Cl NG12 .... 177 E4
enchman Gdns NG14 163 E2
ent Ave NG11 .... 196 B4
ent Bridge
(Nottinghamshire Cty
Cricket Ground) NG2 .. 173 F1
ent Bridge Prim Sch
NG11 .... 185 E4
ent Bridge Sch NG2 .. 173 F1
ent Bvd NG2 .... 174 A1
ent Cl NG23 .... 110 C1
ent Coll NG10 .... 193 E4
ent Cres NG9 .... 183 F2
ent Dr NG15 .... 145 E2
ent Gdns NG14 ...... 164 A2
ent La Besthorpe NG23 . 97 F3
Burton Joyce NG14 .... 164 B2
East Bridgford NG13 .. 165 D2
Kelham NG23 .... 82 C1
Keilham NG23 .... 124 A3
ent La Long Eaton NG10 193 F3
Newark-on-T NG24 .... 125 D1
North Clifton NG23 .... 68 C3
South Clifton NG23 .... 68 B1
ent Port Rd DN21 .... 44 A4
ent Rd Beeston NG9 .. 184 A2
Nottingham NG2 ...... 173 F2
Wellow NG22 .... 78 A2
ent South Ind Pk NG2 . 174 A2
ent St
Gainsborough DN21 .... 24 B4
Long Eaton NG10 ...... 193 F4
Nottingham NG1 ...... 223 F1
Retford DN22 .... 40 A3
Worksop S80 .... 35 F2
ent Vale Rd NG24 .... 124 C1
ent Vale Sch NG9 .... 184 A2
ent Valley View NG5 .. 162 A1
ent View DN21 .... 44 B4
ent View Gdns NG14 .. 176 A3
ent Way NG24 .... 125 D1

Trent Wlk NG19 .... 88 C2
Trentdale Rd NG4 ...... 174 B3
Trentham Dr NG8 ...... 172 B4
Trentham Gdns NG8 .. 172 B4
Trenton Cl NG9 .... 171 D1
Trenton Dr NG10 ...... 194 A4
Trentside NG14 .... 165 D2
Trentside N NG2 ...... 173 F1
Trentview Ct NG2 .... 173 F1
Tressall Cl DE7 .... 170 A4
Treswell Ct NG18 ...... 103 D1
Treswell Rd
Rampton DN22 .... 42 C1
South Leverton DN22 .. 42 B3
Trevelyan Rd NG2 .... 173 F1
Trevino Gdns NG5 .. 147 D1
Trevone Ave NG9 ...... 182 C3
Trevor Rd Beeston NG9 183 F3
West Bridgford NG2 .. 186 A3
Trevose Gdns NG5 .... 161 E2
Treyford Cl NG11 ...... 185 D2
Triangle The DE7 ...... 170 A3
Tricornia Dr NG6 ...... 160 A2
Tring Vale NG5 .... 161 D2
Trinity Ave NG7 .... 222 B1
Trinity Cl DE7 .... 157 F2
Trinity Comp Lower Sch
NG8 .... 172 A4
Trinity Comp Upper Sch
NG8 .... 172 A4
Trinity Cres
East Markham NG22 .. 66 A4
Lambley NG4 .... 163 E4
Wymeswold LE12 ...... 216 A2
Trinity Hospl DN24 .... 39 E4
Trinity Rd
Newark-on-T NG24 .... 140 A2
Retford DN22 .... 29 E1
Southwell NG25 ...... 136 B4
Trinity Sq NG1 .... 223 E3
Trinity St
Gainsborough DN21 .. 24 B4
Loughborough LE11 .. 220 B2
Trinity Wlk NG13 ...... 223 E3
Trinstead Way NG5 .. 161 E4
Triumph Cl NG22 ...... 106 C4
Triumph Rd
Eakring NG22 .... 106 C4
Nottingham NG7 ...... 172 B2
Trivett Sq NG1 .... 223 F2
Troon Cl NG16 .... 158 C4
Trough La NG16 ...... 158 C4
Trough Rd NG16 ...... 159 D4
Troutbeck NG12 ...... 188 A2
Troutbeck Cres NG9 .. 183 E4
Trowell Ave Ilkeston DE7 170 A3
Nottingham NG8 ...... 171 D3
Trowell CE Sch NG9 .. 170 D2
Trowell Cl NG18 ...... 103 D1
Trowell Gr
Long Eaton NG10 ...... 182 B3
Stapleford NG9 .... 170 C2
Trowell La NG10 ...... 213 F4
Trowell Park Dr NG9 .. 170 C1
Trowell Rd
Nottingham NG8 ...... 171 E3
Stapleford NG9 .... 170 B1
True Lovers Wlk LE11 220 A2
Trueman Cl S81 ...... 36 A3
Trueman Gdns NG5 .. 162 A3
Trueman St DE7 ...... 157 F2
Trueman Dr NG15 .... 146 A4
Truman Dr NG15 ...... 146 A3
Truman St Cossall DE7 158 A1
Kimberley NG16 ...... 158 B4
Truman's Rd NG2 .... 173 E1
Truro Cl LE12 .... 205 F1
Truro Cres NG7 ...... 172 C4
Trusley Wlk NG9 ...... 88 C2
Tryst The NG24 ...... 125 D1
Tuckers Cl LE11 ...... 220 B1
Tudor Ave NG18 ...... 102 C4
Tudor Cl Carlton NG4 174 C3
Long Eaton NG10 ...... 182 C1
Tudor Cres NG21 .... 118 A4
Tudor Ct Arnold NG5 .. 162 A3
Hucknall NG15 ...... 145 E3
Tudor Gr NG1 .... 223 D4
Tudor Rd NG2 .... 185 F4
Tudor Sq NG2 .... 185 F4
Tudor St NG17 ...... 100 C1
Tudsbury Terr NG17 .. 101 D2
Tudwal Cl NG5 .... 161 D4
Tudwal Wlk NG5 .... 161 D4
Tulip Ave NG3 .... 173 E4
Tulip Rd NG16 .... 158 A3
Tunnel Rd
Nottingham NG7 ...... 222 C2
Retford DN22 .... 39 F3
Tunstall Cres NG8 .... 160 A1
Tunstall Dr NG5 ...... 160 C2
Tunstall Rd NG5 ...... 161 F4
Turnberry S81 .... 36 A3
Turnberry Ave NG14 114 C4
Turnberry Cl
Beeston NG9 .... 183 D4
Ilkeston DE7 .... 157 E1
Turnberry Ct NG12 .. 186 B2
Turnberry Rd NG6 .. 160 B3
Turner Ave
Langley Mill NG16 .... 143 D2
Loughborough LE11 .. 220 A1
Turner Cl NG9 .... 182 C3
Turner Dr
Eastwood NG16 .... 158 A4
Worksop S81 .... 35 F2

Turner Rd
Long Eaton NG10 ...... 193 E2
Worksop S81 .... 35 F2
Turner St NG15 ...... 146 A4
Turners Croft DN22 .. 42 B4
Turners Ct NG9 ...... 173 E1
Turneys Ct NG2 ...... 173 F1
Turnley Rd DE55 ...... 113 E3
Turnpike La NG9 ...... 184 A4
Turnstone Wharf NG7 172 C1
Turpin Ave NG4 ...... 162 A4
Turpin Cl DN21 .... 15 E1
Turton Cl NG16 ...... 143 D2
Turvey La LE12 .... 212 B1
Tuxford Ave NG20 .... 74 C4
Tuxford Comp Sch NG22 66 A2
Tuxford Ct NG18 ...... 103 D1
Tuxford Prim Sch NG22 .. 65 F2
Tuxford Rd
Boughton NG22 .... 77 F3
East Markham NG22 .. 66 B3
Egmanton NG22 .... 79 F4
Normanton on T NG23 .. 81 F3
Walesby NG22 .... 64 B1
Tuxford Windmill NG22 66 B2
Tuxford WN NG3 ...... 173 F3
Twells Cl NG3 .... 173 F4
Twentylands Dr LE12 205 E1
Twin Oaks Dr NG17 .. 100 B1
Twinyards Cl NG17 .. 100 B1
Twitchell The
Beeston NG9 .... 183 F2
Newark-on-T NG24 .... 139 F3
Sutton in A NG17 .... 100 C1
Two Acres S81 .... 18 A1
Twycross Rd NG6 .... 161 D4
Twyford Gdns NG11 184 C2
Twyford La DN22 .... 50 B2
Tyburn Cl NG5 .... 147 D1
Tylden Rd S80 .... 35 E3
Tylden Way S80 ...... 35 E3
Tynedale Cl
Long Eaton NG10 .... 193 D3
Nottingham NG8 ...... 160 B1
Uldale Ct NG9 .... 183 D2
Ullscarf Cl NG2 ...... 186 B3
Ullswater Cl NG4 .... 162 C1
Ullswater Cres NG9 183 E4
Ullswater Dr NG15 .. 145 F4
Ulster Rd DN21 ...... 15 E1
Underwood Ave DN22 19 D2
Underwood CE Sch
NG16 .... 142 B4
Underwood Gdns S80 .. 35 E2
Union Cl NG15 .... 131 D1
Union Rd NG3 .... 223 F3
Union St Beeston NG9 184 A3
Bingham NG13 .... 177 F2
Long Eaton NG10 .... 193 F4
Loughborough LE11 .. 220 A2
Mansfield NG18 ...... 102 A4
Retford DN22 .... 39 F4
Selston NG16 .... 129 D4
Sutton in A NG17 .... 100 C1
Unity Cres NG3 ...... 162 B1
Unity Rd NG17 .... 115 D4
Univ of Nottingham
Beeston NG9 .... 184 A4
Nottingham NG7 ...... 172 A1
Univ of Nottingham
Department of Ag
Economics LE12 .... 213 D4
Univ of Nottingham
Sutton Bonington
Campus LE12 .... 204 A1
University Bvd NG7 .. 184 B4
Unwin Rd NG17 ...... 101 D2
Unwin St NG17 ...... 100 A2
Uplands Ct NG8 ...... 171 F3
Upminster Dr
Arnold NG5 .... 147 F1
Nuthall NG16 .... 159 E2
Upper Canaan NG11 196 B4
Upper College St NG1 223 D3
Upper Dunstead Rd
NG16 .... 143 D2
Upper Eldon St NG2 .. 173 F2
Upper Mexborough Rd
NG16 .... 129 D4
Upper Orchard St NG9 .. 182 B4
Upper Parliament St
NG1 .... 223 E3
Upper Row NG22 ...... 54 A1
Upper Wellington St
NG10 .... 182 B1
Uppingham Cres NG2 185 E3
Uppingham Gdns NG2 173 E1
Upton Cl DE75 .... 143 D4
Upton Dr NG5 .... 161 E3
Upton Hall NG22 .... 52 A2
Upton Mount NG19 .. 87 F1
Upton Rd Askham NG22 52 A2
Southwell NG25 ...... 122 A1
Upton Wlk DN21 .... 24 C4
Urban Rd NG17 ...... 115 D3
Urnstone Cres NG18 103 E2
Utile Gdns NG6 .... 160 A4

Vale Rd Carlton NG4 .. 174 C3
Mansfield Woodhouse NG19 .. 88 A2
Vale The DE7 .... 157 F2
Valentine Ave NG16 .. 128 C4
Valeside Gdns NG4 .. 174 C3
Valetta Rd NG5 ...... 162 A4
Valiant Rd NG5 ...... 125 F1
Vallance St NG19 .... 88 A2
Valley App NG22 ...... 105 F4
Valley Comp Sch S81 .. 35 F3
Valley Dr NG16 ...... 144 A1
Valley Farm Ct NG4 .. 161 D4
Valley Gdns NG2 .... 186 B3
Valley La NG23 ...... 169 E4
Valley Prospect NG24 139 E3
Valley Rd Beeston NG9 183 D3
Bilsthorpe NG22 ...... 105 F4
Carlton NG4 .... 162 A1
Kimberley NG16 ...... 158 B4
Nottingham NG5 ...... 161 D2
Radcliffe on T NG12 176 B3
Shirebrook NG20 ...... 72 C3
West Bridgford NG2 .. 186 A3
Worksop S81 .... 35 F3
Valmont Ave NG18 .. 103 D3
Valmont Rd Beeston NG9 183 D4
Nottingham NG5 ...... 161 D2
Vancouver Ave NG12 175 F1
Vanessa Dr DN21 .... 15 E2
Vanguard Rd NG10 .. 193 E3
Varden Ave NG9 ...... 172 A1
Varney Rd NG11 ...... 184 C2
Vaughan Ave
Bottesford NG13 ...... 181 E1
Hucknall NG15 .... 131 C1
Vaughan Rd NG9 .... 172 C3
Vaughan Rd NG18 .. 103 D3
Vedonis Pk NG15 .... 146 A3
Vellus Ct NG17 ...... 101 D1
Ventnor Rise NG5 .. 160 C2
Venus Cl NG6 .... 160 C3
Vera Cres NG21 ...... 118 A4
Verbena Cl NG3 .. 173 E4
Verder Gr NG5 ...... 160 C4
Vere Ave NG17 ...... 100 C3
Vere St NG6 .... 160 A4
Verne Cl NG4 .... 174 B4
Verney St NG19 ...... 86 C4
Verney Way NG19 .. 86 C4
Vernon Ave Beeston NG9 183 F3
Nottingham NG6 ...... 160 C2
Vernon Cres NG15 .. 117 D1
Vernon Ct Nuthall NG16 159 F2
Shirebrook NG20 ...... 73 D2
Vernon Dr NG16 .... 159 F2
Vernon Park Dr NG6 160 C2
Vernon Rd
Kirkby in A NG17 .... 114 C3
Nottingham NG6 ...... 160 C2
Vernon St Ilkeston DE7 157 F2
Newark-on-T NG24 .. 140 A4
Nottingham NG1 .... 223 D3
Shirebrook NG20 .... 73 D2
Veron Pk Trad Est NG5 160 C2
Verona Ave NG4 .... 174 C3
Verona Ct NG18 .... 103 D3
Veronica Ct NG8 .... 160 B1
Veronica Dr Carlton NG4 162 B1
Giltbrook NG16 ...... 158 B4
Veronica Wlk NG11 184 B1
Veronne Dr NG17 .. 101 D3
Vesper Ct NG18 .... 102 C4
Vessey Cl NG24 .... 140 B2
Vessey Rd S81 ...... 35 F4
Vexation La NG22 .. 91 F4
Vicar La Misson DN10 .. 4 B2
Tibshelf DE55 .... 99 F3
Vicar Way NG18 .... 103 D4
Vicar's La DN22 .... 43 D1
Vicar's Wlk S80 .... 35 F1
Vicarage Ave
Ilkeston DE7 .... 157 E2
North Leverton w H DN22 42 B4
Vicarage Cl
Collingham NG23 .... 98 A1
North Leverton w H DN22 42 B4
Nottingham, Old Basford
NG5 .... 160 C2
Nottingham, St Ann's NG3 223 E4
Shirebrook NG20 .... 72 C3
Vicarage Ct NG17 .. 100 C4
Vicarage Dr
Burton Joyce NG14 .. 163 F2
Clarborough DN22 .. 30 B3
Vicarage Gn NG12 .. 186 A2
Vicarage La
Beckingham DN10 .. 14 B1
Keyworth NG12 ...... 197 F2
Kneeton NG13 .... 166 B1
North Muskham NG23 110 B2
Radcliffe on T NG12 175 F2
Ruddington NG11 .... 196 B4
Vicarage Rd NG25 .. 136 C4
Vicarage St Beeston NG9 183 F3
Ilkeston DE7 .... 157 E2
Vicarage Way NG17 129 F4
Vicarage Wlk DN22 .. 42 B4
Vicars Ct NG21 ...... 89 F1
Vickers St
Market Warsop NG20 74 A2
Nottingham NG3 .... 173 E4
Vickers Way NG22 .. 105 F4

Victor Cres NG10 .... 182 B2
Victor Terr NG5 .. 161 E1
Victoria Ave
Lowdham NG14 ...... 150 C1
Lowdham NG14 ...... 164 C4
 Nottingham NG2 .. 173 F2
Victoria Cl Arnold NG5 147 F1
Boughton NG22 ...... 77 F3
Gainsborough DN21 24 C3
Victoria Cres NG5 .. 161 E1
Victoria Ct Ilkeston DE7 157 F1
Mansfield NG18 ...... 102 A3
Victoria Rd NG1 .... 223 E3
Victoria Ctr S NG1 .. 223 E3
Victoria Emb NG2 .. 185 E4
Victoria Gdns
Newark-on-T NG24 .. 140 A4
Watnall NG16 .... 145 D1
Victoria Gr NG15 .. 131 D1
Victoria Pk Way NG4 175 D3
Victoria Rd
Bingham NG13 ...... 178 A3
Bunny NG11 .... 196 C1
Carlton NG4 .... 175 D3
Kirkby in A NG17 .. 114 C3
Nottingham NG5 .... 161 D2
Pinxton NG16 .... 113 E2
Retford DN22 .... 39 F3
Sandiacre NG10 .... 182 A3
Selston NG16 .... 129 D4
West Bridgford NG2 185 F4
Worksop S80 .... 35 F1
Victoria Sq S80 .... 35 F1
Victoria St Carlton NG4 162 C1
Hucknall NG15 ...... 146 A4
Ilkeston DE7 .... 157 F2
Kimberley NG16 .... 159 D3
Langley Mill NG16 .. 143 E2
Long Eaton NG10 .. 193 D3
Loughborough LE11 220 A2
Market Warsop NG20 74 A3
Newark-on-T NG24 .. 139 F4
Nottingham NG1 .... 223 E2
Radcliffe on T NG12 175 F2
Selston NG16 .... 129 D4
Shirebrook NG20 .... 72 C2
South Normanton DE55 113 D3
Stanton Hill NG17 .. 100 B3
Stapleford NG9 ...... 182 B4
Sutton in A NG17 .. 100 C1
Victoria Terr DE55 .. 99 D4
Victory Cl
Long Eaton NG10 .. 193 E3
Mansfield Woodhouse NG19 .. 89 D1
Victory Dr NG19 .... 88 C1
Victory Rd NG9 ...... 184 A4
Villa Rd Keyworth NG12 197 F2
Nottingham NG3 .... 173 E4
Villas St NG9 .... 183 F4
Village Cl Farndon NG24 139 D3
West Bridgford NG2 186 C2
Village Farm Cl LE12 204 C1
Village St
Owthorpe NG12 .... 199 F4
West Bridgford NG2 186 A2
Village Way NG24 .. 139 D3
Villas The NG20 .... 59 D2
Villiers Rd Arnold NG5 161 F1
Mansfield NG18 .... 102 C4
West Bridgford NG2 186 A4
Vincent Ave NG9 .. 183 F3
Vincent Gdns NG7 172 C4
Vine Cl NG13 .... 181 D1
Vine Cres NG10 .... 182 A3
Vine Farm Cl NG12 187 F1
Vine Dd DN11 .... 8 B4
Vine Terr NG15 ...... 146 A4
Vine Tree Terr LE12 215 E1
Vine Way NG24 .... 140 A4
Vines Cross NG8 .. 171 F1
Violet Ave NG16 .... 144 A1
Violet Cl NG6 .... 160 A4
Violet Hill NG18 .... 103 D4
Violet Rd Carlton NG4 162 B1
West Bridgford NG2 186 A4
Vista The NG9 ...... 182 C3
Vivian Ave NG5 ...... 173 D4
Voce Ct S81 .... 36 A3
Vulcan Cl NG6 ...... 160 C2
Vulcan Pl S80 .... 35 F2
Vyse Dr NG10 .... 193 E2

Waddington Dr NG2 185 E2
Wade Ave DE7 ...... 170 A4
Wade Cl NG18 ...... 102 B2
Wadham Rd NG5 .. 161 F3
Wadhurst Gdns NG3 223 F4
Wadhurst Gr NG8 .. 171 E1
Wadnal La NG23 .. 80 C2
Wadsworth Rd NG9 182 C2
Wagstaff La NG16 .. 128 B3
Wain Ct S81 .... 36 A4
Wainfleet Cl NG15 131 D1
Wainer Cl NG5 .. 185 D2
Wainwright Ave NG19 101 E4
Wakefield Ave NG12 176 A2
Wakefield Croft DE7 157 E2
Wakeling Cl NG25 .. 136 C4
Walbrook Cl NG8 .. 160 A2
Walcot Cl NG11 .... 184 B1
Walcote Dr NG2 .. 185 E2
Waldeck Rd NG5 .. 161 D1

Waldemar Gr NG9 .... 184 A3
Waldron Cl 28 NG2 .... 173 E1
Walesby CE Prim Sch
NG22 .... 64 A1
Walesby Ct NG18 .... 103 D2
Walesby Dr NG17 .... 115 E3
Walesby La NG22 .... 77 E3
Walford Cl NG13 .... 181 D1
Walgrave Wlk 34 NG5 .... 161 D4
Walk Mill Dr NG19 .... 131 D1
Walk The DN21 .... 24 C4
Walkden St NG18 .... 102 A4
Walker Cl NG4 .... 140 A4
Walker Gr NG9 .... 182 C3
Walker Sq NG5 .... 160 C2
Walker St
Eastwood NG16 .... 144 A2
Nottingham NG2 .... 173 F2
Walkeringham Prim Sch
DN10 .... 13 F3
Walkeringham Rd
Beckingham DN10 .... 14 A1
Gringley on t H DN10 .... 13 D2
Walkerith Rd
Morton DN21 .... 15 D3
Walkerith DN10 .... 14 B4
Walkers Ave NG16 .... 143 F3
Walkers Cl
Bingham NG13 .... 177 F2
Mansfield Woodhouse NG19 .. 89 D1
Walkers Yd NG12 .... 175 F2
Wall St DN21 .... 24 B4
Wallace Ave NG4 .... 174 C4
Wallace Rd LE11 .... 220 A1
Wallace St NG11 .... 195 D1
Wallan St NG7 .... 222 A4
Wallett St NG4 .... 175 D4
Wallett Ave NG9 .... 183 F4
Wallingbrook Rise S80 ...... 35 D1
Wallingwells La S81 .... 25 D3
Wallis Rd NG18 .... 102 B4
Wallis St NG6 .... 160 C2
Walnut Ave
Shireoaks S81 .... 34 C4
Tickhill DN11 .... 8 A4
Walnut Cl
Aslockton NG13 .... 178 C3
Ilkeston DE7 .... 170 A4
Walnut Dr Beeston NG9 ... 183 D4
Calverton NG14 .... 148 C4
Walnut Gr
East Bridgford NG13 .... 165 E1
Radcliffe on T NG12 .... 175 F2
Walnut Paddock LE14 .... 202 A2
Walnut Rd NG13 .... 181 D1
Walnut Tree Cres NG19 .. 89 E1
Walnut Tree Gdns NG6 .. 159 F4
Walnut Tree La NG13 ...... 165 E1
Walsham Cl NG9 .... 183 E1
Walsingham Rd NG5 .... 162 A3
Walter Halls Prim Sch
NG3 .... 161 F1
Walter St NG7 .... 222 C4
Walter's Cl NG24 .... 139 D3
Walters Cres NG8 .... 128 B3
Waltham Cl
Balderton NG24 .... 140 B2
West Bridgford NG2 .... 186 A3
Waltham La Harby LE14 .. 202 A1
Long Clawson LE14 .... 211 F1
Waltham Rd NG11 .... 117 D1
Walton Ave NG3 .... 173 F3
Walton Cl NG19 .... 103 D4
Walton Cres NG4 .... 174 C4
Walton Dr
Keyworth NG12 .... 197 F2
Sutton in A NG17 .... 114 B4
Walton Rd NG5 .... 148 A1
Walton St
Long Eaton NG10 .... 182 B1
Sutton in A NG17 .... 101 D2
Walton's La NG23 .... 110 C2
Wands Cl NG25 .... 136 B4
Wansbeck Cl NG7 .... 222 C3
Wanstead Way NG5 .... 146 C1
Wapping La DN21 .... 44 B4
Warburton St NG24 .... 125 D1
Ward Ave NG15 .... 130 C1
Ward Pl NG18 .... 101 F3
Ward St 18 NG7 .... 172 C4
Ward's End LE11 .... 220 A2
Wardle Gr NG5 .... 162 A4
Wardlow Rd DE7 .... 157 F2
Wareham Cl
Nottingham NG8 .... 160 A2
West Bridgford NG2 .... 185 E3
Warkton Cl NG9 .... 183 E3
Warnadene Rd NG17 ...... 114 C4
Warner Pl LE11 .... 220 B2
Warner St NG7 .... 222 A3
Warrands Cl NG25 .... 136 B4
Warren Ave
Annesley NG15 .... 130 B4
Nottingham NG5 .... 161 D1
Stapleford NG9 .... 182 B4
Warren Ave Extension
NG9 .... 182 B4
Warren Cl
Gainsborough DN21 .... 15 D1
Huthwaite NG17 .... 100 A1
Warren La NG9 .... 182 B4
Warren La
Kegworth DE74 .... 193 D1
Long Eaton DE74 .... 203 D4
Warren Prim Sch NG5 ... 147 D1

Warren Rd
Annesley Woodhouse NG17 115 D1
Hucknall NG15 .... 145 E3
Warren The NG12 .... 187 F1
Warren Way NG19 .... 103 E4
Warrender Cl NG9 .... 171 E1
Warrener Gr NG5 .... 160 C4
Warrenhill Cl NG5 .... 161 D4
Warrington Rd NG6 .... 160 B4
Warser Gate NG1 .... 223 F2
Warsop Cl NG8 .... 159 E1
Warsop La NG21 .... 117 F4
Warsop Rd NG19 .... 88 B2
Warsop Vale Jun Mix &
Inf Sch NG20 .... 73 E2
Warton Ave NG3 .... 173 F4

Warwick Ave
Arnold NG5 .... 161 F3
Beeston NG9 .... 183 F4
Carlton in L S81 .... 25 F3
Warwick Cl NG17 .... 115 E3
Warwick Dr
Mansfield NG18 .... 102 C4
Shipley DE7 .... 157 E2
Warwick Gdns NG12 .... 187 F1
Warwick Rd
Balderton NG24 .... 140 B2
Long Eaton NG10 .... 194 A4
Long Eaton NG10 .... 161 E1
Nottingham NG5 .... 161 E1
Wasdale Cl NG2 .... 186 B3
Wash Pit La NG12 .... 200 B4
Washdyke La NG15 .... 145 F4
Washington Dr
Mansfield NG18 .... 101 F3
Stapleford NG9 .... 170 C1
Washington St DN21 .... 24 B3
Wasnidge Cl NG3 .... 223 F3
Wasnidge Wlk NG3 .... 223 F4
Watchwood Gr NG14 ...... 148 C4
Watcombe Cir NG5 .... 161 E1
Watcombe Rd NG5 .... 161 E1
Watendlath Cl NG2 .... 186 B3

Water La
Carlton in L S81 .... 26 A3
Long Clawson LE14 .... 211 F2
Mansfield NG19 .... 87 D2
Newark-on-T NG24 .... 124 C1
Oxton NG25 .... 134 A2
Radcliffe on T NG12 .... 175 F2
Retford DN22 .... 39 F2
Shelford NG12 .... 164 B1
South Normanton DE55 .... 113 D3
Tickhill DN11 .... 8 A3
Water Mdws S80 .... 35 E1
Water Orton Cl NG9 .... 182 C2
Waterdown Rd NG11 .... 184 B1
Waterford St NG6 .... 160 C2
Waterfurrows La NG12 ... 164 B1
Waterhouse La NG4 .... 163 D1
Waterloo Cl DE55 .... 113 E4
Waterloo Cres NG7 .... 222 C4
Waterloo La NG9 .... 170 C3
Waterloo Prom NG7 .... 222 C4

Waterloo Rd
Beeston NG9 .... 184 A3
Hucknall NG15 .... 131 D1
Nottingham NG7 .... 222 C4
Watermeadow Cl NG19 .. 88 B3
Watermeadows The
NG10 .... 193 D4
Waterside Cl
7 Loughborough LE11 ..... 220 A3
Sandiacre NG10 .... 182 A2
West Bridgford NG2 .... 186 B3
Waterside Gdns NG7 ...... 172 C1
Waterslack Rd DN11 .... 9 D2
Waterson Ave NG18 ...... 102 C2
Waterson Cl NG18 .... 103 D2
Waterson Oaks NG18 .... 102 C2
Waterway St NG2 .... 173 E1
Waterway St W NG2 .... 173 E1
Waterway The NG10 .... 182 B2
Waterworks St DN21 .... 24 B3
Watford Rd NG8 .... 160 A1
Watkin St NG3 .... 223 E4
Watkins La DN22 .... 32 B3
Watnall Cres NG17 .... 101 F4
Watnall Rd
Hucknall NG15 .... 145 F2
Nuthall NG16 .... 159 E3
Watson Ave
Mansfield NG18 .... 102 B4
Nottingham NG3 .... 174 A3
Watson Rd
Ilkeston DE7 .... 157 E1
Worksop S80 .... 35 F1
Watson St NG20 .... 74 A2
Watson's La LE14 .... 202 A2
Wavell Cres DN10 .... 11 D1
Waveney Cl NG5 .... 162 A3

Waverley Ave
Beeston NG9 .... 184 A3
Carlton NG4 .... 163 D1
Waverley Pl S80 .... 47 D4
Waverley Rd NG18 .... 102 A2
Waverley St
Long Eaton NG10 .... 193 F4
Nottingham NG7 .... 223 D4
Tibshelf DE55 .... 99 D4
Waverley Terr NG1 .... 223 D3
Waverley Way S80 .... 47 D4
Waverly Cl NG7 .... 115 E3
Wayford Wlk 7 NG6 .... 160 A4
Wayne Cl NG7 .... 184 C1
Weardale Rd NG5 .... 161 D1
Wearmouth Gdns 5
NG5 .... 147 D1
Weaver Cl LE11 .... 220 A1

Weaver's La
NG15, NG16 .... 129 F2
Weavers Cl LE12 .... 205 F2
Weavers The NG24 .... 139 E3
Weaverthorpe Rd NG5 ... 162 A3
Webb Rd NG8 .... 172 A4
Webster Ave NG16 .... 143 F1
Webster Cl NG21 .... 104 A1
Weedon Cl NG3 .... 174 A3
Weekday Cross NG1 .... 223 E2
Weetman Ave NG20 .... 74 A3
Weetman Gdns 3 NG5 ... 161 D4
Weighbridge Rd NG18 .... 102 B3
Weightman Dr NG16 .... 158 A4

Welbeck Ave
Carlton NG4 .... 162 B1
Newark-on-T NG24 .... 125 D1
Welbeck Cl
Nottingham NG3 .... 223 F4
Sutton in A NG17 .... 100 C3
Welbeck Dr NG21 .... 75 F1

Welbeck Gdns
Beeston NG9 .... 182 C2
Nottingham NG5 .... 162 A2
Welbeck Gr NG13 .... 177 E2
Welbeck Pl NG22 .... 66 A2
Welbeck Prim Sch NG2 .. 173 E1
Welbeck Rd
Harworth DN11 .... 9 D3
Long Eaton NG10 .... 182 B2
Mansfield Woodhouse NG19 88 B2
Radcliffe on T NG12 .... 176 A2
Retford DN22 .... 39 F2
West Bridgford NG2 .... 185 F4
Welbeck St NG17 .... 56 C1
Welbeck Bank NG18 ...... 102 A4
Welbeck Bank Lea NG19 . 88 A1
Welbeck Bank Link NG19 . 88 A1
Welbeck Bank Mews DE74 . 203 E1
Welbeck Bank Wynd NG18 102 A3
Welbeck Bridford
Inf Sch The NG2 .... 185 F4
Welbeck Sq NG17 .... 100 C3
Welbeck St Creswell S80 .. 58 C4
Kirkby in A NG17 .... 115 E3
Mansfield NG18 .... 102 A4
Market Warsop NG20 .... 74 A2
Sutton in A NG17 .... 100 C1
Whitwell S80 .... 45 D3
Worksop S80 .... 35 F2
Welbeck Wlk NG3 .... 223 E4
Welby Ave NG7 .... 222 B2
Welch Ave NG9 .... 182 C4
Weldbank Cl NG9 .... 183 D2
Weldon Sch The NG4 ..... 162 B1
Welfare Cl NG20 .... 72 C2
Welfitt Gr NG20 .... 59 D1
Welham Cres NG5 .... 162 A4
Welham Gr DN22 .... 40 A4
Welham Rd DN22 .... 40 A4
Well Fen La NG23 .... 156 B4
Well La LE14 .... 210 A1

Welland Cl
Newark-on-T NG24 .... 125 D1
Worksop S81 .... 35 F4
Wellcroft Cl NG18 .... 101 F3
Wellesley Cl S81 .... 35 E4
Wellesley Cres NG8 .... 159 F1
Wellin Cl NG12 .... 186 A2
Wellin Ct NG12 .... 186 A2
Wellin La NG12 .... 186 A2
Wellington Cir NG1 .... 223 D2
Wellington Cl NG20 .... 74 A2
Wellington Cres NG2 ...... 185 F4
Wellington Pl NG16 .... 143 F1

Wellington Rd
Burton Joyce NG14 .... 164 A3
Newark-on-T NG24 .... 140 A4
Wellington Sq
Nottingham NG7 .... 222 C3
Retford DN22 .... 39 F4

Wellington St
Eastwood NG16 .... 143 F2
Gainsborough DN21 .... 24 B4
Long Eaton NG10 .... 182 B1
Loughborough LE11 .... 220 B2
Nottingham NG3 .... 223 E4
Retford DN22 .... 39 F4
Stapleford NG9 .... 182 B3
Wellington Terr NG7 .... 222 C3
Wellington Villas NG7 .... 222 C3
Wellow Cl NG17, NG19 .... 101 E4
Wellow Gn NG22 .... 77 F1
Wellow Rd Eakring NG22 .. 92 C1
Wellow NG22 .... 77 E1
Wells Cl NG19 .... 88 B2
Wells Gdns NG3 .... 173 F4
Wells La DN22 .... 43 E3
Wells Road The NG3 .... 161 F1
Wellspring Dale NG9 .... 182 C3
Welshcroft Cl NG17 .... 115 D3
Welstead Ave NG8 .... 160 A1
Welton Gdns NG6 .... 160 A4
Welwyn Ave NG19 .... 88 B3
Welwyn Rd NG8 .... 171 F3
Wembley Gdns NG9 .... 171 D1
Wembley Rd Arnold NG5 . 162 A3
Langold S81 .... 16 C2
Wembley St DN21 .... 24 B4
Wemyss Gdns NG8 .... 172 B2
Wendling Gdns NG5 .... 161 D4
Wendover Dr NG8 .... 160 A1
Wenham La NG17 .... 99 F2
Wenlock Cl NG16 .... 158 B3
Wensley Rd NG5 .... 161 F3
Wensleydale Cl S81 .... 36 A4
Wensleydale Cl
Mansfield NG19 .... 88 C1
Nottingham NG8 .... 160 B2
Wensleydale Rd NG10 .... 193 D3
Wensor Ave NG9 .... 183 F4
Wentbridge Dr NG18 ...... 103 D2
Wentworth Cl NG19 .... 88 C1
Wentworth Cnr NG24 ..... 139 F3
Wentworth Croft DE75 ... 143 D2

Wentworth Ct NG16 .... 158 C3
Wentworth Gn DN22 .... 39 F2
Wentworth Rd
Beeston NG9 .... 183 E3
Kirkby in A NG17 .... 114 C4
Nottingham NG5 .... 161 D1
Wentworth St DE7 .... 158 A1
Wentworth Way NG12 .... 186 B2
Wesley Cl
Balderton NG24 .... 140 B2
Hathern LE12 .... 213 D1
Wesley Gr 17 NG5 .... 161 D1
Wesley Pl NG9 .... 182 C4
Wesley Rd DN22 .... 39 F4

Wesley St
Annesley Woodhouse NG17 130 A4
Ilkeston DE7 .... 157 F2
Langley Mill NG16 .... 143 E2
Nottingham NG5 .... 161 D1
Wesley Way NG11 .... 196 B3
Wesleyan Chapel Wlk
NG9 .... 182 B4
Wessex Cl S81 .... 36 A3
Wessex Rd S81 .... 36 A3
West Ave
Kirkby in A NG17 .... 115 E2
Sandiacre NG10 .... 182 A3
Stapleford NG9 .... 182 C4
West Bridgford NG2 .... 185 F4
West Bank Ave NG18 ...... 102 A4
West Bank Lea NG19 .... 88 A1
West Bank Link NG19 ...... 88 A1
West Bank Mews DE74 ... 203 E1
West Bank Wynd NG18 .. 102 A3
West Bridford
Inf Sch The NG2 .... 185 F4
West Bridgford
Jun Sch The NG2 .... 185 F4
West Bridgford South
Cty Jun Sch NG2 .... 185 F3
West Brook La NG23 ...... 112 A3
West Carr Rd DN22 .... 39 E3
West Cl NG12 .... 197 F1
West Cres Beeston NG9 .. 184 A2
Kirkby in A NG17 .... 115 E2
West Ct DN22 .... 39 E4
West Dr Beeston NG9 ...... 184 A4
Edwinstowe NG21 .... 76 A1
West End Beeston NG9 .... 183 F3
Calverton NG14 .... 148 B4
Farndon NG24 .... 138 C2
Long Clawson LE14 .... 211 E2
Long Whatton LE12 .... 212 A2
Pinxton NG16 .... 113 E2
Sutton in A NG17 .... 100 C1
West End Arc NG1 .... 223 D2
West End Ct NG13 .... 181 D2
West End St NG9 .... 182 B3
West Furlong
Cotgrave NG12 .... 188 A1
Retford DN22 .... 39 E4
West Gate
Long Eaton NG10 .... 193 F4
18 Mansfield NG18 .... 102 A4
Tickhill DN11 .... 8 A4
West Grove Rd DN22 .... 39 F3
West Hill Mansfield NG18 102 A4
Sutton in A NG17 .... 100 B3
West Hill Ave NG18 .... 102 A4
West Hill Dr NG18 .... 102 A4
West Hill Pk NG19 .... 88 A2
West Hill Rd DN22 .... 39 E2
West La
Edwinstowe NG21 .... 76 A1
Girton NG23 .... 82 C1
West Leake La NG11 .... 204 B3
West Leake Rd LE12 .... 205 E1
West Moor NG2 .... 174 B2
West Moor Rd DN10 .... 13 F3
West Notinghamshire
Coll of F Ed
Mansfield NG18 .... 102 A4
Sutton in A NG17 .... 100 B3
West Park Pl DN22 .... 39 E3
West St Arnold NG5 .... 161 F4
Harworth DN11 .... 9 D3
Hucknall NG15 .... 146 A4
Kimberley NG16 .... 159 D2
Langley Mill NG16 .... 143 D2
Misson DN10 .... 4 A1
Morton DN21 .... 15 D2
Nottingham NG2 .... 173 F2
Retford DN22 .... 39 F3
Warsop Vale NG20 .... 73 E2
Whaley Thorns NG20 .... 59 D2
Worksop S80 .... 35 F2
West Terr Hucknall NG15 . 146 A4
8 Ilkeston DE7 .... 157 F1
West Thorpe LE12 .... 217 E4
West View
Carlton in L S81 .... 25 F3
West Bridgford NG2 .... 185 E3
West View Rd NG4 .... 174 C4
West Wells La DN10 .... 12 C1
West Wlk
1 Nottingham NG1 .... 173 F2
Retford DN22 .... 39 E4
West Wood Est DN10 .... 9 F2
Westbourne Cl
Retford DN22 .... 40 A3
Sutton in A NG17 .... 100 B2
Westbourne Rd
Selston NG16 .... 129 D2
Sutton in A NG17 .... 100 B2
Westbourne View NG17 . 100 B2

Westbrecks La DN22 43
Westbrook Ave NG15 116
Westbrook Spccl Sch
NG10 193
Westbury Cl NG9 183
Westbury Rd NG5 161
Westbury Spccl Sch NG8 . 160
Westby La
Awsworth NG16 158
Kimberley NG16 158
Westcliffe Ave
Carlton NG4 162
Radcliffe on T NG12 176
Westcroft Dr LN1 57
Westcross Ave NG9 182
Westdale Ave NG17 101
Westdale Cl NG10 193
Westdale Cres NG4 162
Westdale Ct NG4 162
Westdale Jun & Inf Schs
NG3 162
Westdale La E NG4 162
Westdale La W NG3 162
Westdale Rd
Mansfield NG19 88
Westwood NG16 128
Westerdale S81 36
Westerfield Way NG11 ... 185
Westerham Cl NG8 171
Westerham Rd NG11 196
Westerlands NG9 182
Western Ave
Bingham NG13 177
Kirkby in A NG17 115
Mansfield NG18 101
Saxilby LN1 56
Western Bvd NG8 172
Western Dr NG24 140
Western Fields NG11 196
Western Gdns NG8 172
Western St NG1 223
Western Terr NG7 222
Western Wlk DN10 10
Westfield Cl
Mansfield NG19 101
Sutton in A NG17 100
Westfield Dr
Ilkeston DE7 157
Mansfield NG19 101
Worksop S81 36
Westfield La
Collingham NG23 111
Mansfield NG18, NG19 101
Westfield Rd
Annesley Woodhouse NG17 115
Bingham NG13 177
Retford DN22 39
Westfield Way NG24 139
Westfields La NG14 149
Westgate
Southwell NG25 136
Worksop S80 35
Westgate St NG3 173
Westgate View S80 35
Westglade Jun & Inf Sch
NG5 160
Westhay Ct NG8 172
Westholme Gdns NG8 172
Westhorpe NG25 136
Westhorpe Ave NG3 173
Westhorpe Dr NG10 193
Westhorpe Market Pl
NG25 136
Westland Ave NG15 145
Westland Dr NG16 113
Westleigh NG19 88
Westleigh Rd NG8 159
Westminster Ave
Kirkby in A NG17 115
Stapleford NG10 182
Westminster Cl
Nottingham NG3 173
Worksop S81 36
Westminster Dr NG12 176
Westmoore Cl NG3 162
Westmoreland Ct 18
NG5 173
Westmorland Ct DN11 9
Westmorland Dr S81 25
Westmorland Way NG16 . 128
Weston Ave NG7 172
Weston Cl Arnold NG5 161
Sutton in A NG17 115
Weston La NG23 81
Weston Rd NG22, NG23 80
Weston St DE75 143
Westray Cl NG9 170
Westrivew Ct NG4 174
Westville Dr NG15 145
Westville Gdns NG3 173
Westward Ave NG9 184
Westway Cotgrave NG12 . 187
Worksop S81 36
Westwick Rd NG8 171
Westwick St DE7 170
Westwood Dr S80 35
Westwood Rd NG2 173
Wetherby Cl
Kimberley NG16 158
Nottingham NG8 160
Wetherlam Cl NG2 173
Wetsyke La NG24 140
Whaddon Cl LE11 220
Whaley Bridge Cl NG18 . 103
Whaley Comm S44 58
Whaley Rd NG20 58
Whaley Thorns
Heritage Ctr NG20 59

Wha – Woo 257

haley Thorns Prim Sch
NG20 59 D2
haley Thorns Sta NG20 58 C1
harf La NG12 175 F2
harf Rd
9 Mansfield NG18 102 A3
Misterton DN10 6 C1
Nottingham NG7 223 D1
Pinxton NG16 113 E1
Retford DN22 39 F3
Stanton Hill NG17 100 B3
harf St DN10 10 A4
harfdale Gdns NG18 103 D3
harfdale Rd NG10 193 D3
harfedale
Nottingham NG8 171 D2
Worksop S81 36 A4
harmby Ave NG19 87 E2
harncliffe Rd
Loughborough LE11 220 B2
Retford DN22 39 F2
harton St DN22 40 A3
hatton Ct NG18 103 D2
hatton Rd
Hathern LE12 212 C1
Kegworth DE74 203 E1
hatton Rise NG5 161 E2
heat Cl NG8 171 E3
heat Croft S81 36 A4
heatacre Rd NG7 184 C1
heatcroft View NG2 185 E2
heatfield Cres NG19 88 C3
heatfield Dr DN11 8 A4
heatfield Way NG17 100 C4
heatfields Rd NG3 174 A4
heatgrass Hill
NG25, NG23 122 B2
heatgrass Rd NG9 183 D3
heatland Dr LE11 220 B1
heatley Ave NG17 114 C2
heatley Cl
Mansfield Woodhouse NG19 88 C1
Ruddington NG11 196 B3
heatley Dr NG4 174 B4
heatley Gr NG9 183 F2
heatley La NG23 112 A2
heatley Rd
Clayworth DN22 21 F2
Sturton le S DN22 32 A3
heatsheaf Ct NG14 163 F2
heeldale Cl NG8 171 D2
heeldon St DN21 24 B4
heeler Ave NG16 144 A1
heeler Gate
Nottingham NG1 223 E2
Selston NG16 129 D1
heldon Ave NG4 162 B1
hernside Rd NG5 161 F3
hetstone Cl NG16 159 E2
hickham Ct 24 NG2 173 E1
hilton Cl NG17 101 D3
himsey Pk NG4 174 C3
hinbush La NG14 133 F2
hinfell Cl NG7 184 C1
hinlatter Dr NG2 186 B3
hinleys Rd DN22 31 D1
hinney Bank NG19 88 B2
hinney Hill NG19 88 B2
hinney La NG22 77 E3
hinney Moor Cl DN22 39 F3
hinney Moor La DN22 39 F3
hinney Moor Way
DN22 39 F3
histon Cl NG5 161 D3
hitaker Cl DN22 29 E1
hitbread St NG7 172 C4
hitburn Rd NG9 182 C2
hitby Cl NG8 171 D2
hitby Cres NG5 162 A3
hitby Rd
Eastwood NG16 144 A2
Harworth DN11 9 D3
hitchurch Cl NG5 160 C4
hitcombe Ct DN22 39 E2
hitcombe Gdns
11 NG5 147 D1
hite Ave S81 16 C2
hite Furrows NG12 187 F1
hite Hart La NG23 112 A4
hite Hart St NG18 102 A4
hite Hart Yd S80 35 F1
hite House Rd DN11 9 E2
hite Lodge Gdns NG8 171 E4
hite Post Modern Farm
Ctr NG22 119 D4
hite Rd NG5 160 C2
hite's Ave NG4 174 A3
hite's Wood La DN21 24 C4
hite's Wood Lane
Cty Sch DN21 24 C4
hitebeam Gdns NG6 159 F4
hitechapel St NG6 160 B1
hitegate LE11 220 B3
hitegate Prim Sch
NG11 195 E4
hitegate Vale NG11 184 B1
hitehall Ct DN22 39 F3
hitehall Gdns DN22 39 F3
hitehall Rd DN22 39 F3
hitehead Cl DE7 157 E1
hitehead Dr NG16 143 E4
hitehead La NG17 100 C3
hitehouse Ave LE11 220 B1
hitelands NG12 188 A1
hitely Cl NG9 182 C4
hitemoor Ave 6 NG8 172 B4
hitemoor Ct NG8 172 B4
hitemoor La NG23 112 A2

Whitemoor Prim Sch
NG8 160 B1
Whitemoor Rd NG6 160 B1
Whitemoss Cl NG8 171 F2
Whitestone Cl NG18 103 D2
Whitestub La NG22 106 C3
Whitewater Cl NG22 77 E3
Whitewater La NG22 63 D1
Whitewater Rd NG22 77 E3
Whitewates La S81 18 A3
Whitfield Cl NG11 185 D3
Whitfield St NG24 140 A4
Whiting Ave NG9 182 C1
Whitney Cl NG19 89 D1
Whitsun Dale S81 36 A4
Whittaker Rd
Beeston NG9 183 D2
Rainworth NG21 118 A4
Whittier Rd NG2 174 A2
Whittingham Ct NG3 162 A2
Whittingham Rd NG3 162 A2
Whittle Cl NG24 125 D1
Whitton Cl
4 Beeston NG9 183 E1
19 Nottingham NG5 147 D1
Ranskill DN22 19 D2
Whitwell Cl NG8 159 F1
Whitwell Prim Sch S80 45 D3
Whitwell Rd
Nottingham NG8 159 F1
Thorpe Salvin S80 34 A2
Whitwell Sta S80 45 D3
Whitworth Dr
Carlton NG4 163 E1
Radcliffe on T NG12 175 F1
Whitworth Rise NG5 160 C4
Whomsley Cl NG24 140 B4
Whyburn La NG15 145 E4
Whyburn Prim Sch NG15 145 F4
Whyburn St NG15 146 B3
Whyston Ct NG15 145 E3
Wichnor Cl NG11 184 C2
Wickens Wlk NG3 173 F3
Wickerwood Dr NG17 114 C3
Wicket Gr NG7 222 A2
Wickstead Cl NG5 161 F2
Widdowson Cl NG6 159 F4
Wide La Hathern LE12 213 D1
Wymeswold LE12 217 E2
Wide St LE12 213 D1
Widecombe La NG11 195 E4
Widmerpool La LE12 217 E4
Widmerpool Rd NG12 207 F2
Widmerpool St NG16 113 E1
Wighay Rd NG15 131 D1
Wigley Cl NG3 173 F3
Wigman Rd NG8 171 F4
Wigsley Rd Harby NG23 70 B1
North Scarle LN6 83 E3
Wigthorpe La S81 26 A2
Wigwam Gr NG15 146 B4
Wigwam La NG15 146 B4
Wilberforce Rd NG19 87 E1
Wilcox Ave NG19 88 A3
Wilcox Dr NG16 129 D1
Wild Flower Farm NG13 190 B1
Wild Hill NG17 99 F4
Wilde Cres NG16 129 D3
Wilden Cres NG7 184 C1
Wildman St NG7 222 C4
Wildman Villas DN10 14 A1
Wilford Cl NG24 140 A4
Wilford Cres NG11 196 B4
Wilford Cres E NG2 173 E1
Wilford Cres W NG2 173 E1
Wilford Gr
Nottingham NG2 173 E1
West Bridgford NG2 185 E4
Wilford La NG2 185 E4
Wilford Meadows Sch
NG11 185 E4
Wilford Rd
Mansfield NG18 103 D2
Nottingham NG2 173 D1
Nottingham NG2 223 E1
West Bridgford NG11 185 E1
Wilford Sports Complex
NG2 185 E3
Wilford St NG2 223 E1
Wilfred Ave NG24 140 B2
Wilfrid Gr NG2 185 F2
Wilhallow La NG16 128 C1
Wilkins Gdns NG11 184 B1
Wilkinson Ave NG9 183 F3
Wilkinson Cl NG19 87 D3
Wilkinson Distribution Ctr
S80 48 A4
Wilkinson St NG7 172 C4
Willand Ct DN22 29 F1
Willaston Cl NG6 160 B2
Willbert Rd NG5 148 A1
Willerby Rd NG5 162 A3
Willersley Dr NG2 173 E1
Willesden Gn NG16 159 E2
Willetts Ct NG17 100 C1
Willey La NG16 144 A4
William Ave NG16 143 F1
William Booth Inf Sch The
NG2 173 F2
William Booth Rd NG2 174 A2
William Bradford Cl DN10 3 E1
William Cl NG4 175 D4
William Crane Comp Sch
NG8 160 A1
William Harrison Sch
DN21 24 C3
William & Henry Mews
LN6 84 B2

William Lilley Inf Sch
NG9 182 B3
William Old Ct 10 NG8 172 A3
William Rd
Stapleford NG9 182 B4
West Bridgford NG2 185 F4
William Sharp Comp Sch
NG8 171 E3
William St Hucknall NG15 146 A4
Long Eaton NG10 182 B1
Loughborough LE11 220 A2
Newark-on-T NG24 140 A4
Saxilby LN1 57 D2
Williams Rd NG9 183 D2
Williams St S81 16 C2
Williamson St NG19 101 F4
Willingham Rd DN21 24 C1
Willis Rd NG24 139 F3
Willoughby Ave
Long Eaton NG10 182 B2
Nottingham NG7 222 B2
Willoughby Cl NG7 184 A4
Willoughby Ct
Mansfield NG18 103 D1
Nottingham NG7 222 B1
Willoughby Rd
West Bridgford NG2 185 F3
Widmerpool NG12 208 B2
Willoughby St
Beeston NG9 184 A3
Cossall DE7 158 A1
Gainsborough DN21 24 B4
Nottingham NG7 222 B1
Willoughby Way NG22 64 A1
Willoughby-on-the-
Wolds Prim Sch LE12 217 E4
Willow Ave Carlton NG4 175 D4
Carlton in L S81 25 F4
Hucknall NG15 145 E2
Kirkby in A NG17 114 C3
Long Eaton NG10 182 B1
Mansfield Woodhouse NG19 89 D1
Misterton DN10 6 C1
Shirebrook NG20 72 B3
Stapleford NG9 182 B3
Willow Brook NG12 198 A1
Willow Brook
Cty Prim Sch NG12 198 A1
Willow Cl
Burton Joyce NG14 163 F3
East Leake LE12 214 B4
Gainsborough DN21 15 D2
Radcliffe on T NG12 175 F1
Saxilby LN1 57 D2
Selston NG16 129 D4
South Normanton DE55 113 D3
Worksop S80 35 F1
Willow Cres
Carlton NG4 163 D1
Lambley NG4 163 E4
Sutton in A NG17 100 B2
Willow Ct NG16 129 D1
Willow Dr
Annesley Woodhouse NG15 129 F3
North Muskham NG23 110 C1
Willow Farm Prim Sch
NG4 163 D1
Willow Hill Cl NG6 160 A3
Willow Holt
Lowdham NG14 150 C1
Retford DN22 39 F2
Willow La Carlton NG4 163 D1
Langar NG13 190 B1
Willow Pool La LE12 213 E3
Willow Rd
Bingham NG13 178 A2
Carlton NG4 175 D4
New Balderton NG24 140 B3
Nottingham NG7 172 C1
West Bridgford NG2 185 F2
Willow Rise NG10 182 A3
Willow Tree Cl NG19 89 E1
Willow Wong NG14 163 F3
Willowbridge La NG17 100 B1
Willowbrook Ct 13 NG2 173 E1
Willowdene NG12 188 A2
Willows The
Farndon NG24 139 D2
Nottingham NG8 172 A4
Pleasley NG19 87 D3
Willwell Dr NG2 185 E2
Wilmington Ct LE11 220 B1
Wilmington Gdns NG5 161 E3
Wilmore Way NG19 101 E3
Wilmot La NG9 183 F3
Wilmot St Ilkeston DE7 157 F1
Long Eaton NG10 193 D3
Wilne Ave NG10 193 D2
Wilne Rd NG10 193 D2
Wilsic Rd DN11 8 A4
Wilson Ave NG17 114 C3
Wilson Cl Arnold NG5 162 A3
Everton DN10 11 D1
Mattersey DN10 20 A4
Wilson Rd NG16 143 F1
Wilson St
Gainsborough DN21 15 D1
Newark-on-T NG24 124 C1
Pinxton NG16 113 E2
Radmanthwaite NG19 87 E1
Wilson's La NG25 137 F2
Wilsthorpe Rd
Breaston DE72 193 D4
Long Eaton NG10 193 D3
Wilsthorpe Sch NG10 182 A1
Wilton Ave LE11 220 B1
Wilton Pl DE7 157 F1
Wilton Rd NG7 222 A4

Wilton St
7 Ilkeston DE7 157 F1
Nottingham NG6 160 C2
Wilton Terr NG6 160 C2
Wiltshire Ave NG16 128 A2
Wimbishthorpe Cl NG13 181 D2
Wimbledon Dr NG16 159 F2
Wimbledon Rd NG5 161 D2
Wimborne Cl NG2 185 E3
Wimbourne Rd NG7 222 B4
Wimpole Rd NG9 171 E1
Winborne Cl NG19 101 E3
Winchester Ave NG9 183 F4
Winchester Cl
East Leake LE12 205 F1
Mansfield NG18 103 D2
Worksop S81 36 A4
Winchester Cres DE7 170 A4
Winchester Ct NG5 161 F2
Winchester Dr NG19 88 B2
Winchester St NG5 161 E1
Winchester Terr 7 NG5 161 E2
Winchilsea Ave NG24 140 A4
Windermere Ave DN11 8 C2
Windermere Cl
Carlton NG4 162 C1
West Bridgford NG2 186 B3
Worksop S81 35 F4
Windermere Gdns NG10 182 A1
Windermere Rd
Beeston NG9 183 E4
Hucknall NG15 145 F4
Long Eaton NG10 182 A1
Nottingham NG7 173 D4
Windley Dr DE7 157 E2
Windley Sch NG7 222 C4
Windmill Ave NG15 146 A3
Windmill Cl NG3 173 F3
Windmill Ct NG12 197 F1
Windmill Gr NG15 146 A3
Windmill Hill NG25 134 B3
Windmill La
Mansfield NG18 102 B4
Nottingham NG2 173 F3
Worksop S80 47 D4
Windmill Rd LE11 220 B2
Windmill Ridge Mid Sch
NG18 102 C4
Windmill View NG2 174 A2
Windmill Way DE74 203 D1
Windrush Cl NG9 171 E1
Windsmoor Rd NG16 143 E4
Windsor Ave
Newark-on-T NG24 139 F3
Sutton in A NG17 100 A2
Windsor Cl
Collingham NG23 112 A4
Gringley on t H DN10 12 C1
Hucknall NG15 146 A4
Trowell NG9 170 A3
Windsor Cres
Arnold NG5 162 A3
Stapleford NG9 182 C4
Windsor Ct Bingham NG13 177 E2
Harworth DN11 9 D3
Sandiacre NG10 182 A2
Windsor Dr NG20 74 A2
Windsor Gdns
Carlton in L S81 25 F3
Mansfield NG18 102 B3
Windsor Rd
Carlton in L S81 25 F3
Clipstone NG19 89 E2
Mansfield NG18 102 B3
Newark-on-T NG24 139 F3
Retford DN22 29 E1
Selston NG16 129 D4
Worksop S81 35 E4
Windsor St Beeston NG9 184 A3
Stapleford NG9 182 C4
Windy Ridge NG20 74 B2
Windyridge DN10 11 E2
Wing Alley NG1 223 F2
Wingate Cl NG8 171 F3
Wingbourne Wlk NG6 146 B1
Wingfield Ave S81 36 A3
Wingfield Dr
Beeston NG9 172 A1
Ilkeston DE7 157 E2
Wingfield Rd NG18 103 D2
Wings Dr NG15 145 E2
Winifred Cres NG14 163 F2
Winifred St
Hucknall NG15 146 A3
Rhodesia S80 35 D2
Winkburn La NG22 121 F4
Winkburn Rd NG19 101 F4
Winnery Cl DN11 8 A4
Winrow Gdns NG6 160 B2
Winscale Ave NG5 161 D4
Winscale Gdns 15 NG5 161 D4
Winscombe Mount
NG11 195 F4
Winsford Cl NG8 160 A1
Winster Ave Carlton NG4 162 B1
Ravenshead NG15 117 D2
Winster Cl NG9 171 F1
Winster Gr S81 35 F4
Winster Way NG18 103 E3
Winston Cl Arnold NG3 162 B3
Stapleford NG9 182 C4
Winston Ct NG24 139 F3
Winston Dr NG23 153 F2
Winston Gn DN10 19 F4
Winston Gr DN22 30 A1
Winter Closes NG16 128 C1
Winterbeck Cl NG13 181 D2
Winterbourne Dr NG9 170 C1

Wintern Ct DN21 24 B3
Winterton Cl NG5 161 F3
Winterton Rise NG5 161 D4
Winthorpe Cty Prim Sch
NG24 125 E4
Winthorpe Rd
Arnold NG5 162 A4
Newark-on-T NG24 125 D2
Winthorpe St NG19 101 E3
Wintringham Cres NG5 162 A3
Wire La DE55 99 D2
Wisa Terr NG5 161 E2
Wiseton Rd DN22 21 E3
Wishford Ave NG7 222 A1
Wisley Cl NG2 185 E2
Wistow Cl NG8 172 C4
Witch La NG23 96 C4
Witham Cl NG24 125 D1
Withern Rd NG8 159 F1
Withorn Mews NG19 101 F4
Witney Cl NG5 160 C4
Wittering Cl NG10 193 F3
Wiverton Rd
Bingham NG13 177 F2
Nottingham NG7 173 D4
Woburn Ave NG17 115 E3
Woburn Cl NG2 186 B2
Woburn Croft NG10 182 A2
Woburn La NG19 87 E2
Woburn Pl NG19 87 E2
Woburn Rd NG19 87 E2
Woburn Rise NG5 162 A3
Wodehouse Ave NG11 195 D1
Wolds Dr NG12 197 F2
Wolds Rise NG12 197 F2
Wolfit Ave NG24 140 C3
Wollacombe Cl NG3 162 B3
Wollaton Ave NG4 162 C1
Wollaton Cres NG9 183 F4
Wollaton Ct NG6 160 C3
Wollaton Hall Dr NG8 172 B2
Wollaton Hall (Natural
History Mus) NG8 172 A2
Wollaton Paddocks NG8 171 E2
Wollaton Rd
Beeston NG9 183 F4
Kirkby in A NG17 115 E3
Nottingham NG8 172 B3
Wollaton Rise NG8 171 F1
Wollaton St NG1 223 D3
Wollaton Vale NG8 171 F1
Wolseley Ct NG17 100 C2
Wolsey Ave NG7 222 B3
Wolsey Dr NG17 115 D4
Wolsey Rd NG24 125 D2
Wolsey Way 2 LE11 220 B2
Wong La DN11 8 A4
Wood Ave Creswell S80 58 B4
Sandiacre NG10 182 A3
Wood Cl NG18 102 C4
Wood End Dr NG15 117 D1
Wood Gate LE11 220 A2
Wood Gr NG14 148 C4
Wood Hill LE14 218 C2
Wood La
Barkestone-le-V NG13 192 B1
Beckingham DN10 23 D4
Carlton NG4 163 D1
Creswell S80 58 B4
Egmanton NG22 79 F3
Gringley on t H DN10 12 C2
Grove DN22 41 F2
Hucknall NG15 145 F4
Kersall NG22 94 A1
Kingston-on-S NG11 204 C4
Market Warsop NG20 73 F4
North Wheatley DN22 22 B1
Shirebrook NG20 72 C1
South Scarle NG23 98 C3
Wood Link NG6 159 F4
Wood Nook Cl NG16 128 C3
Wood St Arnold NG5 161 F4
Eastwood NG16 143 F2
Ilkeston DE7 157 F1
Mansfield NG18 102 A4
Market Warsop NG20 74 A3
Newark-on-T NG24 140 A4
Nottingham NG7 222 C3
Wood View NG12 186 A2
Wood View Bsns Ctr 15
NG5 147 D1
Wood's La NG23 153 D1
Woodbank Dr NG8 171 E1
Woodbeck Rise DN22 39 E4
Woodborough La NG5 148 B2
Woodborough Rd
Mansfield NG19 87 F1
Nottingham NG3, NG1 161 F1
Woodbridge Ave NG11 184 C2
Woodchurch Rd NG5 147 D1
Woodcoates Rd NG22 67 D3
Wooden Beck Hill DN10 13 E2
Woodfield Rd
Gainsborough DN21 15 F1
Nottingham NG8 159 F1
Pinxton NG16 113 E2
Woodford Cl NG5 146 C1
Woodford Rd
Arnold NG5 162 A3
Hucknall NG15 146 A3
Woodgate Cl NG12 187 F2
Woodgate Ct NG7 222 C3
Woodgate La
Beckingham LN5 142 C4
Cotgrave NG12 187 E2

Woodgate Rd LE12 .... 214 B4
Woodhall Cl
  🅱 Kirkby in A NG17 .... 114 C4
  Mansfield NG18 .... 102 C4
Woodhall Cres LN1 .... 56 C2
Woodhall Gdns NG18 .... 102 C4
Woodhall Gn DN22 .... 39 E1
Woodhall Rd NG8 .... 172 A3
Woodhead Cl NG21 .... 76 A1
Woodhedge Dr NG3 .... 174 A4
Woodhill Ave DN21 .... 15 F1
Woodhill Rd NG23 .... 98 A1
Woodhouse Ct NG19 .... 88 B1
Woodhouse La
  Carlton in L S81 .... 26 A4
  Sutton in A NG17 .... 101 D4
Woodhouse Pl NG22 .... 66 A1
Woodhouse Rd NG18 .... 102 A4
Woodhouse St NG3 .... 173 F3
Woodhouse Way NG16 .... 159 E2
Woodkirk Rd NG7 .... 184 C1
Woodland Ave
  Gainsborough DN21 .... 15 D2
  Huthwaite NG17 .... 99 F2
  Ilkeston DE7 .... 157 E2
  Worksop S80 .... 36 A1
Woodland Cl
  Clipstone NG21 .... 90 A2
  Cotgrave NG12 .... 187 F1
  Farnsfield NG22 .... 120 A3
  Radcliffe on T NG12 .... 176 A2
Woodland Cres NG18 ...... 102 C2
Woodland Dr
  Mansfield NG18 .... 102 C2
  Nottingham NG3 .... 161 E1
  Nuthall NG16 .... 159 F2
  Southwell NG25 .... 121 E1
  Worksop S81 .... 35 F3
Woodland Gr
  Arnold NG5 .... 161 E2
  Beeston NG9 .... 183 E3
  Carlton NG4 .... 174 C3
  Mansfield Woodhouse NG19 .. 88 B2
  Market Warsop NG20 .... 74 A2
Woodland Rd
  Mansfield NG18 .... 102 C4
  West Bridgford NG2 .... 173 F1
Woodland Rise NG15 ..... 117 D1
Woodland View
  Southwell NG25 .... 136 B4
  Whaley Thorns NG20 .... 59 D2
Woodland Way NG16 ..... 143 F1
Woodland Wlk NG17 ...... 115 E3
Woodlands NG24 .... 125 E4
Woodlands Cl
  Newark-on-T NG24 .... 139 F3
  Wymeswold LE12 .... 216 B2
Woodlands Dr LE11 .... 220 A1

Woodlands Farm Cl
  NG15 .... 145 E2
Woodlands Gr NG15 .... 145 E2
Woodlands Sch NG8 ...... 172 A4
Woodlands The Blyth S81 ... 18 A3
  Mansfield NG19 .... 88 A1
  Nottingham NG6 .... 160 B3
  Whaley Thorns NG20 .... 59 D2
Woodlands Way NG17 .. 100 B1
Woodlane Gdns NG3 ...... 173 F4
Woodleigh NG12 .... 197 F1
Woodley Sq NG6 .... 146 B1
Woodley St NG11 .... 196 B4
Woodruff La NG22 .... 106 A3
Woods Foundation
  CE Sch NG14 .... 149 E2
Woods Hill NG17 .... 100 C1
Woods La NG14 .... 148 C4
Woods Terr DN21 .... 15 E1
Woodsend NG14 .... 163 F2
Woodsetts La S81 .... 25 D1
Woodsford Gr NG7 .... 184 C1
Woodside
  Eastwood NG16 .... 143 F2
  Farnsfield NG22 .... 120 A3
  Retford DN22 .... 39 E4
  Sutton in A NG17 .... 100 C4
Woodside Ave
  Mansfield NG18 .... 102 B2
  Nuthall NG16 .... 159 D3
  Radcliffe on T NG12 .... 176 A2
Woodside Cres
  Ilkeston DE7 .... 157 E3
  Long Eaton NG10 .... 193 D4
Woodside Dr NG5 .... 161 E4
Woodside Rd
  Beeston NG9 .... 183 F4
  Beeston, Chilwell NG9 ...... 183 D2
  Burton Joyce NG14 .... 163 E2
  Radcliffe on T NG12 .... 176 A2
  Ravenshead NG15 .... 116 C2
  Sandiacre NG10 .... 182 A3
  Shirebrook NG20 .... 72 C3
  Shireoaks S81 .... 34 C4
Woodside View DN11 .... 9 D2
Woodstock Ave NG2 .... 222 A4
Woodstock Cl NG24 .... 140 B4
Woodstock Rd NG9 .... 182 C2
Woodstock St NG15 ...... 146 A3
Woodston Wlk NG5 .... 148 A1
Woodthorpe Ave
  Arnold NG5 .... 161 F2
  Loughborough LE11 .... 220 A1
Woodthorpe Ct NG5 ...... 161 F2
Woodthorpe Cty
  Prim Sch The NG5 .... 161 F3
Woodthorpe Dr NG3 ..... 161 F2
Woodthorpe Gdns NG5 .. 161 F2
Woodthorpe Rd
  Loughborough LE11 .... 220 A1
  Nottingham NG3 .... 161 F2

Woodview NG12 .... 188 A1
Woodview Ct NG4 .... 174 B3
Woodview Gdns NG19 ..... 89 E1
Woodville Cl NG9 .... 183 E3
Woodville Dr NG5 .... 161 E2
Woodville Rd 🅱 NG5 ..... 161 E1
Woodward Rd NG2 .... 173 E1
Woodwards The NG24 ... 140 B3
Woodyard La NG8 .... 172 A3
Wooliscroft Way DE7 ..... 157 E1
Woollaton St NG15 .... 146 A4
Woolmer Rd NG2 .... 173 E1
Woolpack La NG1 .... 223 F2
Woolpack St DN22 .... 39 F4
Woolsington Cl NG8 ...... 159 E1
Woolsthorpe Cl 🅱 NG8 .. 172 A3
Wootton Cl NG8 .... 171 E4
Worcester Ave NG19 .... 88 B3
Worcester Cl
  Lowdham NG14 .... 150 C1
  Worksop S81 .... 36 A4
Worcester Gdns NG5 .... 161 F3
Worcester Mews NG19 .. 88 B3
Worcester Rd NG5 .... 161 F3
Wordsworth Ave
  Hucknall NG15 .... 145 E3
  Mansfield Woodhouse NG19 .. 88 A2
  Sutton in A NG17 .... 100 A2
Wordsworth Dr NG24 ... 140 B3
Wordsworth Rd
  Arnold NG5 .... 161 E4
  Awsworth NG16 .... 158 B3
  Nottingham NG7 .... 222 A4
  West Bridgford NG2 .... 185 F3
Worksop Coll S80 .... 47 D4
Worksop Mus S80 .... 35 F1
Worksop Priory
  CE Prim Sch S80 .... 35 F1
Worksop Rd
  Babworth DN22 .... 49 E4
  Blyth S81 .... 18 A1
  Cuckney NG20 .... 60 A2
  Edwinstowe NG21, NG22 .. 76 B3
  Nottingham NG3 .... 173 F3
  Whitwell S80 .... 45 D4
  Woodsetts S81 .... 25 D1
Worksop Sta S80 .... 35 F2
World of Robin Hood The
  DN22 .... 64 A3
Worrall Ave Arnold NG5 .... 161 F4
  Long Eaton NG10 .... 182 C1
Worsborough Cl NG18 .. 101 F3
Worth St NG4 .... 174 C4
Worthington Rd NG24 ... 140 C2
Wortley Ave NG9 .... 170 B2
Wortley Cl DE7 .... 170 A4
Wortley Hall Cl NG7 ...... 172 B1
Worwood Dr NG2 .... 185 E2
Wossock La LE12 .... 204 C2
Woulds Field NG12 .... 187 F1
Wray Cl NG3 .... 173 F3

Wren Ct S81 .... 35 E4
Wrenthorpe Vale NG11 .. 195 F4
Wright St Carlton NG4 ... 175 D4
  Newark-on-T NG24 .... 140 A4
Wright Wilson St DN22 ... 39 F3
Wrights Orch NG12 .... 197 F1
Wrightson Cl NG17 .... 101 D2
Wroot Rd DN9 .... 1 A3
Wroughton Ct NG16 ...... 144 A1
Wroxham Dr NG8 .... 171 E1
Wycar Rd NG22 .... 106 A2
Wychwood Dr NG9 .... 170 B1
Wychwood Rd NG13 ...... 177 E2
Wycliffe Gr NG3 .... 161 F1
Wycliffe St NG7 .... 160 C1
Wycombe Cl NG11 .... 195 E4
Wye Gdns NG7 .... 172 B3
Wyggeston Rd NG13 ..... 181 D2
Wyke La NG24 .... 138 C3
Wykeham Rd NG5 .... 162 A3
Wykes Ave NG4 .... 162 C1
Wymeswold CE Sch
  LE12 .... 216 B2
Wymeswold Ind Est
  LE12 .... 216 A1
Wymeswold Rd
  Hoton LE12 .... 215 F1
  Rempstone LE12 .... 215 F3
  Wysall NG12 .... 207 E1
Wymondham Cl NG5 ..... 162 A3
Wynbreck Dr NG12 .... 197 F2
Wyndale Dr NG18 .... 103 D3
Wyndham Ct NG9 .... 183 D2
Wyndham Mews NG3 ... 173 D4
Wyndings The NG5 .... 161 F2
Wynhill Ct NG13 .... 177 E3
Wynlea Dr S81 .... 16 C3
Wynndale Dr NG5 .... 161 D2
Wynndale Fst Sch NG18 .. 103 D3
Wynward Cl DE7 .... 157 E2
Wynwood Cl NG9 .... 183 D1
Wynwood Rd NG9 .... 183 D1
Wyrale Dr NG8 .... 159 F1
Wysall Cl NG19 .... 87 F1
Wysall La
  Keyworth NG12 .... 207 E4
  Wymeswold LE12 .... 216 B3
Wysall Rd Costock LE12 .. 206 C1
  Keyworth NG12 .... 197 D1
  Rempstone LE12 .... 215 F3
  Widmerpool NG12 .... 208 A2
  Wysall NG12 .... 207 D4
Wyton Cl NG5 .... 161 D3
Wyvelle Cres DE74 .... 203 E2
Wyvern Ave NG10 .... 193 E3
Wyvern Cl NG16 .... 158 A4
Wyville Cl NG7 .... 222 A3

Yalding Dr NG8 .... 171 E2
Yalding Gdns NG8 .... 171 E2
Yarwell Cl NG3 .... 174 B4

Yates Gdns 🅱 NG5 161
Yatesbury Cres NG8 171
Yeoman Ave NG6 146
Yeoman Cl S80 36
Yeoman Park Sch NG19 ... 88
Yeomans Ct NG7 222
Yeovil Ct NG18 103
Yew Barrow Cl NG2 186
Yew Cl East Leake LE12 ... 214
  Nottingham NG5 161
Yew Tree Ave
  🐑 Kirkby in A NG17 114
  Nottingham NG5 161
Yew Tree Cl
  New Ollerton NG22 77
  Radcliffe on T NG12 175
Yew Tree Dr Bawtry DN10 9
  Huthwaite NG17 99
  Shirebrook NG20 72
Yew Tree La
  Carlton NG4 163
  Nottingham NG11 184
Yew Tree Rd
  Elkesley DN22 50
  Hucknall NG15 146
  New Ollerton NG22 77
Yewdale Cl
  Nottingham NG11 195
  West Bridgford NG2 186
Yonge Cl NG12 175
York Ave Beeston NG9 ... 183
  Sandiacre NG10 182
  Westwood NG16 128
York Cl Carlton NG4 162
  East Leake LE12 205
York Dr NG8 159
York Pl S81 34
York Rd Harworth DN11 9
  Long Eaton NG10 182
  Loughborough LE11 220
  Shirebrook NG20 72
  Tickhill DN11 8
York St Carlton NG4 175
  East Markham NG22 65
  Mansfield NG18 102
  Nottingham NG1 223
  Sutton in A NG17 100
York Terr
  Market Warsop NG20 74
  Misterton DN10 7
  Pinxton NG16 113
Yorke Dr NG24 125
Yorke St Hucknall NG15 .. 146
  Mansfield Woodhouse NG19 .. 88
Young Cl NG6 159
Young Cres NG17 101
Yvonne Cres NG4 174

Zouch Rd LE12 213
Zulla Rd NG3 173
Zulu Rd NG7 160

SD	SE	TA	TB
SJ	SK	TF	TG
SO	SP	TL	TM
ST	SU	TQ	TR
SY	SZ	TV	

Any feature in this atlas can be given a unique reference to help you find the same feature on other Ordnance Survey maps of the area, or to help someone else locate you if they do not have a Street Atlas.

The grid squares in this atlas match the Ordnance Survey National Grid and are at 500 metre intervals. The small figures at the bottom and sides of every other grid line are the National Grid kilometre values (**00** to **99** km) and are repeated across the country every 100 km (see left).

SJ	SK
SO	SP

Example Page 128

To give a unique National Grid reference you need to locate where in the country you are. The country is divided into 100 km squares with each square given a unique two-letter reference. The atlas in this example falls across the junction of four such squares. Start by working out on which two-letter square the page falls. The Key map and Administrative map are useful for this.

The bold letters and numbers between each grid line (**A** to **F**, **1** to **8**) are for use within a specific Street Atlas only, and when used with the page number, are a convenient way of referencing these grid squares.

00

ample   *The railway bridge over DARLEY GREEN RD in grid square B1 on page 128*

p 1: Identify the two-letter reference, in this se page 128 is in **SP**

p 2: Identify the 1 km square in which the lway bridge falls. Use the figures in the southwest rner of this square: Eastings **17**, Northings **74**. is gives a unique reference: **SP 17 74**, accurate 1 km.

p 3: To give a more precise reference accurate 100 m you need to estimate how many tenths ong and how many tenths up this 1 km square feature is (to help with this the 1 km square is ided into four 500 m squares). This makes the dge about **8** tenths along and about **1** tenth up m the southwest corner.

is gives a unique reference: **SP 178 741**, accurate 100 m.

Eastings (read from left to right along the bottom) come before Northings (read from bottom to top). If you have trouble remembering say to yourself "Along the hall, THEN up the stairs"!

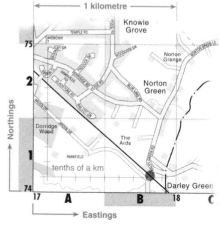

Name and Address	Telephone	Page	Grid Reference

Ordnance Survey

STREET ATLASES

ORDER FORM

The Street Atlases are available from all good bookshops or by mail order direct from th publisher. Orders can be made in the following ways. **By phone** Ring our special Credit Card Hotline on **01933 443863** during office hours (9am to 5pm) or leave a message on the answering machine, quoting your full credit card number plus expiry date and yo full name and address. **By post or fax** Fill out the order form below (you may photoc it) and post it to: **Philip's Direct, 27 Sanders Road, Wellingborough, Northants NN8 4NL** or fax it to: **01933 443849**. Before placing an order by post, by fax or or the answering machine, please telephone to check availability and prices.

COLOUR LOCAL ATLASES		
	PAPERBACK	
	Quantity @ £3.50 each	£ Total
CANNOCK, LICHFIELD, RUGELEY	☐ 0 540 07625 2	➤
DERBY AND BELPER	☐ 0 540 07608 2	➤
NORTHWICH, WINSFORD, MIDDLEWICH	☐ 0 540 07589 2	➤
PEAK DISTRICT TOWNS	☐ 0 540 07609 0	➤
STAFFORD, STONE, UTTOXETER	☐ 0 540 07626 0	➤
WARRINGTON, WIDNES, RUNCORN	☐ 0 540 07588 4	➤

COLOUR REGIONAL ATLASES				
	HARDBACK	SPIRAL	POCKET	
	Quantity @ £10.99 each	Quantity @ £8.99 each	Quantity @ £5.99 each	£ Total
BERKSHIRE	☐ 0 540 06170 0	☐ 0 540 06172 7	☐ 0 540 06173 5	➤
	Quantity @ £10.99 each	Quantity @ £8.99 each	Quantity @ £4.99 each	£ Total
MERSEYSIDE	☐ 0 540 06480 7	☐ 0 540 06481 5	☐ 0 540 06482 3	➤
	Quantity @ £12.99 each	Quantity @ £9.99 each	Quantity @ £4.99 each	£ Total
DURHAM	☐ 0 540 06365 7	☐ 0 540 06366 5	☐ 0 540 06367 3	➤
HERTFORDSHIRE	☐ 0 540 06174 3	☐ 0 540 06175 1	☐ 0 540 06176 X	➤
EAST KENT	☐ 0 540 07483 7	☐ 0 540 07276 1	☐ 0 540 07287 7	➤
WEST KENT	☐ 0 540 07366 0	☐ 0 540 07367 9	☐ 0 540 07369 5	➤
EAST SUSSEX	☐ 0 540 07306 7	☐ 0 540 07307 5	☐ 0 540 07312 1	➤
WEST SUSSEX	☐ 0 540 07319 9	☐ 0 540 07323 7	☐ 0 540 07327 X	➤
SOUTH YORKSHIRE	☐ 0 540 06330 4	☐ 0 540 06331 2	☐ 0 540 06332 0	➤
SURREY	☐ 0 540 06435 1	☐ 0 540 06436 X	☐ 0 540 06438 6	➤
	Quantity @ £12.99 each	Quantity @ £9.99 each	Quantity @ £5.50 each	£ Total
GREATER MANCHESTER	☐ 0 540 06485 8	☐ 0 540 06486 6	☐ 0 540 06487 4	➤
TYNE AND WEAR	☐ 0 540 06370 3	☐ 0 540 06371 1	☐ 0 540 06372 X	➤
	Quantity @ £12.99 each	Quantity @ £9.99 each	Quantity @ £5.99 each	£ Total
BIRMINGHAM & WEST MIDLANDS	☐ 0 540 07603 1	☐ 0 540 07604 X	☐ 0 540 07605 8	➤
BUCKINGHAMSHIRE	☐ 0 540 07466 7	☐ 0 540 07467 5	☐ 0 540 07468 3	➤

PHILIP'S

The best-selling *OS Motoring Atlas Britain* uses unrivalled and up-to-date mapping from the Ordnance Survey digital database. The exceptionally clear mapping is at a large scale of 3 miles to 1 inch (Orkney/Shetland Islands at 5 miles to 1 inch).

A special feature of the atlas is its wealth of tourist and leisure information. It contains comprehensive directories, including descriptions and location details, of the properties of the National Trust in England and Wales, the National Trust for Scotland, English Heritage and Historic Scotland. There is also a useful diary of British Tourist Authority Events listing more than 300 days out around Britain during the year.

Available from all good bookshops or direct from the publisher:
Tel: 01933 443863

The atlas includes:

- 112 pages of fully updated mapping
- 45 city and town plans
- 8 extra-detailed city approach maps
- route-planning maps
- restricted motorway junctions
- local radio information
- distances chart
- county boundaries map
- multi-language legend